THE ROUGH GUIDE TO

ALBANIA

This first edition written and researched by
Marc Di Duca, Owen Morton & Ben O'Donnell

ROUGH GUIDES

Contents

APOLLONIA ARCHAEOLOGICAL PARK

Introduction to **Albania**

Over three decades after throwing off the chains of a particularly suffocating brand of communism, Albania is emerging as an intriguingly multifaceted Balkan travel destination. All but closed to foreigners for half of the twentieth century, this small country now beckons travellers to its world-class beaches, snow-dusted peaks, windswept fortresses and ancient ruins. Although many tourists come for a beach holiday on the riviera, there is more to Albania than its coastline: the country is steeped in culture and history, from Illyrian ruins to medieval castles, Ottoman-era mansions to museums documenting the long, grey years under iron rule. But the secret is out, so come soon.

From the snow-bound peaks of the Albanian Alps to the sun-bleached beaches braiding the Ionian and Adriatic coasts, this small Balkan nation has an astonishing variety of landscapes and experiences for travellers. From April to November, warm weather means you can enjoy **outdoor adventures**, especially in the mountainous north, much of which is still being discovered and made accessible to hikers. The sandy **beaches** of the riviera can be very special when the crowds disperse, though July and August are times to avoid. However, you don't have to venture far from the tourist trail to discover empty wild strands and secluded pebbly coves. In between the coast and the mountains lie fascinating cities: layer-cakes of history built and destroyed by a medley of invaders and settlers, from the ancient Illyrians via Greeks and Romans to the Ottoman Empire and, finally, the paranoid communist regime of **Enver Hoxha**. The bustling capital Tirana is the place to learn the story of Albania's four decades of workers' utopia, its **museums** and **bunkers** preserving the memory of those who suffered under one of Europe's most restrictive dictatorships.

Albania is also still a land of genuinely welcoming hospitality, especially in more rural areas but also in places firmly on the tourist map. The country boasts countless **farm stays** where you can engage with local people, indulge in traditional food and

ALBANIA
NORTH ALBANIAN ALPS
MONTENEGRO
PODGORICA
KOSOVO
PRISTINA
Peja
Kosovo Polje
Gjakova
Ferizaj
Prizren
Thethi
Valbona
Bajram Curri
VALBONA VALLEY NATIONAL PARK
Lekbibaj
Fierza Reservoir
Kruma
Hoti
Lake Skhodra
Kopliku
SHKODËR
Drin
Bar
Shkodra (Shkodër)
Oblika
Puka
Kukësi (Kukës)
KUKËSI
KORAB MOUNTAINS
Mali i Korabit (2764m)
Tetovo
SKOPJE
Gostivar
NORTH MACEDONIA
LEZHA
Shëngjini
Lezha (Lezhë)
A1
Rrësheni
Peshkopia
Laçi
Burreli
DIBËR
Klosi
Debar
Kicevo
Bulqiza
Fushë-Krujë
DURRËSI
Shijaku
Kamza
DAJTI NATIONAL PARK
MARTANESH MOUNTAINS
Durrësi (Durrës)
TIRANA
A3
Bari, Trieste & Ancona
SHEBENIKU-JABLLANICA NATIONAL PARK
Kavaja
Librazhdi
ADRIATIC SEA
Elbasani
Shkumbini
Ohrid
Resen
Bitola
Rrogozhina
Peqini
Cërriku
ELBASANI
Prrenjasi
Lake Ohrid
Karavasta Lagoon
Lushnja
Lake Prespa
DIVJAKA-KARAVASTA NATIONAL PARK
Gramshi
Pogradeci
PRESPA NATIONAL PARK
Seman
Dimali
Kuçova
Devoll
PINDUS MOUNTAINS
FIER
Fieri (Fier)
A2
Berati
BERATI
Maliqi
Zvezda
Flórina
Patosi
TOMORRI MOUNTAIN NATIONAL PARK
Korça (Korçë)
Poliçani
Bilishti
Sazani
Ballshi
Çorovoda
KORÇA
Kastoriá
Brindisi
Vlora
Bay of Vlora
Vjosa
Osumi
FIR OF HOTOVË-DANGËLLI NATIONAL PARK
Erseka
Orikumi
Këlcyra
LLOGARA NATIONAL PARK
Tepelena
GRIBE MOUNTAINS
Përmeti
GREECE
Strait of Otranto
Ionian Coast
VLORA
Çarshovë
Himara
GJIROKASTRA
Gjirokastra
Kónitsa
Delvinë
N
Jorgucati
Kalpáki
Saranda
Ksamili
Butrint
Corfu
Konispoli
Ioánnina
0
30
kilometres
Metres
2000
1500
1000
500
200
0

FACT FILE

- Albania has a **population** of around 2.4 million people, with 598,000 of those living in the capital Tirana. One-third of the country resides in Tirana County.
- Albania has one of the lowest **birthrates** in the world, at an average of 1.21 children per woman.
- Albanian was first recognized as an **Indo-European language** in the 1850s. By the nineteenth century, the tongue was written in at least ten different alphabets – some invented whole-cloth in Albania – before a version of the Latin alphabet was adopted as the standard.
- Dictator Enver Hoxha built somewhere between 150,000 and 750,000 **concrete bunkers** across Albania between the 1960s and 1980s, though not all of them survive to this day. It was possibly the greatest single act of communist paranoia of the late twentieth century.
- Albania is among the most **religiously diverse** countries in Europe: 51 percent of the population identify as Muslim, including five percent in the Sufi Bektashi sect, while sixteen percent are Christians, about equally split between Catholicism and Eastern Orthodoxy. Atheists and unaffiliated believers fill out most of the rest.
- **Famous Albanians** by birth or parentage include Mother Teresa; singers Dua Lipa and Rita Ora; actors Eliza Dushku, John Belushi and Jim Belushi; and ChatGPT developer Mira Murati.
- Albania is having a well-deserved moment in the spotlight for international tourism. In 2024, the country welcomed a record-breaking **11.7 million visitors** – a huge leap from the 3.7 million in 2014 and the 645,000 in in 2004.
- **Mount Korabi** (Maja e Korabit), at 2764m, is the highest peak in Albania and fourth-highest in the Balkans, just a touch below Mount Olympus (2917m) in Greece.
- Albania and its cross-border habitats are home to an unusually high number of **endemic species**, including the Albanian water frog, Ohrid trout (locally called *koran*) and around thirty native plants

unplug from the twenty-first century for a while. However, don't expect much peace and quiet in the busy coastal resorts where mass tourism now operates at full throttle.

And no matter what you may have read or heard, travel to Albania is also safe. The days of the vendetta are pretty much over and the lawlessness and upheaval of the 1990s has been replaced by hope for a peaceful and prosperous future within the European Union (EU). Crime is no longer the issue it once was, and standards of facilities and infrastructure are on the rise.

So, as it will quickly become apparent to anyone who steps off a plane at Tirana International Airport, Albania is undergoing a renaissance, firmly established as a democratic member of NATO and broadly connected to the European and international communities. Still one of Europe's poorest countries, problems obviously persist, but this small Balkan state is irreversibly on the road to better days, with tourism strongly part of the mix.

Where to go

The obvious place to start, **Tirana** is one of Europe's smaller capitals but it's a city that's developing fast, with skyscrapers, hotels and restaurants springing up almost on a daily basis. The Albanian metropolis is a unique and eccentric melange of Ottoman, Italianate, communist and contemporary architecture, and many remnants of its storied past survive, most notably in its museums that offer glimpses

SKANDERBEG STATUE

BARMY BUNKERS

A ubiquitous feature of the landscape across Albania, there are hundreds of thousands of **concrete bunkers** to be found in the country. A legacy of the paranoid communist regime of **Enver Hoxha**, they date across a twenty-year period from 1967 onwards, and were intended to provide civil defence in the event of an invasion by enemy forces. Hoxha took his inspiration from the guerrilla warfare that the Albanian resistance engaged in during **World War II**, in which fighters emerged from heavily defended mountain territory to attack lowland targets.

The bunkers range in size and design, from the smaller and more common installations that could house one or two soldiers to huge shelters for more sizeable units. There were even large networks designed to house the entire government in the event of **nuclear attack**. Their construction used up valuable resources and was **economically crippling**, which meant other infrastructure naturally suffered.

After Hoxha's death, the building scheme ground to a halt, but not before the landscape of Albania had been transformed. Despite bunker removal programmes in the post-communist period, these malevolent-looking concrete edifices still dot the cities and countryside. Some, however, have become quirky landmarks, adorned with playful murals or repurposed to host art installations and cafés. Here are a few particularly worth a visit:

- **Bunk'Art 1 and 2.** Enormous complexes of underground tunnels in Tirana, designed to house Albania's government if the country were invaded or suffered a nuclear attack. They have been converted into fascinating museums detailing the bunkerization programme and the history of Albania under communism, and also house exhibitions of modern art. See pages 63 and 58
- **Pirogoshi.** Found in the Gradeci Canyon near Berati, this military complex burrowed into the mountainside was part of a plan to fortify the region so it could act as a backup headquarters in the event of Tirana's downfall. See page 129
- **Cold War Tunnel, Gjirokastra.** Underneath Gjirokastra Castle, this 1970s design was intended as a place of refuge for local government officials. It contains offices, sleeping quarters and so on, and retains some original furnishings and paraphernalia. It can only be visited on a tour. See page 204
- **Zvërneci.** Hidden beneath the lighthouse on the western cliff of this peninsula is a series of four large, interconnected bunkers, intended for naval defence: inside the first tunnel remains a poster for the inhabitants to use in identifying enemy vessels. The exterior has been decorated with environmentally themed street art. See page 246
- **Phoenice.** These ancient ruins date back about 2500 years, but they occupy such an important strategic position that they were refortified in the communist era. The result is a bizarre combination of crumbling remains dotted with concrete bunkers. See page 261

of life under communism, by turns terrible and fascinating. It's by far the most cosmopolitan place in Albania, with the highest variety of restaurants and cultural offerings. However, in the heat of summer most visitors flock straight to the **riviera**, where long, pebbly beaches rival anything on the Mediterranean. The authorities have vowed to clear the infamous swarms of sun umbrellas, meaning more space to enjoy the beautiful coast (free of charge). Those who head off the beaten track will be rewarded with quieter, more secluded azure vistas and untamed coves untouched by mass tourism. Albania's other natural wonder is its **mountains**, the north a crumpled peakscape with countless hiking and cycling routes through Shangri-La-esque valleys and gorges. The loop from **Shkodra** via **Thethi**, **Valbona** and the **Komani** ferry is becoming a European travel classic.

Almost joined at the hip with Tirana, **Durrësi** is Albania's main port and an Adriatic gem with its ancient amphitheatre, Roman ruins, beaches and kicking nightlife. Further south, the port of **Vlora** is an engaging destination thanks to its worthwhile museums, good beaches and fine restaurants serving boat-fresh seafood.

The 'City of a Thousand Windows', centrally located **Berati** is a historical treasure trove brimming with Ottoman-era architecture and crowned by a dramatic castle. The town of **Korça** in the southeast of the country has lots of idiosyncratic museums to peruse, as well as a vibrant bazaar area given over to food, drink and music, while hillside **Gjirokastra** just shy of the Greek border is a UNESCO-listed tangle of stone-built lanes and storeybook tower houses.

In the far south, squaring up to the Greek island of Corfu across a narrow strait, **Butrint** is Albania's premier archaeological site (one of many, it must be added) and another UNESCO World Heritage Site where visitors can explore an entire town's worth of Greek, Roman and medieval ruins.

AVERAGE MONTHLY TEMPERATURES AND RAINFALL

	Jan	Feb	Mar	Apr	May	Jun	Jul	Aug	Sep	Oct	Nov	Dec
DURRËSI												
Max (°C/°F)	13/55	15/59	18/64	21/70	25/77	30/86	33/91	34/93	29/84	24/75	20/68	15/59
Min (°C/°F)	4/39	6/43	8/46	11/52	14/57	18/64	21/70	21/70	18/64	14/57	10/50	6/43
Rainfall (mm)	130	115	100	95	75	50	30	45	75	110	160	140
TIRANA												
Max (°C/°F)	13/55	14/57	17/63	21/70	25/77	29/84	32/90	33/91	28/82	23/73	18/64	14/57
Min (°C/°F)	2/36	3/37	6/43	9/48	13/55	17/63	19/66	18/64	15/59	11/52	7/45	3/37
Rainfall (mm)	135	150	130	115	120	85	30	30	60	105	210	175
KORÇA												
Max (°C/°F)	5/41	9/48	12/54	17/63	21/70	25/77	29/84	29/84	24/75	19/66	13/55	7/45
Min (°C/°F)	-2/28	1/34	3/37	6/43	10/50	13/55	16/61	16/61	13/55	8/46	4/39	-0.3/31
Rainfall (mm)	70	80	55	60	80	45	25	25	40	80	145	100

When to go

Most visitors travel to Albania in the main **summer season**, between **June and September**. These months are the hottest, with temperatures regularly nudging above 40°C in the country's lower-elevation corridors. This is great weather for swimming in the sea and sunbathing, though not so good for visiting museums and archaeological sites or doing very much at all outdoors. July and August are by far the busiest months, with the beaches often completely chock-a-block and accommodation on the coast booked out. Come to the riviera in **May** or **late September** and early October and you'll find a different scene altogether, with most places open but a fraction of the summer crowds. However, much of the tourist infrastructure along the coast calls it a day between late October and May.

One area of the country you might also want to visit in Albania's **shoulder season** is the mountainous north, though at altitude the edge is taken off extreme summer temperatures. From November through to March and April, trails and access roads can be blocked by snow.

One **year-round destination** is the capital, Tirana. You'll get much more out of the city when the mercury sinks below 25°C, though, so it's best to avoid June through August, when sweltering temperatures might put you off visiting its many excellent (though lacking air-conditioning) museums. Other cities, especially those inland such as Berati and Gjirokastra, have similar issues.

Albania's colourful folk traditions are among the highlights of a visit so you might want to plan a trip to coincide with one of its many festivals. Individual events are listed below and in the individual chapters.

DURRËSI BEACH

Author picks

Our authors have trekked mountainous trails, climbed to hilltop Byzantine monasteries, and consumed far more Albanian wine than is strictly necessary – it's a hard job, but someone's got to do it. Here are some of their top experiences.

Hit the trails The mountainous north of Albania is a hiker's nirvana but the trail between Thethi and Valbona, part of the mighty Peaks of the Balkans (see page 90), is something special.

Bunkering down Bunkers are an almost ubiquitous sight across the land, but the two Tirana Bunk'Art nuclear shelters (see pages 63 and 58) are the most fascinating places in the capital for those with an interest in Albania's long decades under a communist dictatorship.

Hilltop fortresses Albania is dotted with picturesque castles perched atop imposing vantage points: enjoy expansive views from strongholds such as Borshi Castle (see page 254), Gjirokastra Castle (see page 205) and Rozafa Castle (see page 79) near Shkodra.

Marvellous monasteries Beautiful Byzantine churches such as the one at St Mary's Monastery (see page 255) are found across the south of the country, often sheltering medieval frescoes.

Folk culture You are never far from a folk performance in Albania, whether that be iso-polyphony singing (see page 205), the *sazet* music of the south (see page 195) or the Oda Dibrane festival in Peshkopia (see page 99).

Socialist realism art The communist era left behind some marvellously blocky designs, including Vlora's Independence Monument (see page 243), the Drashovica World War II memorial (see page 247), and the mural at the National History Museum in Tirana (see page 56).

Secluded beaches The Albanian riviera is now well and truly on the tourist map, but beaches such as Gjipeja (Gjipe; see page 250) and Lukova (see page 255) still have an undiscovered feel.

Albanian wine Discover Albania's surprising viticultural scene at *Alpeta Agrotourism & Winery* or *Pupa Winery* (see page 125) near Berati.

Our author recommendations don't end here. We've flagged up our favourite places – a perfectly sited hotel, an atmospheric café, a special restaurant – throughout the Guide, highlighted with the ★ symbol.

HAJJI BENDO MOSQUE, BORSHI CASTLE

INDEPENDENCE SQUARE MONUMENT

25

things not to miss

It's impossible to see everything Albania has to offer in one trip – and we don't suggest you try. What follows is a taste of some of the country's highlights: natural wonders and cultural treasures, serene beaches and UNESCO-protected old towns, dramatic drives and adventurous hikes. Each highlight has a page reference to take you straight into the guide, where you can find out more. Coloured numbers refer to chapters in the Guide section.

1

1 MOUNT DAJTI

See page 66

The best day-trip from Tirana is Mount Dajti, just east of the city. Take the cable car to the summit for fine panoramas, meals with a view, and hiking.

2 BUNK'ART 1 AND 2

See pages 63 and 58

A pair of gigantic nuclear bunkers in Tirana reimagined as subterranean museums, Bunk'Art 1 focuses on Albania's twentieth-century history, regaled partially in art installations, while its younger cousin beneath the former Ministry of Internal Affairs is dedicated to communist repression and terror.

3 GJIROKASTRA OLD TOWN

See page 229

The UNESCO-inscribed historical centre of Gjirokastra is a warren of stone houses and narrow lanes in the shadow of a magnificent castle.

4 LAKE KOMANI BOAT TRIP

See page 92

A great way to reach or return from the northern mountains, this scenic reservoir trip is like sailing down a fjord.

5 BLUE EYE

See page 262

This karst hole in Southern Albania shines bright blue in the Balkan sun. It's so deep no one has ever reached the bottom of it.

6

7

8

9

10

6 LLOGARA PASS

See page 250

One of Europe's most dramatic drives, the zigzagging route down from the Llogara Pass provides spectacular views of the Albanian riviera.

7 DURRËSI HISTORIC CENTRE

See page 142

Piece together over two thousand years of history through the architectural jigsaw of this port city's compact core.

8 PËRMETI'S VJOSA RIVERLANDS

See page 229

Whether you want to chase rapids by river raft or luxuriate in thermal springs, the electric-blue waterways of the Vjosa River inspire awe and adventure.

9 FARM STAYS

See page 35

One of the best ways to experience the traditional food and culture of this welcoming Balkan nation is to stay at one of the many rural farms that host guests.

10 NATIONAL MUSEUM OF MEDIEVAL ART

See page 165

Albania is incredibly rich in Orthodox frescoes and icons, and the finest works of its home-grown painters live at this Korça museum.

11 BUTRINT

See page 264

Unveil layers of ancient regional history at the country's leading archaeological site.

12 APOLLONIA ARCHAEOLOGICAL PARK

See page 220

Discover how the Greeks and Romans lived, worked and studied at this amazing ruined city and museum near the city of Fieri.

13 THETHI TO VALBONA HIKE

See page 88

The hiking route between Thethi and Valbona is the most popular in Albania, and for good reason. The view along the Valbona Valley is truly spectacular.

14 CLIMB MOUNT KORABI

See page 101

Mount Korabi is Albania's highest peak, and a fairly easy hike to the summit is a great way to spend a day near Peshkopia.

15 LAKE OHRID

See page 173

Shared with the Republic of North Macedonia, this huge lake is a wonderful summer retreat with crystal-clear waters, laid-back fishing and freshwater seafood galore.

13

14

15

16

17

16 SHEBENIKU-JABLLANICA NATIONAL PARK

See page 171

Hugging the Albanian border with the Republic of North Macedonia, this national park is a remote sprawl of glacial lakes, dense forests and deep valleys.

17 KORÇA OLD BAZAAR

See page 162

A restored historic market area converted into a happening hotspot of bars, restaurants and shops.

18 BASHTOVA CASTLE

See page 152

Arguably Albania's most striking castle, a short trip from Durrësi, it's no surprise its fairy-tale turrets and battlements are on UNESCO's tentative list.

19 SKANDERBEG SQUARE

See page 56

Tirana's epicentre boasts some of the capital's most recognizable landmarks and bustles from morning until night with strolling locals and tourists.

20 BERATI MEDIEVAL CORE

See page 111

Unfurling just beneath the castle, the Ottoman centre of Berati has earned the town its moniker 'City of a Thousand Windows'.

18

19

20

21

22

23

24

25

21 LAKE SHKODRA

See page 86

Albania has a share of the biggest lake in the Balkans, best accessed from the town of Shiroka near Shkodra.

22 BLLOKU

See page 61

The former gated Tirana neighbourhood for communist party bigwigs, Blloku has reinvented itself as a hip place of cool restaurants, bars and hotels. Nearby, Piramida is the city's wildest communist relic.

23 KRUJA BAZAAR AND CASTLE

See page 73

Just 30km from Tirana, the evocative medieval hilltop town of Kruja celebrates Skanderbeg, the national hero for his leading role in Albanian resistance against the Ottomans.

24 THE RIVIERA

See page 236

Tourist magnet and the Mediterranean's latest up-and-coming destination, the resorts and hidden coves of the Albanian riviera are laced by some exquisite beaches.

25 OSUMI CANYON

See page 128

One of Albania's most spectacular natural attractions, this gorge plummets 150m in some places. At points it is only a few metres wide, flanked by soaring limestone walls.

Itineraries

Albania might be small, but you'll still need at least a month to scratch beneath the surface of this fascinating country. There's just enough infrastructure to get you between big cities but you'll definitely need your own car or even a 4WD (and/or guide) to reach smaller places and remote locations.

THE GRAND TOUR

Culture-packed cities, Roman ruins, UNESCO wonders, Ottoman-era architecture: Albania has an embarrassment of riches. With your own car, this grand tour might take anything from ten days to two weeks depending on how long you spend in each place.

❶ **Shkodra** Hooked around the shores of Lake Shkodra – the biggest natural body of water in the Balkans – this culturally engaging city is a wonderful launchpad for trips into the surrounding region and for a wider tour of the country. See page 86

❷ **Lezha** It's a short drive from Shkodra to Lezha, a small town with big connections, most notably to the Albanians' national hero Skanderbeg, whose mausoleum is the main calling card here. See page 102

❸ **Tirana** The motorway starts at Lezha, meaning you reach Tirana in no time. You could easily spend a week in and around the Albanian capital visiting the communism-examining museums, feasting on the country's most varied food, and climbing Mount Dajti for fine city views. See page 50

❹ **Durrësi** Albania's main port city is a short journey from Tirana and is well worth a visit for its Roman ruins, inviting beaches and excellent seafood restaurants strung along the sand. See page 139

❺ **Berati** A mere 90km of decent road separates the coast from one of the highlights of Central Albania: the historical town of Berati with its mighty castle and clusters of well-preserved Ottoman-era buildings. See page 110

❻ **Gjirokastra** There's no direct route to the next stop, the road bucking and weaving south to Gjirokastra, a stone-built, UNESCO-protected wonder with heaps of Ottoman architecture and narrow cobbled lanes. See page 200

❼ **Butrint** From Gjirokastra it's a slow 70km drive towards the coast to reach Butrint, Albania's most impressive archaeological site. Exploring the ruins of this Greek and Roman city transports you back into the ancient past. See page 264

COASTAL ADVENTURE

Albania's coastline is not only fringed with sandy beaches, it is also home to ancient Greek ruins, fine seafood restaurants and one of Europe's most breathtaking drives. A hire car is a must to make the most of this trip, which could take anything from a week to a fortnight, depending on how long it takes to rouse yourself from your sun-drunk reverie.

❶ **Durrësi** Start in Albania's principal port, the ancient city of Durrësi with its Roman amphitheatre and long beaches. Ferries dock here from Italy, making it a natural entry point for those touring in their own vehicle. See page 139

❷ **Apollonia** It's just over an hour's drive south to Apollonia, one of the most significant archaeological sites in Albania with its Greek and Roman ruins scattered over green hillsides. See page 220

❸ **Vlora** Just thirty minutes by car separate Apollonia from Vlora, the northern gateway to the glittering riviera. Albania's third city has a vibrant, renovated centre and some excellent eating options. See page 238

❹ **Llogara Pass** Though a tunnel now bores through the mountain, the Llogara Pass is one of Europe's most exhilarating drives, with switchbacks, downhill slaloms and the most amazing views in Albania. See page 250

❺ **Himara** Further along the coast is the riviera's principal resort: Himara. Hooking around a gleaming bay, the town has everything you need for a do-nothing beach break. See page 252

❻ **Qeparoi** A short hop south, this unsung Ionian village is surrounded by an azure bay, with magical coastal castles and an alluring old town. See page 254

❼ **Saranda** Decent, if well-frequented, roads lead to Saranda, another major beach resort town. Ferries leave from here to Corfu. See page 256

MOUNTAINS OF THE NORTH

This northern odyssey could take fit hikers and intrepid travellers anything from a week to a month depending on how many side treks take your fancy.

❶ **Shkodra** Gateway to the north, Shkodra is definitely worth a few days of your time to explore Lake Shkodra and the city's museums. See page 86

❷ **Thethi** A two-hour white-knuckle ride over the Buni i Thorës Pass (1704m) brings you to the picturesque village of Thethi, until recently a lost world surrounded by high peaks. Several hiking routes run from here. See page 86

❸ **Valbona** One of those trails from Thethi is Albania's most popular hike, wending 18km through an alpine wonderland to the equally remote village of Valbona. See page 89

❹ **Bajram Curri** It's a 24km bus or taxi ride to Bajram Curri, a major service centre for the northern mountains. It's a great place to stock up, chill out and repair or replace gear. See page 90

❺ **Kukësi** It's a tortuous journey across rough terrain by 4WD from Bajram Curri to Kukësi and you should allow a day to complete the route. The town has a sprinkling of interesting sights and is a launch pad for adventures in the mountainscape beyond. See page 94

❻ **Puka** By road the journey from Kukësi to Puka takes around two hours along twisting roads through the peaks. Puka has a unique combination of skiing, hiking and craft beer to enjoy, before returning to lower altitudes for some R&R. See page 91

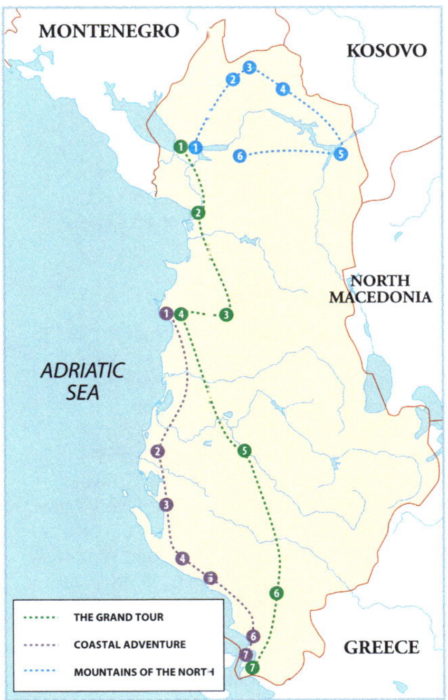

Sustainable travel

Albanians are working hard to promote sustainable travel and preserve the beauty of their country and their rich cultural heritage. Here's what you can do to help them succeed.

A country just emerging into the mass tourism limelight, Albania has a good chance to get things right from the outset when it comes to sustainability. However, the country has inherited many bad practices from the decades of communism and chaos of its aftermath, and it lacks a lot of essential infrastructure, especially when it comes to waste management and water treatment. A flurry of rampant development along the coast along with a controversial new airport in the ecologically important habitat of Vlora (see page 238) has placed the environment under heavy strain, but NGOs and local businesses have tirelessly campaigned to protect the land and promote ecotourism. Plus, there are several things that travellers can do to limit their impact while still enjoying their trip to the full.

LEAVE NO TRACE

The number one topic when it comes to the environment in Albania is waste management. The sad reality is that few other countries in Europe are as strewn with litter as Albania. Outside Tirana and a couple of other big cities, refuse collection is very patchy and in rural communities hardly exists at all. To avoid exacerbating the problem, try to limit your waste production and never throw rubbish out of your car window (sadly, this is not uncommon with locals in Albania). If travelling in your own car, crush plastic bottles and take them home with you, where you can dispose of them in an environmentally sound way. Tirana now has recycling facilities so make sure you use them.

ECOALBANIA

A decade ago, professors from Tirana University teamed up with an environmental NGO to create EcoAlbania (www.ecoalbania.org), an organization that engages in green projects across the land. It has successfully campaigned to make the Vjosa waterways (see page 229) a national park amid plans to dam the river and create hydropower plants. Other projects include conservation of the endangered Albanian water frog, developing a school curriculum in environmental issues, and clean-up campaigns in Osumi Canyon (see page 128). There are limited opportunities to participate in volunteer work and you can apply to take part online.

FARM STAYS

Choosing a farm stay (*agroturizëm*) is a great way to sample local food and hospitality and the money you spend at this type of accommodation usually stays in the community. Hosting paying guests helps farms preserve traditional food production, supports livestock husbandry and could encourage young people to stay and work in rural areas. It is also an excellent opportunity to engage with local people and get to know Albanians beyond tourist-weary hotel receptionists and waiters. Learn more about agritourism in Albania at www.agrotourism.gov.al.

AGROPUKA

This Puka-based NGO (www.agropuka.org) supports mostly women food producers in

MANY ALBANIAN CITIES ARE BIKE-FRIENDLY

rural areas. It created three social enterprise cooperatives to help female farmers produce, process and sell their products, helping to increase the income for remote communities. The team provided training in business start-ups, marketing and self-financing, and helped to set up food markets and fairs across Puka (see page 91). Seek out produce from AgroPuka members to support efforts to keep traditional food production alive and to preserve ancient ways of life in the mountains of Albania.

SHOP SENSIBLY SOLIDARITY SHOP

There is a growing crop of sustainable shops that travellers can support during their time in Albania. Berati-based Solidarity Shop (see page 118) is packed with locally produced handicrafts and preserved foods from the Berati region, serving as a marketplace for local farmers and artisans who might not have access to their own storefront. Gratuities are used to support families in need within rural communities. Initiatives in 2024 included food deliveries, holiday-gift campaigns and building homes for families displaced by an earthquake. In Elbasani, Tradita ime Artizanale (see page 138) is the best place in town for authentic handicrafts. What's more, you can shop with a conscience as this local shop is the outlet for a social entrepreneurship organization that enables impoverished women to sell their traditional craftwork.

BEACHES

In late 2024, it was rumoured that authorities were going to make an attempt to rid Albania's beaches of the forests of sunbeds and umbrellas that have become the scourge of every seaside town in the land. It will no longer be possible for any and every local business to rent a patch of sand, and hotels will only be able to set up as many sunbeds as they have room for. The sardine-packed sunbaker phenomenon is one of the main reasons holidaymakers don't return to Albania's riviera: the experience of lying twenty rows back, unable to even see the sea and breathing in billowing cigarette smoke, is not a particularly memorable or enjoyable one. If the problem persists despite changes to the law, don't encourage illegal beach grabs and unfurl your towel elsewhere, ideally where there are no sun umbrellas.

CYCLING

It may come a surprise to many, but Albanians often get around by bike. This is a legacy of the communist era when personal vehicle ownership was essentially banned. Tirana, Korça and a few other towns and cities have excellent cycle lanes and bike facilities, though the number of cycle-hire places is lacking and as of autumn 2024 there were no shared-bike schemes in operation. Hitting the marked cycling trails of the northern mountains makes for a sustainable holiday you'll long remember. There are also lengthy road-cycling itineraries around the south of Albania; a guide is recommended for these.

SUSTAINABILITY-FOCUSED TOUR OPERATORS

Wilderness adventure and conservation go hand in hand, so it's little surprise that tour operators specializing in trekking, biking, rafting, kayaking, climbing, yoga and village visits practice sustainability and promote responsible rural development. Either through their companies or affiliated nonprofits, the founders and employees of these organizations mark and maintain trails, clean up litter, partner with family restaurants or guesthouses in impoverished areas and raise awareness of environmental threats. Even if you skip a trip, virtually all such outfits will clue you in to volunteer opportunities. Leaders include Tirana-based Active Albania (www.activealbania.com), Përmeti-based Vjosa Explorer (www.vjosaexplorer.com) and AvenTour Albania, the travel arm of nonprofit Korça Alpin (www.korcaalpin.org).

TIRANA: THE MAIN GATEWAY TO ALBANIA

Basics

Getting there

Most people who visit Albania arrive by plane, which is typically the easiest and cheapest way to travel. Tirana International Airport Nënë Tereza (Mother Teresa) is the only operational international airport in Albania. As of 2024, a total of 23 airlines serve the airport, linking the Albanian capital with many parts of Central, Eastern and Western Europe. Destinations reflect the largest markets for Albania's tourist industry – such as Germany, Italy, the Czech Republic, Austria and Poland – as well as where the biggest diasporas of Albanians and Kosovan Albanians live (Italy, Greece, the UK, Germany and Austria). The only destinations served outside Europe are the UAE and Turkey, with only seasonal holiday beyond Istanbul. Albania-bound travellers also have the option of flying to Podgorica, Montenegro; Pristina, Kosovo; Thessaloniki, Greece; or Ohrid, North Macedonia, and crossing the border by land.

Most flights are now year-round, though some services are paused or reduced in frequency over the European winter. Another international airport is due to open in Vlora on Albania's Adriatic coastline in 2025, though it's mired in controversy due to concerns over its environmental impact on the surrounding wetlands that shelter dozens of endangered birds. A third airport, Kukës International Airport Zayed in northeast Albania, opened in 2021 but had ceased service by 2024; it is not yet clear when or if flights will resume. Other ways of getting to Albania include by ferry from southern Italy and Corfu, or by bus or car from countries in continental Europe.

Flights from the UK and Ireland

There are **several daily nonstop flights** between **London** and Tirana International Airport (www.tirana-airport.com), taking around three hours and costing from £15 in low season and from £100 at the height of summer. Hungarian low-cost airline **Wizz Air** (www.wizzair.com) links Luton with Tirana up to three times a day, while **Ryanair** (www.ryanair.com) flies out of Stansted thrice-daily, from Manchester thrice-weekly and from Bristol and Edinburgh twice-weekly over the summer season. British Airways (www.britishairways.com) operates services out of London Heathrow. More flights from regional airports across the UK are certain to start up over the coming years.

There are **no direct flights from Ireland** to Albania, your best bet is to fly to London or to mainland Europe (Munich, Frankfurt or Milan are possible routings) and connect to another flight from there.

Flights from mainland Europe

Many **European cities now have direct flights to Tirana**, some operated by budget airlines. There are daily flights to Frankfurt and several other regional airports in Germany, Rome and many other cities in Italy, Athens, Istanbul, Brussels, Zurich, Vienna, Valencia, Barcelona, Budapest, Belgrade, Madrid and Malmö. A large share of these are operated by Ryanair and Wizz Air. In 2021, a second international airport opened in Kukësi in northeast Albania, offering flights to European cities, including Zurich and Istanbul, but the airport is no longer in service as of 2025. Check Kukës International Airport Zayed's website (www.kuiport.al) for developments.

Flights from the US and Canada

As of 2024 there were **no direct flights between Albania and North America**, and travellers from the US and Canada have to **fly via London, Munich, Frankfurt, Vienna or Zurich**. From many major cities all around the continental US, the best routing might be with United Airlines (www.united.com) and its codeshare partners: Austrian Airlines (www.austrian.com) via Vienna; Lufthansa (www.lufthansa.com) or Discover (www.discover-airlines.com) via Frankfurt; or Swiss Air (www.swissair.com) via Zurich. The routes usually entail a flight time of around fourteen hours,

A BETTER KIND OF TRAVEL

At Rough Guides we are passionately committed to travel. We believe it helps us understand the world we live in and the people we share it with – and of course tourism is vital to many developing economies. But the scale of modern tourism has also damaged some places irreparably, and climate change is accelerated by most forms of transport, especially flying. We encourage all our authors to consider the carbon footprint of the journeys they make in the course of researching our guides.

though a handful of quicker connections have begun to appear. Another popular option is via **Istanbul** with Turkish Airlines (www.turkishairlines.com). **Return fares** start at around US$700 regardless of which routing you choose. There are whispers, however, that a US airline will be commencing direct flights to/from New York in 2025.

From Canada, Austrian Airlines and Air Canada (www.aircanada.com) codeshare via Vienna from Toronto and Montreal. Lufthansa and Air Canada do the same out of Vancouver via Frankfurt and Munich. Fares start at around US$950.

Flights from Australia, New Zealand and South Africa

There are **no direct flights** between Albania and Australia, New Zealand or South Africa. From Australia, the most convenient service is from Melbourne via Dubai (25hr) with Emirates (www.emirates.com). All other routes require two connections: the first in Asia – Singapore or Bangkok, for instance – and the second in a major European hub like Frankfurt or London. The same applies when travelling to Albania from New Zealand. Flights start at roughly AU$1700 from Australia and NZ$3000 from New Zealand, with **flight times** ranging from 22–35 hours depending on connections.

If you're travelling from South Africa to Tirana, the best routings are from Johannesburg or Cape Town via Dubai or Istanbul, with fares starting at around ZAR15,000 return, more often than not with Emirates.

Trains

No matter what you might read online, Albania is not linked to any of its neighbours by rail. The **nearest you can get to Albania by train is Bar** in Montenegro, from where it is possible to continue by bus over the border to Shkodra. The railway journey to Bar is a tortuous if scenic trip from the Serbian capital Belgrade, which is connected to a number of European cities (including Vienna and Budapest) but may not be entirely safe for Western travellers as of 2024. However, if you really are determined to travel by train, the Belgrade–Bar service runs twice daily and includes the seasonal day train Tara (mid-June to mid-September; 11hr; tickets from €24) and the overnight sleeper Lovćen, which departs at 8.20pm and takes ten hours (add €6–20 for a shared six-bed couchette up to a three-bed compartment). Tickets must be bought at the station.

From Athens, you can take the Hellenic Train to Thessaloniki (several daily; 5hr; tickets from €43), from where bus services connect to multiple cities in Albania (see Buses). Check schedules at www.hellenictrain.gr.

From the UK, it is possible to travel to Bari in Italy by train then take the ferry to Albania, though this is a long and complicated journey. There is just one London–Bari rail itinerary: Eurostar to Paris then TGV to Milan, where you board the Frecciarossa to Bari. The total journey time is around nineteen hours, though the route requires an overnight stop in Milan. In all likelihood, this won't save you money compared to flying, but it is far more environmentally friendly and provides a chance to stop off in other countries along the way. Alternatively, a longer overland route trundles from Paris via Stuttgart, the night train to Zagreb, and onwards by bus to Belgrade, where you hop on the night train to the Montenegrin capital Podgorica. Regular buses link Podgorica with Shkodra and Tirana.

It's certainly simpler and more cost-effective to buy a rail pass (see below), invest in an international rail timetable and plan your own itinerary, than to try to purchase a return ticket: most agents deal exclusively with premier express services, and fares often work out way more expensive than flying. The high cost is at least partly explained by the fact that almost all through-tickets from London to European destinations use very expensive Eurostar services.

Rail passes

If you're planning to visit Albania as part of a more extensive trip around Europe, it may be worth buying a rail pass. Italy, Croatia and neighbouring Montenegro are covered in the **Interrail** scheme, which is available to European residents. Interrail passes can be bought through the likes of Trainseurope and Eurail in the UK (see below) and come in two categories: one for those aged 26 and over, and the (cheaper) under-26 version. There is a range of passes offering different durations, from four days' travel in a one-month period, which will just about suffice for a trip to Albania and back; although a more leisurely approach would require a pass for seven days' travel within one month, or ten days within two months. Interrail passes do not include travel between Britain and the continent, although pass-holders are eligible for discounts on rail travel in the UK and on cross-Channel ferries.

Non-European residents qualify for the **Eurail Global pass**, which must be purchased before arrival in Europe from selected agents in North America, Australia and New Zealand or from Trainseurope or Voyages SNCF in London. The pass allows unlimited train travel in twenty European countries, including

Belgium and Germany. Passes for those aged 28 and over are for first-class travel only; the under-28s pass comes with a second-class option. There's an extensive choice of time periods. Further details of these passes can be found on www.eurail.com.

RAIL CONTACTS

Deutsche Bahn www.bahn.com. Timetable information and through-ticketing on some European routes.
Eurostar www.eurostar.com. Trains from London to France, Belgium and the Netherlands.
Eurail www.eurail.com. Global agents for Eurail and individual European rail tickets on some routes.
The Man in Seat 61 www.seat61.com. Train enthusiast-run site packed with information on all aspects of international rail travel. Far more reliable than many official sites.
Trainseurope www.trainseurope.co.uk. Interrail passes and through-tickets on European routes.

Buses

As there are no train services in or out of Albania, the only way to reach neighbouring Balkan states over land, if you are not driving, is by bus. Tirana and other Albanian cities are well connected with destinations in Greece, North Macedonia, Kosovo and Montenegro. Budget operator **FlixBus** (www.flixbus.com) offers direct bus services between **Shkodra and Podgorica** (1hr 35min), which makes flying into the Montenegrin capital and crossing the Albanian border by bus an option if you are visiting the northern mountains.

A host of bus companies link **Tirana with Pristina**, the capital of Kosovo, with direct services hourly and a journey time of four hours. There are also direct buses in the morning and evening to **Skopje**, the capital of North Macedonia (7hr).

Leaving Greece, you can catch buses from Athens, Thessaloniki, Patras, Piraeus, Larissa, Argos, Ioannina, Chalcis, Corinth, Sparta and other cities, as far afield as Heraklion in Crete, and reach various destinations in Albania, including Tirana, Durrësi, Shkodra, Vlora, Berati, Elbasani, Gjirokastra, Korça and Pogradeci. Routes from major cities and those near the border run daily, sometimes multiple times. Alb Trans (tel: 069 400 4079), Star Travel (tel: 069 960 5501), Alvavel (tel: 067 604 2191) and Metro-Euro (www.metroeuro.travel) cover Greece thoroughly. Alvavel and Metro-Euro also make trips most days to Istanbul, and many of the above companies serve a handful of cities in other countries too.

You can reach Albania via day-long or overnight trips from surprisingly far out in continental Europe. Arjani Travel (www.arjanitravel.com), Hak Bus (www.hakbus.net), Firenze Lines (www.firenzelines.com) and Alb Trans (tel: 069 400 4079) are among the operators offering broad coverage between multiple Albanian destinations and cities large and small in **Germany**, **Italy** and **Switzerland** as well as **Serbia**, **Montenegro** and **North Macedonia**.

There is no official website for all bus information, but a helpful source is www.travel.gjirafa.com, though be aware that it isn't one hundred percent reliable. Timetables occasionally change without warning and services can run late or be cancelled at the last minute. If you can't find a specific route, date, time and price online (or want to confirm details), try calling or messaging the bus service on WhatsApp and an operator will be able to give you guidance.

Ferry

Visitors from Northern Europe might find flying to Corfu and taking the hydrofoil to Saranda the cheapest and easiest way to reach Southern Albania. Finikas Lines (www.finikas-lines.com) and Ionian Seaways (www.ionianseaways.com) operate a sometimes-chaotic timetable of ferry and catamaran services between **Corfu and Saranda**. There are up to thirteen sailings a day in the summer and at least one service year-round, with a **journey time** of anything between thirty and ninety minutes. A one-way ticket on a standard ferry costs around €15.

It is also possible to reach Albania **from Italy by sea**. Ventouris Ferries (www.ventourisferries.com) and GNV (www.gnv.it) connect **Durrësi with Bari**. There are two (overnight) sailings a day (10hr) and the return trip costs around €120 for a foot passenger or approximately €450 for a family of four with a car. Adria Ferries (www.adriaferries.com) offers one overnight service (16hr) between **Ancona and Durrësi**, with tickets from €160 for a foot passenger and considerably more if you're taking a car.

Starlines (www.starlines.it) sails from **Brindisi to Vlora** four days a week year-round and daily in the high season (7hr; tickets from €100). A-Ships (www.a-ships.com) operates the same route five days a week from June to September. In the past, there have been services connecting Italy with Saranda, which may restart in coming years. Check www.traghetti.com for more information on ferry routes between Italy and Albania.

If you're travelling with a vehicle in July and August, it's wise to book months in advance for all ferries in the region.

FERRY CONTACTS

Adria Ferries www.adriaferries.com; Ancona–Durrësi.
A-Ships www.a-ships.com; Brindisi–Vlora.

Finikas Lines www.finikas-lines.com; Corfu–Saranda.
GNV www.gnv.it; Bari–Durrësi.
Ionian Seaways www.ionianseaways.com; Corfu–Saranda.
Ventouris Ferries www.ventourisferries.com; Bari–Durrësi.
Starlines www.starlines.it; Brindisi–Vlora.

Visas and entry requirements

All visitors to Albania must have a **valid passport** for the duration of their stay. Citizens of the UK, EU, Canada, Australia, New Zealand, Japan and Israel are allowed to enter Albania without a visa for stays of up to ninety days in any 180-day period. United States citizens can enter ad stay without a visa for one year. Those from other countries should check visa requirements online or with their Albanian embassy or consulate before leaving home. You can find more information in English about visa requirements on the Albanian Foreign Ministry website www.punetejashtme.gov.al.

If you plan to stay longer than ninety days, you will need a **long-stay visa** and sometimes a **residence permit** (and a bureaucratically provable reason to obtain that permit such as work, marriage and so on). If you overstay the allotted time, you will be fined on departure according to how many additional days you remained in the country. Find more information on all visa types and how to apply at www.e-visa.al.

Border crossing checks for visitors travelling into and out of Albania by land (see box) are normally quick and painless.

There are no **customs restrictions** on personal belongings, though you are limited to two hundred cigarettes, one litre of spirits and 500g of coffee. It's a good idea to declare major items – televisions and other electronic equipment – to ensure that you can take them out of the country when you leave. Pets are allowed in to the country, providing you have a recent vaccination certificate.

BORDER CROSSINGS

The main border crossings into Albania if you are driving or travelling by bus are:

- Muriqani–Sukobin for Montenegro (near Shkodra).
- Morina–Vërmica, between Kukësi and Prizreni, for Kosovo.
- Qafë-Thana–Kjafasan, on the main road to Ohrid.
- Tushemishti–Sveti Naum, near Pogradeci, for North Macedonia.
- Kakavija–Ktismata, between Gjirokastra and Ioannina, for Greece.
- Qafë-Bota–Sagiada, to follow the Ionian coast from Saranda into Greece.

ALBANIAN EMBASSIES AND CONSULATES ABROAD

The full list of Albanian embassies and consulates can be found at www.punetejashtme.gov.al/en/perfaqesite-shqiptare-ne-bote.
Australia 13 Culgoa Circuit, O'Malley, ACT 2606, Canberra; www.ambasadat.gov.al/australia/en.
Canada 130 Albert Street, Suite 302 Ottawa, ON, K1P 5G4; https://ambasadat.gov.al/canada.
China Guang Hua Lu, 28, Beijing; www.ambasadat.gov.al/china.
South Africa (Consulate General) Shop G57, Fourways Mall, Bryanston 2055, P O Box 87393, Houghton 2041, Johannesburg.
Switzerland Pourtalesstrasse 45 A, CH-3074 Muri bei, Bern; www.ambasadat.gov.al/switzerland.
UK 33 St George's Drive, London SW1V 4DG; www.ambasadat.gov.al/united-kingdom.
US 2100 S Street, NW; Washington DC 20008; www.ambasadat.gov.al/usa.

Arrival

By plane

Tirana International Airport is located 17km northwest of central Tirana and 32km northeast of Durrësi city centre. The **Rinas Express** shuttle-bus service to Tirana (400 lek/€4; www.luna.al) runs on the hour, every hour, 24 hours a day. Tickets can be booked online in advance or bought on board from the driver using cash or card payment. To find the buses, exit the airport terminal and walk 100m straight through the uncovered car park.

Other buses from here make regular trips to Durrësi, Fieri, Shkodra and Vlora, with no ticket costing more than €12. Find up-to-date schedules and information at www.tirana-airport.com/en/transport-and-directions/15/By-Bus.

The journey by **taxi** into Tirana takes around 25–40 minutes and is set at a fixed price of €22 as of 2024. The trip to Durrësi takes 35–50 minutes and costs €30 for the city centre or €35 for the beach. A taxi to Shkodra will set you back €70, and to Vlora €110. The approved airport service Tia Taxi has a rank outside the arrivals hall (tel: 069 999 9300, www.tiataxi.al). When you're returning to the airport, indicate 'aeroporti' or 'Rinas' as your destination to the driver.

By ferry

Many visitors arriving by ferry are heading for **the riviera**, and all three ports are no further than a 3hr drive from the main resorts along this stretch. If you're making your way to the capital from the coast, it's around a 40min–1hr drive or taxi ride from the Durrësi ferry port to Tirana but almost 4hr from Saranda.

By bus

Tirana has four bus terminals. Most domestic buses use the **South and North Regional Terminal**, which is located just over 4km northwest of the city centre (where Rruga Kastrioti parts from the motorway) and a ten-minute taxi ride. Bus services to and from Elbasani, Korça and other points southeast of Tirana use the **Southeast Regional Bus Terminal** (called 'Student City', or *Qyteti Studenti*), around 2km from the centre near where Rruga e Elbasanit meets Rruga Arben Broci.

Most international buses come and go from the **East Bus Terminal** next to the TEG shopping centre, about 8km southeast of the centre (15–20min by taxi). As of 2024, only a few cross-border bus services still stop at the old **International Station**, 1.8km northwest of the centre (behind the Asllan Rusi Sports Palace just after the big roundabout on Rruga Dritan Hoxha) and within walking distance.

From 7am until 11pm, an hourly shuttle bus (400 lek/€4) from the airport travels to the **Airport Bus Stop**, just behind the Palace of Culture on Skanderbeg Square, dropping passengers at intermediate locations en route by request.

By car

There are only **three motorways** running through Albania – the A1, which links Tirana with Pristina in neighbouring Kosovo; the A2, which runs the short distance between Fieri and Vlora; and the A3, which connects Tirana with Elbasani in Central Albania. Entering Albania by car (see box, page 30 for border crossings) is pretty unexciting these days thanks to improved conditions on the main routes.

As of 2024, there are just a handful of tollbooths in the country, all on the A1, including one between Tirana International Airport and the SH2 to Tirana or Durrësi (€2.50)

By train

A train line between Tirana and Durrësi and Tirana International Airport is currently **under construction**, with no set slated for completion in 2026.

Getting around

Getting around Albania is all part of the adventure. Driving is generally the best way to explore the country, taking the inadequate public transport network out of the equation and allowing you to venture away from the main cities and beach resorts to remoter destinations. Massive improvements to the national road network have made driving much easier than it once was, with many former dirt and rocky tracks now surfaced. Even so, getting from A to B remains time-consuming: many roads are still narrow and bumpy, while winter weather conditions play havoc with transport; snowfall can block routes in the mountains altogether. Traffic in and around Tirana is often borderline dystopian, the streets clogged for kilometres on end. But if you don't have your own wheels, you'll be forced to rely on the country's bus network – not altogether impossible, but the root cause of many a traveller's headache.

By bus

If you don't bring your own car or rent a vehicle, then you'll have to tackle Albania's **bus system**. There is no national carrier; instead, myriad local companies run fleets of buses of all configurations to a somewhat chaotic and uncoordinated timetable. The main cities and towns have bus networks, though finding information online is hit and miss. It might be worth checking the Visit Albania website (www.albania.al), which has limited details on country-wide travel, or one of its regional alternatives, though bear in mind details might not have been updated in some years. Otherwise, you could check the website of the town hall (search '*bashkia*' plus the destination name), which occasionally lists transport details. But probably the best way to find out whether a bus goes where you want it to is to enquire about routes and timetables at your hotel or the local tourist information centre – if there is one. On the plus side, bus tickets are cheap, **tickets** can be bought on board from the driver and once you're on the road, travel is a breeze If your itinerary is focused on major tourist destinations and you arrive in the summer, when service is most reliable, you may find that the bus system spares you a great deal of money and aggravation compared to driving.

If you're venturing further afield to remoter towns and outlying villages (not to mention places in between), you'll likely have to ask around on the ground. With some exceptions, most villages are connected to the nearest municipal centre by a bus that runs once a day in each direction: usually to the village at midday and back to the city early in the morning (around 6 or 7am). Another option is to take an inexpensive **shared minivan or minibus** (*furgon*), which (sometimes) ostensibly runs to a timetable (ask at tourist information centres or bus terminals for up-to-date schedules) but more often than not simply departs when it's full.

There are two websites providing information on routes and departure times: www.etransport.al is the official site, launched by the General Directorate of Road Transport Services in 2024. At the time of writing, it remains clunky to use and incomplete in places, but updates are continuing. An unofficial site, www.travel.gjirafa.com, is generally more accurate, especially if you are travelling in and out of Tirana.

Most cities have intercity buses as well, though you'd most likely only need them in the sprawl of Tirana, Durrësi and Vlora, along with a few other spots noted throughout this Guide. Fares are, across the board, well under 100 lek/€1, but they will be collected, in cash.

By train

The only train service you are likely to use in Albania in coming years is the line between **Tirana and Durrësi** and (more usefully) to Tirana International Airport. That entire stretch of railway was under construction at the time of writing. The state-owned Albanian Railways (Hekurudha Shqiptare) estimates the project to be completed in 2026 and chugs along with regular social media updates in the meantime; find more information at www.hekurudha.al. Until that line is complete, rail service is intermittently available on other routes, such as Elbasani to Durrësi Beach on Fridays, Saturdays and Sundays in summer. Those rides are slow, more for the novelty or nostalgia of the experience than efficient travel, but kids and train enthusiasts may enjoy them. Keep an eye on the Hekurudha Shqiptare Facebook and Instagram pages (linked via website above) for the posting of new schedules and destinations.

By car

On paper, driving is by far the best of getting around Albania. Whether you hire a car or bring your own, having your own wheels saves time hunting for unmarked bus stops and waiting around wondering if a bus is going to show up. But you should brace yourself for an intense experience behind the wheel. **Road conditions** are generally fine until you deviate from the main routes. Steep, winding mountain roads; sudden unpaved sections; animals wandering across the road; and, anywhere in the backcountry, roads only suitable for 4WDs are all common. These are not particularly obvious from maps, though navigation apps like Google Maps, www.mapy.cz and www.maps.me might give some indication of problematic areas (note that Apple Maps is lagging behind, though www.openstreetmap.org is another generally up-to-date resource). Nonetheless, always research where you are going beforehand. If a road looks like a too-good-to-be-true shortcut – it is. Stick to main roads. There is also the added threat of **flash flooding** throughout the year in the northern mountains, while **snowfall and ice** can block or endanger mountain routes around the country between December and March. Rockfall, even on good roads, in the highlands is also a risk. Lighting is generally poor at night, even on newer motorways. Other drivers frequently disregard road rules in favour of a Mario Kart-esque motoring adventure.

City driving presents a fresh set of frustrations. Traffic in Tirana is unrelenting, especially around rush hour, all year. The coast road along the riviera also gets very busy during the summer and clogs up in the areas around the main resort towns; allow extra time for any journey along this stretch. Ditto for summer driving in Durrësi, Berati and Gjirokastra. Beware of unmarked one-way streets and speed bumps, potholes, broken stoplights at major intersections, cyclists or walking dawdling in the street and loiterers who park in traffic lanes.

To drive in Albania, you'll need a **driving licence** and **registration documents** if taking your own car, plus a **Green Card**. Be aware that Kosovo is not part of the Green Card system – you will need to buy fifteen days' insurance at the border if driving a foreign-registered vehicle. If renting a car, you may also need a **1968 International Driving Permit (IDP)**, which UK drivers can easily pick up from the post office for a small fee. International permits are available to US and Canadian travellers through their automobile associations – the AAA and CAA, respectively.

Petrol and parking

Petrol stations are plentiful near most cities, towns and older highways, but be aware that long stretches of rural road – such as in the remote northern mountains – and new highways may lack them. Many stations are open 24 hours a day; in rural areas, there may only be one that remains open at night. However, driving in Albania certainly won't save you any money. **Fuel prices** in late 2024 were some of the highest in Europe (around €1.80 for petrol and diesel), mostly due to high taxes charged by the government. North Americans especially would do well to note that the Albanian for petrol or gasoline is *benzinë*. The much cheaper *gaz* is liquefied petroleum gas, which will not work in your car unless you have a specialized fuel tank for it. (*Dizel* is diesel.)

Parking is not a problem outside of the main cities and popular destinations, where it very much *is* a problem. If driving into Tirana any time of the year or into Durrësi, Berati, Gjirokastra, Vlora or Saranda in the summer, it's strongly advisable to know in advance where the most suitable car parks are and to navigate to one directly (we list some of the best in specific chapters of the Guide).

Don't be tempted to park on the street for free and walk into the centre – car theft and robberies of personal belongings from vehicles are still a problem in Albania. More likely, you'll just get frustrated and/or fined, and most car parks will cost less than five euros for an afternoon (or even a day). **Hotels** often offer free parking to guests.

However, be aware that many short-term rental owners may claim to provide parking, but when you pull up in your three-ton Mercedes-Benz Vito you'll be confronted with a space designed for a Fiat 500 in the late 1980s, likely on a 1 in 5 gradient with nowhere to turn at the top. Never drive up a steep, rocky road without scouting ahead first.

Rules of the road

Like the rest of continental Europe, you drive on the right in Albania. **Speed limits** are relatively low in Albania and generally well signposted but, if not, as a general rule they are typically 40kph in towns, 80–90kph on main roads and highways and 110kph on motorways. It is illegal to drive with more than 0.01 percent alcohol in your bloodstream.

Traffic police are a fairly common presence, and an office will flag you down with a handheld sign; failure to stop will earn you a harsher penalty.

Breakdowns and emergencies

Even if you drive an EU-registered car, make sure your third-party **insurance** covers Albania (it usually does). If you **break down**, contact your insurance company first as many now have agreements with Albanian recovery services (check your policy). Be aware, however, that you may wait a long time for assistance outside Tirana. If you think you have only a minor fault, taking your vehicle to the local village *auto servis* (**mechanic**) can work out a lot quicker, especially with older cars. In rural areas, most Albanians will drop everything to help someone in need, so don't panic. Your best bet is often to walk to the nearest house and rattle off an explanation including the words *makinë* (car) and *problem*. A jump-start, tractor-pull or whatever else you need can often be arranged. If you have mobile data, you can also search a map app and call a nearby *karrotrec* (towing service).

It is worth taking with you an **emergency kit**, including a jack, spare wheel, fan belts, wiper blades, water and overnight food. If you are involved in an **accident**, you'll need to speak to the police (tel: 112).

Car rental

Hiring a car to drive yourself around Albania is not particularly cheap, but it is by far the best way to ensure that you'll be able to take in everything you want to see. **Car rental** here differs from elsewhere else in Europe mainly in that most agencies are single small businesses, so scout local reviews for reputable ones (we've recommended many throughout the Guide). The biggest issue is availability of smaller cars in July and August, so **book well ahead**. The major international chains have offices at Tirana International Airport. On the riviera there are many local hire places if you just need a car for a day or two. Try to take a small car if you plan on city driving or a 4WD if you're intending to venture off paved roads, and don't skimp on price for a robust vehicle or a feature you prefer, such as automatic transmission. Most independent rental offices will only provide insurance coverage for an accident in which the other driver is at fault and scratches or dings you put on the car are often settled with a cash payment. (If you're willing to spend the time, your accommodation host can sometimes help you find a fairer price from a local mechanic.) Be aware that driving off road or on unpaved tracks normally invalidates your insurance policy. If you want to cross from Albania into a neighbouring country, check with the rental agency that your car has the necessary permits, and ask if they can help you obtain a Green Card certificate. The latter you can also purchase yourself at any insurance office, typically for under €20. If you wait until you reach the border crossing, it'll set you back much more.

Taxis

Unless you are driving, you are highly likely to need a taxi at some point. These are mostly inexpensive but best booked through your hotel or restaurant. (In Tirana, you're generally fine to flag one down or find a taxi rank.) Always make sure the meter is switched on before you even think of reaching for the seatbelt. Or, for longer journeys, agree on both a price and a pick-up time and place for your return if necessary: there won't be any cabs to hail in that picturesque hilltop village.

If your stop isn't a popularly known location, you can either show your driver the address on a map or name a nearby toponym, such as a museum, square, large hotel or university building. Uber doesn't exist in Albania, but there are **taxi apps** such as Speed Taxi, UPs Taxi and Taxi.al. Note, though, coverage is not extensive outside the big cities. Find the numbers of reputable local services throughout the Guide. One firm worth remembering in Tirana is Green Taxi (www.green.al), a company with an EV (electric vehicle) fleet that offers fixed prices on trips from the city to the airport, Durrësi and its beaches, Kruja and other nearby destinations, typically at significantly lower prices than others. Because of government subsidies, EV taxis in general are a more cost-effective option. Tips are never required but always appreciated.

Private transfers

If you are looking to traverse a common route, such as from Tirana to the coast, you may be able to pick up a **shared taxi** from outside bus stations. These offer a quicker and more convenient way to travel than by bus, and may only cost a little more money. You can also find details for these services on the Visit Albania website or through your hotel (ask at reception).

By bike

You might be surprised to see just how many locals get around **Tirana** by pedal power. However, this is less the result of environmental awareness, but more a hangover from the days of communist dictatorship when private car ownership was essentially forbidden. It is possible to navigate the capital by bike – in the centre, at least, there is around 20km of well-maintained **cycle paths**. Grand Park in particular is a great place to cycle. There are a couple of **bike-hire places** (see page 68), though other cities and towns are hit or miss. Bikes can be rented in Shkodra, Durrësi, Pogradeci and Berati. Elsewhere, you'll probably need your own two-wheeler, or ask at your hotel if they have bikes available for guests to rent or borrow.

Mountain biking in the northern mountains is becoming increasingly popular and is a great way to see the region. Experienced bikers tackle the **Peaks of the Balkans** trail, typically breaking the 190km circuit into manageable 40–50km sections and taking around five days to complete the entire route. It's challenging but rewarding; take plenty of spare inner tubes, essential parts, basic tools and snack foods.

Other forms of transport

The only other forms of transport you might find yourself aboard is the **cable car** in Tirana and the **ferry** along Lake Komani. One of northern Albania's highlights, in fact, is the Komani–Fierza ferry ride, a serene three-hour 30km cruise along narrow, fjord-like Lake Komani, passing farms and sleepy hamlets tucked into the folds of 1500m-high mountains. Three car ferries shuttle across the lake in summer, with smaller passenger boats stopping off at isolated homesteads – best of which is the half-bus, half-boat Dragobia ferry. Other reliable operators include Komani Lake Ferry (www.komanilakeferry.com), Komani Ferry (www.komaniferry.al) and Alpin (www.alpin.al). Some accept online bookings and offer pick-up and drop-off in Tirana and Shkodra; one-way tickets from 2000 lek/€20. You might also use the **Dajti Ekspres cable car** to scale Mount Dajti (www.dajtiekspres.com), which connects the eastern suburbs of Tirana to the mountain's 1613m-high summit; a return ticket costs €14. There are no domestic flights within Albania.

Accommodation

Albania now has a full range of accommodation, from basic backpacker hostels to luxury five-star international hotels, rustic farm stays to boutique B&Bs. With mass tourism arriving in the country over the past decade, the supply has mushroomed to meet demand, with a flurry of hotels springing up, especially along the riviera. Costs are still relatively low, with the highest rates unsurprisingly at the beach resort hotels on the riviera, which peak during the European summer holidays. In low season, a simple guesthouse in a small town costs peanuts, keeping the destination within the reach of budget travellers – for now. Standards vary erratically, so scour online reviews before making a decision. Use popular booking sites where possible for peace of mind that payment methods are secure.

Hotels

Hotels in Albania range from newly built five-star luxury (such as the new *Tirana Marriott*) to half-renovated communist-era hotels with dodgy plumbing and odd whiffs. There are no national standards, and with such a mixed bag out there it's a good idea to read reviews before booking. **Breakfast** is almost ubiquitous and usually included in the price. Make sure your hotel has **air conditioning** if arriving in

ACCOMMODATION PRICE CODES

Each accommodation reviewed in this Guide is accompanied by a price category, based on the cost of a standard double room in high season. For camping, prices are given per pitch, while for hostels, prices are based on a dorm bed.

€ = Under €35
€€ = €35–60
€€€ = €60–90
€€€€ = Over €90

summer, and note that many coastal hotels close from around October to April.

Guesthouses

A **guesthouse** in Albania can be anything from a converted historical *kulla* (fortified stone tower house) in the north or Gjirokastra to a boutique lodge in Tirana or an Italianate-style city abode in Durrësi. (Especially in rural places or historic houses, a guesthouse is called a *bujtinë*.) Almost all are family-run, with the owners often on site to answer questions and offer advice. Breakfast is usually served – and might be the highlight of your day. In more remote areas, dinner is often offered at a fine price, too. This type of accommodation usually offers a more personal experience, with the chance to engage with locals, taste **home-made food** and gain a better understanding of life in Albania than you might otherwise in a hotel.

Farm stays

The Albanian authorities encourage start-up **farm stays**, called agritourism (*agroturizëm*) here as elsewhere. These promote rural and ideally sustainable development, make sure some of the money tourists bring into the country stays in the local economy and provide new opportunities for struggling farms and villages facing depopulation. Today, farm stays form a significant chunk of the country's accommodation offering. They are, by their very nature, found almost exclusively in the **countryside**. The actual accommodation can differ wildly, from purpose-built luxe chalets to spare rooms in a farmhouse. The biggest plus at these places is usually the food: almost always **home-cooked traditional fare** using the freshest in-season produce. *Agroturizëm* is a great way for visitors to interact with the Albanian community and contribute directly to the local economy. Larger or more established farms may offer guided hikes, horseriding, live traditional music and even massage and other wellness treatments. Some farm stays adhere to national standards set by the government and checked annually by the local tourism board; others simply follow their own family practices. Formerly cheap, some of these places have begun to charge almost Western European prices, but most travellers still find the experience a fulfilling one and good value for money considering the high-quality farm-fresh food, home-made libations and idyllic locations. A digital resource, www.agrotourism.gov.al, can help you find a spot that's your speed.

Hostels

Albania has some great **hostels** that have retained something of the backpacker vibe of yore. As you might expect, the largest concentration is found in cities with a large tourist footfall (Tirana, Shkodra, Berati, Saranda) and they are typically open year-round. Albania's hostels are great places to pick up travel tips, book transfers and meet like-minded buddies. **Facilities** are usually of a decent standard and often include a shared kitchen, laundry service, common areas, wi-fi and even bars and cafés. If you're visiting in summer, make sure dorms have air conditioning – it's pretty essential. Also, try to **book direct** for the best prices.

Camping

Campsites are a relatively new concept in Albania and there certainly aren't anywhere near as many as you find in other Adriatic countries such as Croatia and Slovenia. They are only just beginning to crop up along the riviera, but they have become well established in the northern mountains and some parts of the southeast; **Thethi**, **Valbona** and the **Pogradeci** area of Lake Ohrid have large campsites with both tent pitches and campervan sites with hook-up. **Facilities** range from very basic to modern and comprehensive with shower blocks, self-catering kitchens, wi-fi and waste-disposal points and water for campervans. Many have an attached eatery. Standards really do vary wildly so read reviews.

TOP 5 BACKPACKER HOSTELS

Berat Backpackers Hostel see page 122
Stone City Hostel see page 211
Tirana Backpacker Hostel see page 69
Vlora Backpackers Hostel see page 245
The Wanderers see page 84

Short-term rentals

You'll find an abundance of **short-term rentals** across Albania via the usual suspects, like Airbnb and Booking.com, with typically low rates. However, it's essential to check reviews, particularly for flats and apartments: though interiors tend to be decent, the condition of the buildings and the neighbourhoods in which they reside are not always conducive to holiday bliss. It's debatable how much you are contributing to the local economy by staying in a short-term rental, especially on the riviera where many owners are foreigners. The situation is better in **Tirana**, where a one-bedroom flat in the city centre will cost between €35 and €100 a night on Airbnb. Beware of cheap deals outside the centre where standards could be very low.

Food and drink

Albanian cuisine may not be the world's best known or most celebrated, but food and eating out can provide some of the most memorable experiences you'll have in this country. Outside Tirana and a couple of other big centres, Albanian cooking in restaurants doesn't have to try very hard to remain locally sourced and seasonal – the natural larder of the countryside and sea is bountiful. Dishes are often meat-leaning and hearty, with lamb, beef, chicken and goat as local favourites. Best of all, it's about community and connection, sharing conversation over convivial meals with friends and family.

Albanian cooking has all the elements of Mediterranean and Balkan cuisine, with fresh fruit and veg, olive oil and grilled meats playing a major role on menus and in kitchens across the land. A culinary crossroads for millennia with wild geographic diversity, Albania's table offers Turkish-influenced pastries, Adriatic Italian-style seafood places and more than a few entirely home-grown recipes. Lunch is still generally regarded as the main meal – families often gather for long, leisurely meals in the middle of the day. However, restaurants are set up for tourists for whom it's more convenient to eat a big meal after the sightseeing day is done. On the riviera and in Tirana and other major cities and towns, staff will at the very least be able to discuss the menu in English and some may be able to talk in more detail about dishes and ingredients. Both on and off the tourist track, price doesn't track neatly with quality, and the best spots in town may be incredibly inexpensive. Likewise, don't write off joints with simply, kitschy or tourist decor. In resorts along the coast, expect many restaurants to shutter from October to April.

Albanian specialities

Albanian cuisine is a tasty fusion of Mediterranean and Balkan influences, and if there's one thing the Balkans can agree on, it's ***byrek***, a ubiquitous savoury flaky pastry usually filled with spinach, cheese or minced meat. This can be a snack on the go or part of a meal in a restaurant. Another iconic Albanian dish is ***tavë kosi***, a warming and comforting baked lamb and yoghurt casserole. Tender lamb, marinated with garlic and spices, is combined with a tangy yoghurt and rice mixture, then baked to golden perfection. *Tavë kosi* is regarded as a national dish of Albania and is found throughout the country, especially during festive occasions and family gatherings. ***Fërgesë***, a belly-filling mix of piping-hot ricotta-style cheese, tomatoes, onions and spices, often with bell peppers, beef or liver depending on the region, is another must-try when eating out in Albania. It is often served with crisp, freshly baked bread. The classic Albanian dessert is ***bakllava***, a layered dessert of nuts, honey and filo pastry, very similar to that found in Turkey, Greece and across the Middle East, though usually slightly less sugary. At certain addresses, you can still find some real old-school stuff on the menu, like roast head of lamb or organ-meat soup.

Regional specialities are listed in relevant chapters throughout the Guide.

EATING OUT PRICE CODES

Each restaurant and café reviewed in this Guide is accompanied by a price category, based on the cost of a two-course meal (or similar) for one, including a non-alcoholic drink.

€ = under 1000 lek/under €10
€€ = 1000–2000 lek/€10–20
€€€ = 2000–3000 lek/€20–30
€€€€ = over 3000 lek/over €30

Breakfast

For Albanians, **breakfast** tends to be light to make space for lunch, typically the largest meal of the day in their culture. However, as you will soon discover, hotels and guesthouses cater for foreign sensibilities and often put on a huge spread including pastries such as *byrek*, bread, soft cheese, jams, marmalades, *gliko* (fruit preserved in syrup) fresh fruit and salad. Most accommodation in Albania provides breakfast. In hotels this is normally a buffet where you might find pretty much what you would expect anywhere in Europe but with other Albanian foodstuffs offered as well. In smaller guesthouses breakfast might be cooked to order.

Farm stays can offer an absurdly lavish affair, with dish after dish of home-produced fare. Albanians drink coffee with breakfast, usually an ***ekspres*** (espresso). In the unlikely event your accommodation doesn't supply breakfast, most towns and villages have a café of some description where you can pick up pastries and coffee for a few hundred lek. These open fairly early, typically between 7am and 8am.

Lunch

For locals, the main meal of the day is **lunch**, typically eaten between noon and 2pm, either at home or in a work canteen or nearby restaurant. It can be anything from lamb stew, bean soup or meatballs to pilaf rice, salads and myriad pastry-based dishes. However, tourists might prefer to grab a lighter option like a sandwich, pastry or salad from a local café or taverna. *Byrek* is a popular choice, a filling pastry stuffed with cheese, spinach or meat.

Dinner and eating out

Albanian **restaurants** (*restorant* or *taverna*) differ little from those found across the Balkans and Southern Europe. They range from informal pizza places open from noon till late, to more formal affairs that may only open in the evening. In Tirana you can find all kinds of international cuisine, from Asian fusion to fish and chips, local grilled meat to regional Italian food. Outside the capital there is far less variety. Eating out is still very affordable but not the bargain it was five years ago. A two-course meal in an inexpensive restaurant typically costs between 1000 lek and 2000 lek (€10–25). A traditional dinner or lunch experience is usually well more than two courses, however, often including salad; a *meze* plate of different cheeses, spreads or veggies; another of pastries; one or several hot appetizers like stuffed peppers (*speca të mbushura*) or baked cheese (*djathë në furrë*); and a dish of meat on the bone. Often, which meat you want is the only choice you need to make, and each platter is intended to be shared among two to four.

Albanians tend to see **dining out** as a leisurely experience and waiters may give you more time to consume what you've ordered than you are used to. Many tourists complain of being 'ignored' by waiting staff, but this is likely just down to servers allowing patrons the time they typically would for Albanian guests. Simply flag down a waiter when you're ready to pay.

Dinner is usually eaten later in the evening, somewhere between 8pm and 10pm, with some families dining as late as 11pm. The exact time depends on the region and family traditions, but generally, Albanians linger over dinner, often accompanied by socializing and multiple courses. Nonetheless, restaurants cater to both early-bird tourists and late family gatherings. Reservations are only necessary at popular places in Tirana over the weekend and on the riviera during peak season.

Desserts

Albanian menus are not huge on **desserts** – local puddings and treats are more typically picked up at bakeries and patisseries instead. Perhaps the most popular is *bakllava*, thin layers of filo pastry filled with nuts and honey (cheaper versions use sugar syrup). *Tullumbë* is like an Albanian doughnut soaked in syrup, while *kadaif* consists of shredded dough with a sweet

TOP 5 PLACES TO EAT LIKE A LOCAL

Mrizi i Zanave Agroturizëm Near Lezha, this agrotourism restaurant combines farm-to-table dining, eco-friendly practices and bucolic views. See page 104

Agroturizëm Gjepali Just outside Durrësi, this professionally run farm stay offers a stylishly countryside restaurant and wine cellar. See page 148

Mësonjëtorja Some of the tastiest takes on traditional Southeast Albanian cuisine can be found at this photo-filled restaurant in Korça. See page 169

Taverna e Kasapit The home-made food here is as typically Albanian as you can find in the capital. See page 70

Fig and Olive Arguably the best place to eat in the holiday resort of Himara. See page 253

REGIONAL CUISINE

Although many Albanian restaurants now offer a standard version of what is regarded as Albanian cuisine, local and traditional dishes reflect regional differences that have been shaped by geography, climate, cultural influences and invaders. In **the north**, the cooking is hearty, featuring **meat-based dishes** like *tavë kosi* (baked lamb with yogurt). The colder climate means more preserved meats and full-fat dairy. More influenced by **Ottoman cuisine**, the **central regions** of Albania are known for their **stews** and **rice dishes**. Along the **coast**, particularly to the south, the focus is firmly on **seafood**, **olive oil**, and more **Mediterranean flavours**. The dishes found in the **far south** also show **Greek influences**, using more **vegetables**, **herbs** and **cheeses** like feta. One ubiquitous dish you will find everywhere is *picë* (**pizza**), which is almost as good as in its native Italy, thanks to many Albanian pizza chefs learning their trade there.

filling. *Trileçe* is the Albanian take on chilled tres leches cake, available to go in most bakeries. *Shëndetlie* is a honey and walnut cake served on festive occasions. *Çorbë* is a rice and milk dish often made as a dessert, sometimes flavoured with rosewater. *Pite* is a layered pastry filled with pumpkin or apple, a kind of sweet *byrek*, though savoury versions are also available.

Drinks

Albania offers the full range of Western **soft drinks** as well as local sodas of varying quality. For a more traditional non-alcoholic beverage, opt for fresh **fruit juices**, often made with local pomegranates, citrus, berries, peaches and melons. As a rule, never drink tap water or ask for it in restaurants, especially in large towns and cities – **bottled water** is widely available and cheap.

Wine

Albanian **wine** has a history going back thousands of years so they must be doing something right. Local winemakers use both indigenous grape varieties such as Shesh i Bardhë, Shesh i Zi, Pulës, Dëbinë and Kallmet as well as better-known Cabernet Sauvignon, Merlot and Sangiovese. With its hot summers and long, warm autumns, the country's Mediterranean climate provides ideal conditions for viticulture. The areas around **Berati** (see page 125), **Durrësi**, **Lezha** and **Përmeti** are known for producing some of the best wines in the country. However, foreign wines are increasingly available in many restaurants, especially cheap plonk from other former communist countries and Italy.

Beer

It may be interesting to discover that Albania produces some very drinkable **beers**. Some of the most popular brands include Tirana, from the country's largest brewery, founded in 1960, known for its light, refreshing lagers, and Korça, from the city of the same name. In recent years, there has also been surge in craft beer, with microbreweries producing all manner of concoctions for the supping public. One of the best is from Puka in the mountainous north. In big cities, imported beers are making inroads, with brews from Italy, Scandinavia, the Netherlands, the Czech Republic and Ireland often available on tap.

Coffee

Coffee is a big part of everyday life for Albanians and is widely available in cafés, restaurants and from kiosks. At home, many prepare coffee in a traditional copper *xhezve*, bringing the mixture of finely ground Arabica, sugar and water to the boil several times to intensify the flavour; locals often sweeten the brew with lots of sugar but rarely add milk. However, on the streets you are not that likely to come across this kind of traditional 'Turkish' coffee, with Italian-style espresso (*ekspres*) having taken over completely. Many Albanians have lived and worked in Italy which greatly influences their coffee choices these days. Cappuccino and macchiato are available at almost any café.

Raki

Of all the drinks you'll come across in Albania, ***raki*** is probably the best known, not to be confused with anise-flavoured Turkish *rakı*. Most Balkan countries have a version of this brandy, but Albanian *raki* is special. It is distilled from a range of fruits but mainly grapes. However, in some places you might find plum, mulberry and even walnut variations. At between forty to fifty percent volume, this is strong stuff – the alcohol content of home-made *raki* can be as high as eighty percent; you've been warned. Unlike vodka in Poland or *slivovice* in the Czech Republic, *raki* is sipped, not downed in one. It is always served neat, never with ice. A recent development is the *raki* cocktail which you may now come across in hip bars in big cities. Traditionally, the spirit is drunk at celebrations, to toast guests and as a digestif. A bottle of good-quality Albanian *raki* makes for a superb souvenir from your trip – these are available from supermarkets and souvenir shops, though the best examples come home-made from agritourism outfits. See page 184 to learn more about *raki*.

The media

Along with the public broadcaster RTSH, there are a few privately owned major media outfits – including Top Channel, TV Klan and Vizion Plus – not to mention a plethora of local stations. In terms of radio, RTSH channels jostle for Albanians' attention with two national commercial stations and lots of smaller local outfits. The BBC broadcasts on 103.9FM in Tirana.

Although an independent body regulates public broadcasters alongside a self-regulating press, there are concerns over the power wielded by a handful of companies who own much of the media landscape. Private media outlets often have links to the political world through lucrative industries like construction, and these business interests compromise **press freedom and independence**. In 2024, Albania was ranked 99th in the World Press Freedom Index, a huge drop from its 84th position in 2020. This drop is hardly surprising when owners of television channels often dictate editorial content and acts of intimidation against journalists are not uncommon. Independent outlets have reported that their work in hampered by a lack of transparency from the government.

Albanians have a **strong online profile**, with around 76 percent of the population online by 2022; Facebook tops the list of social networks, with Instagram snapping at its heels.

Newspapers, magazines and online news

There are plenty of local newspapers and news websites. Not many are published in English, but most are online, and articles can easily be translated. In terms of keeping up with the news in Albania on your travels, *Tirana Times* is an **English-language weekly** worth reading, or you can check the English-language **website** *Albanian Daily News*. Also online, *Euronews Albania* maintains and complete and comprehensive English-language edition. In Tirana you might be able to pick up the foreign press a day or two later, but this is now rare and expensive.

Television and radio

There are very few Engl sh-language television and radio channels in Albania.

Festivals

Albania hosts a truly impressive number of festivals and events throughout the year, large and small, which tend to celebrate culture and traditions and offer an opportunity to try local food and drink. Some are low-key affairs, but others – such as the Tirana International Film Festival and Gjirokastra's National Folk Festival – can be wonderfully boisterous, featuring national dance, street performances and an abundance of wine and beer stalls. Some festivals are also public holidays, which may result in the closure of tourist attractions and affect public transport. Accommodation can be sparse and traffic plentiful during long weekends. The major festive occasions of Albania's four primary religions – Sunni Islam, Catholicism, Orthodox Christianity and Bektashi (Sufi) Islam – are all public holidays.

Festival calendar

JANUARY–MARCH

New Year's Eve and Day The last night and first day of the year can be a boisterous affair with lots of festivities. As a formerly atheist communist country with a penchant for fireworks, Albania counts New Year's as the biggest bash of all.

Summer Day Somewhat confusingly, Summer Day is in fact a spring holiday in March. An ancient pagan Albanian celebration that endures around the country, it is marked by bonfires, feasts, special costumes and desserts.

APRIL–JUNE

Easter The biggest event in the Christian calendar, with processions on the evening of Good Friday, midnight Mass on Easter Eve, and lots of eating, drinking and games on Easter Sunday and Monday.

South Outdoor Festival https://southoutdoor.al. Major riviera festival with DJs, concerts, guided outdoor activities, sports and food. April or May; Borschi.

Swing Marathon www.hemingway.al. Three-day jazz marathon at Tirana's *Hemingway Bar* and on a vintage train to Shkodra. April; Tirana and Shkodra.

International Cultural Weeks https://www.jkn.al. Seven-month-long festival that sees the capital celebrate the culture of a different country every week. May–November; Tirana.

National Folk Festival www.gjirokaster.al. Gjirokastra's biggest party is the National Folk Festival of traditional song and dance, held in the castle every five years. It draws thousands from across every region of the country. June; Gjirokastra.

Unum Festival www.unumfestival.com. One of the longer-running and bigger-ticket beachfront EDM festivals among several in Albania, Unum goes all day, all night, all week, with internation and local turntable talent on stage. June; Shëngjini.

JULY AND AUGUST

Korça Beer Fest www.festaebirres.com. Albania's answer to Oktoberfest takes place in Korça and is the country's top ale bash. August; Korça.

Porto Palermo Festival www.portopalermofestival.com. Musical performances held in the atmospheric fort of Porto Palermo. August; Porto Palermo.

Solar Festival https://solarfestival.al. International DJs bring the party tunes to Saranda's seafront, with pulsing sets lasting into the night. July or August; Saranda.

SEPTEMBER AND OCTOBER

Tirana Marathon www.tiranamarathon.com. Albania's top running event featuring a full-blown marathon, half-marathon, a 10k and a fun run. October; Tirana.

Oda Dibrane Music Festival www.albania.al. Big folk festival attracting ensembles from across the Albanian-speaking world. October; Peshkopia.

Wine & Stories Festival www.berat.al. Week-long food and wine festival on Berati's Bulevardi Republika, the most popular wine fest and competition in Albania. October; Berati.

Harvest festivals Towns and villages across Albania have weekends devoted to celebrating the harvest, for tomatoes, apples, walnuts, olives, cherries and much more. Expect food, drink, music and DIY fruit-picking. September to November.

NOVEMBER AND DECEMBER

Tirana International Film Festival www.tiranafilmfest.org. A candidate for Tirana's biggest festival, with domestic and international film screenings. November; Tirana.

Christmas Albanians of all faiths celebrate the Christmas season, with major festive and winter markets and citywide cheer in Tirana, Berati, Korça and beyond. On 25 December, families gather to give gifts and share meals. Some hotels and restaurants shutter for the winter holiday week, but it's always festive.

Sports and outdoor activities

Albania is on the radar of in-the-know travellers for its varied landscapes and the opportunities for adventure within them. There are plentiful outdoor activities on offer, from hiking and mountain biking in the northern mountains to snorkelling on the riviera and river rafting on the Vjosa or Osumi. As Albania grows in popularity as a tourist destination, it is undoubtable that more and more adventure operators will jump on the bandwagon, making these experiences more accessible than ever.

Hiking

The northern mountains are the obvious venue for a hiking-focused trip in Albania. The route between Thethi and Valbona is the best-known, and the **Peaks of the Balkans** trail passes through the area, but there are countless other paths in the region and the infrastructure to bed and feed hikers. Other good areas for hiking are around Peshkopia where you can make a day ascent of **Mount Korabi**, Albania's highest peak, and around the bases of **Kukësi** and **Bajram Curri**. There are also excellent routes of varying length and intensity between upland villages of the **riviera**; in the **Drino Valley** of the southwest; around the **Prespa Lakes** and **Shebeniku-Jabllanica National Park** in the southeast; through the **canyons** of **Osumi**, **Holta**, **Nivica** and **Lëngarica**; and even in the mountains ringing **Tirana**. Hikes in the north are easy to organize and safe enough to attempt without a guide, even with limited experience of hiking in mountainous terrain, but other highlands, such as **Mount Tomorri**, are best tackled with someone who knows the lay of the land. All Albania's mountainous regions are remote and can experience harsh weather in winter, with some mountain passes closing due to heavy snowfall between December and March so it's best to ask around locally about conditions and keep an eye on the weather forecast. Late spring and autumn are the best times for high-altitude hikes in terms of manageable temperatures. The hiking app of choice in Albania is **Wikiloc** (www.wikiloc.com), and it's worth subscribing to access maps and routes offline. As anywhere, hike with a buddy if you plan to be out for a spell or tackling challenging terrain.

Cycling

Mountain biking is increasing in popularity, particularly in the north, with many marked trails and growing infrastructure to keep cyclists pedalling. Some of the best routes are around **Thethi** (essentially following hiking routes) and in the **Dajti Mountain National Park**, but there are countless other options such as a circuit of Butrint National Park, a cruise around Himara on the riviera or a loop around Lake Ohrid, which takes bikers into North Macedonia. The only problem is that you'll need to **bring your own mountain bike** as outside Tirana there are precious few rental outfits. However, if you are without wheels and looking to hire a bike, the best places to start are tourist information centres and backpacker hostels.

When it comes to using bikes to get around, Tirana has a surprisingly good cycle-path network, and many locals use two-wheelers to travel around the city. The capital has a number of hire centres, even for e-bikes (see page 68).

Watersports

On the riviera watersports aren't a huge part of the holiday mix but in some of the main resorts such as **Himara** and **Saranda** there are operators and hire places. If you specifically want to try **windsurfing**, stand-up **paddleboarding** (SUP) or SUP yoga, **Velipoja**, near Shkodra, is a good destination to head for; try Albanian Watersports (www.albanianwatersports.com) for guided tours, lessons and gear. Beaches north of Durrësi can get ideal conditions for surf, too. **Swimming** is an obvious water-based activity you can organize yourself. The finest **snorkelling** spots are along the Karaburuni Peninsula and Sazani Island, reachable by boat from Vlora or Dhërmiu.

Running

Running is an activity that is only just taking off in Albania. The top running event in the country is the **Tirana Marathon** in October, but other minor races are being added every year.

If you are a trail runner, the northern mountains are a superb place to train, with hundreds of kilometres of vert and lots of rewarding routes especially out of the remote villages of Thethi and Valbona. In recent years, more and more trail runners have become aware of the allure of the **Peaks of the Balkans** (see page 90).

Other activities

Even inland, water lovers are becoming spoiled for choice in Albania, and **river rafting** has become a popular way to spend an afternoon. Unless you're lucky (or unlucky?), you likely won't catch wild, thrashing rapids, but the best spots to rush along are the **Vjosa River** near Përmeti, the **Osumi River** near Berati and the **Shkumbini River** near Elbasani. Trained guides provide good-quality gear and rafts, usually with high safety standards.

There are many **thermal springs** that bring up warm, soothing, therapeutic waters, especially in the **Lëngarica Canyon** near Përmeti, **Sarandapori** in the far southeast and **Peshkopia** in the northeast.

For **fishing**, it's hard to wrong with **Lake Ohrid**, while **birdwatching** opportunities abound between winter and late spring. **Divjaka-Karavasta National Park** has a wealth of biodiversity, particularly in the skies, but most protected lakes and lagoons in Albania will delight ornithologists. Alight on **Butrint Lagoon**

TOP 3 NATIONAL PARKS

Albania has a total of twelve national parks, the newest signed into law in 2023. Acquiring reliable information on Albania's national parks in advance is difficult, with a sparsity of logistical detail even on the website of the National Agency of Protected Areas (Agjencia Kombëtare e Zonave të Mbrojtura; www.akzm.gov.al).

Dajti Mountain National Park Lying just outside Tirana's cityscape and linked to the eastern suburbs by cable car, the Dajti Mountain National Park (Parku Kombëtar Mali i Dajtit) is Albania's most accessible. Sprawling across three hundred square kilometres, the park is crisscrossed with hiking trails and mountain-bike routes that encourage tourists to discover the regional flora and fauna without damaging it. The highlight is Lake Bovilla (Ligeni i Bovillës), a vivid turquoise-hued reservoir that provides household water for the capital. See page 66

Alps of Albania National Park An amalgamation of the Thethi and Valbona Valley national parks, the mountainous Alps of Albania National Park (Parku Kombëtar Alpet e Shqipërisë) is by far Albania's most dramatic. Offering the country's best altitude hiking, its untouched landscapes take in isolated valleys and high passes framing fine views. Thethi and Valbona are the main service centres, both now accessible by road. See page 87

Butrint National Park In the far south of the country, this wild pocket of lakes, marshes, reedbeds and islands is an important habitat for birds and many other species that thrive in wetlands. The highlights of Butrint National Park (Parku Kombëtar i Butrintit) for visitors are the Ksamili Islands and the Butrint archaeological site. See page 264 south of the riviera or **Lake Prespa** in the southeast with your binoculars.

In a country where you can hardly avoid tripping over phenomenal mountain ranges, **climbing** is gaining traction, and the number of routes with bolts and fixed pins is increasing. Climbers gravitate, naturally, to the **Albanian Alps** around Thethi and Valbona, but the canyon behind **Gjipeja (Gjipe) Beach** on the riviera near Vunoi is also an emerging destination. Find more detailed information at www.climbingalbania.com.

If you're less surefooted, perhaps opt for **horseback treks** instead. You can take riding lessons, hacks into the highlands and even multiday excursions from ranches and farms around **Korça** and **Kolonja** in the southeast, and from **Gjirokastra** and **Përmeti** in the southwest.

And believe it or not, there's **skiing** here too in the winter. The only full-service piste is near **Dardha** in the southeast, as well as a slope in **Puka** in the north.

Shopping

Handicrafts, raki, wine, olive oil, honey, mountain tea, *qilim* (kilim) rugs, local art, Skanderbeg statues, Albanian flags, bunker fridge magnets and communist-era trinkets are just some of the items that weigh down suitcases in the departures hall at Tirana International Airport. Prices for most souvenirs are the same as in Western Europe. On the riviera there's an increasing amount of tat for sale, some of it made god knows where or by whom. At the same time, the overall quality and availably of traditional Albanian take-homes has shot up, and artisanal keepsakes are replacing mass-produced knickknacks in souvenir shops. Haggling will probably get you nowhere these days.

Foodies can pick up some excellent gourmand finds to take home with them, such as Albanian **honey**, particularly from the mountains of Southeast Albania or the Valbona Valley, where it's renowned for its purity and intense flavour. Varieties include meadow, chestnut and forest honey. **Jams and preserves** made from local figs, cherries, plums and berries and **bakllava** are also wonderful souvenirs to take home with you. **Olive oil** (*vaj ulliri*) is another worthwhile buy, produced across Albania and of reasonable quality; buy direct from local makers to reduce the risk of it being cut with other inferior oils.

You might also like to pick up a bottle or two of **wine** from Albania's top viticultural regions – most notably Berati and Durrësi – which are of high quality and pretty much unavailable outside the country's borders. Look for wine made using Albania's native grape varieties – Shesh i Bardhë (White Shesh), Shesh i Zi (Black Shesh) and Kallmet. **Raki** is another option, which you can easily pick up from supermarkets though any home-made stuff your agritourism host plies you with will be far superior.

Notable artisanal shops are highlighted throughout this Guide, if you're in the market for lace, stone carvings, oil paintings, wool rugs, folk garments and more. There are now clusters of vendors selling fine made-in-Albania goods in Tirana Castle, the Gjirokastra Bazaar and the Kruja Bazaar. For other shopping – say for food or everyday items – Albania has plenty of supermarkets and small convenience stores. The Italian supermarket chain Conad has outlets in Tirana and a handful of bigger cities. Interspar also has a presence. Tirana has a number of Western-standard shopping centres (see page 71).

Markets are disappointing in Albania – they're rarely the Mediterranean bazaars overflowing with fresh produce that most expect. Very often stalls are given over to cheap, low-grade clothing and footwear and battered second-hand clothes.

Travelling with children

Albania is unlikely to present problems to travellers with children. Shops in the main cities are full of anything you might need to buy for your kids and locals are very welcoming to families. While Tirana's communism-themed museums, bunkers and art museums will bore young kids to tears, a ride on the cable car to the top of Mount Dajti or days on the beach by the Adriatic will form memorable and enjoyable experiences.

Albania has lots of food little ones will enjoy (and lots they won't), there are animals galore to spot in the wild and in general there's plenty to do to stimulate young minds. You may need to keep a more attentive eye on children than back home – researching this Guide we saw holes at Rozafa Castle down which a small child could fall and never be recovered. Safety in general across Albania can be woeful, so it's essential to keep a beady eye on where tots wander – and where you step, too.

Children under 5 travel free on ferries and **public transport**, while under-16s pay half-fare. **Hotels** charge by the room, with a small supplement for an additional bed or cot, and many offer family rooms. Some Tirana **restaurants** offer children's menus at a reduced price, though this is rare in the countryside. In terms of practicalities, **disposable nappies** are available at most pharmacies and supermarkets in Tirana and larger towns, but less available elsewhere. Same for **baby foods** and **milk powders**, so bring your own if this is likely to be a concern. Breastfeeding in public, even discreetly, is likely to draw stares. You'll be hard-pressed to find highchairs and dedicated changing facilities in remoter locations, though you might come across them in more modern cafés and restaurants in Tirana and the main cities.

Culture and etiquette

There are very few cultural pitfalls to watch out for in Albania. The country is generally a relaxed place where people don't mind too much what you do. Even if you do accidentally commit a social faux pas, locals are unlikely to take enormous offence. However, there are a handful of things to be aware of to ensure your trip runs smoothly.

Clothing

Things are fairly liberal when it comes to **clothing** in Albania. The only time you should adjust your apparel is when visiting active mosques, Bektashi shrines and churches. Before entering mosques and shrines, you'll need to remove your shoes, and in both churches and mosques you should dress conservatively; women should cover their heads, shoulders and legs. Men should not wear a hat in Orthodox or Catholic places of worship.

Elderly and children

Albanians show much respect to the **elderly**. Travelling with **children** opens up a whole new dimension and will bring you into closer contact with locals.

Smoking

There is a **smoking ban** in all enclosed spaces, but this is often ignored – mainly in bars, almost never in restaurants or hotels. People tend to observe the ban on public transport.

Other customs

Always **remove your shoes** when you enter a home, including in short-term rentals like Airbnb. English-speaking Albanians like to engage foreigners in conversation on a whole variety of topics, though it is best to **avoid political discussions**, especially around the status of Kosovo, Serbia, LGBTQ+ rights and so on. Even with strangers, Albanians will gladly go to town on the absolute state of the government and economy, and sometimes like to chat religion and international affairs. No cause for alarm, but debate respectfully, stick to what you know and don't air judgment on things you may not. Finally, don't be taken aback by forthright-seeming questions, which are friendly in intent: what's your job, how old are you, are you married – well, why not?

Travel essentials

Accessible travel

It must be said that Albania is decades behind the rest of Europe when it comes to **accessibility**. Only the newest of hotels in big cities have any disabled facilities whatsoever; the odd museum may have ramps and lift access. Albania's cities are cobbled with lots of steps and unexpected rough and uneven ground. As of 2024, very few companies offered tours for those needing accessible facilities and assistance, but this may be changing. That being said, locals are extremely helpful towards anyone with a disability and will go out of their way to assist where possible. It's a good idea, however, to stick to **newer hotels** on the riviera or in Tirana where facilities are in better shape generally. When it comes to public transport, Albania must be one of Europe's worst countries for accessibility and it is advisable to arrange **private transfers** when moving around.

Costs

Albania is perceived as a 'cheap' destination and if you are travelling from Zurich or Los Angeles, it probably is. However, it's definitely not the bargain trip it was just a few short years ago. Albanians are now well aware of how much money people in Western Europe pay for things and charge accordingly. But it is still possible to come across excellent deals, especially off the beaten path or outside the peak tourist season.

If you stay in a **backpacker hostel**, use public transport and buy locally made food, you could in theory spend less than €40/4000 lek a day. Staying in

ROUGH GUIDES TRAVEL INSURANCE

Looking for travel insurance? Rough Guides partners with top providers worldwide to offer you the best coverage. Policies are available to residents of anywhere in the world, with a range of options whether you are looking for single-trip, multi-country or long-stay insurance. There's coverage for a wide range of adventure sports, 24-hour emergency assistance, high levels of medical and evacuation cover and a stream of travel safety information. Even better, roughguides.com users can take advantage of these policies online 24/7, from anywhere in the world – even if you're already travelling. To make the most of your travels and ensure a smoother experience, it's always good to be prepared for when things don't go according to plan. For more information go to http://roughguides.com/bookings/insurance.

a **midrange hotel** or farm stay, eating one restaurant meal a day and travelling by taxi would push costs over the €100/10,000 lek mark per day. Sleeping in **upmarket hotels**, eating out every meal and using taxis and private transfers will cost upwards of €200/20,000 lek per day, though the sky is the limit in Tirana and on the coast. All of the above are estimates – how much you spend on holiday is a purely personal matter.

Crime and personal safety

Despite what you might have seen in the movies or read on the internet, Albania is a generally **safe destination**. Albania's crime index is on the same level as Canada's and lower than most European big cities. However, **theft** is an issue in some places, especially along the riviera and in crowded locations in Tirana. As in all big cities, it is best to be vigilant and follow the usual safety precautions: don't flash expensive gear on your person (especially newer smartphones); don't carry large sums of cash; leave at least one debit card in your hotel safe; and avoid wandering around unsafe neighbourhoods at night.

Drinking water

Most tap water in Albania is **not drinkable**, though not dangerous for rinsing or brushing your teeth. Especially if you're visiting in the hot summer months, **always keep bottled water to hand**. You may find it most convenient to buy it as Albanians do, by the 7-litre or 10-litre jug, refilling your own bottles as necessary and cutting down on plastic waste. Certain high-elevation cities near water sources, such as Korça, do have safe, drinkable tap water. You may see springs with fountains near trails or roads in mountain areas; such spring water is also clean and refreshing.

EMERGENCY PHONE NUMBERS

General emergency number 112
Police 129 (state police) or 126 (traffic police)
Ambulance 127
Fire 128
Lifeguard 125
Emergency at sea 125

Electricity

Albania uses 230V/50Hz. Visitors from the UK and the US will need a **two-pin adapter**. Occasionally in older properties there are non-standard two-pin sockets where the holes are too small for modern European plugs, but this is now relatively rare.

Health

Most travellers to Albania will have **no required vaccinations**, but check your embassy's website for the latest information. It is always wise to be up to date with your polio, tetanus, typhoid and hepatitis inoculations. Most public hospitals (found in cities and major towns) have Accident and Emergency departments, which provide free emergency treatment to all. More routine treatment will have to be paid for so **travel insurance** is highly recommended. Neither the European Health Insurance Card (EHIC) nor the Global Health Insurance Card (GHIC) are valid in Albania. There are **hospitals and clinics** in most of the major cities and towns, though those in Tirana are generally the best equipped. To access **emergency care**, call 112 or 127. Most towns will have at least one **pharmacy** for dealing with common minor complaints and ailments, and staff usually speak a little English.

There are certain health issues you need to be aware of in Albania. You may encounter large dogs, especially in the mountains, but a bite from one of these, while nasty, carries little danger of rabies. A greater danger comes from brushing up against ticks, which can pass on encephalitis, in grassy, forested areas. It's always a good idea to be vaccinated against this if you travel often to Central and Eastern Europe. Sunstroke is a risk that can be easily avoided by staying out of direct sun and staying hydrated. Inevitably, a combination of heat and eating foods you may not be used to can result in a bout of travellers' tummy. This usually clears up within a couple of days but if symptoms persist for any longer, Imodium should do the trick. Finally, try to **avoid swallowing any seawater** while swimming in the sea. Albania still pumps sewage into the sea and bacteria in the water can give you a very nasty stomach bug indeed. Air quality is generally fine to good around the country, but if you're sensitive to pollutants, it may be worth checking a daily index online for Tirana. **Road traffic** remains a higher cause of injury and death than in most European countries, but road safety is improving.

Internet

High-speed internet is as ubiquitous in Albania as it is everywhere in Europe. Rare is the guesthouse or hotel that doesn't have free guest access. The only exceptions are places in the mountains where there is poor signal, though these are becoming rarer.

LGBTQ+ travellers

Albania has comprehensive anti-discrimination laws, though same-sex marriage sadly remains illegal. The gay and lesbian communities are not very visible, general attitudes are conservative and it's rare to come across self-declared gay bars/clubs or LGBTQ+ organizations. That said, Tirana's alternative **nightlife scene** is increasingly **inclusive** of the queer community. But in general, as in much of the Balkans, LGBTIQ+ travellers are generally advised to exercise discretion and caution.

Maps

Probably the best offline (and online) map app to use in Albania is the Czech **Mapy.cz** (https://en.mapy.cz), which shows the country in superb detail and makes navigation easy. Google Maps may be better for searching for specific businesses. Paper maps for Albania can be problematic as the country is changing faster than publishers can update cartography. **Maps.me** and **OpenStreetMap** (www.openstreetmap.org) are also reliable. For hiking and outdoor trails, **Wikiloc** (www.wikiloc.com) is the most comprehensive.

Money

The Albanian currency is the **lek**. There are 5, 10, 20, 50, 100 lek coins and 200, 500, 1000, 2000, 5000 and (rare) 10,000 lek notes. Euros are widely accepted at most businesses and vendors that primarily serve tourists; dollars and other currencies less so.

ATMs

In cities, **ATMs** (cash machines) can be found in banks and in places with heavy footfall. In Tirana they are as frequent as any other capital city in Western Europe, but in smaller towns, there may be only one, and in villages, none. There are virtually no ATMs in the northern mountains or rural southeast so make sure you take cash with you. As always, shield your hand when entering your PIN to protect your card details. It's also preferable to use ATMs within banks, which are monitored by CCTV. There's no escaping high withdrawal fees (often upwards of 500 lek/€5), but always decline the operating bank's suggested currency conversion rate if given the option.

Cards vs cash

Cash is king in Albania, and you do need to **carry some money** in Albania, especially when visiting markets, buying drinks or snacks from kiosks and travelling via taxi or bus. Beyond Tirana, expect to pay in cash at small restaurants, guesthouses, markets, some hotels and even petrol stations, and if you're heading somewhere rural, be sure to **withdraw enough cash to cover your expenses** while you have access to an ATM. Some businesses may advertise credit or debit card payments, but card readers are known to break. Carry some euro notes to avoid withdrawing or exchanging money at the airport on arrival, and don't forget to spend or exchange your lek notes before you return home.

Opening hours and public holidays

In the main cities, **shops** are usually open between 8am and 7pm in the summer, though smaller towns and villages might close in the afternoon for a **siesta** (any time between noon and 4pm). Most shops are closed on Sundays. **Banks** are typically open Monday to Friday between 9am and 3pm; government offices also typically close by mid-afternoon. On the main **public holidays**, banks and shops are usually closed (see box). **Cafés** tend to follow longer hours, opening at 8am for morning coffees and pastries and staying open any time up until midnight for serving dinners and drinks. **Restaurants**, too, serve patrons late into the evening though will usually open later, around

PUBLIC HOLIDAYS

January 1 New Year's Day
January 2 New Year's Holiday
March 14 Summer Day
March 22 Nevruz Day
March/April Easter
April Eid al-Fitr (End of Ramadan)
May 1 International Worker's Day
April/May Orthodox Easter
June 16 Eid al-Adha (Feast of Sacrifice)
September 5 Saint Teresa Sanctification Day
November 22 Alphabet Day
November 28 Flag and Independence Day
November 29 Liberation Day
December 8 National Youth Day
December 25 Christmas Day
Varies Eid al-Fitr (End of Ramadan)
Varies Eid al-Adha (Feast of Sacrifice)

11am in time for lunch. Outside Tirana, opening hours for businesses and attractions, especially smaller ones, can be frustratingly arbitrary. If you have your heart set on a visit, call ahead.

Phones

In order to use your **mobile phone** in Albania, check with your service provider first. Many European and North American companies enable customers to use their phone in Albania as at home, but UK companies may not. In this case, an **e-SIM** may be the answer; Airalo is one of the most reliable on the market. Buying an Albanian SIM to use temporarily in your phone may seem like a good idea, but you could lose access to services and contacts you need by doing so. This is only advisable if you are staying for an extended period in the country. Prepaid SIM cards for tourists can be purchased inexpensively from Vodafone or ONE Telecom stores. Virtually every person and business in Albania with a mobile uses WhatsApp.

GSM signal is not as widespread as you may be used to. In mountainous areas, service may be limited to villages and towns only.

Photography

There are no specific rules around where you can or cannot take photos in Albania. Though, obviously, a little caution should be exerted around **active mosques**, **monasteries** and **military installations**. Always ask local people for **permission** before you photograph them. Some stallholders in markets may not be too happy about you snapping their produce.

Post

In the unlikely event you need send a letter or postcard, every small town has at least one branch of **Posta Shqiptare** (Albanian Post; www.postashqiptare.al). Postage stamps are only available from post offices. If you want to send a parcel home, you can find an international DHL service point in nearly every sizeable city, plus FedEx and UPS in Tirana. For sending or receiving international mail, these are far more reliable options than the national post.

Time

Albania is in **Central European Time** (CET), which is one hour ahead of GMT and six hours ahead of EST, with the clocks going forward in spring for summertime and back again in autumn.

Tipping

It's customary and polite to tip staff at cafés, bars and restaurants, and for guided tours. It's appreciated, if less expected, to tip taxi drivers and food delivery staff as well. Small change suffices at a café, and a few lek notes (around ten percent) is typical for sit-in drinks and meals. Outstanding service with extra dishes comped should be recognized with more. Though tipping is not mandatory, remember that wages are very low in Albania; the cost of living is outpacing residents; and a small amount in your country will go a long way in many parts of this one.

Tourist information

Albania's **tourist service** is patchy and erratic. Each municipality chooses whether to fund a tourist information centre and any accompanying services such as websites, publications and so on. Some towns have fully functioning visitor centres; others have nothing whatsoever. We have listed tourist information centres for specific cities and towns, where available, throughout the Guide.

Visit Albania (www.albania.al) is the official national tourism ministry's website for visitors, and it may offer inspiration. Other local websites can be AI-generated chaff with no specifics or helpful information. Emails to tourist offices go largely ignored, but staff are helpful enough if you turn up in person.

CALLING HOME FROM ABROAD

To make an international call, dial the international access code (00), then the destination's country code, before the rest of the number. Note that the initial zero is omitted from the area code when dialling the UK, Ireland, Australia and New Zealand from abroad.

Australia international access code + 61
New Zealand international access code + 64
UK international access code + 44
US and Canada international access code + 1
Ireland international access code + 353
South Africa international access code + 27

Often, better sources of information are Facebook pages, Instagram accounts, traveller blogs and even hotel, hostel and tour-operator websites and social media pages. If you are venturing beyond Tirana and the riviera, it's best not to rely on Tripadvisor, which can be extremely out of date and inaccurate for remote destinations. Always check the year that customer reviews were posted to ensure the business is still active. Google Maps and Booking.com are used regularly in the country, and do usually provide up-to-date crowdsourced reviews.

GOVERNMENT WEBSITES

Australian Department of Foreign Affairs www.dfat.gov.au
British Foreign & Commonwealth Office redirects to www.gov.uk
Canadian Department of Foreign Affairs www.international.gc.ca
Irish Department of Foreign Affairs www.dfa.ie
New Zealand Ministry of Foreign Affairs www.mfat.govt.nz
US State Department www.state.gov
South African Department of Foreign Affairs www.dirco.gov.za

Tirana and around

NATIONAL HISTORY MUSEUM

1

Tirana and around

Albania's capital is a fascinating blend of old and new, a rapidly modernizing city underscored by ever-present reminders of a storied historic legacy. Dotted with Ottoman-era architecture, sprinkled with lively cafés and bustling with local markets, Tirana offers a special mix of history, culture and modern, youthful energy. Explore iconic landmarks like Skanderbeg Square and the famous Pyramid (Piramida), sample traditional cuisine and dive into the weird-and-not-so-wonderful world of Albanian communism at world-class museums. Three decades of open borders and a flurry of budget flights mean Tirana is not the mystery it once was, but it's still a city that will keep you captivated until you move on north, south or to the coast.

The nation's capital and its cultural and political epicentre, **Tirana** has come a long way since the fall of communism in 1991. Forward-looking and youthful, trendy and traditional, Tirana feels like a city bigger than its half a million would suggest. It's a lively place with crowds bustling through the streets, incessant traffic swarming along its boulevards and life lived out on the pavements.

Those expecting a drab communist-era cityscape will be disappointed (or relieved) – over thirty years of Balkan wild capitalism has created a modern, bright place where only the odd reminder of the city's troubled past pokes through the bristle of new tower blocks, advertising hoardings and shopping centres. There are cycle lanes and recycling bins (unheard of outside the capital), urban buses and police directing traffic. Fashionably dressed kids whizz by on e-scooters and university students hurry to lectures. It's a surprisingly leafy place with mature trees casting much-welcome shade on the concrete pavements.

But despite the rapid modernization of Tirana, the city's tourist offerings make much of the four decades of communism that Albania endured, much more than, say, Warsaw or Prague. The two **Bunk'Art museums** examine the communist leaders' suffocating paranoia while the **House of Leaves** proves just how thoroughly the regime stamped down on even the slightest hint of opposition. Albanian communist dictator (1944–1985) **Enver Hoxha's villa** remains virtually untouched in the **Blloku** neighbourhood, an erstwhile gated community for the chosen communist few.

And when you are done with the city's unique set of attractions, the capital's **dining scene** is second to none, with restaurant owners putting as much thought and attention to detail into their interior spaces as they do into their menus. And these days that food can be traditional Albanian grilled meats, Italian desserts or Adriatic seafood fused with sushi. There really is plenty of choice, though vegetarians and vegans may struggle a little.

Summer is not the best time to turn up in Tirana as temperatures can creep over 40°C in July and August, when many locals escape for the coast. Come in the shoulder seasons for more enjoyable conditions. In the sweltering heat, when the sweat drips from the tip of your nose on a bus with broken air-con, it can be difficult to imagine that Tirana regularly dips below freezing levels on winter nights. Snow in the surrounding highlands is not uncommon, hanging around longest on **Mount Dajti**, the best half-day trip from the city and reachable by cable car.

Brief history

Tirana, the capital and largest city of Albania, is a fairly new arrival on the scene, only founded in 1614 by Sulejman Pasha Bargjini, an Ottoman general. The city's

BUNK'ART 2

Highlights

❶ **Skanderbeg Square** The city's epicentre surrounded by buildings old and new, including Albania's premier history museum. See page 56

❷ **National History Museum** Albania's top history museum regales the nation's fascinating story from the very beginning. See page 56

❸ **Bunk'Art 2** In a late-1980s bunker hidden beneath the former Ministry of Internal Affairs, this chilling museum reveals how the communist dictatorship kept the population in a constant state of fear. See page 58

❹ **House of Leaves** Based in the Sigurimi's state security listening station, the excellent Museum of Secret Surveillance shows how the communist-era secret police tried to spy on anyone they saw as a potential threat to their grip on power. See page 59

❺ **Bunk'Art 1** A huge subterranean bunker built for the paranoid communist elite, but which now houses exhibitions on Albania's twentieth-century history and a curation of contemporary art installations. See page 63

❻ **Grand Park** Tirana's green lung, a place for rest and a great escape from the super-heated city concrete in the summer. See page 64

❼ **Mount Dajti** The most popular day-trip from Tirana, this 1613m-high mountain can be scaled by cable car. See page 66

HIGHLIGHTS ARE MARKED ON THE MAPS ON PAGES 52 AND 54

1

development was closely tied to the influence of the Ottoman Empire, which controlled the region for several centuries. However, there is very little Ottoman architecture remaining, mainly because succeeding Italian and communist rulers overlaid much of the city centre and beyond with the stern limestone facades and concrete that defined twentieth-century socialism.

Early history and Ottoman era

Before the city was officially established, the land on which Tirana now stands was sparsely populated, primarily by farmers. The name Tirana is believed to have derived from the ancient Greek 'Theranda', which was used loosely for this region during antiquity. Another theory suggests that the moniker originates from 'Tirkan', a Byzantine-era castle built on Mount Dajti, overlooking the present-day capital.

The establishment of Tirana in 1614 marked the beginning of its emergence as an urban centre. Albanian general and Ottoman governor **Sulejman Bargjini** built a mosque, a hammam (Turkish bath) and a bakery, which formed the foundations of

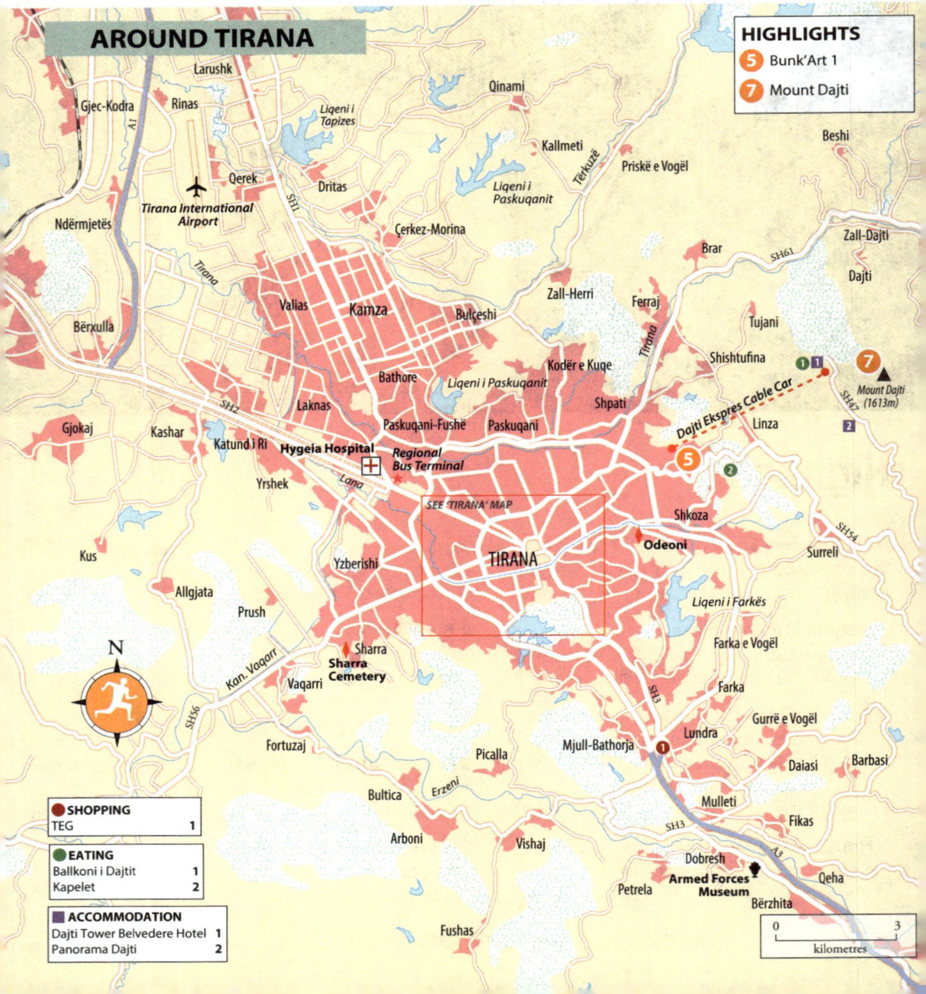

the settlement's early infrastructure. The town gradually grew as it became a hub for commerce, due to its favourable position on an important **trading route** between the Adriatic coast and inland regions of the Balkans.

Under **Ottoman rule**, Tirana remained a modest settlement but continued to expand steadily. By the nineteenth century, it had developed into a small town with a handful of mosques, a bazaar and a few thousand inhabitants, though it was a long way from capital status. If you look carefully, the influence of the Ottoman Empire is still evident in Tirana's architecture and urban layout, with a handful of historical mosques and buildings from that era surviving to this day.

Independence and early twentieth century

The early twentieth century was a turbulent period for Tirana, as it was for much of Albania and the wider region. In 1912, Albania declared its **independence** from the Ottoman Empire, and the country began to navigate its way through the challenges of building a nation. Tirana, still a small fish in the Albanian pond, was not the obvious choice for the capital. However, due to its central location and potential for growth, it was declared the provisional **capital** on February 8, 1920, during the Congress of Lushnja. The decision was made official in 1925, cementing Tirana's status as the political and administrative heart of the country, which it remains to this day.

In the interwar period, Tirana witnessed rapid modernization **Zog I**, who ruled Albania as king from 1928 to 1939, played a significant role in the city's changing face. Italian architects were commissioned to design grand government buildings, wide boulevards and new infrastructure, giving the streets a blend of European pizzazz and traditional Albanian architecture.

World War II and the communist era

During **World War II**, Tirana was occupied by Italian forces in 1939 and later by Nazi Germany in 1943. The city became a focal point of resistance against the invaders, and in 1944 communist partisans, led by Albanian communist revolutionary **Enver Hoxha**, eventually seized control of the capital.

The establishment of a **communist government** triggered a series of significant changes for Tirana. Leader Enver Hoxha's regime (1944–1985) focused on industrializing the city and creating a socialist utopia. The architecture of this period is characterized by utilitarian buildings, large public squares and thundering thoroughfares. Countless historical landmarks were demolished at this time, including a number of religious sites in line with Hoxha's atheist policies. Needless to say, this was a tough time for Tirana's residents. Forty years of **oppression** ensued, with ruthless state control over even the smallest aspects of everyday life; famously, private car ownership was prohibited. All acts of resistance and protest were met with brutal repression.

1991 to the present day

The **fall of communism** in 1991 sparked a period of monumental political, economic, and social upheaval, the effects of which still resonate today. Tirana experienced rapid urbanization, with a surge in population and a chaotic spate of construction, much of it unregulated development. The 1990s were plagued by instability but the city slowly stabilized and began to settle into its role as a confident European capital.

Today, Tirana is an energetic city with the highest standard of living in the country. It has reestablished itself as a centre of culture, education and economy, blending its Ottoman heritage, Italian influences and communist past with the aspirations of a contemporary European metropolis. The city's dynamic transformation continues as it seeks to balance its historical legacy with the demands of the twenty-first century.

1

TIRANA
HIGHLIGHTS
1 Skanderbeg Square
2 National History Museum
3 Bunk'Art 2
4 House of Leaves
6 Grand Park of Tirana
SHOPPING
Illyrian Bloodline 1
EATING
Balbi 35 6
Era 2
Lakror'Ane 4
Mullixhiu 7
Taverna e Kasapit 5
Ujvara 1
Xheni Fast 3
ACCOMMODATION
Freddy's Hotel 1
Habitat Hotel 3
Iliria Boutique Hotel 6
Rogner Hotel Tirana 4
Tirana Backpacker Hostel 2
Tirana Marriott 5
DRINKING & NIGHTLIFE
Bunker 1944 1
Lake View Bar 5
Mon Cheri 2
My Favourite Tirana 6
Radio 3
Sophie Caffe 4
0 400
metres
N
Regional Bus Terminal (1.2km) & Hygeia Hospital (1.4km)
LAPRAKË
21 DHJETORI
KOMUNA E PARISIT
Our Lady of Good Counsel Catholic Hospital
Tirana International Bus Terminal
Ring Center Shopping Mall
British Embassy
Tirana Mosaic
Police station
Stadium "Selman Stermasi"
Aquadromi
Botanical Garden
Zoo
Lana
Parku 1 Kilometër
RRUGA DRITAN HOXHA
RRUGA ASIM VOKSHI
RRUGA E KAVAJËS
MUHAMET GJOLLESHA
BULEVARDI GJERGJ FISHTA
BULEVARDI BAJRAM CURRI
RRUGA FRANG BARDHI
RRUGA IRFAN TOMINI
RRUGA TEODOR KEKO
RRUGA E DURRËSIT
RRUGA MINE PEZA
RRUGA E KOSOVAREVE
UNAZA E MADHE (A3)
RRUGA MUHAREM BUTKA
RRUGA EGNATIA
RRUGA DON BOSKO
RRUGA JORDAN MISJA
RRUGA PANORAMA
RRUGA HYSNI GERBOLLI
RRUGA ALBANOPOLI
RR. ANDROKLI KOSTALLARI
RR. E. FRASHERI
RRUGA ARTAN LENJA
RRUGA NDRE MJEDA
RRUGA FROSINA PLAKU
RRUGA KONGRESI I LUSHNJES
RRUGA YLBERE BYLYKBASHI
RR. MUHEDIN LLAGANI
RR. SHEFQET MUSARAJ
RRUGA SALI BUTKA
RRUGA NIKOLLA JORGA
RRUGA NIKOLLA LENA
RR. SULEJMAN PITARKA
RR. MYSLYM SHYRI
RRUGA SKENDERBEG
FREDERIK SHIROKA
RRUGA QEMAL BUTKA
RRUGA DHIMITER SHUTERIQI
RR. HASAN ALLA
RRUGA XHON KENEDI
RR. KODRA E DIELLIT
RRUGA ISUF ELEZI
RRUGA REXHEP JELLA
RR. IBRAHIM DERVISHI
RRUGA ANTON LUFI
RR. SULEJMAN DELVINA
RRUGA ZEF JUBANI
RR. M. TUTULANI
RR. ANDON ZAKO ÇAJUPI

STACIONI I TRENIT
BULEVARDI I RI
RRUGA FERIT XHAJKO
RRUGA S MAJI
RR. E DIBRËS
RRUGA BARDHYL
Nënë Tereza Hospital
RRUGA KONGRESI I MANASTIRIT
RR. BESIM ZYMA
RRUGA ALI BAUSHI
RRUGA SIRI KODRA
RRUGA RIZA CEROVA
RRUGA RESHIT PETRELA
HYSEN DALLIU
RR. MAHMUT FORTUZI
RR. THANAS ZIKO
RRUGA 4 DËSHMORËT
RRUGA BARDHYL
XHAMLLIKU
RR. XHANFIZE KEKO
RRUGA E DIBRËS
BULEVARDI ZOGU I
RRUGA E BARRIKADAVE
RRUGA TAFAJ
RR. ALI PASHË GUCIA
RRUGA DERVISH HEKALI
RRUGA ARKITEKT SINANI
RR. FORTUZI
RR. QEMAL STAFA
RR. ARKITEKT KASEMI
SEE 'CENTRAL TIRANA' MAP
ABC Clinic
RR. BARDHOK BIBA
RR. QEMAL STAFA
Kokonozi Mosque
RR. HOXHA TAHSIM
BULEVARDI ZHAN D'ARK
RR. VLLAZËN LUTA
Ismail Kadare House Museum
National History Museum
Theatre of Opera & Ballet
AVNI RUSTEMI SQUARE
RR. TEFTA TASHKO-KOÇO
SKANDERBEG SQUARE
RR. LUIGJ GURAKUQI
Lana
BULEVARDI BAJRAM CURRI
RR. KONT L. BERTOLD
RRUGA ALI DEMI
RR. E KAVAJËS
RRUGA IBRAHIM RUGOVA
Skanderbeg Statue
Farmaci Ditë e Natë
ALI DEMI
RR. IDRIZ DOLLAKU
Et'hem Bej Mosque
RR. GEORGE W. BUSH
RRUGA ALI DEMI
RR. ÇAMËRIA
Bunk'Art 2
SHËTITORJA MURAT TOPTANI
BULEVARDI ZHAN D'ARK
RRUGA SHYQYRI ISHMI
House of Leaves
Kinema Millennium
Museum of Natural Sciences Sabiha Kasimati
National Gallery of Arts
RR. PETRO NINI LUARASI
RRUGA SALI NIVICA
RR. MYSLYM SHYRI
Independence Memorial
Mosque of Namazgah
RR. MIHAL GRAMENO
European Trade Centre
RRUGA MIHAL GRAMENO
RRUGA TODI SHKURTI
BULEVARDI GJERGJ FISHTA
BULEVARDI BAJRAM CURRI
BULEVARDI DËSHMORËT E KOMBIT
RR. E ELBASANIT
RR. PJETER BUDI
RR. ALI VISHA
RRUGA ALI VISHA
RR. KRISTAQ CAPO
RR. VASO PASHA
RR. IBRAHIM RUGOVA
RR. UKRAINE LIRË
Piramida
RRUGA PAPA GJON PALI II
RR. DRAGO SILIQI
RR. REXHEP HAMIT DEMI
RR. JORGJIA TRUJA
RR. PJETER BUDI
RR. ISMAIL QEMALI
RRUGA PJETER BUDI
RRUGA PJETER BUDI
Hoxha's Residence
THEMISTOKLI GËRMENJI
US Embassy
QYTETI STUDENTI
Postbllok - Checkpoint Monument
ASIM ZENELI
RR. STAVRO VINJAU
RR. SOTIR KOLEA
RRUGA ARBEN BROCI
RRUGA ARBEN BROCI
BLLOKU
Convention Center
Air Albania Arena
RR. ABDYL FRASHËRI
Presidential Palace
AHMET PAZARI
RR. SHEH
REXHEPI
RR. PERLAT
RR. JANOS HUNYADI
MOTHER TERESA SQUARE
National Archaeological Museum
RRUGA FAIK KONICA
RRUGA GRAMOZ PASHKO
University of Arts
RR. LEK DUKAGJINI
RR. GJENERAL NIKOLS
RR. MAHMUT DACI
RRUGA FUAT TOPTANI
RRUGA SAMI FRASHËRI
RR. LIDHJA E PRIZRENIT
RR. GJENERAL NIKOLS
RRUGA 3 VELLEZERIT KONDI
RRUGA E ELBASANIT
RR. DORA D'ISTRIA VILA
St Procopius Church
RR. HAKI SHEHU
Luna Park
Amphitheatre
Grand Park of Tirana
K. LUARASI
Palace of Brigades
RRUGA VIENA
RRUGA XIBRAKEVE
Martyrs' Cemetery

1 Skanderbeg Square and around

At Tirana's centre is **Skanderbeg Square** (Sheshi Skënderbej), the very heart of the capital and, it could be said, the whole of Albania. It's by far the city's most iconic and historically significant public space, surrounded by a cluster of landmark buildings – the vast majority of visitors will gravitate here at some point during their stay. Named after the Albanian national hero Gjergj Kastrioti – AKA Skanderbeg (Albanian: Skënderbeu or Skënderbej) – who led the resistance against the Ottoman Empire in the fifteenth century, the square is a focal point of civic pride and identity. Originally created during the era of Italian influence in the 1930s, its design was heavily inspired by the fascist architectural style. However, the space has undergone significant revamps over the decades. Brussels-based architect firm 51N4E spearheaded the most recent transformation, scooping the 2018 European Prize for Urban Public Space for its efforts. The design features a large open area paved with multicoloured stones carted in from different regions across Albania, an act meant to symbolize the unity of the country.

Some of Albania's most interesting museums can be found on and around the square, including the **National History Museum**, the **House of Leaves** and **Bunk'Art 2**. It is home to the **National Theatre of Opera and Ballet**, the National Bank and the **Et'hem Bej Mosque**, each building a historic piece in the capital's architectural jigsaw. The area also has more than its fair share of decent **restaurants** and **hotels**. These days, there's always something going on here, from folk festivities to cultural exhibitions.

National History Museum

Sheshi Skënderbej 7 • Charge • www.mhk.gov.al

The biggest attraction on Skanderbeg Square, dominating its northern flank, is the **National History Museum** (Muzeu Historik Kombëtar). The mosaic above the entrance, dating from 1981 and simply entitled 'The Albanians', is worth pausing to admire before you step inside. It depicts an ideologically sound (for those times) version of Albanian history, complete with Illyrian warriors, brave intellectuals and armed partisans in national costume, all striding confidently forth beneath the country's striking flag (which essentially remained the same during communism and after). The mosaic was entirely restored tile by tile, with guidance from surviving original artists, and unveiled afresh in 2023. The rest of the museum was closed in 2024 for an equally ambitious overhaul; a reopening date has not yet been set.

Prehistoric and Illyrian era

The museum starts in the same way so many from the former communist world did (and still do) – at the very beginning. **Prehistoric** finds from Stone Age to Iron Age are followed by exhibits on the Illyrians, the first named inhabitants of these lands. Two items stand out: **Goddess of Butrint** (or the Head of Apollo), an elegant marble bust believed to date to the first century BC; and the first mosaic ever discovered in the country depicting a woman's head, the '**Durrës Beauty**', from the fourth century BC.

Ottoman rule to independence

The second floor explores the medieval feudal system and the centuries that Albania spent under **Ottoman** rule. Skanderbeg naturally receives an entire room to himself, examining in detail his role in the struggle against the pesky Ottomans. On the third floor you'll find displays on the **national reawakening** and the renaissance of Albanian culture which led to the declaration of independence in November of 1912. An ethnographical exhibition includes icons and nineteenth-century textiles.

World War II and communist reign

One of the most fascinating sections of the museum deals with **World War II**. The role of the communist resistance is still the main focus, but exhibitions on the impact of Albanian factions like the Balli Kombëtar (National Front) and the Lëvizja e Legalitetit (Legality Movement), as well as the British secret army Special Operations Executive, on the course of the war in the southern Balkans now tell the wider story. The following room looks at the four decades of **communism** Albania suffered and the events that led to its collapse.

Most exhibits have English-language labels. You'll need around two hours to see everything in the museum.

Et'hem Bej Mosque

Sheshi Skënderbej 1 • Free

Built between 1790 and 1821, first by Ottoman-Albanian religious leader Molla Bej and then later his son, Haxhi Et'hem Bej, the **Et'hem Bej Mosque** (Xhamia e Haxhi Et'hem Beut) is the foremost example of Ottoman-era architecture in Tirana. Tucked into the southeast corner of Skanderbeg Square, its elegant design features a combination of intricate frescoes, Arabic calligraphy and floral motifs, which adorn both the interior and exterior walls.

The mosque is renowned not just for its architectural beauty but also for its survival story. During the decades of communist rule, Albania was officially atheist, and all religious practices were banned. Countless churches, mosques and other holy sites were destroyed, closed or repurposed.

However, the Et'hem Bej Mosque miraculously survived and in 1991, it became a symbol of freedom when thousands of worshippers gathered here to perform prayers for the first time in decades and incredibly faced no reprisal from the authorities, marking the end of religious repression in the country.

Skanderbeg Statue

Sheshi Skënderbej • Free

On the southern flank of Skanderbeg Square looms Tirana's most iconic **statue** – Albania's national hero gallantly astride his mighty steed. The 11m-high monument was erected in 1968 to commemorate the 500th anniversary of the death of Gjergj Kastrioti, commonly known by his honorific name Skanderbeg (Albanian: Skënderbeu or Skënderbej), and remains a powerful symbol of freedom and independence to this day. Until 1991, Skanderbeg had company on the square: an imposing 10m-high bronze Enver Hoxha. The two parted ways when the communist dictator was forcibly demounted and carted off by a crowd of rejoicing locals, never to return.

Behind the statue is a cheesy selfie spot, a pink heart bearing the words 'You are happy, you are in Tirana', where tourists like to take a snap with Skanderbeg in the background.

Clock Tower

Sheshi Skënderbej • Charge

Rising 35m into the air behind the Et'hem Bej Mosque, Tirana's **Clock Tower** (Kulla e Sahatit) dates back to 1822 and was first erected by the Ottoman general Haxhi Et'hem Bej (1783–1846). Amazingly, this was the highest structure in the Albanian capital for most of the twentieth century but is now dwarfed by apartment blocks, many still under construction at the time of writing. Climbing the ninety steps to the top is almost compulsory – the views across the patchwork square are just about worth the exertion.

National Gallery of Arts

Bulevardi Dëshmorët e Kombit • Charge • www.facebook.com/GaleriaKombetareArteve

The 4500-strong collection at the **National Gallery of Arts** (Galeria Kombëtare e Arteve) spans Albanian painting from the early nineteenth century to the late twentieth century. The most interesting are those created during the communist era, with a special emphasis on Albania's take on socialist realism. Besides the countless determined-looking collective farm workers and moustached freedom fighters, there are many works by artists who were imprisoned for their creative endeavours in the 1960s and 1970s. More twentieth-century excesses can be found behind the communist-era structure in the shape of monuments in storage, which includes a couple of rare Stalins. At the time of writing, the museum was closed for renovation after sustaining damage during a 2019 earthquake, with no reopening date yet set.

Resurrection of Christ Orthodox Cathedral

Rruga Dëshmorët e 4 Shkurtit 5 • Free

Just off Skanderbeg Square, the **Resurrection of Christ Orthodox Cathedral** (Katedralja Ngjallja e Krishtit) was only built in 2012 as a symbol of religious resurrection. The primary cathedral of the Albanian Orthodox Church is a thoroughly modern, somewhat bland structure, designed by a New York architectural company, though inside you'll discover some beautiful frescoes alongside the usual array of haloed icons.

Bunk'Art 2

Rruga Abdi Toptani • Charge • www.bunkart.al

The younger cousin of Bunk'Art 1 (see page 63), **Bunk'Art 2** is housed in a communist-era bunker and network of underground tunnels beneath the Ministry of

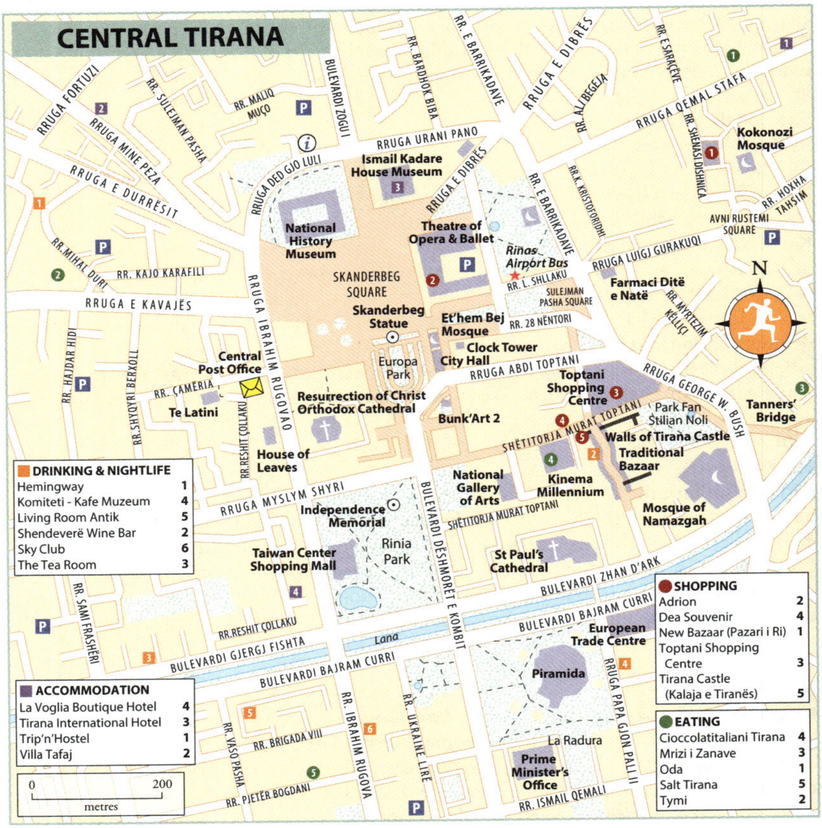

Internal Affairs, the government department that once oversaw the feared Sigurimi, the Albanian equivalent of East Germany's Stasi or Moscow's KGB. The huge edifice, built in the early 1980s and measuring around one thousand square metres, was one of Hoxha's final acts of paranoia and is interesting in its own right, with many of its spaces left exactly as they were found in 1991. The walls are made from 2.5m-thick slabs of concrete, sturdy enough to shelter the ministry honchos in a Soviet/NATO nuclear attack that never came.

Room after room contains haunting exhibitions on the ways in which the state kept Albanians frozen in a permanent state of fear and liquidated those who presented any kind of protest. There are mock-ups of prison cells, lots of brutal-looking weapons and secret rooms where the communist elite would have hidden in the case of invasion. Despite the odd clunky piece of late-twentieth-century tech, the displays are very text-heavy, great if you're interested in the period and have plenty of time to while away here. Some rooms are not suitable for children and are marked as such.

Tanners' Bridge

Rruga Refik Toptani • Free

There aren't too many reminders in Tirana of the centuries the city spent under Ottoman rule, but the **Tanners' Bridge** (Ura e Tabakëve), an ancient-looking stone affair just off the riverside boulevard, is one of them. It's not much to look at, just a strip of well-polished rocks on a couple of arches that leap over nothing in particular, but it is an interesting nod to Tirana's past in a rapidly modernizing cityscape. How the delicate structure has survived in such a central spot from the nineteenth century is anyone's guess. You can still walk over the bridge if you like, though a (busy) road now bypasses it.

House of Leaves

Rruga Ibrahim Rugova • Charge • www.muzeugjethi.gov.al

If you have any interest in Albania's communist past, the **House of Leaves** (Shtëpia me Gjethe), or Museum of Secret Surveillance, is essential viewing. Between 1944 and 1991, this was the headquarters of the secret police – the much-feared Sigurimi – though the creeper-choked building itself began life as a maternity hospital, built by King Zog I's doctor in 1931.

It was from here that state security spied on private conversations in individuals' flats, embassies and hotels. The ground-floor rooms display the surveillance equipment used, from tiny microphones and cameras to various bugs and amplifiers. There's even a training manual showing officers how to insert miniscule listening devices into walls, picture frames and the soles of people's shoes. On the first floor, displays examine just who the repressive state saw as an enemy (all foreigners, those with connections to foreigners and so on), political trials and transcripts of intercepted conversations. The museum provides a truly fascinating overview of how meticulous the Hoxha regime was in preserving its isolation by keeping tabs on anyone it considered a risk. Allow at least two hours to do the place justice.

Ismail Kadare House Museum

Rruga e Dibrës 25 • Charge • https://shtepiakadare.tirana.al

Gjirokastra-born **Ismail Kadare** (1936–2024) was the greatest novelist, poet, screenwriter, and playwright Albania has ever produced (see box). A kind of Albanian Havel, Kadare wrote throughout the communist period using clever, subtle ways of masking criticism of the regime to fool the strict censors. His allegorical novels examined contemporary society under the shadow of dictator Hoxha, including *The General of the Dead Army* and *The Siege*. He lived with his wife Elena in an apartment in a Bauhaus tenement block until he fled to Paris in 1990 only months before the communist regime fell. Even though he was asked to serve as president of post-communist Albania, he declined though he continued to revisit the country in his fiction. He only returned to Tirana in the last few years of his life.

The latter has been transformed into the **Ismail Kadare House Museum** (Muzeu Kadare – Shtëpia Studio e Shkrimtarit Ismail Kadare). Several rooms have been left almost as they would have been in the 1970s and 1980s, and Kadare's library remains intact. The tour (in English) includes a film showing life in Tirana in the 1970s, a rare and intriguing insight.

If you've never read a Kadare book, after visiting his quarters, you'll certainly be tempted to seek out a translation or two. Kadare died in Tirana in 2024 at the age of 88. His importance to Albanians is underlined by the fact that two days of mourning were declared in Albania, one in Kosovo.

Rinia Park

Bulevardi Dëshmorët e Kombit • Free

Translating as 'Youth', **Rinia** is the city centre's most popular **green space**, occupying around seventy acres directly to the south of Skanderbeg Square. It was created in 1950 to celebrate the liberation of Tirana during World War II. The park, which underwent a revamp in 2020, is a great place to picnic and just relax between Tirana's emotionally charged museums. As well as a peaceful retreat from the city's hustle and bustle, **Parku Rinia** also shelters an important site – the **Independence Monument**, which can be found in its northeast corner.

Dating from 2012, it was erected to mark a century of Albanian self-rule. Created by architects Visar Obrija and Kai Kiklas, it comprises a pair of 6.5m-high illuminated pillars; one represents repression, the other freedom. The two concrete slabs joined together would make a single rectangular tower (if they didn't weigh fifteen tons, that is); its deconstructed design symbolizes Albania's openness to independence.

In 2016 another attraction sprang up just outside the park, in front of the National Gallery of Arts – **The Cloud** by Japanese architect Sou Fujimoto. This delicate-looking art installation is made from a lattice of white steel poles that form a kind of Minecraft-esque cloud. The grid varies in density so that it frames or obscures the surrounding park as people move around it. The transparent structure is particularly impressive when illuminated after dark.

THE LIFE AND WORK OF ISMAIL KADARE

Ismail Kadare (1936–2024) was Albania's most celebrated author, renowned inside and outside the country for his contributions to literature. Born in 1936 in Gjirokastra, Kadare studied literature at the University of Tirana and later in Moscow.

Kadare's works, often set against the backdrop of Albania's disturbed and knotted history, explore themes of dictatorship, human resilience and the clash between tradition and modernity. His most famous novel, *The General of the Dead Army* (1963), depicting the sombre task of an Italian general retrieving the remains of fallen soldiers from Albania after World War II, catapulted him to international fame.

Throughout his career, Kadare's narrative style blended realism with elements of myth and folklore, examining Albania's complex sociopolitical landscape through a unique lens. His criticism of totalitarian regimes, often veiled in allegory, earned him both acclaim from readers and critics and the attention of the security apparatus during the communist era. Strangely, he was never imprisoned, and Enver Hoxha himself allegedly intervened several times to stop Kadare's persecution.

Kadare's illustrious, sixty-plus-year career has been recognized on the international literary stage. He was awarded the inaugural Man Booker International Prize in 2005 and was nominated for the Nobel Peace Prize in Literature a record fifteen times. When Kadare died on 1 July 2024, Albania mourned the passing of its greatest literary figure.

South of the Lana River

South of the **Lana River** (Përroi i Lanës) that flows through the capital, the cityscape is dominated by two areas – the parkland around the **Pyramid of Tirana**, built essentially as a museum dedicated to Enver Hoxha but now a multivenue hub and little-used cultural centre, and **Blloku**, the former gated enclave for communist party bigwigs that since the 1990s has reinvented itself as a trendy and desirable neighbourhood. Hoxha's villa stands there, though at the time of writing it wasn't open for the public to visit. The modern forward-looking face of Albania can be seen in the shape of the dramatic **National Stadium**.

Pyramid of Tirana

Bulevardi Dëshmorët e Kombit and Bulevardi Bajram Curri • Free • www.piramida.edu.al

The landmark **Pyramid of Tirana** (Piramida e Tiranës) was built in 1988 originally as a museum dedicated to the life of Albanian leader Enver Hoxha, who for four decades until his death in 1985 ran an increasingly isolated communist state in which religion and private property were banned, not to mention colour televisions and typewriters. The then-futuristic 21m-high concrete cone, designed by a team of architects that included Hoxha's daughter and son-in-law, was intended to symbolize Albania's transition into modernity under his rule. (It also looks like Albania's symbolic eagle from above – or that was the idea, anyway.)

However, when the regime was overthrown in 1991, a museum dedicated to a communist dictator was most definitely surplus to requirements. The structure saw several reincarnations, including stints as a conference centre, nightclub, and radio station. However, in the late 1990s it fell into disrepair, becoming little more than a blank canvas for graffiti artists and a rundown brutalist symbol of Albania's inability to develop as a country. A rite of passage for backpackers at the time was to scramble up its flank to the summit and slide down – many discovered the shortcomings of the Albanian healthcare system as a result.

Fast forward twenty years and the pyramid of old has essentially gone. Dutch architecture studio MVRDV added a stepped roof and brightly coloured cubes to the monument and it gained a new lease of life as a multivenue hub. The only attraction here currently for tourists is the chance to climb the steps to the top for great city views. There are a few cafés around the base of the pyramid and various statues and monuments dot the grounds.

Blloku

An off-limits precinct for the ruling party's top brass during the communist decades, the **Blloku** district to the southwest of the Pyramid of Tirana is now one of the city's hottest postcodes hosting the city's hippest bars and restaurants and snazzy hotels. Under Enver Hoxha's dictatorship, ordinary citizens were forbidden to enter Blloku, and the streets and buildings were unmarked on city maps. When the regime was overthrown in 1991, this district was in excellent shape compared to the city's other impoverished neighbourhoods, hardly surprising considering this is where Hoxha himself lived.

Hoxha's villa

Rruga Ismail Qemali and Rruga Ibrahim Rugova

Hoxha's villa, on Rruga Ismail Qemali, still stands: a relatively modest three-storey abode by today's standards and nothing compared to the residences of many of Eastern Europe's communist madmen. But Albania had one of the poorest populations in the world in the latter half of the twentieth century, which meant a villa in its own palm-shaded grounds with multiple bathrooms, a library and Persian rugs throughout was a

1

pipe dream for its citizens. Hoxha lived here for decades, and his wife Nexhmije Hoxha continued to live here for years after his death in 1985.

Sadly, it isn't possible to peek inside at the untouched retro interior, which is mostly just as it was when Nexhmije was evicted in 1991. Walls are hung with socialist realist art, and a series of living rooms are centred around clunky television sets. There's a swimming pool in the basement and an escape door opening onto a tunnel that led to an underground bunker in which a paranoid Hoxha could hide in case of attack. While the villa is currently closed to the public, there are rumours that this might soon change – watch this space.

Mother Teresa Square

Just over a kilometre south of Skanderbeg Square is another piazza, dedicated to an Albanian possibly better known overseas than the other national hero (see page 57) – **Mother Teresa**, who was born in Skopje, in what's now North Macedonia, in 1910. The austere **Sheshi Nënë Tereza** is flanked by three noble institutions. On its eastern edge, the grand, colonnaded National Archaeological Museum, famously the first museum created in Albania (1948) after World War II, shares a home with the Institute of Archaeology. On the south side of the square rises the Polytechnic University of Tirana, whose stern facade is an Italian fascist-era addition dating from 1940, while the western fringe is dominated by another sombre building in the same style, the University of Arts.

National Archaeological Museum

Sheshi Nënë Tereza 3 • Charge • www.akad.gov.al/muzeu-arkeologjik

The **National Archaeological Museum** (Muzeu Arkeologjik Kombëtar) covers in impressive depth all bases, from the Stone Age to the Ottoman Empire via the Illyrians, Greeks and Romans. The five halls are organized in chronological order, but there are no labels (or tours) in English and very few even in Albanian, so if archaeology is not your field, the objects on show may have only limited aesthetic value.

National Stadium

Sheshi Italia

Completed in 2019, the **National Stadium** (other names bandied about include Air Albania Stadium, National Arena, Arena Kombëtare – take your pick) is the Albanian national football team's hallowed turf and one of the most significant new architectural landmarks in the country. With a seating capacity of around 22,500, it is the largest stadium in the country. The striking design is the work of Italian architects Archea Associati and stands, somewhat aptly, on Italy Square. The thousands of red-and-black panels that cover the entire structure reflect Albania's national colours. Not only is the stadium used for football matches involving Albania's men and women's national teams (and some of Tirana's professional teams), it is also planned to host concerts and other large events. In 2022 this was the venue for the first-ever UEFA Conference League final between AS Roma and Feyenoord.

Postbllok – Checkpoint Monument

Bulevardi Dëshmorët e Kombit • Free

Located in Lulishte Ismail Qemali, a small park between Blloku and the Pyramid of Tirana, **Postbllok – Checkpoint Monument** was erected in 2013 by Albanian dissident and artist Fatos Lubonja as a reminder of the atrocities committed by the Hoxha-era regime and those who died at its hands. Despite Albania being known as a country of bunkers (Hoxha had well upwards of 150,000 underground shelters built during an eight-year period, inspired by a visit to North Korea), the typical domed concrete structures are missing from central Tirana (the one at the entrance to Bunk'Art 2 is a controversial replica). Lubonja brought one of the original edifices here to incorporate into the sculptural installation along with a piece of the Berlin Wall and twisted concrete supports from the Spaçi Prison where political prisoners, including Lubonja, were held. The name of the monument is a nod to its proximity to one of the erstwhile entrances to Blloku (see page 61), the neighbourhood sealed off by the secret service and home to communist party elites until 1991.

Aquadromi

Rruga Anton Ashta • Charge

Tirana seriously overheats in the summer months, but some respite comes in the form of **Aquadromi**, situated near the northern edge of the lake in Grand Park. It's all a touch dated, but as you dive into the 50m-long pool or shoot down one of the waterslides you give a felt hat. There is a café on site and lots of cooling grass and sun loungers. Understandably, crowds descend on the waterpark when the heat is on, but it closes between November and April.

Beyond the city centre

Scattered around the immediate city centre are several worthwhile **attractions** once you've seen everything super-central. Many of these can be reached on foot – when this is not the case, public transport details are given.

Bunk'Art 1

Rruga Fadil Deliu, 5.5km northeast of Skanderbeg Square • Charge • www.bunkart.al • Take bus #11 (Porcelan–Qendër) to the Bunk'Art 1 stop

In the far northeast of the city, near the Dajti Ekspres cable car lower station (most visitors combine the two attractions into a single day-trip), **Bunk'Art 1** is a must-see for anyone visiting the Albanian capital (and a great way to escape the summer heat).

TIRANA'S MURALS

You won't be in Tirana long before you notice the abundance of art murals adorning the sides of communist-era tenement blocks and other buildings. The bland facades have been turned into monster canvases, splashing the drab urban landscape with colour and character. In the past, the city has hosted a mural festival, inviting an international band of street artists to work their magic on the streets. The result: an outdoor gallery of around fifty works of art. Here is some of the best street art and where to find it:

Mother Rruga Komuna e Parisit. This almost photo-like mural of an elderly lady peering at a mobile phone is by Uruguayan street artist Theic Camilo Nuñe.

Do not judge Rruga Myslym Shyri. Depicting a guy appearing to steal a bike, this mural by Serbian artist Artez certainly brightens up a dishevelled neighbourhood.

Sister Tone Rruga Mustafa Lleshi. English artist Harriet Wood, or 'Miss Hazard', created this huge take on *Motra Tone* (Sister Tone), an iconic 1883 painting by renowned Albanian painter Kolë Idromeno (1860–1939).

Girls just wanna have fun Sheshi Demokracia. Italian street artist Bifido painted this incredibly life-like mural of a girl peeking through her fingers in the Qyteti Studenti area, as a comment of female oppression in a patriarchal society.

Spider-Man 'I have to go' Rruga Muhamet Gjollesha. One of Tirana's most striking pieces of street art, a mammoth cartoon Spider-Man speaking on the phone next to an Art Nouveau-styled female.

Spread across five levels and containing over a hundred rooms, this was the daddy of all Hoxha's bunkers, the place he, his family and the party inner circle would have seen out a nuclear attack. This makes it one of the greatest physical expressions of Stalinist paranoia anywhere in the former communist world. Discovered by locals when the regime came crashing down in 1991, the complex now hosts exhibits that combine the recent history of Albania with contemporary art installations.

The entrance to Bunk'Art 1 is an experience in itself: an opening in a rock face leading to a long tunnel that eventually opens out into a large courtyard, where the museum begins. After passing through the radiation decontamination facility, room upon room, corridor upon narrow corridor awaits in this subterranean labyrinth, much of it an eerie time-warp in its original Cold War state. Some contain works of contemporary art by international and Albanian artists, often based on a political theme.

Highlights include a full-blown underground cinema, a mock-up of a socialist-era flat with chunky analogue TV and brown furniture, and a stretch of border fence entangled with barbed wire and set to a barking-dog soundtrack. There is also a comprehensive exhibition on the communist resistance, a monument to all those who died excavating such bunkers for the party elite, a photographic montage of interesting bunkers – right next to a mosque, turned into a fast-food kiosk, upside down on a beach – and countless other exhibits. You could spend three hours here if you wanted to see everything.

Martyrs' Cemetery

Rruga e Elbasanit • Free • Take bus #8 to the Pallati i Brigadave (Palace of Brigades) stop

The **Martyrs' Cemetery** (Varrezat e Dëshmorëve të Kombit) was established in 1971 during the communist era and serves as the final resting place for over nine hundred partisans who fought against fascist forces during World War II, contributing to Albania's liberation from Italian and German occupation. The most prominent feature of the cemetery is the Mother Albania statue, a 12m-tall monument that represents the nation's grieving mother. This towering figure stands as a guardian over the graves, some belonging to notable figures from Albania's communist decades. Enver Hoxha himself was buried here in 1985 but after the fall of communism his body was relocated to the Sharra cemetery (see page 65), also in Tirana, in 1992, as the government did not think the dictator should rest in peace alongside those who had paid the ultimate price for their country's freedom.

Palace of Brigades

Rruga e Elbasanit • Free • Take bus #8 to the Pallati i Brigadave (Palace of Brigades) stop

Located opposite the Martyrs' Cemetery, the **Palace of Brigades** (Pallati i Brigadave) is a storied piece of Tirana architecture. Built between 1936 and 1941 in the Italian rationalist style as a Royal Palace for King Zog I, the completed building was never seen by Zog, who fled during the Italian invasion of Albania in 1939. After World War II it served as a military headquarters, hence its current name. Today, it is the **Presidential Palace** for Albania's elected head and used for high-level government and state functions. It is set amid opulent 180-acre gardens containing thousands of trees, colourful flowerbeds and statues. The complex is only open at weekends for the public to wander the palace gardens. Sadly, there are no guided tours of its interiors.

Grand Park

Parku i Tiranës • Free

The Presidential Palace crouches on the eastern edge of a huge chunk of parkland that unfurls south of the National Stadium. Created in the 1950s out of existing woodland, Tirana's **Grand Park** (Parku i Madh) stretches across some 750 acres, making it one of the largest city parks in Europe. In the 1990s this was an unpleasant place, strewn with rubbish and dangerous after dark. Though it's still not perfect, steps have been taken to make this a more agreeable spot. There are cycle paths, walkways, newly designed sculptures, kids' playgrounds, a summer outdoor cinema and a handful of places to enjoy a drink. The main focus of the park is the **artificial lake**, actually a reservoir that prevents the River Lana from flooding the city centre. The waterside paths are a great place to train for the Tirana Marathon (see page 71) or enjoy an easy bike ride.

There are two major monuments within the park. The first is the **Holocaust Memorial** at the entrance near the university, erected in 2020. Designed by late architect and Buchenwald concentration camp survivor Stephen Jacobs (1939–2021), the three stone plaques – in Albanian, Hebrew and English – pay homage to the victims of the Holocaust and the Albanians who protected Jews from the Nazis (see page 114). Nearby, the **Memorial Cemetery** contains the graves of 47 British soldiers who died on Albanian soil during World War II.

Be aware that it is advisable to avoid venturing into the less-frequented parts of the park after dark.

Sharra Cemetery

Rruga Lekë Zaharia • Free

Tirana's **Sharra Cemetery** (Varrezat e Sharrës), located on the city's southwest outskirts, is the largest and most significant burial site in the entire country. Laid out in the late twentieth century, it's the final resting place for thousands of individuals, reflecting a cross-section of Albania's modern history. Many prominent figures have been laid to rest here – journalist and patriot Sali Nivica, author and politician Haki Stërmilli and writer and political dissident Musine Kokalari among them – but the most-visited grave here belongs to one person many Albanians would like to forget: Enver Hoxha.

The communist dictator who ruled the country from 1944 until his death in 1985 was originally buried in the Martyrs' Cemetery (see page 64). But in 1992 his body was disinterred and reburied here. His grave is made up of a red marble tombstone between two concrete pillars that flank a metal sculpture of the black double-headed eagle from the Albanian flag. Sometimes, the eagle is hard to see through the clouds of flowers hanging from it – yes, diehards still come here to honour one of Europe's worst dictators. If you want to visit, be aware that Hoxha's grave is not that easy to find. Try putting the GPS coordinates 41°18'455"N 19°45'707"E into your phone or smartwatch and you should get there.

Tirana Mosaic

Rruga Sandër Prosi • Free • Bus #16A to Karl Topia

Those interested in Roman remains and with an hour to spare should head to the eastern suburb of Zogu i Zi to seek out the **Mozaiku i Tiranës**, one of the few **mosaics** in Albania that you can still see in its original location. This one was discovered during construction work in 1972 and has been preserved ever since as a national monument. It's thought to have formed the floor of a large villa that stood here in the first century AD and belonged to local vintners.

Finding the mosaic can be tricky. From the large roundabout at the end of Rruga e Durrësit it is around 400m south amid blocks of flats; follow signs.

Bektashi World Centre

Rruga Hysen Loci • Free

Tirana is home to the world headquarters of a Muslim sect called Bektashi (Kryegjyshata Botërore Bektashiane), a branch of Sufism that was expelled from Turkey almost a century ago. The central temple here is called the **Odeoni**, the main prayer room of which was opened in 2015 and can be visited by the public. It's an ornate space filled with gleaming marble, graceful columns and pools of natural light. The impressive sight is a reminder that half of Albania's population is Muslim (though the country has no official religion). Beneath the temple is a museum of Bektashism, though there's precious little here in English. Visitors can also wander the gardens and grounds of the campus, and find the *tyrbes* (tombs) of Bektashi leaders. In 2024, Prime Minister Edi Rama announced to the United Nations that he'd seek to recognize the small enclave as a sovereign nation, Vatican-style. Even if plans don't pan out, bring a passport or other ID to enter.

Armed Forces Museum

Near Bërzhita, 15km southeast of the city centre on the Tirana–Elbasani Highway • Charge • www.muzeu-fa.gov.al

Opening in a new and improved venue in 2023, the **Armed Forces Museum** (Muzeu i Forcave të Armatosura) is Albania's biggest new tourist attraction in years. Located around twenty minutes by car along the Tirana–Elbasani Highway out of town, fans of obscure military history should make the effort to see it.

In typical post-communist style, this museum is thorough, starting the rundown of Albania's military history with the Illyrians. However, it's the outdoor display of heavily armoured vehicles that many will find most interesting. The quickest and easiest way to reach the museum is to take a taxi from central Tirana. This should cost around 3000 lek.

Mount Dajti

The best day-trip from Tirana is an ascent of **Mount Dajti** (Mali i Dajtit), which rises 1613m above sea level around twenty kilometres northeast of the city centre. It's commonly combined with a snoop around Bunk'Art 1 (see page 63), which is right next to the lower station for the Dajti Ekspres cable car, an Austrian-built *teleferik* providing a quick and easy way of reaching the top. You can drive to the top of Mount Dajti but it is really not advised – the road is steep and twisting.

Various attractions await at the top, mostly aimed at families and tourists. There's a minigolf course with one hole that looks like a Hoxha-era bunker; the *Ballkoni i Dajtit Restaurant* (see page 69) with unrivalled views and quality food; a children's playground; viewing platforms; a self-serve café for refreshments; a place for newlyweds to attach a padlock; and other minor distractions. But it is the views are the main calling card, with the whole of Tirana unfolding before you.

The mountain forms part of the **Mount Dajti National Park** (see box, page 67), which has some hiking possibilities. From the upper cable car station, you can walk to Mount Dajti's 1613m peak via a steep path and 4km trail. For something a little more challenging you can then continue southeast along the Dajti Ridge Trail until you reach the road at the Qafa e Priskës mountain pass, where you could arrange for a taxi to pick you up or hitchhike back into Tirana.

Dajti Ekspres cable car

Charge • www.dajtiekspres.com • Take bus #11 (Porcelan–Qendër) from Tirana city centre and alight at the last stop; from here it's a short uphill walk to the cable-car station (follow the brown tourist signs)

Most people ascend Mount Dajti via the **Dajti Ekspres cable car**. On its slow, steady climb up the mountain, the scruffy suburbs outside soon give way to green wooded slopes. The ride takes around fifteen minutes and drops passengers at an activity area beneath the main peak. At this altitude it can be refreshingly cooler in summer, and in winter the summit is often dusted in snow long after it's cleared from the streets of Tirana below. Buy your return ticket (unless you are determined to walk back down)

MOUNT DAJTI NATIONAL PARK

Covering almost three hundred square kilometres northeast of Tirana, **Mount Dajti National Park** (Parku Kombëtar Mali i Dajtit) has been a protected natural area since 1966. The visitor information centre is on the SH47 road that leads from Tirana's eastern extremities to the upper cable-car station. The park is known for its rugged, impenetrable terrain where various ecosystems thrive undisturbed by humans. Oak and beech forests dominate, providing habitat for elusive **wildlife** such as brown bears, wild boars, golden eagles and the endangered Balkan lynx. There aren't many marked trails in the area, making **hiking** and **mountain biking** a bit of an adventure, though the map app www.mapy.cz can help navigating the region easier. One of the most beautiful sights in the park is **Lake Bovilla**, a reservoir whose waters shine turquoise in the sun. By far the best views of this natural wonder can be taken in from the *Bovilla Restaurant*, where tables flank a glass facade high above the lake. Dammed in the 1990s, Bovilla provides Tirana with a source of drinking water and is a common destination for guided hiking excursions from the capital.

but before you climb aboard, always check what time the last service runs; note the cable car doesn't usually run on Tuesdays.

ARRIVAL AND DEPARTURE — TIRANA

By plane The modern Tirana International Airport Nënë Tereza (www.tirana-airport.com) is located near Rinasi, 17km northwest of the city. The airport arrivals hall has a tourist information desk, car rental services, bureaux de change, ATMs and outlets to acquire an Albanian SIM card. Wizz Air, Ryanair and British Airways serve the UK and Western Europe from here, including London Stansted, Luton and Heathrow, Munich, Frankfurt and Milan. Austrian Airlines provides links to Vienna, Lufthansa connects Frankfurt and Turkish Airlines offers flights to Istanbul. In 2021, a second international airport opened in Kukësi (https://www.kuiport.al), connecting northeast Albania with a small number of European cities, including Zurich and Istanbul, but it was inactive at the time of writing. Another international airport is due to open in Vlora in 2025, offering direct access to Albania's Adriatic coastline.

To/from Tirana International Airport Nënë Tereza To reach the centre, take the Rinas Express shuttle bus (400 lek/€4; www.luna.al) which runs hourly, 24hr a day. At the time of writing, Tia Taxi (tel: 069 999 9300, www.tiataxi.al) was the only authorized operator and has a taxi rank outside the arrivals hall. Bus services from Tirana to the airport depart from the Airport Bus Stop near the National Theatre of Opera and Ballet. The journey by taxi takes around 25–40min and costs approximately 3500 lek/€35 to the city, usually less returning. Another option is to have your hotel arrange a car, a much more secure choice.

By bus Tirana is linked by bus services to every large city and most towns and villages around the country. For timetable information, the websites www.etransport.al and www.travel.gjirafa.com are handy but by no means comprehensive. There is no single bus terminus in Tirana – instead services leave from various points just outside the city centre. Domestic buses use the South and North Regional Bus Terminal, around 4km northwest of the city centre and a 10min taxi ride; or the Southeast Regional Bus Terminal, 2km southeast of the centre. Most bus services from neighbouring countries stop at the East Bus Terminal outside the city, about 8km southeast of the centre (15–20min by taxi). The Rinas Express shuttle bus to/from the airport uses the Airport Bus Stop, just behind the Palace of Culture on Skanderbeg Square. Buses also connect the airport with Durrësi, Fieri, Shkodra and Vlora, though services are not as frequent.

By car Driving to Tirana is an experience you might just want to pass on. Roads are often chaotic, though not as bad as even just a decade ago. Rental cars are available at the airport and from outlets in the city centre. Only the capital's more upmarket hotels have secure parking, though there is a handful of underground and guarded car parks in the centre. Note that there's little free parking – you'll need to pay using the ticket machines on the street or, more often, via text with an Albanian phone number, but charges are relatively cheap.

If you bring your car into the city you'll likely arrive either by the A1 from the north and west or the A3 road from the south, which skirts the city to the east and then joins to the A1, which becomes Rruga e Elbasanit and heads into the centre. The inner city centre has a ring road, on which traffic can be heavy but orderly.

By train It isn't possible to reach Tirana by train. The railway station was demolished in 2013 and the line from Durrësi closed. However, works are currently underway to reopen the route, with plans in the pipeline to extend it to the airport. The line is expected to reopen in 2026.

See Basics (page 27) for more on arrival to Albania and transit information and tips

1

GETTING AROUND

By foot The centre of Tirana is small enough to explore on foot without having to work out the city's public bus system. Most visitors choose to walk around the city, only resorting to a bus or taxi to reach the cable car for Mount Dajti, Bunk'Art 1 or other sites outside the immediate centre.

By bus Tirana has a bus network of fourteen lines at the last count. Bus travel is very cheap for a European capital: a single fare is 40 lek/€0.40. You can buy tickets on board from the conductor or purchase a travel pass at a kiosk. Services run frequently (every 3–10min) and vehicles are relatively new (some are even electric). Sadly, with very few dedicated bus lanes, hopelessly long traffic jams are common. Visit https://tirana.al/pikat-e-interesit/linjat-urbane to see the full map.

By taxi There are countless taxi companies in Tirana, though not all of them are reliable. A few recommended firms include Black Taxi (tel: 068 687 8500), Blue Taxi (www.bluetaxi.al), Green Taxi (www.green.al) or Bee Taxi (tel: 080 080 80). Note that most taxi drivers fancy themselves as tour guides, but they'll also be the friendliest captive audience you'll find if you want to practice a little chitchat in basic Albanian. Be sure to agree a price for journeys in advance if you don't want to be landed with a hefty bill, though the risk of rip-off is much lower in Tirana than coastal cities. Currently, Uber and Bolt do not operate in Albania, though VrapOn (www.vrapon.al) is a similar taxi-booking app that works in Tirana and other large cities. Trips within the centre should cost 400–600 lek (€4–6), with cash usually needed.

By bicycle It may come a surprise to learn that Tirana is a bike-friendly city. There are cycle lanes running through the centre and many locals do use them. It may be a legacy of communist days when only party hobnobs were able to drive and the populace had no choice but to get around on cheap bikes. Concrete plant pots prevent cars from parking in the bike lanes, though drivers can be unforgiving, straddling road markings in their chunky 4WDs and SUVs. To rent a two-wheeler, contact Absolute Bike (Rruga Naim Frashëri Pallati 24; www.absolutebikestirana.com), which also offers repairs. You can rent e-bikes in Tirana now too; try LikSad on Rruga Margarita Tutulani, near the Grand Park (www.liksad.al). If you bring your own bike, be sure to pack a sturdy lock.

By car If you plan on staying in Tirana, there is no point picking up a rental car at the airport as you won't need it to explore the city and it will be money down the drain. If you intend travelling elsewhere in Albania, hiring a car in the capital before you leave is a good idea.

By cable car A cable car runs between the western suburbs and the summit of Mount Dajti, payable by card and cash.

INFORMATION

Tourist information Just behind the National History Museum, Tirana's tourist point (Rruga Ded Gjo Luli, tel: 355 422 233 13; Mon–Fri 8am–4pm) is helmed by helpful and friendly staff who all speak English. The Albanian National Tourist Board's website (www.albania.al) has interesting background on the country but is far from comprehensive.

Listings The website of the city's tourism board, Visit Tirana (www.visit-tirana.com), has limited information on sights, restaurants, bars, festivals and events.

Tours Green Tirana (www.greentirana.com) is a travel company that specializes in sustainable tours, from guided walks and bike rides to local cultural experiences. The website lists other green initiatives in and around Tirana, though keep an eye out for greenwash.

ACCOMMODATION

SEE MAPS PAGES 52, 54 AND 58

Tirana has accommodation to suit every budget, from five-star luxury to backpacker hostels. When choosing a place to stay, make sure you are within walking distance of the centre – as Tirana is not a big place, this shouldn't be difficult. Short-term rental sites such as Airbnb and Booking.com have some great deals on entire flats which can be as low as €50 a night.

HOTELS

Dajti Tower Belvedere Hotel Upper cable car station on Mount Dajti; www.dajtiekspres.com/facilities/dajti-tower-hotel. We're not sure who would want to stay at the top of Mount Dajti as it would make exploring Tirana very inconvenient. But if all you want to do is relax, stroll the forests and enjoy the views, then this lofty hotel is for you. **€€**

Freddy's Hotel Rruga Bardhok Biba 75; www.freddyshotel.com. Traditionally one of the cheapest sleeps in town, *Freddy's* prices have crept up in recent years but the air-conditioned, centrally located (if small) rooms here are still a good deal. **€**

Habitat Hotel Kompleksi Delijorgji, Rruga e Kavajës; www.habitathotel.al. The decor at this relatively new hotel (2021) looks a bit DIY store, but rooms are comfortable and clean, the breakfast is worth getting out of bed for, and the location just over 2km west of Skanderbeg Square is manageable as lots of buses pass this way. **€€**

Iliria Boutique Hotel Rruga e Elbasanit 1; www.iliriahoteltirana.com. Situated just behind the Pyramid of Tirana, this upmarket fifteen-room boutique hotel has bags of minimalist style but manages to retain a colourful character at the same time. Think muted rooms with pops of pastel and lots of clean lines. The entire interior is a study in restrained elegance, infused with a cool Scandi edge. **€€€**

La Voglia Boutique Hotel Rruga Reshit Çollaku 5; www.lavogliaboutiquehotel.com. With just seven rooms, this small, personally run guesthouse near Rinia Park is the perfect hideaway. Rooms are on the tight side, but the location is peaceful and the decor soothing. Breakfast included. **€€**

Rogner Hotel Tirana Bulevardi Dëshmorët e Kombit; www.hotel-europapark.com. Very popular choice of digs with a central location, upmarket facilities including its own tennis courts and pool, and impeccably regimented staff. It's a little expat haven of calm amid the capital's bustle. €€€€

Tirana International Hotel Sheshi Skënderbej; www.tiranainternational.com. You really can't get more central than the *Tirana International*: the boxy behemoth rises above the north side of Skanderbeg Square, next to the National History Museum. Rooms are twenty-first-century business class but with a dash of design flair and colour, there are two restaurants and a bar plus all the other services and facilities you'd expect to find in a hotel of this category. €€€

Tirana Marriott Sheshi Italia; www.marriott.com. The skyscraper that sprang up during the reconstruction of the National Stadium is now the *Tirana Marriott*, one of the capital's best places to stay. The standard of rooms is high, the staff attentive and the whole experience a smooth one. One bonus is that some rooms have views over the pitch so you might just have the opportunity to watch the national or Tirana pro teams play their home games. It might, however, not be a bonus if there's a noisy concert on. €€€€

★ **Villa Tafaj** Rruga Mine Peza 86; www.villatafaj.com. Owned by the Tafaj family, one of Tirana's oldest clans, this 1920s villa is a delightful and characterful place to lay your head. Rooms are individually furnished in an antique style; there's a bar and restaurant; and you can even park your car here for the duration of your stay. Breakfast is included. Book well ahead. €€

HOSTELS

Albanian hostels still have the remnants of the authentic backpacker vibe that's often now a thing of the past in Europe. They are great places to pick up information, arrange ad-hoc tours and even make the odd travel buddy.

★ **Tirana Backpacker Hostel** Rruga e Bogdanëve 3; www.tiranahostel.com. Seems incredible that Tirana only got its first backpacker hostel in 2005. What's even more unbelievable is that the original survives to this day. It offers six-bed dorms as well as doubles and singles, breakfast is included and there's a bar, kitchen and a vegetarian dinner nightly (extra). €

Trip'n'Hostel Rruga Musa Maçi 1; www.tripnhostel.com. Cool backpacker hostel a short walk east of Skanderbeg Square, with dorms sleeping between four and twelve, air conditioning, 24hr reception, free breakfast and welcoming staff. There's also a kitchen and a bar with a happening vibe on summer evenings. €

CAMPING

There are campsites dotted around Tirana, but very few have much in the way of facilities. If you're determined to spend the night under rustling nylon, a good place could be **Panorama Dajti** on the road up to Mount Dajti which offers marvellous views of the city and is located near a bus stop. Campervanners should check out **Park4Night** (www.park4night.com) for other suitable spots.

EATING

SEE MAPS PAGES 52, 54 AND 58

Tirana has the best dining scene in Albania with a variety of restaurants not found in any other city. Blloku is the place to head for contemporary dining with Albanian food fused to many other types of cuisine. More traditional and long-established places are dotted around the wider city centre.

Balbi 35 Rruga Gjeneral Nikols; tel: 068 564 6043. One of the best places in Albania for pizza (and the capital isn't short on decent pizzerias), located just beyond the National Stadium. Offers several vegetarian and vegan options too. €€

Ballkoni i Dajtit Mount Dajti; www.dajtiekspres.com. One of a handful of places to eat at the top of Mount Dajti, this highly praised restaurant has arguably the best views of any eatery in Albania. There's a long list of international-inspired mains, all served with a side of mountain panoramas. €€

Cioccolatitaliani Tirana Rruga Ibrahim Rugova; www.facebook.com/cioccolatitaliani.tirana. Standout dessert palace situated in the Blloku neighbourhood. Watch the chocolatiers and gelatistas at work in the open kitchen before tucking into genuine gelato, chocolate cake, pastries, pancakes and countless other tooth-rotters. It's a great place to bring the kids. Part of a Italian chain. €

Era Rruga Ismail Qemali; www.era.al. At the heart of Blloku, this Albanian-Italian restaurant is a very popular choice for its shabby-chic dining room and well-executed blend of traditional cooking and Italian favourites. The long menu lists everything from imaginative salads to pastas to steaks, and the service is swift and friendly. It's the more casual sibling of the excellent *Era Vila* on Rruga Papa Gjon Pali II. €€

★ **Kapelet** Rruga Hasan Bastari; www.facebook.com/kapeletrestaurant. High in the hills to the east of Tirana, this spectacular restaurant has the wow factor, both in the dining room and on the plate. The interior evokes Southeast Asia with lots of bamboo and rattan. The limited menu takes the best of regional Albanian cuisine, meaning lots of grilled meats, cheeses, olives and vegetables. But this place really comes into its own on warm summer evenings when from the outside tables the whole of Tirana lights up below you. Simply magic. €€

Lakror'Ane Rruga Viktor Eftimiu; www.instagram.com/lakrorane1. The attention to detail at this family-owned Albanian restaurant sets it apart from others in the city. The dining room is an antique-bedecked village house with eclectic furniture and lots of charm. Ingredients are sourced locally where possible. Traditional salads and pickles, meatballs, cheeses and grilled meats are washed down with Albanian wines and excellent *raki* (fruit brandy). Located around two kilometres on foot from Skanderbeg Square. €€

Mrizi i Zanave Bulevardi Zhan D'Ark; www.mriziizanave.al.

1

Near Tanners' Bridge, this classic restaurant serves up Albanian fair with a large dollop of heroic folklore. Try the *tavë dheu*, veal stewed with vegetables in a clay pot; roast goat with potatoes; or blueberry-dyed tagliatelle with double cream. A real gem of a place, but reservations in advance are advised. Also offers a god-save kids' menu involving chips. €€€

★ **Mullixhiu** Shëtitorja Lasgush Poradeci, near the artificial lake in Parku i Madh; www.mullixhiu.al. Earthy restaurant in Blloku that invokes the feeling of eating in an abandoned barn, but beyond the acres of wood panelling and glass cabinets piled high with corn-on-the-cob, *Mullixhiu* plates up a slow-food menu of traditional Albanian dishes using local ingredients. Prices are low for this standard of food. €€

Oda Rruga Luigj Gurakuqi; www.facebook.com/oda.tirane. No rundown of places to eat in Tirana would be complete without a mention of *Oda*. The experience here is like eating at someone's house – a house, that is, where there is nightly live folk music. Book a table in the courtyard for a magical evening in the city centre. Recent reviews suggest the classic Albanian cuisine may have gone off message a little. €

★ **Salt Tirana** Rruga Pjetër Bogdani; www.salt.al/tirana. A typically urbane Blloku affair, *Salt Tirana* is a Mediterranean-Asian fusion restaurant serving delicious seafood and a range of other dishes. The sushi comes in for high praise, paired with Albanian wines by clued-up staff. The cocktails are some of the best in Blloku. What's more, this multitiered place is huge so you don't need to worry about table reservations. €€€

★ **Taverna e Kasapit** Rruga Perlat Rexhepi 12. Wonderfully homely tavern where the family cooks for its guests as if they are visiting for the weekend. The food is pure Albanian so expect lots of grilled meat, cheese, pastries, salads and veg. The cooks suggest dishes according to what produce they have fresh in that day and it's always a good idea to follow their recommendations. €€

★ **Tymi** Rruga e Kavajës; www.facebook.com/TymiVerReci. A few steps off Skanderbeg Square, *Tymi* takes eclectic interiors to the next level, with everything from Tiffany lamps to old vinyl records, retro guitars and global beer bottles packing out the intimate space. The food is excellent: grilled meats, huge salads, soups, meatballs – everything is fresh and cooked to order. Download the menu from a Facebook QR code before you arrive. €€€

Ujvara Rruga Gjin Bue Shpata; www.facebook.com/ujvara.tirane. South of the river, the low-lit and atmospherically modern *Ujvara* plates up a very successful combination of Mediterranean classics and Asian fusion. Think sushi with truffle risotto, all washed down with Albanian wine for a multinational dining experience. Good service. €€

Xheni Fast Rruga Sami Frashëri 6–17. The incredibly cheap eats here, particularly considering its location in upmarket Blloku, are filling and tasty. There's *qofte*, grilled chicken, pasta, stewed beef and many other dishes, some costing as little as 100 lek. The dining space is simple (though the exposed lightbulbs are bit '2015 hipster' – we can forgive). It's a great option for a meal on the go or just a cup of coffee. Cash only (euros accepted). €

DRINKING & NIGHTLIFE

SEE MAPS PAGES 54 AND 58

Tirana and especially the Blloku district has plenty of places to enjoy cocktails, a coffee or a beer.

★ **Bunker 1944** Rruga Andon Zako Çajupi. This retro bar in a former air-raid shelter is furnished with jumble-sale tables, random chairs and lamps, all meant to evoke the year of Albania's liberation from the Nazis – 1944. Staff put on a real party with traditional music, dancing and basic meals.

Hemingway Rruga Kont Urani; www.hemingway.al. This cosy hangout ten minutes' walk east of Skanderbeg Square is a great place for a post-sightseeing drink. Occasional jazz and other live music.

★ **Komiteti – Kafe Muzeum** Rruga Papa Gjon Pali II; www.facebook.com/komiteti.kafemuzeum. The team behind *Komiteti* have taken the 'café-museum' concept to the next level, packing out their colourful premises with over three thousand artefacts from around Albania. And if you have acquired a taste for *raki*, the bar stocks many varieties of the fruit brandy and serving staff are knowledgeable about local tipples as well as being able to mix international cocktails. A superb place to hang out, day or night. The *Komiteti* recipe has been a hit around Albania, and you can find outposts with quirky local flavour in several other cities too.

Lake View Bar Next to the lake in Grand Park. A scenic spot to relax in Grand Park. The coffees and other drinks are pretty standard, and there are breakfasts and other light meals which are enjoyed with lake views.

Living Room Antik Rruga Vaso Pasha. Very trendy and chic cocktail bar in the north of Blloku, whose interiors are sprinkled with carefully curated antiques and lots of eclectic seating. The cocktails come in for high praise. Some claim this place only really gets going after midnight – you be the judge.

Mon Cheri Branches across Tirana; www.moncheri.al. This café chain has at least sixteen branches across the city and is a good fallback option when all you want is a coffee to go.

My Favourite Tirana Parku i Madh. Head here after dark for twinkling views of illuminated Tirana across the lake. Sink into a beanbag and kick back with a well-earned beer after a day on your feet sightseeing.

★ **Radio** Rruga Ismail Qemali 29/1; www.radio.al. A charming time-warp, *Radio* in the Blloku neighbourhood is cluttered with vintage radios, TVs, 1970s furniture and socialist realism posters. It's a fascinating collection of historical objects, and the cocktails aren't bad either. Have the bar staff mix you a Tirana Mule – Albanian gin with ginger, lemon, lime, sherbet and cucumber.

Shendeverë Wine Bar Shëtitorja Murat Toptani. This superb wine bar in Tirana Castle serves bubbly, reds and whites from the owners' own Çobo vineyards. There's plenty

TIRANA'S CULTURAL CALENDAR

The Albanian capital is not a big on festivals and it's certainly not worth planning a trip around Tirana's events calendar. However, if you are in town, the following can provide an interesting distraction from all the Cold War horror. Find updated listings at www.visit-tirana.com/events.

Swing Marathon April. This three-day jazz extravaganza is held at the *Hemingway* bar and continues in the carriages of a vintage train to Shkodra. www.hemingway.al.

International Cultural Weeks early May to Nov. Over seven months, Tirana embraces the culture of a different country each week through exhibitions, film, music and food. www.jkn.al.

Tirana Marathon Oct. Albania's top athletics event sees runners pounding the streets every October. There's also a half marathon, a 10k and a fun run. www.tiranamarathon.com.

Tirana International Film Festival early Nov. Arguably the biggest single festival in the capital, TIFF features successful international pictures as well as new cinematic works from Albanian filmmakers. www.tiranafilmfest.org.

Winter Festival and Christmas markets Dec to Jan. Albanians of all faiths love Christmas, and no town decks the halls quite like Tirana. Shop for handmade gifts, try hearty snacks and take in the dazzling lights strung around Skanderbeg Square. www.visit-tirana.com.

of tasty morsels to pair with your wine, and the serving staff are very knowledgeable.

Sky Club Sky Tower, Rruga Ibrahim Rugova; www.facebook.com/skyclubtirana. If you like your drinks with a view, there's no better place than this lofty bar at the top of the Sky Tower. The whole thing slowly rotates, providing a 360-degree panorama of the city, best savoured at sunset. Some complain of pricey drinks and inattentive service.

Sophie Caffe Sheshi Wilson; www.sophiecaffe.com. Good for a pastry breakfast, a light sandwich lunch or a cuppa any time, this friendly, youthful café just off the southwest corner of Blloku is a sure-fire bet. Also cocktails and wine by the glass in the evening. Part of a chain around Tirana and beyond.

The Tea Room Bulevardi Gjergj Fishta 4. Wholly un-Albanian, the tea and cakes served at this English-style parlour are second to none. Decor is twee, with frilly wall lights and flowery wallpaper. The cheesecake is excellent.

ENTERTAINMENT

Hemingway Rruga Kont Urani; www.hemingway.al. The cosy *Hemingway* bar is one of the places in central Tirana where you are most likely to catch live jazz at the weekend.

Kinema Millennium Rruga Murat Toptani; www.kinemamillennium.com. Be sure not to miss the latest blockbuster releases while on your travels by visiting Kinema Millennium next to the Toptani Shopping Centre. Also shows the odd Albanian and obscure European film.

National Puppet Theatre Southwest corner of Sheshi Skënderbej; www.facebook.com/teatrikukullavefaqjazyrtare. Extravagant, theatrical puppet shows were a cherished (or at least tolerated) part of childhood during communism, and Tirana's theatre reopened in late 2024 after extensive renovations to the 1924 Italianate building, once the chamber of Albania's parliament. Nearly a hundred fantastical vintage puppets have also been restored and displayed, a unique bygone craft that may intrigue kids (and adults).

National Stadium Sheshi Italia; www.facebook.com/arena.kombetare. It's definitely worth checking out what's on at the National Stadium (though it doesn't actually have its own website) as in addition to the Red and Blacks playing their home games there, there are occasionally rock and other concerts on the agenda. Some of Albania's biggest music stars perform there.

National Theatre of Opera and Ballet Sheshi Skënderbej; www.tkob.gov.al. Looking out over Skanderbeg Square, the communist-era National Theatre of Opera and Ballet puts on a more varied programme of shows than you might think. An international opera performance one night might be followed by a Michael Jackson tribute act or folk dance show the next. Check the website for the current programme or simply drop by to see what's on.

Te Latini Rruga Çamëria; www.facebook.com/telatini. You may not have travelled to Albania purely to try Latin dancing, but with a distinct lack of clubs in the capital, you might just be tempted to hit the dancefloor here. There are cocktails galore, the staff are fun and it's an atmospheric place to hang out, even if you have two left feet.

SHOPPING

SEE MAPS PAGES 52, 54 AND 58

Thirty years ago, the idea of shopping in Tirana would have been absurd. These days you can buy almost anything in the Albanian capital, with huge malls sprouting in the suburbs that are as good as anything in Europe's richer nations.

1

However, you might be more interested in souvenirs than perusing the same brands from back home, and the city centre is better for local handicrafts and independent boutiques. Tirana's markets are not the chaotic free-for-all they once were but are still interesting and colourful places to peruse.

Adrion Sheshi Skënderbej; www.adrionltd.com. Albania's biggest bookstore, housed conveniently in the National Theatre of Opera and Ballet on Skanderbeg Square, has a fine collection of Albania-themed books as well as many books in English. Also sells souvenirs and claims to be open 24hr a day (we haven't tested the validity of this).

Dea Souvenir Shëtitorja Murat Toptani. Packed to the rafters with eclectic mementos, this is a solid option if all you want is a bunker fridge magnet, an olive wood chopping board or a miniature bottle of *raki*.

Illyrian Bloodline Qëndra Tregtare, National Stadium; www.illyrianbloodline.com. This urban fashion brand is the brainchild of hip-hop artist Rigels Rajku, known as Noizy. Also has stores located in three other Albanian cities and in Kosovo.

New Bazaar (Pazari i Ri) Sheshi Avni Rustemi; www.pazariiri.com. The New Bazaar (not actually new at all), a 500m stroll from Skanderbeg Square, is not the wild Balkan haggle fest it once was. Investment in the city market has produced some decent eateries and an altogether calmer shopping experience. It's still a great place to pick up some of Albania's amazing fruit and veg as well as local arts and crafts. There are also concerts and cultural events organized here, plus a seasonal open-air cinema.

TEG Rruga Nacionale; www.teg.al; buses #2 and #8 from the centre. Albania's top mall lies to the southeast of the city on the Tirana–Elbasan Highway. As good as any shopping centre you'll find in Western Europe, this is a one-stop shop for anything you might need as well as most things you don't.

Tirana Castle Shëtitorja Murat Toptani; www.kalajaetiranes.al. In the ruins of a Byzantine-era fortress sometimes attributed to the emperor Justinian I, Tirana Castle (Kalaja e Tiranës) is now an upscale shopping area, with a handful of the city's top shops for picking up high-quality souvenirs such as wine, *gliko* (fruit preserve), woodcarvings, jewellery, mountain tea, olive oil, *qilims* and more.

Toptani Shopping Centre Rruga Abdi Toptani; www.toptani.com.al. This relatively upmarket shopping mall provides one of the glitziest retail experiences in Albania and is home to many brands you'll know and countless ones you definitely won't. Drop in for a Tissot watch or a loaf of bread from the Conad supermarket.

DIRECTORY

Banks and exchanges Exchange offices are dotted around the centre, but a reliable stretch is along Rruga Ibrahim Rugova opposite Parku Rinia; the Iliria '98 chain generally has good rates too. ATMs can be found all over town; Abi Bank and Raiffeisen Bank have slightly lower withdrawal fees. OTP Albania, Intesa Sanpaolo, Banka Kombëtare Tregtare (BKT), Credins and Tirana Bank are also safe, secure banks for withdrawing and present everywhere.

Embassies Canada, Rruga Ibrahim Rugova 42 (tel: 4 225 7274, www.international.gc.ca/country-pays/albania-albanie/tirana.aspx); France, Rruga Skënderbej 14 (tel: 454 0703, https://al.ambafrance.org); Germany, Rruga Skënderbej 17 (tel: 4 227 4505, https://tirana.diplo.de); UK, Rruga Skënderbej 12 (tel: 4 223 4973, www.gov.uk/world/organisations/british-embassy-tirana); USA, Rruga Stavro Vinjau 14 (tel: 4 224 7285, https://al.usembassy.gov).

Emergencies Police, ambulance and fire, tel: 112.

Hospitals ABC Health (Rruga Qemal Stafa 260; tel: 069 409 6078, www.abchealth.org) is a private clinic with English-speaking doctors and a wide range of medical services. University Hospital Center Mother Teresa (Nënë Tereza; Rruga e Dibrës 372; tel: 04 237 3835, www.qsut.gov.al) is a large public hospital, while Hygeia (off the Tirana–Durrësi Highway, SH2, near the Northern and Southern Albania Regional Bus Terminal; tel: 04 239 0000, www.hygeia.al) is a private hospital with a 24hr emergency department.

Pharmacies Farmaci Ditë e Natë (tel: 04 454 1237, www.ditenate.al) has branches across Tirana, including at Rruga Mine Peza, Rruga Kongresi i Manastirit 44/11 and Rruga Luigj Gurakuqi. As the name ('Day and Night') implies, it is open 24hr and staff should speak some English.

Post office The central post office (www.postashqiptare.al) is at Rruga Reshit Çollaku 4, just a few steps off Skanderbeg Square. The most convenient options for sending international mail are the DHL and UPS service points on Rruga Ismail Qemali in Blloku.

Kruja

KRUJA, just 32km from Tirana, became the seat of the first autonomous Albanian principality of the Middle Ages, **Arbanon**, and the stronghold of the last one, the **League of Lezha** (see page 276). Deceptively mighty, the small hilltop city held out against the full pressure of the Ottoman Empire during three long, brutal sieges under the direction of Albanian national hero Gjergj Kastrioti Skënderbeu (or Skënderbej; Skanderbeg). Since that era, Kruja has held a place in the Albanian imagination, a doomed but defiant symbol of resistance like Troy, Carthage or Masada.

Kruja has long been an alluring day-trip from the capital thanks to its **bazaar** (Pazari i Krujës), a charming huddle of wood-and-terracotta-eaved storefronts selling local olive oil and hand-woven *qilims*. Nearby, **Kruja Castle** (Kalaja e Krujës) is home to the **National Ethnographic Museum**, thoroughly renovated in 2024.

Kruja Bazaar

Rruga Albanopolis • Free

The **Pazari i Krujës** or **Pazari i Vjetër** (Old Bazaar) was up and running as early as the fifteenth century, but it began to take its current form – timber-clad stalls along cobblestone streets, perched on a broad ledge adjoining the castle – in the eighteenth century. Most of the shops today run along one L-shaped pedestrianized street, and there's more variety and better quality in what's sold here than you'll find in many other tourist towns. Browse handmade wood carvings, *qilims*, felt caps, folk costumes, preserved treats from local farms, copperware, communist-era odds and ends, and more.

Kruja Castle

Rruga Kala • Free

The **Kalaja e Krujës**, like the bazaar, is a modest affair but it's the most storied stronghold in Albania. Its surviving foundations date to the fifth and sixth centuries AD, and it proved much trickier to topple than most of Albania's heavyweight citadels when the Ottoman Empire came knocking. Frustrating sieges in 1450, 1466 and 1467, the fortress only fell in 1478 after a yearlong blockade starved its inhabitants out. Like other medieval citadels, Kruja Castle and Kruja town were formerly one and the same: the ramparts enclosed homes, shops, places of worship and, in the Ottoman era, lavish villas. People still live and work here today. Nearby are the ruins of the Sultan Mehmed Fatih Mosque (Xhamia e Fatihut), built shortly after the Ottoman conquest; a terracotta-roofed hammam; and the small 1779 Dollma Tekke (Teqeja e Dollmës) of the Bektashi order.

Gjergj Kastrioti Skënderbeu National Museum

Kalaja e Krujës • Charge • www.muzeumet-kruje.com

The **Muzeu Kombëtar Gjergj Kastrioti Skënderbeu** is a two-for-one showcase of medieval and modern history, one of the last sizable museums in the country that retains its communist-era layout and presentation. The building is loosely based on a true castle but unmistakably eighties in style, Enver Hoxha's answer to Disney World's Cinderella Castle; its architects would design the Pyramid of Tirana a few years later. Inside, the museum preserves the intended vibe of hallowed shrine to the great Albanian hero, with a hall of bronze busts of Skanderbeg and his lieutenants and several superb wall-sized socialist realist murals of Skanderbeg's military and diplomatic exploits. Bibliophiles will also appreciate the substantial collection of volumes here.

Ethnographic Museum

Kalaja e Krujës • Charge • www.muzeumet-kruje.com

Built by the wealthy Toptani family in 1764, this handsome two-level *konak* was restored in 2024, and now shelters the **Ethnographic Museum**. Look out for the original frescoes across the frieze of the upstairs living rooms, intricate woodcarvings, stonework around the fireplaces and sumptuously decorated trunks, tables and rugs. On the lower floor, learn about olive oil pressing and *raki* distillation. In one salon you can don VR goggles to watch folk dancers appear at a wedding, or 'try on' digital folk costumes in another.

ARRIVAL AND GETTING AROUND — KRUJA

By bus Hourly buses run from Tirana (1hr), dropping you right by the bazaar.

By car Kruja is a 50min drive from Tirana and Durrësi, with plenty of paid parking available.

The north

HIKERS IN THE VALBONA VALLEY

The north

The north of Albania is all about dramatic peaks, high-altitude hikes, jaw-dropping views and the warm hospitality of local communities. The rugged beauty of the northern mountains with their vertiginous passes, remote villages and rich cultural heritage is a secret just beginning to be revealed. Some of the trekking in the region is top-drawer, transporting hikers to the Europe of yesteryear. But when you've had your fill of summits and valleys, the coast beckons with low-key resorts, high dunes and vibrant cities such as Shkodra and Lezha that are awash with history.

The mountainous north is one of the most memorable parts of Albania, especially for those into lacing up hiking boots and gripping trekking poles. No other region of the country offers so many opportunities for **outdoor adventures**. The sheer amount of natural beauty on show in the peaks is astounding and yet the region receives a trickle of visitors compared to similar locations in the Austrian or Slovenian Alps.

The **Albanian Alps**, also known as the Accursed Mountains, are the star of the show, a rugged limestone range stretching across Northern Albania and into neighbouring countries. Jaw-dropping landscapes, lost-in-time villages, glacial rivers, deep valleys and well-marked trails are the aspects of the region travellers come to experience. The **Valbona Valley** and the village of **Thethi**, now joined together in a single national park, are by far the two most-visited destinations in the massif, and the trail between them is Albania's most popular hike, though it's by no means a stroll in the park.

Thethi and Valbona aren't the only places you should seek out, though. To really escape the crowds, head to emerging service centres such as Kukësi, Puka and Peshkopia where the trails are just being discovered. From Peshkopia you can make a day ascent of Albania's highest peak, **Mount Korabi**. And when you've had your fill of the high life, Albania offers a novel way of descending back down to the lowlands. A cascade of dams forms a series of huge reservoirs all the way from the highlands almost to the coast, and a **boat ride** along one of these (from Fierza to Komani) is a must-do experience. The small ferries pass through the often narrow, fjord-like gorge of the Drini River, giving travellers a chance to relax after their exertions.

The north isn't all about wilderness and lonely trails – urban attractions abound in the city of **Shkodra**, often dubbed the gateway to the north. One of the oldest cities in the Balkans, it is enticingly located near – though not entirely on the banks of – **Lake Shkodra** (Liqeni i Shkodrës), the biggest natural lake in the Balkans. Perched on a hill overlooking the city is **Rozafa Castle** (Kalaja e Rozafës), one of Albania's more interesting castles. Shkodra is also known for its vibrant arts scene, with numerous **galleries** and cultural events. The **Marubi National Museum of Photography** (Muzeu Kombëtar i Fotografisë Marubi), housing one of the largest collections of historical photographs in the Balkans, offers a fascinating glimpse of lost Albanian ways of life in the nineteenth and twentieth centuries.

One unique cultural aspect of the region is the **Kanun** (see page 101), a traditional set of laws that governed the social and legal life of the highlanders. While not widely practiced today, the Kanun's cultural legacy affects everything from family structures to hospitality and architecture. Many visitors find it fascinating to learn about these traditions while staying in guesthouses that were once defensive towers, where those who had committed murder hid out the vendetta.

The **best time to visit** the plains of Northern Albania is in **April**, **May** and **October**. The flats south of Shkodra and around Lake Shkodra are some of the hottest places in

EBU BEKËR MOSQUE

Highlights

❶ **Shkodra** The north's biggest city, boasting a spectacular lakeside location, one of Albania's top castles and a lively city centre. See page 79

❷ **Lake Shkodra** The Balkans' biggest natural lake is a highly protected habitat for birds, against a mountainous backdrop. See page 86

❸ **Thethi** Lost in the northern mountains, Thethi's stone houses and lonely location has enchanted travellers for years, though a new road makes it much easier to reach. See page 86

❹ **Thethi to Valbona hike** Albania's most popular hike is a jaw-dropping route over a high pass into the Himalayan-like Valbona Valley. See page 88

❺ **Peaks of the Balkans** This epic long-distance trail rollercoasters its way across the mountainscape of three countries – Albania, Kosovo and Montenegro. See page 90

❻ **Lake Komani boat trip** An easy escape from the high-altitude adventure is via a slow boat journey along Lake Komani. See page 92

❼ **Mount Korabi** Ascend the region's highest mountain, which is shared between Albania and North Macedonia. See page 101

❽ **Mrizi i Zanave Agroturizëm** Widely considered Albania's top *agroturizëm* experience with unusually bold architecture and top-notch slow food. See page 104

HIGHLIGHTS ARE MARKED ON THE MAP ON PAGE 78

a country that gets unbearably hot and sticky in July and August. However, some relief from the scorching temperatures and mugginess can be found at altitude in summer, though the best time to hit the mountains is arguably early autumn when the leaves begin to turn.

Winter is a magical time: the 40°C of summer is a distance memory as you watch the snow fall outside the window of a cosy alpine guesthouse. However, most of the trails are snowed over at this time of year.

Shkodra

One of the most rewarding and diverse cities in Albania, **SHKODRA (SHKODËR)** should be on every visitor's itinerary. You could easily spend at least five days in this lively and historical city, exploring all its museums, mosques, churches and **Rozafa Castle** (Kalaja e Rozafës), with a spot of shopping and lots of outdoor cafés in between. Apart from hopping on the bus to reach Rozafa in the far south of the city, the centre can largely be navigated on foot. Shkodra is also the jumping-off point for several natural attractions in the north, namely **Lake Shkodra** (Liqeni i Shkodrës; sometimes referred to as Lake Skadar) and the **Accursed Mountains** (Bjeshkët e Nemuna), and there are many tour agencies and minibus owners willing to help you reach both.

Shkodra is not a place you want to visit between June and September. The northern plains experience some of the highest temperatures in Albania with the mercury climbing over 40°C daily and high humidity making city sightseeing a sweat bath. Come in May or October to get the most out of this cultured, highly enjoyable and multifaceted city.

Brief history

One of Europe's oldest cities and arguably Albania's most culturally significant settlement, Shkodra has a long and eventful history dating back over two millennia. Its position in Northwestern Albania, near the shores of Lake Shkodra and close to the Adriatic, has made it a strategic hub for several Balkan civilizations.

The city's origins can be traced back to the Illyrians – Shkodra was actually the capital of the alliance of Illyrian territories under King Gentius in the third century BC. 'Scodra', as its first recorded name was back then, served as a centre of trade. In 168 BC, the city fell under Roman control after the Illyrians were defeated in the Third Illyrian War. Shkodra became the capital of Praevalitana, an ancient Roman province that included parts of present-day Albania, Montenegro and Serbia, and was developed as a city.

Following the decline of the Western Roman Empire, Shkodra continued under Byzantine rule. During the medieval period, it became contested territory, caught between competing powers such as the Byzantine Empire, the Slavs encroaching from the north, and the Venetians. From the eleventh to the fourteenth century, the city saw periods of stability under local Albanian rulers and the establishment of the Balsha (or Balšić) family's control. However, by 1396, the Venetians took control of Scutari, as they called it, recognizing its strategic importance on the Adriatic coast.

In the late fifteenth century, the Ottoman Empire pressed its conquest of the Balkans, with Shkodra a primary target. The Siege of Shkodra from 1478 to 1479 was one of the most significant battles between the Ottomans and the Venetians. Despite fierce resistance, the city fell to the Ottomans in 1479. Under Ottoman rule, Shkodra became an important administrative and military centre, as well as a vibrant cultural and trade hub.

In the nineteenth century, Shkodra played a pivotal role in the Albanian National Awakening (Rilindja), a movement that promoted Albanian identity, autonomy and eventually freedom from Ottoman rule. It became a lodestar for Albanian culture, education and resistance. By 1912, Albania declared its independence, and Shkodra became an integral part of the new state. During the communist period Shkodra's architectural heritage was left to crumble but since 1991 preservation has been ongoing.

Rozafa Castle

Rruga e Kalasë • Charge

Dramatically perched on a promontory above the southern reaches of Shkodra, 3.5km south of the city centre, **Rozafa Castle** (Kalaja e Rozafës) is top billing as far as attractions are concerned. It's an obviously strategic point, established by the Illyrians at the confluence of the Buna and Drini rivers.

Legend swirls around the castle and the origins of its name. As the story goes, it's said that the three brothers who built the castle couldn't get the walls to stand firm. A wise old man advised them to brick up one of their wives as a human sacrifice – the one who brought the men food next day was to become the unlucky lady. The two elder siblings had warned their spouses of the danger, but the younger brother stuck to his promise of secrecy and, of course, it was his wife Rozafa who turned up. It's said she had one request – to leave a breast protruding so that she could feed her baby son. Some locals still believe the walls weep milk.

Tales aside, the fortress has been fought over and controlled by a long list of empires and rulers. Some of the walls date back to the Illyrians and the fourth century BC. The Venetians added a church, which was then converted into a mosque by the Ottomans after the Siege of Shkodra in 1479. Today the castle is in ruins, with only the small **museum** a functional building. Visitors can scramble around the whole caboodle but be aware that health and safety is not much of a priority, and you should take care especially if you have children. There are some deep holes that little ones could fall into.

The crumbling limestone battlements and turbulent history are interesting enough, but it's the views from Rozafa that will linger longest in the memory. The scene is truly a dramatic one with the rivers glistening in the sunlight below, Shkodra's mountain-backed urban sprawl extending to the north and the blue of Lake Shkodra almost reaching the horizon to the northwest. The hazy blue mountains on the eastern shoreline of the lake belong to Montenegro.

If driving to Rozafa, it's best to leave your car at the bottom of the hill as the tiny car park at the top fills almost instantly. The best way to reach the fortress is to take a taxi from central Shkodra (10min) which can drop you at the top, saving you the hard, sweaty climb up. You can then either walk back into town or organize another taxi. Sturdy shoes are advised.

Site of Witness and Memory

Bulevardi Skënderbeu • Charge

This building started life as a Franciscan seminary, but during the communist decades it served as the local headquarters of the state security and secret police – the much-feared Sigurimi. Since the 1990s it has been turned into a **museum** documenting the unimaginable horrors that the building witnessed. The various displays and artefacts tell the story of how the local security services arrested, interrogated, tortured and murdered thousands here. The exhibition spaces are a mix of dramatically modern and authentically preserved – the contrast between the two makes it all the starker. The cells are particularly disturbing, as are the walls of photographs of those who were imprisoned here. Many find Shkodra's **Site of Witness and Memory** more moving even than Tirana's Bunk'Art museums (see pages 63 and 58) and House of Leaves (see page 59).

History Museum

Rruga Oso Kuka • Charge • www.muzeuhistorikshkoder.org

Shkodra's tiny **History Museum** (Muzeu Historik) is as interesting for the building it occupies as for the exhibits inside. The striking villa was the nineteenth-century home of Oso Kuka, a member of the border force who died in a battle with the Montenegrins in 1861. The perfectly preserved Ottoman-era abode is a typical Shkodra house from the period with many architectural features once specific to the area, such as a large stucco fireplace and a separate living room for womenfolk.

The displays are divided into two parts. Downstairs are **archaeological finds** from the Shkodra district including Roman coins, Bronze Age artefacts and pieces of carved stonework from Rozafa Castle (see page 79). Upstairs awaits the more interesting

ethnographical collection with several colourful costumes belonging to Muslims and Catholics, demonstrating the erstwhile ethnic diversity of the region.

Rruga Kolë Idromeno

Between Sheshi Nënë Tereza and Sheshi Dugajët e Reja, **Rruga Kolë Idromeno** is Shkodra's most pleasant street: a pedestrianized thoroughfare lined with outdoor cafés, galleries, small shops and the odd museum. This is the city's place to see and be seen,

with locals gathering for their evening *passeggiata* (stroll) once the temperature falls to bearable levels. Some of the main attractions are here, too, including the Ebu Bekër Mosque and the Marubi National Museum of Photography.

Marubi National Museum of Photography

Rruga Kolë Idromeno 32 • Charge • www.marubi.gov.al

2

The unique **Marubi National Museum of Photography** (Muzeu Kombëtar i Fotografisë Marubi) displays the work of Albania's most prominent photographic dynasty. The archive includes Albania's first photograph, taken in 1858 by Italian refugee Pietro Marubbi (1834–1903), who spent most of his life in Shkodra and later changed his name to its Albanian translation – Pjetër Marubi. Just as photography was becoming fashionable, Marubi set up a studio on Rruga Kolë Idromeno, the street later named after one of Albania's most celebrated artists – Idromeno studied at Marubi's creative space and created Albania's first film in 1912. Marubi's adopted son, Kel, became the official photographer for King Zog I in the 1930s. Kel's son, Gegë, continued the artistic tradition but went on to collaborate with the Sigurimi, shooting footage that helped the secret police arrest and even execute people. However, it was Gegë who dedicated the archive to the state in 1970, a collection that makes up part of this fascinating museum.

The images on show provide a literal snapshot of life in the north of Albania in the late nineteenth and early twentieth centuries taken by various photographers from the Shkodra region over the decades. There are mountain folk in shaggy costumes, boys from well-to-do families in sailor outfits, moustached Ottoman officials in myriad uniforms, and spartan communist-era scenes. The museum also regularly hosts temporary exhibitions put together from its half-a-million photography archive.

You could spend at least two hours here. Almost all the captions are in English.

Ebu Bekër Mosque

Rruga Fushë Çelë 1 • Free

You could certainly say Shkodra's main mosque, **Ebu Bekër Mosque** (Xhamia Ebu Bekër), just off the central Democracy Square (Sheshi Demokracia), has had a turbulent past. The original was destroyed by an earthquake in 1905, its replacement was demolished by the communists in the 1960s. What you see today is a Saudi-financed design dating from 1995. The simple, light interior, decorated in white-and-blue geometrical patterns, can hold over a thousand worshippers (it rarely does).

Statue of Mother Teresa

Sheshi Nënë Tereza • Free

Just 100m south of the Ebu Bekër Mosque, on Mother Teresa Square (Sheshi Nënë Tereza), stands a **bronze statue** of Albania's most famous nun. Many agree this is not the most attractive image of **Mother Teresa**, her arms crossed and an expression of misery on her face. Each October local Catholics lay wreaths at her feet.

Cathedral of St Stephen

Sheshi Gjon Pali II • free

A symbol of Shkodra's religious plurality and tolerance, the **Cathedral of St Stephen** on John Paul II Square (Sheshi Gjon Pali II) was once an island of Christianity in a sea of Ottoman Islam. Built in the late 1850s, the place of worship is a fairly new arrival on the scene. Inside you'll find ceiling paintings by Kolë Idromeno, one of Albania's most celebrated artists, but otherwise it's a pretty plain affair. This could be down to the fact that from 1967 until 1991 it was put to use as a sports hall. Reconsecrated as the cathedral of the Archdiocese of Shkodra-Pult in 1991 in the presence of Mother Teresa, it received a visit from Pope John Paul II in 1993.

MASKS MADE IN SHKODRA

It may come as a surprise to learn that many of those decorative masks you see at Italy's world-famous Venice Carnival are, in fact, made in Shkodra. The **Venice Art Mask Factory** (Rruga Inxh. Gjovalin Gjadri, tel: 068 406 7481) on the outskirts of town is where skilled local artisans handcraft the *baùta* from paper mâché. Contact the factory direct for a tour, after which you can buy a souvenir in the shop to take home (or to Venice) with you.

2

ARRIVAL AND DEPARTURE

SHKODRA

By plane If you want an alternative to Tirana Airport, the nearest airport to Shkodra as the crow flies is in Podgorica (www.montenegroairports.com, TGD), the capital of Montenegro, 60km to the northwest. There are flights here from several European capitals including London and Manchester. FlixBus (www.flixbus.com) runs coaches to Shkodra from Podgorica two or three times a day (1hr 50min; €25) and there are other bus services available, too. Tivat Airport, near Kotor in Montenegro, is too far away (over 100km/2hr 30min drive) and there are no direct connections from there.

By bus As the capital of the north and Albania's fifth-largest city, Shkodra is well connected to Tirana by bus. Services leave every 30min or so from the capital's South and North Regional Terminal (2hr 30min; 400 lek/€4). These services also stop en route in Lezha (45min). You can come or go by bus to Tirana Airport (several daily; 2hr), other major cities in Western Albania, and towns in the north too: Durrësi (several daily; 2hr 25min) and Vlora (1 daily; 4hr 30min), as well as Kukësi (several daily; 2hr), Peshkopia (several daily; 4hr) and Puka (several daily; 1hr 20min). To reach Thethi you'll need to take a minibus (around €12). These can be organized through your hotel or hostel.

By car If arriving from Montenegro by car, the nearest border crossing in the south is Muriqani–Sukobin, just 17km from Shkodra city centre. Coming from Podgorica to the north you cross at Božaj–Hani i Hotit. Formalities are usually over very quickly. If driving from Tirana, the motorway runs out at Laçi but the last 50km is on a decent, two-way road. The whole journey is around 100km. Roads within Shkodra can be slightly chaotic and in the old centre very narrow. There's very little parking in the centre.

GETTING AROUND

On foot Shkodra is a very walkable city with most of the sights concentrated in the centre around the central Democracy Square (Sheshi Demokracia), which is actually a huge roundabout.

By bus Buses leave from near Democracy Square for Rozafa Castle (15min) and Shiroka (20min) on a rolling basis. Fares are cheap (30 lek/€0.30), and services run all day.

INFORMATION

Tourist information Visit Shkodër (www.visitshkoder.org) may or may not operate a tiny kiosk just off Democracy Square, and a very 'work in progress' website. The agency does run tours to Thethi and several other locations.

ACCOMMODATION

SEE MAP PAGE 81

There's certainly no shortage of places to stay in Shkodra, with everything from campsites on the shores of Lake Shkodra to five-star hotels right in the city centre to choose from.

Colosseo Rruga Kolë Idromeno; www.colosseohotel.com. Arguably Shkodra's top hotel, this five-star chunk of swank sits right on the most popular pedestrian thoroughfare, the surrounding modest townhouses crouching in its blue-tinted glass shadow. Inside, rooms are crisp and air-conditioned, if unimaginative; staff are polite; there's a gym, a restaurant, three bars and – possibly the least relevant to travellers – sparkling conference facilities. €€€€

★ **Hotel Tradita Geg & Tosk** Rruga Edith Durham 25; www.traditagt.com. Based in a house dating back to 1694, this hotel-guesthouse is the most characterful place to sleep in all of Shkodra. Rooms range from basic but charming to grand, antique-filled affairs with beamed ceilings and four-poster beds. The restaurant is as traditional as they come. €€

★ **Lake Shkodra Resort** 10km north of Shkodra towards Kopliku; www.lakeshkodraresort.com. This is a professionally run Western-style campsite with pitches for tents and campervans right on the banks of Lake Shkodra. There's tons of space here, and the only campsite on this side of the Balkans' largest lake understandably attracts lots of international number plates. There's also a very good restaurant, a shop and decent facilities. Staff speak English. €

Red Bricks Hotel Sheshi Demokracia; www.theredbricks-al.com. Super central, the *Red Bricks Hotel* is a top-class haunt with some of the crispest rooms in town, very well-drilled staff and a superb buffet breakfast in a light-filled dining room. The location on Democracy Square puts you right at the heart of the Shkodra action. €€

2

EDITH DURHAM – QUEEN OF THE HIGHLANDERS

Mary Edith Durham (1863–1944) was a pioneering **British traveller** and **anthropologist** who played a significant role in documenting the culture and history of the Albanian Highlands during the early twentieth century. Born in London to a surgeon father, Durham initially studied art, but her passion for the Balkans, particularly Albania, became the defining feature of her life's work. She first visited the region in 1900, initially to recover from an illness, but was quickly drawn to the rugged landscapes and complex political dynamics of the area.

Although initially attracted to Serbia, Durham became deeply fascinated by the **Albanian people** who, at the time, were under the rule of the Ottoman Empire. Albania was a region fraught with tribal conflicts and tensions, but Durham earned the trust and respect of many locals, particularly in the northern highlands. Her travels were extensive, and she often ventured into areas that few foreigners had ever seen. Durham's ethnographic observations are valuable records of Albanian **customs**, **beliefs** and **ways of life** at the time, many of which were rapidly disappearing due to modernization and political upheaval. Her work was a snapshot of a culture that was largely obliterated during the communist reign of the latter half of the twentieth century.

Her most famous book, *High Albania* (1909), is a vivid account of her experiences in the mountainous north. She describes the fierce independence of the Albanian tribes, their elaborate code of honour (Kanun) and their ancient traditions. Durham also delved into **political advocacy**, supporting Albanian independence and frequently writing in favour of Albanian rights in European newspapers. She saw Albania as an underdog in the region, frequently overshadowed by its neighbours, and used her platform to bring attention to its plight. She drew some criticism at home for her stances, especially when it came to Serbia. During the Balkan Wars (1912–1913) and the collapse of the Ottoman Empire, Durham bravely continued her travels in Albania, acting as a **humanitarian** and documenting the impact of the wars on the Albanian population. Her writings are filled with empathy for the suffering of the locals, as she witnessed firsthand the destruction of villages, displacement of people, and the harsh realities of conflict.

Known to the Albanians as 'Mbretëresha e Malësorëve' (Queen of the Highlanders), Durham is remembered as a passionate advocate for Albania and its people. She was admired by King Zog I in exile and in 2004 was described by Albanian president Alfred Moisiu as "one of the most distinguished personalities of the Albanian world during the last century". Her work, mostly held by the Royal Anthropological Institute in London, remains an invaluable historical resource, capturing a critical period in Albanian history. Her collections from the region are in the safe keeping of the British Museum and are occasionally displayed as part of exhibitions.

Rose Garden Hotel Rruga Justin Godard 18; www.rosegardenhotel.al. In a restored mansion, the *Rose Garden Hotel* has clean rooms, some with writing desks and antique touches. The whole set-up is very comfortable, and the secret garden out back is a wonderful place to relax after a day on the road. Also has its own restaurant. €€

★Shkodra Backpackers – Mi Casa es Tu Casa Bulevardi Skënderbeu 26; www.micasaestucasa.it. *My House is Your House* is Shkodra's original backpacker hostel. It can be found in the centre of Shkodra and is a wonderfully bohemian, colourful place. The house has a lot of history (ask the owner) and contains dorms and private rooms, all individually decorated. This is also a great place to organize onward travel to Thethi and Valbona. €

The Wanderers Hostel Rruga Gjuhadol; www.thewanderershostel.com. Albania's hostels have really kept that backpacker vibe and there's no better example in the north than *The Wanderers*. A great place to stay with a large outdoor seating area and a bar, though the dorms are a little bland. It's one of the best places to arrange transfers into the mountains. Breakfast is included. €

EATING

SEE MAP PAGE 81

Aroma Bulevardi Skënderbeu; www.facebook.com/AromaRestorant. *Aroma* tries to please every palate with its steaks, pizzas, healthy options and traditional Albanian dishes, and certainly keeps wallets heavy thanks to its very reasonable prices. The dining room is a study in twenty-first-century cool with low-strung lighting, plants and retro veneer. A great fall-back option, whatever you fancy. €

Atelier Rruga 28 Nëntori 6; https://atelier.al. The stone-walled dining room of this popular place is adorned with antiques, and the walled garden out back is Shkodra's cosiest. The menu is a mixed bag of seafood, Albanian meat dishes and pasta, all superbly executed. The English-speaking staff come in for high praise. €€€

★ **Idromeno** Rruga Besnik Sykja 2; www.idromeno.al. *Idromeno* is named after the famous Albanian artist, and the food at this relative newcomer is also a work of art. Try the beef cheek in dark chocolate sauce or the rabbit rolls with potato, rounded off with chamomile mousse and olive oil cream. The staff are polite; the ambience understated. €€€

Pasta te Zenga Rruga 28 Nëntori; tel: 069 253 0662. Shkodra's best Italian job is this very modern affair a short stroll from the Ebu Bekër Mosque. The pastas, risottos, seafood and salads use local ingredients and burst with flavour. Wash it all down with Albanian wines. €€

Scutari Garden Rruga Vaso Kadia. Located in the parkland to the northeast of Democracy Square, this small place is earning a name for itself among foreign visitors for its egg dishes, wraps, fruit salads and great coffees. It's a soothing place to start the day if your hotel doesn't do breakfast. €

Tradita Geg & Tosk Rruga Edith Durham 25; www.traditagt.com. Top restaurant at the top hotel in town, plating up the most traditional fare in the entire north of Albania. The stone-walled dining room and heavy beamed ceilings set the scene for the excellent lamb, grilled meats, stews and other hearty dishes. There's live music most nights. Some complain of overbearing service. €€

Vila Bekteshi Rruga Hasan Riza Pasha 33; www.cocja.com. One of Shkodra's oldest restaurants, this beautifully traditional villa creates a fitting backdrop for special meals involving Adriatic seafood and highland staples. Choose between the courtyard or indoor dining space. English-speaking staff, but some diners have reported fluctuations in the quality of the dishes. €€

2

DRINKING AND NIGHTLIFE

SEE MAP PAGE 81

Baza Bulevardi Zogu I. Low lit pub with flavoursome cocktails, decent grub and lots of games, all enjoyed in god-sent air-conditioned premises with punkish flashes of graffiti-esque colour.

Il Sole Caffe Rruga Hafiz Sabri Bushati; www.ilsolecaffe.com. From your first espresso to your last cocktail and everything in between, this café is one of the city's best hangouts, whatever time of day you show up. There's cheap and tasty food and snacks using locally sourced ingredients where possible, and the ambience is very chilled out.

Shega e Egër Rruga Gjuhadol; tel: 066 619 6553. Fresh juices, smoothies and healthy food in a casual joint – think upcycled palette tables and tree-trunk stools – that attracts a backpacker crowd. Great place to chill if you are melting on the oven-hot streets. Also holds various events.

SHOPPING

SEE MAP PAGE 81

Venice Art Mask Factory Rruga Inxh. Gjovalin Gjadri; tel: 068 406 7481. Although masks fake and real are sold across town, the only guarantee of handmade authenticity is to visit the factory shop where they are made. It might seem a curious souvenir to bring back from Albania, but the quality of these masks is higher than you'll find in Venice itself.

DIRECTORY

Banks There's no shortage of branches of Albania's major banks, with ATMs, in the centre, both around Sheshi Demokracia and on Rruga Kolë Idromeno.

Emergencies Tel: 127, tel: 129 or tel: 112.

Hospital Spitali Rajonal i Shkodrës (Shkodra Regional Hospital) is at Rruga Kolë Heqimi 11. Located in the east of town, this is the state hospital and by all accounts provides a better service than the private facilities that are nearby.

Pharmacies Farmacia Jote (tel: 069 279 4663) is on Rruga Studenti, right next to Democracy Square. Out of all the city's pharmacies, this one keeps the longest hours and should have some English-speaking staff members.

Post office The city's main post office can be found at Rruga 28 Nëntori 3. There's a DHL service point on Bulevardi Skënderbeu near Sheshi Nënë Tereza.

Kiri Valley

With a car, one of the most rewarding day-trips from Shkodra is the **KIRI VALLEY**, to the northeast. The **Kiri River** (Lumi i Kirit) beats a path through 2000m-high mountains between Shkodra and Thethi, before wending south to the foot of the rocky promontory supporting Rozafa Castle, at which point it merges with the Drini River. The road that traces the river is driveable for around 20km from

Shkodra as far as Prekali, with several places to pull in along the way. The first worthwhile stop is the **Mesi Bridge** (Ura e Mesit), one of Northern Albania's most photographed sites. Where the old road parts from the newer highway, an ancient humpback stone bridge leaps over the Kiri in one wide arch. This was once the only way over the river and was used for transporting wood down from the mountains. It served its purpose until the 1960s, when the main road was built.

From the bridge, take the old road to the village of Drishti where **Drishti Castle** (Kalaja e Drishtit; free) looms high above the houses. The bishops of Shkodra lived here until the ninth century, and the fortress was used to guard the area north of Shkodra right up until the nineteenth century. It's quite an uphill hike through the rough limestone and bushes to reach the ruins from Drishti, but the views across the river and the mountains beyond are worth the effort.

Unfortunately, the only way to press forward from Drishti on to Prekali is to double back to the Mesi Bridge and then rejoin the highway as it climbs into the valley. Tiny villages, the odd restaurant and wild swimming spots appear randomly as the road narrows ever further. Finally, you arrive at the village of **Prekali**, cradled among the peaks. There's a **church** and a **bar** here as well as some great places to bathe in the silky jade-green waters of the Kiri. Rough **mountain-bike trails** push on into the peaks.

Lake Shkodra

It has to be said that when it came to sharing out **LAKE SHKODRA** (Liqeni i Shkodrës), Montenegro was handed the lion's share of noteworthy beaches. The shoreline to the north of Shkodra is marshy and agricultural, and there are no settlements actually on the lakeside, evidently due to flooding. Only the *Lake Shkodra Resort* (see page 83) – the region's best campsite – has decent access. To cool down in the summer, head 6.5km along the southern shore of the lake to the small town of **Shiroka**, which is draped across a rocky ledge between the steep mountainsides and the water. Here you'll find a modernized seafront, with parking and other facilities, which gives onto a stretch of **pebble beach**. The huge pedestrian area is an impressive sight with cobbles laid out in folksy patterns, lots of imaginatively designed seating and a cluster of **food trucks** and kiosks. There are also plenty of **restaurants**, cafés and several waterfront places to stay. It makes for a great half-day trip or just an evening jaunt to watch the sunset.

The Albanian Highlands

The Dinaric Alps, the Great Highlands, the Accursed Mountains – call them what you will but the peaks and valleys of the northern mountains are nothing short of spectacular. If you're interested in hiking and nature, then this is where you should come. After Tirana and the riviera, the **ALBANIAN HIGHLANDS** are one of the biggest attractions this small Balkan nation has to offer. Shkodra is the jumping-off point for the mountains of Albania's north and the best place to organize tours and transport.

Thethi

"I think no place where human beings live has given me such an impression of majestic isolation from all the world".

Edith Durham in *High Albania*

The most popular spot in the Albanian Highlands is **Thethi**, a two-hour drive north of Shkodra. Although now almost entirely given over to the needs of tourists, this mountain village still has that same Shangri-La feel it did back when Edith Durham (see box, page 84) penned *High Albania*, its stone-built, shingle-roofed houses cradled in the belly of a yawning valley, all set against a backdrop of snow-capped peaks. The saw-toothed mountains, rising to heights of 2000m, wrap around Thethi on all sides, creating a feel of the Alps as they once were – wild and untouched. And although twenty-first-century tourism has indisputably arrived here, it is still remote enough to preserve a semblance of its previous isolation. In summer, temperatures are lower than in Shkodra, but the days can still be hot. Come in autumn for a quieter, cooler, more colourful experience as the valley blazes gold and red.

2

In the village, aimless wandering brings a bounty of rewards. The stoic grey-stone **church** dating from 1892 is one of Albania's most photographed edifices, its lonely tower stark against the wall of cragged mountains behind. The building was repaired in 2005 using funds from Albanians abroad. Notice there is no mosque in Thethi – the locals are Catholic, not Muslim. Near the church is the village **museum**, set in a traditional house with curious architectural features, including holes through which dwellers would shoot at approaching enemies and a special opening for expelling waste without setting foot outside. This is vendetta country, after all.

You'll notice other buildings in the village fortified with defensive towers where male family members could wait out a feud – the best-preserved is the **Safe Tower**, which has been converted into a museum. If a man committed murder, his elders had fourteen days to negotiate with the victim's family to agree on compensation. Otherwise, he would be killed by one of the bereaved relatives. For a fraught two weeks, the perpetrator would take refuge on the first floor of the edifice, hence the name. These towers were once a feature of almost every Albanian village and were still being built in the early part of the twentieth century, but King Zog I had many demolished in an effort to modernize. Those that survived, such as the one in Thethi, are now national monuments.

Alps of Albania National Park

Thethi once lay at the centre of the old Thethi National Park, but in 2022 this was amalgamated with the Valbona Valley National Park and the Gashi Nature Reserve to create the **Alps of Albania National Park** (Parku Kombëtar Alpet e Shqipërisë). The area surrounding Thethi is rich in natural wonders that you don't have to be a seasoned hiker to reach. An easy 3km walk south of the village centre, the **Grunasi Waterfall** cascades 30m into a pool whose waters are icy cold even in summer. Some 6.5km further south, near the village of Ndërlysa (or Ndërlysaj), the **Blue Eye** (Syri i Kaltër) is a surreal turquoise sink pool fed by a tumbling waterfall. Unfortunately, it's a victim of its own beauty and on hot days you definitely won't be alone. There are other similar pools nearby worth seeking out for a quieter experience. You can visit both Grunasi Waterfall and the Blue Eye on a single out-and-back day hike (13km each way); sturdy footwear is advised.

Like elsewhere across Albania, sadly Thethi and the surrounding landscape has a waste-management problem. As always, tourists should leave no trace, taking all of their rubbish with them back to a city where they can dispose of it properly.

ARRIVAL AND DEPARTURE — THETHI

By bus Minibuses leave Shkodra for Thethi on an ad-hoc basis. Contact the village hostels for details or ask at your hotel. The journey takes just over 2hr (around €12) and there's usually a stop at the Thora Pass (Qafa e Thorës). You can now easily visit Thethi as part of a day-trip with a guide; ask in the city's hostels for more information.

By car The paved road from Shkodra used to end at the Thora Pass and the final stretch to Thethi was only possible in a 4WD, but that changed in 2021 with the development of a fully asphalted road all the way from Shkodra to Thethi. This obviously made it much easier to reach the remote mountain village, sparking a flurry of visitors to a region once essentially cut off from the rest of the country (by road at least). Most drivers still stop at the Thora Pass to admire the incredible views. There's also a restaurant there for a bite to eat en route.

2

INFORMATION

Tourist information There's a tourist office (tel: 067 204 9837; daily 8am–6pm) right in the centre of Thethi.

ACCOMMODATION AND EATING

Thethi certainly has no shortage of places to sleep, with seemingly every stone dwelling converted into accommodation of some kind. Be sure to book ahead, especially late and early in the season when some village families have already left for, or not yet returned from, their city homes and therefore fewer places are open. All the hotels listed below will be willing to arrange guides, tours and transfers, and even the campsite has a restaurant.

Hotel Alpet Rruga Nikgjonaj; tel: 069 459 0407. Thethi's most happening accommodation, with a lively restaurant that spills out into the grounds and cosy wood-clad rooms. It's one of the places that stays open year-round and has the heating system to prove it. Spending a winter night here as the snow falls outside is an experience that will live long in the memory. €€

Kamping Zorgji Rruga Fushë; tel: 0682 319 610. This large campsite occupies the central section of the village and can accommodate hundreds of people (don't worry, it never does). Facilities are basic. €

Thethi Paradise Rruga Gjeçaj; www.thethiparadise.com. Situated on the route down from the Thora Pass into Thethi, the five timber villas that make up this much-lauded accommodation enjoy some of the best views from any bedroom in the land. However, the location is away from the action down in the valley and the chalets are newbuilds that lack the character of Thethi's stone properties. The restaurant is a welcome sight at the end of a day's hiking. €€

★ **Villa Gjeçaj** Rruga Nikgjonaj; www.villagjecaj.com. One of the most characterful places to stay in Thethi, this family-run guesthouse occupies a tall stone-built villa and a newer residence. Room decor is understated – all wood accents and cream tones – and the views are stupendous. Your hosts are always on hand to offer advice, and the restaurant is one of Thethi's best. €€

THETHI–VALBONA HIKE

Possibly the most popular long-distance hike in all of Albania is the **trek from Thethi to Valbona** (some tackle the walk the other way, but here we describe the route from Thethi). Dramatic, steep and quite exposed in places, this isn't a route for novice hikers. That said, the majority of people who can walk the distance between the villages (around 18km) should be able to manage this trail if they're prepared for steep slopes and rough ground. It takes around six to eight hours to complete the hike, which is a section of the **Peaks of the Balkans**, a 192km circular trek through the borderlands of Montenegro, Albania and Kosovo. Be sure to prebook accommodation for Valbona so you can flop down as soon as you arrive and pack emergency food, a first-aid kit and plenty of water – especially in summer.

The trail starts at the road bridge across the Thethi River and heads northwest. After around a kilometre, the path to Vusanje in Montenegro continues straight on, but you should turn right. Almost immediately you begin to climb through stunted fir trees, ascending almost 1000m over the next six kilometres. The highest point on the walk is the **Valbona Pass** (Qafa e Valbonës) at 1795m, from where there are fantastic views across Albania's northern mountainscape. To the northeast looms **Mount Jezerca**, the highest peak in the Dinaric Alps at 2694m. If you've brought a picnic lunch, this is the place to eat. The **Valbona Valley**, formed millions of years ago by a glacier, yawns below you. Most of the rest of the trail is downhill. Around 10km into the hike, you arrive in the hamlet of **Rragami**, where there is a cluster of cafés. The next jumble of houses is **Llomi**, which has an unofficial campsite. At the 14km mark, the limestone path gives way to paved road, which leads you into **Valbona**.

The route is supposedly **closed** between November and May but that really depends on **weather** conditions. If it snows on the pass, do not attempt to hike it without proper winter gear. Although the route is now well marked, having an offline map facility on your smartphone is a good backup. Obviously, there is no mobile signal.

It should be stressed that if you're travelling by car and want to take on this hike, you should leave your vehicle in Shkodra and ask your accommodation in Shkodra, Thethi or Valbona to help you arrange transport into and out of the mountains. There are no roads between Thethi and Valbona, so if you bring a car to one village, you'll have to hike back another day to retrieve it. See box, opposite page, for a suggested itinerary loop.

A SCENIC BOAT RIDE

With around three or four days to spare, you might want to attempt to strike out on a loop around the Albanian Highland's best destinations. Beginning in **Shkodra**, ask around the hostels for the next available minibus to **Thethi** and stay the night. The next day, enjoy some light **hiking** in the valley and a hearty meal. After a good night's sleep, trek from Thethi to **Valbona** (see box, page 88) and **overnight** there. On the final day, hop on a bus to **Fierza** and then board the **ferry** (1000 lek/€10 per person) down dramatic **Lake Komani** to **Komani** (3hr), from where minibuses run back to Shkodra (2hr). It's the classic circuit and many hostels and hotels in Shkodra can arrange the whole thing for you.

2

Valbona

VALBONA is probably the second most-visited village in the area though a pretty small place that essentially shuts up shop over the winter. The **Peaks of the Balkans** (POB) trail runs right through the village and where there are hikers, there's food and beds.

Valbona doesn't have Thethi's showstopping setting, but it is a very pleasant place to rest up and chill out between hikes. The POB heads north from here to Vusanje in Montenegro, a slightly more demanding hike than the Thethi–Valbona trail. With the right gear (tent and provisions), it is possible to loop back to Thethi via Montenegro (from Llomi), but this is a lonely route and only for experienced hikers used to spending nights out in the wilds and carrying everything with them.

ARRIVAL AND DEPARTURE — VALBONA

By bus Obviously no bus runs back to Thethi as the only way to reach the village is by hiking over the Valbona Pass, but there are minivans constantly arriving from and leaving for Bajram Curri (1hr) and Fierza (1hr 40min), with some going as far as Shkodra and even Tirana.

By car Valbona is easier to reach by car than Thethi, though the road between Kukësi and Fierza is a rollercoaster, albeit a scenic one. There are no petrol stations after Bajram Curri so fill up in advance. Most accommodation has some form of free parking for guests.

ACCOMMODATION AND EATING

Hotel Margjeka Valbona; www.hotelmargjeka.al. Occupying a typically tall stone building a couple of kilometres outside the village, the smartness of this hotel contrasts starkly with the rugged mountains outside. It has arguably one of the best hotel restaurants in Valbona and is a very popular choice, so book ahead. **€€**

Jezerca Guesthouse Valbona; tel: 067 309 3406. A series of wooden chalets gazes out across the river at the mountains beyond – the fine view you can enjoy from your bed every morning. The kitchen here turns out filling mountain fare, just the job to set you up for a day's hiking. The chalets themselves are well heated and have crisply modern bathrooms. **€**

★ **Quku i Valbonës** Valbona; www.facebook.com/JourneytoValbona. This is the umbrella name for three accommodations – the legendary backpacker haunt *Farmhouse Hostel*; the *Rezidenca* luxury guesthouse; and the *Rilindja Hotel*, some distance away. There are dorms, a restaurant, a hiking information centre and heaps of advice on offer to all who stay here

DIRECTORY

Tour companies Catherine Bohne at Journey to Valbona (Bajram Curri; tel: 068 360 5795, www.facebook.com/JourneytoValbona) has been in the business of promoting tourism to Valbona and helping travellers for over twenty years, and the staff here are the best people to contact for accommodation, tours, transport and local colour. She is heavily involved with *Quku i Valbones* (see above), sells local produce, runs the TOKA conservation NGO in Bajram Curri (see page 90) and is generally a mine of information on the area and what it has to offer.

Vermoshi and Lëpushi

In the far north of the region, surrounded by high peaks and huddled tight against the border with Montenegro, the valley village of **VERMOSHI** is the end of the line as far as the Albanian part of the Accursed Mountains is concerned. Thethi it may not be – the

PEAKS OF THE BALKANS

The Peaks of the Balkans is a challenging 192km hiking route across the rugged mountainous landscapes of Albania, Kosovo, and Montenegro. Renowned for its natural beauty, the route offers hikers a unique opportunity to explore the pristine wilderness of the Western Balkans, with its towering peaks, deep valleys, glacial lakes and remote mountain villages.

The trek takes adventurers through the heart of the **Accursed Mountains**, a mountain range characterized by its dramatic and jagged contours. The highest point of the walk is **Mount Jezerca** (Maja e Jezercës) in Albania, standing at 2694m. The trail weaves through a diverse range of terrains, from lush alpine meadows to steep, rocky ascents, all in some of the most untouched and remote areas of Europe.

One of the most appealing aspects of the Peaks of the Balkans is its cultural richness. The route connects several traditional villages, where visitors can enjoy Albanian hospitality. Hikers often stay in guesthouses or mountain huts run by local families, offering a glimpse into everyday life in this part of the world. This cultural exchange, combined with the natural beauty, makes for an unforgettable experience. **Thethi** and **Valbona** in Albania, and **Vusanje** in Montenegro are all on the route.

The trail is also rich in biodiversity. Hikers may encounter a variety of **wildlife**, including chamois, lynx, eagles and even brown bears. The route passes through several national parks, including **Prokletije National Park in Montenegro** and the **Alps of Albania National Park** (see page 87), both of which aim to preserve the region's unique ecosystems and native species.

While the Peaks of the Balkans is gaining popularity, it remains relatively uncrowded compared to other major European trekking routes, making it ideal for those seeking solitude and adventure. However, the trail can be demanding, with its remote locations, high elevations and often-challenging weather conditions, making it suitable for those with at least some experience of multiday hiking.

setting not as dramatic – but there are fewer tourists here and the surrounding trails are nowhere near as heavily frequented. The village has several guesthouses.

LËPUSHI, 11km to the south just off the SH20, is another lost-in-time village, its stone and timber houses dotting a wide, rugged valley. The village's guesthouses, chalets and rooms make for a good launchpad for hiking. Buses run here from Shkodra, 85km to the south.

You can then strike out on a two-day 40km hike south to **Vukli** (Vukël) and **Nikçi**, fuel up on local food in a traditional restaurant and spend the night in a guesthouse, then press on to **Thethi** (see page 86).

Bajram Curri

With its 7500 inhabitants, post office, shops, blocks of flats and sports facilities, **BAJRAM CURRI**, the administrative centre of the Tropoja region, is a metropolis compared with the valley villages of the Accursed Mountains. It is named after a prominent Albanian nationalist and freedom fighter, Bajram Curri (1862–1925), who played a key role in the Albanian struggle for independence from the Ottoman Empire and later opposed the Serbian occupation of Albania. He was murdered in these mountains on the orders of King Zog I, but the communists renamed this small settlement in his honour. The town later grew into the regional capital.

Bajram isn't really the sort of place you'd want to hang around in for very long, though some of its central streets have been modernized. It is essentially a service centre and launchpad for hikes and other outdoor adventures in the surrounding mountains. The place to turn to for information and advice is **Journey to Valbona** (www.facebook.com/JourneytoValbona), whose owner Catherine Bohne operates a shop and information centre for hikers and tourists and runs conservation NGO **TOKA** (Rruga Sylejman Vokshi) just out of town. TOKA has been involved in many projects that aim to promote and protect the environment of the Albanian Alps and the social and economic well-being of those who live within its folds; it occasionally has some limited volunteer opportunities.

ARRIVAL AND DEPARTURE — BAJRAM CURRI

By bus Buses run to Bajram Curri from Shkodra around six times a day. The journey takes a tortuous 6–7hr at least. There are regular buses and minibuses to and from Tirana (departures from outside the Palace of Culture; buy tickets on board), with a journey time of around 6hr.

By car As there is no direct route through the mountains, the distance between Bajram Curri and Shkodra is greater than it appears on the map (240km). The journey takes 5–6hr, and the road is winding and slow-going. The route goes via Puka. Driving from Tirana (4hr) it's around the same distance as from Shkodra, but the first 144km are on the fast(er) A1 highway. There are plenty of places to park in Bajram Curri.

INFORMATION

Tourist information Journey to Valbona operates a hiking information centre and small shop in Bajram Curri (Rruga Sylejman Vokshi; tel: 067 301 4638, www.facebook.com/JourneytoValbona).

ACCOMMODATION

Black Mountain Hotel Rruga Sylejman Vokshi; tel: 069 401 0525. This central hotel wins plenty of praise for its well-maintained facilities and helpful staff. Rooms are crisply up to date with monochrome bathrooms and cool, fresh linen. A/C throughout, but warm in winter. €€

Eurobushi Hotel Rruga Bylbyl Breçani; tel: 069 779 8777. You'd be excused for thinking you'd entered a Finnish sauna upon stepping inside this purpose-built hotel, as the whole caboodle – from corridors to rooms – is wood-clad. But the bedrooms are stylishly done out and are very comfortable and cosy. €€

Hotel Shkelzeni Rruga Fatmir Hasadandoci; www.hotelshkelzeni.com. Bajram Curri's top hotel has generously proportioned light and airy rooms with fancy antique-style furniture. Like most hotels of this size and stature in Albania, the *Shkelzeni* has a slightly over-formal restaurant so prise off those hiking boots before you head out for dinner. €€€

EATING

Caka Rruga Sylejman Vokshi; tel: 067 736 9513. Run singlehandedly by a female chef, the food at this central restaurant is simple, no-nonsense Albanian fare such as grilled meats, salads and hearty soups. It's arguably the best non-hotel eatery in town. €

DIRECTORY

Pharmacy Nezaj is situated on Rruga Sylejman Vokshi.

Post office The main post office is on Rruga Mic Sokoli.

Puka

An hour or so drive from Shkodra along the old road to Kukësi (see page 94), scenic little **PUKA** makes for an interesting day-trip or overnighter on the way into the higher mountains further north, or even Tirana. With its small-town vibe, genuinely open locals and an unexpectedly renovated centre, Puka may even tempt you to stay longer than you expected.

At around 800m above sea level and cradled among low peaks, the town has emerged as a hiking centre in its own right. In warmer weather there are several worthwhile trips you can take from the town into the surrounding area, using Puka as a cosy and convenient service hub and base. Even in winter, the high-altitude fun continues when Albania's miniscule skiing industry comes to life.

Brief history

The town's name (a source of mirth to some British visitors – Puka or Pukë, take your pick) is believed to originate from an Illyrian word meaning 'high place', fitting for

2

LAKE KOMANI

Lake Komani (Liqeni i Komanit) is an artificial **reservoir** located in Northern Albania, around 140km away from Tirana (3hr by car) and 60km from Shkodra (1hr 30min), formed by the damming of the Drini River. Wending its way between the towering limestone walls of the **Albanian Alps**, it is one of the most picturesque aspects of the region, albeit a wholly manmade one. The lake was created in the 1970s when the Komani Hydroelectric Power Station was constructed, a part of the Drini River Cascade, a series of six large reservoirs (including two in Vau i Dejës and Fierza) and five hydroelectric power plants in Albania and North Macedonia. Lake Komani plays a crucial role in Albania's energy production, generating a significant portion of its electricity.

However, Lake Komani is not only known for its energy sources but also for its breathtaking **natural beauty**. The lake is often described as a fjord-like landscape due to its steep forest-covered slopes plunging straight into emerald-green waters. The scenery is dramatic, with narrow gorges, cliffs and isolated villages dotting the surrounding terrain. It has become a popular destination for adventurers seeking to experience Albania's wild and relatively untouched landscapes.

Essentially, the only way to explore Lake Komani is by taking a **boat trip**. Regular ferry services operate on the lake, connecting the towns of **Komani** in the south and **Fierza** in the north. The journey is possibly one of the most scenic boat rides you'll ever take inland, offering panoramic views of the mountains, secluded beaches and crystal-clear waters. Along the route, passengers can also spot small Albanian villages, many of which are inaccessible by road, preserving a unique and traditional way of life.

A **shorter boat trip** from Komani into the **Shala River** (Lumi i Shalës) tributary of the reservoir is also a popular detour, but its Instagram-friendly clear waters, riverfront 'beaches' and time-etched canyon faces have made it an attraction, and you'll likely find it far from secluded in the high season.

its lofty mountainous surrounds. It once stood on an ancient trade route used by the Romans but during the Ottoman period it became an important administrative centre. However, the area also played a role in resistance against Ottoman rule as its rugged topography was difficult for outside powers to penetrate and exert complete control, and so Puka became known for its strong sense of independence.

The twentieth century witnessed significant changes, particularly during the communist era when efforts were made to industrialize and modernize the region. The town became a centre for wood-processing and agriculture, and its historical churches and mosques were razed to the ground.

Many of the characterful old stone houses were replaced with soulless concrete blocks. Having shaken off the economic woes of the 1990s, today Puka strives to develop its obvious tourism potential – outdoor adventures, hiking, skiing, local food. It's still a work in progress as it struggles to compete with bigger names on the Albanian tourism scene.

The town itself has a smattering of sights, which you can see in a couple of hours. After that you'll have to find transport out into the sticks or pull on your hiking boots and get planning.

Puka Museum

Sheshi Tërbuni • Free

Puka's small **museum** is part of the cultural centre in the middle of town. It has an interesting exhibition, especially if you are into colourful Balkan folk costume – the examples on display are particularly decorative (and old).

There's also a small section on Albanian musical instruments and displays on local history, from cavemen to the Ottomans.

Puka Lake

Just south of the town centre, the pretty **Puka Lake** (Liqeni i Pukës) is a lovely spot for a picnic with views of the wooded hills and snow-dusted mountains beyond. In summer there are often boats to hire and kiosks selling food.

Puka ski slope

Tel: 069 221 9985

Puka is regarded as offering the best **skiing** in the land, though it doesn't have much serious competition, it must be said. The **slope** itself (*pistë e skive*) lies to the south of town and isn't very long (around half a kilometre). The lift is a basic affair. Sadly, you won't find any information about the place online, but we were assured there is ski hire available and an instructor on hand.

ARRIVAL AND DEPARTURE — PUKA

By bus There's a bus service around every hour or two from Tirana to Puka, with a journey time of 2hr 40min. Two middle-of-the-day buses make the run up here from Shkodra (1hr 20min).

By car Puka is not quite halfway between Shkodra and Kukësi; the road to both is winding and sometimes quite steep with plenty of switchbacks and narrow sections. It takes a lot longer to drive (2hr to Shkodra, 3hr to Kukësi) than your GPS might suggest.

ACCOMMODATION AND EATING

Agroturizëm Devin Qerreti; tel: 069 920 3082. Run by a local woman and her daughters, this small farm stay (three rooms) in the village of Qerreti is comfortable enough, but the real plus here is the personal approach and the meals the family lay on for guests using local produce. The storeroom is an Aladdin's cave of goodies, from pickles to *raki*, dried fruit to cherry liqueur. It's located around 7km west of Puka. €€

Hotel Turizëm Puka Qendër (centre); tel: 067 207 0306. The epicentral *Hotel Turizëm* is a one-stop shop for travellers, with a clutch of modern rooms and a bar and restaurant serving the beer it makes out back, plus it doubles up as an unofficial tourist information centre. There's plenty of parking nearby. €€

★ **N'konak Guesthouse** Rruga Ymer Puka 44; tel: 069 454 1410. For warm and authentic Albanian hospitality, book ahead for this three-room guesthouse located in the north of the town. It has beds made of pallets, the breakfast is of such generous proportions you won't want to eat for the rest of the day, and the friendly owners are full of tips and local information. There's also a small retro-museum in the house. €

★ **Përparim Laçi Guesthouse** Rruga Ismet Uke Laçi; tel: 068 205 6472. Run by the local ski instructor, this traditional stone-built guesthouse with a cluster of alpine-looking timber chalets opposite is set near the ski slope, a short walk south of town. There's an inviting restaurant serving traditional Albanian dishes on the premises, ski hire and a warm, personal welcome by the owners and their staff. Nicely heated in winter. €€

SHOPPING

AgroPuka Lagjja e Re; tel: 069 606 6909, www.agropuka.org. This NGO (non-government organization) was established twenty years ago to bring together small producers, especially women, in the rural backwaters of the Puka area. Over three hundred members make dried fruit and mushrooms and all manner of other preserves, pickles and condiments, which you can buy at the organization's shop. Call ahead.

Agroturizëm Devin Qerreti; tel: 069 920 3082. The family at the Devin guesthouse sell all kinds of preserves, jams, *raki*, syrups and dried fruit. These make for great local souvenirs or snacks on the trails when you need to refuel.

BIRRA PUKA

Forget Korça and Tirana, Puka makes some of the best **beer** in the country – namely **Birra Puka** (www.facebook.com/pukabeer). The secret may be the pristine spring water the small brewery uses in the production of its three types of amber-coloured lager. The facility is located in the centre of town, behind the *Hotel Turizëm* – ask there for a **tour** of the brewery and a **tasting session**. And if you see Puka's beer anywhere on tap across the rest of Albania, don't hesitate to order a pint.

DIRECTORY

Pharmacy Farmaci Seferi, the town's main pharmacy, can be found at Sheshi Tërbuni opposite the town hall.

Post The post office is located next to the Hotel Turizëm in the centre of Puka.

Kukësi

2

Despite not being the most attractive town around, **KUKËSI** is redeemed by a scenic location overhung by immense peaks and its views of the huge reservoirs created by damming two rivers that merge nearby. Close to the Albania-Kosovo border, Kukësi has fast highway links to both capitals – Pristina and Tirana – along with an international airport (little used as yet).

There's not much to see in town and there's nothing old here (see below), but Kukësi shows great potential as a centre of tourism – it's easy to reach and a good base for a couple of days' rest before striking out into the wilderness.

With its easygoing vibe, it's clear to see why this town (pop. 16,000) has become a gateway to the northern mountains.

Brief history

The reason there is nothing predating the 1970s in Kukësi is because, in fact, it used to be located somewhere else. The original was submerged in 1976 by the manmade Fierza Reservoir, created between 1971 and 1978 through the damming of the Drini River. As a result, **New Kukësi** (Kukësi i Ri) was built on higher ground to accommodate the community of displaced residents. When the water in the artificial lake is low, you can still spot the roofs of the lonely old stone houses poking sadly above the surface.

The other significant moment for the town came in the late 1990s during the Kosovo War. Around half a million Kosovan refugees fled over the border into Albania to escape the Serbs, and Kukësi – despite its size and economic hardship of the times – looked after them remarkably well. For its efforts, in 2000, it became the first city ever to be nominated for a Nobel Peace Prize (it lost out to South Korea's president, Kim Dae-jung, who won on account of his efforts to improve relations with North Korea).

Rruga Eksod '99

Rruga Eksod '99

In the evenings the traffic grinds to a halt on **Rruga Eksod '99** and seemingly the whole town turns out for the evening *passeggiata* (stroll). Children whizz around on bikes, groups of teenagers flaunt their best togs and parents push prams through the rapidly cooling mountain air.

It's the best time to be on the streets and join the locals. It is also home to a couple of key attractions, including the **Ethnographic Museum of Kukësi** and the **Memorial Tower** in honour of the locals' support to Kosovan refugees in 1999.

Ethnographic Museum of Kukësi

Rruga Eksod '99 • Free • www.kukesi.gov.al

Like many small Albanian towns, Kukësi has a worthwhile local museum. Located near the town hall, the **Ethnographic Museum of Kukësi** (Muzeu Etnografik Kukës) is divided into three pavilions examining ethnography, archaeology and biodiversity. The entire exhibition highlights the uniqueness of the region, from the 750 types of medicinal plant found in the terrain to the early Kuksian civilization that dominated the area eight thousand years ago to the regional folk costume that differs from others in Albania.

Interestingly, the museum is located on the 'Exodus of '99' Street, a reference to the refugee crisis (see page 94) during the Kosovo War.

Memorial Tower

Rruga Eksod '99

Right next to the Ethnographic Museum of Kukësi, the 23.5m-high **Memorial Tower** was built in 2009 to commemorate the half a million **Kosovan refugees** who flooded into Kukësi in 1999. The structure was financed by Kosovo as a gesture of gratitude to the people of Kukësi who received international recognition for their efforts. The small exhibition inside examines the Kosovo War.

Radio Kukësi

Rruga Gjalica 13

Radio Kukësi was founded by dictator Enver Hoxha to spread political propaganda, but it also played its part in the Kosovo conflict, broadcasting the names of those who had escaped to safety to families and friends still in Kosovo. Today, the large socialist realist bas-relief above the entrance to the building is a reminder of the forty years of iron rule: a rugged worker holding what looks like a torch, a communist star over his right shoulder, the Albanian flag fluttering over his left.

Inside, a small **museum** contains dusty analogue-broadcasting equipment and photos from the Kosovan refugee exodus of 1999.

ARRIVAL AND DEPARTURE — KUKËSI

By bus Twice-daily buses services connect Kukësi and Shkodra with a journey time of 2hr. You can take a bus to and from Tirana twice an hour at some times of the day and the journey to the capital takes 2hr. There are many services a day to/from Bajram Curri (1hr 40min) and there's at least one daily scheduled bus to Kosovan capital Prishtina (1hr

40min). Services depart from the bus station where Rruga Islam Spahiu meets the main road through town; buy tickets from the driver.

By car Kukësi lies just 26km from the border with Kosovo. The A1 Tirana–Prishtina highway (we refrain from calling this a motorway) passes along the southwest edge of Kukësi, meaning you can be in the Albanian capital in under 2hr and in Prishtina in around the same time due to potential queues at the border. The best way to travel here from Shkodra is to head down the coast to Laçi and join the A1 there. Driving via Puka and the twisting, bucking road through the mountains makes it a very long journey indeed. Once in Kukësi, parking is not usually a problem though it is always safer to arrange through your accommodation rather than leaving vehicles on the street.

By plane Kukësi may have an international airport (www.kuiport.al), 3.5 km south of the city centre, but at the time of writing it was not in use.

ACCOMMODATION

SEE MAP PAGE 95

For a town of its size, Kukësi has no shortage of beds, and standards of accommodation have crept up in recent years.

Amerika Rruga Eksod '99; tel: 068 203 2007. This newbuild hotel puts you right on the promenade and has well-appointed rooms and an owner for whom nothing seems to be too much trouble. Cleanliness is maintained throughout, and the breakfast comes in for high praise. €€

Baz'hur Boutique Hotel Rruga Mahmut Daci; tel: 069 979 1160. Opened in 2023, this very crisply appointed hotel in a purpose-built block is set to dominate in future years. The rooms are impeccable, the staff well drilled, and the whole place generally expertly managed. €€€

Hotel Gjallica Rruga Dituria; tel: 024 222 527. Communist-era hotel with spruced-up facilities but still a whiff of socialist hospitality in places. Nonetheless, standards are generally high, largely as the *Gjallica* now has competition on the hotel scene. Rooms come with twenty-first-century bathrooms and contemporary decor. The restaurant is particularly welcoming after a day out sightseeing. €€

Sky View Hotel Rruga Dëshmorët; tel: 068 507 8991. Kukësi's newest hotel is in a glass-and-steel tower block with some of the best views you'll find without climbing a local mountain. Rooms have modern decor and there's an Italian restaurant. €€€€

EATING

SEE MAP PAGE 95

The larger hotels in town have restaurants you can fall back on if need be. There is also a few street-food stalls and kiosks in Kukësi, especially on the promenade in the evenings.

Lugina e Drinit Rruga e Kombit; tel: 069 861 5769. Visitors generally agree that the Drini Valley restaurant is the town's best. The location is spectacular, with far-reaching views across the reservoir formed by the Black Drini River to the south. The food, mainly hearty Albanian staples, with a few local extras such as freshwater fish thrown in, is tasty and will not bust your budget. The service here is impeccable. €€

Pizzeria Jamaica Rruga Zogu i Parë; www.facebook.com/jamaicapizzeri. Pretty much the best pizza in town is served at this very un-Adriatic-sounding place on the pedestrian precinct. The vague Caribbean theme may be completely out of sync with what's outside the front door, but the pizzas come fast and filling. €

Xhamlliku Rruga Islam Spahiu; www.facebook.com/restorant.xhamlliku. This Greco-Albanian restaurant in the centre of town plates up grilled meat, salads, fish and rice dishes in a super-modern glass-plated building that looks like it has landed in the hills of Albania from a different planet. Also does takeaway and pizza. €€

DIRECTORY

Health Spitali Rajonal Kukës, on Rruga Spitali, is the primary hospital of the broader Kukësi region covering much of Northeast Albania.

Pharmacy Farmaci 24, on Rruga Spitali, is open Mon–Sat 8am–9.30pm, Sun until 8pm.

Post The post office is located on Rruga Dituria.

Shishtaveci

Thirty kilometres southeast of Kukësi, the alpine village of **SHISHTAVECI** is poised at a lofty altitude of 1300m, just half a kilometre short of the Albania-Kosovo border. The lonely road from Kukësi climbs through the dramatic canyon of the Vana River and across the high ground to this erstwhile ski resort, now a place for half-day trips. When there's a dusting of snow on the surrounding peaks and you look across at Shishtaveci, with its pointed mosque and squat cottages, it's hard to believe you are still in Europe. The locals are Slavic-speaking Muslims called Gorani, who eke out a living in this often-harsh corner of the Balkans.

There are around 60,000 Gorani living in Albania, Kosovo and the Republic of North Macedonia, though the number in Kosovo has fallen since the late 1990s. The

LURA LAKES: A SECLUDED IDYLL

"Who has not seen Lura, has not seen Albania."

Gjergj Fishta, Albanian poet and politician

Popular with domestic tourists, the **Lura Lakes** are an area of outstanding natural beauty set amid the mountains along the eastern border with North Macedonia. Protected as far back as 1966, the parkland is known for its idyllic alpine lakes, thick forests and wealth of biodiversity. The former Lura Lakes National Park is now part of the larger **Lura-Mount Deja National Park** (Parku Kombëtar Lurë-Mali i Dejës), which covers an area of 193 square kilometres. This remote corner of Albania is sufficiently difficult to reach to keep all but the most dedicated visitors away, rewarding those that do make the effort with a wealth of unspoiled beauty.

GEOGRAPHY AND LANDSCAPE

The park's main calling card is its group of glacial lakes, collectively known as the **Lura Lakes** (Liqenet e Lurës). There are twelve main lakes in the park, scattered across the landscape at altitudes ranging from 1350m to 1700m above sea level. These alpine pools are renowned for their crystal-clear waters, which mirror the surrounding peaks and forests.

Among the most notable are the **Great Lake** (Liqeni i Madh), the largest in the set and ringed dramatically by forested slopes; the **Black Lake** (Liqeni i Zi), with its dark depths and wall of thick vegetation; and the **Lake of Flowers** (Liqeni i Luleve), carpeted with water lilies in the summer months. What is remarkable is that although the lakes are all in the same location, each one has its own unique character.

Beyond its watery attractions, the terrain is a mix of rugged peaks, alpine meadows and dense forests, all watched over by the imposing 2118m-high **Lura Mountain** (Kunora e Lurës), which offers panoramic views across the wilderness from its summit. The higher altitudes provide habitat for coniferous trees such as pines and firs, while the lower folds and foothills are cloaked in oak and beech forests. The changing landscape throughout the park provides a dynamic biosphere for both flora and fauna.

CONSERVATION

Despite its natural beauty and ecological significance, the Lura Lakes area faces several **environmental challenges**. In the past, **illegal logging** and **deforestation** have damaged parts of the park, threatening its biodiversity and landscape. Additionally, the area has been impacted by other human activities like unregulated grazing and **tourism**.

Efforts to restore and protect the park are ongoing, with **reforestation projects** and **stricter regulations** being implemented to curb illegal activities. In recent years, there has been a growing awareness of the park's value, and local and national authorities, along with environmental organizations, are working to preserve this unique ecosystem.

VISITING LURA LAKES

To reach the Lura Lakes, you will have to rough it a bit. The area is usually accessed from the villages of Fushë-Lura and Lura e Vjetër, north of the lakes, themselves tricky to reach due to their remote location. Rough tracks and trails head to the Great Lake and then connect to the other eleven. If you wanted to see them all on foot, it would make a 16km route in one direction. With a tent and supplies this could make for a great overnight hike, sleeping somewhere near the southernmost lake.

main calling card here is the sublime location of the village, cradled amid the looming peaks, though be careful not to wander too far from the marked walking trails as there are almost certainly unexploded land mines in the area. Note that you'll need a car to reach Shishtaveci.

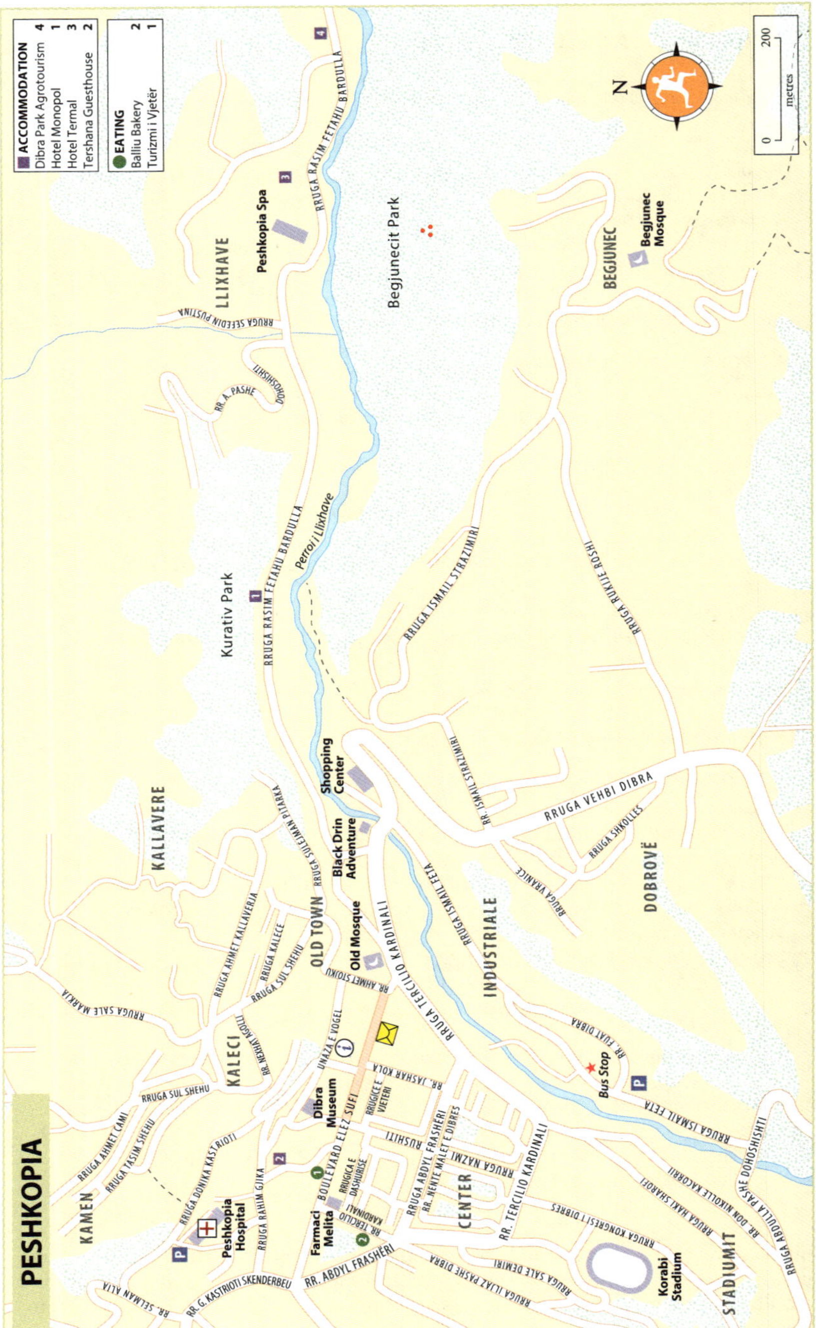
PESHKOPIA
ACCOMMODATION
Dibra Park Agrotourism 4
Hotel Monopol 1
Hotel Termal 3
Tershana Guesthouse 2
EATING
Balliu Bakery 2
Turizmi i Vjetër 1
N
0
200
metres
Peshkopia Spa
LLIXHAVE
Begjunecit Park
BEGJUNEC
Begjunec Mosque
Kurativ Park
Perroi i Llixhave
Shopping Center
Black Drin Adventure
KALLAVERE
OLD TOWN
Old Mosque
INDUSTRIALE
DOBROVË
KALECI
Dibra Museum
Bus Stop
Farmaci Melita
Peshkopia Hospital
KAMEN
CENTER
Korabi Stadium
STADIUMIT
RRUGA RASIM FETAHU BARDULLA
RRUGA SEFEDIN PUSTINA
RR. A. PASHE
DOHOSHISHTI
RRUGA ISMAIL STRAZIMIRI
RRUGA RUKIJE ROSHI
RR. ISMAIL STRAZIMIRI
RRUGA VEHBI DIBRA
RRUGA SHKOLLES
RRUGA VRANICE
RRUGA SULEJMAN PITARKA
RRUGA AHMET KALLAVERJA
RRUGA KALECE
RRUGA SUL SHEHU
RRUGA TERCILIO KARDINALI
RRUGA ISMAIL FETA
RR. AHMET STOJKU
RRUGA SALE MARKJA
UNAZA E VOGEL
RR. NEXHAT AGOLLI
RR. FUAT DIBRA
RR. JASHAR KOLA
BOULEVARD ELEZ SUFI
RRUGICE E VJETERI
RUSHITI
RRUGA ABDYL FRASHËRI
RR. NENTE MALET E DIBRES
RRUGA NAZMI
RR. TERCILIO KARDINALI
RRUGA AHMET CAMI
RRUGA TASIM SHEHU
RRUGA DONIKA KASTRIOTI
RRUGA RAHIM GJIKA
RRUGICA E DASHURISE
RR. SELMAN ALIA
RR. G. KASTRIOTI SKENDERBEU
RR. ABDYL FRASHËRI
RRUGA ILIAZ PASHE DIBRA
RRUGA SALE DEMIRI
RRUGA KONGRESI I DIBRES
RRUGA HAKI SHAROFI
RR. DON NIKOLLE KACORRI
RR. ABDULLA PASHE DOHOSHISHTI

Spaçi Prison

SH40, Kodër-Spaçi • Free • www.spacprison.com

Roughly midway between Kukësi in the east and Lezha by the coast lies **Spaçi Prison** (Burgu i Spaçit), the decaying complex of Enver Hoxha's most notorious prison and forced labour camp. When it was built in the 1960s, it was so hopelessly remote in the mountains of the barren Mirdita region that walls were not even deemed necessary, only fences and watchtowers, for containing the 1400 inmates. Those interned here toiled in the mines, working in sweltering heat and toxic air; most were political prisoners, especially artists and intellectuals.

2

Today, the abandoned huddle of administrative buildings, cell blocks, isolation chambers and rusted mining equipment has been left to slowly degrade. Conservation and remembrance groups have helped to add Albanian- and English-language signage and collect testimonies from surviving convicts, including recollections of a two-day uprising in 1973, when prisoners seized control of the compound and raised the Albanian flag sans communist star.

While Albania is not shy about memorializing horrors of recent history, no other place brings home the inescapability of totalitarianism like this bleak spot in the country's harshest landscape.

From the A1, you'll need to drive north about 7.5km on hard-packed (but not paved) roads through the mountains. It'll take at least thirty minutes from the highway.

Peshkopia

Capital of the wider Dibra region with just over 13,000 inhabitants, **PESHKOPIA** is slowly making a name for itself in the world of Albanian mountain tourism. Cut off from much of the rest of the country for centuries, invaded by a motley band of empires on the rise and fall, and then shunned during the communist decades as a backwater, the city is finally on the rise.

A pleasant city cradled among the high peaks of the Korabi mountain range (**Mount Korabi** is the fourth-highest peak in the Balkans at 2764m), Peshkopia has become popular, at least among home-grown tourists, for its **hiking** and **thermal springs**.

Foreign visitors might want to stop here to strike out on some off-the-map treks, soothe aching muscles in the chalky, mineral-rich baths and generally enjoy a beautiful place in Europe that has – as yet – remained gloriously under the radar of mass tourism.

Dibra Museum

Rruga Safet Zhulali • Charge

The **Dibra Museum** (Muzeu i Dibrës), set in a colonnaded, almost classical-looking building just off the pedestrianized Bulevardi Elez Isufi, is worth popping into during the week (it closes at the weekend), perhaps on a rainy day, to peruse the delightfully old-fashioned displays of archaeological finds, traditional cookware, folk costumes,

ODA DIBRANE FOLK FESTIVAL

Held over a weekend in October, the **Oda Dibrane** is the largest annual **folk festival** in the Albanian-speaking world, attracting ensembles from Albania, Kosovo, North Macedonia and Montenegro for two days of **dance**, **music**, **food** and general merriment. A lot of the action takes place seemingly ad-hoc on the pedestrianized streets of the town but there is a more organized part at the **cultural centre** (Rruga Suf Xhelili). The colour and tradition on show is worth making a special trip for, but accommodation is at a premium during the event (with hiked prices to show for it). As is often the case in Albania, finding any detailed information on the programme, venue etc, even in Albanian, is near-impossible.

Illyrian jewellery and black-and-white photos of felt-hatted freedom fighters from yesteryear. It's all a bit sparse and there's nothing in English, but if you are interested in Albanian history, it can slot a piece or two into the cultural jigsaw.

Boulevard Elez Isufi

Also known as the Boulevard of the Linden Trees, **Bulevardi Elez Isufi** is the very pleasant, pedestrianized street that runs almost the entire width of the town from east to west. It is entirely hemmed by rows of Linden trees that throw welcome shade onto the stone and cobbled walkways. The thoroughfare is lined with shops, cafés and bars and is, yes you guessed it, the scene of the evening *passeggiata* (stroll).

Old Town

Rruga Shehat Shehu

Often referred to as the **Bazaar** (Pazari), behind the New Mosque – a large, impressive structure hinting at the religious leanings of the local population – lies the **Old Town**. The attraction here is the historic architecture that has survived despite years under the rule of Serbs, Nazis and communists.

Peshkopia Spa

Rruga e Llixhave • Charge

One of the most pleasant things you can do in Peshkopia is take the road east into the gorge of the Perroi i Llixhave to reach the **hot springs**, around 2km upstream. The spa complex here was only built at the end of the 1980s but the sulphurous hot springs have been known and used for centuries. Wallow in mineral-rich water naturally heated by the earth's volcanic activity to almost 40°C or sign up for a skin-nourishing mud treatment.

There are plenty of hotels located along the road leading out to the spa, which is open year-round.

ARRIVAL AND DEPARTURE — PESHKOPIA

By bus Buses from Tirana run throughout the day until around 5pm and make the journey to Peshkopia in around 4hr. There are three daily scheduled bus services running to Kukësi (2hr).

By car It is actually less than 100km from Tirana to Peshkopia but it feels like a lot more when you drive. The road bucks and twists through the Dajti Mountain National Park (Parku Kombëtar Mali i Dajtit) then passes through a constant ribbon of tiny villages and small towns with low speed limits.

INFORMATION

Tourist information The local tourist board runs a small visitor information office on Bulevardi Peshkopi (www.visitdiber.com), near the Skanderbeg monument. You can download excellent hiking maps from the website, including one that describes the trek to the top of Mount Korabi, Albania's highest.

ACCOMMODATION

SEE MAP PAGE 98

Peshkopia has sufficient places to stay though most hotels are situated out on the road to the hot springs. The town has witnessed a few attempts at backpacker hostels in the past but at the time of writing there were none.

★ **Dibra Park Agrotourism** Rruga e Llixhave; tel: 069 878 3544. One of the best places to stay in all Northern Albania, this imaginatively fitted-out place has a variety of living spaces, from an alpine cottage to a stone-built round tower with a circular bed. The staff are genuinely friendly and the food here is top-notch. One of the biggest pluses here is that it boasts its own thermal pool for guests' exclusive use. €€

Hotel Monopol Rruga e Llixhave; www.facebook.com/HoteliMonopol. Commendably crisp and modern hotel on the road out to the hot springs. The style is twenty-first-century white and beige, with artwork on the walls adding a splash of colour. There's a decent restaurant and bar on the premises. Bathrooms are squeaky clean. €€

Hotel Termal Rruga e Llixhave; www.hoteltermal.al. The main hotel at the spa, the *Termal* has been welcoming guests for over thirty years. It's all a little dated with a jumble of 1990s sofas, thin mattresses and flowery bedspreads, but the price is good and if all you are looking for is a crash-pad the night before a hike, it's a survivable option. €

THE KULLA OF NORTHERN ALBANIA

When touring Albania, you cannot fail to notice the *kulla* (or *kullë*), a traditional **Albanian tower house** peculiar to the northern mountains. Mostly dating back to the seventeenth and eighteenth centuries, these stone-built structures were designed primarily for defensive purposes in a time of tribal conflict and *gjakmarrje* (Albanian blood feud). The *kulla* typically consists of two or three storeys, with thick stone walls and small windows to provide protection from enemies.

The ground floor often housed livestock, while the upper floors were reserved for living quarters. A key element of a *kulla's* design was the fortified second floor, which included slit-like windows that allowed the residents to shoot at approaching enemies. The towers also served as symbols of clan pride and were passed down from generation to generation.

Culturally, the *kulla* reflects the strict codes of the *besa* (or *besë*), an Albanian concept of honour – or a specific pledge – as well as the Kanun, a traditional set of laws governing social conduct. *Kullas* played a significant role in upholding these values, providing refuge to families during feuds or conflicts.

Though many *kullas* have fallen into disrepair over time, they remain an important part of Albania's cultural heritage. Some have been restored, and there is growing interest in preserving these iconic structures as a reminder of Albania's rich history and traditions. A unique combination of practicality, defence and cultural significance makes them a fascinating feature of Albanian heritage.

Tershana Guesthouse Rruga Rahim Gjika; tel: 021 820 306. This central guesthouse is one of the most characterful places to stay, with antique-styled, individually decorated rooms, a cooked breakfast and a friendly welcome from the hosts who really do make their guests feel as though they are at home. €

EATING

SEE MAP PAGE 98

Two local dishes you should look out for in Peshkopia's eateries are *jufka* (a local pasta) and *sheqerpare* (a kind of baked dumpling in sugar syrup), which are specialities of the region.

Balliu Bakery Rruga Tercilio Kardinali. The best bakery in town is this modern glass cube selling fresh bread, cakes and sandwiches. It's a great pitstop or place to stock up.

Turizmi i Vjetër Bulevardi Peshkopi 17; tel: 069 917 7343. Located on the main boulevard through town, this lovely restaurant offers Albanian and Mediterranean cooking as well as local pasta and pizzas. €€

DIRECTORY

Health The broader Dibra region's hospital is Spitali Rajonal Peshkopi (Dibër) on Rruga Rrahim Gjika.

Pharmacy Farmaci Melita, located on Rruga Tercilio Kardinali, is open daily 8am–8pm.

Post The post office is on Bulevardi Peshkopi.

Mount Korabi

At 2764m, **MOUNT KORABI** is Albania's highest peak, though it's actually shared with North Macedonia (it is that country's highest mountain, too). If you are a hiker, an ascent is a must-do and it's not too hard to achieve. The tourist office has downloadable trail maps and route descriptions that point you in the right direction. The trails to the summit of Korabi start at the village of Radomira, around 30km north of Peshkopia. A **circular route** up via Fusha e Korabit and back down the valley of the Veleshica (or the other way round) comes in at around 26km. There's virtually no shade on the trail, which means great views but prolonged sun exposure in summer (wear a hat and sunscreen or visit in spring/autumn).

The route is fairly easy to follow, though the only people you might meet on the way are a few shepherds. At the peak, the **view** is nothing short of spectacular, standing on the roof of both North Macedonia and Albania, the legions of mountains marching away into the haze as far as the eye can see.

This is remote backcountry hiking, so take emergency food, warm clothing even in summer, a first-aid kit, waterproofs and a water bottle (there's plenty of water on the route). Tell someone in Peshkopia where you are going and when you will be back. There's no mobile signal beyond the road.

Lezha

Not many tourists take the trouble to call into **LEZHA** on their way to or from Shkodra, Tirana or the riviera, passing swiftly through the western suburbs on the road across the superheated flatlands south of Shkodra to or from the motorway. But a short stop here pays dividends, especially if you have an interest in Albanian history. This is the final resting place of the national hero **Gjergj Kastrioti**, immortalized as Skanderbeg (Albanian: Skënderbeu or Skënderbej) – the scourge of the Ottoman Empire. Although his body is long lost, a dramatic memorial rises over the spot where he was buried. **Lezha Castle** (Kalaja e Lezhës) is poised high above the town, though in these parts even 170m is lofty.

Brief history

Lezha has roots dating back to antiquity – and boasts the stone remnants to prove it. Founded as the Illyrian town of **Lissus** in the fourth century BC, it is one of the longest-inhabited places in Albania. Lezha occupied a strategic location near the Adriatic Sea, lending it importance as a military and trade centre.

One of Lezha's most notable historical events was the 1444 **League of Lezha** (Lidhja e Lezhës), which saw national hero Skanderbeg uniting Albanian clans to resist the Ottoman invasion. This political and military alliance is considered a pivotal moment in Albanian history. Skanderbeg later died in Lezha in 1468 and was buried in the local cathedral.

Built on a hill overlooking the city, Lezha Castle was an important point for the Venetian Republic and played a role during the centuries of Ottoman occupation.

Skanderbeg Memorial

Sheshi Gjergj Kastrioti • Free

Most Albanians know Lezha for one reason: the town was the last resting place of the national hero Skanderbeg. It was here that Skanderbeg managed to unite and galvanize local clans to fight against the Ottoman invasion and it was here that Skanderbeg died in 1468, after two decades of struggle and brilliant victories against long odds.

When Skanderbeg died, the local tribes immediately buried him in the cathedral. But when the Ottomans finally took Lezha in 1479, they destroyed the grave and turned the cathedral into a mosque. Between 1880 and 1905, the place of worship served the local Bektashi population who, to this day, believe that Skanderbeg converted to their religion before he died. In 1968, the ownership of the mosque was passed to the state, the minaret pulled down and the structure was repurposed as the **Skanderbeg Memorial**. Columns were erected all around the crumbling old ruins and a huge glass roof balanced atop them, protecting the monument from the wrath of the elements.

Once inside, you'll find the hero's stern bronze bust staring back at you, behind him a defiant Albanian flag. A glass case holds a replica of his sword and helmet.

The memorial is located in parkland in the town centre riddled with the remnants of the ancient Illyrian town of Lissus, which date back almost two-and-a-half millennia.

Gjergj Fishta Monument

Rruga e Kallmetit • Free

One of Albania's best-known literary figures, the poet **Gjergj Fishta** (1871–1940) was born in the small village of **Fishta**, 15km the north of Lezha, where you can visit the house in which he was born. The town is rightly proud of its connection to the Shkodra MP, priest, diplomat and writer who penned *The Highland Lute,* an epic 1937 poem based around Albania's struggle for independence.

The **monument** stands a symbolic stone's throw from the Skanderbeg Memorial and depicts Fishta as a priest in church robes. Behind him is the library named in his memory, where you can find many books on Albanology as well as a section containing books in English (and other languages).

Lezha Castle

Rruga e Kalasë • Charge

Another must-see are the crumbling ruins of **Lezha Castle** (Kalaja e Lezhës) high above the town. It's a 1.7km walk up to the fortress from the Skanderbeg Memorial – the two places are, in fact, linked as the national hero sent signals from Lezha Castle to Rozafa Castle (see page 79) in Shkodra.

Despite lying unused and neglected for over a century, sections of the defensive walls are remarkably intact. It's the views, however, that steal the limelight, overlooking the series of bridges of Lezha straddling the Drini River on the final furlong of its long journey from North Macedonia. Beyond is the glittering Adriatic, while the Dinaric Alps ripple inland.

ARRIVAL AND DEPARTURE — LEZHA

By bus At the busiest times of the day, several buses an hour depart for, or arrive from, Tirana (1hr) and Shkodra (50min). Lezha city bus services trundle to coastal town Shëngjini, which is around 7km northwest of the city, on a rolling basis.

By car Lezha lies 60km north of Tirana, with the A1 highway connecting the two settlements (1hr 30min). Shkodra is around an hour's drive north of Lezha on ordinary A roads. It takes around the same time to reach Durrësi by car.

INFORMATION

Tourist information The tourist information office for Lezha is located at Sheshi Gjergj Kastrioti, near the Skanderbeg Memorial.

ACCOMMODATION — SEE MAP PAGE 102

Hotel Liss Shëtitorja Gjergj Fishta; tel: 067 200 9841. The old communist-era lumpen hotel has been renovated into a 39-room, mid-range option with air-conditioned rooms, lots of dark wood and neat, modern bathrooms. Little reminders of the past lurk in places but, all in all, this is a decent place to sleep. €€

Ishull Lezha Campsite Rruga Lezhë–Shënkoll; tel: 069 669 9676. This campsite was only established in 2024 and has clean, fresh facilities, a bar, shady spots and nice views of the mountains. It's on the road south. €

Jolly Hotel Shëtitorja Gjergj Fishta; tel: 021 522 017. You are sure to leave in a jolly mood after staying at this glass-and-steel high-rise in the centre of Lezha. Most rooms have stupendous views over the town, and the top-floor restaurant is a welcome sight at the end of the day. Decor is business class with various works of art adding dashes of colour. €€

EATING

SEE MAP PAGE 102

2

Akuarium Ishull-Shëngjini; tel: 069 555 5919. Out on the main road in the Ishull Shëngjini suburb, this family-run seafood restaurant is well worth making the trip out of town to experience. Housed in a modern purpose-built cube, the interior is crisply twenty-first century; the seafood and fish dishes very well executed; and the wine list impressive. €€

★ **Bistro Serrani** Rruga Luigj Gurakuqi; tel: 068 407 4808. This modern little bistro by the Drini River is claimed by many to serve the best food in town. The menu fuses Italian favourites with sushi, and everything is presented and served with real panache. €€

★ **Mrizi i Zanave** Fishta; www.mrizizanave.al. Regularly rated as one of Albania's top *agroturizëms*, this place is named after Gjergj Fishta's poem, *The Fairies' Hideaway* – and you could say a meal here is a fairy-tale slow-food experience. There's no set menu and not all of the dishes are necessarily traditional Albanian recipes, but all ingredients used are organic, local and seasonal. The actual farmhouse (where you can stay) stars in many promotional materials for tourism to Albania – one corner of the traditional stone house is famously cut away and replaced with glass. Very much worth the trip out to the village of Fishta, though you'll have to book at least a week in advance to secure a table. €€€

Restorant Peshkatari Ishull-Shëngjini; tel: 069 392 5744. This excellent restaurant on the coast, an eight-minute drive from central Lezha, has seating poised almost over the lagoon, small private garden pavilions, a modern interior, impeccable and knowledgeable service, some of the best seafood you'll taste on this stretch of the Adriatic, and a generally welcoming atmosphere. €€€

DIRECTORY

Hospitals Lezha has a large hospital (Rruga e Spitalit; tel: 054 445 3564) that serves the wider region.

Pharmacy Farmaci Ditë e Natë, in Lagjja Nënë Tereza, just over the bridge on the west bank of the Drini, is part of a nation-wide chain. Open daily 8am–11pm.

Post The post office is in central Lezha on Sheshi Gjergj Kastrioti.

Shëngjini

Essentially now joined at the hip with Lezha, the port town of **SHËNGJINI** has reinvented itself since the 1990s as a beach destination and now boasts the most popular stretch of sand north of the Durrësi area. On hot days it seems most of Shkodra is packed like sardines onto the beach and many Tiranas holiday here instead of on the riviera, where prices are now too high. Sadly, there's precious little space to unfurl a towel for free as many local hotels and businesses rent parts of the beach and charge visitors for the pleasure of hiring a sun lounger and shade. Ever-increasing numbers of flashy hotels are springing up along the shoreline, some still under construction at the time of writing.

However, not all is lost. Outside July and August, some owners of the beach rentals pack up for winter, and a short bike or taxi ride further north reveals huge swathes of wild, untamed dunes that couldn't be crowded even if the whole of Tirana showed up at once.

Brief history

Shëngjini has been a vital port for Albania's north since Roman times and is still a major gateway for goods arriving from Italy and other Mediterranean trade hubs. Italian occupiers changed its name to San Giovanni di Medua in 1939, but it reverted to its original moniker after World War II. Since 1990, the town has added tourism as a revenue stream to its port, building more hotels on the waterfront than any other town north of the capital.

Shëngjini Beach

Seafront • Charge

Shëngjini's **main beach** stretches 6km south from the port in a patchwork quilt of rented sun loungers (many broken) packed twenty deep. If lying in the shade in 40°C, shoulder-to-shoulder with other sunbakers and with no view of the sea, isn't your idea of a blissful day, walk south until you reach the part where local businesses no longer regard it profitable to privatize the beach. There, you can unfurl your towel wherever you like. The sea is shallow all along the strand.

The beach is backed by high-rise hotels and a wall of dramatic mountains – a scene not unlike the Italian riviera.

Rana e Hedhun

6km north of Shëngjini • Free

An out-of-bounds military zone until the 1990s, the beach and dunes at **Rana e Hedhun** are much wilder and infinitely more pleasant than the town's main beach. A 50m wall of powdery sand drops steeply to a thin strip of beach. The tide sadly often washes up litter but if the beach is clean, it can be a magical spot. Some locals sandboard on the dunes, an interesting activity to watch. Unlike in town, there are no hotels or restaurants here, so bring a picnic if you intend to spend the day here.

ARRIVAL AND DEPARTURE — SHËNGJINI

By bus City buses shuttle between Shëngjini and Lezha very regularly (1hr 15min) and stop at various points along the seafront.

By car Shëngjini is just 6km from the centre of Lezha. If you want to head straight for the 'unrented' (lounger-free) stretches of the beach, take the left turn at around 4km into the drive. Parking can come at a premium in summer, though in the shoulder season you'll have no problem finding a spot. You can reach Rana e Hedhun by car (30min) along narrow tracks.

INFORMATION

Tourist information The tourist office in Lezha (see page 103) also takes care of Shëngjini, providing local information and maps to visitors.

ACCOMMODATION

Shëngjini has more hotels than you can shake a broken sun umbrella at, though in July and August the whole lot can be booked solid.

Domus Hotel & Apartments Rruga Kënallë–Kunë; www.domus.al. This hotel of recent vintage is at the quieter southern end of the beach. Most rooms have sea views, the decor is relaxingly beige and white, and there's an excellent restaurant on the premises. €€

Hotel Guri Shëngjin Rruga Lezhë–Shëngjin; tel: 034 952 20691. This beautiful stone building on the road out to Lezha has understatedly spartan rooms, a good restaurant and a location convenient for both Lezha and Shëngjini. It's a stylish alternative to Shëngjini's beachfront newbuilds. €€

EATING

Ara Shëngjin Rruga Fran Ivanaj; tel: 069 487 1644. New trendy place just back from the sands offering seafood platters, often served on olive wood, and cocktails. There's indoor seating or you can pick an umbrella-shaded table outside with views of the Adriatic only partially obstructed by sun loungers. €€€

Detari Vjetër Bulevardi Nënë Tereza; tel: 069 668 3473. Long-established seafood joint on the main road through town with a crisply nautical dining room and traditionally prepared dishes. Large portions and lots of wine to choose from. €€€

Molla Rruga Fran Ivanaj; tel: 067 294 1241. At the southern, less touristy end of the beach, this great seafood restaurant connected to a hotel of the same name has a frontline location and is one of the most romantic spots to dine at sunset. €€

DIRECTORY

Pharmacy Farmaci Eva, on Rruga Fran Ivanaj, is (allegedly) open 24hr a day.

Berati, Durrësi and Central Albania

OSUMI CANYON

Berati, Durrësi and Central Albania

From the mountains to the valleys to the sea, Central Albania is the country's spiritual heartland. It's where Albanians actually live, home to the three most-populous counties outside Tirana County. Here, too, is Mount Tomorri, the holy mountain sacred in Albanian mythology, and Berati, a bewitching, beautiful UNESCO-listed city that's being reinvigorated with youthful energy. The long, sandy Adriatic beaches and cragged riverine canyons in this corner of the country have long beckoned sunseekers and adventure chasers. Ancient and medieval hubs like Durrësi and Elbasani are finding intriguing and inventive ways to spotlight their respective Roman and Ottoman heritage. In this part of Albania, you can don a VR headset to watch gladiators duel one day and swim in a remote alpine lake severed from civilization another. With a landscape spanning wetland to winelands, there's palpable excitement about what the future could hold here, and a new generation of smart, ambitious Albanians who won't hesitate to tell you about it.

Freestyle exploration is hit or miss here: there are incredible gems far off the beaten path and big cities with not much to see. Two towns with illustrious but distinct histories can provide visitors with an understanding of the complicated melee of past (and present) influences on the region. **Berati**, capital of the Pashalik of Berati, offers a glimpse into what Albania was like at the height of the Ottoman Empire's power here, from the fifteenth to the nineteenth centuries. The grandeur of the period is well preserved in mosques and mansions, a nod to the strong influence of Islam in Albania. **Durrësi**, formerly Dyrrachium, was a Roman, Byzantine and Venetian capital; its prominence still broadcast by its crumbling amphitheatre, forum, fortress and archaeological museum.

Around seventeen kilometres east of Berati Castle, transcendent **Mount Tomorri** (Mali i Tomorrit) remains a holy site for the hundreds of thousands of Bektashi Muslims who pilgrimage to the mountaintop shrine to Abaz Ali, a paragon of courage in the Sufi sect.Tucked into the crumpled folds of Tomorri Mountain National Park, foothills villages like **Roshniku** and **Droboniku**, and the **Osumi Canyon** (Kanioni i Osumit) are blessed with some of Albania's most enchanting natural scenery, and all are easy, popular day-trips from Berati.

East of the mountain, **Gramshi** offers quieter escapes into nature, with azure lakes, waterfalls and the spectacular vistas of Grabova e Sipërme and Valamara Massif (Mali i Valamarës), a place lost in time.

Approaching Tirana to the north, **Elbasani** is a city where austere medieval ramparts and post-communist chaos collide. The Adriatic coast to the west has lost some favour among Tirana's young and fashionable crowd, but it's full of surprises if you know where to look: the bluff-backed coves and tidepools of beaches like **Plazhi i Gjeneralit** entice when summer crowds thin out, while **Divjaka-Karavasta National Park** (Parku Kombëtar Divjakë-Karavasta) has tranquil hideaways for hikers, beachgoers and birdwatchers year-round.

And everyone should sample whole-grilled *levrek* (seabass), *merluc* (hake) and *kocë* (dorade) fresh from the sea and lagoon. Tender seafood is served in hole-of-the-wall spots up and down the coast.

DURRËSI

Highlights

❶ **Islamic heritage** The ornate mosques of Berati unveil a proud heritage; Central Albania's Bektashi shrines and post-communist masjids continue the story. See page 114

❷ **Berati Castle** An intimidating citadel from below, it's a living castle inside, with cheery tavernas and evocative ruins shoulder to shoulder. See page 119

❸ **Mount Tomorri** This mighty 2416m-high mountain commands awe from every angle. Journey to the sacred summit. See page 124

❹ **Berati wine tasting** Explore vineyards and try wines made from ancient grapes native to Albania – you might be surprised. See page 125

❺ **Osumi Canyon** Broad, majestic and inviting, the Osumi River's gorges are a natural treasure. Hike, raft or wallow in the sun. See page 128

❻ **Grabova e Sipërme and Valamara** From a remote medieval village, trek to an otherworldly landscape far from civilization. See page 132

❼ **Durrësi** Through innovative restoration projects, the capital of age-old civilizations is coming back to life. See page 139

❽ **Bashtova Castle** An enormous, mysterious, largely intact castle – what's it doing in the middle of nowhere? See page 152

HIGHLIGHTS ARE MARKED ON THE MAP ON PAGE 110

Berati

As the story goes, **BERATI** was the place that Baba Tomorri – the father of gods and humans in Albanian folklore – showered with his affections. And it is indeed an easy place to love. The whitewashed Ottoman houses that crowd the craggy face of its castle hill, with the lustrous Osumi River (Lumi i Osumit) below, complete the quintessential postcard picture of Albania. The walls of the **Berati Castle** (Kalaja e Beratit) reveal layers of history: Ottoman blocks atop Roman and Byzantine masonry atop ancient Illyrian stones. Tavernas, bars and promenades spill over with chatter and tunes. Dried figs, cherries, sweets, grilled meats, cheeses and, above all, **wine** have made this agriculturally rich area a **culinary hotspot**. Tourists bring international energy, and the Beratas, with their outsized hospitality, welcome it.

Sweltering in the summer, set away from Albania's cardinal highways and some distance from the coast, Berati has not always topped the destination hotlist for Albanian visitors and could feel unapproachable to foreign ones. That has changed. There are now plenty of restaurants, hotels, English-language digital resources and tour operators weaving creative routes through the city and well into the hills and valleys beyond.

Berati's UNESCO World Heritage Site status, inscribed in 2008, covers three historic neighbourhoods: **Kalaja** (or Kala), inside the sprawling hilltop citadel, where around a hundred people still live; **Mangalemi**, the prosperous Ottoman centre in the eighteenth and nineteenth centuries, at the base of the hill; and the old Orthodox Christian quarter of **Gorica**, across the river. The riverfront axis where Rruga Antipatrea, Shëtitorja Osumi and the pedestrianized Bulevardi Republika meet, in front of the Bachelors' Mosque (Xhamia e Beqarëve), is the centrepoint from which you can walk to the main attractions in the old city. There's a lot to see here, but the old city is reasonably compact; you'll only break a sweat walking up to the castle.

Brief history

In Albania, it often seems like the **Illyrians** fortified every hill they could climb, and both the Kalaja area of Berati and the hill behind Gorica were no exception. Alexander the Great and his Macedonian successors skirmished with the Illyrians around Berati on and off, naming it Antipatrea, until it was taken over by the **Romans** in 200 BC. Several centuries of relative peace ensued, as Berati occupied a useful position for overland trade.

From 860 AD until its final **Ottoman** conquest in 1417, Berati was contested by the Bulgarian Byzantine, Angevin, Serbian and Ottoman Empires, roughly in that order, often through regional proxies and armies that weren't above switching sides when opportunities arose. Among the medieval power players were the Albanian **Muzaka family**, whose principality stretched from the Adriatic to Kastoria in modern-day Greece, with Berati as capital. The last Muzaka ruler allied with Skanderbeg (Gjergj Kastrioti Skënderbeu, or Skënderbej) in a failed attempt to retake the city in 1455, a costly setback for the national hero, not to mention the Muzakas.

But Berati slowly, then rapidly, gained importance under Ottoman rule. The outstanding King Mosque (Xhamia Mbret), a 1494 gift from Sultan Bayezid II, was an early sign of attention from Istanbul. The city's golden era was relatively brief, but glorious. Ahmet Kurt Pasha, an Albanian Ottoman official, manoeuvred his way to control over the region, solidified with the creation of the Pashalik of Berati in 1774. A vigorous builder, his fingerprints can be seen all over the city's landmarks. Among his architectural creations was a lavish palace complex, though only the Gate of the Pasha (Porta e Pashait) survives from that. In the late eighteenth and early nineteenth centuries, the Mangalemi and Gorica neighbourhoods began to take their current shape, and Berati's bazaar became the leading shopping centre in Albania. Muslims, Christians and around a hundred Jewish families tolerated each other while there was money to be made.

It all came crashing down in 1851, however, when an earthquake wrecked the city. But Berati rebuilt, and Enver Hoxha's government kept much of the historic city intact. Taken by the shine of the White City, Hoxha added his own contribution in stone: the letters ENVER across the face of Mount Shpiragu (Mali i Shpiragut) for all of Berati to see. In 2012, a group of local artists edited the mountain to read 'NEVER'. The stone letters have since been taken down.

Mangalemi and the medieval centre

Most likely, you'll arrive in the **Mangalemi** quarter, the part that gives Berati its moniker, the 'City of a thousand windows'. After Ahmet Kurt Pasha's palace was cleared out around the nineteenth century, wealthy families built *konaks* (traditional houses) here, squeezed between the Kalaja hill, the river and the former bazaar area (now Bulevardi Republika). Less grandiose than Gjirokastra's hulking mansions, the vernacular ones here are unique in their own way.

The windows were designed to let in what little sunshine reached Berati during its chilly, dark winters; the light grey masonry is simply the local limestone, and the little house-shaped chimneys were mostly for impressing the neighbours. Incidentally, because of all its reflective stone surfaces, Berati reaches temperatures of up to 10°C hotter than in nearby villages.

The streets and steps here are just a hair's width in some places, crowded by the second-floor bulge of Ottoman-era living quarters, but when you're on Rruga Antipatrea, it's hard to get lost. The road curves east at the ruins of the Vrioni Seraglio

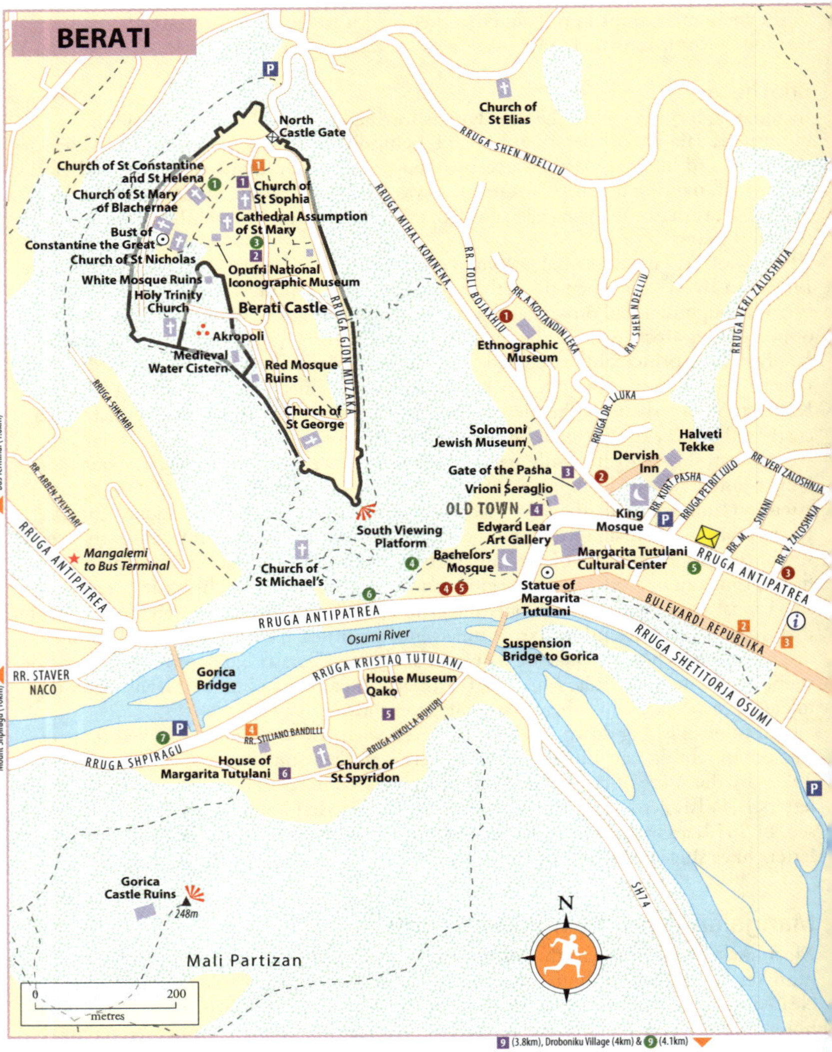

(Sarajet e Vrionasve), fronted by a neo-Romanesque arcade. The square next to it, finished in 2024, preserves sections of masonry from the older Ahmet Kurt Pasha palace as well as the Gate of the Pasha, livened up with elegant carved rosettes and floral motifs.

To the northwest, you'll huff and puff 900m up Rruga Mihal Komnena to the gate of the Kalaja, a steep twenty-minute push. In the other direction around the south side of the hill, a trail from Rruga Antipatrea leads up to the fourteenth-century Church of St Michael (Kisha e Shën Mëhillit), one of the city's two superbly picturesque late-Byzantine churches. Don't miss taking in a view of Mangalemi from one of the nearby boulevards and bridges at night.

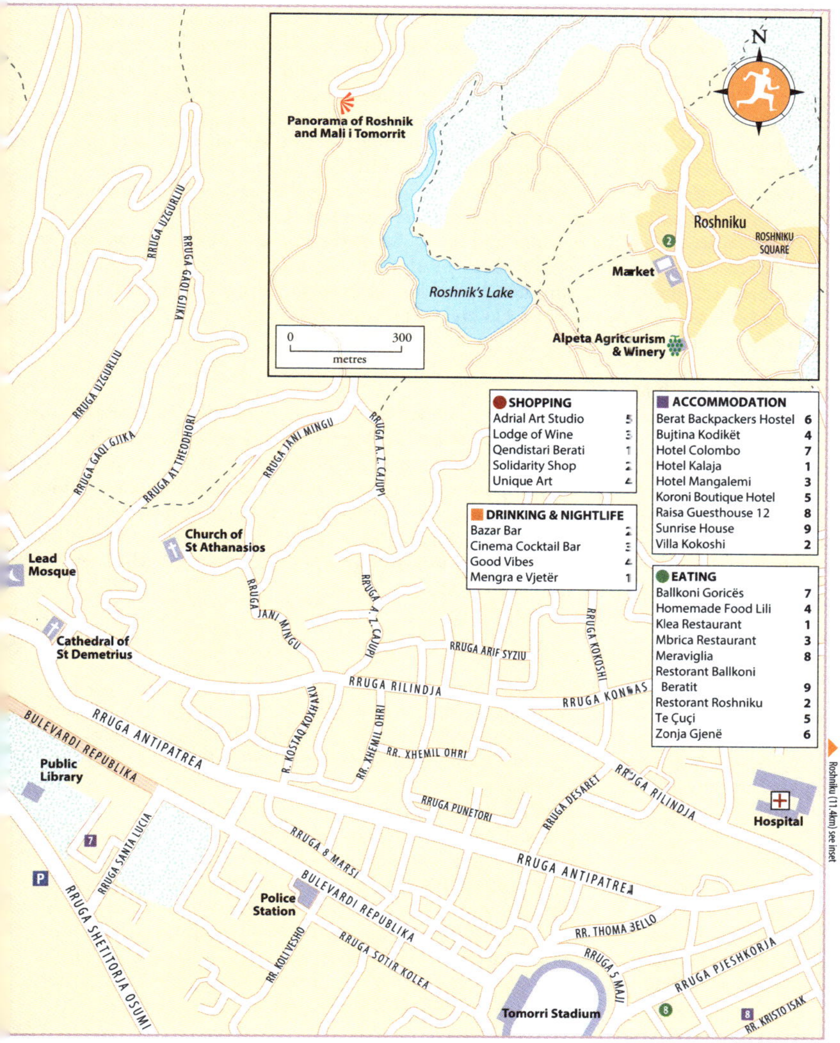

Bachelors' Mosque

Rruga Antipatrea, across from Bulevardi Republika

Front and centre in Mangalemi facing the long-gone bazaar is one of Berati's signature sights, the **Bachelors' Mosque** (Xhamia e Beqarëve). A sop to the city's young merchants who put careers before family – but sent plenty to its tax coffers – the mosque was built in 1827 and restored in 2019. Non-worshippers can't usually visit the interior, but the exterior frescoes beneath the eaves of the roof are a rare and vibrant display of Islamic figurative art. On the northeast wall, look for the scene depicting warships swarming a walled city on a cape, which is either the Siege of Constantinople or quite a coincidence.

King Mosque

Corner of Rruga Mihal Komnena and Rruga Kurt Pasha • Free

The original 1494-built **King Mosque** (Xhamia Mbret) was reconstructed in 1833 and restored in 2021. It may appear dressed-down from the exterior, but the mosque is well worth a look inside: its coffered wood ceiling, inlaid with octagons, triangles and other geometric patterns, sports vivid reds and greens. Visitors (of any gender) can climb up to the women's balcony outside prayer times for a superior view of the nineteenth-century ceiling, mihrab and minbar. Behind the mosque to the northeast is the small medieval square, bounded by the Halveti Tekke (Teqeja e Halvetive) and an old dervish inn. The *teqe* (or *teqeja*; tekke) once served Berati's Bektashi community, but the current structure dates to a 1782 building programme of Ahmet Kurt Pasha, the founder and first ruler of the Pashalik of Berati. Even more ornamented than the King Mosque, its interior balcony and ceiling are decked out with Baroque curves, flutes and floral patterns, and crosshatching designed to look like gold filigree. The inn, a typical caravanserai (roadside lodgings for travellers), is not open to visitors.

Solomoni Jewish Museum

Corner of Rruga Mihal Komnena and Rruga Kol Myzeqari • Free; donations • Informal tours • www.facebook.com/muzeu.solomoni

The simple one-room **Solomoni Jewish Museum** (Muzeu Solomoni) has been Albania's only Jewish museum since its opening in 2018, though new ones are planned in Vlora and Tirana. A collection of letters, photos, documents and the research of late founder Simon Vrusho, this gallery space tells two stories: that of Jews who lived in Berati, and that of those who sheltered here during World War II. Vrusho's widow, Angjelina, will be happy to show you around; other visitors have included an Israeli Minister of Culture and many amateur genealogy tracers.

JEWS IN ALBANIA

Very few Jews live in Albania today, but it's not for lack of ancestral connection. Jews began arriving in Berati in numbers in the **sixteenth century**, descendants of those expelled during the Spanish Inquisition, and Rruga Hebrentjë (Jew Street) marks the historic location of a small **Jewish quarter** a few blocks from the Muzeu Solomoni. For centuries, a few hundred Jewish residents lived in and around Berati, the largest population in Ottoman Albania. Simon Vrusho's research led him to identify an abandoned village near Tomorri called Davidhi.

In the eighteenth and nineteenth centuries, more Jews emigrated here, now from Greece to Vlora. But the most noteworthy chapter of Judaism in Albania came a few decades after Albanian independence, at the outbreak of **World War II**. Honouring the code of the *besa* (or *besë*) and violently unenthusiastic about the Nazi occupation of their country, Albanians took in Jews fleeing from all corners of Europe, falsifying identities and paperwork for them and **saving an estimated 600 to 1800 lives** during the Holocaust. By Vrusho's count, 63 families in Berati alone, both Christian and Muslim, protected Jews during the war. Albania was the only country in Europe with more Jewish residents at the end of the war than the start.

Ethnographic Museum

Rruga Toli Bojaxhiu • Charge • www.muzeumet-berat.al/en/ethnographic-museum

Berati has many sights, but the **Ethnographic Museum** (Muzeu Etnografik) is its only museum detailing Beratas' history, heirlooms, culture and everyday life, providing helpful context for what went on behind all those windows and walls. In one of the grandest eighteenth-century *konaks* remaining in the city, the gallery displays 1400 artifacts, including some of the finery produced by the region's excellent craftspeople – embroiderers, goldsmiths, coppersmiths and dresswear designers chief among them. It's scheduled to reopen in 2025 after renovation works, which involved restoration of the living chambers and a replica of a typical contemporary bazaar street.

Bulevardi Republika and eastern Berati

From the Bachelors' Mosque and suspension bridge, pedestrianized **Bulevardi Republika** runs 750m east, snaking between a long park and Rruga Antipatrea – the entire area was once the bazaar of Berati. Street vendors selling fresh fruit and grilled corn fringe the park's edge, while the bars and restaurants on the opposite side come to life after night.

From the west, the first landmark is a statue of **Margarita Tutulani** (1925–1943), a Gorica local who joined the communist party in 1942 and became active in the antifascist movement against the occupying Italian government, participating in high-profile protests in Berati. She was captured, tortured and executed at just 18 years old, enraging the city and galvanizing many more people to join the resistance movement. The socialist realist building behind her houses the **Margarita Tutulani Cultural Center** and the **Galeria e Arteve Edward Lear**, a modest gallery showcasing modern art from around Europe (Rruga Antipatrea; www.facebook.com/edwardlear.galeri). At the eastern end, the pedestrianized boulevard opens up onto **Sheshi Teodor Muzaka**, home to the excellent tourist information centre (see page 116), and **Sheshi Iliaz Vrioni**; the adjacent public squares are a popular meeting place for locals and host to many city concerts and festivals (an underground car park opened here in 2024, highly improving the appearance of the street level). On the east side of Iliaz Vrioni Square stands the post-communist Cathedral of St Demetrius (Katedralja e Shën Dhimitrit), and to the north, the architecturally exquisite sixteenth-century **Lead Mosque** (Xhamia e Plumbit), so named for the covering of its dome; enter from Rruga Gaqi Gjika.

3

ARRIVAL AND DEPARTURE — BERATI

By bus/minibus The Berati main terminal runs services to most major and mid-sized cities south of Tirana, though some connections are only once a day; the infrequent buses to Saranda and Gjirokastra fill up quickly before the scheduled departure time, though unscheduled early-morning *furgons* (minibuses) may also drive these routes. The availability and reliability of buses is somewhat notorious, and you'd be smart to seek out intel from your accommodation. There are also daily buses to some of the nearby villages; they leave around midday and return early in the morning. The terminal is on SH72 (Rruga Antipatrea), 2.9km north of the city (urban buses connect to the centre roughly every 30min). You can buy tickets on board the bus from the driver; having the exact cash is most convenient.

For international travel, buses depart from the main Berati bus terminal for destinations in Greece, Turkey, Germany and Italy. Ticket offices are at the station. Agencies include Arjani Travel (tel: 069 272 6870, www.arjanitravel.com), Firenze Lines (tel: 069 203 3056, www.firenzelines.com) and AlbGreece/A.A. Travel (tel: 069 955 7750).

Domestic destinations Çorovoda (listed as Skrapari; many daily; 1hr 30min); Droboniku (1 daily; 20min); Durrësi (many daily; 1hr 50min); Elbasani (many daily; 1hr 45min); Fieri (many daily; 1hr 25min); Karkanjozi (1 daily; 40min); Korça (several daily; 4hr); Gjirokastra (1 daily; 3hr); Gramshi (several daily; 1hr 50min); Librazhdi (several daily; 2hr 10min); Lushnja (many daily; 1hr); Përmeti (1 daily; 3hr); Pogradeci (several daily; 3hr 10min); Poliçani (many daily; 35min); Roshniku (1 daily; 40min); Saranda (several daily; 4hr 5min); Tepelena (1 daily; 3hr 25min); Tirana (many daily; 2hr 30min); Tomori village (1 daily; 1hr 30min); Vlora (many daily; 2hr 5min).

By car The SH72 is the only way in and out of Berati from other major cities. Traffic chokes a bit on Rruga Antipatrea and Rruga Staver Naco approaching the city, as they're the only two roads leading to the centre. To reach Gorica by car, you need to head south on the Ura e Re over the river, then turn left and proceed on Rruga Shpiragu; the nearer bridges are pedestrian-only. In late 2025 or 2026, a paved road around the north slope of Mount Tomorri is expected to be completed, which will link Berati to Gramshi going east, though it will likely remain a slow journey. The Rruga Nacionale toward Çorovoda, southeast of Berati, is asphalted – not well, mind you – and becomes a dirt road some kilometres beyond Çorovoda. **Do not** take it as a shortcut to Përmeti.

GETTING AROUND

By bus The city bus runs from the bus terminal along Rruga Antipatrea to the east of the city, and back. The stop near the communist-era Dëshmorët e Kombit World War II memorial puts you near both Gorica and Mangalemi.

By car A car is generally a hindrance in Berati but can be an asset for travelling to natural attractions beyond the city. There are inexpensive paid parking lots near the centre. The underground car park under Sheshi Teodor Muzaka has its entrance on Shëtitorja Osumi. There's another, slightly pricier, car park beneath the Conad supermarket at Rruga Antipatrea and Rruga Petrit Lulo. Some spots are available near and around the north gate of the Berati Castle, at the end of Rruga Mihal Komnena. Decent options for rental cars include Berat Car Rental (Rruga Antipatrea near Rruga Migjeni; tel: 069 375 8350), Your Car Rental (Rruga Antipatrea, 300m north of the bus terminal; tel: 068 807 0046) and Rental Car Makina me Qera Berat (Rruga Antipatrea, 500m south of the terminal; tel: 068 363 5110).

By taxi There's a taxi rank at the bus terminal and another on Rruga Gaqi Gjika next to the Lead Mosque (Xhamia e Plumbit). Fares within the city are inexpensive. To arrange trips to and from Roshniku, Droboniku or Bogova, call or message a reputable service like Taxi Berat (tel: 069 254 9415) or Taxi Edi (tel: 069 967 8759).

By bike For forays into the countryside, a sturdy bike can be a good companion here. You can rent both road and mountain bikes from 1001 Albanian Adventures (Rruga Mihal Komnena across the street from the Gate of the Pasha (Porta e Pashait); www.1001albanianadventures.com).

3

INFORMATION

Tourist information The tourist information centre is a freestanding building on Berati's central square, Sheshi Teodor Muzaka, near Rruga Antipatrea (Mon–Fri 8am–6pm, Sat 8am–4pm; www.berat.al). It is staffed by friendly,

GUIDED TOURS IN AND AROUND BERATI

While Berati has generally outstanding tourism infrastructure, some of the city's sites can be sparse on informational signage, which makes a walking tour a valuable addition. Tours are also a handy way to access landmarks that may be locked up outside the peak season. The greater Berati-Tomorri area has some of the most incredible natural attractions in Albania – but accessibility ranges from fairly difficult through to near impossible, even with a car, and most trails and sites are poorly marked. Day-trips leaving from Berati to Mount Tomorri, the Osumi Canyon, local wineries and more hidden spots are generally the safest and most rewarding way to explore these places. Most are very reasonably priced and include food and transport. Here are some of the best:

1001 Albanian Adventures Rruga Mihal Komnena, across the street from the Porta e Pashait; www.1001albanianadventures.com. Offers a range of interesting hiking, trekking and mule-riding tours, with destinations including Droboniku and Pirogoshi Cave (Shpella e Pirogoshit). Visit its sister store, the Solidarity Shop, to buy local wine, olive oil and handmade jewellery.

Albania Rafting Group SH74, southeast of Gorica, in *Hotel Castle Park*; www.albrafting.org. One of Albania's top adventure specialists is based in Berati, and its tours make the most of the natural wonder of the region, spanning lake-kayaking, rafting on the Osumi, e-bike riding, canyoning, and snowshoeing on Tomorri in the winter.

Berat City Tours by Visit Albania Tour Operator (VATO) Rruga Mihal Komnena, next to the King Mosque; www.beratcitytours.com. Provides ready-made and bespoke tours of the city and the surrounding region. Founded by brothers Isuf and Alket Braho in 2017, the company offers highly educational guided city walks, cooking classes and wine tasting and combined hiking, 4WD and quad-bike excursions to hard-to-reach places of interest like the Mount Tomorri north summit. A leader in the city for offbeat experiences, the company also rents camping gear and off-road vehicles.

knowledgeable city experts who are fluent in English. They're able to answer any queries and provide information about restaurants, hotels, events, tours, logistics and local sights. The centre is well stocked with up-to-date, easy-to-understand maps, along with additional brochures. It's probably the best municipal tourist information office in the country.

Websites www.berat.al; www.bashkiaberat.gov.al.

Festivals Every October, regional and national producers showcase their wine, *raki*, cheese, *gliko* and olive oil from stalls on Bulevardi Republika as part of the Wine & Stories Festival. This week-long shindig includes live music performances, storytelling and other festivities and events held throughout the city. It's become the most popular wine festival in Albania, culminating in a blind-tasting competition to determine the best-in-show wine. Berati keeps its Christmas Market up for a full two months, from November through early January. Festive decorations and booths selling mulled wine, winter snacks, ornaments and other handicrafts are set up around Bulevardi Republika and Sheshi Teodor Muzaka.

ACCOMMODATION

SEE MAP PAGE 112

The joke in Berati now is that anyone will honour the Albanian code of hospitality and welcome a stranger into their home – you just need to book it on Airbnb first. Some hotels and guesthouses have been around since the 2000s or earlier, but there's been a major boom in accommodation since 2022, with a more diverse offering now than ever before – and there's likely to be more and more openings in the coming years. In addition to the below, the Alpeta, Pupa and Nurellari wineries (see page 125) offer high-end rooms in the Berati region.

Bujtina Kodikët Rruga Llambi Guxhumani and Rruga Kostaq Stefa; www.facebook.com/BujtinaKodiketTheCodexInn. A budget-friendly traditional home at the centre of everything in old Mangalemi, *Bujtina Kodikët* charms with stone fireplaces, exposed timber beams and heirloom furniture; some rooms have Ottoman-style bench sofas. The guesthouse is run by a welcoming host, who makes a very nice traditional Beratas breakfast. €€

Hotel Colombo Rruga Santa Lucia and Shëtitorja Osumi; www.hotel-colombo.al. The gigantic new-looking Neoclassical building at the eastern end of Bulevardi Republika shelters this 118-room hotel, the Beratas take on an international luxury megahotel. Rooms and suites can accommodate up to four, and perks include all the usual conveniences of bigger hotels: 24hr reception, concierge service, daily housekeeping, free parking, a spa (charge) and a swimming pool (charge). €€€€

★ **Hotel Mangalemi** Rruga Mihal Komnena, next to the Porta e Pashait; www.mangalemihotel.com. The first private hotel in Berati after the fall of communism, *Mangalemi* is built on the ruins of Ahmet Kurt Pasha's eighteenth-century palace in an unbeatable location. Rooms are spacious and comfortable, and despite the palatial digs and years of upgrades, the hotel has managed to cling onto a dash of its 1993 quirk: rotary phones in some rooms, recreation room-style wood-panelled walls in others. The rooftop terrace has excellent views, the restaurant is decent, the Ottoman-style *çardaks* (enclosed balconies) offer spots to curl up and watch passersby, and staff are professional and proud. €€€

Raisa Guesthouse 12 Two blocks from Rruga Pjeshkorja; tel: 067 686 6161. A terrific choice for budget travellers looking for peace and space, this loft just east of the city centre is eclectically decorated by the family who live downstairs – a personal interpretation of an Ottoman wood-panelled sitting room. The room has a fireplace, minifridge, views to the Tomorri foothills and on-site parking. The excellent home-made Beratas breakfast isn't too heavy in the summer heat, and the hosts go above and beyond with hospitality. €

EATING

SEE MAP PAGE 112

Beratas cuisine is season-led: in summer dishes are lighter with an emphasis on vegetarian recipes, and more traditionally meat-centric in winter. In addition to the grapes that give the region an abundance of wine and *raki*, the wider area is fertile for Cornelian cherries, figs, plums and olives. Dishes to look out for include *patëllxhanë të mbushur* (stuffed eggplant) and *speca të mbushurs* (filled peppers); *pispili*, a spinach and leek pie spiked with mint; *vienez*, a veal, pork or chicken schnitzel stuffed with cheese. Prices are pretty standardized (and fairly low) for both refined and rustic places.

★ **Home-made Food Lili** Rruga Llambi Guxhumani; tel: 069 234 9362. Six time-worn wooden tables on a covered patio behind a modest Mangalemi villa – that's about the scope of one of Berati's hottest addresses. Tables are shared, and the vibe is very much casual dinner party: Lili is a gregarious host, his father makes the wine and *raki*, and his wife prepares hearty portions of delicious Beratas favourites, including *patëllxhanë të mbushur* (stuffed eggplant), *vienez* (cheese-filled schnitzel), *byrek* (savoury filo pastries) and *gjizë* (Albanian ricotta-style cheese). You can't go wrong with the menu, which is limited to just a few chef specials. The prices are tough to beat, vegetarians will eat well, and reservations are a must. €€

Meraviglia Rruga Pjeshkorja near Rruga 5 Maji; tel: 068 255 6258. The best place in town for seafood. A passion project of the chef-owner, *Meraviglia* is a cosy space with nautical decor and a comfy outdoor dining space. Order superlative whole-grilled fish, crudo, fried calamari and less common options like salt-baked shrimp – a must-try. For top-tier seafood barely above market prices, this is well worth the twenty-minute walk from the centre. €€

★ **Te Çuçi** Rruga Antipatrea and Rruga e Shatervanit; tel: 069 667 6004. A small place frequented by both tourists and locals, *Te Çuçi* is Berati's popular local lunch spot. You can easily fill your belly with soups, cheeses and other small plates, but all the Beratas staples are here. Spy some old-timey Albanian dishes that are hard to find on menus, like *paçe koke* (stew made with the head of a cow) or *paçe plënci* (tripe soup). A less intimidating but no less traditional option is *tasqebap*, a beef stew that was once the main culinary event at weddings in this part of Albania. €

Zonja Gjenë Rruga Antipatrea near Rruga Andrea Vrusho; tel: 068 559 2745. In a gorgeously restored 1915 Ottoman-style house right in the heart of Mangalemi, this is a top choice for classic Albanian dishes like *fërgesë* (melted cheese with peppers), stuffed eggplant, *pispili* (spinach and leek pie), *tavë kosi* (lamb and rice dish baked with yoghurt and eggs), and kebab, plus some more Italian-inflected pasta and antipasti. The setting feels fine-dining elegance – without the steep prices. Check out live music here too. €€

DRINKING AND NIGHTLIFE

SEE MAP PAGE 112

3

Berati is not a big city, but there are spots that can get lively in the summer evenings, mostly along Bulevardi Republika and in Gorica, near the Ura e Goricës (Gorica Bridge). For live music, you may have better luck in some of the larger restaurants or, over the weekends, in Sheshi Teodor Muzaka. It's also always worth seeing what the Qendra Kulturore is putting on.

Bazar Bar Bulevardi Republika near Sheshi Teodor Muzaka; www.facebook.com/bazarberat. The pedestrianized promenade is lined with bars and cafés, some better than others. This bar mixes extra-large glasses of all the classic cocktails, plus some Albanian house specialties. A variation on a nostalgic Albanian college-kid drink, *kaçurrel*, mixes fernet and punch, or the convivial staff are always happy to rustle up something creative for you. It's lively but not rowdy.

Cinema Cocktail Bar Sheshi Teodor Muzaka and Bulevardi Republika; tel: 069 214 4056. Probably the closest thing Berati has to a nightclub, in that it has live music, DJs and dancing, this lounge is comfortable and spacious, spilling out to Sheshi Teodor Muzaka. Bartenders keep the cocktails tasty and the vibe chill. Not a folklore spot, but a great place to hear Albanian pop.

ENTERTAINMENT

Qendra Kulturore Margarita Tutulani Rruga Antipatrea, Pallati i Kulturës building. The local Qendra Kulturore has a small auditorium for ballet, piano recitals, classical music and plays. It also hosts poetry and book readings both here and at the Biblioteka Vexhi Buharaja on Shëtitorja Osumi. But most of the events it helps to organize are held outdoors, including folk song and dance shows, marching band parades and rock concerts. The main venues are in front of the Sarajet e Vrionasve (Vrioni Seraglio; see page 112) and Sheshi Teodor Muzaka (see page 115).

SHOPPING

SEE MAP PAGE 112

Souvenir shops come and go in Berati, and you'll find little in the way of window or street shopping here compared to Gjirokastra. There are vendors around the Kalaja who are swapping out mass-produced trinkets for locally made laces, linens and kilims, mostly near the Akropoli (see page 120) and Onufri National Iconographic Museum (see page 120).

Adrial Art Studio Rruga Antipatrea across the street and west of the suspension bridge; tel: 069 460 5992. Find expressive and eye-catching original paintings of Berati and Mount Tomorri by local artists at Adrial Art Studio, as well as commissioned landscapes and portraits. Alongside the showpiece oil-on-canvas artwork you'll find smaller, framed scenes of Mangalemi alleys, Kalaja landmarks and Orthodox icons, with acrylics, watercolours, lithography and more.

Lodge of Wine Rruga Veli Zaloshnja in the *Hotel Berati*; www.hotelberati.al/lodge-of-wine. Berati's specialty stop for Albanian wine and spirits, this has a broad selection of both big names (in Albania) and less common bottlings, including aged vintage *raki* and Albanian gin.

★ **Qendistari Berati** Rruga Toli Bojaxhiu next to the Muzeu Etnografik; tel: 069 458 8313. Lots of souvenir vendors in Berati sell lace, but this is the place to buy it. A tiny storefront owned by a family of lacemakers, this shop has curtains, window valances, tablecloths, table runners, centrepieces and other frothy pieces of beautiful decor, sewed on site with evident pride (you can also see their handiwork in some of the city's high-end historic hotels). The team who run this shop also specialize in embroidery, which you can find adorning linens and folkloric costumes, as well as woven handbags, placemats and kilims.

Solidarity Shop Rruga Mihal Komnena and Rruga Doktor Lluka; tel: 069 883 1536. One-stop shop for handicrafts and speciality foods made in the Berati area, a storefront for farmers and artisans who wouldn't otherwise have one. Find funky and traditional designs for jewellery, embroidered tote bags, woven handbags, ornaments and more, plus local wine and *gliko* (fruit preserve). All gratuities go toward providing necessities for impoverished families in rural communities.

Unique Art Rruga Antipatrea across the street and west of the suspension bridge; tel: 069 531 4235. The place to go for exceptional woodcarving, whether you're interested in a Mangalemi cityscape carved in olive wood or something more whimsical. Icons, keychains, jewellery and bespoke pieces are also available.

DIRECTORY

Banks and currency exchange Most of the major Albanian banks have branches and ATMs along Bulevardi Republika and Sheshi Teodor Muzaka. There are also a few Western Unions in the centre, including one on Bulevardi Republika and another next to the Bachelors' Mosque (Xhamia e Beqarëve). Find currency exchanges in the same area, along Rruga Antipatrea between Mangalemi and Sheshi Teodor Muzaka.

Emergencies Ambulance (tel: 127 or tel: 112), police (tel: 129 or tel: 112).

Hospital The hospital, Spitali Rajonal Berat, is on Rruga Rilindja where it meets Rruga Antipatrea in the east of the city (tel: 03 223 4237).

Pharmacies Good, easy-to-find pharmacies in the centre include Farmaci Igli on Rruga Antipatrea (tel: 069 634 3356) and Farmaci Mone on Rruga Gaqi Gjika, both near Sheshi Teodor Muzaka.

Police The police station is on Bulevardi Republika and Rruga Koli Vesho (tel: 03 223 4280).

Post office There's a DHL service point on the first floor of the Pallati i Kulturës Margarita Tutulani, on the Rruga Antipatrea side (tel: 04 240 6666). The Posta Shqiptare office in the centre is on Rruga Antipatrea just east of Rruga Petrit Lilo.

3

Kalaja

Berati Castle (Kalaja e Beratit) is more a fortified town than a stronghold and, since people still live there, it is also a neighbourhood, too called 'castle': **KALAJA** – or 'Kala', the spelling, which you will see on signs across town. It's one of Albania's must-visit sights but never feels terribly crowded – it spans 25 acres – and its refreshingly low on kitsch shops and touristy restaurants. After centuries of use, abuse and disuse, the ancient ramparts hold strong, but most of the medieval interior is in ruins, partially built over with eighteenth- and nineteenth-century houses – more Les Baux-de-Provence than Neuschwanstein, if you will. Within its ancient ramparts you will find cobbled streets, frescoed **Byzantine churches**, the puzzling **Red Mosque**, the **Onufri National Iconographic Museum**, plus a handful of apartments and restaurants.

Berati Castle

Kalaja • Free

The evolution of **Berati Castle** (Kalaja e Beratit) is most visible outside the north gate: Illyrian-era orthogonal blocks lay the foundation; strata of brick, stone and mortar are Byzantine, mostly from sixth and thirteenth centuries AD; and the finishing touches to the ramparts and the crenellations and cannon loopholes are Ottoman. The landmarks of the castle are scattered around Kalaja. You can dive inside the walled town or follow the circuit of the ramparts, but don't miss the **viewing platform** at the southernmost rampart, which provides spectacular views of Gorica, Mangalemi, twentieth-century Berati, the Osumi River below and Mount Tomorri in the distance. Besides that, there's no right or wrong way to meander through the castle. Around every corner, you'll discover delightful relics of art and architecture spanning millennia of civilizations.

Churches of St Mary of Blachernae and St Nicholas

Donation requested

From the north gate, a narrow passage leads past a seventeenth-century church and giant bust of Constantine the Great, a near-replica of the one in Rome. According to some sources, the first Christian emperor had Illyrian ancestry, if you're wondering what he's doing here. On your left, the **Church of St Mary of Blachernae** (Kisha e Shën Mari Vllahernës) is a trinket-box Byzantine church dating to the thirteenth or fourteenth century, but its interior frescoes are a later addition by Nikolla Onufri, son of Albania's most renowned iconographic painter. Next to it, the sixteenth-century **Church of St Nicholas** (Kisha e Shën Kollit; free) was painted by the more famous Onufri – Nikolla's father – but it's only open on special occasions. For historical context, visit the excellent Onufri National Iconographic Museum (see page 120) nearby.

Acropolis

Free

Take the path behind the Church of St Nicholas to the Onufri National Iconographic Museum (Muzeu Kombëtar Ikonografik Onufri), then turn right onto Rrugica Mbrica or Rrugica Shën Triadha and follow the signs to the **Acropolis** (Akropoli), once the bastion of the ruling families of Berati and free to enter. Here, you'll see a parade ground, stables and the ruins of the White Mosque (Xhamia e Bardhë) along the way. Pause to take in views of Mount Shpiragu, to the west, then continue south through a gate in the wall to the castle's innermost keep. Little remains here but a somewhat forlorn archway and a twelfth-century cistern that hydrated the population of Kalaja. The cistern is still plastered, and it still holds (stagnant) water.

Holy Trinity Church

3

To the west of the Akropoli, the **Holy Trinity Church** (Kisha e Shën Triadhës) is a Berati icon, set against the castle wall, and one of the finest examples of late-Byzantine architecture in Albania. Dating to the early fourteenth century, its interior is decorated with frescoes and *spolia* — columns and capitals plucked from ancient Antipatrea.

Red Mosque

Rrugica Mbrica

South of the Akropoli, you'll find the ruins of the **Red Mosque** (Xhamia e Kuqe), a puzzling structure that may have predated the Ottoman conquest of the city. It's a brick construction, characteristic of Byzantine masonry, and the minaret, typically rising to the right of the entrance during that period, is on the left here. Regardless of propriety, that tower is all that still stands.

Church of St George

Rrugica Mbrica

Last up on Rrugica Mbrica before the viewing platform is the **Church of St George** (Kisha e Shën Gjergjit), repurposed as a canteen for Enver Hoxha and his deputies. The boss could admire his name on the flank of Mount Shpiragu from the balcony here, but the building is closed to visitors now.

Onufri National Iconographic Museum

Rrugica Shën Triadha near Rrugica Mbrica; follow signs • Charge • www.muzeumet-berat.al/en/onufri-iconographic-museum

One of Albania's two excellent collections of medieval and post-Byzantine art, along with the Muzeu Kombëtar i Artit Mesjetar (National Museum of Medieval Art) in Korça (see page 165), the **Onufri National Iconographic Museum** (Muzeu Kombëtar Ikonografik Onufri) showcases the work of the country's most famous iconographic painter, whose workshop was here in Berati. A high-ranking priest in the mid-sixteenth century, Onufri injected drama, colour and realism into iconography. At a time when most churchgoers couldn't read, icons and murals brought the stories and sermons of the Bible to life, and Onufri seemed to understand the importance of provoking emotion through religious art. Even casual appreciators can see how his paintings pop with greens, pinks, blues and what is now called 'Onufri red'. See page 188 for more on Onufri and other post-Byzantine artists.

The museum occupies the **Cathedral of the Dormition of St Mary** (Katedralja Fjetja e Shën Mërisë), built in 1797. A small assemblage of two hundred artworks and religious objects, it's very much worth a stop. Some of Onufri's most celebrated tempera-on-wood works from churches around the Berati region are preserved here, including a blue-winged and defiant *St John the Baptist*; *St Mary with Jesus*, draped in his signature red in contrast with the Christ Child swaddled in bright orange; and *Deisis*, a Gothic-influenced series of panels in gold, centred on a throned pink-clad Christ. Later works show Onufri's long influence. Two takes on St Demetrius in battle show

how techniques (and talents) diverged: eighteenth-century icon painter Kostandin Shpataraku splashed his canvas with bright red and blue, while a 1781 version from brothers Gjergji and Johani Çetiri is more subdued.

Gorica

South of the Osumi River, reached on foot via a modern suspension bridge or the stone-built Gorica Bridge (Ura e Goricës), is Berati's old Orthodox Christian quarter of **Gorica**. Squaring up to Mangalemi across the river, Gorica has the same eighteenth- and nineteenth-century architecture as that of its northern sibling but with one obvious difference: church campaniles contour the skyline instead of minarets. Plus, its riverfront promenade is much more walkable than the traffic bottleneck of Rruga Antipatrea on the opposite bank. By day, Gorica is a peaceful neighbourhood to wander. Keep an eye out for placards on houses commemorating their moonlighting as hideouts and meeting places of the National Liberation Movement (Lëvizja Antifashiste Nacional-Çlirimtare; LANÇ); one was the former home of Beratase antifascist hero Margarita Tutulani (see page 115). Another hidden gem worth seeking out is the eighteenth-century **House Museum Qako** (Rruga Jani Kosta; tel: 069 474 8002; charge), a private residence with wonderfully preserved floral frescoes, coffered ceilings and original fireplace. The owners also offer visitors the chance to taste their home-made *raki* and *gliko* (fruit preserve).

By night, Gorica rollicks (a little) more. There is a smattering of peppy restaurants, bars and hostels in the district, especially around the Gorica Bridge. It's also the jumping-off point for some of Berati's more picturesque hikes, including a scenic loop from the Gorica Bridge up to the ruined Gorica Castle (Kalaja e Goricës) and down to the suspension bridge. Both trailheads are on Rruga Nikolla Buhuri.

3

Gorica Bridge

Connects Rruga Antipatrea and Rruga Kristaq Tutulani • Free

Originally a wooden bridge, the one that stands today is based on a 1778 stone construction by Ahmet Kurt Pasha. Largely rebuilt after a flood in 1880 and turned over to pedestrians in the 1930s, **Gorica Bridge** (Ura e Goricës) is among the longest and most elegant Ottoman bridges surviving in the country, an impressive nine-arched feat of engineering designed to withstand what used to be a viciously fickle river.

Church of St Spyridon

Rruga e Kishës • Free

With much of its present structure dating to 1864, the **Church of St Spyridon** (Kisha e Shën Spiridhonit) is an interesting contrast to the older Byzantine churches in the Kalaja and Mangalemi: those are almost chapel-esque in size and stature and frilled with decorative brickwork, cupolas and terracotta shingles. If the older churches are cupcakes, St Spyridon is a pound cake: long, plain and brown. Still, the three-aisled basilica, which follows the transition to post-Byzantine architecture under Ottoman rule, maintains an attractive portico and campanile, and it's a welcome surprise to emerge on the manicured green lawn (a nod to its stint as a zoological and botanical museum under the communist regime).

ARRIVAL AND DEPARTURE — KALAJA (BERATI CASTLE) AND GORICA

KALAJA (BERATI CASTLE)

By foot You can enter the citadel complex one of two ways (safely, anyway): Rruga Mihal Komnena leads straight from Mangalemi to the north gate (main entrance), a 20min walk uphill from the Porta e Pashait; or a left turn off Rruga Mihal Komnena, about 250m past Muzeu Solomoni, provides a steep shortcut to a ruined rampart on the east side, shaving 5–10min off the trek.

By car or taxi You can take a cab to prevent slogging up Rruga Mihal Komnena on foot, or drive and park in one of the few spaces just outside or inside the north gate. Note, though, parking spots are limited, with some reserved for residents or hotel guests in the castle, and it can be tricky to maneuver a car if you have to turn back.

GORICA

By foot From the Mangalemi quarter, it's a quick jaunt to Gorica, over the suspension bridge in Berati centre or the Ura e Goricës. Both are pedestrian-only.

By bus Buses leave at midday from Gorica for the villages southwest of Berati. The pick-up point is the car park next to the Ura e Goricës and Rruga Kristaq Tutulani.

Destinations Malinati (several daily; 1hr 5min); Sinja (1 daily; 40min); Tërpani (1 daily; 1hr 20min).

By car To reach Gorica from the Berati neighbourhoods north of the Osumi River by car, head south on the Ura e Re over the river, then turn left and proceed on Rruga Shpiragu.

By taxi There's a taxi rank in Gorica next to the Ura e Goricës. Reputable taxi firms that service Gorica include Taxi Berat (tel: 069 254 9415) and Taxi Edi (tel: 069 967 8759).

INFORMATION

KALAJA (BERATI CASTLE)

Tours Berat Backpackers Tours, run by *Berat Backpackers Hostel* (Rruga Nikolla Buhuri 295; www.beratbackpackers.com), is a fun and budget-friendly operator focusing on the two most popular excursions from the city: the Osumi Canyon (see page 128) and Roshniku (see page 124) for tastings of local wine and *raki*.

3

ACCOMMODATION

SEE MAP PAGE 112

KALAJA (BERATI CASTLE)

Since 2022, Kalaja has witnessed a surge in accommodation openings. Houses in the citadel that have been renovated and reimagined as lodgings tend to be single-unit villa-apartments, so best for self-catered stays.

Hotel Kalaja Rrugica Mbrica; www.facebook.com/hotelkalajaberat. One of the first and biggest (relatively speaking – it has three rooms) of the historic villas transformed into accommodation in the castle, this is a comfortable, atmospheric spot for those who want to be high up on the rock and near parking. Rooms are simply but tastefully furnished, with superb views of the ancient surroundings. €€

Villa Kokoshi Rrugica Mbrica near Rrugica Shën Triadha; tel: 069 271 3787. A one-bedroom villa that can sleep up to five, the Kokoshi family's property is an architecturally striking mansion built in 1900 and renovated into a boutique cottage stay. It has plenty of original charm in the furnishings – kilims, dark-wood bedframes, sliding wood shutters – but is modern where it counts, with a rainfall shower, washing machine and full kitchen. There's a very nice restaurant here as well. €€€

GORICA

In the past few years, there has been a flurry of new openings in Gorica, to suit every budget and style preference.

Berat Backpackers Hostel Rruga Nikolla Buhuri 295; www.beratbackpackers.com. The first hostel to open in Berati and the second in the whole of Albania, this has become a Gorica staple for its adventure-traveller social scene, with a spacious hangout room and vine-shaded patio for drinks, cards and ping-pong. Set in an eighteenth-century Ottoman house, the hostel offers clean, comfortable dorms for six to eight, as well as a handful of private rooms, all with modern amenities and some with excellent views over the old city. You can also camp here and book tours to Osumi Canyon or local wineries. Dorms €

★ **Koroni Boutique Hotel** Rruga Jani Kosta; https://koroniboutiquehotel.albania-hotel.top/en. One of the stateliest *konaks* in Gorica was expertly renovated and opened as a hotel in 2023, preserving some of the original stone and woodwork in the rooms and adding modern amenities. Owners go out of their way to be accommodating and welcoming, and breakfast is excellent. It's centrally located yet quiet – a top-value pick. €€

EATING

SEE MAP PAGE 112

KALAJA (BERATI CASTLE)

Klea Restaurant Rrugica Shën Sofia, near the Kalaja north gate; tel: 069 768 4861. The restaurant of *Hotel Klea*, this is one of the best dining spots in the castle. Expect traditional cuisine in an atmospheric villa with a lovely garden terrace for balmy evenings. Stuffed eggplant and oven-baked cheese are among the Albanian dishes to go for, but *Klea* also throws in some Greek options like *dolmadakia* (stuffed vine leaves) with tzatziki, and moussaka. €€

★ **Mbrica Restaurant** Rrugica Mbrica; tel: 069 364 3995. Not named for the street it resides on but rather the family after which the street is named, *Mbrica* is a restaurant, guesthouse and private museum in one, owned by the Mbricas. The view over Berati alone warrants a visit, but this is also a good place to feast on grilled meats like lamb and veal, and to try fig and cherry *gliko* (fruit preserve). You may also catch live music, and the museum is worth a peek, displaying the tools, workshop and finished product in the craft of silversmithing, the original business of the family. €€

GORICA

Ballkoni Goricës Rruga Shpiragu near the Ura e Goricës; tel: 068 363 0005. Opened in 2024, this lovely restaurant does indeed boast a marvellous balcony; in fact, the rooftop here has the best view in town of the Ura e Goricës at golden hour. It's a good place for a drink, but the kitchen does a line in fine renditions of Beratas staples and international picks. Staff are very friendly, and the kitchen excels with meat dishes like *vienez* (cheese-stuffed schnitzel) and *qofte* (meatballs). €€

DRINKING AND NIGHTLIFE **SEE MAP PAGE 112**

KALAJA (BERATI CASTLE)

★ **Mengra e Vjetër** Rrugica Shën Triadha near the Kalaja north gate. Opened in 2024, this wine bar in an old stable block, the "Old Manger" is a unique spot in the castle. The cosy arched stone interior looks just how it sounds, and a small outdoor area is dotted with oak-barrel tables in keeping with the main calling card here: Albanian wine. Staff are all connoisseurs, and they'll happily guide you through a tasting of some local favourites, including reds, whites and rosés from indigenous grape varieties like Pulës and Serinë, as well as Cabernet Sauvignon, Sangiovese and blends. An excellent venue for sampling wines (and cheeses) from different parts of the country in one place.

GORICA

Good Vibes Rruga Kristaq Tutulani and Rruga Stiliano Bandilli. Laidback place with tiki touches and a playlist of ambient house music. Skittles-coloured decor and a big patio encourage people to relax and mingle, making this a popular spot with the hostel crowd. The cocktail quality remains high, though, and top-shelf drinks are very reasonably priced.

3

Around Berati

The countryside around Berati is all hills, valleys, canyons and fields – an appropriate landscape for Albania's heartland. Unfortunately, with a few exceptions, it's difficult to explore on your own. The villages of Gjeroveni, Sinja, Osmenzeza, Gllava and Tërpani, south of Berati, have rustic appeal, orchard-fresh produce and placid lakes, but the unpaved, rocky roads are inaccessible without an off-road vehicle or tour guide. There is, however, a green, monster-sized off-road bus that carts passengers to and from Tërpani. Even Malinati, a leading viticultural region supplying Enver Hoxha's crew with wine, calls for a car with high clearance or a decent mountain bike. A guided excursion to any of these places is well worth a day-trip; see page 116 for information on tours. Anyone, however, can easily reach **Roshniku** and **Droboniku**.

Droboniku

Droboniku, a sleepy village directly south of Berati, has little left to regale its history, but it does feature some of the most amazing views of both the city and Mount Tomorri – all reachable on foot. On the Gorica trail to the ruined Gorica Castle (Kalaja e Goricës), you can press on to Droboniku, about 4.5km one-way. It's steep in places and not the easiest path to follow, but the tourist information office or the trail app Wikiloc (www.wikiloc.com) can help you out. The reward is acres of cherry orchards, making this an exceptional diversion during blooming season, and a smattering of traditional restaurants.

ARRIVAL AND DEPARTURE **DROBONIKU**

By car or taxi Droboniku is located 7.5km (10min) by road south of Berati centre via Rruga Kristaq Tutulani, then SH74. Berati taxis will also take you (see page 116).

By bus A village bus departs from Berati's main terminal at midday and returns early in the morning (1 daily; 20min).

ACCOMMODATION AND EATING **SEE MAP PAGE 112**

Restorant Ballkoni Beratit Droboniku centre; tel: 069 624 2434. From the street, it looks like a dozy village hangout, but its quiet facade belies an eatery with a smart, updated interior – and energetic TikTok presence. Spit-roasted lamb and chicken over *petka* (home-made pasta) cooked in a *saç* oven (lidded metal pan set over hot coals) are made to be shared. The balconies, especially the rooftop one, give unobstructed panoramas of Berati city, the Osumi valley and Mount Tomorri. €€

Sunrise House Off SH74; tel: 069 332 8440. This luxury villa opened in 2024, comprising a pair of two-bedroom apartments sleeping five and seven. Floor-to-ceiling windows overlook a private pool, which in turn frames views of the Osumi valley. The distinctive A-frame house is modern, but the furnishings are heirloom and antique. Find an upright piano, firepit and French-style *boiserie* (wooden panelling) in the downstairs apartment; upstairs, the lofted pad has its own balcony. €€€€

Roshniku

The road to **Roshniku** is one of the most spectacular short drives in Albania. A one-lane road that manages to somehow function as a two-lane road and veers sharply around more than a few blind mountain corners, it's a sure-fire hit – for whoever's not driving. Pull over where the paved road meets the dirt path to Roshnik i Vogël for a panorama of Tomorri tumbling down to Roshniku village. You'll take in sublime views of olive groves and vineyards and, finally, the Lake of Roshniku (Liqeni i Roshnikut) cradled in the belly of the valley.

3

Before the road was paved, Roshniku was undiscovered by outsiders. And it is hardly busy today, with one exception: the **Alpeta Agritourism & Winery** (see page 125), perched on the southernmost ledge of the village. Even if you don't visit the winery, you're sure to be enamoured with the sight of the vine-combed landscapes and figs drying on mats in the sun.

ARRIVAL AND DEPARTURE — ROSHNIKU

By car Roshniku is 13.5km northeast of Berati centre via Rruga Migjeni, then Rruga e Duhanasit. Drive 25min or take a taxi. You can park in the car park next to *Alpeta Agritourism & Winery* or in Sheshi Roshnik, but don't attempt to drive beyond the main road through town or the road to the square unless you have a small 4WD.

By bus A village bus departs from Berati's main terminal at midday and returns early in the morning (1 daily; 40min).

EATING AND DRINKING — SEE MAP PAGE 112

Restorant Roshniku Roshniku village centre; tel: 069 240 9401. Perched on a Roshniku valley overlook, both indoor tables and outdoor terraces here give diners a feeling of being tucked within the folds of the foothills. The simplest ingredients straight from the farm are the star of the show: fresh figs, grapes and olives. But you can go all-in with slabs of lamb on the bone, or even the full shank if you're part of a bigger party. This and Alpeta Agritourism (see page 125) are the places to taste the bounty of Berati's natural larder. €€€

Mount Tomorri

Once upon a time, there were two brothers: Tomorri and Shpiragu. According to legend, they loved the same woman, or the same city, or in some retellings, the woman *is* the city – Kalaja, the hill of Berati. In other versions, she is the manifestation of Earthly Beauty, sister of Sea Beauty. Regardless, the situation became untenable, and the brothers came to blows. As the story goes, Tomorri, armed with a sword, and Shpiragu, with his cudgel (or possibly a cannon), mortally wounded each other, turning into the mountains we see on opposite sides of Berati today – Mount Tomorri (Mali i Tomorrit), with its pockmarked scars, and Mount Shpiragu (Mali i Shpiragut), scored with deep slashes from head to foot. The woman drowned in her tears – the Osumi River.

Baba Tomorri is generally the father of all gods in Central Albanian folklore, but Tomorri is also the 'Olympus', where all the gods lived. Old Albanian scholarship also suggests the mountain, perhaps somewhat wishfully, as the site of Dodona, the oracle of the Pelasgians, the ancient pre-Hellenic inhabitants of Greece. Though the date Mount Tomorri was first settled is uncertain, the remnants of Tomorri Castle (Kalaja e Tomorrit) at the foot of the mountain are credibly dated to at least the

WINE IN BERATI

Albania might not spring to mind as a leading wine region, but locals have in fact been making the most of the bounty of the vines for thousands of years. From the Bronze Age on – and through the Ottoman and the communist periods – Albanians tended home vineyards and sometimes made wine on a larger scale.

Since the 1990s, winemakers have worked to better understand their grapes and terroirs, many spending stints in Italy to learn the international standards of viticulture. Some producers have found success with varieties like Merlot, Cabernet Sauvignon and Sangiovese, but one of the distinguishing qualities of Albanian wine is just how much of it is still made with grapes indigenous to the area or the wider Balkans. Shesh i Zi, Kallmet, Vlosh, Vranac, Mavrud, Serinë e Zezë and Debinë e Zezë are the red varieties to remember, while whites to watch for are Shesh i Bardhë, Cerrujë, Debinë e Bardhë and Pulës (also called Puls, Pulsi, Pulëz and Pulësi). Century-old vines untouched by the historic phylloxera epidemic are not unheard of.

There's no consensus on the best wine region in Albania, but the wineries you can visit are mostly in the Berati foothills, the Lezha hills in the northwest, the rolling lowlands between Tirana and Durrësi, and the southeastern highlands around Kolonja and Përmeti. Of these, Berati has more visitor-friendly vineyards than anywhere else, and it's become known as Albania's leading wine destination.

Unlike Napa or Bordeaux's Left Bank, you won't find a neat row of premier châteaux side by side here. Here, wineries are scattered across the region, and some are easier to find than others. A wine-tasting tour can really add value to learning the ins and outs of Albanian wine and will save you time in transit (see page 116 for tour operators). The weeklong Wine & Stories Festival in Berati city every October also brings together most of the best producers in one place. These are some of the finest oenophile addresses around Berati.

Alpeta Agritourism & Winery Southernmost point of the main road through Roshniku; https://alpeta.al. The Fiska family began making small quantities of wine in Roshniku in 1994. You can taste reds, whites, rosés and *raki*, learn about the winemaking process and trundle through the vineyards – some of the most scenic in Albania. Reds are mostly Cabernet-Merlot blends, and the white is Pulës. *Alpeta* also has an excellent restaurant and two guesthouses on the property. It gets very busy and books up well in advance in the high season.

Çobo Winery SH72 northwest of Berati, Ura Vajgurore; www.cobowine.com. Oenophile Muharrem Çobo has grown his winery into a modest viticultural empire, in part on the back of his Shendeverë sparkling wine, made from Pulës in the traditional (ie. Champagne-style) method. At the tasting room, you can sample red blends; Sheshi (both i Zi and i Bardhë); bubbly and *raki*. You can also try Çobo at the *Shendeverë Wine Bar* in the Tirana Castle (Kalaja e Tiranës).

Edoni Winery SH91 toward Kuçova, Kuçova; www.edoniwinery.com. With a focus on local grape varieties, *Edoni* makes delicious reds (Sheshi i Zi), whites (Sheshi i Bardhë and Pulës) and a Vranac rosé. The winery is easy to reach but less well known than others in the region, with an excellent farm-to-table restaurant.

Vila Hadaj Malinati village; www.facebook.com/vilahadaj. Way out in the sticks in Malinati, the favoured wine region of the communist elite, *Vila Hadaj* can only be reached by bike or 4WD. The seclusion, however, is part of the appeal, along with the panoramas and the local cuisine. A lovely place to try red blends and Pulës with historic pedigree.

Nurellari Winery 1km south off Rruga Nacionale between Berati and Çorovoda (follow signs), Fushë-Peshtani; www.facebook.com/kantinanurellari. With a modern, impressive tasting room and barrel cellar, *Nurellari* has come a long way since the family first began making wine in a warehouse in 1995. Reds from Montepulciano, Cabernet Sauvignon, Shesh i Zi and Serinë e Zezë are standouts. There's also a guesthouse for overnight stays; book well in advance.

Pupa Winery On Rruga Nacionale between Berati and Çorovoda, Fushë-Peshtani; www.pupawinery.com. In 2022, *Pupa* undertook a major revamp, resulting in a new restaurant and guesthouse, along with an aristocratic barrel cellar. Tastings are very reasonably priced, and you can visit vineyards in the Tomorri foothills. The focus is exclusively on ancient Albanian grapes, including white and red Serinë and Debinë, and a rosé from the rare Birvo i variety.

eleventh century AD. Gjergj Kastrioti Skënderbeu (or Skënderbej; Skanderbeg) scored a significant victory against the Ottomans here in 1457, and the mountain took on spiritual significance for both Orthodox Christians and Sufi Muslims. Every August, hundreds of thousands of Bektashi Muslims make a pilgrimage up the mountain to the Tyrbja e Abaz Aliut (Shrine of Abbas ibn Ali) on the south summit.

Mount Tomorri National Park

Charge

Mount Tomorri National Park (Parku Kombëtar Mali i Tomorrit) covers around 260 square kilometres of meadows, shrubland, forests, springs and surreal karst and limestone formations. It bristles with life: there are several species of newt and snake, including vipers, and around 140 bird species, among them eagles, hornbills and honey buzzards, which eat wasp larvae. Wild boars, goats, bears and deer roam the foothills too. Unless you're an experienced trekker and navigator with proper equipment and a truck, the road to the Tyrbja e Abaz Aliut (Shrine of Abbas ibn Ali) is really the only accessible hike on Tomorri. The mountain is almost always either shrouded in cloud or painfully exposed to the sun, and trails to the 2400m-high north summit, **Çuka e Partizanit**, are strenuous and/or nonexistent. With a guide, however, that journey can be accomplished in a day if you're accustomed to alpine hiking (see page 116 for guides). Nonetheless, Tomorri is wondrous, rising above a cluster of lesser peaks, and it's obvious why it holds such a place of reverence in the national imagination.

3

The northern slopes

Thanks to road improvements, Tomorri is a good mountain to drive, to a point. From Fushë-Peshtani along the Rruga Nacionale between Berati and Çorovoda, the twenty-minute drive to the village of **Karkanjozi** is a scenic route full of harrowing blind corners that should amply prepare you for the even more scenic, even more terrifying drive around the southern slope of Tomorri. From Karkanjozi, you can hike, bike or drive by 4WD around 6.5km (2hr hiking one-way) to **Tomori i Madh**, the last village before the mountain ascends and the vantage point for **Koprinishta**, the dramatic outcropping on which the crumbling Tomorri Castle (Kalaja e Tomorrit) is poised.

With an off-road vehicle, you can also reach a trail to the castle from the north, out of the village of **Dardha** (1.7km), around which are plentiful opportunities for hiking, picnicking and camping. A paved road through this area, connecting to the **Gramshi** municipality on the east side of the mountain, is slated for completion in 2025 or 2026. It'll make the northern foothills significantly easier to explore.

Teqeja dhe Tyrbja e Abaz Aliut

Every year (20–25 August), people flock to the southeastern slope of Mount Tomorri from all over Albania and the world to take part in the annual pilgrimage to the **Tyrbja e Abaz Aliut**. Tomorri is spiritually significant to Albanians of all stripes, but on these days, it's the religious epicentre for followers of Bektashism, a sect of Sufi Islam that first took hold in Albania and the Ottoman Balkans in the fifteenth century. August is when the spirit of Abaz Aliu (see page 127) is said to return to the mountain each year.

The **pilgrimage** is holy, rowdy and sometimes bloody. It can involve visiting some of the 'footsteps' of Abaz Aliu in the rock formations around the mountain, the sacrifice of thousands of sheep, and a two-hour hike up a 6.8km dirt road to the south summit to pay respects at the *tyrbe* (or *tyrbja*, a shrine or tomb). Throughout, meat is grilled, *raki* is consumed into the small hours, and the area is filled with music and dancing. Some Bektashis – and anyone else who wants to join – camp out for days.

The shrine and *teqe* (or *teqeja*), a house of worship for Bektashis, were not originally designed to accommodate today's 800,000 pilgrims but the complex has expanded over the years. It's likely that a Bektashi shrine has existed on the south summit since at least the fifteenth century, but the current *tyrbe* was built around 1880: a small cylindrical structure with polygonal stone walls and a green metal roof, surrounded by a stone terrace with fine views over Central Albania. The *teqe* below, dating to 1916, tumbles across a series of huge stone terraces on the southeastern slope of the mountain. There's lots of parking, a café, another *teqe* where several Bektashi dervishes are buried and a tremendous panorama over forested peaks. A dirt road connects the *teqe* and *tyrbe* and climbs to the summit – it's not exactly wilderness immersion, but the hike and its destination are unlike any other in Albania. All visitors are welcome in any season.

Bogova Waterfall

The easiest diversion into Mount Tomorri National Park is the twenty-minute walk to **Bogova Waterfall** (Ujëvara e Bogovës), near Bogova village on the Rruga Nacionale between Berati and Çorovoda. At 20m high, it may not be the most imposing of waterfalls, but a splash in the frigid pool below is a bracing way to cool off on a sweaty summer day. There's a small bar nearby, and it's a popular weekend spot for locals. Coming from Berati, you'll pass the town of Poliçani on your right. Look out for the massive complex of now-abandoned weapons and munitions factories that Enver Hoxha built here as part of his project to make the Tomorri area a military stronghold.

ARRIVAL AND DEPARTURE — MOUNT TOMORRI

From Berati, there are only a few ways to reach Mount Tomorri National Park (Parku Kombëtar Mali i Tomorrit) on your own that are uncomplicated.

By bus or minibus There are village buses that leave

ABAZ ALIU AND THE BEKTASHI ORDER IN ALBANIA

Abaz Aliu (Abbas ibn Ali) was the son of the son-in-law of the Prophet Muhammad, Ali ibn Abi Talib, the first Shia imam. Born in Medina in the mid-seventh century, Abaz was killed in the **680 AD Battle of Karbala**, a small uprising against a new caliph who had been controversially appointed. According to the story, the rebels and their families were cut off from water for days, and Abaz undertook a daring expedition to the Euphrates River alone. There, he was ambushed, and he came to be revered for his courage and self-sacrifice. He is buried at the princely Al-Abbas Shrine in Karbala, in what is now central Iraq. How he came to Albania is shrouded in legend; perhaps he journeyed here to protect Berati, perhaps he flew to Tomorri on a white horse after his martyrdom.

In the thirteenth century, a Sufi mystic named **Sari Salltiku** spread the early teachings that would go on to become **Bektashism**, perhaps as far as the Balkans (there is a *tyrbe* devoted to him in Kruja). As a mystical, heterodox faith emphasizing the pursuit of oneness, self-knowledge, human harmony and higher truth, Bektashism was fairly compatible with medieval Albanian folk beliefs, Orthodox Christianity and even rural animism. There were – and are – no prohibitions on drinking, dancing, singing and mixed-sex prayer, nor dress codes for laypeople. Unsurprisingly, Bektashism became popular among the Ottoman Janissary infantry, many of whom were Balkan-born subjects of the empire, converts to Islam taken to faraway Istanbul.

In nineteenth-century Albania, Bektashism became strongly intertwined with nationalism and the **Albanian Rilindja**, especially through the literary works of the Frashëri brothers (see page 111), born into a Bektashi-affiliated family. When the new government of Turkey shut down Bektashi lodges in its 1925 secularization campaign, the headquarters of the *tarikat* (*tariqa*, or order) moved to Tirana. In 1930, work began in the Albanian capital on the **Bektashi World Centre** (*Kryegjyshata Botërore Bektashiane*). During the communist era, Albanians practiced in secret and kept the faith alive abroad, particularly at a *teqe* in suburban Michigan. Today, Nevruz (*Nowruz*), a commemoration of Abaz Aliu's family in the Shia and Sufi faiths, is a public holiday observed on 22 March.

from the main Berati terminal to the mountain villages of Karkanjozi, Tomori, Lybesha and Kapinova in Tomorri's northwestern foothills at around midday, returning early in the morning. The bus to Çorovoda from Berati (many daily; see page 115) can drop you off at Bogova for the Bogova Waterfall (Ujëvara e Bogovës) if you request the stop. There's no bus to the Teqeja e Abaz Aliut, but the Berati tourist information office can point you in the direction of any *furgons* (minibuses) that may head there on a given day.

By car Drivers can reach Karkanjozi, Bogova and the Teqeja e Abaz Aliut from Berati via the Rruga Nacionale southeast towards Çorovoda. The road is not dangerous or scary, but it's in disrepair, so be mindful of potholes and avoid driving after dark. To reach Karkanjozi, take the left turning (north) just before Pupa Winery; it's about a 45min drive from Berati in total. For the Bogova Waterfall car park, turn left (east) at Bogova village and continue around 600m; it takes around an hour to drive here from central Berati. To reach the Teqeja e Abaz Aliut, take the left (north) after the Gega Oil petrol station west of Poliçani. The next 30–45min of road are profoundly beautiful and extremely hairy, especially if you're not fond of heights. The road is well asphalted, but it's a one-lane passage with two-way traffic tracing the full southern slope of Tomorri, often without guardrails. The *teqe* is about 1hr 30min from Berati.

By taxi Berati city taxis can take you to Karkanjozi, Bogova or the *teqe*, but be mindful of distances and nail down rates and return times in advance. See page 116 for information on reputable taxi services.

3

INFORMATION

Tourist information At the time of writing, there is no visitor centre, and information for navigating Mount Tomorri National Park is sparse. Be aware that several of the park's roadside maps indicate 'you are here', where you are, in fact, not 'here'. Unless you want to spend several days exploring Tomorri on your own, consider taking a guided tour from Berati (see page 116).

ACCOMMODATION AND EATING

The village of Ujaniku, around 3.5km northeast of the Teqeja e Abaz Aliut via paved road, is the only place inside Mount Tomorri National Park with more than one guesthouse, and it only has a few. There are a handful of others scattered around the slopes of the mountain, and you can also pitch a tent anywhere, though there are no facilities. All guesthouses listed also serve breakfast and dinner.

Bujtina Kapinova Kapinova village; tel: 069 555 5579. Opened in 2024, this cluster of luxury cabins on the west side of the mountain offers gorgeous views and creature comforts like flatscreen TVs, wi-fi and rainfall showers. The property has helped develop some easy-to-follow trails around the area, and that's what you're here for. €€€€

★ **Bujtina Qafë-Dardha** Qafë-Dardha village; tel: 068 518 7071. A rural retreat on the north slope of Tomorri, this five-room guesthouse is a cut above thanks to the hospitality of the owners. *Bujtina Qafë-Dardha* is surrounded by breathtaking trails, vistas, lakes and peaks, but you need to know the lay of the land. Proprietor Batjar Koçi can orient you and even leads hikes up the mountain; he'll also pick guests up in Berati at a fair price (at the time of writing, a 4WD is needed to reach the property). Rooms are simple and comfortable and can accommodate up to four. The team also make dinner – and *raki*. €€

Café at Teqeja e Abaz Aliut Near the *teqe*, next to the dirt road to the summit; www.kryegjyshataboterorebektashiane.org. Thousands of people grill meat, eat and drink here during the annual August pilgrimage, but the pleasant café on the Bektashi campus serves snacks and drinks to all visitors, any time. The terrace overlooking the lesser mountains is a lovely place to relax after hiking back down from the south summit of Tomorri. €

Hani Baba Tomorr Ujaniku village; tel: 068 512 3123. This highly welcoming family-run place has comfortable rooms and enough space to accommodate larger groups who want to sleep or dine here; you can also pitch a tent on the property for a small fee. There's a terrace for outdoor dining; chickens and dogs roam the property; and the common room draped in furs has a cosy winter lodge vibe. Excellent home-made breakfast and dinner. €€

Osumi Canyon

The Osumi River (Lumi i Osumit) beats a path through the mountains west of Korça, merging into the Semani River (Lumi i Semanit) northwest of Berati. But Berati claims the river – and the river claims Berati. In the spring, snowmelt from the many mountains it passes by causes water levels to rise – often quickly and dangerously. Berati city used to flood when the waterway brought with it a powerful arsenal of rocks, trees and mud; the iconic stone Gorica Bridge (Ura e Goricës; see page 121) was overwhelmed and largely destroyed in 1880.

Millions of years ago, erosion and glacial activity upstream of Berati carved a canyon up to 150m deep along the river's course. The 26km-long **Osumi Canyon** (Kanioni i Osumit) starts near the town of Çorovoda, about fifty kilometres southeast of Berati by road. Its magnificent limestone formations – orange-brown pillars streaked with grey – are a natural treasure of Central Albania, and the turquoise water demands a swim when the weather is hot. It's a magical place, and you don't need to be a hardy type to enjoy it. Plenty of people come in the summer just to lounge and splash around in the calm, cooling shallows. In July and August, you can walk and swim long stretches of the river and riverbed in the canyon (bring water shoes). While the Osumi is usually tamer now than it was a century ago, its power still fluctuates dramatically between seasons, so in spring and fall, you'll have more adventurous experiences to try, like **rafting** or **gorge hiking**. There are trails along the canyon ledges you can follow on your own during most of the year.

There are several **viewpoints**, wild swimming spots and seasonal food shacks along the Rruga Nacionale southeast of Çorovoda. A shaded viewing platform around 4km past Çorovoda provides a panorama that reveals the true scope of the canyon. After another 2.7km, you reach the '**Bride's Hole**', a divot in the ledge where, according to legend, an unwilling bride-to-be prayed to the canyon that she be saved from marriage. Obliging, the rock swallowed her up and hid her forever. It's a great photo opportunity, but you shouldn't jump in the hole. One of the last and best spots to reach the river is near the **Old Zabërzani Bridge** (Ura e Vjetër e Zabërzanit), a rickety gorge crossing.

Kasabashi Bridge and Gradeci Canyon

Rruga Arkitekt Kasemi, Çorovoda • Free

Near the Osumi Canyon, just northeast of Çorovoda town, you'll find the **Kasabashi Bridge** (Ura e Kasabashit), a small but architecturally splendid Ottoman bridge built in the sixteenth or seventeenth century. With its single-arched design, it's a miniature design of the elegant style of bridge seen, most famously, in Mostar, Bosnia and Herzegovina. A caravan route from Berati once crossed this landscape.

In this area, you can hike the **Gradeci Canyon** (Kanioni i Gradecit), which narrows to only 1.5m wide in places, making it much narrower than Osumi's gorge, and much deeper, with its limestone walls nudging 200m. You'll pass a series of derelict **communist military installations**, **bunkers** and **tunnels** drilled into the mountains for storage of weapons and armoured vehicles. In the 1960s, Enver Hoxha decided to fortify Tomorri into a sprawling – but secret – military complex: Poliçani was the centre for arsenal manufacturing, and this area, Pirogoshi, was a base. It's just a tiny sliver of something much bigger. On the southeast slope of Tomorri, Hoxha built a small city's worth of cave bunkers and tunnels to act as offices, living quarters and a command headquarters in case Tirana ever came under attack. Most of that complex was ripped apart during the 1997 unrest – supposedly, a vast treasury was locked away here – and it's inaccessible now. Another trail, up along the canyon ridge, leads to the wide-mouthed limestone **Pirogoshi Cave** (Shpella e Pirogoshit).

The canyons aren't hard to explore, but they're deceptively far from Berati. Unless you want to spend a few days here, consider taking a guided trip from the city (see page 116).

ARRIVAL AND DEPARTURE — OSUMI CANYON

By car You can enter the Osumi Canyon at a few points. Follow the twisty and poorly maintained Rruga Nacionale from Berati southeast to Çorovoda (1hr 30min). A small 'beach' near Sharova village, 2.5km south on paved roads, is the starting point for a short hike south into the canyon. The Old Zabërzani Bridge entry point is around 11km south of Çorovoda on the Rruga Nacionale; look out for a small parking area along with a few summer snack bars. Dipping in here and wading south, you'll soon see the bridge. Alternatively, around 2km northeast of Çorovoda on Rruga

Arkitekt Kasemi, you'll find a path to Gradeci Canyon, and 2.5km up dirt roads from Kasabashi Bridge is the trailhead for Pirogoshi Cave.

By bus Buses from the Berati main terminal run to Çorovoda (many daily; 1hr 30min). The municipality is called Skrapari, which is the destination name at the bus terminal. From the Çorovoda bus stop, it is a 30min walk to both the Sharova entrance to the Osumi Canyon and to the Kasabashi Bridge. You may be able to find taxis or *furgons* (minibuses) in Çorovoda to continue to the Old Zabërzani Bridge entry point to the canyon.

ACCOMMODATION

The vast majority of visitors to the Osumi Canyon are day-trippers from Berati. There is a handful of hotels in the area for the few folk spending multiple days in the area, though they aren't really anything special other than their proximity to the canyon.

Hotel Kanione Rruga Hysen Zaloshnja (SH72), Çerenishti village; https://kanionehotel.com. Not exactly a rustic retreat, the fairly modern *Kanione* offers the space and convenience of a large hotel, despite its rural setting. Rooms sleep one to four, there's 24hr reception, breakfast is included, and dinner can be taken overlooking the Osumi valley. The hotel also organizes canyon hikes. €€€

Hotel Shpëtimi Rruga Sadush Myftari, Çorovoda; tel: 069 574 8924. This brightly furnished budget hotel in Çorovoda has singles, doubles and family rooms sleeping four. Parking and a light breakfast are available. Located right across the street from Çorovoda's main square and a pedestrianized street dotted with restaurants and cafés. €

EATING

Summer Bar and Restaurant 11km south of Çorovoda on the Rruga Nacionale; tel: 068 267 7409. A solid seasonal snack spot right next to the Zabërzani jump-in point to the Osumi Canyon. Grilled pork ribs, fries, salad, whole-grilled fish and *qofte* (meatballs) are standouts, and, of course, the riverside digs are unbeatable. Friendly staff – and prices. €

★ **Zani's Grill & Bar** Rruga Nacionale, Zabërzani village. Find a fresh, filling organic meal at an old-fashioned price at this spot down near the southeastern point of the gorge (asphalted in 2024). All vegetables are grown in the kitchen-garden of this family-run operation, so don't skip the salad, and be sure to try bruschetta or stuffed peppers. Lamb and goat on the bone, served with hand-cut fries, should satisfy even the heartiest of eaters. €€

Gramshi and the Devolli River valley

The part of Central Albania curving around the highlands north of Mount Tomorri roughly traces the **Devolli River** (Lumi i Devollit) from Berati north to the Elbasani area, then presses further south on the east side of the mountains. It's a quiet landscape of lakes, valleys and gentle hills until you reach **Gramshi**, where Tomorri again looms to the west. The 90km trip by car from Berati to Gramshi takes around one hour and 45 minutes via motorway (some portions of which are neglected country roads). You'll pass through the lake-pocked, low-key township of **Belshi**, where a short detour to **Seferani Lake** (Liqeni i Seferanit) makes for a pleasant pitstop to grab a meal or a more leisurely diversion thanks to its hiking, fishing and swimming opportunities. At 900m wide and 80m deep, the much bigger **Banja Lake** (Liqueni i Banjës) on the Gramshi side, bounded by pine-forested hills and crags, looks so perfectly and uniformly turquoise it could be fake – in fact, it is. The reservoir was formed by the Banja dam, which interrupts the Devolli with a hydropower plant that was built in 2016. Accessed via SH59 and SH89, the majestic lake is only an hour's drive from Tirana, making it an easy escape for the capital's urban crowd. There are boat trips across its glittering surface.

The road to Gramshi, via snaking but well-paved roads and modern bridges, is one of Albania's easier scenic routes, and there are pockets of paradise to be discovered deep in the Devolli hills.

Gramshi town

The town of **Gramshi** doesn't have ancient pedigree, but it was an important manufacturing centre during the communist era, with plants dedicated to the

THE COMMUNIST CITY SQUARE

Enver Hoxha built **new squares** in virtually every Albanian municipality, first following the architectural blueprints of the Soviet Union and, later, his own idiosyncratic philosophies of urban planning. Here were the *pallat* (large offices or chambers) buildings of civic administration, austere and impersonal white, grey or brownish structures that **communicated power** and often radically diverged from the existing town's appearance. Typically, on or near the city square, you'd find the municipal or regional seat of governmental authority, the palace of culture, the local treasury building, a state-run hotel and the party headquarters. Some squares also had cinemas, theatres, museums, libraries and smaller banks, as well as **heroic statues** in the socialist realist style (sometimes, of course, the 'hero' was Enver Hoxha). In the 1950s, Hoxha emulated the crisp though lightly ornamented architectural style of Stalinism for his *pallat* designs. After Albania's fallout with the USSR, Hoxha's style became sparser, though the emphasis on **grand-scale buildings** and boulevards remained. Today, many of the major squares have been modified beyond recognition, at least to outsiders. In some places, like Durrësi (see page 139) and Tirana (see page 56), the general outline remains obvious and some of the original buildings have found new uses – but more modern development still encroaches. In only a few towns, including Gramshi, does the square look essentially the same now as in the 1980s.

3

production of soft drinks, alcohol, canned goods and weapons like the Kalashnikov assault rifle. But the collectivization of farms severely damaged the existing economy of rural agriculture. The main point of interest is the town square, whose buildings have been mostly preserved in both form and function since the communist years.

Kamber Dërmyshi Central Square of Gramshi

Now called **Kamber Dërmyshi Central Square of Gramshi** (Sheshi Qendror i Gramshit Kamber Dërmyshi), the town square is an architectural jigsaw of twentieth-century Albanian socialist architecture. A 1946-built prefecture-level office sits on the northeast side. On the north end is the former Komiteti Qendror i Partisë (Party Committee Headquarters), completed in 1966 and now the Gramshi municipality office. The faded building on the west, dating to the same time, was once the palace of culture before being turned into a museum in the 1970s, though it is not usually open. **Hotel Tomorri** (see page 132) on the south side, built in 1971, retains its original role.

ARRIVAL AND GETTING AROUND — GRAMSHI

By bus The main bus stop is around 500m north of the Kamber Dërmyshi Central Square of Gramshi on SH71, across the street from Rruga e Konservimit. Village buses are less than 100m up the road (south); find the once-a-day bus to Lenia for Valamara there.

Destinations Berati (several daily; 1hr 30min); Durrësi (several daily; 2hr 30min); Elbasani (many daily; 1hr); Fieri (1 daily; 2hr 20min); Korça (1 daily; 2hr 40min); Lenia (1 daily; 2hr); Lushnja (1 daily; 2hr 40min); Tirana (several daily; 1hr 50min); Vlora (1 daily; 2hr 55min).

By car The SH71 cuts right through Gramshi. Roads are well paved but twisty, both north and south, and there's minimal traffic anywhere. Roads in the town are a little rougher. Street parking is fine.

INFORMATION

Tourist information Look for a freestanding sign displaying tourist information in the north part of the main square, in front of the Bashkia Gramsh. You can see maps and details about the town and the wider region, in English.

ACCOMMODATION

★ **Hani i Taulant Shahinit** 13.5km south of Gramshi via SH71, Kodovjati; https://hani.al. With chickens flapping out back and an old tractor in the hills, this farm and guesthouse isn't instantly recognizable as a 1960s military office. In a little village between the Gramshi region's far-flung sights, this upscale lodge has five ultra-comfortable rooms overlooking the Devolli and the garden, all outfitted with polished wood floors and antique furniture. Fresh, local food is a passion of the owners, and anyone can stop by to chow down on *pispili* (spinach and leek pie), liver over rice, hard and soft cheeses, and spit-roasted lamb. €€€

Hotel Latifi SH71; tel: 067 652 7663. You won't find many new hotels in this part of Albania, but this place is modern enough that you'll be comfortable. Within walking distance of the centre, it offers excellent mountain views across the Devolli, fast wi-fi and a very welcoming owner. *Latifi* is simple, clean and offers great value for money. €

Hotel Tomorri Sheshi Kamber Dërmyshi; tel: 069 217 8921. If you want a central hotel, this local stalwart has been going strong for fifty years. On the main square and close to restaurants, markets and the bus station, it's a budget option with basic amenities and clean rooms – the best with terrific views over the town and out to Tomorri. €€

EATING

Redi Rruga Hamit Dollani and Rruga Xhile Liçi. Albania's small towns are full of unassuming little spots where you'll eat big and enjoy every dish plonked down in front of you – and this is one. *Redi* serves up traditional salads and *mezes*, along with king-sized plates of grilled veal and lamb. A great place to fill up after a day exploring the countryside. €

Restaurant Altini Rruga Rinia; 069 223 4440. House-made wine, plus heaping plates of grilled lamb, T-bone veal steak, vegetables, *pispili* (spinach pie) and other Gramshi specialties liven up the table at this local spot south of the centre. Decor is simple but tasteful, service is friendly. Be sure to try fresh fruit for dessert. €€

3

Holta Canyon

Unnamed road, Çekini village • Free

Holding its own against some of the best canyons in the country (and there are plenty), **Holta** (Kanioni i Holtës) offers a much more intimate experience than its better-known siblings. Under an hour's drive from Gramshi, the gorge is backdropped by the southwestern taper of the Polis Mountains (Mali i Polisit), whose stark and jagged landscape has been sculpted by ancient seismic activity and years of erosion. Holta Canyon funnels through narrow points just one metre wide and yawning chasms up to 150m high. Along its wending course, trickling waterfalls wash the limestone walls, which have been smoothed by time and the flow of the Devolli River tributary. In the narrowest passageways that only see the sun briefly, the water becomes an almost spectral hue of blue. Though the water is mostly frigid, occasionally you'll stumble across an unexpected (and blissfully welcome) warm pool where underground thermal activity has heated the riverbed.

The canyon is easy to find and there's only one way in from the road. You'll need to wade to explore it, so bring water shoes. This is a summer spot, as the river rises dangerously high by the end of September. Come early to avoid Tirana tour buses.

ARRIVAL AND GETTING AROUND — HOLTA CANYON

By car Follow SH71 north from Gramshi for 8km, then turn right towards Gjergjovina and Holta. The road becomes unpaved, but any car can make it to the canyon mouth. The journey takes 1hr. You can park (and camp) by the canyon.

EATING

Bar Restorant Kanioni i Holtës Main road near the canyon entrance; tel: 068 237 9648. Despite having limited competition for Holta dining, the food and prices here are pleasant. Most of the standard Albanian grilled meats are available – pork, lamb, chicken, goat – accompanied by salads and fries. €€

Grabova e Sipërme and the Valamara Mountains

There are many places of otherworldly beauty in Albania that still require a degree of determination to find, and **Grabova e Sipërme** has to be near the top of the list. The remote village is the gateway to the **Valamara** (Mali i Valamarës), a 2400m-high massif that separates Gramshi and Central Albania from Pogradeci and Eastern Albania. But Grabova itself has no gateway – or an easily accessible one, at least. Once an established city with an estimated 12,000 inhabitants, today the village has a few-dozen residents at most – and even fewer visitors. It is only reachable by a long, gnarled dirt and gravel road best tackled by 4WD, bike or a combination of bus and hiking. The reward, however, is more than worth the effort: a trip back in time to an entirely unspoiled landscape of **glacial lakes** and wild Cretaceous rock formations, 1000-year-old bridges, and proud stone churches.

Like **Voskopoja** in Korça (see page 187), it was a busy haven for Orthodox Christians before and during Ottoman times, and the two cities were once linked by a well-trafficked trade route. There are seven medieval bridges still standing, which may be as old as the tenth or eleventh century AD, but Grabova's heyday peaked in the seventeenth century, the period in which the Aromanian (Vlach) population built the post-Byzantine **churches of St Nicholas** (Shën Kolli) and St Paraskevi (Shën e Premte) – and are still being restored by the Aromanians today. Perhaps there was a touch of the divine in the making of the Kopaçi Rock (Shkëmbi i Kopaçit) too: towering over the landscape, it is cloven in two, forming a giant horseshoe – with Mount Tomorri floating in the distance between the two crests.

The 11km round hike from Grabova to the summit of Valamara is long but not difficult, rewarding hikers with a view of untamed alpine shrubland and the two glacial **Lakes of Valamara** (Liqenet i Valamarës).

If you've made it this far with a hardy car, consider adding the **Sotira Waterfall** (Ujëvara e Sotirës) to your itinerary. On the west side of the Devolli, it's tough to reach, but the falls are sublime in the late spring and early summer.

ARRIVAL AND DEPARTURE — GRABOVA E SIPËRME AND THE VALAMARA MOUNTAINS

By car As of 2025, you can make it to Grabova e Sipërme in a car with high ground clearance, though a 4WD is definitely recommended, especially in anything less than stellar weather. From Gramshi, follow SH71 about 16.5km south. There's a short bridge after the village of Kodovjati and two turnings off-road – **ignore these**, and instead take a sharp left (north) another 2km down. Follow signs for Lenia (Lenië) and Grabova e Sipërme. You'll be on unpaved mountain roads for about 1hr 30min.

By bus A village bus leaves the Gramshi bus stop at SH71 and Rruga Holta at noon for Lenia village (1 daily; 2hr) and returns early in the morning. From Lenia, it's a fairly steep, rocky 1hr 30min hike to Grabova e Sipërme.

ACCOMMODATION

Hotel Grabova Rruga e Pacollareve, Grabova e Sipërme; tel: 61 481 975 919. A Bavarian-style mountain lodge just a short walk from the village, this is your best – only – option for an overnight stay in Grabova e Sipërme. Rooms are straightforward but cosy, dinner is fresh from local ingredients, there's often a fire warming the common room, and the owner can tell you all about Valamara and Grabova. Rooms fill up weeks or even months in advance. €€

Elbasani

One could make a case that **ELBASANI** is the true historic midpoint of Albania. The Shkumbini River (Lumi i Shkumbinit) flows just south of the city, and the river traditionally marks the split between the country's northern Gegërishtja (Gheg) and southern Toskërishtja (Tosk) dialects. The Roman **Via Egnatia** between Dyrrachium (Durrësi) and Byzantium shoots straight through the middle of Elbasani's old town (see page 143). For hundreds of years, Christians lived north of the Via Egnatia and Muslims, south.

Today, thanks to the A3, you can technically travel door to door from Tirana in 45 minutes. However, the roads just outside and within Elbasani are poorly maintained and often clogged with traffic, and there's only one easy, central car park. Saying

3

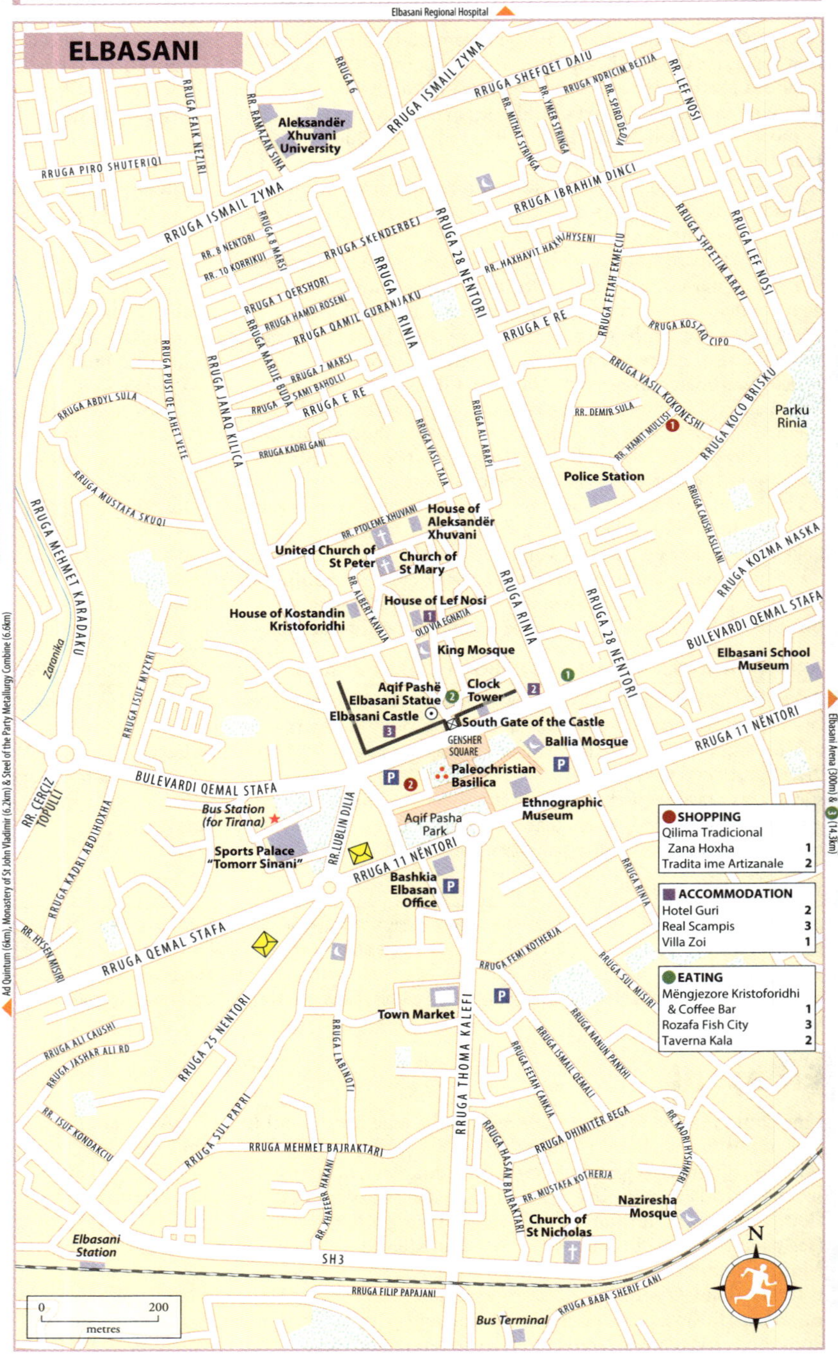
Elbasani Regional Hospital
ELBASANI
Aleksandër Xhuvani University
Police Station
Parku Rinia
House of Aleksandër Xhuvani
United Church of St Peter
Church of St Mary
House of Lef Nosi
House of Kostandin Kristoforidhi
OLD VIA EGNATIA
King Mosque
Aqif Pashë Elbasani Statue
Clock Tower
Elbasani Castle
South Gate of the Castle
GENSHER SQUARE
Ballia Mosque
Paleochristian Basilica
Ethnographic Museum
Elbasani School Museum
Bus Station (for Tirana)
Sports Palace "Tomorr Sinani"
Aqif Pasha Park
Bashkia Elbasan Office
Town Market
Naziresha Mosque
Church of St Nicholas
Elbasani Station
Bus Terminal
Zaranika
RRUGA ISMAIL ZYMA
RRUGA SHEFQET DAIU
RRUGA LEF NOSI
RRUGA 28 NËNTORI
RRUGA RINIA
RRUGA SKENDERBEJ
RRUGA IBRAHIM DINCI
RRUGA E RE
RRUGA JANAQ KILICA
RRUGA MEHMET KARADAKU
BULEVARDI QEMAL STAFA
RRUGA 11 NËNTORI
RRUGA QEMAL STAFA
RRUGA 25 NËNTORI
RRUGA THOMA KALEFI
RRUGA SUL PAPRI
RRUGA MEHMET BAJRAKTARI
RRUGA KOZMA NASKA
RRUGA KOCO BRISKU
RRUGA VASIL KOKONESHI
RRUGA DHIMITËR BEGA
RRUGA FILIP PAPAJANI
RRUGA BABA SHERIF CANI
SH3
SHOPPING
Qilima Tradicional Zana Hoxha 1
Tradita ime Artizanale 2
ACCOMMODATION
Hotel Guri 2
Real Scampis 3
Villa Zoi 1
EATING
Mëngjezore Kristoforidhi & Coffee Bar 1
Rozafa Fish City 3
Taverna Kala 2
Ad Quintum (6km), Monastery of St John Vladimir (6.2km) & Steel of the Party Metallurgy Combine (6.6km)
Elbasani Arena (300m) & 3 (14.3km)
0 200 metres
N

that, it's well worth a day-trip, best accessed by bus to remove the stress and hassle of driving. Forty kilometres southeast of Tirana, the **castle city** is sheltered within medieval ramparts and home to fine **Ottoman mansions** and a superlative **ethnographic museum**. While it lacks the obvious excitement of Tirana or the cachet of Berati, Elbasani is a biggish city that feels like a small town and a snapshot of urban Albania circa 2010, in both interesting and frustrating ways. Every morning, people shop for clothes, groceries, jewellery and electronics in the stalls along Rruga Thoma Kalefi, bazaar-style, darting across the street whenever they see an opening. Hotels are few, and folks are friendly; you might meet the mayor making his rounds. There is even a functioning train to Durrësi; the trip takes three hours. You'll see very few tourists in the historic walled **Kalaja district**, or anywhere else. It likely won't be this way forever.

Brief history

Elbasani first began to take shape as **Mansio Scampa**, or Scampis, a Roman outpost in the second century BC that evolved into a walled city. Even with the jumble of houses, shops, churches and mosques that has since mushroomed across the streets, the Kalaja clearly follows the rectangular shape of the typical Roman planned town. The north–south lines of the grid are muddled now, but the east–west thoroughfare is impossible to miss: **Rruga Egnatia** bisects the old city as it has for 2200 years. In 1466, Sultan Mehmed II rebuilt the walls, and **Elbasani Castle** (Kalaja e Elbasanit) was the biggest fortress in Albania on flat ground.

3

During the Albanian National Awakening (Rilindja) and early years of independence, the city effectively functioned as the crossroads of what Albanian culture was and what it could be. Elbasani-born translator **Kostandin Kristoforidhi** – sometimes called the father of Albanian grammar – published the New Testament in both Gheg and Tosk (see page 286), and the first modern dictionary of Albanian. The closest thing to a Gheg-Tosk hybrid, the Elbasani dialect became the standard administrative form of Albanian after independence, a humble persuasion by scholar Aleksandër Xhuvani, who happened to hail from here. Elbasani even experimented with religious unification. In 1928, an Orthodox priest teamed up with the Catholic Church to build the **United Church of St Peter** (Kisha Unite e Shën Pjetrit). The place of worship remains, though the idea never took off.

Elbasani first became a craft and manufacturing leader from the seventeenth to nineteenth centuries, highly regarded for silk weaving, pipe carving, silversmithing, bellfounding and soapmaking. The products of its gunsmiths were the toast of Albania's independence fighters. Enver Hoxha had even bigger ambitions for the area, ordering the construction of a huge metallurgical complex for the production of metals, dubbed the 'Steel of the Party' (Çeliku i Partisë), which spanned twelve factories, 670 acres and 47km of on-campus railway tracks. Built with the help of the Chinese during Albania's short-lived alliance with China, it was inaugurated in 1978 – and began to fall into disuse just a dozen years later. Its furnaces and smokestacks now glower and rust about 4km from the city, to the delight of urban spelunkers.

Elbasani Castle

Kalaja • Free

With its imposing walls nudging nine metres in places, the enormous **Elbasani Castle** (Kalaja e Elbasanit) is the first thing to grab your attention in town. When it was rebuilt in 1466, it had 26 of the hefty rounded towers you see along the south wall. It is a living, inhabited castle, filled with beguiling eighteenth- and nineteenth-century Ottoman-style houses and alleys, but it feels empty. The activity in the city is elsewhere, but the heritage – some of it crumbling – lingers here.

The **Clock Tower** (Kulla e Sahatit) is the most prominent landmark, an 1899 augmentation rising nearly twenty metres, and it marks the primary entrance at the nearby south gate on Bulevardi Aqif Pasha. It's next to the statue of Aqif Pashë Elbasani, a nationalist who first raised the flag of independent Albania over Elbasani in 1912. Inside, you can't miss Rruga Egnatia, but it's a bit of a scavenger hunt to find the houses of Kostandin Kristoforidhi (see page 135) on Rruga Vasil Moisiu near Rruga Jani Todri; and Aleksandër Xhuvani (see page 135) at Rruga Ptolome Xhuvani 30. Note that they are rarely open to the public. The dignified Italianate **mansion of Lef Nosi**, a signer of the Albanian Declaration of Independence and the country's first Minister of Post-Telegraphs is being renovated into a museum of communications and technology (Rruga Egnatia and Rruga Tajar Guranjaku).

King Mosque

Rruga Xhaferr Kongoli 12 • Free

One of the first and finest mosques in Albania, Elbasani's **King Mosque** (Xhamia Mbret) beckons as you proceed from the south gate of the castle up Rruga Xhaferr Kongoli. Built in 1492, it's a classic example of early Ottoman religious architecture, with an expansive porch, clean rectangular plan and single minaret. It's just one of three fifteenth-century mosques that survive in Albania; the others are in Berati (see page 114) and Korça (see page 162).

Church of St Mary

Rruga Saveta Mishta • Free

Elbasani is primarily Sunni Muslim today, but this church is a reminder that it was once more or less divided, and Orthodoxy held sway here too. You'll find the **Church of St Mary** (Kisha e Shën Mërisë) if you follow the central Rruga Tajar Guranjaku north, past Rruga Egnatia. Built in 1556 and once decorated by Albania's most revered icon painter, **Onufri** (see page 188), and Orthodox icon and fresco artist **David Selenica** (see page 188), it burned down and was reconstructed in 1833. The mishmash of Orthodox styles and influences is worth checking out, particularly the magnificent iconostasis, which took forty woodcarvers ten years to finish.

The newer centre and around

Gensher Square (Sheshi Gensher), directly across the street from Elbasani Castle's south gate, is where the old city starts to merge into the newer. On the southwest side, you'll find the foundations of a substantial paleochristian basilica, only discovered in 2007, and the small Parku Aqif Pasha south of that. To the east, on a pedestrianized street connecting the heavily trafficked Bulevardi Aqif Pasha and Rruga Qemal Stafa, there are usually a number of stalls selling handmade lace along with mass-produced Albania kitsch. Nearby is a small museum in what was the first Albanian secondary school, the **Shkolla Normale e Elbasanit** (Rruga Qemal Stafa, across from Rruga Refik Serica; www.shkollanormale.al).

Just east of Gensher Square is the **Ballia Mosque** (Xhamia e Ballies; Bulevardi Aqif Pasha), a contemporary take on the central mosque, inaugurated in 2022. The rather galactic architecture looks striking and a little outré from outside, but the four-floor, 1900-square-metre interior, with its origami-spiral apertured dome, is undeniably awe-inspiring. It's not a tourist site; ask before taking photos inside.

Just under seven kilometres from the city centre via the SH7, you'll find **Ad Quintum**, the ruins of a Roman bathhouse for travellers from the second or third century AD, originally built at the point where the Via Egnatia passed west of the city.

Ethnographic Museum

Entrance on the pedestrian passage between Rruga Qemal Stafa and Sheshi Gensher • Charge • www.facebook.com/muzeuetnografikelb

Of Albania's many ethnographic museums, the one in Elbasani is one of the best, in its excellent preservation, quality of period furnishings, breadth of English-language information and just sheer opulence. It's also well organized and easy to understand, providing visitors with a full picture here of how wealthy Albanians lived in the eighteenth and nineteenth centuries. The **ground floor**, once the storage rooms, is now devoted to Elbasani's exceptional crafts. Admire smoking pipes, ceramic pottery, copper and bronze coffee pots, silver jewellery, rifles and intricately carved wooden trunks and wall fixtures. On the **first floor**, find the 'women's room' and 'men's room', both arranged in the classic style with bench couches around the walls; the former has outstanding woodcarving on the ceiling and recessed-cupboard doors, and the latter preserves original sapphire-blue, floral-patterned wall frescoes. The museum also hosts poetry readings, art shows and photo exhibitions, and artisans from the area are sometimes invited to sell handmade jewellery, linens and clothing here.

Monastery of St John Vladimir

7.3km by road northwest of Elbasani via SH3, Shijoni village; follow signs • Free • 15min drive or take a taxi • www.facebook.com/manastirishenjoanvladimiri

An unusual relic of a chaotic time in Albanian history, the **Church of St John Vladimir** (Kisha e Shën Joan (or Gjon) Vladimirit) dates to 1381. For less than a century, Durrësi, Elbasani and Kruja were held, with some difficulty, by the Topia (Thopia) family of Albanian nobles. Their Principality of Albania (Principata e Arbërisë) warred and allied with the Venetians, Serbs, Angevins, Ottomans and other Albanian ruling families like the Muzakas of Berati (see page 111).

When the powerful Karl Topia conquered Durrësi, he acquired the relics of the canonized eleventh-century Serbian prince Jovan (John) Vladmir and built this big, boxy basilica to house the saint's tomb; the singular architectural style incorporates influences from both Catholicism and Orthodoxy. Jovan Vladimir was eventually moved to Tirana, but his reliquary and coffin are still here, and some original frescoes are preserved in the apse. Ask around the **monastery** (Manastiri i Shën Joan Vladimirit), and someone from the order will pull back the curtain to show you.

ARRIVAL AND GETTING AROUND — ELBASANI

By bus Like all populous Central Albanian cities, Elbasani is well connected to much of Albania (and beyond), but its bus system is an enigma to outsiders. Elbasani has two main domestic stations, and some cities connect to both, at different times. One station primarily serves Tirana; it can be found near Rruga Kadri Hoxha, next to the large Pallati Sportit Tomorr Sinani, less than 400m from the Kalaja's south gate. The main terminal, which connects to most other cities, is on Rruga Nikolla Puka, near Rruga Thoma Kalefi, around 1km from the Kalaja via Thoma Kalefi.

Destinations Berati (many daily; 1hr 45min); Dhërmiu (several daily; 3hr 5min); Durrësi (many daily; 1hr 25min); Erseka (several daily; 3hr 10min); Fieri (many daily; 1hr 50min); Gjirokastra (several daily; 3hr 30min); Golemi (several daily; 1hr 30min); Gramshi (many daily; 1hr); Himara (several daily; 3hr 30min); Korça (many daily; 2hr 15min); Kukësi (several daily; 2hr 30min); Librazhdi (many daily; 30min); Lushnja (many daily; 1hr 10min); Peshkopia (1 daily, 4hr 45min); Pogradeci (many daily; 1hr 25min); Saranda (several daily; 4hr 25min); Shkodra (several daily; 2hr 20min); Tepelena (several daily; 3hr 5min); Tirana (many daily; 50min); Vlora (many daily; 2hr 30min).

By car Elbasani is located around 40km from Tirana centre and 56km from Tirana International Airport and technically the drive should take 45min and 1hr, respectively, via the A3 (Tirana–Elbasani Highway). However, those timeframes can vary wildly, especially as traffic always grinds to a halt along the SH3 to Elbasani city during rush hour. Roads within the city are a mess: major intersections with no stoplights, cars idling in the street, and so on. The best car park is located in front of *Hotel Skampa*, at the intersection of Rruga Janaq Kilica and Bulevardi Aqif Pasha, right in the centre and with minimal fees.

By taxi There's not much in Elbasani that calls for a taxi, but the central taxi stand is on Rruga Qemal Stafa next to the Ethnographic Museum.

By train Elbasani to Durrësi is one of the only operational passenger train routes in the country. It is decidedly low-speed rail travel, but much beloved as a nostalgic experience. The train stops at both Golemi and in Durrësi during the summer (Durrësi Beach (Plazhi i Durrësit) only, at the time of writing), plus some other towns. It runs on Fridays, Saturdays and Sundays, leaving Elbasani at 6am and reaching Durrësi at 9am. It departs Durrësi at 3pm and arrives at Elbasani at 6pm. The Elbasani train station is located on the corner of SH3 and Rruga Shefikat Sefa, and the rail service posts its new schedules each season at www.facebook.com/TRAINSINALBANIA.

3

INFORMATION

Tourist information There is no tourist information centre, but staff at the Bashkia Elbasan (Town Hall) may be able to find a map for you. It's at Rruga Qemal Stafa near Rruga Thoma Kalefi.

Maps Tourist information signs and maps with details of points of interest in and around the city, in English, can be found next to the south gate of Elbasani Castle and across the street on Gensher Square.

Websites www.elbasani.gov.al; www.qarkuelbasan.gov.al; www.elbasani.org.

ACCOMMODATION

SEE MAP PAGE 134

Hotel Guri Bulevardi Aqif Pasha and Rruga Isuf Ibershimi; tel: 069 208 3089. The upscale *Hotel Guri* is well appointed with elegant wallpapering and rococo-style furniture. Staff are attentive, breakfast is included, rooms are clean, and the guests can enjoy a coffee – and full city views – at the property's *Kafe Kalaja*, atop the southeast tower of the Kalaja. €€€

Real Scampis Rruga Janaq Kilica, west Kalaja entrance; www.realscampis.com. This hotel-restaurant-café hybrid has the hottest postcode in Elbasani, next to the southwest tower of the Kalaja, with terraces overlooking a garden of sculpted hedges on one side and the wilder vines growing through the castle walls on the other. Rooms are simple but comfortable. The restaurant is among the livelier places in town and one of the best spots to catch live music. €€

★ **Villa Zoi** Rruga Egnatia and Rruga Kol Popa; www.zoi.al. Mikel Tarousa has lived all over Europe, but his family home is in the Kalaja, next door to independence-era leader Lef Nosi's. In 2024, Mikel and his wife, Zoi, opened a sharp six-bedroom guesthouse here, preserving the original nineteenth-century walls that wrap around the garden and villa. A top choice in the heart of the castle with top-end modern amenities. Mikel also leads interested guests on tours around historic Elbasani and even to the metallurgy combine (see page 135). €€

EATING AND DRINKING

SEE MAP PAGE 134

★ **Mëngjezore Kristoforidhi & Coffee Bar** Rruga Rinia and Bulevardi Aqif Pasha; www.mengjezorekristoforidhi.eu. A breakfast spot that's evolved into an all-day dining joint and evening hangout, this is among the best places to try the Elbasanas classic *tavë kosi*, a casserole of lamb and rice baked in yoghurt and egg. Pilaf – with lamb, veal or meatballs – is another top choice, and diners who are feeling the spirit can shoot for *tavë* with liver, or grilled or fried veal tongue or brains. Simple decor, incredible prices. €

Rozafa Fish City 7km northeast of Elbasani via SH3, Labinot-Fusha; www.rozafa.al. Rozafa Fish is an international fishing and seafood juggernaut, headquartered right here in *Fish City*, a sort of Albanian nautical theme park, with industrial-sized busts of Skanderbeg and other heroes; murals of Jim Morrison and Picasso painting *Guernica*; a replica lighthouse, a hotel, cinema and various fish-processing facilities, all arranged around the tunnels of a former military depot. There is the seafood restaurant, too, which does pretty much everything with shrimp, salmon, tuna, calamari and more. €€

Taverna Kala Rruga Xhaferr Kongoli; tel: 069 455 2951. The first place on the right inside the south gate of the castle, this atmospheric little taverna is crammed with old trinkets and vintage items – clocks, cameras, dolls – and serves up imperial-sized portions of traditional Elbasanas favourites, with a focus on tasty *tavë* casserole dishes (meat and rice baked in yoghurt and egg). You can opt for the classic *tavë kosi* with lamb, or try a *tavë* with veal, white beans or okra. €€

SHOPPING

SEE MAP PAGE 134

Qilima Tradicional Zana Hoxha Rruga Hamit Mullisi near Rruga Koço Brisku; tel: 068 475 8798. One of the most esteemed workshops for hand-loomed kilims (*qilims*) in the country, Zana Hoxha's is an essential stop if you're in the market for a serious-quality traditional patterned Albanian rug. Weavers incorporate styles from all over the country and create more contemporary designs too. As it's more a workshop than a storefront, it's probably worth calling ahead.

★ **Tradita ime Artizanale** Shopping centre on the plaza directly west of the paleochristian basilica; tel: 067 644 6966. A small but comprehensive shop showcasing handmade products from local craftspeople, Tradita ime Artizanale is a terrific shop for finding authentic Albanian goods. Peruse felt caps, woven handbags, socks, folk costumes and kilims to fit all sizes and budgets, mostly in traditional patterns of the region. The shop is the storefront of a social enterprise organization that employs impoverished women in craftwork.

DIRECTORY

Banks and currency exchange Most of the nationwide banks have branches around Parku Aqif Pasha south of the Kalaja; many are clustered along Rruga Qemal Stafa between the Rruga Lublin Dilja roundabout and Rruga Rinia. There's a Western Union on Rruga Qemal Stafa near Rruga Rinia. Another, which also has a currency exchange,

is located on Rruga Qemal Stafa and Rruga 25 Nëntori, near the roundabout.
Emergencies Ambulance (tel: 127 or tel: 112), police (tel: 129 or tel: 112).
Hospital The Spitali Rajonal Elbasan is a big hospital with an urgent care and several specialist wards. The main entrance is on Rruga Petrit Gaçe (tel: 05 425 8644).
Pharmacies Farmaci Roma (tel: 069 363 7216) is on Rruga Qemal Stafa, at the west end of Parku Aqif Pasha, and there's a FarmaBlend (tel: 069 404 0455) in *Hotel Skampa* on Bulevardi Aqif Pasha.
Police The police station is on Rruga Koço Brisku near Rruga 28 Nëntori.
Post office A DHL service point is on the ground floor of the nine-storey building near the roundabout intersection of Rruga 25 Nëntori and Rruga Qemal Stafa (tel: 04 240 6666). On the other side of the roundabout, Posta Shqiptare is on Rruga Qemal Stafa.

Durrësi

3

For better and worse, **DURRËSI** has been the prize of Greeks, Romans, Byzantines, Bulgarians, Serbs, Angevins, Albanians, Venetians, Albanians, Italians and Albanians once more, over the past 2600 years. It was the capital of Roman Albania, Byzantine Albania, Venetian Albania and even independent Albania for a few years. A primary port of the eastern Adriatic, the city has prospered tremendously and been caught in world-historical clashes. The remnants of its eventful history are easy to see, yet often overlooked by visitors to the country.

Today, Durrësi is Albania's second city and the only one you can enter directly by car, bus, boat and train. Most of those options are slow-going, mind you, when you're jostling with the 1.5 million other travellers who pass through here. But to appreciate Durrësi, it does help shift down a few gears and embrace the unhurried pace of local life. Older Durrsak gentlemen take their daily dips in the Mediterranean or dangle fishing lines from makeshift benches over the water, while students chitchat on the 'Sphinx' ('Sfinksi') terraced pier after class.

Sundown brings a thriving cultural scene of **film**, **theatre** – and karaoke. Parks and pedestrian areas have been created, expanded and beautified in the past decade, and the city's **museums** and monuments are being restored and modernized after a deadly earthquake struck Central Albania in 2019. Most heritage projects that aren't yet completed will be by 2026. Durrësi may be less fashionable than the Albanian riviera, but it is the crown of the coast.

You'll find most of Durrësi's points of interest in three neighbourhoods: the centre, where ancient and interwar Italian influences echo in colossal ruins and colourful aspiring *palazzos*; neighbouring **Vollga**, an expanse of promenades, piers, restaurants and curious sculptures; and the **Plazhi** east of downtown, a beach curving 12km south, where the Adriatic ebbs out to a long horizon.

Brief history

Greek chroniclers tell us the settlement that would become Durrësi was founded in either 627 or 625 BC by Hellenic colonists. **Epidamnos**, as it was then called, rapidly became wealthy, and with more money came more problems. Aristotle described its government as a sort of constitutional oligarchy in which a democratic faction eventually gained power. This rather contentious system eventually led to a crisis that brought in Corinth and Corfu, somehow escalated to Athens and Sparta, and helped trigger the **Peloponnesian War**. This little affair in Albania served as the backdrop for a Roman play that **Shakespeare** adapted into – if you can imagine – *The Comedy of Errors*.

The Roman republic first conquered the coast in 229 BC and made the city the main eastern connection to Brundisium (Brindisi) across the Adriatic. Now called **Dyrrachium**, it witnessed a confrontation between the armies of **Julius Caesar** and **Gnaeus Pompey** in 48 BC.

Pompey won the battle but, of course, lost the Roman civil war. The Romans built a huge **amphitheatre** in Dyrrachium, the western terminus of the **Via Egnatia** road that

DURRËSI
ACCOMMODATION
Adriatik Hotel 1
Art Gallery Boutique Hotel 5
Colombia Apartments & Rooms 6
Gent's Inn 3
Hostel Durrës 4
Hotel Kloest 7
Wave Beachfront Apartments 2
EATING
Agroturizëm Gjepali 2
Banesa 23 5
Dyrrah Mare 1
Gusto di Mare & Sushi Time 4
Peshk i Freskët Bracja 3
SHOPPING
Marigo Souvenirs and Gift Shop 1
DRINKING & NIGHTLIFE
Bistro Mol 3
Cinco Cavalli Summer Club 2
Kantina Gjergj Kastrioti Skënderbeu 1
Vinum Wine Bar 4
Hospital
Medical are Lami
Niko Dovana Stadium
Police Office (Regional)
Mausoleum of Martyrs
British Children's Library of Durrësi
Bus Stop
Bus Terminal
Sheshi Demokracia
Durrësi Train Station (Center)
Ferry Terminal
Peeping Tourist
Durrësi "Old Doors Trail" Houses
Byzantine Forum
Termet (Roman Baths)
Aleksandër Moisiu Theater and Cultural Center
King Zog's Royal Villa
Great Mosque
Liria Square
Durrësi Municipality Building
Police Station (City)
Archaeological Museum of Durrësi
Walls, Castle of Durrësi
Durrësi Amphitheater
Fatih Mosque
Venetian Tower Heritage Information Center
House-Museum of Aleksandër Moisiu
Medieval Hammam
Albanian State Bank
Volga Park
Gladiator Statues
Unknown Soldier Monument
Veliera
Children's Cultural Center
Sphinx
Sport Center
Taulantia Promenade
Volga Promenade
Redon Sculpture
Sheshi Mujo Ulqinaku
Tina Turner, John Lennon, Bob Dylan and Mick Jagger Statues
Immigration and Visas (DVKM Office)
Durrësi Port
ADRIATIC SEA
N
0 250 metres
2 (1.2km)
Rruga Mujo Ulqinaku
Rruga Laguna
Rruga Kastrioti
Rruga Eqerem Shijaku
Rruga Aleksander Goga
Rruga Kristo Sotiri
Rruga Agimi
Rruga Hysen Kertusha
Rruga Isuf Ferra
Rruga Isuf Molla
Rr. Prokop Meksi
Rruga Hysen Myshketa
Rruga Mustafa Cara
Rr. Vasil Mici
Rruga Murat Sefa
Rruga Andon Naçi
Rruga Ibrahim Bushiqi
Rruga Hajdar Dushi
Rruga e Dëshmorëve
Rruga 17 Janari
Rr. Kuvendi i Vlorës
Rruga e Moisive
Rruga Ulliri i Cel Islamit
Rruga Kont Urani
Rruga Currila
Rr. Telha Cela
Bulevardi Dyrrah
Rruga Egnatia
Rruga e Doganës
Rr. A. Durrsaku
Rr. Adrianet
Rruga Taulantia
Bulevardi Epidamn
Rr. Grigor Durrsaku
Rruga Abaz Çelkupa
Rruga Marta Buda
Rr. Horizonti
Rr. Shekulli XXI
Rruga Glaukia
Rruga Sulejman Pitarka
Rruga Mbreti Gert
Rr. Trajan

Tirana (36km)
Train Station (Plazhi i Durrësit)
Church of St Dominic
Town Market
Durrësi Beach
Bay of Durrësi
0
250
metres
N
Shkozet Train Station
Wellness Medical Services Albania at Ansi Lab
Yachts & Marina
Bay of Durrësi
1 (1.9km) & 2 (10km)
Train Station (Plazhi i Durrësit, 1.2km) & Plepa (3.4km)
Ancona, Bari, Trieste
RR. SHKEMBI I KAVAJES
RR. FADIL HOXHA
RRUGA GLAUKIA
RRUGA ZEF SEREMBE
RRUGA ASDRENI
RRUGA TAHSIM KELLIÇI
RR. SHEN CEZARI
RRUGA SHEN GJERGJI
RRUGA JUBA
RRUGA VELLAZERIMI
RRUGA STAVRI FRASHERI
RR. RINIA DURRSAKE
RR. ARDENICA
RRUGA BISHT KAMZA
RRUGA DIELLI
RRUGA LIQENI I POGRADECIT
RRUGA LIQENI I SHKODRES
RR. LUKANI
RRUGA SHQIPONJA E MALIT
RR. PORTA E DIJES
RR. ADEM HOXHOLLI
RRUGA NATO
RR. SABRI DERMANI
RR. ENVER KOTORRI
RR. MANSKURIA
RR. PELLAZGU
RR. AHMEL LULI
RR. MILI GOGA
RRUGA DRENICA
RR. DRITA E. DITURISE
RR. FARI I DURRESIT
RRUGA POLUMBARI
RR. AHMET DAKLI
RR. STEFAN KACULINI
RRUGA DALIP PEZA
RRUGA ADRIA
RRUGA E DOGANËS
SH2
RR. BAJRAM TUSHA
RRUGA E ENKELEJVE
RRUGA PAVARËSIA
RR. ANDON BOSHNJAKU
RRUGA TEUTA
RR. D. SELENICA
BEACH PROMENADE
RR. DEMOKRACIA
RR. DHIMITER KRAJA
RRUGA TURGUT OZAL
RR. JUSUF MYZYRI
RRUGA BAJRAM CURRI
RR. MBRETI ARBERIT
RR. LULE BORE
RRUGA AGAVEVE
RR. BAJRAM CURRI
RRUGA DAUNIA
RR. D. KULLA
RRUGA QAFE BOTE
RRUGA VENECIA
RR. BRINDISI
RRUGA PORTA E DETIT

3

connected the Adriatic to Byzantium (later Constantinople). The heavyset **city walls** standing today were raised by Byzantine emperor **Anastasius I**, probably in the late fifth century AD. He was, incidentally, an Illyrian Roman born in this city – a local boy made good.

For the next thousand years or so, medieval Europe's big fish, little fish and equally matched fish nipped at each other around Durrësi, sometimes even splitting rulership of the city. The **Venetians** ultimately ceded Durrësi to the Ottoman Empire in 1501 and, for a change, the city shrank and lost prominence. But the Italians returned, first with soft power.

In the 1920s and 1930s, the fanciest facades in the city took their stylistic cues from Italian Neoclassical and rationalist currents, and their funding from Italian financiers. The royal villa of **King Zog I** is the most ornate of them all. It was completed in 1937, giving Zog just a few summers to enjoy it before Benito Mussolini's battalions landed on Durrësi's piers.

The centre

Despite, or perhaps because of, its eventful history, Durrësi has a fairly small surviving historic centre. It starts at a triangular point seaward between the port to the east and Vollga to the west. There, you'll see the **Veliera** public space, a gargantuan convex dome suspended above a pedestrian overpass, with the highway beneath it. After years of delay, the 60m by 40m steel-framed 'sail' was declared finished in 2024 – you be the judge of how well it meshes with the ancient city walls and 1920s downtown behind it.

From here, the centre is simple to navigate: it follows Bulevardi Epidamn north, meets Sheshi Liria, the main square, and then splits into a 'Y' – Bulevardi Dyrrah shoots northeast and Rruga Aleksandër Goga northwest. The first landmark you'll come across is the **Venetian Tower** (Kulla Veneciane), dating to its namesake republic's fifteenth-century reign. The **Byzantine city walls**, just over two metres thick, meet the tower here. They once circuited for around 3.5km; only 500m still stand. You can best admire the pointy pentagonal towers from Rruga Anastas Durrsaku, just to the west of Epidamn.

Before heading up Bulevardi Epidamn, divert one block east to catch a glimpse of the **Albanian State Bank** (Banka e Shtetit Shqiptar), one of the finer buildings Italian architects designed for the city. White with rouge trim, just a touch Baroque and guarded over by a statue of wealth and victory personified, it looks pretty cheerful for a bank, but that's how the world was feeling about money when it first opened its doors in 1928.

Heading north up Bulevardi Epidamn, you'll pass a lot of wonderful architecture of that era: svelte three- and four-floor buildings veer between Italianate styles, but the pastel blues, yellows, pinks, creams and reds borrow most of all from Venice. Huge palms and cafés line both sides of the boulevard. To the right on Rruga Stefan Vokopola, find a fifteenth-century **hammam**, restored and opened as a small museum in 2024, and to the left near Rruga Xhamia, you can see the **Fatih Mosque** (Xhamia Fatih), a small 1503 Ottoman contribution. Nearby is the stone mansion where 1910s pan-European stage sensation **Aleksandër Moisiu** spent his childhood, slated for restoration in 2025.

At the end of Epidamn, you'll reach **Sheshi Liria**, certainly the cheeriest communist square in the country with its squad of palms and rows of little jet fountains. The modernist triumph here is the **Teatri Aleksandër Moisiu**, opened in 1953, at the north end of the plaza, while the reddish *bashkia* (Town Hall), at the south, is actually a 1929 joint. Behind the theatre, to the north, you'll see the ruins of a curved portico and marble flooring, a **Byzantine forum**, and nearby, several of the proud though faded early-twentieth-century gates of the Durrësi 'Old Doors Trail' (www.theolddoorstrail.com).

Venetian Tower heritage information centre

Rruga Anastas Durrsaku and Bulevardi Epidamn • Charge • www.museums.al/#/venetian-tower • English-language animation screenings at 1pm and 6pm

An emblem of Durrësi, the **Venetian Tower** (Kulla Veneciane), at 9m high and 16m wide, does not feel particularly domineering compared to Albania's heavyweight castles. It's what's inside that counts, though. Today's tower is a fifteenth-century design, repaired after the 2019 earthquake, and now home to a digital and VR **heritage information centre**. Projector screens on the interior brick dome take you on an animated journey through the Greek and Roman history of the city and on to future Durrësi (it will surely have flying cars).

Donning **VR headsets**, you can join the action as a spectator at the gladiatorial games in the amphitheatre, poke around the Byzantine forum and, perhaps most interestingly, ponder the fortress as it looked in its Ottoman dotage, based on 1848 paintings by English traveller Edward Lear.

Climb up to the top for a view over the old and new Durrësi, and try to make it all out for yourself. **Digital periscopes** pointing towards the Adriatic show a video

THE VIA EGNATIA

Today we see the mighty Roman legacy in huge amphitheatres and lofty triumphal arches, but the empire was established and maintained through an even bigger, though far less sexy, feat of engineering: an ever-growing network of roads around the Mediterranean. One of the most important, the artery along which legions and merchants flowed between the **Adriatic Sea** and **Byzantium**, was the **Via Egnatia**. It worked like this: over on the Italian peninsula, the Via Appia linked Rome to Brundisium (Brindisi). From there, the Adriatic provided a sea passage to **Dyrrachium**, and Via Egnatia slotted in the third piece of the route connecting the western capital of the empire with what would become its eastern capital.

The first lengths of the road were laid down in the second century BC, shortly after the Romans subdued the western Illyrians and Macedonians, and while they were still battling the Dalmatians (Illyrians to the northwest), Dardanians (Illyrians to the northeast), Thracians (to the east) and others. Efficient roads like the Egnatia helped **Augustus**' armies bring much of the Balkans to heel in the first century AD, and by then Dyrrachium had already become a frenetic trading port, '**Hadriae tabernam**', as the poet Catullus called it – the meeting place of the Adriatic.

Like most major Roman roads of the republic, the Via Egnatia was constructed with large polygonal stone slabs and extended about six metres wide. It eventually stretched over 1100km in length, and archaeological evidence suggests it ran parallel to a sewer for rain and waste runoff. The road was accompanied by milestones and rest stops, called *mansio*, where travellers could sleep, eat, bathe and stock up on provisions for themselves and their horses or oxen. (Elbasani started out as a Mansio Scampa, for example, and a town sprouted around it.)

East from Dyrrachium, the Via Egnatia passed through today's Kavaja, Elbasani, the Jabllanica mountain range and north around Lake Ohrid (Liqeni i Ohrit), then pressed on to Thessaloniki, Philippi and finally Byzantium. In Albania, it almost certainly connected with **Apollonia** (see page 152) and, by the sixth century AD, **Aulona** (Vlora) and **Byllis** (Bylisi). The exact path of the Egnatia in Albania is unknown, but the territory would have been crisscrossed by Roman and Byzantine roads. Many ancient byways in Central Albania are referred to as the Via Egnatia in informational literature – and they might have been. Or they were alternative routes and thoroughfares along the big road; we don't have street signs to identify them now.

Caesar and **Pompey** both marched on the Via Egnatia while clashing at Dyrrachium. The legions of **Augustus** and **Marc Antony** slowly squelched Caesar's assassins from strategic positions near Philippi. The **Apostle Paul** travelled the Egnatia too, and countless Byzantine traders, soldiers and monks later trafficked the highway. The Via Egnatia is long gone, but Durrësi port remains Albania's busiest hub of maritime trade, with more than 3.5 million tons of goods moving in and out every year.

of Julius Caesar's triremes sailing toward the coast and footage of Mussolini's troops landing there two thousand years later.

Durrësi has a long, confusing history and only a few fragmented information placards around the city, so even if you're indifferent to digital razzmatazz, the tower is a must-stop to learn about the city and understand its legacy.

Durrësi Amphitheatre

Rruga e Kalasë, entrance on the west side • Charge • www.facebook.com/p/Qendra-Muzeore-Durrës-100069329044622

In 1966, Albanian archaeologist Vangjel Toçi was having a look around the city walls when he saw a fig tree had fallen into a pit a few metres below ground level. He'd stumbled across a historic marvel: a 136m-high, 20,000-capacity arena that had simply – and incredibly – been lost. Most likely built during the reign of the emperor Trajan in the early second century AD, the **Durrësi Amphitheatre** (Amfiteatri i Durrësit) was similar in size to its Mediterranean cousins that still stand in Nîmes (France) and Pula (Croatia), other imperial centres of power.

3

The northern and western parts of the amphitheatre are the best preserved, but the south curve reveals what archaeologists have most recently excavated on digs in the 2020s. As was the fashion of those days, this arena would have staged gladiatorial combat, beast hunts, public executions and the occasional nonviolent spectacle. You can walk through the arched corridors where animals were once corralled and led out to the arena; the seating is elevated around 2.5m above so lions, tigers and bears could not reach the braying crowds.

Most of the stands are now rubble, but the passageways beneath are fun to explore. Look out for the **chapel** built into the wall, an odd little thing with its apse protruding into the arena. Inside, **mosaics** on the walls depict the Virgin Mary, in robes of royalty, flanked by angels and the figures of Wisdom and Peace (both female, for what it's worth). It was probably a funerary chapel, added sometime between the sixth and eleventh centuries AD. In 2024, new informational signage was installed around the site, and the amphitheatre now hosts regular opera, orchestral and folk performances. It's a welcome glow-up, but there's no museum sadly. Walk around and above the amphitheater on Rruga Sotir Noka for the best views.

The Great Mosque

Sheshi Liria, west side • Free • www.facebook.com/xhamiadurres

The **Great Mosque** (Xhamia e Madhe) on the west side of Sheshi Liria, is the rare masjid that's neither medieval nor modern. After an earthquake destroyed the original, **King Zog I** set about replacing it with something more in keeping with his style. A suave white building with pineapple accents, it was the biggest mosque in the Balkans when it was completed in 1938. But Zog was in exile when it was inaugurated in 1939 by the new Italian Fascist government, which sought to make a big, ingratiating show of how welcoming it would be toward the faiths of its newly conquered protectorate. **Enver Hoxha** did not share these sensitivities; he lopped off the dome and spiked the minaret. Restored to its intended purpose and appearance, it now blends in with the grandiose communist buildings that joined it on the square.

Peeping Tourist

Rruga Mustafa Varoshi • Free • www.peepingtourists.com • Guided tours

This fascinating **exhibition** tells the unique tale of how a communist government turned Albania into a tourist destination. From the mid-twentieth century up until the fall of communism, international visitors had to apply to visit, but this didn't put holidaygoers off: by the late 1980s, more than 15,000 Italians, Brits, Norwegians, Russians and Chinese vacationed here every year. Check out mid-century modern china with the logo of **Albturist**, the **state-run travel agency**, and hotel ashtrays that were bugged with microphones, though it's the stories that bring it all to life. Video interviews reveal former Albturist guides and tourists regaling the sometimes-farcical outcomes of a tightly controlled regime trying to run all-inclusive travel packages – one shaggy tourist is whisked off to have his noncompliant beard shaved; a guide's glasses are fumbled, and a micro-recording device pops out. But it wasn't all spy games. State tourism employees put proud work into creating informative guidebooks in seven languages, snappy illustrated maps and posters, and reams of fabulous postcards. It's a more nuanced picture of the 'closed-off' country, and the delightful retro photos are enough to make you want to book a trip back in time – almost.

Mausoleum of Martyrs

Rruga Aleksandër Goga and Rruga e Dëshmorëve • Free

The U-shaped **Mausoleum of Martyrs** (Mauzoleu i Dëshmorëve), about 500m north of Sheshi Liria up Rruga Aleksandër Goga, should interest twentieth-century history and architecture buffs. Construction on the distinctive monument began in 1949, and the vaults on the ground floor contain the remains of the Durrsak men who were killed in World War II. The large **mosaic** on one terrace of the grand perron staircase adds a happier scene: soldiers, wives, kids and musicians celebrating the liberation of Durrësi in 1944 (spot the Venetian Tower in the background). Installed in 1976, it must be among the smiliest socialist realist artworks in Albania. Upstairs is the unexpected **British Children's Library of Durrësi**. You can take in fine views from here, or ask to see the archives in the back. Pick a random tome labelled *monumentet* (monuments) or *kultura popullore* (popular culture), and thumb through the yellowed pages and time-faded colour photos of magazines and journals from the 1950s through the 1980s, many preserved nowhere else.

3

Vollga

Immediately west of the Venetian Tower, between Durrësi hill and the sea, is the **Vollga** district, where locals flock in the evening after work or school. The **Shëtitorja Vollga**, a large park and promenade along the waterfront, fills much of it. At the west end, the **Sphinx** (Sfinksi), a rocky outcropping converted into a terraced hump, is a prime sunset hangout with fine Adriatic views. Another pier supports two complexes of restaurants and bars hovering over the water, which look like UFOs attempting to dock.

The park is peppered with an abundance of wacky **statues**. There's **Redon** (or Rodon), the Illyrian sea god with his trident, guarding a roundabout. Two **gladiators** the size of trees face off awkwardly, their broken swords rendering them useless. The **Unknown Soldier** (Ushtari i Panjohur) leaps valiantly from his platform, rifle aloft, but from a different angle – when you're walking closer to the water – he appears to be intruding on a sculptural jamming session between Tina Turner, John Lennon, Bob Dylan and Mick Jagger.

From the hilltop above, **King Zog I's Royal Villa** (Pallati i Mbretit Zog I) peers imperiously over the whole bizarre scene. The summer residence of King Zog I and Queen Géraldine, completed in 1937, the cream-and-violet palace cuts a fine figure. It's a bona fide architectural treasure: Neoclassical, rationalist, Italianate, Mediterranean and Albanian all in one, with an unusual truncated-triangle facade forming the wings of an eagle. You can trek up the hill for a closer look and a view over the Vollga, but the palace and esplanade is only open once in a blue moon for special events.

Archaeological Museum of Durrësi

Rruga Taulantia 32 • Charge • www.facebook.com/muzeuarkeologjikdurres

Albania's premier museum of archaeology naturally belongs in Albania's ancient metropolis. Sadly, though, it was severely damaged in the 2019 earthquake and closed in 2022 for repairs and upgrades. No reopening date has been set yet, but work could be completed by 2026. Occupying a three-storey building, with more than three thousand exhibits in its collection, the **Archaeological Museum of Durrësi** (Muzeu

Arkeologjik Durrës) primarily highlights Illyrian, Greek, Roman and Byzantine finds from Epidamnos/Dyrrhachium, including red- and black-figure ceramics, coins from an imperial-era Roman hoard, amphorae, columns, plinths, mosaics, life-sized statues, iron slave shackles and much more. Some displays set the museum apart with region-specific art and artefacts, like epigraphs inscribed with Illyrian names (in Greek script) and lead pipes for a Roman aqueduct 'signed' by a local workshop. Plans for the new museum to expand its scope to medieval, Venetian and Ottoman displays, as well as new finds from 2020s underwater excavations, have also been announced.

Durrësi Beach

Free • The beach starts 2km from the Stacioni i Trenit bus terminal, and it's reachable from the centre via a sidewalk and bike lane that eventually meets the Shëtitorja e Plazhit

Though there is a string of beaches in Durrësi city, to the west and north of Vollga, this is what folks mean when they say 'Durrës Plazh'. **Durrësi Beach** (Plazhi i Durrësit) starts to the east of the port and curves southeast in a crescent shape, spanning around 12km of sand, sun beds and traffic snarls. New comforts and conveniences – aparthotels, e-bike rentals – sit side by side with discarded and corroded tourist attractions of yesteryear. The **Shëtitorja e Plazhit** beach promenade, bustling with locals and visiting couples, families and kids, is built up with condos, hotels and resorts, a mix of shiny new projects and 2000s concrete junkers with peeling paint and wind-ravaged clotheslines.

The yawning beach is 200m wide in places, though sadly the sand is almost completely carpeted by sun beds and umbrellas (charge) in the summer. The water is warm, calm, shallow though decidedly not clear – any weather disturbance dredges up muck, and you're just downstream of Albania's busiest port – but it's perfectly pleasant for wading, floating, swimming or tooling around on a pedalboat or jet ski. When autumn kicks in, conditions are good for kitesurfing, windsurfing and parasailing. The promenade is peppered with restaurants serving excellent fresh seafood (see page 148). It's all much more civilized than one block over on Rruga Pavarësia (SH4) – the neighborhood's only major street – which heaves with cars from Tirana, Pristina, Hungary, Switzerland and beyond.

Nonetheless, Plazhi i Durrësit is very much an urban beach, with all the amenities and drawbacks that entails. Seclusion seekers might have more luck along the **beaches northwest of Vollga**, where the hilly part of Durrësi creates smaller coves and there's no natural breakwater against the Adriatic. **Currila**, **Kallmi** and **Portezi** are worth checking out. But even as late into the year as June and then again as early as September, all the city's beaches can be quite peaceful.

ARRIVAL AND DEPARTURE — DURRËSI

By plane Tirana International Airport is actually located between Tirana and Durrësi, and Durrësi centre is not much further from the airport than the capital. Taxis outside the arrivals hall have fixed rates for Durrësi centre and Plazhi i Durrësit. Buses and minibuses also leave from the airport bus stop for Durrësi around every two hours (several daily; 40min). See page 67 for more Tirana airport information.

By bus and minibus Durrësi has two bus terminals, which are a little chaotic and not too centrally located, though they are sort of intuitive. Most international and Northern Albania buses (including from/for Tirana and the airport) arrive at, and depart from, Durrësi via the Stacioni i Trenit terminal (Rruga Adria at the Sheshi 26 Nëntori roundabout), 1.2km (20min walk) from the Venetian Tower. The other station, Plepa (southern end of Durrësi Beach, where the SH4 and SH56 go under the SH85 (Rruga Martin Camaj), mostly serves domestic destinations south of Durrësi (Berati, Korça, Vlora, etc) – *unless* the buses are coming from Tirana and continuing. At the time of writing, some or all Vlora- and Saranda-bound minibuses stop about 100m south of Plepa station on Rruga Pavarësia. Golemi-bound city buses also stop on Rruga Pavarësia, just opposite the station, though they continue into Durrësi as well. This information could change, so don't hesitate to ask for help. You can buy international bus or ferry tickets from agencies at the Stacioni i Trenit bus terminal. Buses connect to Kosovo, North Macedonia, Montenegro, Greece, Italy, Germany, etc. Some options include Ideal Travel (tel: 067 216 2135), Ariel Travel (tel: 069 313 7296), Riva Travel/Star Travel (tel: 069 694 0914), Xhoni Travel/Hak Bus (tel: 069 550 6173).

Destinations Bajram Curri (several daily; 4hr 15min); Berati (many daily; 2hr); Çorovoda (several daily; 3hr 30min);

Elbasani (many daily; 1hr 30min); Erseka (several daily; 4hr 50min); Fieri (many daily; 1hr 45min); Golemi (many daily; 30–45min); Gjirokastra (many daily; 3hr 40min); Gramshi (several daily; 2hr 40min); Korça (several daily; 4hr); Kruja (several daily; 40min); Kukësi (many daily; 2hr 10min); Lezha (several daily; 1hr 40min); Librazhdi (many daily; 1hr 40min); Lushnja (many daily; 1hr); Përmeti (many daily; 3hr 55min); Peshkopia (several daily, 4hr 20min); Pogradeci (several daily; 3hr); Shkodra (several daily; 2hr 25min); Tepelena (many daily; 3hr); Tirana (many daily; 40min); Tirana International Airport (several daily; 40min); Vlora (several daily; 2hr 30min).

By car Driving from Tirana via the SH2, when you reach Durrësi, signs clearly point toward the exits for the centre, Plazhi and port, though be aware the turn-offs come in rapid succession. From the south, you'll arrive via the SH4 and exit left toward Plazhi and then centre. The highways are fine but could use some attention in both directions, so be mindful as always.

By boat Ferries between Bari (Italy) and Durrësi run daily year-round. Most are overnight (9–10hr), but in high season there are additional midday departures. Adria Ferries (www.adriaferries.com) also runs overnight ferries (16hr) between Ancona (Italy) and Durrësi, which run nightly in the high season, and on alternating nights the rest of the year. The ferry port is on Rruga e Doganës, which can be reached via a pedestrian bridge next to the Stacioni i Trenit bus terminal.

By train On the other side of Stacioni i Trenit bus terminal, on Rruga Adria, the Stacioni i Trenit train station is being rebuilt. It will link Tirana to Durrësi by train and is scheduled to open in 2026. Until then, the station is not in use, though the Plazhi i Durrësit station on Rruga Dhimitër Kraja runs passenger trains to Elbasani every Friday, Saturday and Sunday. See information on page 137.

3

GETTING AROUND

By bus There are five city bus lines in Durrësi, but you probably won't need more than two. One connects the Stacioni i Trenit bus terminal to the centre and Vollga, the other runs from the bus terminal to the Plazhi i Durrësit, including a stop at the Plepa bus station. Check the transport map at www.visitdurres.al/harta-e-transportit-publik.

By car Durrësi is fairly bad for driving most of the year, but in July and August, it's abysmal. The beach boulevard, Rruga Pavarësia, can add thirty minutes to your trip. Even the 'secret' beach road for Durrësi experts (starts along Rruga e Enkelejve) is gnarled. The centre is choked. Street parking is hell – though mostly free! There's a large car park near the Venetian Tower; take the south exit off the statue of Redon roundabout from Rruga Egnatia. A pricey but convenient car park can be found on Rruga Kolonel Tomson, one block from Bulevardi Epidamn. The Plazhi area is tougher; there are a few paid car parks on Rruga Venecia open in the summer, and usually a spot can be found on the street if you drive far enough.

A car can admittedly be handy if you need to travel to Tirana and back, or if you want to drive to near-ish places not well served by public transit, like the Cape of Rodoni or old Kruja. There are loads of small car-rental places in Durrësi, and prices are fairly uniform. Reputable options include Elyan Agency in Plazhi (Rruga Pavarësia side street; tel: 069 664 9444), Ekorent Auto in the centre (Bulevardi Epidamn; tel: 069 364 0568) and Makina me Qira Kryemadhi near the Stacioni i Trenit terminal (Rruga Adria; tel: 069 769 2100).

By taxi Be especially careful with taxis in Durrësi, particularly in highly touristed areas. If you must hail one, request they turn the meter on or negotiate a price in advance. You can find taxi ranks all over the city, including one at the southern entrance to Bulevardi Epidamn just past the Venetian Tower, and several along the first few blocks of Rruga Pavarësia in Plazhi i Durrësit.

There are trustworthy car services in town, if you want to call a cab. BS Taxi guarantees its drivers uses their meters, and it's fast and reliable (tel: 069 635 6682). Koli's Taxi is also a good bet, especially for a fixed price on a longer ride (tel: 069 880 8643); likewise, Eli Taxi (tel: 068 323 0023).

By bike or scooter With good bike paths almost the entire way from the end of Plazhi i Durrësit to Vollga, cycling is one of best ways to navigate Durrësi. There are now several e-bike and scooter rentals in the Plazhi area, including Demo Rent-a-Bike on Rruga Pavarësia (tel: 069 206 6046) and Eco Venture Albania, at the far end of the strip (Rruga Venecia; tel: 069 242 0388). Find cycling itineraries at www.visitdurres.al.

INFORMATION

Tourist information There is no visitor centre in Durrësi. It does have a couple of tourist information signs with a map and points of interest: one on Sheshi Liria next to the theatre building; another at the Plepa bus station. You can also find plentiful English-language online resources with maps, walking trails, bike routes and details of places of cultural and natural interest. See below.

Websites www.visitdurres.al; www.museums.al; www.facebook.com/p/Qendra-Muzeore-Durrës-100069329044622; www.3e-routes.al/category/cultural-monuments-durres; www.theolddoorstrail.com; www.durres.gov.al.

ACCOMMODATION

SEE MAP PAGE 140

In Durrësi you will find every type of hotel: big and small, new and old, good and bad, and the worst won't have changed anything in years except their prices. You'll pay a premium for desirable areas in the high season, but there

3

are deals to be found, especially if you visit outside July and August and look for accommodation just off the shore. There are still cosy, family-run places all over the city that provide that personal touch of famed Albanian hospitality, and there are also new or improved splurge spots that earn their price tags.

★ **Adriatik Hotel** Rruga Pavarësia across the street from Shkolla Bajram Curri; www.adriatikhotel.com. When *Adriatik* was opened in 1957, it was *the* hotel on Plazhi i Durrësit – the only one for international visitors and the choice of party elite for a breezy beach getaway. It's now under the Best Western Hotels & Resorts umbrella, but it retains some mid-century charm, with blown-up vintage photos of Albania landmarks across the walls of most rooms. There's a large spa, sauna, indoor and outdoor swimming pools, a private beach, gym, two restaurants and accessible rooms. Breakfast is excellent, and staff are internationally trained pros. **€€€€**

Art Gallery Boutique Hotel Rruga e Kalasë; www.artgalleryboutiquehotel.com. An intimate nineteen-room bolthole, this is the pacesetter for luxury and elegance in the Bulevardi Epidamn area, though set off from the busy street. Opened in 2024, it has the crushed velvet accents, the fluffy pillows, the rainfall showers and the Nespresso machines in each room, but what really sets it a cut above the rest is its location overlooking the amphitheatre. You can take your coffee on your balcony and dine on the rooftop restaurant for some of the best views in town. **€€€€**

Colombia Apartments & Rooms Shëtitorja Taulantia opposite Ventus Harbour pier; tel: 069 305 0783. A great budget-friendly option in Vollga, this cute aparthotel has seven units that can sleep two or a family of four-plus. Rooms are clean, colourful and comfortable, and the wi-fi is very fast. Breakfast is included at the bakery next door, and you're almost right on the promenade. **€€**

Gent's Inn Rruga Pavarësia across the street from Rruga Shën Mëhilli; tel: 069 279 1944. Six recently renovated one-bedroom apartments right on the sand and above a restaurant run by the same owners – it's the best you can do at this price for beachfront views and vibes. Parking is included, and the spacious units have full kitchens and washing machines. You can also park yourself on a beach lounger beneath a parasol at Gent's Beach, also included. **€€**

Hostel Durrës Sheshi Liria at Rruga Ramazan Jella; www.facebook.com/hosteldurres. The original hostel in town finds itself in what is now a very choice location right on Sheshi Liria. There's a lively scene here, with a spacious patio, outdoor grill, brightly painted common area, live music at the bar next door, group yoga and other hangout activities. Breakfast is included, and there are both dorms and doubles with private bathrooms. Fans but no A/C. **€**

Hotel Kloest Rruga At Erazmi; www.hotelkloest.com. Durrësi now has a gaggle of pricey hotels near Bulevardi Epidamn that look historic, but *Kloest* actually was built in the King Zog I era, 1932, and it's fittingly kitted out with period furniture, embossed wallpaper and other bits and bobs of aristocracy without going over the top. All amenities are modern; staff are warm and professional; and the higher rooms and balconies have a fine view over the Venetian Tower. Usually not in the price stratosphere of similar-standard hotels. **€€€€**

★ **Wave Beachfront Apartments** Rruga Venecia; www.wave-beach.com. Available for short or long stays, this twenty-unit aparthotel has suites for one- and two-bedroom apartments that can sleep a family of four or more, plus pets. Rooms have all the necessary amenities, plus kitchens, parking and – what you came for – floor-to-ceiling windows and glass-doored balconies overlooking the Adriatic. Welcoming, responsive hosts help you make the most of Durrësi. **€€€**

EATING

SEE MAP PAGE 140

One thing that sets the Plazhi i Durrësit apart is its food. You can pick pretty much any restaurant along the promenade and be rewarded with the freshest, finest seafood at affordable prices. For whole fish, there's the whole Mediterranean gamut: *levruk* (seabass), *kocë* (dorade), *merluc* (hake), *barbun* (mullet), *dental* (snapper), *romb (turbot)* and more. Seafood carpaccio or crudo of white and red prawns, shrimp, octopus, calamari and salmon, with peppercorns and soaked in olive oil, is a can't-miss dish. Some places will let you pick out fish, shrimp and anything else at the counter, and prepare it however you like. If you prefer fried, plump for shrimp or calamari. It's worth noting that many Plazhi restaurants close from late autumn until spring.

★ **Agroturizëm Gjepali** 17km from Durrësi centre via SH2 or Rruga Bajram Tusha, following signs toward Shijaku and the restaurant; www.agroturizemgjepali.com. A Tuscan-style villa in the suburb of Shijaku, this is the realized dream of chef-owner Fundim Gjepali, who spent years in the kitchen at Rome's *Antico Arco* before returning home to revive the family farm. Elegant but well priced, with a seasonal set menu and ingredients from local producers and farmers, the restaurant makes light work of staples like *byrek* (savoury filo pastries) and *fërgesë* (peppers and tomatoes baked with cheese). For mains, there are plenty of gamey and meaty options like roasted quail and chicken. The Albanian wine selection is comprehensive too. **€€€**

Banesa 23 Rruga Kolonel Tomson. This quiet, cosy dinner spot in a stylish exposed-brick setting, hidden just behind the bustle of Bulevardi Epidamn, specializes in traditional north-central Albanian cuisine. Start with big *meze* plates of *fasule* (white beans) and several types of *gjizë* (local ricotta-style cheese), then move on to *fërgesë* (melted cheese with peppers) and grilled veal steaks. Service is top-notch, the drinks selection is broad, there's live music, and be sure to peep at the archival black-and-white photos of old Durrësi on the walls. Plenty of vegetarian options. €€

Dyrrah Mare Shëtitorja e Plazhit, 100m south of Adriatik Hotel; tel: 069 366 4675. You're in good hands for seafood at this upscale beachfront spot. The carpaccio is excellent, the fish is fresh and delicious (ask the waiter for a recommendation), the seafood pasta and risotto are done just right, and you can watch the sunset from your table. There are light bites too, such as shrimp tacos with cheese, peppers and onions. Open all year. €€€

Gusto di Mare & Sushi Time Shëtitorja Taulantia; tel: 069 348 4210. A locals' favourite on the Vollga promenade, next to another, *Restorant Gogo*. The latter still pulls off a seafood crudo that might just change your life, but come to *Gusto di Mare* for the full Vollga night experience: an outdoor promenade-side dining scene that hums from afternoon till late, heaving platters of whole-grilled *levruk* (seabass), octopus and vegetables drizzled in vinegar; and enthusiastic service. €€€

★ **Peshk i Freskët Bracja** Rruga Pavarësia, two blocks east of Rruga David Selenica; tel: 69 607 4763. A friendly hole-in-the-wall seafood counter where you can pick out any fish you like, have it prepared to order and pay near-market prices – *Peshk i Freskët Braçja* is a gem. As far as fish goes, ask what's good on the day you visit, and pick that. The staff are super-friendly and take pride in what they do. Don't deny yourself a mixed plate of crispy fried shrimp, calamari and *barbun* (mullet). Order to go or dine at one of the tables on the sidewalk. €

DRINKING AND NIGHTLIFE

SEE MAP PAGE 140

Bistro Mol Shëtitorja e Plazhit opposite the Kompleksi Teuta pier; tel: 069 938 5020. This is your Aperol Spritz spot on the Plazhi i Durrësit. Right on the sand with an unobstructed sea view and a cabana-style patio, *Bistro Mol* leans more refined than rowdy. But you can still watch a game or order a pizza here. Cocktails are expertly made and generous, and the place is open year-round.

Cinco Cavalli Summer Club Rruga Currila; tel: 068 555 0861. You may or may not be up for dress codes, pricey bottle service and arbitrary treatment at the door, but what's not up for debate is that every summer season, the most famous DJs and pop stars in Albania perform here. Pretty much every weekend and throughout the week, the venue is packed to capacity until the wee hours. If it's your scene, it's the place to be seen. Reserve ahead.

Kantina Gjergj Kastrioti Skënderbeu Rruga Bajram Tusha 14; tel: 068 209 1886. Founded in 1933, this distillery is where all that Skënderbeu brandy you see in supermarkets is made. You can also try the smoother, barrel-aged version and upwards of a dozen different wines, but the facility itself is the real point of intrigue. See the phalanx of monolithic concrete fermentation vats from the communist era in action and experience how an industrial-sized state-run factory would have operated. Call ahead.

★ **Vinum Wine Bar** Rruga Taulantia 1; www.vinumdurres.com. *Vinum* is a cosy and classy spot in Vollga, with abstract art on the walls and an intimate outdoor patio that encourages mingling with your neighbours. The main calling card, though, is the Albanian wine list, with reds, whites and rosés from around the country, but especially the Durrësi area. Almost everything is available by the glass, and there are guided tastings of up to nine different wines and *rakis*, every night – a devious offering for a place that then puts a mic in your hand for karaoke. There's live (professional) music too.

ENTERTAINMENT

Qendra Kulturore e Fëmijëve (Children's Cultural Centre) Rruga At Erazmi; www.facebook.com/QkfDurres. This venue opened in a renovated building in 2024 and, yes, it's mostly for kids. But the space also hosts panel discussions, literary forums, festivals and seminars.

Teatri Aleksandër Moisiu (Aleksandër Moisiu Theatre and Cultural Centre) Sheshi Liria; tel: 068 391 3813. A multifunctional arts centre and theatre putting on opera, comedy, drama, ballet, classical music performances, folklore shows, kids' shows, concerts and festivals; also hosts related cultural events at Sheshi Liria and in the amphitheatre. You can stop by to see what's happening. Behind the building, find some ruins of a Roman bathhouse.

SHOPPING

SEE MAP PAGE 140

Marigo Souvenirs and Gift Shop Bulevardi Epidamn near Rruga Dom Nikollë Kaçorri; tel: 068 332 1101. Marigo does have Durrësi-themed shirts, mugs, plates and keychains, if you're just looking to grab an easy souvenir, but it's also a small emporium for more unusual and interesting handmade products by local artisans. Find ceramics, cross-stitching, jewellery, small woodwork items, honey, tea, wine and other Durrësi keepsakes.

DIRECTORY

Banks and currency exchange In the centre, you'll find a few banks with ATMs on the south side of the statue of Redon roundabout, plus a handful on Sheshi Liria, but most are along Rruga Egnatia. In Plazhi i Durrësit, they are mainly located on Rruga Pavarësia between Rruga 3 Vëllezërit Thanasi and Rruga Bajram Curri. Durrësi has many Western Unions, including on Bulevardi Epidamn and Rruga Pavarësia. Currency exchanges can be found all along Rruga Pavarësia in Plazhi, and in the centre, clustered around the area where Rruga Kristaq Rama and Bulevardi Dyrrah meet. Rates for all financial services may be worse near the beach; use ATMs that allow you to decline the host bank's conversion rate.

Emergencies Tel: 127, tel:129 or tel: 112.

Hospital The primary hospital, Spitali Rajonal Durrës, is a big complex with an emergency room and a cluster of specialist offices – public and private – in the area (Rruga Telat Noga; enter the ER from Rruga Aleksandër Goga and the parking from Rruga Kastrioti; tel: 05 222 2222). Medical Care Lami is probably the city's best English-speaking private clinic for both mild and serious medical conditions (Rruga Ahmet Ramzoti, near Rruga Aleksandër Goga; tel: 068 299 9444). In the Plazhi area, Wellness Medical Services Albania at Ansi Lab is a good option (Rruga Pavarësia next to *Palace Hotel*; tel: 069 446 6774).

Immigration and visas For visa issues, visit the DVKM office on Bulevardi Epidamn inside the port complex south of the Veliera, next to the Autoriteti Portual Durrës (Durrësi Port Authority) building (tel: 069 411 0255).

Pharmacies Ansi Farma on Rruga Pavarësia in Plazhi is a quality pharmacy (tel: 069 224 4828), but there are many pharmacies on Rruga Pavarësia. In the centre, try Farmaci Sula (Bulevardi Epidamn, near Rruga Doktor Ismail Tartari).

Police The city police station is on Rruga e Doganës near the meeting point with Rruga Egnatia (tel: 05 223 2250). The regional police HQ is at Rruga Hysen Kertusha and Rruga Aleksandër Goga (tel: 05 222 2266).

Post office The DHL service point is on Rruga Fetah Bllaca near the intersection with Rruga Egnatia (tel: 04 240 6666). Find the central Posta Shqiptare on Rruga Ismail Beja, Sheshi Demokracia (tel: 068 204 4707).

South of Durrësi

The Kavaja municipality immediately south of Durrësi is mostly visited for its beaches. **Golemi**, a continuation of the **Bay of Durrësi** (Gjiri i Durrësit) brings more long, sandy stretches, but it can also be busy. Less developed beaches crop up as the coast proceeds south. The Kavaja coastline meets the **Shkumbini River** (Lumi i Shkumbinit) due west of Elbasani, and there stands one of Albania's most extraordinary and startling monuments, the **Bashtova Castle** (Kalaja e Bashtovës). Another repository of Albanian heritage, Kavaja city's **Ethnographic Museum** (Muzeu Etnografik; Rruga Skuraj near Rruga Taulantia) may also be of interest. In contrast to the stone-built houses of mountainous Berati and Gjirokastra, the museum occupies a low-slung adobe structure built in the nineteenth century by the Ottomans to withstand a humid, stormy coastal region. It reopened in 2024 following a complete restoration.

The beaches

The coast south of Durrësi is not immediately exciting. But press on and eventually the landscape turns marshy, before giving way to sandy stretches against a backdrop of ever-craggier ridges. Here, rock formations in the water create shallow tidepools, and the highway recedes east.

Golemi Beach

Bulevardi i Pishave, Golemi • Free, with charge for sun beds and umbrellas

Around 5km long and crescent-shaped, **Golemi Beach** (Plazhi i Golemit) is a little broader than Durrësi's, and the town itself a little quieter. The sea is warm and shallow in high season, but beware of jellyfish. Golemi has a swanky reputation going back some years, and much of the waterfront is given over to large resort hotels with sky-high prices and low-tier service. However, smaller, more authentic places (at more palatable prices) can be found, especially if you move away from the centre. The scene itself is fun if you're looking for beachy vibes mixed with poolside lounging, spa treatments and all-night cavorting. South of Golemi proper but still in the bay, there are some hard-to-reach coves tucked between coastal ridges, some of which now have great facilities for camping.

General's Beach

Unnamed road, Bardhori village • Free, with charge for sun beds and umbrellas

Green hills shelter a small cove beach at the **General's Beach** (Plazhi i Gjeneralit), supposedly named for an Italian general who took a shine to it in the 1930s. A sandy arc gives way to a pebbly and shell-strewn seabed, with **tidepools** burbling around eroded rock formations. The surf is clearer than nearby beaches, protected from the bay. There is only a smattering of bungalows and a **bar-restaurant**, but the beach is also small – arrive early on August weekends if you want to secure a spot. But, because it's hard to reach, the beach is generally quiet and pleasant the rest of the year. If you have proper footwear to traverse rocks, shells and tree debris, wander south of the beach to discover remoter, quieter spots. Then again, away from the main beach, no one cleans up the copious litter people leave.

Spilleja Beach

Along Rruga e Pishave, Spilleja • Free, with charge for sun beds and umbrellas

Spilleja Beach (also: Spille), or Plazhi i Spillesë, is long, shallow and sandy. The coastal landscape here is not going to knock your socks off, but it's a relatively uncrowded stretch with cheap parasols, easy access, pine forests, lax rules on throwing down your own towel, and a few seafood shacks to keep your energy up after a game of beach football.

3

Spilleja has a much more rustic vibe than most beaches on the Adriatic coast without losing points for comfort and convenience.

ARRIVAL AND GETTING AROUND — THE BEACHES

GOLEMI BEACH

By bus or minibus Buses to/from Durrësi Stacioni i Trenit stop every 30min (very roughly) at points along the Durrësi and Golemi coastline in the summer, with the last stop at the central Golemi roundabout, on Rruga Kryemëdhej-Golem. From here, it's around a 500m walk west to the beach. Look for a big red city bus or a minibus with a 'Durrës–Golem' sign in the window.

By taxi Any Durrësi taxi will cart you to Golemi (20–40min, depending on season and time of day), but ask for the price before you set off, and decide if it's worth it to you. Tirana and airport taxis will also take you; Green Taxi (tel: 069 800 2000) charges €25 from Tirana centre, and airport taxis bump on another €10 for the privilege.

By car Driving south from Durrësi, leave the SH4 highway at the exit for Golemi, near the south of town. Driving north, you need to exit north of Kavaja town; look for signs. In high season, there's substantial traffic on all the little streets in and out of Golemi. Find a paid car park on Rruga e Plazhit near Rruga Roma.

GENERAL'S BEACH

By car Leave the SH4 at the Rrakulli exit, near Kavaja town. Follow signs southwest toward Bagoja (signposted 'Bago'), Bardhori and Plazhi i Gjeneralit. Most of the roads off the highway are dirt, poorly maintained and traverse some hills. It's doable in any car if you drive slowly, but the journey will take 1hr-plus from Durrësi.

SPILLEJA BEACH

By car From the SH4, exit west toward Luzi i Vogël and continue straight toward Spilleja (signposted 'Spille'), about 14km from the highway. Roads are paved, and parking is easy to find. Factor in around 1hr from Durrësi.

ACCOMMODATION

GOLEMI BEACH

★ **Comfort Suites** Rruga Qerret-Plazh; www.comfort-suites.al. This beachfront spot goes the extra mile: the owner is hands-on, and the staff are super-friendly and attentive. The pool area is chic, with adorable fringed bamboo umbrellas that look like flat-topped banyan trees. Rooms here include simpler, less pricey options, and suites with hot tubs, balconies, rainfall showers and so forth. A rooftop restaurant with excellent fresh seafood is a nice plus, and the beach bar, *Moai*, mixes incredible cocktails. €€€€

Camping Plazhi i Bardhë Unnamed road, Bagoja village; www.campingplazhibardhe.com. Like most unspoiled beaches, Plazhi i Bardhë is not easy to reach, but a lot of love has gone into making this little cove worth the trip. The campground offers waterfront spots for vans and tents, with good sanitation, an on-site restaurant, a sauna, washing machines, loungers and umbrellas. Message the staff in advance for directions. €

EATING

GOLEMI BEACH

Flower Restaurant Rruga Ahmet Çaçi; www.hotel-flower.com/flower-restaurant. *Flower* raised the stakes for upscale accommodation and dining when it opened in 2016, and it has grown into something of a destination now. Dining by the pool in the twilight is an experience; groups from all over the world chat, laugh, smoke cigars and celebrate the luxe life, if only for a few hours. The many, many superb desserts, from raspberry cream-dolloped brownies to *bakllava*, might be the highlight – order for the table and share. €€€€

DRINKING AND NIGHTLIFE

GOLEMI BEACH

Nao Beach Bar Rruga e Kompleksit; tel: 069 687 9018. If you're trying to sleep in a hotel nearby, too bad for you: *Nao* plays it loud and goes all night. Attracting a well-heeled crowd doesn't set *Nao* apart but complementing that scene with top-tier live musicians leading the party does. There's trance and house, sure, but also pop acts, rock bands and even some Albanian slow jams thrown into the mix.

3

Bashtova Castle

Rruga e Plazhit, Vilë-Bashtova village • Charge

You're driving around the barely inhabited Adriatic flatlands south of Durrësi in a (perhaps futile) search for an untouched beach, and – bam: a huge castle with 12m-high ramparts looms up before you in the middle of nowhere. Welcome to the **Bashtova Castle** (Kalaja e Bashtovës), the most striking and least-touristed major fortress in Albania. Highlights include a pair of stout circular towers, an imposing gate and three crenellated 9m-high sandstone walls preserved almost as they were over five hundred years ago. In the middle of four walls (one was rebuilt later), there's nothing – an eerily empty, grassy expanse. Climb the walls near the corner towers to see Bashtova at once stark and extravagant.

It was, indeed, extravagant to construct a fortress like this from scratch in the fifteenth century. It is not certain who built it or why. At the time, the area was a centre of the grain trade and located at a strategic point – near both the **Via Egnatia** trading route and the **Shkumbini River** (Lumi i Shkumbinit). Most likely, Bashtova was a Venetian project. From Durrësi, Venetians took hold of these plains in the late 1300s, and within a century, lost them to the Ottomans. Excavations in 2022 involved drilling and clearing two metres of accumulated sediment to reach the original ground level, where archaeologists discovered deposits of **cannonballs**, smaller ballistics and **ceramics**. The castle has since been meticulously restored, and there are now stairs and guardrails so visitors can walk the walls safely. The fortress is scheduled to reopen, with a new **visitor centre** and **museum**, in 2025.

ARRIVAL AND GETTING AROUND — BASHTOVA CASTLE

By car Whether you're driving from the north or south, follow the SH4 to the village of Gosa, and exit the highway to Rruga e Plazhit. Follow the road 12km (keep left when it forks with Rruga e Boshtovës), and you can't fail to see the castle. It's around a 45min drive from Durrësi or 35min from Lushnja.

ACCOMMODATION AND EATING

Kodra e Godenve Rruga e Plazhit, Vilë-Bashtova; www.kodraegodenve.com. *Kodra e Godenve* looks a bit like a citadel, perhaps appropriate to its location though less suited to its billing as a 'bio resort', though it is indeed a place full of horses, rabbits and birds, surrounded by farmland. Rooms are fairly basic but designed with families in mind; the largest accommodate up to seven. A pool and a garden crawling with critters will please the kids, while the very fine Italian-Albanian cuisine should keep the grown-ups in line. €€€

Divjaka-Karavasta National Park

With extraordinary biodiversity, a broad sandy coast and just a 1hr 30min drive from Tirana, **Divjaka-Karavasta National Park** (Parku Kombëtar Divjakë-Karavasta) has all the raw materials to be an incredible destination for nature lovers. But in a country blessed with awe-inspiring canyons and actual Alps, wetlands are just not as outwardly impressive. The Adriatic waters are thick with reedy detritus, and the tourist town and beach bars are an eyesore. It takes effort to reach the most pristine areas of the **Karavasta Lagoon** (definite form: Karavastaja; Laguna e Karavastasë), and only then does it click that there's real magic here.

The park is home to around 260 species of bird, with an estimated 51,000 feathered residents – temporary and permanent – a year, more than anywhere else in Albania. Most of the guys who'll pique ornithologists' interest come in the winter and stay through June, including the **Dalmatian pelican**, a huge bird that can grow to 1.8m in height and whose wingspan can reach 3.5m – the size of a small car. You might also spot great white herons, brown herons, ducks, geese, pygmy cormorants, collared pratincoles and the occasional troupe of strutting **pink flamingos**. Thousands of amorous avians come here to breed, and hundreds to nest. **Sea turtles** also started nesting on these shores around 2018.

To navigate the park, which encompasses over 220 square kilometres, you need to reach the **visitor centre**, on a paved road directly west of Divjaka town. Next to the centre, you can climb the 230 steps to the top of the **360° Tower** (Kulla 360°) for fine views over the lagoon, marshlands and the sea (charge). Maps indicate the trailheads to various hikes over boardwalks and through scrubland, pines, poplars and cedars. Paths wend through the ethereal swampy landscape and are rarely crowded. For the best panorama of the entire lagoon, find the less-than-snappily-named 'trail of the tower by the first lagoon channel', marked on the map in pink.

3

If you arrive at the tower at sunrise or sunset and clamber up the rickety stairs to the top, you'll be rewarded with a magnificent view over the rippling 42-square-kilometre lagoon, the reddish-gold marsh scrubland riven by brackish rivulets. You'll spot birds dodging and dashing and maybe a lone fisherman or kayaker. Bring binoculars if you have any.

ARRIVAL AND GETTING DIVJAKA-KARAVASTA NATIONAL PARK

By car The visitor centre is 4km from Divjaka town, and the park's tourist village starts about 1km further south on the same paved road. To reach the channel observation point, you'll need to drive on the beach (not through town) near the forest towards the end of the beach bars, and you should see a left turning with a small signpost to 'Ura e Vaut'. A car with high clearance can continue; otherwise, you'll need to walk (20min). The sand is hard-packed and navigable in any car if you follow the tyre tracks. Ignore your GPS.

By bus or minibus There are morning buses from Lushnja to Divjaka (several daily; 30min), and minibuses from Lushnja shuttle visitors to the visitor centre and back.

On foot Following trails from the visitor centre, you can reach one of the park's observation towers via the 3.3km 'trail of the pelican' in around 30min. The channel observation tower is 5.3km away and is a 1hr hike.

ACCOMMODATION

Olive Guesthouse (Fori Vodo) Rruga Xengut, Divjaka; tel: 068 253 0438. Hosts Naja and Fori Vodo light up their guesthouse with warmth and generous hospitality. Rooms are comfortable and clean, and the tasteful decor adds a personal touch. A hearty breakfast includes home-made pastries and pies, eggs, fresh fruit and vegetables, and coffee taken in Naja's kitchen. A fantastic deal, all in all. €

Pelikan Unnamed road, Divjaka tourist village; www.facebook.com/p/Bar-Restorant-Hotel-Pelikan-100063488863806. A solid option if you want to stay in the park proper, this hotel and restaurant has friendly staff, simple but clean rooms, modern amenities and all-important mosquito netting. You're only separated from the beach by a row of pines. €€

EATING

★ **Bar Restorant Beni Rrudho** Unnamed road, Divjaka tourist village; tel: 068 827 0066. A best-in-class place tucked away in Divjaka-Karavasta National Park, *Beni Rrudho* is partially hidden in the forest on the road toward the tourist village. The food here is precisely what the coast is all about: fresh, delicious, caught-that-day seafood. Find shrimp and squid on kebabs, whole *levreku* (seabass) and *ngjala* (eel) grilled over coals and served with seasonal vegetables. It's real fisherfolk food in a peaceful spot nestled in the pines. €€

Korça and Southeast Albania

NATIONAL MUSEUM OF MEDIEVAL ART

Korça and Southeastern Albania

In culture, climate and topography, Southeastern Albania is the real-deal Balkans. A proudly meat-eating, beer-drinking, guitar-strumming, tabletop-dancing type of place, hundreds or thousands of metres above sea level, the region feels (and is) much closer to the mountains and monasteries of Northern Greece than the sun loungers and Instagram cocktails of the Mediterranean coast. Just a few decades ago, it took a full day of travel to reach Korça – the region's largest city – from Tirana, and the longtime geographical isolation of the area gives it a flavour unique from the rest of the country. The formidable fir-coated mountains and ancient lakes that (literally) set the region apart also grace it with some of the most beautiful natural scenery in Albania, especially in the winter when the landscapes glitter beneath a blanket of fresh snow. A cultural crossroads for thousands of years, Southeastern Albania was already settled by Neolithic peoples eight millennia ago – when agriculture was just reaching Europe – and its collections of medieval Orthodox art and architecture are the finest in the country.

Korça, the most dashing city in Albania, has the liveliest historic core of any city here year-round. Terracotta-roofed villas, Italianate mansions and Ottoman *konak*-style houses line leafy boulevards and cobblestone alleys. It is a city of museums, but not a museum city: locals and visitors gather to dine, drink and chat in the cafés and restaurants along **Bulevardi Republika** and in the **Korça Bazaar** (Pazari i Korçës) every night.

The journey from Tirana, now an easy one, is well worth it, and most of the Southeast's top sights can be reached from Korça on well-maintained roads in under an hour. In the north toward Dibra, **Shebeniku-Jabllanica National Park** (Parku Kombëtar Shebenik-Jabllanicë) is a playground for hikers, climbers and critter-spotters, and is part of a transnational UNESCO World Heritage Site of ancient forests. Travelling southeast, **Lake Ohrid** (Liqeni i Ohrit) and the **Prespa Lakes** (Liqenet e Prespës) both reward kayakers, campers, fishers and birdwatchers with cool, clear waters and soaring mountain panoramas. **Ohrid** (Albanian: Ohri or Ohër) was first settled at least 7900 years ago and preserves important Illyrian and paleo-Christian ruins, and today is one of the most laidback and budget-friendly beach destinations in Albania. Prespa reveals fascinating cave churches from the late Byzantine era. East and south of Korça, the crests, foothills, forests and farmlands of the **Morava** (Mali i Moravës) and **Gramos Mountain** (Mali i Gramozit) offer sumptuous views and fine food.

While Albania isn't short on evocative villages, the Southeast boasts some of its finest settlements, frozen in amber and exuding century-old charm thanks to mindful historic preservation. **Voskopoja**, a crucible of trade, learning and Orthodox faith in the eighteenth century, holds the grandest collection of post-Byzantine fresco art in Albania, if not the world. Iconography hidden or saved from the atheistic crackdown during communism now shines bright in Korça's **National Museum of Medieval Art** (Muzeu Kombëtar i Artit Mesjetar). The stately stone mansions of **Dardha** and **Rehova** are historic spaces in which to feast on traditional meals made from local ingredients. Lamb, goat, pastries, mulberries, cherries, honey, tea, wine and *raki* elevate the farm-to-table experience in agritourism stays from Morava south through **Kolonja**. Here, too, the **Vjosa River** (Lumi i Vjosa) shimmies onto the scene at the Albania-Greece

PRESPA LAKES

Highlights

1 Pazari i Korçës by night After dark, Korça's historic bazaar thrums with live music in trendy bars and traditional tavernas. See page 162

2 National Museum of Medieval Art The best and most diverse collection of Albanian Orthodox art shines a light on iconography – and helps you decipher it. See page 165

3 Pogradeci's art scene A laidback city with a gorgeous setting inspires artists to work (and play) in its lively studios and galleries. See page 174

4 Prespa Lakes Kayak to medieval cave churches on the most idyllic and unspoiled of the country's great lakes, then hike in the surrounding hills. See page 181

5 Boboshtica raki Rare and green in hue, mulberry *raki* is the most delicate expression of Albania's national spirit; try it in the restaurants and farmhouses of Boboshtica. See page 184

6 Frescoes of Voskopoja An eighteenth-century cosmopolis reduced to a village, Voskopoja conceals some of the Balkans' most magnificent frescoes inside its churches. See page 187

7 Kolonja farm stays The agritourism farms of the far southeast are a nature-lover's playground for hiking, camping, horseriding and, most of all, eating well. See page 192

HIGHLIGHTS ARE MARKED ON THE MAPS ON PAGES 158 AND 160

SOUTHEAST ALBANIA
N
Prevalla
Stebleva
SHEBENIKU-JABLLANICA NATIONAL PARK
Dorëz
Qerreti
Librazhdi
Botun
Brezhani
Veleshta
Ohrid St Paul the Apostle Airport
Struga
Ohrid
NORTH MACEDONIA
Spathar
Shkumbini
Sutaj
Xhyra
Rrajcë
SH3
A2
Lini
Resen
ELBASANI
Katjel
NATIONAL PARK GALICICA
Lake Ohrid
Monumental Tombs of Selca e Poshtme
Peshtani
Zavalina
REZERVAT NATYROR I MENAXHUAR "LIQENI POGRADECIT"
Krani
Driza
Bishnica
Poroçan
Ljubanishta
3
Kalivaçi
Pogradeci (Pogradec)
Tushemishti
PRESPA NATIONAL PARK
4
Lake Prespa
SH71
Gramshi
Dollna Gorica
Grabovica
Zamshë
Podgoria
Kodovajti
Stërkanji
Maja e Valamarës (2373m)
SH3
Devol
KORÇA
Pili
Small Prespa Lake
Zaroshka
Tomorrica
Moglica
Maliqi
Rëmbeci
Zëmblaku
Shipska
Church of St George
Plasa
Dushari
Monastery of St John the Baptist
MORAVA MOUNTAINS
Morava Cross
Korça
SH3
Krystallopigi
Bilishti
Voskopoja
6
Church of St Elijah
Gjerbësi
Maja Shëndëllisë (1365m)
Poloska
BERATI
5
Dërsniki
Boboshtica
Maja Faqekuqit (2352m)
Kamenica Tumulus
Vithkuqi
Leshnja
Polyánemo
Çorovoda
Dardha
SH72
Osumi
Vidohova
Panariti
Helmas
Maja Llofkës (1879m)
Trílofo
Qafzezi
Kaltanji
Osum
Nestório
Radovicka
GREECE
Erseka
Frashëri
Tsarka Petsik (2523m)
FIR OF HOTOVA-DANGËLLIA NATIONAL PARK
Këlcyra
Aetomilítsa
Néa Kotíli
SH75
Piskova
Barmashi
GRAMOZ MOUNTAINS
Plikáti
SH75
Vjosa
Lëngarica
Limari
Përmeti
7
GJIROKASTRA
Petrani
Mastorochória
Leusa
DHËMBELI MOUNTAIN
Erindi
Maja Zgurës (2091m)
Loutrá
Leskoviku
NEMËRÇKA MOUNTAIN
Poliçani
Maja e Papingut (2482m)
0
10
kilometres
Çarshova
HIGHLIGHTS
3 Pogradeci's art scene
4 Prespa Lakes
5 Boboshtica raki
6 Frescoes of Voskopoja
7 Kolonja farm stays

border, creating a fertile soil not only for growing ingredients but also for inspiring poets, linguists, educators, journalists and other intellectuals who formed part of the pro-independence **Albanian National Awakening**, or **Rilindja**.

Korça

The home of the first Albanian-language school, the first Albanian brewery and even, briefly, an early autonomous Albanian republic with its own coin mint, the city of **KORÇA** has long been ahead of the curve. More recently, Korça has enjoyed a decade-long revitalization while other urban centres are just catching up. The city is clean, green and has a thriving cultural and restaurant scene. The historic core gleams, with its cobblestone alleys and pedestrianized boulevards restored to their late nineteenth- and early-twentieth-century lustre. The villas, shops, schools and cafés of Korça's "**Little Paris**" era have transformed into museums, boutique hotels, restaurants, galleries and, again, cafés. The **Birra Korça** brewery, established in 1928, is still going strong.

About 165km southeast of Tirana by road, Korça has a population of around 130,000. The city sprawls across the **Korça Plain** (Fusha e Korçës), a flat basin sheltered by mountains. Don't be deceived, though: at about 870m above sea level, it sits at a higher altitude than Mendoza in the Argentinian Andes. Korça is Albania's only sizeable city that experiences regular snowfall. But in July and August, you'll relish the pleasantly cool evenings, a real reprieve if you're travelling in the high season.

The city plan is shaped like a half-moon, with the Morava Mountain (Mali i Moravës) rising immediately to the east behind Korça's **Martyrs' Cemetery** (Varrezat e Dëshmorëve). Most of its attractions are clustered in the **Old Bazaar** (Pazari i Vjetër), also called the Korça Bazaar (Pazari i Korçës); along **Bulevardi Republika** and the pedestrianized **Bulevardi Shën Gjergji**; and **Bulevardi Fan Noli**. From the bazaar area, you can walk to the end of Bulevardi Republika in about 25 minutes. You'll want at least a day to explore Korça on foot, more to visit all six of the city's **museums**. As many of Southeastern Albania's points of interest, from Ohrid in the north to Kolonja further south, are within an hour's bus ride, Korça is a natural base for exploring the region.

Brief history

Like Ohrid and Kolonja, the Korça Plain (Fusha e Korçës) has been inhabited since Neolithic times, but Korça city is new by European standards, a project of Ottoman Albanian military commander and governor **Iljaz Bej Mirahori** in the late fifteenth century. Born in this region, Iljaz rose to prominence in the Ottoman Empire, distinguishing himself in the 1453 Conquest of Constantinople, and was appointed head administrator of his home *sanjak* (district). He commissioned the Iljaz Bej Mirahori Mosque (Xhamia e Iljaz Mirahorit), finished in 1496, as well as a madrasa (place of study), a hammam and the bazaar. In the ensuing centuries, Korça mushroomed, especially after the destruction of Voskopoja in the late eighteenth century, making space for Albanians, Aromanians (Vlachs) and Greeks practicing both Islam and Orthodox Christianity.

The period of the **Albanian National Awakening** (Rilindja) and years following Albanian independence were especially turbulent – and prosperous. In 1845, Naum Veqilharxhi, a lawyer from nearby Vithkuqi, published an Albanian-language alphabet that could be taught to, and read by, anyone, in an early attempt to create a unified Albanian language (see page 290). This helped ignite intellectual fervour in Korça, and in 1887, a teacher and publisher named **Pandeli Sotiri** opened the first modern **Albanian-language school**, carefully navigating the strong misgivings of both Ottoman and Greek authorities. Other schools around the region and the future country rapidly followed.

Korçars began emigrating in droves to Bucharest, Vienna, Istanbul and Boston, sending money home to their families and spreading dangerous ideas about liberty and

Bus Terminal (International), ESP Group/Alvavel Office (250m)
KORÇA
N
Bus Terminal
Rruga 1 Maji
Rruga
Rruga Insan Korça
Markata e Shijes
Church of St Mary
St Mary's Flower Garden
Rruga Midhi Kostani
Rruga Kiço Greço
Rr. Kristo Luarasi
1 (2.3km)
DHL Service Point
Rruga Loni Llogori
Rruga Ajet Xhindolli
Rruga Viktimat e 7 Shkurtit
Teatri Andon Zako Çajupi
Sheshi i Teatrit
Rruga Kiço Greço
Rruga Edit Durham
Panoramic Tower
Pazari i Korçës
Korça Bazaar
Rr. Spase Pema
Rrugica Jovan Spiro Kosturi
Bulevardi Fan Noli
Rruga Ismail Qemali
Rruga Ajet Xhindolli
Rruga Nevruz Nure
Rr. Asllan Sala
Rruga Bari Zylali
Rrugica Jovan Spiro Kosturi
Rr. Asllan Sala
Rruga Insan Korça
Rrugica Ilia Avalea
Rruga Xhavit Dishnica
Clock Tower
Iljaz Bej Mirahori Mosque
Vangjush Mio Park
Rruga Sabaudin Kacidhja
Rruga Hamid Mani
Rruga Ramadan Isak
Rruga Floresha Myteveli
Rr. Mehmet Afezolli
Rruga Vangjel Koçi Lemi
Rruga Mehmet Afezolli
Police Station
Rruga Xhafer Cenko Lubonja
Rruga 28 Nëntori
Rruga Bajram Curri
Rruga Iliaz Bej Mirahori
Rruga 6 Deshmoret
Rruga Riza Cerova
Rruga Demir Progri
Intermedical Clinic
Rr. Don Gjok Buzuku
Rruga Gaqo Qeleshi
Rruga Qybra Sokoli
Rr. 28 Nëntori
Rruga Kristaq Prifti
SHOPPING
Etnoart 2
Studio Romeo Kallço 3
Thurje Handmade 1
Vasi Kolevica Art Studio 4
EATING
FindFour 3
Fix si Qëmoti 4
Mësonjëtorja 6
Mik Mak 2
Shtëpia e Birrës 7
Taverna Vasili 1
Vila Borgjeze 5
DRINKING & NIGHTLIFE
C'era Una Volta Pub & Bar 1
Sa!kõ Cocktail Bar 2
Vila Alketi 3
ACCOMMODATION
At Home Hostel 6
Bujtina Leon 8
Hani i Gjelit Hotel 4
Hani i Pazarit Boutique Hotel 3
Hotel Pazari & Apartments 7
Park Plazza 2
Shtëpia e Kuajve (House of Horses) 1
Trésor Art Boutique 5
Kamenica Tumulus (10km)

4

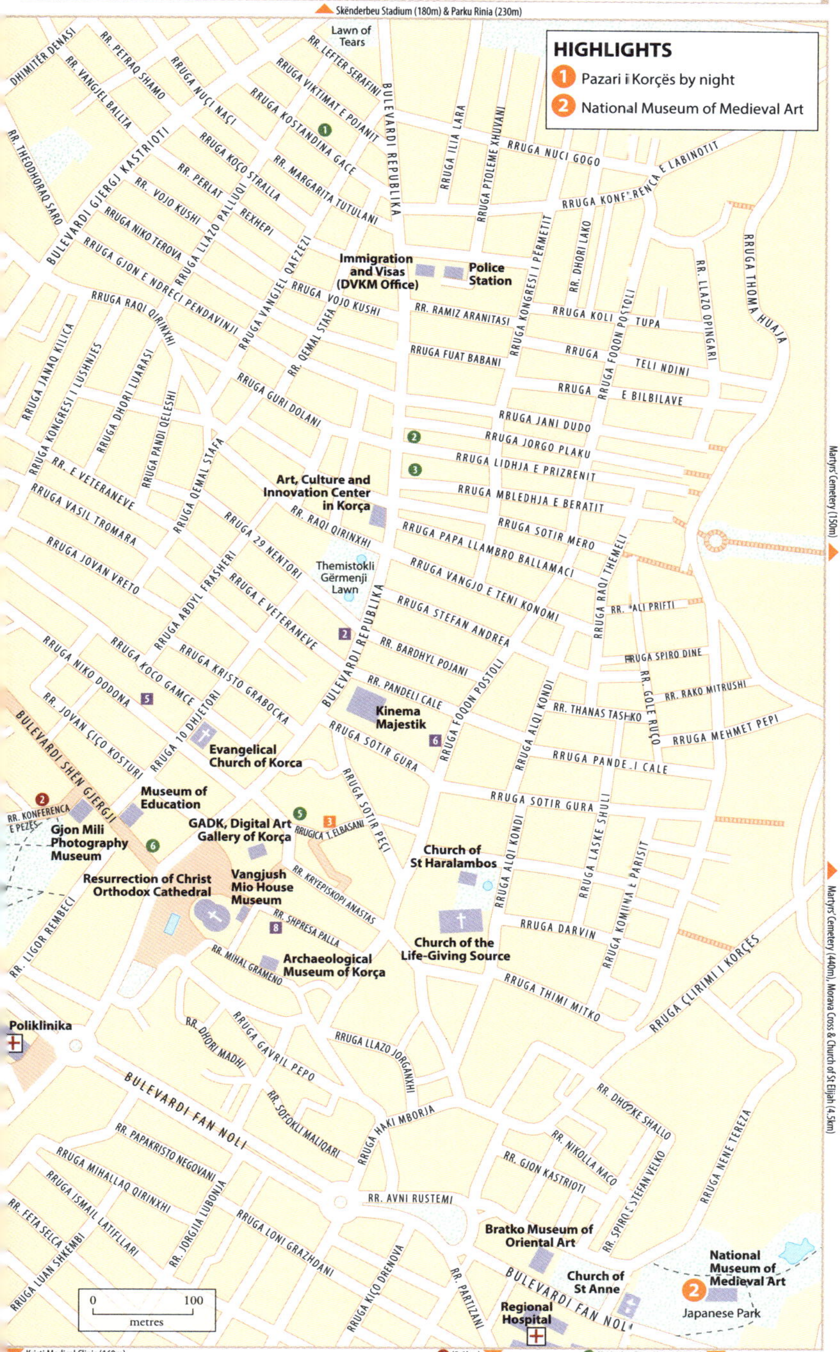

Skënderbeu Stadium (180m) & Parku Rinia (230m)
HIGHLIGHTS
1 Pazari i Korçës by night
2 National Museum of Medieval Art
Lawn of Tears
Immigration and Visas (DVKM Office)
Police Station
Art, Culture and Innovation Center in Korça
Themistokli Gërmenji Lawn
Kinema Majestik
Evangelical Church of Korca
Museum of Education
Gjon Mili Photography Museum
GADK, Digital Art Gallery of Korça
Resurrection of Christ Orthodox Cathedral
Vangjush Mio House Museum
Archaeological Museum of Korça
Church of St Haralambos
Church of the Life-Giving Source
Poliklinika
Bratko Museum of Oriental Art
Church of St Anne
Regional Hospital
National Museum of Medieval Art
Japanese Park
Martyrs' Cemetery (150m)
Martyrs' Cemetery (440m), Morava Cross & Church of St Elijah (4.5km)
4
Kristi Medical Clinic (160m)
4 (2.1km)
7 (240m); Birra Korça (270m)
0 100 metres
DHIMITËR DENASI
RR. PETRAQ SHAMO
RR. VANGJEL BALLTA
RR. THEODHORAQ SARO
RRUGA NUÇI NAÇI
RR. LEFTER SERAFINI
RRUGA VIKTIMAT E POJANIT
RRUGA KOSTANDINA GACE
RRUGA KOÇO STRALLA
RR. MARGARITA TUTULANI
BULEVARDI REPUBLIKA
RRUGA ILIA LARA
RRUGA PTOLEME XHUVANI
RRUGA NUCI GOGO
RRUGA KONFERENCA E LABINOTIT
BULEVARDI GJERGJ KASTRIOTI
RR. PERLAT REXHEPI
RR. VOJO KUSHI
RRUGA NIKO TEROVA
RRUGA LLAZO PALLUQI
RRUGA GJON E NDRECI PENDAVINJI
RRUGA VANGJEL QAFEZEZI
RRUGA VOJO KUSHI
RR. QEMAL STAFA
RR. RAMIZ ARANITASI
RRUGA KONGRESI I PERMETIT
RR. DHORI LAKO
RRUGA KOLI TUPA
RRUGA FOQON POSTOLI
RR. LLAZO OPINGARI
RRUGA THOMA HUAJA
RRUGA FUAT BABANI
RRUGA TELI NDINI
RRUGA E BILBILAVE
RRUGA RAQI QIRINXHI
RRUGA JANAQ KILICA
RRUGA KONGRESI I LUSHNJES
RRUGA DHORI LUARASI
RRUGA PANDI QELESHI
RRUGA QEMAL STAFA
RRUGA GURI DOLANI
RRUGA JANI DUDO
RRUGA JORGO PLAKU
RRUGA LIDHJA E PRIZRENIT
RRUGA MBLEDHJA E BERATIT
RR. E VETERANEVE
RRUGA VASIL TROMARA
RRUGA JOVAN VRETO
RRUGA 29 NENTORI
RR. RAQI QIRINXHI
RRUGA PAPA LLAMBRO BALLAMACI
RRUGA SOTIR MERO
RRUGA RAQI THEMELI
RRUGA VANGJO E TENI KONOMI
RRUGA ABDYL FRASHERI
RRUGA E VETERANEVE
RRUGA STEFAN ANDREA
RR. ALI PRIFTI
RR. BARDHYL POJANI
RRUGA SPIRO DINE
RRUGA NIKO DODONA
RRUGA KOCO GAMCE
RRUGA KRISTO GRABOCKA
RR. PANDELI CALE
RRUGA FOQON POSTOLI
RRUGA ALQI KONDI
RR. THANAS TASHKO
RR. GOLE RUÇO
RR. RAKO MITRUSHI
RRUGA MEHMET PEPI
RR. JOVAN ÇIÇO KOSTURI
RRUGA 10 DHJETORI
RRUGA SOTIR GURA
RRUGA PANDE I CALE
BULEVARDI SHEN GJERGJI
RR. KONFERENCA E PEZES
RRUGA SOTIR PEÇI
RRUGICA T. ELBASANI
RRUGA LASKE SHULI
RR. KRYEPISKOPI ANASTAS
RRUGA ALQI KONDI
RRUGA KOMUNA E PARISIT
RR. LIGOR REMBECI
RR. SHPRESA PALLA
RRUGA DARVIN
RR. MIHAL GRAMENO
RRUGA THIMI MITKO
RRUGA ÇLIRIMI I KORÇËS
RR. DHORI MADHI
RRUGA GAVRIL PEPO
RRUGA LLAZO JORGANXHI
BULEVARDI FAN NOLI
RR. SOFOKLI MALIQARI
RRUGA HAKI MBORJA
RR. DHOSKE SHALLO
RR. NIKOLLA NACO
RR. GJON KASTRIOTI
RR. SPIRO STEFAN VELKO
RRUGA NENE TEREZA
RR. PAPAKRISTO NEGOVANI
RRUGA MIHALLAQ QIRINXHI
RRUGA ISMAIL LATIFLLARI
RR. FETA SELCA
RRUGA LUAN SHKEMBI
RR. JORGJIA LUBONJA
RRUGA LONI GRAZHDANI
RR. AVNI RUSTEMI
RRUGA KIÇO DRENOVA
RR. PARTIZANI
BULEVARDI FAN NOLI

nationalism. Following Albania's **declaration of independence**, Greece, Bulgaria and France occupied Korça in quick succession in the heat of **World War I**. Finally, Albanian fighters managed to negotiate the creation of the coin-minting **Autonomous Albanian Republic of Korça** (Republika Autonome Shqiptare e Korçës) in 1916, led by activist and Rilindja leader Themistokli Gërmenji under French protection. Korça became an industrial powerhouse during the communist period, though its religious institutions were stamped out and many of its emigrants never had the chance to return home. But the city's uniquely strong international ties, particularly to the United States and France, persisted. In 1994, descendants of the Korça diaspora helped fund the construction of the Resurrection of Christ Orthodox Cathedral (Katedralja Ortodokse Ringjallja e Krishtit), among the largest in the country, signalling the return of religious freedom to Albania. Korça's ongoing renaissance got underway soon after.

Korça Bazaar

The original city centre no longer functions as a marketplace, but it is the buzziest of Albania's historic bazaar districts. Once the frenzied stomping ground of around a thousand vendors buying and selling from Ottoman, Greek and Venetian merchants, **Korça Bazaar** (Pazari i Korçës) now comes alive at night. Restored nineteenth-century caravanserais (roadside inns) have been reimagined as luxe hotels, and the main square is surrounded by chic bars, lounges and family-friendly eateries. Bars play international and Albanian pop and rock from the 1980s, 1990s and today. Swing by on public holidays, at the weekend and during Korça's many festivals to experience the square in its element, packed with revellers and filled with live music. Together with the cluster of streets behind the nearby **Resurrection of Christ Orthodox Cathedral** (Katedralja Ortodokse Ringjallja e Krishtit), the Pazari i Korçës neighbourhood has the finest nineteenth-century Ottoman architecture in Southeastern Albania. It's particularly worth a peek into the fine courtyard of what is now **Hani i Pazarit Boutique Hotel**.

Iljaz Bej Mirahori Mosque

Rruga Floresha Myteveli 12 at Rruga Asim Voksha • Free • www.facebook.com/xhamiailjazbejmirahori

Like many Albanians of his time, Iljaz Bej Mirahori joined the Ottoman military; unlike others, he married a daughter of Sultan Mehmed II. Iljaz was eventually granted administration of the Korça region and is said to have lived past 100 years of age, long enough to see his mosque completed in 1496. Among the oldest

SERENATA KORÇARE

All you really need for a **serenata** (serenade) is a guitar and a heart full of yearning. Korça's most famous homegrown folk music, the *serenata* (sometimes *serenatë*) started gaining popularity in the 1920s and has since established itself as a lasting genre: Songs about heartbreak, desire, pain, grief and lasting turned out to be particularly resonant throughout the turmoil and hardship of twentieth-century Albania.

The traditional calling for a *serenata* would have supposedly been on the street, in the snow, under the balcony of a woman one pines for – an allegedly successful way of wooing Korçare girls a century ago. Today, *serenatas* are usually performed by duos and trios – men and women – with guitars and mandolins, in tavernas around Korça and villages like **Dardha** (see page 185) and **Boboshtica** (see page 184). The venues around the bazaar bring in singers regularly, and **Birrari Panda** (Bulevardi Fan Noli next to the National Museum of Medieval Art; www.facebook.com/Birrari) schedules acts every weekend. The restaurant at the **Barba Boutique Hotel** is another good place to catch a performance (Rruga Antoni Athanas and Rruga Ilia Mitrusha; tel: 069 249 2755), as is the **Alpin House Restaurant** (SH90 between Boboshtica and Dardha; tel: 069 316 2484).

buildings standing in Korça – and one of the oldest mosques in Albania – the **Iljaz Bej Mirahori Mosque** (Xhamia e Iljaz Mirahorit) is a terrifically preserved specimen of early Ottoman architecture, almost entirely original. Only the lead covering of the domes, an innovation to protect from inclement weather, was added a century later, and the building survived the 1960 earthquake that brought down both the minaret and eighteenth-century clock tower, as well as its misuse as a warehouse during communism. Peer inside to see **eighteenth-century fresco work** preserved in the dome and interior corner vaults. The tombs of Iljaz and his family were destroyed during the multiple Greek occupations of Korça between 1912 and 1916, but the clock tower was rebuilt in 2015.

Bulevardi Republika and Bulevardi Shën Gjergji

From the bazaar, cross Bulevardi Fan Noli and head east on Rruga Edit Durham, and you'll reach **Theatre Square** (Sheshi i Teatrit) one block away. The red-capped stone slab here is the **Panoramic Tower** (Kulla Panoramike), which you can climb to the top for a fine vantage point. On the east side, the **Andon Zako Çajupi Theatre** (Teatri Andon Zako Çajupi) is a curious edifice affixed with the masks of Comedy (looking devious) and Tragedy (looking annoyed at Comedy). Exit the square onto **Bulevardi Shën Gjergji**, a tree-shaded pedestrian street lined with municipality offices, museums, restaurants, crêperies and ice-cream stands. The first thing you'll see on the boulevard is a 1:1 scale outline, on the ground, of a church facade. It's a reminder of the Korça that didn't survive: on this site, the **Church of St George** (Kisha e Shën Gjergjit) stood until it was torn down following the Hoxha regime's antireligion edicts of 1967.

4

Bulevardi Shën Gjergji culminates at the **Unknown Soldier** (Ushtari i Panjohur) statue and then hits Bulevardi Republika, a leafy thoroughfare that's been the main drag of the city for over a century. In the 1920s and 1930s heyday of Korça, citizens would dress in their evening finest and promenade up and down the street, and it remains a choice avenue for swanning and gawking. Korçars flaunted their wealth here, too, and many of the Italianate houses of the well-heeled crowd remain. Walking north, you'll pass a few landmarks: At Bulevardi Republika 12, the **Kinema Majestik** is the most obvious testament to Korça's American connection, an Art Deco-style movie theatre built in the late 1920s. **Themistokli Gërmenji Lawn** (Lulishtja Themistokli Gërmenji) honours the guerilla fighter-turned-statesman with a statue. Trendy hotels, restaurants and bar-lounges cluster along the rest of the boulevard to the **Lawn of Tears** (Lëndina e Lotëve), formerly the city's fringes. When husbands and sons departed for faraway places to find work, their families would bid farewell to them here.

Gjon Mili Photography Museum

Rruga Konferenca e Pezës and Bulevardi Shën Gjergji • Charge • www.facebook.com/p/Muzeu-i-Fotografisë-Gjon-Mili-100064703288057

Housed in a 1930s Romanian Revival-style mansion, the **Gjon Mili Photography Museum** (Muzeu Gjon Mili) celebrates the life and work of Albanian-American photographer Gjon Mili. Born in Korça in 1904, Mili was both an experimental and popular photographer in his four-decade career, mostly published in the American magazine, *Life*. A graduate of the Massachusetts Institute of Technology (MIT), Mili helped pioneer the use of flash and strobe-lit photography for capturing moving objects The most arresting photos in this small but interesting gallery capture ballerinas, gymnasts, actors and jugglers in stop-motion sequences – a revolutionary style in the 1940s.

Museum of Education

Bulevardi Shën Gjergji and Rruga 10 Dhjetori • Charge • www.facebook.com/MuzeuiArsimit

You'll likely hear or read about Albanian schools a few times on your travels here. What's the fuss? During the *Rilindja*, leaders recognized the importance of passing on the stories, values and culture of an Albanian identity if the dream of a nation were ever to be achieved. Ottoman and Greek powers-that-be recognized it too, and the first Albanian educators undertook a dangerous mission.

The first modern Albanian-language school opened in this building in 1887, now the **Museum of Education** (Muzeu i Arsimit). Through original textbooks, audio-recordings, photos and personal effects of teacher-directors like **Pandeli Sotiri**, **Petro Nini Luarasi** and sisters **Sevasti** and **Parashqevi Qiriazi**, the museum traces the founding of the school, its challenges and the lives of some notable alums. Notably, when the school opened, it emphasized a secular education, and boys, girls, Christians, Muslims, rich and poor students learned side by side – mixing religions in school was not just progressive but illegal. Appropriately, the museum is dense with information (in English) and a little overwhelming for those not already invested in the topic, but it's worth a short visit to get up to speed on an achievement that remains a point of pride for Albanians today.

Around the cathedral and Bulevardi Fan Noli

The centrepiece of Korça, **the Resurrection of Christ Orthodox Cathedral** (Katedralja Ortodokse Ringjallja e Krishtit), rises above its neighbours on the east side of Bulevardi Republika. Fronted by a plaza, the cathedral is a few steps from Shën Gjergji and Bulevardi Fan Noli, making it the hinge point of the city. From the intersection of Republika and Fan Noli, you can walk the latter about 1km east to the **Birra Korça** brewery. In this southeast corner of the city, a warren of impressive early-nineteenth-century Ottoman *konak* houses conceals the **Vangjush Mio House Museum** (Vangjush Mio Shtëpia e Muze) and the **Church of the Life-Giving Source** (Kisha Burimi Jetëdhënës), once the city's magnificent metropolitan church, now slowly being reconstructed after its partial demolition around 1980. Catch construction workers at the entrance (Rruga Sotir Peçi and Rruga Thimi Mitko) on their lunch break, and they'll let you in to take a glimpse at the shell of the lofty nave, whose stones are etched with the history of Orthodoxy in Albania. As Bulevardi Fan Noli pushes east, the historic centre gives way to the newer city and one of Albania's cultural big-hitters – the **National Museum of Medieval Art** (Muzeu Kombëtar i Artit Mesjetar). After, unwind with a visit to the historic **Birra Korça factory** down the street, which gives free guided tours and tastings until 2pm (Bulevardi Fan Noli 1; www.birrakorca.com.al), or head to its **Shtëpia e Birrës** beer garden (see page 169).

Resurrection of Christ Orthodox Cathedral

Bulevardi Republika • Free • www.mitropoliaeshenjtekorce.com

Construction on Korça's new **Resurrection of Christ Orthodox Cathedral** (Katedralja Ortodokse Ringjallja e Krishtit) began in 1994 to replace the cathedrals that had been crippled or toppled in the preceding decades. A towering **Byzantine Revival** structure in buttery stone with terracotta domes and trim, the basilica is almost always open for the devout and the curious to stop in, and Albania's most venerated saints are splashed across the frescoes up and down the golden walls of the nave, aisles and apses. But the church and its square really come alive during Christmas (*Krishtlindje*) and, especially, Easter (*Pashkë*), when a city-wide procession arrives to watch a solemn liturgy that erupts into bells, cheers and fireworks at midnight.

GADK, Digital Art Gallery of Korça

Bulevardi Republika and Rruga Kryepiskopi Anastas, behind the library • Charge • www.gadk.al

The imaginative **GADK**, or **Digital Art Gallery of Korça** (Galeria e Arteve Digjitale Korçë), opened in 2024 in the former city archives building. Twenty-minute audiovisual shows unfold on the walls, ceiling and floor as you sit or walk around. The immersive experiences take you on a journey through a show of your choice, for example, 'Van Gogh' or 'Albanian Iconography: The Great Masters'. It's great for kids who might grow bored of too much of the real thing. The space also hosts piano concerts, poetry nights and other cultural events.

Vangjush Mio House Museum

Rruga Spiro Ballkameni • Charge • www.instagram.com/vangjushmiomuseum

Vangjush Mio, alongside Androniqi Antoniu and her sister Sofia Papadhimitri, was among the first Impressionist painters in Albania, all born in Korça and celebrated during their lifetimes. Mio's house and studio survives, renovated by his daughter in 2010. Directly behind the cathedral, the **Vangjush Mio House Museum** (Vangjush Mio Shtëpia e Muze) displays oil paintings and drawings made by the artist between 1915 and his death in 1957, including still lifes, landscapes of Korça, and lots of nudes. Only open on weekends.

Archaeological Museum of Korça

Rruga Mihal Grameno 19 • Charge • www.facebook.com/arkeologjiakorce

An 1842 *konak* behind the cathedral houses the region's **Archaeological Museum of Korça** (Muzeu Arkeologjik i Korçës). Unfortunately, at the time of writing, it's in very shabby condition compared to Korça's other museums. The small collection encompasses artifacts from eight thousand years ago to the thirteenth century AD, as well as some interesting photos of early excavations in the Korça Plain. The Neolithic displays, including bone and ceramic tools and vessels are the most interesting, and there's a pair of skeletons from the **Tumulus of Kamenica** (Tuma e Kamenicës), if you don't have a chance to visit that site (see page 166).

4

Bratko Museum of Oriental Art

Bulevardi Fan Noli 57 • Charge • www.facebook.com/Bratkomuseumoforientalart

The idiosyncratic **Bratko Museum of Oriental Art** (Muzeu i Artit Oriental Bratko) presents the collection of Albanian-American photographer **Dhimitër Mborja**. Fascinated by Asian cultures, Mborja collected Chinese silk screens, Hindu and Buddhist statuettes and a suit of samurai armour. But if you didn't come to Albania to see Asian art, focus on Mborja's own photos instead. Working with the UN in the aftermath of World War II, he captured scenes of General Douglas MacArthur and the postwar rebuilding effort in Japan.

National Museum of Medieval Art

Bulevardi Fan Noli 59 • Charge • www.facebook.com/MuzeuiArtitMesjetar • Tours via audioguide and app ('MKAM' in the Google Play Store and Apple App Store)

This is Korça's cultural heavyweight, a treasure trove of Albanian religious art unrivalled in the country. The avant-garde contemporary **National Museum of Medieval Art** (Muzeu Kombëtar i Artit Mesjetar) opened in 2016, though the museum has existed since 1980. The permanent exhibition is tightly focused and highly informative: four hundred objects on display, mostly icons, spanning six hundred years, from the thirteenth through the nineteenth centuries. The highlights of the collection are unquestionably the icons of the **post-Byzantine masters**, with **Onufri**, **Kostandin Shpataraku** and brothers **Kostandin and Athanas Zografi** (see page 188) especially well represented. But other works help to fill in the gaps, telling the story of an Orthodox artistic tradition that was often hard to maintain under Ottoman dominion; more primitive and derivative works are also given space here. If you, understandably, find it hard to distinguish stylistic differences between various Orthodox icons and frescoes, the information labels are fantastically instructive.

The museum continues to receive and restore artworks discovered around Albania, hidden beneath floorboards or blackened and turned into doors during communism. If you plan to explore the country's historic Orthodox churches, the exhibitions here will help you slot together the pieces of the cultural jigsaw. The total collection of eight thousand pieces, some of which are rotated regularly, draws on pieces from **Voskopoja**, **Vithkuqi**, **Prespa** and **Kolonja**, nearby, as well as **Berati**, **Elbasani**, **Delvina** and beyond.

After the impressive two-storey Golden Hall, the museum follows a chronological path. The first balcony displays Byzantine icons painted before the Ottoman conquest, and a standout is the *Archangel Michael*, depicted in full battle armour, the commander of his celestial army. Then you're on to Onufri, and many of his most intricate scenes are here. The *Nativity of Christ*, *Baptism of Christ* and *Descent to Hell* show the maestro's fearlessness with colour and contrast. Eccentric secondary details feel like Easter eggs: in the corner of the *Baptism*, Poseidon, mounted on a pink dolphin, looks on despondently. Across the hall, a collection from the **Church of the Archangels** (Kisha e Shën Mëhillit; see page 191) in Vithkuqi offers a contrast from later, seventeenth-century artists – the portraiture is simple, the perspective is flat and the colour palette is more limited.

Finally, admire the complete nineteenth-century iconostasis from the **Church of St Nicholas** (Kisha e Shën Nikollës; see page 193) in Rehova, but linger with the portable icons of the **Zografi brothers**, by turns action-packed and emotive.

Beyond the centre

On the **outskirts** of the city and within a few kilometres' drive, Korça has one of the better urban parks in Albania, the affecting **Martyrs' Cemetery**, and one of the largest and oldest **burial sites** in the country – the only one of its kind you can easily visit.

4

Rinia Park

Bulevardi Rilindasit • Free

Korça's **Rinia Park** (Parku Rinia), which translates as Youth Park, isn't just for kids. If you're strapped for time and won't be able to venture into Albania's remote wilderness, then come here for an autumn stroll or a splash through winter slush and snow. It might scratch the nature itch – just. Fountains and pines abound, but also be sure to check out the procession of modern sculptures on Bulevardi Rilindasit, both formal and fantastical. A new one is added every year.

Martyrs' Cemetery

Rruga Konferenca e Labinotit • Free

The stairs ascending to the **Martyrs' Cemetery**, Korça's monument and memorial to its World War II fallen begin just 300m east of Bulevardi Republika via Rruga Mbledhja e Beratit, but the burial site feels a world away from the bustling boulevard. A larger-than-life statue of a soldier with fist upraised stands in the centre, surrounded by the graves of Korçar partisans killed during the fight against Axis occupation. Like many communist-era memorials, this one is not well maintained; watch your step if you take the staircase. At the southeast corner of the graveyard, you can exit to a **trail** that leads up into the **Morava Mountain** (Mali i Moravës) for the best panorama of the city and the Korça Plain you'll find anywhere. It follows Rruga Çlirimi i Korçës until the foot of the mountain, where the road curves away while the trail veers north, then southeast, up one of Morava's ridges to the giant **Morava Cross** (Kryqi i Moravës), a huge post-communist landmark, and a small chapel. It's about a 3.4km hike each way and takes around an hour to climb to the summit. You can also drive there.

A few longer, more arduous treks up the western slope of Morava can be undertaken from trailheads in the village of **Drenova**, 5km southeast of Korça via the SH75; follow signs.

Tumulus of Kamenica

10.5km south of Korça by road on the SH75, Kamenica village; follow signs • Charge • Drive or take a taxi 15min

The **Tumulus of Kamenica** (Tuma e Kamenicës) is one of the biggest *tumuli* (mound burials) excavated in the Balkans. The earliest burials found here date to the thirteenth century BC, and more than four hundred graves and 440 skeletons have been discovered. The tumulus itself requires a stroke of imagination to appreciate, but the **museum** displaying and explaining its finds is an eye-opener. Skeletons and replicas of grave goods are laid out, and informational panels highlight what they revealed to archaeologists. One skull had a wound from trepanation, primitive cranial surgery, but the lesion had healed, meaning the individual survived the procedure.

ARRIVAL AND DEPARTURE — KORÇA

By bus or minibus The intercity bus station on Rruga Midhi Kostani, near the intersection with SH75, has direct lines to most decent-sized Albanian cities, plus local village lines to Voskopoja, Vithkuqi and Pusteci (Prespa). It's about 700m (10min walk) from the bazaar area via Rruga Kiço Greco. You can also find taxis and city buses here.

Destinations Berati (several daily; 4hr); Durrësi (many daily; 3hr 40min); Elbasani (many daily; 2hr 15min); Erseka (many daily; 55min); Fieri (several daily; 4hr); Gjirokastra (1 daily; 4hr 20min); Leskoviku (several daily; 2hr); Librazdhi (many daily; 1hr 50min); Lushnja (several daily; 3hr 20min); Përmeti (several daily, 3hr 15min); Pogradeci (many daily; 50min); Pusteci (1 daily; 35 min); Saranda (1 daily; 5hr 20min); Tirana (many daily; 3hr); Vithkuqi (1 daily; 40min); Vlora (1 daily; 4hr 40min); Voskopoja (several daily; 30min).

Around 250m up the SH3, there's another bus station at Rruga Muzakajt 17, which connects Korça with international destinations, outside the ESP Group/Alvavel office. Destinations include Thessaloniki, Athens and Istanbul. You can purchase ESP/Alvavel tickets in person or try an agency by phone. Alvavel (tel: 08 224 2847), Metro-Euro (tel: 08 224 5111), Arjani Travel (tel: 068 482 5926) and Alba-Trans (tel: 069 406 0001) are options.

By car Traffic coming into Korça from Tirana and Pogradeci via the SH3 from the northwest is generally light compared to other cities in Albania, as is traffic coming in from Erseka to the south via the SH75. Highways in both directions are in good shape overall but require tackling a few tight mountain switchbacks. Some drivers take them fast.

GETTING AROUND

You won't need more than your own two feet to explore Korça but finding a reliable taxi or renting a car for a couple of days makes the broader region more accessible to you.

By bus The urban buses in Korça run along the major traffic arteries, including Rruga Kiço Greco, Rruga Fan Noli and Bulevardi Gjergj Kastrioti, making stops near the intercity bus station, the bazaar area and Birra Korça, among others.

By car If driving, stick to the main arteries and avoid routes that take you into small cobblestone streets. Finding parking on the Bulevardi Republika can be a challenge; Bulevardi Fan Noli is easier. In the Pazari i Korçës zone, there's inexpensive 24hr paid parking at Rruga Ajet Gjindolli and Rruga Rexhep Satka, and also at Rrugica Skënder Çaci and Rrugica Jovan Spiro Kosturi (tel: 069 214 6845). Your best bet is to ask your hotel for tips on where to park.

Reputable car-rental agencies include Makina me Qera Eiffel (Rruga Pandeli Vangjeli 10; tel: 069 574 0100), Makina me Qera Andrea (Bulevardi Gjergj Kastrioti and Rruga Raqi Qirinxhi; tel: 069 976 2903) and Enterprise (Bulevardi Republika and Rruga Kajo Karafili; tel: 067 600 0900).

By taxi Buses do not serve the Morava villages – Drenova, Boboshtica, Dardha and Sinica – at all, and there is only one bus service a day to the Prespa area and to Vithkuqi. However, all are within a 45min drive of Korça, and most city cabs will take you for a reasonable price. If you're leaving the city for a few hours or the day, be sure to communicate that to your driver, and arrange any necessary return trips and confirm prices in advance, especially if you're heading to Prespa or Vithkuqi, where there are fewer restaurants or hotels to help if you get stuck. You can call or message a reliable service like Taxi Pali (tel: 069 893 6811) to make arrangements ahead. Otherwise, find taxis on Rruga Midhi Kostani in front of the main bus station. There's also a more central taxi stand near Sheshi i Teatrit on Rruga Edit Durham.

By bike Korça has expansive parks and well-paved roads leading to charming villages in every direction. Biking is encouraged and the municipality even put together nineteen routes of the city and region for cyclists (www.issuu.com/bashkiakorce/docs/korca_bike_print_fin_eng_2_opt_opt).

INFORMATION

Tourist information The tourist information centre is located in Sheshi i Teatrit, next to the Panoramic Tower (Kulla Panoramike). It is supposed to reopen in 2025 with staff to provide maps and brochures for information and attractions in the city and the nearby villages (tel: 08 225 7803). There's a city map on the exterior of the building, and QR codes provide maps of cycling routes. If the office is closed, you can pivot to Bulevardi Shën Gjergji and take the stairs at the outline of the church to the *bashkia* (town hall), where someone should be able to rustle up some materials for you.

Websites www.facebook.com/p/korca-Tourism-61554081772703; www.instagram.com/korcatourism; www.linktr.ee/bashkiakorce; www.bashkiakorce.gov.al.

TOUR OPERATORS

Korça Alpin (AvenTour Albania) A nonprofit with an emphasis on environment stewardship in the Korça region and beyond, Korça Alpin marks and maintains trails and cleans up litter. The group's travel arm, AvenTour Albania (Rrugica Jovan Spiro Kosturi and Rrugica Ilia Avalea; www.aventouralbania.com), has put together packages in the Korça region with a focus on trekking, biking, climbing, kayaking and yoga near villages like Vithkuqi, Voskopoja and Bozdoveci.

Korça Free Walking Tours Travel pro Juxhin Shishko set up shop in his hometown in 2021 and now offers the definitive free walking tour of the city, both informative and entertaining. Shishko also leads day-trips to Voskopoja and Prespa (www.facebook.com/KorçaFreeWalkingTour).

ACCOMMODATION

SEE MAP PAGE 160

Korça has the full gamut of family-run guesthouses, backpacker hostels, business hotels and a few genuinely unique and splurge-worthy experiences. During the high season, prices stay well below those of Tirana and the coast; doubles can be found for under €80 in all but the swankiest spots. However, Korça also sees higher demand during autumn and winter, and prices and availability reflect that.

At Home Hostel Rruga Foqon Postoli 68; www.instagram.com/athomehostelsince2011. With three- and four-bed dorms, both women-only and mixed, this is a convivial place to stay near the nightlife spots on Republika. There's a bar on site and a hammock, balcony, terrace and barbecue for communal use. Dorms €

Bujtina Leon Rruga Shpresa Palla 3; tel: 069 436 6504. A faithful reconstruction of an Ottoman *konak*, inside and out, this six-room guesthouse right behind the cathedral has rooms with wood-panelled ceilings, dark wood trim and intricate kilims on the floors. Parking, and breakfast in the courtyard under trellised grapevines, are included. Beds are very comfortable, and budget-minded solo travellers can book single rooms. €€

Hani i Gjelit Hotel Pazari i Korçës square; www.hanigjelit.com. A historic Italianate building right in the bustle of the main bazaar square, reimagined as a chic five-room hotel for comfort-conscious travellers or special-occasion stays. Some rooms have Jacuzzis and fireplaces, and all have excellent wi-fi and flatscreen TVs. €€€

Hani i Pazarit Boutique Hotel Pazari i Korçës and Bulevardi Fan Noli; www.hanipazarit.com. In a restored nineteenth-century Ottoman caravanserai (inn), this hotel has gained a reputation for outstanding service, cuisine and amenities in one of the city's most atmospheric locations. The balcony overlooks the courtyard where travellers 'checking in' two hundred years ago tethered their mules and horses. Rooms downstairs follow the contours of the stables, with exposed-brick barrel vaulting. The excellent restaurant on site frequently has live music. €€€

★ Hotel Pazari & Apartments Bulevardi Fan Noli and Rrugica Jovan Spiro Kosturi; www.hotelpazari.al. A modern, highly comfortable bolthole a cut above other hotels in its price bracket. With a friendly, helpful 24hr reception, free parking, fast wi-fi and breakfast included, it's a very fine base for exploring the city and region. Some rooms have balconies with mountain and city views. The company also rents apartments and villas for up to ten guests. €

Park Plazza Bulevardi Republika and Rruga 29 Nëntori; www.park-plazza.com. An international-style twenty-room hotel with a high standard of service and a reliable reputation, *Park Plazza* has the classic comforts you'd expect of a four-star: 24hr reception, fast wi-fi, LED-lit mirrors, an airport shuttle and most anything else you'd need to take care of business. €€€

★ Shtëpia e Kuajve (House of Horses) 2.9km from Korça west on SH3 (Rruga Desaretët), Turani village; tel: 069 470 7888. The passion project of a former champion jockey and horse trainer who moved back to his home village, this ranch is one of the best places to stay in the region for horseback riding, whether you're a first-timer or a cowboy. The hotel and stables have twelve rooms (for humans), thirty horses and a restaurant on site; the owners grow some of the produce and purchase other ingredients from neighbours in the village. You can arrange guided hour-long horseback jaunts, day-trips to a nearby waterfall and multiday horseback and camping excursions into the Voskopoja highlands. €€€

★ Trésor Art Boutique Rruga Niko Dodona 20; www.tresorartboutique.al. One of the ritziest postcodes in Korça, this seven-room hotel occupies a 1933 villa. Each room is unique, and the owners have restored original paintings by Zografi family members, descendants of the famous post-Byzantine painters (see page 188). Several bedrooms and sitting rooms are decorated with floor-to-ceiling trompe-l'œil scenes. The restaurant here serves steakhouse favourites like dry-aged Fiorentina and other cuts of beef that are typically hard to find in Albania. €€€€

4

EATING

SEE MAP PAGE 160

Many of Korça's hotels and guesthouses also operate top-flight restaurants on the premises, open to anyone; *Trésor Art Boutique* and *Hani i Pazarit* are standouts. The best of the rest includes traditional tavernas serving Korçar menus, plus a handful of spots that cater to more international tastes. High-quality dining remains relatively inexpensive. In Korça, as elsewhere, price and taste of decor don't necessarily correlate with taste of food.

★ FindFour Bulevardi Republika and Rruga Mbledhja e Beratit; tel: 067 622 2555. Four-floor *FindFour* is a beloved

KORÇA CUISINE

The hearty, rib-sticking food of the greater Korça region is reason alone to visit Southeastern Albania, and Korçar restaurants have been exported to Tirana, Durrësi and beyond. Individual villages have their own specialties, and Albanian favourites like roasted and grilled lamb, goat and chicken are as good as, or better than, anywhere else. But there are also region-specific dishes you need to try.

Lakror is the carb that powers Korça. You might think of *lakror* as the thin-crust pizza to *byrek*'s deep-dish pie. Two thin sheets of fresh dough are rolled precariously thin, with the filling of choice stuffed between them. Cheese, spinach, onions, tomatoes and potatoes are all classics. It's then cooked in an oven called a *saç* – an iron dome hung from a hook over a metal tray atop coals – until the *lakror* is crispy on the outside and gooey on the inside.

Kërnacë, or *kërnackë*, is a small sausage made from minced beef or pork mixed with onions, garlic and spices like oregano.

Petka (also called *rosnica*) is found throughout Albania, but you're most likely to see it in the casseroles of Korça and Kolonja. It's a simple pasta made from flour, eggs, milk and salt, dried for days and broken into small pieces. It's often served with chicken, eggplant or mushrooms.

Petanik is a type of *byrek* made with layers of noodles. In the region, the classic filling is *fasule*, boiled beans.

Trahana is the breakfast of champions here, and a bit like oatmeal in flavour and texture. The dough is made with either milk or *kos* (yogurt), dried, and sifted or crushed into a powder. Usually served in a bowl, it's then topped with either sweet or savoury additions: cheese, tomatoes, olives, raisins, fresh fruit, cinnamon, nuts, etc.

Korça and the surrounding villages have food festivals from summer till winter, most of which bring together some combination of local restaurants, food producers large and small, and live music performances. The main one to watch for, especially when making hotel bookings (reserve well in advance), is the **Festa e Birrës** (Korça Beer Fest) in August (www.festaebirres.com). Other fun ones include the **Festa e Lakrorit** (Lakror Festival) in the village of Polena, also in August; the **Festa e Mollës** (Apple Festival) in Dvorani in September/October; and the **Festivali i Dimrit** (Winter Festival) in Korça city throughout December, where you can chow down on baked apples and roasted chestnuts, and drink mulled wine.

4

all-day hangout for indoor and outdoor dining and drinking. Big, frothy cappuccinos; crispy waffles and crêpes; and sweet and savoury varieties of *trahana* (Albanian version of porridge) bring people in early. It's also a standout in for its vast menu of pizzas, pastas, pork ribs, Albanian standards, vegetarian dishes, well-crafted desserts and creative cocktails. In a restored Italianate mansion on Republika, it's scheduled to reopen in 2025 after a kitchen upgrade. €€

Fix si Qëmoti Pazari i Korçës square; www.fixpro.al/fix-si-qemoti. The *Fix* brand of packaged sandwich meats and sausages can be found in supermarkets throughout Albania, and the Korça-based company operates a few restaurants and deli counters in town too. This one, a mid-range family-friendly spot for meat lovers, has pride of place on the bazaar square. Order a platter of grilled chops, ribs and sausages in true Balkan fashion, or go a la carte. *Llukanik*, a highlands smoked sausage, is a good bet. You can also guarantee a decent burger here. €€

★ **Mësonjëtorja** Bulevardi Shën Gjergji; www.restorantmesonjetorja.com. Opened in 2024 next to the Museum of Education (Muzeu i Arsimit), *Mësonjëtorja* ('The School') plays homage to Korça history inside the former home of Pandeli Cale, a Korçar freedom fighter, mayor and signer of the Albanian Declaration of Independence. More adventurous dishes include *të brendëshme*, the Albanian platter of organ meats, but the mouthwatering house specialty is steamed pork belly and shank with dried apricots and walnuts. While you wait for your starter, peruse the archival photos of nineteenth-century Korça on the walls, a who's-who and what's-what of the old city. €€

Mik Mak Bulevardi Republika and Rruga Jorgo Plaku; tel: 069 523 2371. A fast-food stand on Bulevardi Republika, *Mik Mak* mainly does one thing, and it does it darn well: *lakror në saç* (see page 169). Hot, crispy and gooey with cheese, order to go and eat it in the park down the street. You can also opt for other traditional fillings like spinach, tomato or onion. €

Shtëpia e Birrës Bulevardi Fan Noli, entrance 70m west of Birra Korça's; www.birrakorca.com.al/restoranti. The 'Beer House' is the beer garden of home-grown brewery Birra Korça (see page 164). It's a Bavarian-sized outdoor space next to a gastropub, and the star of the show is, of course, the Birra Korça lineup: blonde, dark, '01' lager and golden ale are all on draft, and pints are poured for less than a euro. The pub fare – sausages, kebabs, fries – soaks up the excesses, and there's live music every night in summer. €

Taverna Vasili Rruga Kostandina Gaçe and Rruga Llazo Palluqi; www.facebook.com/taverna.vasili. A big space with big plates, this taverna spins all the hits. Come for *këmackë* (sausages), *petanik* (noodly byrek), *lakror* (pies), grilled pork, ribs, schnitzel, chicken and more, all washed down with Birra Korça. The service is convivial and the vibe is congenial, especially on Saturday nights when local musicians play live and loud. €€

★ **Vila Borgjeze** Rruga Kryepeshkopi Anastas off Bulevardi Republika; www.vilaborgjeze.com. An Italian-inspired steakhouse, *Vila Borgjeze* is in the running for Korça's best fine-dining spot. The grand building and its frescoes may strike you as a bit much, but the food is exceptional and not particularly pricey for the standard of food. The 'Hammer of Thor' is the restaurant's signature take on pork knuckle; baked and glazed to fall off the bone. Veal steak and racks of pork ribs are excellent choices, but the kitchen also makes sushi, if that's what you're craving. The hotel is just as luxe, with breakfast and room service from the kitchen. €€€

DRINKING AND NIGHTLIFE

SEE MAP PAGE 160

Like elsewhere in Albania, some of Korça's popular restaurants tend to blur the line with nightlife after 10pm or so. For more creative cocktails, music and dancing, head to the Pazari i Korçës, especially the square where live performances happen most weekends. But don't expect to find all-night parties or a club scene here.

★ **C'era Una Volta Pub & Bar** Pazari i Korçës square; https://www.facebook.com/nelondi. All about the music, *C'era Una Volta* has a full bar, beer on tap and stays open late (2am). On weekends, it's standing room only in the indoor-outdoor space, and Albanian pop and rock from the early 2000s gets the crowd singing along. On Fri, Sat and holidays, the bar books live acts and DJs. On quieter nights, you can enjoy the decor, as you won't see 'dive bar meets Ottoman-era bazaar stall' in many other establishments.

4

Sa!kō Cocktail Bar Rrugica Jovan Spiro Kosturi and Rrugica Ilia Avalea; www.instagram.com/saikococktailbar. *Sa!kō* is somewhere between tiki bar and sushi counter in vibe. Think rattan chairs and lampshades paired with tropical plants and vines, in an Italianate building near the bazaar square. The cocktails are more impressive in the glass than on the menu; the signature Sa!kō combines gin, lavender, lime juice and cream, garnished with a violet blossom, but bartenders are happy to share new concoctions too. Live music and DJs on weekends.

Vila Alketi Rruga Kryepeshkopi Anastas 50m east off Bulevardi Republika; www.instagram.com/bujtinaalketi. All dark wood and grey stone, with vintage photos, *qilims*, bicycles, record players, folk costumes, musical instruments, military helmets and, most of all, guns, stuffed in every cranny and hung on every wall, this is very much an old-school type of place for beer drinkers and hell raisers (there's a playground out front for them). It's also a decent restaurant.

ENTERTAINMENT

Qendra e Artit, Kulturës dhe Inovacionit në Korçës Bulevardi Republika and and Rruga 4 Shkurti; www.facebook.com/qak.korce.3. Inaugurated in 2024, the Art, Culture and Innovation Centre of Korça combines a gallery of visual art and a stage for folkloric and modern music and dance. It's also the new home of the Korça Symphony Orchestra.

Teatri Andon Zako Çajupi Sheshi i Teatrit; www.facebook.com/teatriAZKKorce. The place to go for drama, opera, comedy, orchestral music, ballet and classical concerts in Southeastern Albania. The curtain lifts for both Albanian and international compositions and performers. It's also simply called the Teatri Korçë.

SHOPPING

SEE MAP PAGE 160

Korça is not a great place to shop for trinkets, but it's a pretty good place to find high-quality original art and handicrafts – some traditional, some modern.

★ **Etnoart** Rruga Konferenca e Pezës and Bulevardi Shën Gjergji; www.instagram.com/lirikapojani_artcrafts. Among the best places in Albania to shop for traditional costumes, Etnoart opened in 2024 as the brick-and-mortar shop of designer Lirika Pojani. Buy embroidered vests and shirts, shawls, felt hats, knitted socks and other classic garments here, either ready-made or bespoke. Etnoart also features a small 'museum' with a tableau of a twentieth-century Albanian interior and mannequins fitted with Pojani's handiwork.

Studio Romeo Kallço Rrugica Ilia Avalea near Rrugica Jovan Spiro Kosturi; www.facebook.com/romeo.kallco. Korça artist Romeo Kallço is primarily an oil-on-canvas painter, but also works as a restorer of icons. Using thick, Impressionistic brushstrokes and vivid colours, he paints still lifes and landscapes but also city scenes, especially of Korça's historic plazas and hidden streets. Fantastic original art of the region, from the region.

Thurje Handmade Pazari i Korçës square; www.thurjehandmade.com. Specializing in rugs, Thurje's products are, indeed, made by hand, on looms right here in the shop. Designs are all originals by founder-sisters Mikaela and Xhorxhia Maçka, some incorporating traditional motifs.

Rugs, wall hangings and accessories are for sale, made from Albanian sheep wool, flaxseed and twine.

Vasi Kolevica Art Studio 3.4km southeast of Korça on Rruga e Drenovës; www.facebook.com/vasikolevicaart. Ceramic artist Vasillaq Kolevica throws vases, bowls, pots and sculptures large and small here, many glazed and painted in his trademark neon and pastel colours. Occasionally, the studio hosts arts workshops open to all too.

DIRECTORY

Banks and currency exchange Most of Albania's major banks have branches and ATMs right on Bulevardi Republika, between the intersection with Bulevardi Fan Noli and Themistokli Gërmenji Lawn (Lulishtja Themistokli Gërmenji); a few also have branches on Rruga Midhi Kostani between the bus station and Sheshi i Teatrit. There are also a handful of Western Unions, including one on Bulevardi Republika next to Credins Bank. Several currency exchanges are on Rruga Edit Durham, right between the bazaar area and Sheshi i Teatrit.

Emergencies Tel: 127 or tel: 112 for medical; tel: 129 or tel: 112 for police.

Hospital The biggest hospital in Southeastern Albania, the Spitali Rajonal Korçë is at Bulevardi Fan Noli 48 (tel: 08 224 2755), across the street from the National Museum of Medieval Art (Muzeu Kombëtar i Artit Mesjetar). General and specialist private clinics include Klinika Intermedical Korçë (Rruga 28 Nëntori and Rrugica Qamil Panariti; tel: 069 995 5773) and Klinika Mjekesore Kristi (KMK, Rruga Rexhep Telhaj/Kristaq Prifti 13, H.4; tel: 08 225 0771).

Immigration and visas For visa issues, visit the DVKM office on Bulevardi Republika and Rruga Dhimitër Rëmbeci; tel: 069 411 0259.

Pharmacies In the centre, there's an Orange Farmaci on Bulevardi Republika (tel: 069 403 0070) across the street from the cathedral, and several well-stocked pharmacies behind the hospital. Try Farmaci Nial (Rruga Todi Vogli and Rruga Kristaq Isak; tel: 069 549 1619).

Police The city police station is at Rruga Dhimitër Rembeci 4 (tel: 08 225 9100), next to the DVKM office, and the regional police station is at Rruga Floresha Myteveli 17 (tel: 08 224 2500), directly behind the Iljaz Bej Mirahori Mosque (Xhamia e Iljaz Mirahorit).

Post office There's a DHL service point at Bulevardi Gjergj Kastrioti, Pallati 2, Kati 1 (tel: 04 240 6666). The Posta Shqiptare in the centre is just south down the street in Sheshi i Teatrit, next to the theatre.

4

Shebeniku-Jabllanica National Park

At around 345 square kilometres, **SHEBENIKU-JABLLANICA NATIONAL PARK** (Parku Kombëtar Shebenik-Jabllanicë) is the third-largest national park in Albania. It might be overshadowed by some of the other big-hitters, but that's only because it's unknown, a true backcountry barely touched by development.

During the communist period, most of this wilderness was entirely off-limits as a restricted military zone. It snows here well into April and rains throughout the rest of the year, which makes for tricky travel on unpaved roads.

EXPLORING SHEBENIKU-JABLLANICA

You don't have to hike for days or climb for hours to reach the treasures of the park, although you certainly can should you wish to. The rolling hills and meadows surrounding **Fushë-Studna Lake** (Liqeni i Fushë-Studës) and the **Deer Lawn** (Lendina e Kaprollit) are just a 1.5km easy walk east from the trailhead near the Fushë-Studna **visitor centre**. The **Ice Cave** (Shpella e Akullit), with some evocative stalactite formations and superb panoramas, can be reached on foot via a 2.7km trail. Other soul-stirring locations, like the peaks of **Shebeniku**, **Kallkani** and **Raduçi**, and the **Seat and Stairs of Skanderbeg** (Sofra e Skënderbeut and Shkalla e Skënderbeut), where legend has it the national hero rested his troops and plotted his next move, require a little more footwork.

You can rent bikes at the Fushë-Studna visitor centre, but for a full-day or multiday excursion including camping, kayaking, snowshoeing or star charting, consider a guided expedition. Shebenik Egnatia Explorers (tel: 069 487 8598, www.instagram.com/shebenik_egnatia_explorers) and Shebenik Adventure (tel: 067 430 6495, www.facebook.com/p/Shebenik-Adventure-100064185636811) operate in all seasons.

But thanks to some road improvements, many trailheads are now quite accessible, some of them less than a ninety-minute drive from Tirana. From Librazhdi, the town that serves as the gateway to the park, you can slowly meander 25km north to the park's main **visitor centre** in the village of **Fushë-Studna**.

With or without a hired guide, this remote corner of the country is ripe for hiking, mountain biking, camping and stargazing. Its peaks, in the **Shebeniku massif** and **Jabllanica range**, reach nearly 2300m in elevation. Glacial activity in the last Ice Age has contoured the mountains into rugged ridges, sharp precipices and fourteen glacial lakes. More than twenty square kilometres of the park are now protected as part of the multicountry UNESCO World Heritage Site with a wordy title – the Ancient and Primeval Beech Forests of the Carpathians and Other Regions of Europe.

The giant, ancient European beech trees, Bosnian pines and silver firs are a highlight for would-be botanists, but the park is also a habitat for wildlife like the golden eagle, brown bear, Balkan chamois and critically endangered Balkan lynx. And as for humans? The sacred **Eremite Cave of Koshorishti** (Shpella Eremite e Kosharishtit), which can be reached on foot, contains a fresco of unknown date painted by a very determined hermit.

ARRIVAL AND GETTING AROUND SHEBENIKU-JABLLANICA NATIONAL PARK

By bus and minibus Librazhdi is easy to reach. The bus terminal on Rruga Unaza, just off the SH3, connects directly to many central cities. Fushë-Studna is more challenging: a bus departs Librazhdi daily at midday, stopping at villages along the way and reaching the visitor centre in about 1hr 30min. It returns along the route in the early morning.

Destinations Berati (several daily; 2hr 10min); Durrësi (many daily; 2hr); Elbasani (many daily; 25min); Erseka (several daily; 2hr 40min); Fieri (several daily; 2hr 15min); Korça (many daily; 1hr 50min); Lushnja (many daily; 1hr 30min); Pogradeci (many daily; 1hr); Tirana (many daily; 1hr 15min); Vlora (several daily; 2hr 50min).

By car In this area, it may be more convenient to have your own wheels, especially if you want to drive into the park. From Librazhdi, it will take about an hour to reach Fushë-Studna in a 4WD via the partially paved Rruga Nacionale of Librazhdi, and a bit longer in a normal car, though it's very doable. The fully paved stretches of road to trailheads in the closer villages of Togëzi and Zgoshti are easy to traverse. An off-road vehicle is recommended for other roads into the park. Send your accommodation a photo of your car and ask if it can handle the trip.

INFORMATION

Tourist information The visitor centre in Fushë-Studna is right on the Rruga Nacionale and open consistently throughout the summer. Staff can provide maps and tips. The Librazhdi Tourist Information Office on Rruga Hekurudha can also help you find your way more generally, and placards in that centre's courtyard provide information about flora, fauna and points of interest in the park, in English.

Maps Trail maps created by park employees can be found at every trailhead, and online at www.linktr.ee/explorelibrazhd.

Websites www.facebook.com/AdZMElbasan; www.linktr.ee/explorelibrazhd; www.facebook.com/fushestuden.

ACCOMMODATION

Like most rural guesthouses, these also serve both breakfast and traditional Albanian dinner on site or at a sister property nearby.

★ **Bujtina Kael** Rruga e Qarrishtës, Dorëzi village; www.instagram.com/bujtina_kael. In the mountains, an arduous day earns a decadent stay, right? Rustic-chic *Bujtina Kael* spares no comfort. The three-suite guesthouse located in the foothill village of Dorëzi makes the most of its setting, with large balconies and floor-to-ceiling windows overlooking the undulating fields and peaks, plus a hot tub for relaxing sore legs, a gazebo and a hearty home-made breakfast. €€

Joen Village Fushë-Studna; www.joenvillage.com. A large property for the area, *Joen* has rooms for two, apartments for four and villas that can accommodate parties of up to thirteen. All have central heating, minifridges and wi-fi. Convenient to all Fushë-Studna trails, the hotel also offers mountain bikes to rent, and has a gaggle of sports equipment, games and activities for kids, including rainy-day savers like dominoes and puzzles. €€€

EATING AND NIGHTLIFE

Jon Ceku Traditional Restaurant Rruga Kodra e Pepajve, Dorëzi village; tel: 069 816 3983. Sister property to *Bujtina Kael* (see above) and just down the street, this is where the party's at. Catch live music, knock back a *raki* and hit the dance floor. If this all sounds too exuberant, then grab a table and tuck into the huge portions of roasted lamb and veal, *kulaç* soda bread and village salad from greens grown by local farmers. Tomatoes, grapes and green apples from these hills are very succulent. €€

Lake Ohrid

Shared between Albania and North Macedonia, **LAKE OHRID** (Liqeni i Ohrit) has much to recommend it. In fact, it always has. Excavations on the Albanian side starting in 2021 have revealed that a Neolithic settlement existed here at least 7900 years ago, among the oldest of its kind in Europe. It is as worth plopping down on the banks of **Ohrid** (Albanian: Ohri or Ohër) now as then. The water here is crystalline, the vibe

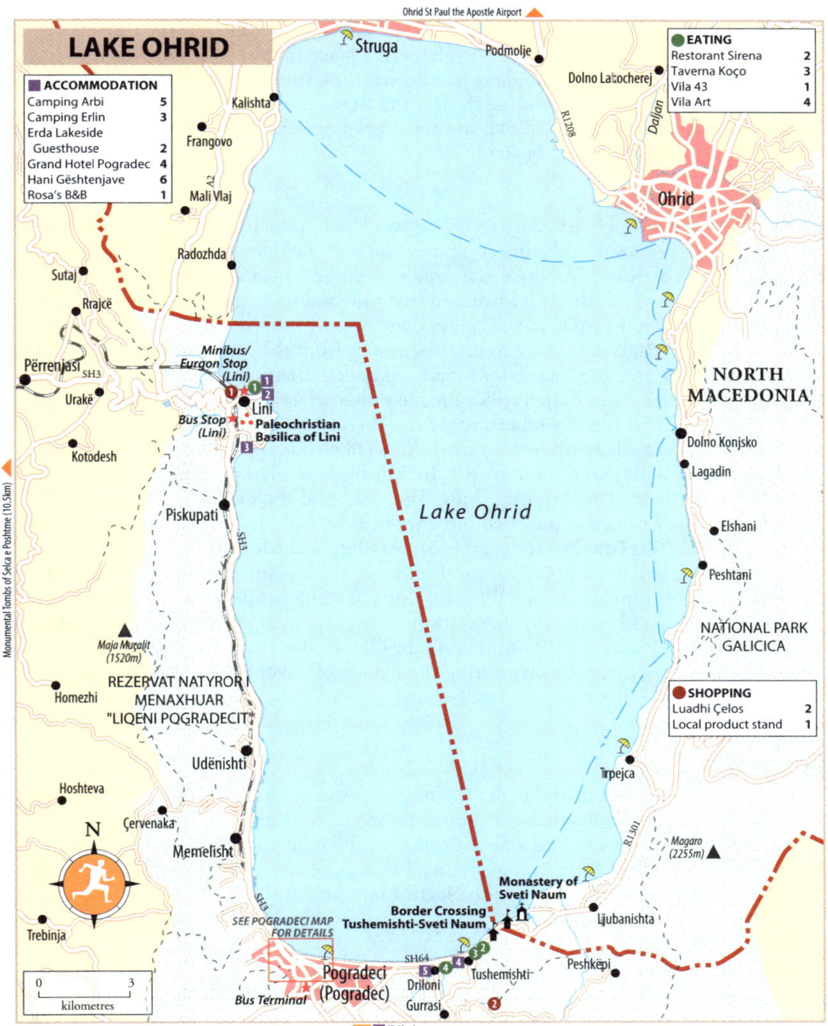

tranquil, and the weather mild. Freshwater fishing, paddling, hiking and lounging in the sun remain favourite pastimes. Arriving from the hot, hectic Mediterranean coast or Tirana, you may imagine a change in the air (and your blood pressure) as soon as you cross the **Qafë-Thana** mountain pass and the lake hovers into view.

A cross-border UNESCO World Heritage Site for both natural and cultural distinction, Ohrid is one of the oldest lakes on the planet, formed two to three million years ago, as well as the deepest in the Balkans. The Albanian side is a teardrop-shaped slice to the southwest, while the Macedonian side – the northeast chunk of the lake – has the lion's share. Its waters cover nearly 360 square kilometres and are home to some two hundred species of plants, animals and other organisms, including seventeen endemic species of fish. King among them is the *koran* trout, which local restaurants serve grilled or baked. *Belushkë*, a smaller trout species, and *krap* (carp) are also delicacies.

If you stick to the main tourist boulevards of the mid-sized city of **Pogradeci**, you'll find urban parks, beaches, restaurants and fantastic vistas, but little in the way of architecture, monuments and museums. It's a fine place to drop a fishing line in the water (no permit required), take a paddleboat for a spin or snap photos of the brightly painted rowboats on the beach. But the shore and hinterland reward deeper exploration: to the springs of **Driloni**, the alluring village of **Lini**, the Illyrian **royal tombs of Selca e Poshtme** and beyond.

Brief history

Eight thousand years ago, inhabitants of the area lived, quite literally, on the water – in 'pile dwellings', houses on stilts hovering over the lake. Underwater excavations at a site called **Buqeza**, near Lini, revealed a sizable seven-acre **palafitte village** that likely homed between two hundred and five hundred inhabitants at that time. The **Museum of Pogradeci** (Muzeu i Pogradecit) displays fragments of the wooden piles, stone fishing weights, arrowheads, bone tools and ceramic vessels from the early Neolithic era, along with photos from ongoing excavations. Such lakeside settlements continued to flourish through the Bronze Age. Illyrian tribes fortified themselves on nearby hilltops between around 2000 BC and the second century BC – the earliest Illyrians to get a mention in the historical record. From fortress towns like **Enkelana**, populations farmed, worshipped and built grand monuments. In 335 BC, the Illyrians clashed with the army of **Alexander the Great** in these hills. They lost, and the mantle of Illyrian power shifted west. The Romans subjugated but enriched the region, creating an important passage along the **Via Egnatia** (see page 143). Starting in the fourth century AD, Ohrid also became a notable ecclesiastical centre in the Byzantine Empire, as the sixth-century basilica at Lini attests to. Following Albania's independence and World War I, Ohrid became a rather swanky destination. If you squint at photos of the Pogradeci waterfront in the 1920s and 1930s, it could be Como. But Pogradeci's proximity to Yugoslavia put a strain on the city during the regime of **Enver Hoxha**, who visited all too frequently and militarized the area heavily.

Pogradeci city

Pogradeci is clean, modern and chill. The massive waves of international tourism in Albania haven't broken here – yet. Home to one of Albania's premier-league restaurants, *Rosa e Tymosur*, and a historic quarter full of artists' studios and galleries, it's the rare place where you can lounge on a beach against a backdrop of snow-capped mountains – the Galičica range on the North Macedonian side.

Pogradeci Beach

Along Shëtitorja 1 Maji boardwalk and Rruga Harmonia • Free

About 1.2km of vanilla-brown sand fronts the lake at **Pogradeci Beach** (Plazhi i Pogradecit), where the water slowly darkens from clear to green to blue as the lakebed

drops below. In the summer, Ohrid stays calm and shallow enough for kids to enjoy, though it also stays quite cool. Umbrellas and sun loungers can be rented, as can paddleboats, for taking a spin out on the water. A **park** runs between the beach's long pedestrianized boardwalk and Rruga Dëshmorët e Pojskës, the lakeshore road packed with hotels, restaurants and bars. That thoroughfare is turned over to foot traffic after 6pm in the summer, bringing the whole town out for evening saunters and the occasional modest block party.

Square of Roses

Lakefront and Rruga Reshit Çollaku • Free

At the meeting point of the beach, the historic quarter and the communist-era square, the **Square of Roses** (Sheshi i Trëndafilave) marks the centre of Pogradeci. The plaza of some four thousand roses honours poet **Lasgush Poradeci** and literary journal founder **Mitrush Kuteli** with statues. Both sons of Pogradeci, they wrote about nature, love, death and Ohrid in the 1930s and 1940s. Like many literary figures, both suffered under communism; Kuteli was imprisoned for fifteen years. Benches shaped like curled books are painted with snippets of their work, including Poradeci's *Old Age Song*. Adjacent to the square, the **Odeoni** hosts concerts, dance shows and theatre performances, mostly in the summer. Its Ionic-style colonnade was erected in 2021 to mirror the facade of a tomb at Selca e Poshtme (see page 181).

Historic quarter

Rruga Naim Frashëri, Rruga Çeta e Mokrës and Rruga Mësenjtorja • Free

Across the street from the Odeoni, a tangle of cobblestones and Italianate mansions from the early twentieth century signal the entrance to the **historic quarter**, which isn't much compared to its Korça counterpart but worth a detour, in a city that otherwise cuts a pretty 1990s and aughts figure. Many of the villas have been converted into bars, restaurants and hotels, but most remain residential. In the 2020s, restoration began on some of the finest houses here, like those of poet **Lasgush Poradeci** and the **Içka**

brothers, who were renowned woodcarvers, on Rruga Çeta e Mokrës; the latter is an eye-catching expression of a nineteenth-century Ottoman exterior.

The neighbourhood is also where the city's visual arts community works. Pogradeci claims an outsized share of Albania's most accomplished living painters, sculptors, woodcarvers and sketch artists, both young talent and veterans of the creative scene who came up during communism. Not all the studios and galleries have shops, but visits can usually be arranged (see page 176).

Pogradeci Castle

Rruga e Kalasë, at the top of the hill • Free • 50min walk from the Odeoni

Only scant stone foundations remain from the fourth-century BC Illyrian fortress of Enkelana, the town that would become Pogradeci. Though there isn't much to see, the views over the town and lake make this short hike to **Pogradeci Castle** (Kalaja e Pogradecit) worthwhile on a bluebird day.

Museum of Pogradeci

Rruga Reshit Çollaku 88 • Charge • www.facebook.com/Pogradec2022

A quick visit to the **Muzeu i Pogradecit**, a small museum of history, archaeology and ethnography, will pay off if you plan to spend a few days rambling around Ohrid's archaeological sites, which are otherwise somewhat lacking in contextual information. Revamped and reopened in 2023 to foreground the Neolithic discoveries at Buqeza (see page 174), the gallery has the best collection of Stone Age artefacts in Albania. Placards in English explain the Illyrian, Roman, Ottoman and *Rilindja* exhibits, and staff are happy to take you around for an impromptu tour of the three hundred objects on display. The wooden beams that held up Buqeza's Neolithic stilt houses are here, as are the very intact iron and bronze armaments of Illyrian soldiers, including two helmets, spear tips, swords (for stabbing) and more swords (for throwing).

ARRIVAL AND GETTING AROUND — POGRADECI

By bus Opened in mid-2024, Pogradeci's new bus terminal at the intersection of Rruga Unaza and Rruga Industriale is about a 20min walk from the centre or the beach. From here, regular buses depart every 20–30 min to Lini (30min) and the other Ohrid villages, except Tushemishti, for which you can catch the hourly bus four blocks north at Rruga Reshit Çollaku 53 (many daily; 15min).

Destinations Berati (several daily; 3hr 15min); Durrësi (several daily; 3hr); Elbasani (many daily; 1hr 30min); Erseka (several daily; 2hr); Fieri (several daily; 3hr 15min); Korça (many daily; 45min); Librazhdi (many daily; 1hr); Lushnja (several daily; 2hr 30min); Tirana (many daily, 2hr 30min); Vlora (1 daily; 4hr).

By car Parking on the street is mostly free and generally easy to find in Pogradeci centre. There's occasional congestion on Rruga Reshit Çollaku and Rruga Kajo Karafili during busy hours.

By taxi The city's main taxi rank is located near the intersection of Rruga Kajo Karafili and Rruga Rinia, and drivers are happy to pick you up and drop you off anywhere in the Ohrid region (Lini, Driloni, Tushemishti, etc) on the Albanian side.

By bike Ohrid generally rewards cyclists. The roads by the lake are mostly paved and flat, and the distances between destinations are manageable. Hinterland excursions and cross-border trips are often easier on two wheels than four. Bicikleta me Qera Pogradec rents road and mountain bikes (side street near the intersection of Rruga Kajo Karafili and Rruga Nositi; www.facebook.com/p/Bicikleta-Me-Qera-Pogradec-100044247387336).

INFORMATION

Tourist information The tourist information kiosk is on the main square across the street from the Sheshi i Trëndafilave, in front of Biblioteka Mitrush Kuteli. It is open for a few hours around midday during the summer, and English-speaking staff can provide up-to-date maps and brochures for Pogradeci city and the greater Ohrid region, along with restaurant and hotel recommendations. QR codes stamped on the kiosk provide maps for hiking and cycling excursions beyond the city.

Maps Suggested hiking and cycling routes can be found around Pogradeci, Lini, Tushemishti and Driloni, including distance, length and difficulty, in English.

Websites www.go2pogradec.al; www.facebook.com/visitpogradec; www.bashkiapogradec.gov.al.

ACCOMMODATION

SEE MAP PAGE 175

Elite Hotel Rruga Dëshmorët e Pojskës and Rruga 1 Qershori; www.facebook.com/elitepogradec. There is a number of large, somewhat soulless, beachfront hotels in Pogradeci, though this one gains points for being both reliably comfortable and reasonably priced. Rooms sleeping one to three people are well appointed, many with balconies framing an unobstructed view over Ohrid. A decent breakfast is included. €€€

★ **Hani Gështenjave** 10km driving southeast of Pogradeci on SH3 to the village of Stropcka; tel: 069 295 0881. A gorgeous agritourism guesthouse and restaurant that opened in 2024, *Hani Gështenjave*'s rooms come with all the bells and whistles: rainfall showers, raw-edge wood headboards, *qilims* with traditional patterns, and glass sliding doors opening to balconies with views over the farm, the property's lake, Pogradeci city and Lake Ohrid. The farm-to-table restaurant is worth a trip even if you don't spend the night. €€€

Old Town Inn Rruga Çeta e Mokrës; tel: 069 459 5950. This comfortable, modern hotel in the historic district puts you close to the centre, with rooms for one to four guests, some lofted. Private balconies and modern art upgrade the place, though parking and wi-fi are not available. €

★ **Seven Cafe & Hotel** Rruga Reshit Çollaku 56; tel: 067 629 3603. A 1920s Italianate villa reopened as a B&B, *Seven* is among the best of the bunch near the lake. Rooms for one to four people are outfitted with heirloom wood furniture, upholstered chairs and other elegant touches, while guests (and non-guests) can take breakfast, lunch and dinner on the terrace out front, right across the street from the Sheshi i Trëndafilave gardens. Lake and garden views both beguile. €€€

EATING

SEE MAP PAGE 175

Pogradeci's eating and drinking scene on the lakeshore boulevard, Rruga Dëshmorët e Pojskës, has levelled up, and many places now serve international dishes alongside fresh Ohrid fish plates. Some plate up very nice preparations of grilled fish – *koran*, *belushkë* and *krap* typically – but for a more traditional foray into Lake Ohrid cuisine, you may want to venture to the nearby villages of Lini or Tushemishti. Ohrid is the only natural habitat of *koran* on Earth, and commercial fishing is restricted, so expect to shell out a bit more for the privilege.

Bizantin Restaurant Rruga Dëshmorët e Pojskës 86; tel: 069 202 3909. Try interesting old-school Ohrid dishes like oven-baked salted fish, or something more modern, like sixty-day dry-aged T-bone steak. This is an upscale international spot with serious culinary chops, an ambitious project that opened on the lakeshore drive in 2024. Pistachio lava cake en flambé is a flashy way to finish. The wine list and spirits selection are also strong. €€€€

Casa di Pizza Rruga Dëshmorët e Pojskës near Rruga Mihal Ballkameno; tel: 067 752 1111. The best pizzeria-Italian-seafood restaurant in town, so rarely without a queue of hopeful diners. The seafood pizza is a good bet, and linguine with *koran* puts a local spin on an Italian favourite. The pasta is home-made, and outdoor tables overlook the lake. €€

Restorant Poradeci Rruga Naim Frashëri across from Rruga 24 Maj; www.facebook.com/restorantporadeci. This small eatery, where the owner is the chef and server, has been a Pogradeci staple for more than thirty years. It looks more like a family dining room than a restaurant, and the cuisine matches the vibe. *Tavë* (soured milk casserole) of *koran* and *belushkë* are cooked with onions, walnuts or vinegar. And if you're feeling up for it, try one of the old recipes for organ meat like *tavë kasapi*, made with cow heart and liver. €€

★ **Rosa e Tymosur** Rruga Dëshmorët e Pojskës and Rruga 1 Qershori; www.facebook.com/rosaetymosur.al. The name means 'Smoked Duck', and this is the signature dish here. Smoked duck with *petka* (local pasta), smoked duck with plum sauce, smoked duck flambéed at the table – the speciality comes every which way. Once you've tried the stuff, you'll see why Albanians take the time to detour here on the drive from Tirana to Korça. Big loaves of *kulaç* soda bread studded with olives and pickled peppers fill you up before the starters even arrive, and the atmosphere is cosier than most, with dark-wood decor and exposed-brick walls. Prices are very good for the quality of food. Reserve ahead to prevent disappointment. €€€

4

DRINKING AND NIGHTLIFE

SEE MAP PAGE 175

Den Rruga Naim Frashëri and Rruga Kajo Karafili; www.instagram.com/den__o8. A funky restaurant and wine/cocktail/craft beer bar in the historic quarter, *Den* has a cosy all-weather atmosphere, with raw-edge wood tables, colourfully upholstered booths and abstract murals on the walls. Creative cocktails set this place apart, and mixologists will prepare delicious non-alcoholic varieties too. *Den Marine Lounge* is its lakeside outpost, on Rruga Dëshmorët e Pojskës.

Sherlock Irish Pub Rruga Dëshmorët e Pojskës and Rruga 1 Qershori; www.sherlockirishpub.com. There are more than a few beach bars, beach-adjacent bars and big party lounges on the main lakeshore road in Pogradeci, but this one is the friendliest and often the liveliest. *Sherlock* has a broad selection of brown spirits and European beers, including Pogradeci's own craft brew Birra e Gjyshit. The outdoor area becomes an after-hours hotspot when the bar puts on live rock acts.

★ **Triada Inn** Rruga 1 Janari near Rruga Reshit Çollaku; www.instagram.com/triada_inn. A 2024 addition to the Pogradeci scene, *Triada* serves both classic and creative cocktails and mocktails, changing the menu up with the seasons. A cosy, unassuming bistro in a small side street near the centre, *Triada* also has live music year-round: everything from classic Albanian tunes to acoustic covers of 1990s staples.

ENTERTAINMENT

Qendra Kulturore Lasgush Poradeci Rruga Reshit Çollaku, across the street from the Sheshi i Trëndafilave; www.facebook.com/KultureSportArtTrashegimi. Now encompassing the 1954 Mitrush Kuteli Library (Biblioteka Mitrush Kuteli), an art gallery and a performing arts space, the Lasgush Poradeci Cultural Centre organizes orchestral concerts, folkloric performances, interpretive dance, DJ sets and more, some held in the complex, some in the Odeoni and some in the nearby villages of Lini and Tushesmishti. Stop by to see what's on.

Teatri i Kukullave Piro Xëci Rruga 1 Qershori near Rruga Dëshmorët e Pojskës. Most of the puppet theatres from the communist era have shuttered, but Pogradeci's Piro Xëci Puppet Theatre, established in 1952, was renovated and reopened for puppet shows in 2024.

SHOPPING

SEE MAP PAGE 175

4

With its beautiful natural setting, it's no surprise that Pogradeci has a robust, generations-long tradition of visual arts. The historic quarter hosts the studios of quite a few excellent painters, woodcarvers and sculptors; some are known names in Albanian art, others are up-and-comers. Many don't have shops, but they'll welcome you into their workspaces and showrooms. Contact them in advance, or just try knocking. Painter and engraver Anastas 'Taso' Kostandini (www.facebook.com/anastaskostandini), painter Vangjo Vasili (www.facebook.com/vangjo.vasili), woodcarver Pirro Içka (tel: 069 252 2017), painter Enxhel Gegprifti (www.instagram.com/enxhel25gegprifti) and multimedia artist Ina Cici (www.instagram.com/ciciina) are names to watch.

★ **Ahrid Atelier** Rruga Naim Frashëri and Rruga Kajo Karafili; www.instagram.com/ahrid_atelier. Young artists Ina Cici and Zhaklina Gjolla work in a dizzying variety of media, but they opened this shop in 2024 to showcase their drawings and ceramics inspired by the city and its Illyrian heritage. If you want an artisan-quality Illyrian-style two-handled wine jug or vase to take home, enquire here. Cici's sketches of the historic quarter are also wonderful.

Atelie Taso Rruga 24 Maj; www.facebook.com/anastaskostandini. One of Pogradeci's most versatile artists, Anastas Kostandini created the ironwork panel and the mosaic on the facade of the city's *bashkia* (town hall) in the main square – and was among the original artists behind the monumental 1981 socialist realist mosaic on the facade of Tirana's Muzeu Historik Kombëtar (see page 56). He's also a prolific painter of Pogradeci and Ohrid, creating lively scenes in vivid colours.

★ **ShpellArt** Rruga Reshit Çollaku and Rruga 24 Maj; www.facebook.com/shpellart. Much more than just an art studio, ShpellArt is a hybrid gallery, bar, hangout, library, and music and poetry performance space. The brainchild of painter Henri Shkurti, it opened in 2022 with the goal to provide a welcoming place for anyone with a creative spirit, and it's a great spot to see what's new and cool on the Pogradeci art, music and literature scene. Pop by to take in the vibe or a performance, even if you're not interested in buying.

Shtëpia e Miqve Rruga Naim Frashëri near Rruga 1 Janari; www.facebook.com/miqtenepogradec. The 'House of Friends' is a café, bookstore, studio and gallery where you can sip home-made botanical-infused liquor, read a book off the shelf and peruse handmade souvenirs, from hairpins to keychains, made by local artists.

DIRECTORY

Banks and currency exchange Most of the major banks in Albania have branches and ATMs in Pogradeci centre, near the triangle where Rruga Reshit Çollaku, Rruga Dëshmorët e Pojskës and Rruga Rinia intersect; there's also a Western Union and a currency exchange. Several more currency exchanges nearby are clustered around the cross of Rruga Rinia and Rruga Kajo Karafili.

Emergencies Call tel: 127 or tel: 112 for medical emergencies, or tel: 129 or tel: 112 for police.

Hospitals The main hospital, Spitali Bashkiak Pogradec, is at Rruga Islam Dani and Rruga Unaza (tel: 08 322 4444). There is also the Qendra Shëndetësore Verore, a 24/7 clinic set up during the summer season for minor medical issues or injuries, on the beach promenade (Rruga Harmonia; tel: 068 806 6419).

Pharmacies The city has many pharmacies; try Farmaci Keti, open late every day (Rruga Kajo Karafili and Rruga Çeta e Mokrës; tel: 069 837 1381) or Bjopharma (Rruga Gani Butko near Rruga Ismail Qemali; tel: 067 637 8938).

Police The station is at Rruga Dëshmorët e Pojskës 10.

Post office DHL has a service point at Rruga Reshit Çollaku, Pallati 164 (tel: 04 240 6666). The Posta Shqiptare in the centre is across the street at Rruga Reshit Çollaku and Rruga Rinia (tel: 068 204 4707).

Lini

Lini drapes across a peninsula jutting into Lake Ohrid and captures the attention shortly after you cross the Qafë-Thana mountain pass and begin winding your way down towards the lake. It's well worth a stop or stay in this charming little village. Orange-shingled nineteenth and early-twentieth-century houses jumble up against a bluff, and shopkeepers in the centre will treat you to plum or grape *raki*, and cherry or watermelon *reçel* (jam). A smattering of romantic B&Bs overlooks the lake, and there are fine campsites for pitching a tent. You can hike and kayak in solitude here, and the big city is just down the motorway. The most historically significant site in Lini is its **paleo-Christian basilica**, poised atop the peninsula's bluff, lording over the whole lake. Not much is left of the structure, but coins found during excavations date its origins to the sixth century AD. Some of Albania's finest **late Roman mosaics** lie under the tarps on the basilica floor. One panel centres on a Eucharist cup and fans out to a full wine-and-vine tableau of grape clusters, amphorae, birds and geometric patterns. Call the number on the gate to access the church (currently tel: 067 639 9436) and ask to see some of the mosaics if possible. Follow signs east up the hill from Lini centre 600m; it's a ten-minute walk.

ARRIVAL AND GETTING AROUND — LINI

By bus or furgon Buses depart the main Pogradeci bus terminal every 20–30 min to Lini and the other Ohrid villages north of Pogradeci (many daily; 30min). The Lini bus stop, on the motorway, is about a 1km (15min) walk from Lini centre. *Furgons* (minibuses) departing from the Pogradeci terminal will take you directly to the centre, pulling in at the point where the SH87 meets a small three-way roundabout.

By car It's a straight, mostly flat drive from Pogradeci to Lini, 20min total. Follow the SH3 north, then turn east (right) to SH87 (Rruga e Linit) into the village.

By taxi Any taxi in Pogradeci will also take you to Lini. In Lini centre, there are usually taxis waiting to take you back. You can try Taxi Klodi (tel: 069 296 6888).

4

ACCOMMODATION — SEE MAP PAGE 173

Camping Erlin 2.4km south of Lini, via SH3; tel: 068 406 6666. Secluded but well developed, *Camping Erlin* has a camper-van lot, a private beach with sun loungers and umbrellas, and an on-site restaurant serving lake fish. Facilities are clean, wi-fi is good, and you can walk to Lini village in under 30min. €

Erda Lakeside Guesthouse SH87 (Rruga e Linit); tel: 069 725 2348. This family-run lakeside spot is hard to beat in the area on quality-to-price ratio. Rooms are simple but cheerful, with balconies overlooking the lake. The garden and terrace area is a picture-perfect spot to take breakfast or stop by for dinner. €€

★ **Rosa's B&B** SH87 (Rruga e Linit); www.facebook.com/Rosasbedandbreakfast. Among Lini's lakefront guesthouses, *Rosa's B&B* is a cut above. The patio on the lake is a dreamy place to nap on sun loungers or read a book in an armchair in the summer. Rooms are clean and comfortable, some open directly to the lake terrace. Rosa makes you feel at home; laundry and boat rides can be arranged. It's also a top dining destination for fresh catches in Lini. €€

EATING — SEE MAP PAGE 173

Vila 43 SH87 (Rruga e Linit); www.facebook.com/p/Vila-43-Lin-100025107251092. Right on the lake – you can dock a small boat here – *Vila 43* is Lini's premier seafood spot, with a compact menu focusing on the catch of the day. *Koran* and *belushkë* are prepared in the traditional Ohrid style, grilled whole or in fillets in a dish with wine reduction, dried fruits, nuts or whatever's fresh. There's also a nice guesthouse. €€€

SHOPPING — SEE MAP PAGE 173

Local product stand Lini centre roundabout; tel: 069 523 6231. There are a few souvenir shops in Lini, but this stand is the best for buying locally grown and made products. The shopkeeper will let you try before you buy his plum and grape *raki*, and you can find excellent cherry and apple *reçel* and *gliko* (fruit preserves) as well as less common flavours like watermelon and pumpkin.

Tushemishti and Driloni-Tushemishti Springs Park

Tushemishti is close enough to Pogradeci that sun-seekers and seafood-noshers often opt to stay here instead. *Koran* (Ohrid trout) is plentiful, sun loungers and paddleboats are available on the beach and the wooden walking pier over the lake is a perfectly peachy spot to cast a fishing line.

The village abuts **Driloni-Tushemishti Springs Park** (Parku Ujor Drilon-Tushemisht), 500m west on the SH64. The park's karstic springs are one of the primary water sources for Ohrid lake, and this unique terrain evokes the lakelands of Central Florida. Kick back beneath a willow tree and watch the swans, ducks, peacocks and tortoises. Tushemishti is also near the **Sveti Naum monastery complex** (Shën Naumi), 2.5km east. Across the border in North Macedonia, the monastery was actually part of Albania until 1925. The soon-to-be King Zog I gifted it to Yugoslavia for unclear reasons, but a few months earlier, the Yugoslav army had backed his return to power in Albania.

ARRIVAL AND GETTING AROUND — TUSHEMISHTI

By bus Take a bus (hourly) to Tushemishti from the stop at Rruga Reshit Çollaku 53 in Pogradeci.

By car or taxi Drive 5km east of Pogradeci centre on the SH64; Tushemishti is 15min, at most, by car via a flat, easy road. Alternatively, take a taxi (see page 176).

Tourist information A new tourist information centre for Tushemishti and Driloni-Tushemishti Springs Park is slated to open in 2025 or 2026 on the SH64 and Rruga e Drilonit.

ACCOMMODATION — SEE MAP PAGE 173

Camping Arbi SH64 near Rruga e Drilonit; tel: 069 206 1121. Well kept, spacious and right on the lake, with an uncrowded, uncluttered sandy beach just across the street, *Camping Arbi* has both convenience and charm. The wi-fi is decent, beach loungers are free to use, facilities are very clean and there's a great restaurant on site. Open April through October. €

Grand Hotel Pogradec SH64; www.facebook.com/grandhotelpogradec. One of the newer and better big resort-style hotels on the lake, the *Grand Hotel Pogradec* has a wide selection of rooms, suites and apartments sleeping one to six people. There's a private beach; a pool with sun loungers; balconies in all rooms; parking; and a high standard of cleanliness. Excellent restaurant too. €€€

4

EATING — SEE MAP PAGE 173

★ **Restorant Sirena** SH64; www.facebook.com/HotelSirenaPogradec. Following a kitchen upgrade in 2024, *Sirena* has become one of the top spots on the lake to order fresh-caught *koran, belushkë and krap*. The restaurant specializes in simple, herb-rubbed whole-grilled fish, though you can opt for heavier, more traditional *tavë* (casserole) preparations too. Salads are fresh, the wine list is solid and the large, shaded outdoor seating area is just across the street from the lake. The hotel is a clean, convenient budget option in the area. €€€

Taverna Koço SH64; www.facebook.com/restoranttushemishtikoco. This lakefront taverna

VISITING OHRID TOWN AND SVETI NAUM FROM POGRADECI

A scenic drive tracing the perimeter of Lake Ohrid, which only takes about two hours, is a grand idea – in theory. With its half-timbered houses, cobblestone alleys and lakefront cafés, **Ohrid** is the most romantic city on the waterfront; **Sveti Naum** is among the most awe-inspiring medieval churches in Eastern Europe; and the whole circuit is packed with picture-perfect lake vistas and picnic spots. However, it's not as easy as setting off for a leisurely pootle: the route requires a bit of advance planning and involves crossing two busy border checkpoints.

With a rental car, passage to the **North Macedonian** side is easy enough, provided you have the necessary permits and insurance. Check with the rental agency about permits; the insurance you can quickly purchase at any insurance office in Albania with your license, registration and passport (note, though, it will be cheaper in town than at the checkpoint). Most taxis can't cross the border, but there is a number of specialty services in Pogradeci that can take you. **Taxi Pogradec Gezim** (tel: 069 235 0098) and **Taxi Pogradec Nori** (tel: 069 354 2381) both offer fair rates.

Alternatively, from Tushemishti you can simply **walk or bike to the monastery**. It's a pleasant forty-minute stroll, and there's a shortcut to the complex. You'll skip the line of cars at the border and be on your way with just your passport.

entices seafood lovers with both simple and traditional preparations of *koran*, *belushkë* and *krap*. The *tavë koran* here, with onions, bay leaves and nuts, is worth trying to experience traditional Ohrid fish done right. Also has tasty sweet and savoury breakfast options. €€

Vila Art Rruga e Drilonit, Driloni; tel: 069 869 3666. Order an old-school favourite like *tavë koran* (trout casserole) with lemon and tomato, or just sit for coffee and gaze over the Driloni springs. *Vila Art* may not be the best restaurant in the Tushemishti area, but it has a certain pedigree: The modernist-lodge aesthetic dates to the time when this building was Enver Hoxha's lake retreat. €€

SHOPPING

SEE MAP PAGE 173

Luadhi Çelos 6km southeast of Tushemishti centre via Rruga e Drilonit towards Gurrasi; www.instagram.com/luadhi.celos.agroturizem. Wedged between the bare mountains and the glittering lake, the Ohrid area is mostly agricultural land, and this 650-acre farm grows just about everything you can in these hills. Honey, *reçel* (jam), *gliko* (preserve), pickled vegetables, wine, *raki* and many more goodies can be both tasted and purchased at the shop on the farm here. Call ahead to arrange a full lunch or dinner.

Monumental Tombs of Selca e Poshtme

Selca e Poshtme village • Free

The five **Monumental Tombs of Selca e Poshtme** (Varret Monumentale të Selcës së Poshtme) are unique in Albanian archaeology, one of the few Illyrian sites that was not built over by conquerors who succeeded them. As such, the hillside royal tombs are perhaps the clearest window into how the Illyrians communicated grandeur and power in stone. The mausoleums were part of a larger settlement inhabited from Neolithic times, and they were built between the fourth and third centuries BC, when the Ohrid region was controlled by the Dassaretii Illyrians. Four are carved from the rock face, with simple facades and a few architectonic elements resembling doors and windows. But the fifth is fitted with a semicircular stone entrance, with fluted pilasters topped by Ionic capitals, ornaments you'd find in Hellenic tombs and temples of the era. The view over the hilly Mokra countryside of the Ohrid hinterland is fit for a king – or perhaps a picnic.

ARRIVAL AND DEPARTURE — MONUMENTAL TOMBS OF SELCA E POSHTME

By car Freshly asphalted roads make this site easier to access – though still not to find – than in the past. Follow the SH3 from Pogradeci past Lini and over the Qafë-Thana mountain pass to the west. Turn south at signs to Uraka and remain on the paved road for 11km before the turnoff east (left) toward Selca e Poshtme, which is also, somewhat confusingly, called Gradishta. The road is unpaved from here, but not especially difficult, and signs toward the tombs read 'Varrezat Ilire'. It's about 1hr by car from Pogradeci.

Prespa Lakes

The **PRESPA LAKES** (Liqenet e Prespës) are graced with the most idyllic waterfront in Albania. Though the surrounding landscape is another jewel in the Southeast's crown. Thanks to upgraded roads, the tourist information point for the **Prespa National Park** (Parku Kombëtar Prespë) is now only a 24km (30min) drive north from the centre of Korça. Within the park, there are at least five incredible 700-year-old cave churches, and one of them is on an island best reached by kayak. The beautiful natural scenes – alpine grasslands, gentle hills, ancient oaks and mirrorlike waters – are like a slice of Scotland in Albania.

There are two Prespa Lakes, and together they are not much smaller than Ohrid. **Great Prespa Lake** (Liqeni i Prespës së Madhe) is split between Albania, North Macedonia and Greece, while **Little Prespa Lake** (Liqeni i Prespës së Vogël) only has a tiny spur in Albania. But very few people live here: only three thousand or so in Albania's handful of Prespa shorefront villages. There are no resorts or beach bars (or beaches). The park service has put hard graft into mapping and marking **eleven hiking**

trails around the banks and slopes of the lakes, though it is just as tempting to lose yourself in the soul-stirring landscapes. It is all very, very quiet.

Prespa is separated from Ohrid by just 10km and one massif, the **Dry Mountain** (Mali i Thatë), which rises to nearly 2300m east of Pogradeci. The Prespa National Park takes in the mountain's eastern slope, giving way to tundra meadows of yellow-blossoming Albanian lilies, Macedonian oak forests, the two tectonic lakes and reedy floodplains. Dalmatian pelicans, among the biggest freshwater birds in the world, migrate here in the summer, and more than 25 species of bat live in the many caves.

Brief history

Traces of Neolithic, Bronze Age, ancient Macedonian and Roman inhabitation have been unearthed around the shores and on the islands of both Prespa Lakes. Despite its sleepy vibe, the region was in fact a seat of power in the tenth century AD, when **Tsar Samuel**, emperor of Bulgaria and scourge of the Byzantines, built a fortress and church complex on the island of Agios Achillios, now in the Greek part of Prespa e Vogël.

Apparently fond of the area and clued in to the advantages of a lake protected by a wall of mountains, Samuel is also said to have built a pleasure palace to holiday in on **Maligradi Island** (Ishulli i Maligradit), or 'Little Town Island', in what is now the Albanian corner of Prespa e Madhe. Little of ancient Maligradi remains visible, but excavations are still ongoing.

The Byzantines and their proxies retook the area after Samuel's death, and it became a faith centre for a certain sort of Orthodox adherent: the **eremite**, or hermit. From the twelfth to the fourteenth centuries, the anonymous and the powerful alike contributed churches here, some hewn directly from cliffsides and others freestanding within existing caves. Demographically, the small population of this enclave today is almost entirely Macedonian.

4

Maligradi Island

10min by motorboat or about 45min by kayak from the dock in Pusteci across the street from Kisha e Shën Thanasit • Charge for boat (tour included)

The jewel in Prespa e Madhe's crown is **Maligradi Island** (Ishulli i Maligradit), a tadpole-shaped speck that hides a secret: the finest Byzantine-era fresco art in Albania. Built in 1345 inside the shallow 'Cave of Doves' on the south side of the island, the **Church of St Mary** (Kisha e Shën Mërisë) is covered in paintings, inside and out. Those in the chapel have largely been protected over the centuries and restored to their fourteenth-century lustre.

The earliest frescoes belong to the **Palaeologan Renaissance** style of Byzantine art and iconography, with an emphasis on multiple smaller panels over grand murals. The busy biblical scenes and masterful portraiture are textbook late-Byzantine artistry. The life of Christ takes prominence on the vaulted ceiling, but Mary is front and centre on the exterior above the entrance.

It's well worth the modest cost of hiring a small boat or taking a guided tour with someone who can unlock the chapel.

ARRIVAL AND GETTING AROUND — PRESPA LAKES

By bus Pusteci is the name of the municipality and biggest village, and its bus stop is near the main square and post-communist church. The Prespa bus leaves from the bus terminal in Korça, stopping along the SH79 for the villages up to the border with North Macedonia; the destination on the bus sign may read 'Pustec' or 'Goricë-Dogana'. But it's a daily village bus, leaving Korça around noon and returning early in the morning (1 daily; 40min to Pusteci).

By car or taxi The road from Korça to Prespa Lakes is well paved, but it does include a short series of head-spinning switchbacks. Follow the SH3 north to the SH79. It's about 24km (30min drive) from Korça centre to reach Prespa National Park's tourist information point and 28km (35min) to Pusteci, usually with little traffic beyond Korça. Taxis will also take you; see page 167 for Korça taxi information and prices.

EXPLORING PRESPA NATIONAL PARK

Prespa National Park (Parku Kombëtar Prespë) is generally an approachable park, suitable for folks of all ages and fitness levels looking to escape into nature. Its trailheads are well marked with placards explaining the routes, distances, difficulty levels and expected length of time to hike. Its **visitor centre** is informative and encourages dawdling and drooling over views. You can bike, camp, climb, birdwatch, kayak and even stand-up paddleboard in the lake when the weather permits. If you have your own car, you can easily explore it without a guide. Staff have gathered most trails on Wikiloc (along with a few non-Prespa trails); see www.wikiloc.com/wikiloc/user.do?id=4304509.

But you may want to enlist the services of a tour operator for a more insightful trip, easier access to waterfront sights and transport from Korça. **Explore Prespa Lake Tours** (tel: 069 783 2673; www.instagram.com/exploreprespalaketours) can set you up with a boat to Maligradi or around the Albanian shores of the lake. This is the quickest way to see more primitive cave churches like St Nicholas (Shën Nikollës), Bllashtojna and the Archangelloti church, the latter two dramatically drilled right into the rock face back in the fourteenth century and accessible by ladder. **Nature Experience Albania** specializes in guided hikes (www.nature-experience-albania.com). This is one of Albania's best places to kayak, and **Kayak Albania Paddle Club** can help you get afloat (www.instagram.com/kayak.albania). It's best to arrange a few days in advance.

4

INFORMATION

Tourist information The Prespa National Park visitor centre is the new-looking yellow building on the right side of the SH79 coming from Korça with the big 'Parku Kombëtar Prespë' sign out front – you can't miss it. Find brochures and reams of information in English about the natural, historical and cultural significance of the Prespa region. It's only open in the summer, but even if the centre is closed, the maps, placards and QR codes in the car park are helpful. Don't forget to admire the view.

Maps and signs with trail-specific details in English can be found at all 'official' trailheads. The Pusteci municipality info-point sign is also useful, with a few maps and information. It's posted in the centre, by the square in front of the church.

Websites https://cdn.me-qr.com/jpg/5562034.jpg; www.wikiloc.com/wikiloc/user.do?id=4304509; www.bashkiapustec.gov.al; www.roadstoculture.eu/en/destinations-pustec-2.

ACCOMMODATION

Guest House Mitre Around 100m east of the square on Pusteci's main road; tel: 068 204 0404. This is a simply decorated but comfortable place with a superb view of the lake from the terrace, warm hospitality, home cooking and home-made wine and *raki*. Hosts can pick you up from Tirana Airport. €€

★ **Prespa's Balcony Guesthouse** 350m from the turnoff from SH79 into Gorica e Vogël village; www.instagram.com/prespas_balcony_guesthouse. The most atmospheric boutique guesthouse in Prespa National Park, this clean and cosy three-room villa is a labour of love by mother-daughter duo Zana and Cveta Trajce. *Qilims* and black-and-white family photos feel homely, and the guesthouse also maintains a small personal ethnographic 'museum' representing the Macedonian-Albanian culture of Prespa. Some artisanal handicrafts are for sale, too. Home-made dinner and breakfast include veggie-friendly options, and the English-speaking hosts can help you plan Prespa excursions. Note the rooms share a bathroom. €

EATING AND DRINKING

★ **Bar Restaurant Kristi** 4.7km from the SH79 turnoff to Leska, toward Zaroshka village; tel: 068 242 7469. This vies for the title of Prespa's go-to place for traditional preparations of freshly caught fish. They're all here: *Prespa krap* (carp), *tavë peshku* (carp casserole), *cirona* (grilled belvica trout) and *peshk i thatë* (dried and salted belvica trout). There's outdoor seating and plenty of space for kids to run around. €€

Bar Restorant Panorama 1.2km from Pusteci on the main road just east of the town; tel: 069 962 1688. It's hard to go wrong at this fish restaurant. If you're with a group, order by the kilo or plump for a king-sized pot of *tavë peshku* (carp casserole). There's also a variety of grilled meats, sausages, peppers and sweets. Huge portions, great prices. Right on the lake, it's the liveliest spot in Pusteci by night. €

Morava Mountain villages

Korça crouches at the foot of the **MORAVA MOUNTAIN** (Mali i Moravës) massif, and from the city side, the faces look scrubbed of life – even vegetation. But people live in these hills, which give way to green landscapes on the east-facing slopes, a winter paradise of firs, pines and beeches. The villages south and southeast of Korça are not immune to rural problems with infrastructure and emigration, but they still captivate. **Boboshtica** is only separated from the city by a few kilometres of farmland, while **Dardha** and **Sinica** are nestled higher up in the mountains. The three share some similarities, such as postcard-perfect views and sturdy stone churches, but each brings something unique to the table. None are served by public transport, but all are less than 25km from the centre of Korça.

Boboshtica

The village of **Boboshtica** has attractive views of the Korça plain and a smattering of nineteenth-century landmarks, but its interesting cultural and religious heritage was largely destroyed during the Hoxha years. Now, most people visit for one reason: to eat. Traditional Korçar food is at its finest in here. So, too, is a rare and delicate variety of **raki.**

ARRIVAL AND GETTING AROUND — BOBOSHTICA

By car or taxi Drive or take a taxi from Korça 7.5km southeast via the SH75, then follow the left fork to the SH90 (15min total). Park on the street or in the central square, between Taverna Shën Maria and the abandoned factory. See page 167 for Korça taxi information.

By bike It's an easy, mostly flat cycle ride from Korça.

4

ACCOMMODATION AND EATING

Rosicat Main road into Boboshtica, 200m before reaching the centre; tel: 069 229 5446. A longtime favourite for group get-togethers and live music, this is the place to catch *serenatë* (see page 162) tunes most weekends. *Rosicat* is

RAKI

Raki in Albania is not the same as rakı, the Turkish national drink. It does not taste like liquorice, nor does it turn cloudy when mixed with water. Albanian *raki* is simply unaged or lightly aged brandy (eau de vie), clear liquor distilled from fermented fruit. Production methods are not codified, but *raki* is traditionally distilled in a copper still called a **kazan**, and clocks in pretty strong at 40–60 percent ABV. Albanians take it neat and often pair the tipple with olives, with *gjizë* (ricotta-style curded cheese), with harder cheese like *kaçkavall*, with cured meats such as *proshutë crudo* or *sallam milanez*, and with morning coffee. You will be offered a taste in most rural areas, especially at someone's home or farm. If you abstain, you might offer to try or buy the person's home-made **gliko** (fruit preserve) or **kompot** (fruit drink or dessert) instead.

Most commonly derived from grapes (**raki rrushi**), *raki* can also be made with plums (**raki kumbulle**), cherries, Cornelian cherries, pears, walnuts, juniper berries, blackberries, quinces and raspberries – whatever fruit or nut is most bountiful in a particular region. In Boboshtica, mulberries reign supreme, and the resulting spirit (**raki mani**) is especially prized, with mountain fruit and herbal aromas. It is also, unusually, light green in colour. If you've been burned by supermarket *raki*, this is the place to give the spirit another chance.

More than a hundred families here distil their own *raki*, and many have both mulberry trees and grapevines at home. You can try a small flight if you're keen to test your taste buds: mulberry versus grape *raki*; single- versus double-distilled; barrel-aged versus unaged. The **Festa e Rakisë** (Raki Festival) held here in September is the place to dive in; other towns, like **Gjirokastra**, have also begun doing local takes on the boozy event. Boboshtica village leader **Kostandin Xhoxhi** does the *raki* tradition proud year-round (tel: 069 248 7313), and all the best restaurants in town can offer something to cure what ails you.

cosy and brightly painted, and its menu is formidable. In addition to staples like *lakror* (Albanian pies) and *petka* (local pasta) dishes, you can also opt for very good whole fish or kebabs. €€€

Shtëpia e Traditës 1.5km from where the SH90 towards Boboshtica splits off the SH75; www.shtepiaetradites.com. This family-run taverna ties it all together: mouthwatering traditional dishes, hospitable service, a peaceful pondside setting and fair prices. The lineup of lamb, pork and chicken includes ribs, fillet cuts and organ meat; some grilled, others with less common preparations, like pork baked in a clay oven. Fresh salads are top-notch, and grape, plum and blackberry *raki* give tipplers a spectrum of options. €€

★ **Vila Melko** Main road into town just past where the SH90 turns towards Dardha; www.facebook.com/p/Vila-Melko-100029263826927. A one-stop shop for traditional food, revelry and take-home products, *Vila Melko* is an excellent introduction to Korçar cuisine and hospitality. Ordering *lakror* (Albanian pie) is a given, and staff here can roll it for you tableside if you ask; try it with tomato and onion. Roasted meat – especially lamb or goat – elevates this place a cut above its competitors. There's often live music. Buy cherry *reçel* (jam), butter, honey or mulberry *raki* from the farm. A nine-room guesthouse with heirloom furnishings and walnut trim opened here in 2024. €€€

Dardha

Dardha might just be the handsomest village in the country. Set steeply against an east-facing slope in the **Mali i Moravës**, Dardha is a slice of the Pyrénées in Albania. Stately stone mansions with heavy wooden shutters, slate-shingled roofs and wrought-iron balconies mostly date to the late nineteenth and early twentieth centuries, and day-trippers bring their kids in the autumn to tramp through the fallen leaves around the cobblestone boulevard. At around 1300m in altitude, it snows copiously here, and Dardha has Albania's only full-service **ski slope** and resort.

By the turn of the twentieth century, the village was primed for emigration, as many of its families already worked elsewhere during the harsh winters. The United States would be the primary destination, and local history has it that the first car in Albania arrived here in the 1910s – a Ford. Money flowed back into the village, and in the years following independence, word spread that it was a winter wonderland.

The village and its lofty surroundings are the main calling card, but you can also visit the post-Byzantine **Church of St George** (Kisha e Shën Gjergjit) near the village centre, built in 1838 and retaining few original decorations. The nearby **Muzeu Foto Historik** in a 1924 schoolhouse is rarely, if ever, open.

Sinica

Around five kilometres east of Dardha, there's an even smaller village, **Sinica**. This hilly area of Morava is made for the great outdoors, so it's best enjoyed via an easy hike (1hr 15min) or bike ride from Dardha, though the road between the two villages is paved. You'll feel pretty far from civilization here, but you can spot a few post-Byzantine churches standing sentinel by the road, and a detour up to the **Vala e Madhe Waterfall** (Ujëvara Vala e Madhe) is a worthwhile diversion for its excellent views.

ARRIVAL AND GETTING AROUND — DARDHA

By car or taxi Drive or take a taxi 9km (18km total) southeastof Korça, via the SH75, then joining the SH90 (35min). Roads are well paved, but expect mountain switchbacks, and don't attempt the drive in wet or icy winter conditions unless you have winter tyres. The village streets are cobblestone, but you can find a parking area above the town, just before the bend to *Hotel Dardha*. See page 167 for Korça taxi information.

ACCOMMODATION AND EATING

Dardha is a coveted spot during certain times of year, and you'll want to book in advance in winter. Some of the better restaurants are just outside the village in either direction.

★ **Alpin House** 6.6km northwest of Dardha on SH90; www.facebook.com/Alpinvillage. *Alpin House* gives a creative spin to mountain cuisine. Roast pork with quince and *petulla* (fried dough) with walnuts are specialties, or adventurous diners can order roast head of lamb, once a national favourite but hard to come by today. Kilometres away from anything else and gorgeous in all seasons, it's a fun place to linger after dark, catch live music, dance and drink mulberry, plum and grape *raki*. €€

Bujtina Vatra Sinicare Main road, Dardha to Sinica; www.facebook.com/bujtinavatrasiniciare. A charming restaurant near the Vala e Madhe Waterfall that exudes family pride, this eatery has an outdoor balcony with panoramic views for the fresh seasons and a cosy stone indoors for the snowy ones. Succulent pork ribs, and cherries, strawberries and greens from around the property, make it Sinica's top spot. €€

Guest House Ktona Dardha village south of centre; tel: 068 464 4614. If Dardha feels a little polished for a Balkan village, stay at this more rustic stone cottage, a restored country home built in 1890. With rocking chairs on the terrace, a garden, a full kitchen, an iron furnace for cool nights, *qilims* and floral-upholstered armchairs, it feels like the perfect mountain hideaway. €€

Hotel Dardha SH90 just before the descent into the village; www.facebook.com/hotel.dardha.5. Somewhat out of place in a village of this size, the 24-room *Hotel Dardha* is nonetheless where you'll stay if everything else is booked up. But it does have features and amenities to recommend it: a spa with a hot tub, a billiards table, on-site parking and exceptional views of the mountains from most rooms. €€

ACTIVITIES

SKIING

Ski-Pista Bigëll 3.6km by road west of Dardha centre, on the way from Korça; www.facebook.com/SkiPistaBigell. It may not be Vail or Chamonix, but Dardha has the only skiing piste in Albania with a lift, a lodge, equipment to rent, an après-ski restaurant and chalets. The food is good, the hospitality is warm, the slope is well kept, and that's about all you really need for a leisurely day mucking around in the snow.

4

The Voskopoja Highlands

From the late seventeenth to the late eighteenth centuries, **VOSKOPOJA** was one of the most powerful and prosperous cities in all of what is now Albania, but the village that remains today doesn't appear especially marvellous – at first. A quick 20km trip from Korça but sequestered in the mountains to the west, Voskopoja fills up with weekenders seeking fresh air amid the black pines. But the glory of the eighteenth-century Enlightenment of learning and art in the Greek-speaking Orthodox world echoes through its five surviving churches adorned with magnificent frescoes, most of them invisible to passersby.

The village of **Shipska**, 5km north, holds another mid-seventeenth-century church whose floor-to-dome frescoes have been restored to pristine condition, while **Vithkuqi**, 20km south of Voskopoja, adds still more churches decorated in the same exuberant post-Byzantine style. Together, these places of worship preserve arguably the greatest concentration of eighteenth-century **Orthodox fresco art** in the world, rivalled only by the Mount Athos monastery complex in Greece.

Unlike those at Athos, the Albanian churches can be visited by both men and women, Orthodox or not.

Brief history

Voskopoja, called Moschopolis by Greeks, grew from a smattering of shepherds to a city of 20,000 to 60,000 Albanians, Greeks, Aromanians (Vlachs), Bulgarians and others in a remarkably short period of time around the mid-seventeenth century. Only a century later, it would be reduced to rubble almost as quickly and decisively.

The meteoric rise and fall of a populous centre of trade, art and education – almost entirely Christian in the Ottoman Empire – has bestowed Voskopoja almost mythical status. The area, owned and protected by the sultan's mother, controlled a critical overland trade route between the Adriatic and Istanbul. As a moneymaker for the empire, Voskopoja was given unusual freedom to promulgate and celebrate Orthodox ideas, faith and art.

The **New Academy**, an incubator of East-meets-West ideas, was founded in 1744; scholars taught philosophy, theology and poetry, Descartes, Locke and Leibniz. For a time, the only **printing press** in the empire operated here, along with a vast library. Contemporary foreign visitors counted twenty-plus churches, and the city's wealth and prestige lured the **post-Byzantine masters**, including the **Zografi brothers** (see page 188) and **David Selenica** (see page 188), to paint its houses of worship. (Ottoman authorities tolerated such lavish displays of Orthodox iconography – so long as they were inside.) In 1769, marauders ransacked the city, and it was razed twice more in the span of two decades. Most survivors took the hint and fled.

On a more triumphant note, the first assault brigade of the **Lëvizja Antifashiste Nacional-Çlirimtare** (LANÇ; the National Liberation Movement) the partisan Communist resistance to the Axis occupation of Albania, formed and trained on Makërza field near Vithkuqi in August 1943. Enver Hoxha exhorted eight hundred soldiers there to 'be a terror for the enemy and hope for the people', and the brigade would go on to fight in virtually every important battle until the liberation of Albania.

Voskopoja

Fewer than a thousand people live in **Voskopoja**, a knot of cobblestone passages lined with century-old homes, traditional guesthouses and excellent restaurants and tavernas. The five surviving frescoed churches from Voskopoja's eighteenth-century heyday are mostly on the periphery of the village or outside it, testament to the size of the city that once was.

The **Church of St Nicholas** (Kisha e Shën Kollit), near the present-day centre, and the **Monastery of St John the Baptist** (Manastiri i Shën Prodhromit), two kilometres up a hill to the northeast of town, are the only ones that keep their doors – or, at the least, grounds – open during relatively fixed hours, but a visit to some combination of the other four can usually be arranged by calling tel: 069 995 5149 (if that fails, try texting Anxhela Zguri, a docent and owner of the excellent guesthouse *Bujtina Liana*, on tel: 069 473 0344).

The churches are slowly being restored. Some have been severely vandalized – mostly after communism, as recently as the 2010s – and all have suffered neglect and weather damage. Not all are always accessible, but docents who live in town will open up the ones that are, giving a brief guided tour and overview of the art and architecture of each, in English.

Church of St Nicholas

Rruga Shën Kolli and Rruga Koste Cekani • Free

The **Church of St Nicholas** (Kisha e Shën Kollit) is the perfect introduction to the Voskopoja church ensemble. It's in the centre of the village, it holds weekly services and… well, just look inside – the interior is resplendent in painter **David Selenica**'s golds, reds, greens, whites and, most of all, blues, completed in 1726. Every surface that's not floor or furniture is frescoed. Coming from a bright sunny day into the rather dimly lit, sooty shrine feels like crossing into another, mystical dimension. Dozens of scenes here portray both beloved and bizarre stories from the Bible and the adventures of St Nicholas. On the south transept wall, find one panel where the saint captains a ship laden with suspiciously modern-looking cannons; on another, he outwits the Greek goddess Artemis.

The church is architecturally similar to its Voskopoja siblings and other post-Byzantine churches around Southern Albania: an elongated basilica shape instead of the Byzantine cross-in-square plan, with a nave, aisles, a broad narthex, a series of domes and a portico, all hidden within a fairly humdrum stone exterior. Don't miss the portico frescoes, finished by the **Zografi brothers** in 1750, which are characteristically graphic. St Ignatius here looks not so much terrified or angry, more disappointed, to be mauled by lions. It's worth inquiring here about the spectacular **Church of the Archangels** (Kisha e Shën Mëhillit) down the street, which will hopefully reopen sooner rather than later.

4

POST-BYZANTINE PAINTING

By the year 1501, almost all of Albania and mainland Greece had been conquered by the Ottoman Empire, but the region's residents were largely Christian. When the Renaissance and then the Enlightenment caught fire in Western Europe, the ideas swirling about philosophy, philology and art spread east to cosmopolitan Orthodox centres like Ioannina and Kastoria, now in Greece, and Voskopoja. Nowhere is that influence more visible now than in the paintings of what came to be called the **post-Byzantine** tradition.

Not much is known about the lives of the master painters. **Onufri**, one of the first and most ingenious, was born in the early sixteenth century, wrote in Greek, likely trained in Venice and founded a school of painting in Berati. Along the way, he came up with ideas about colour, composition and figurative representation that would define the post-Byzantine style – always firmly rooted in the visual language of Orthodox iconography, but incorporating innovations and techniques of **Western Gothic** and **Renaissance** styles. Onufri was meticulous about detail; some of his panels tell multiple stories across the frame and make even more allusions. He was also – well – unorthodox about colour. His vivid 'Onufri red' pigment is considered his signature shade, but he also applied pink and teal, often contrasting like with like on the same canvas or shading one hue into another.

Nikolla Onufri, his son, worked in his father's tradition, and the Central Albanian lineage of iconographers continued with **Kostandin Shpataraku**, born near Elbasani in the first half of the eighteenth century. Shpataraku had an eye for dynamic motion and liked to dress up his biblical scenes with the clothes, buildings and even food of his own time. For instance, in his *Last Supper*, now in Korça's National Museum of Medieval Art (see page 165), the disciples are reclining, gesticulating and reaching across the table, which is laden with Albanian meats, cheeses and breads that may look familiar.

4

Also in the early eighteenth century, the so-called **School of Korça** ignited. Kolonja-born **David Selenica** painted big, bold and all over the Greek Orthodox world, but the **Church of St Nicholas** (Kisha e Shën Kollit) in Voskopoja is his masterpiece, done up floor to dome by Selenica and his workshop between 1722 and 1726. A look inside makes it clear why he's considered for blue what Onufri was for red. Selenica did not hesitate to inject anachronisms and even humour into his scenes, and he achieved a mastery of portraiture unmatched by other post-Byzantine artists. The faces of his saints and angels are probably the likenesses of ordinary cityfolk in the towns where he worked. Selenica's younger Korçar contemporaries, the Baroque-inspired brothers **Kostandin and Athanas Zografi**, debuted on the art scene at the peak of Voskopoja's creative energy, and their signatures can be found in several churches there. They excelled in both fine details and broad landscape elements – the ruffling of tunics and the cast of glances; flowers, birds, buildings, happy cities and imploding cities that had wronged God.

Church of the Dormition of St Mary

Rruga Shën Maria • Charge • Guided tour with admission

The largest of the surviving five and once a cathedral, the **Church of the Dormition of St Mary** (Kisha Fjetja e Shën Marisë) in the north of the village is generally open to visitors who telephone (see page 190), though time has been unkind to it. Completed around 1699, the complex may have held as many as one thousand worshippers at once. As to be expected, the fragmentary frescoes here celebrate the Holy Virgin, and a closer look pays off with some Bible lore they don't teach in Sunday school. Notice, under the bed where Mary lies in rest, a grabby little guy reaching for her. The Archangel Michael swoops in to lop off his hands.

Church of St Athanasius

650m walking west, then north, of Kisha Fjetja e Shën Marisë • Charge • Guided tour with admission

Near Shën Marisë and usually closed, the **Church of St Athanasius** (Kisha e Shën Thanasit) is still worth a look for its portico frescoes, painted by the **Zografi brothers**

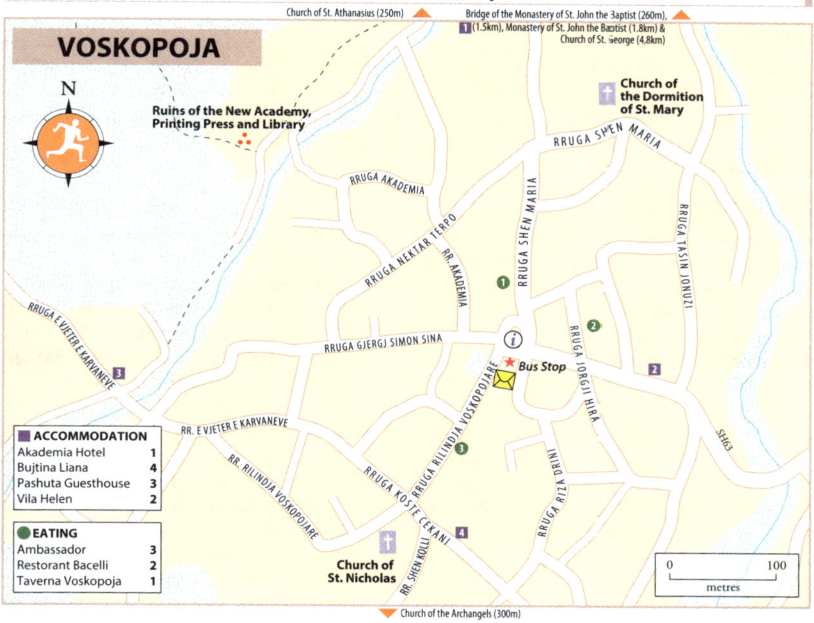

in 1745. The pair leaned into apocalyptic scenes from Revelation here. In one lunette painting, the towers of Babylon collapse on an unfortunate crowd, while in another, angels turn the rivers and springs to blood. But otherwise, it's a peaceful spot at the edge of the village.

Monastery of St John the Baptist

2.4km northeast of Voskopoja up Rruga Shën Prodhromi • Free • Walk from the centre in 30–40min

A hike (or drive) uphill out of town through a conifer corridor leads to the tranquil **Monastery of St John the Baptist** (Manastiri i Shën Prodhromit), a favourite local picnic spot that really flaunts the natural beauty of this corner of Albania, especially in the autumn when leaves blaze brilliant yellow and orange. The frescoes in the modest church, which dates to 1632, are of some interest, as the first of them may have been painted by the monks themselves. You'll also cross or pass the Ura e Manastirit të Shën Prodhromit, an attractive cobblestone bridge from the same period linking the monastery to the town.

New Academy, printing press and library

Rruga Akademia • Free

On a dirt road at the western edge of town, a sign reads 'New Academy and library of the city, 1742. In this area stood the 1720 printing press'. Crumbling stone foundations and rubble heaps are scattered around the area and into pastureland well beyond the existing village. It's all that remains of the great university.

ARRIVAL AND GETTING AROUND — VOSKOPOJA

By bus Buses travel from the Korça bus terminal to Voskopoja (and vice versa) every two hours until late afternoon (several daily; 30min). The village stop is at the informal central square of Voskopoja, the intersection of Rruga Shën Maria and Rruga Rilindja Voskopojare, next to the tourist info centre.

By car or taxi The 20km road to Korça, the SH63, has some manageable zigzags, but it's paved and well maintained (journey time 30min). If you don't have your own car, Korça taxis ply the route frequently; see page 167 for information. Most guesthouses here will also be happy to offer advice on transport.

4

INFORMATION

Tourist information The tourist information centre in the central square is rarely, if ever, open. However, a map of the village and points of interest, as well as placards with some history in English and engravings of eighteenth-century Voskopoja, can be found nearby. Call tel: 069 995 5149 to book a guide for visits to the churches. Korça tour operators also offer itineraries for Voskopoja (see page 167). Note: there are no ATMs, petrol stations or pharmacies in Voskopoja; bring cash.

ACCOMMODATION

SEE MAP PAGE 189

In Voskopoja, every house is a guesthouse, it seems. Fortunately, most of them maintain high standards and have appealing restaurants. If you have your own car and crave slumber in a sleepy village, Voskopoja can be a serviceable base for exploring greater Korça.

Akademia Hotel 2km from Voskopoja, up Rruga Shën Prodhromi toward the monastery; www.akademiahotel.com. In the 1950s, the state built Voskopoja's first nature retreat, now the atmospheric *Akademia Hotel*. Restored to its slightly offbeat glory, it has sixteen rooms, plus thirteen villas in the forest. There's a restaurant with plentiful indoor and outdoor seating, and reception can arrange hiking, horseback rides and even weddings on site. A nice place to linger over a hot drink on a crisp day, even if you don't sleep over. €€

4

Bujtina Liana Rruga Koste Cekani; tel: 069 473 0343. This cosy guesthouse right across the street from the Church of St Nicholas faithfully replicates the historic villa style. Rooms sleeping one to four people have modern amenities and exposed stone walls; the pick of the bunch come with fireplaces and balconies. Co-owner Anxhela Zguri is a docent for the churches and highly knowledgeable about Voskopoja history, art and architecture. €€

Pashuta Guesthouse Rruga e Vjetër e Karvanëve; www.facebook.com/hotelpashuta. A consistently popular eight-room guesthouse that has kept its prices modest, *Pashuta* has a collection of modern, comfortable rooms, the best with stone fireplaces and Jacuzzi bathtubs. Near the centre of Voskopoja, it maintains a rustic feeling with a lawn, playground and kitchen-garden of fresh produce for its traditional restaurant. €€

★ **Vila Helen** SH63 and Rruga Shën Prodhromi; www.instagram.com/thevillahelen. The luxe suites at *Vila Helen* are ideal for couples or families and equipped with top-flight amenities. Fireplaces, Jacuzzi bathtubs and stylish decor set against stone walls make it the most romantic spot in town, great for a special-occasion getaway. Expect abstract art, exposed wood beams, raw-edge wood tables, flower petals on the bed, incense sticks, that sort of thing. The bar serves excellent *petulla* (Albanian puffy doughnuts), French toast with mascarpone and other breakfast treats. €€€

EATING

SEE MAP PAGE 189

★ **Ambassador** Rruga Rilindja Voskopojare; www.facebook.com/restorantambassador. Serving up hearty traditional cuisine in the heart of the village, *Ambassador* has become a staple on the Voskopoja dining scene. Decked out with dark wood and an imposing hearth, it looks the part to host a Balkan winter feast. Spit-roasted lamb, lamb offal and roasted veal are the standout mains, but fried cheese with honey and sesame, washed down with home-made *raki* is a fine way to start the night. Grilled and pickled vegetables, and yoghurt with walnuts, help round out the regional delicacies. Catch live music here on weekends. €€

Restorant Bacelli SH63 and Rruga Jorgji Hira; www.facebook.com/hotelbacellivoskopoje. A very fine restaurant on the first floor of a very fine hotel, *Bacelli* is hard to miss thanks to its rather ostentatious colonnaded archway that beckons from the street. Inside, the space is cosy and simple, though. Roasted 'village' (free-range) chicken over *petka* (local pasta) is a Voskopoja specialty. A solid selection of Albanian and Italian wines is also available. €€

Taverna Voskopoja Rruga Shën Maria; www.facebook.com/p/Taverna-Voskopoja-100051259556294. A large, lively space, *Taverna Voskopoja* can put on a simple lunch or a boisterous party. It's easy to cram a table with chunks of roasted veal, pork and lamb, and plates of pastries like home-made *lakror*. If getting two pies feels daunting, try one with half spinach and half tomatoes and onions. €

Shipska

A pleasant, mild hike along the old road north from Voskopoja brings you to **Shipska**, a modest huddle of houses with a grand church, the **Kisha e Shën Gjergjit** (St George). The three-storey, double-porticoed basilica was reconstructed and restored from near-ruin in 2004, by architects hoping to provide a blueprint for the preservation of other post-Byzantine churches in the region. None have yet matched the success here, though. With the naos, narthex, portico, bell tower and frescoes returned to their mid-eighteenth-century glory, this church is the best way to see Orthodox art and architecture as the Albanian, Aromanian and Greek Christians of the 1700s would have. Probably best to ask your church guide in Voskopoja if it's unlocked before heading off.

ARRIVAL AND GETTING AROUND — SHIPSKA

On foot Only 5km north of Voskopoja, it's probably easiest and definitely most enjoyable to simply walk to Shipska (follow signs from Rruga Shën Prodhromi; 1hr 15min).

Vithkuqi

The rise and fall of **Vithkuqi** more or less dovetailed with that of Voskopoja. At its peak in the late eighteenth century, Vithkuqi may have had as many as 15,000 residents and more than fifteen churches and monasteries. While it lacks the 'lost city' mythos and tourist cachet of Voskopoja, the village, spread along three hilltops, arguably has a more sublime setting and can be reached via a picturesque drive past the azure **Gjançi reservoir** (Rezervuari i Gjançit).

Monastery of Sts Peter and Paul

3.1km by road northeast of Vithkuqi • Free • Turn left after crossing the Ura e Zotos bridge, keep right, and continue on foot (10min) after the road becomes rough

A hidden gem in the hills outside town, the **Monastery of Sts Peter and Paul** (Manastiri i Shën Pjetrit dhe Palit) is worth exploring even when the church is locked. (If there's someone at Kisha e Shën Mëhillit in town, they may be able to arrange for you to peek inside this one.) There is actually a pair of churches here: that of the two apostles, and the **Chapel of Sts Cosmas and Damian** (Kapela i Shën Kozmai dhe Damjanoi). Construction began in 1709, and the frescoes are owed to the workshop of **Kostandin and Athanas Zografi**, who enlisted local Vithkuqi talent to execute much of the composition; some of the most intricate paintings can be seen in the unusual single-domed porch through which the larger church is entered.

The monks here lived in the chapel – and here they remain. Ask to visit the ossuary beneath the chapel, where the skulls and bones of quite a few nameless brothers are stacked, boxed and scattered (or don't).

4

Church of the Archangel Michael

1.2km northwest from Vithkuqi along the main town thoroughfare • Free • 20min walk

A rather large post-Byzantine basilica, once the diocesan centre of Vithkuqi, the **Church of the Archangel Michael** (Kisha e Shën Mëhillit) most likely dates to the late seventeenth century. With three aisles, three domes, barrel vaulting and a preserved portico, it's a church you can take your time in.

ARRIVAL AND GETTING AROUND — VITHKUQI

By car or taxi Vithkuqi is 27km (35min) southwest of Korça via the SH75 (Rruga Insan Korça), on paved roads that are mostly straight. See page 167 for important information on Korça taxis.

By bus There is one bus to Vithkuqi from Korça each day, departing at midday and returning in the early morning (1 daily; 40min).

ACCOMMODATION AND EATING

Bar Restorant Andoni First right entering Vithkuqi on the main village thoroughfare from the south; tel: 068 526 6990. An easy-going spot near the centre of Vithkuqi, *Andoni* is a decent place to grab an *ekspres* (espresso) or dig into a *lakror* (Albanian pie), a fresh salad or walnuts, a delicacy of this particular village. €

Guest House Tona Main road, 200m east of the Kisha e Shën Mëhillit; www.instagram.com/guest_house_tona. This small stone villa has an old-fashioned iron furnace heater, an heirloom *qilim* and large windows framing views of the pine-blanketed hills, often dusted in snow come winter. A cute, cosy place in the style of the homes that many Korçars still live in. €€

Kolonja and Gramos Mountain

The far southeast of Albania follows the SH75 along a fishing hook shape – south from Korça and then west to Përmeti. Long a remote corner of Albania, **KOLONJA** is much more than a destination for the hardiest of backpackers or communist-era asylum-seekers fleeing to Greece over the mountains. The area has benefited from its solitary location, in some ways, developing slowly yet smartly. A farmer first kicked the dirt on a patch that would become what we now call **agritourism**, in 1998. One of Albania's quaintest and quietest historic villages, **Rehova**, has been protected and preserved. Today, much of the main road is freshly asphalted, with a new motorway impending in 2025.

Saying that, Kolonja thankfully hasn't changed too much: it's still an overwhelmingly rural place where scruffy men herd sheep up scraggly peaks. And, though the trip from Korça or Përmeti has never been easier, navigating the region by car still requires nerves of steel. Kolonja lies on a plateau around 1100m above sea level, where the landscape – and the road – begins fitfully tilting and climbing and careening down again to the Vjosa River (Lumi i Vjosës).

You may find it difficult to pinpoint 'Kolonja' on a map. The seat of the municipality is Erseka, a 38km drive south of Korça, with the town of Leskoviku 44km further south. The Greek border is only around 10km east of Erseka as the crow flies, and you can indeed hike it – to the highest peak of the **Gramos Mountain** (Mali i Gramozit) massif, **Çuka e Peçit**.

Brief history

Kolonjars and Greeks have long been courteous neighbours. The earliest evidence of trade with Thessaly dates to the third millennium BC: a copper chisel and vessel discovered in the settlement of **Kamniku**, whose people were masters of pottery. When the site was excavated, archaeologists found painted vases in fantastical shapes, with bulbs protruding like Winnie-the-Pooh ears. During the late Bronze and Iron Ages, the Illyrians of Kolonja rendezvoused with folks as far south as Attica. A hoard of coins found in the region was minted near Athens in the sixth or fifth century BC – the era of Athenian democracy, Solon and Pericles. Around the same time, the Illyrians began burying their dead in the **Tumulus of Rehova** (see page 193), one of the largest burial mounds in the region, with 285 graves found.

On 6 July, 1943, Kolonja suffered one of the worst war crimes in **World War II Albania**. Wehrmacht soldiers on their way to Axis-occupied Greece massacred the village of **Borova** with flamethrowers, executing 107 civilians. Today, a simple, poignant memorial stands on a small hill: a circular stone wall surrounding smaller circles of headstones, with individual families of the victims occupying each circle.

Erseka

The capital of the Kolonja municipality, **Erseka** is home to fewer than four thousand people, with a handful of unassuming but bright Italianate and communist-era buildings arranged around **Sheshi Rilindja**. Its main attraction is the **Muzeu Jorgji Qirjako**, a municipal museum named after one of Albania's best translators, which could appear drably rationalist from the outside, if not for a pair of large, jazzy *qilim*-patterned signs reading 'As e vogel' and 'As e madhe'. Together, they translate as 'Neither small nor big', the name of a popular Kolonjare folk song and an apt tagline for the region.

Jorgji Qirjako Museum

Rruga Pali Prifti on Sheshi Rilindja • Charge • Tel: 069 745 4143

Built in 1962, the **Jorgji Qirjako Museum** (Muzeu Jorgji Qirjako) is the main cultural centre in Kolonja (also called Muzeu Historik Ersekë). The collection is pretty small, though its remit is wide-reaching, and its upkeep is sharper than you'll see in many municipal museums. Spanning eight thousand years of Kolonja, exhibits cover the archaeology, history, ethnography and art of the region.

Be sure to check out the replicas of the Kamniku ritual ceramics and admire the geometric patterns on original pottery. The recently rediscovered collection of early twentieth-century photos by Albanian photographer **Dhimitër Vangjeli** (1872–1957) is of particular interest, capturing everyday life from a century ago – men showing off their furs and cars, women testing out Singer sewing machines. As in Dardha, rural meant refined.

Rehova

2.2km from Sheshi Rilindja, directly east on Rruga Pali Prifti • Free • 35min walk on sidewalk or cycle via bike path on the paved street

Easily reachable by car, bike or even on foot, **Rehova** nonetheless feels extremely secluded – at least for now. It is set in stone: streets, walls and roof tiles match the slate-grey of the Mali i Gramozit rising to the east. The village begins at the Rehova Gate (Porta e Rehovës) and adjacent square, where visitors can find a tourist information point (unstaffed).

Climb the sloping cobblestone Rruga Pali Prifti to the **Church of St Nicholas** (Kisha e Shën Nikollës), the original home of the nineteenth-century iconostasis now on show in the **National Museum of Medieval Art** (see page 165) in Korça. You'll find some signs in the church and in the café next door.

The village's courtly two-storey 'American'-style villas date to the early twentieth century, when men emigrated to the United States and sent earnings back to their families; several have now been converted into comfortable guesthouses. It's a good overnight option for hikers keen to strike out on the 9km day trek to the highest peak of Gramos Mountain (Çuka e Peçit).

ARRIVAL AND GETTING AROUND — ERSEKA AND REHOVA

By bus Erseka is well served by buses from Korça's main bus terminal (many daily; 55min); the bus station at Sheshi 20 Tetori is 400m from the main square, Sheshi Rilindja, on the SH75.

Destinations Durrësi (several daily; 4hr 50min); Leskoviku (several daily; 1hr 10min); Gjirokastra (1 daily; 3hr 30min); Përmeti (several daily; 2hr 20min); Pogradeci (several daily; 1hr 45min); Tirana (several daily; 4hr); Saranda (1 daily; 4hr 30min).

By car or taxi Erseka, Rehova and Borova are easy to reach by car on roads that are in good condition going both north and south. All are well signed and hard to miss. A straighter route to Korça on the SH75 that skips hilly switchbacks will be completed in 2025, but south to Leskoviku and Përmeti is formidably steep, narrow and curvy. Taxis from Korça will generally take you to Erseka or nearby villages; see information on page 167. Taxis can also be found in Erseka if you're continuing south.

INFORMATION

Tourist information There is no visitor centre in Erseka, but the Bashkia Kolonjë town hall on the east side of Sheshi Rilindja, next to Muzeu Jorgji Qirjako, can offer maps and brochures if it has them. In Rehova, the tourist info point at the Rehova Gate (Porta e Rehovës) is usually unstaffed, but hiking maps, general information about the village and contact details for local accommodation are all posted on the windows.

Websites www.kolonja.gov.al; www.facebook.com/p/Bashkia-Kolonjë-100064822352848.

Tour operators Explorer Albania (Rruga Mujo Ulqinaku, Pall. 5, Kati 1, Tirana; www.explorer-albania.al) is helmed by experienced local guides, siblings Marjen, Eva and Anila Rama. The eight-day Folkloric Tour in the South of Albania takes in Korça, Kolonja, Gjirokastra and Përmeti, focusing on farm visits, cooking classes, regional handicrafts and traditional song and dance performances. Tours are customizable in length, focus and starting point, and a shorter option is the particularly excellent two- or three-day excursion through the highlights of Kolonja.

ACCOMMODATION

★ **Bujtina Cakuli** Rruga Pali Prifti, Rehova; www.instagram.com/bujtina_cakuli_rehove. Valentina and Gjergji Cakuli have created a serene scene indeed at their year-round Rehova guesthouse, a traditional stone villa upgraded and updated by their architect daughter. The couple have four rooms with modern amenities around a shared living room, and food is a priority: cherries, tomatoes, plums, peppers and much more from the garden are channelled into Valentina's vegetarian-friendly cooking. The Cakulis also make *raki*, offer cooking classes and help hikers plot their paths up Mali i Gramozit. €€

Hotel Borova Sheshi Rilindja and Rruga Pali Prifti, Erseka; tel: 069 910 8388. A larger hotel, by Kolonja standards, this clean, comfortable option was converted from a communist-era lodge. Fully refurbished and reopened in 2024 with brand-new amenities and fresh decor, it offers family-friendly rooms and the best view in town of Sheshi Rilindja (and the rest of Erseka, for that matter). €€

Shtëpia Koço Thomollari Rruga Shën Gjergji, Rehova; tel: 068 399 4585. Lavdëria and husband Koço Thomollari have hosted visitors in one of Rehova's oldest houses for more than a decade, offering an inviting bed-and-breakfast stay in their three rooms. The couple also prepare casseroles, *lakror*, meat dishes and more for those who want dinner, providing guests with a glimpse of traditional, friendly village life and hospitality. €

EATING

Borova Agroturizëm 3.2km south of Erseka on SH75; www.facebook.com/hotelrestorantborova. A fine establishment for regional ingredients and dishes, including fresh salad, roast chicken and, sometimes, *kukurec* – lamb wrapped around seasoned offal, including tripe and sweetbreads, tied to a spit and roasted. There's outdoor seating and sometimes live music, if you're looking to party in Erseka. €€

DIRECTORY

Banks and currency exchange There's a Western Union on the SH75 in the centre of Erseka near the bus station and Rruga Ahmet Bektashi.

Medical Call tel: 112 or tel: 127 for emergencies. The municipal hospital, Spitali Kolonjë Shaniko Jupasi, is on Rruga Gani Butka and SH75.

4

Gramos Mountain and Gërmenji-Sheleguri Nature Reserve

Part of the Pindus range in Northern Greece and Southern Albania, **Gramos Mountain** (Mali i Gramozit) is not simply a single mountain but a long limestone range that provides the backdrop for and sculpts the landscape of Kolonja. Rising to 2500m, it has the highest peak in the south of Albania, but it can be hiked comfortably enough in a day, and the slopes aren't so steep that they can't be ascended by mountain or dirt bikes.

Moderately challenging trails lead to **Çuka e Peçit**, the crowning summit, as well as the glacial **Gramos Lake** (Liqeni i Gramozit). You're more likely to stumble across mountain goats than fellow tourists on treks. Along the way expect the unexpected: tea infused with locally grown herbs; a Bektashi *teqe* (place of worship); or the ruins of a communist-era military border guard post. Rehova is a popular launchpad for hikes, but Çuka e Peçit can be reached more quickly from the villages of Starjeja (or Starje) or Hodallari. This isn't a national park, and some trails can be tricky to follow, so download the Wikiloc (www.wikiloc.com) app to navigate routes or enlist the help of your guesthouse. Both Bujtina Cakuli (see page 193) in Rehova and Sofra Kolonjare (see page 195) near Erseka can point you in the right direction or arrange a guide.

The **Gërmenji-Sheleguri Nature Reserve** (Rezervati Natyror Gërmenj-Shelegur), tucked into the folds of the foothills south of Mali i Gramozit, is a nature-lover's wonderland, densely forested with oak, fir and black pine, gorgeous in all seasons. With its relatively cool climate, the natural larder of Kolonja brims with apples, tomatoes, onions and more. Rabbits, boars and lamb grow small and lean here, and two of the standout agritourism farms in Albania, **Farma Sotira** (see page 195) and **Sofra Kolonjare** (see page 195), honour the culinary traditions of the region with flair.

ARRIVAL AND GETTING AROUND — GRAMOS MOUNTAIN

By bus Buses between Korça, Erseka, Leskoviku and Përmeti will stop at the major agritourism farms along the SH75, including *Farma Sotira* and *Sofra Kolonjare*, if you ask the driver.

By car Starjeja, Hodallari and Rehova, the usual hiking start points, are all less than 3km from the SH75; follow signs. Most larger agritourism restaurants and farm stays are directly off the motorway between villages.

ACCOMMODATION AND EATING

★ **Farma Sotira** SH75, 16km northeast of Leskoviku; www.farmasotira.com. Despite the natural bounty of the surrounding land, *Farma Sotira* started life in 1998 as a fish farm, and concrete trout beds still crisscross the property. Owners Toni and Jonida Hida were hosting a friend for a late night of *raki*, who noted there was nowhere even remotely nearby to sleep off the boozy excesses – and the idea for a campground was born. Pitches were later joined by eleven rustic bungalows. *Sotira* is a working farm, with three hundred sheep, seventy cows, chickens, ducks and fifty beehives. It's an unabashedly outdoorsy place, eschewing luxury trappings and offering soul-stirring activities like swimming, volleyball, hiking and evening horseback rides up the slopes of Gërmenji-Sheleguri, as well as an 'apitherapy' room where you can strap on a mask and breathe through a beehive. Camping €; rooms and bungalows €€€

★ **Sofra Kolonjare** SH75, 14km north of Erseka; www.sofrakolonjare.al. Brothers Edi and Xhensil Bilo, along with their families, pull together all the strands of Kolonjar farming, food, hospitality and folklore at *Sofra Kolonjare*, a multigenerational project that started in 2002 with the opening of the main lodge. *Sofra* is serious about old-school gastronomy. You might, for instance, have the chance to watch *petka* (pasta) being rolled out on mats on the lawn by women singing traditional *petka*-making songs (in praise of hardworking women). *Copranik*, a Kolonjar pie with corn, cheese, green onions and chicken, is the speciality to try here, but seasonal dishes featuring lamb, *lakror*, *kompot* and other Southeastern Albanian treats are all executed expertly. The team also leads hikes into the Mali i Gramozit foothills. Overnighters can camp, stay in the agritourism lodge or upgrade to one of eight rooms in the luxury villa opened in 2024. Camping €; hotel €€€

Leskoviku

Once an Ottoman outpost of some importance, **Leskoviku** is now a tiny but beautifully situated town 44km south of Erseka with a reputation for excellence in three important realms: music, booze and thermal baths. **Sazet music**, or *saze*, usually played by a band with polyphonic singers, lutes, a clarinet, an accordion and sometimes a violin, first came on the scene in the late nineteenth century, and Leskoviku is among the best places to catch a live performance – ideally while enjoying a glass of red wine from the Balkan grape variety Mavrud.

To unwind in warm mineral-rich pools overlooking the Vjosa, far from, well, everything, drive and hike 14km south and east to **Sarandapori Thermal Springs**, or Sarandaporo (Burimet Termale Sarandaporo). There are no resorts or complexes here; simply hop in.

4

ARRIVAL AND GETTING AROUND — LESKOVIKU

By bus The bus stop is in the centre of Leskoviku, next to Melesin Distillery.

Destinations Erseka (several daily; 1hr 10min); Gjirokastra (1 daily; 2hr 20min); Korça (several daily; 2hr); Përmeti (several daily; 1hr 10min); Saranda (1 daily; 3hr 20min); Tirana (1 daily; 5hr).

By car The roads to Leskoviku are beautiful, well-asphalted and safe, but difficult even by Albanian standards, especially if you're prone to carsickness. Driving east from Përmeti, take the SH80 southeast via Tre Urat, then the SH65 north (1hr 15min). South from Erseka, you need to follow the SH75 for 1hr. If you're driving to or from Korça, the 2hr journey is a dizzying series of seemingly endless zigzags. Check your petrol before you set off.

DRINKING AND ENTERTAINMENT

★ **Melesin Distillery** Rruga Faik Konica 5; www.instagram.com/melesin.distillery. A combination distillery-restaurant-hotel-music venue, *Melesin* makes *raki* finished in oak and cherry barrels, as well as gin and wine. The copper column and pot stills can be seen in the dining area of the repurposed historic building. Exposed stone walls, archival photos and judicious use of Albanian motifs give the place a minimalist-chic vibe. The Sazet e Leskovikut band of Kristi Konica (see below) plays here every week.

Sazet e Leskovikut tel: 069 751 5275. The Leskoviku-based four-man band of clarinettist Kristi Konica performs around Kolonja; they're your best chance to catch *sazet* music live in the region. With songs about loving, dancing and Leskoviku, the traditional *sazet* repertoire is a little more upbeat and up-tempo than Korça's *serenatas* (see page 162) and you're encouraged to hit the dancefloor and work on your *valle* moves.

Southwest Albania

GJIROKASTRA CASTLE

5

Southwest Albania

A historically harsh and unforgiving place, Albania's inland south forged fearless, fearsome, shrewd and poetic figures who shaped the culture and trajectory of the nation. The folktales of this region often seem to end in tears – as do many of its real-life stories. A seventeenth-century traveller referred to Gjirokastra – the heart of the far south – as 'the city of lamentation' for its loud, frequent mourning rituals. From the slate-shingled towns and isolated mountain villages came some of the most celebrated and notoriously uncelebrated Albanians in modern history who inflicted tragedy or bore it: Ali Pasha, the freethinking warlord; paranoid dictator Enver Hoxha; Abdyl, Naim and Sami Frashëri, the forward-thinking brothers and leaders of the Albanian National Awakening; genius, wily novelist Ismail Kadare; and Musine Kokalari, the brave, persecuted voice of democracy. In Gjirokastra, Përmeti, the Dangëllia uplands, the Myzeqeja plain, and the Vjosa and Drino river valleys, there is not only astonishing natural beauty, but also a rich history rooted in the triumphant but bittersweet story of its people. While the Southwest technically encompasses the Albanian riviera, in this Guide we have covered the coastal stretch in chapter six (see page 236).

Gjirokastra, the storybook UNESCO World Heritage city, is unmissable for its Gordian knot of cobblestone streets and alleys, its towering sharp-edged castle and its lofty, lordly fortified mansions. It's a place where you can buy bespoke bas-reliefs carved from stone on the spot in the bazaar, ride a vintage Mercedes on rough roads, and watch generations of singers and dancers unite in traditional folk performances. The Drino Valley (Lugina e Drinos), stretching from Gjirokastra to the Greek border 28km south, is imprinted with the architectural fingerprints of civilizations spanning over two millennia. First came the Chaonian Greeks at **Antigonea** and the Imperial-era Romans at **Hadrianopolis**, both now preserved as archaeological parks. Later, medieval Orthodox believers added monasteries and churches at **Labova e Kryqit** and around the **Gjerë Mountain** (Mali i Gjerë, meaning 'Wide Mountain'), and the communist regime bore tunnels and bunkers into the countryside. Approximately 150km north of Gjirokastra by road, you'll find the post-Byzantine churches and Roman ruins of Apollonia in the Myzeqeja plain around Fieri, and south of that, Albania's most tranquil grand ruins at **Byllis** (Bylisi), once a powerful Illyrian hub and cultural centre, perched over the Vjosa River (Lumi i Vjosës).

Where the Vjosa meets the Drino at **Tepelena**, you can explore the remnants of a newer, but no less intriguing, kind of empire: the early-nineteenth-century pashalik of **Ali Pasha**, a clan chief who became a European power player. The crumbling remnants are all that remain of his once-mighty fortress, palace, bridge and aqueduct. To the southwest, the desolate canyonlands around **Nivica** open up like a dusty treasure chest revealing unexpected natural gems. The **Vjosa**, Europe's first Wild River National Park (2023), beats a path across Southern Albania, becoming the font for the lush greenery that embraces **Përmeti**, a little city in a big paradise of mountains, ravines, waterfalls and thermal springs. Raft, hike, climb, horseride, bike or just soak in the mineral-rich pools. Simply cross the river from town to the breathtakingly quiet **Fir of Hotova-Dangëllia National Park** (Parku Kombëtar Bredhi i Hotovës-Dangëlli).

NATIONAL FOLK FESTIVAL, GJIROKASTRA CASTLE

Highlights

❶ **Iso-polyphony** Part dirge, part ballad, part drone – this age-old Albanian folk music is recognized by UNESCO for its cultural significance. Follow the entrancing sound to Gjirokastra. See page 205

❷ **Gjirokastra's tower houses** Magnificent and absurd, the fortified mansions in Gjirokastra's steep hills showcase Albania's most wonderful home-grown architecture. See page 206

❸ **Villains and verse** Gjirokastra, the city of dreamers, dissidents and dictators, weaves together the stories of its complex cast of characters through the years in several excellent museums. See page 208

❹ **Byllis and Apollonia** The Illyrians, Greeks, Romans and Byzantines cherished these sites, now the most enchanting of Albania's archaeological parks. See page 221

❺ **On the trail of Ali Pasha** His appetite for conquest was legendary, but Ali was a vigorous, innovative builder too. Trace the ruins of his realm around Tepelena's highlands. See page 224

❻ **Watery adventures in Përmeti** Raft the gorges of the Vjosa or luxuriate in Bënja's thermal springs. See page 229

❼ **Sweet treats** Satiate sugar cravings with the South's Albanian-Greek sweet treats; don't miss Përmeti's syrupy candied fruits. See page 230

HIGHLIGHTS ARE MARKED ON THE MAPS ON PAGES 200 AND 202

5

Gjirokastra

It is sometimes said that Albania is one big village, figuratively. **GJIROKASTRA (GJIROKASTËR)** is one big village – literally. Fewer than 20,000 live in Gjirokastra, and of those, many come from families that have been there for ten-plus generations. Beyond the main square, the **old city** climbs the steep hillside amid a tangle of cobblestone, where you won't find any banks, pharmacies, taxi ranks or supermarkets. Year-round residents sip coffee in pavement cafés and chip at their latest stone carving in workshops or on the street. If you visit in the summer or during a festival, the vibe is very different. Around the **Gjirokastra Bazaar** (Pazari i Gjirokastrës), the

alleys pulsate with singing, dancing, drums and even turntables, and artisans set up pavement stalls showcasing their sculptures, engravings, kilim (*qilim*) rugs and ceramics. The revelry runs late.

But whatever the season, the stone city never fails to cast its spell on visitors. The **medieval castle**, sometimes described as a great ship parting the slopes around it, floats on a promontory above the town – the entire city once lived inside its walls. Around and below, a cluster of whitewashed, wood-beamed houses tumble down the hillside. In the well-heeled **Palorto**, **Dunavati** and **Manalati** neighbourhoods, the stern and stylish nineteenth-century tower houses – part Ottoman villa and part family fortress – eye the scene watchfully from their positions on the wings of the Gjerë Mountain. Gjirokastra's great twentieth-century novelist, **Ismail Kadare**, once described the city as 'resembling an eagle that is ready to fly'.

Brief history

Gjirokastra has always been an in-between place, where rough riders from what's now Northern Greece, Southern Albania and beyond slugged it out in hard times, settling in as minor nobles and major merchants when the winds calmed.

The setting of the city looks like a prime spot for a primitive ancient hilltop fortress, but for one problem: no water. Though a small one did exist here, the Chaonian Greeks preferred to turn east to establish **Antigonea**, while the Romans diverted south for **Hadrianopolis**. The Byzantines or their proxies built a fortress at Gjirokastra (then Argyrókastro) between the ninth and tenth centuries AD, but Gjirokastra only started to make waves in 1386, when Albanian headman **Gjin Zenebishi** seized the castle and made the city his capital, fending off the Ottoman-allied Florentine ruler of Epirus (now mostly in Greece). Upon Zenebishi's death in 1418, the Ottomans besieged and successfully captured the city, making it a stronghold of the new Sanjak of Albania. The region's craftspeople got to work, trading jewellery, leather, clothing and guns. In 1811, **Ali Pasha Tepelena** claimed Gjirokastra for his pashalik, building much of the current castle fortification, along with the clock tower and a massive aqueduct.

The twentieth century was a fraught time for Gjirokastra, molding some of the most steadfast and ruthless Albanians of modern history. Among other contributions to the Albanian National Awakening (Rilindja), Gjirokastra yielded local brothers **Çerçiz** and **Bajo Topulli**, guerilla fighters who assassinated both the local Ottoman military chief and the Greek Orthodox bishop of Korça. In 1908, **Enver Hoxha** was born here to a middle-class family in the Palorto neighbourhood. Once Hoxha and his communist faction prevailed toward the end of **World War II**, they began eliminating anyone of influence outside their ranks. One Gjirokastra politician – a certain Bahri Omari – who'd backed the Germans was executed in 1945, no matter that he was Hoxha's brother-in-law. Young Gjirokastrite writer **Musine Kokalari** (1917–1983), who founded a democratic opposition party, was imprisoned and exiled until her death.

Gjirokastra Bazaar

Old Gjirokastra is a vertiginous, disorienting knot of haywire streets and cobblestone alleys that flout both common sense and reason – it's part of the charm. It's a smart idea to start your explorations in **Çerçiz Topulli Square** (Sheshi Çerçiz Topulli), beneath which is a conveniently located car park if you're driving. The historic core is walkable, though it can be a bit of a workout. Facing the hills, with the castle looming above to your left, you'll find the tourist information centre and so-called **Cold War Tunnel** on your left.

From here, you can walk up Rruga Gjin Zenebishti to the heart of the **Gjirokastra Bazaar** (Pazari i Gjirokastrës), a chicken-foot-shaped five-way intersection called the Bazaar Pass or 'Neck' (Qafa e Pazarit), the most recognizable spot in Gjirokastra. Note the peculiar three-sided building with a cantilevered five-sided top floor that

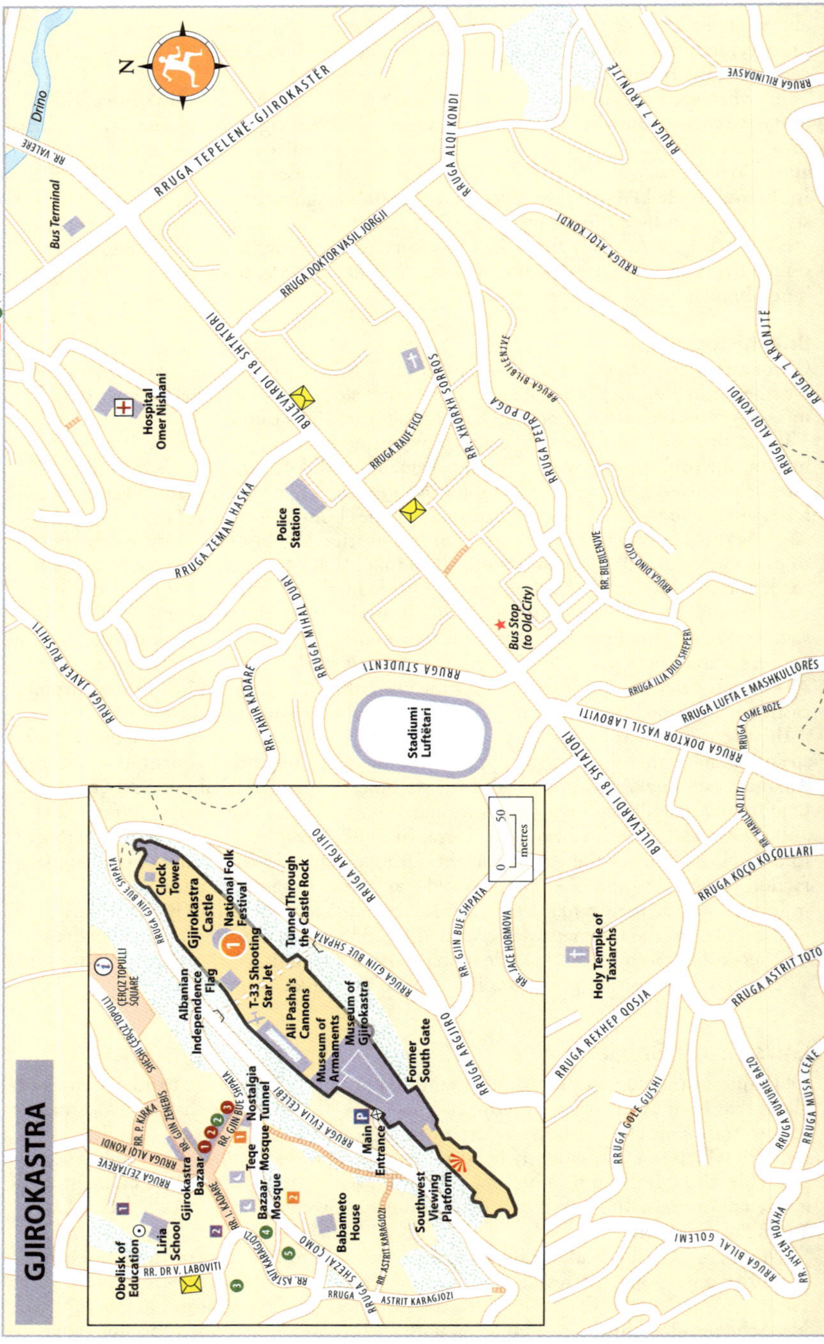
GJIROKASTRA
N
Drino
(3.5km)
Bus Terminal
Hospital Omer Nishani
Police Station
Stadiumi Luftëtari
Bus Stop (to Old City)
Holy Temple of Taxiarchs
RR. VALERE
RRUGA TEPELENË-GJIROKASTËR
RRUGA ALQI KONDI
RRUGA DOKTOR VASIL JORGJI
BULEVARDI 18 SHTATORI
RRUGA ZEMAN HASKA
RRUGA RAUF FICO
RR. XHORXH SORROS
RRUGA PETRO POGA
RRUGA BILBILENJVE
RR. BILBILENJVE
RRUGA DINO CICO
RRUGA ILIA DILO SHEPERI
RRUGA 7 KRONJTË
RRUGA RILINDASVE
RRUGA JAVER RUSHITI
RRUGA MIHAL DURI
RR. TAHIR KADARE
RRUGA STUDENTI
RRUGA LUFTA E MASHKULLORËS
RRUGA DOKTOR VASIL LABOVITI
RRUGA COME ROZE
RR. HARILLA LITI
RRUGA KOÇO KOÇOLLARI
RRUGA ASTRIT TOTO
RRUGA REXHEP QOSJA
RRUGA GOLE GUSHI
RRUGA BUKURIE BAZO
RRUGA MUSA ÇENE
RRUGA BILAL GOLEMI
RR. HYSEN HOXHA
RRUGA ARGJIRO
RR. GJIN BUE SHPATA
RR. JACE HORMOVA
RRUGA GJIN BUE SHPATA
RRUGA EVLIA CELEBI
RRUGA SHEZAI ÇOMO
RR. ASTRIT KARAGJOZI
RRUGA ASTRIT KARAGJOZI
RR. DR V. LABOVITI
RRUGA ZEJTAREVE
RR. I. KADARE
RR. P. KIRKA
RR. GJIN ZENEBIS
SHESHI ÇERÇIZ TOPULLI
ÇERÇIZ TOPULLI SQUARE
Clock Tower
Gjirokastra Castle
National Folk Festival
Albanian Independence Flag
T-33 Shooting Star Jet
Tunnel Through the Castle Rock
Ali Pasha's Cannons
Museum of Armaments
Museum of Gjirokastra
Former South Gate
Main Entrance
Southwest Viewing Platform
Nostalgia Tunnel
Teqe Mosque
Bazaar Mosque
Babameto House
Gjirokastra Bazaar
Liria School
Obelisk of Education
0
50
metres

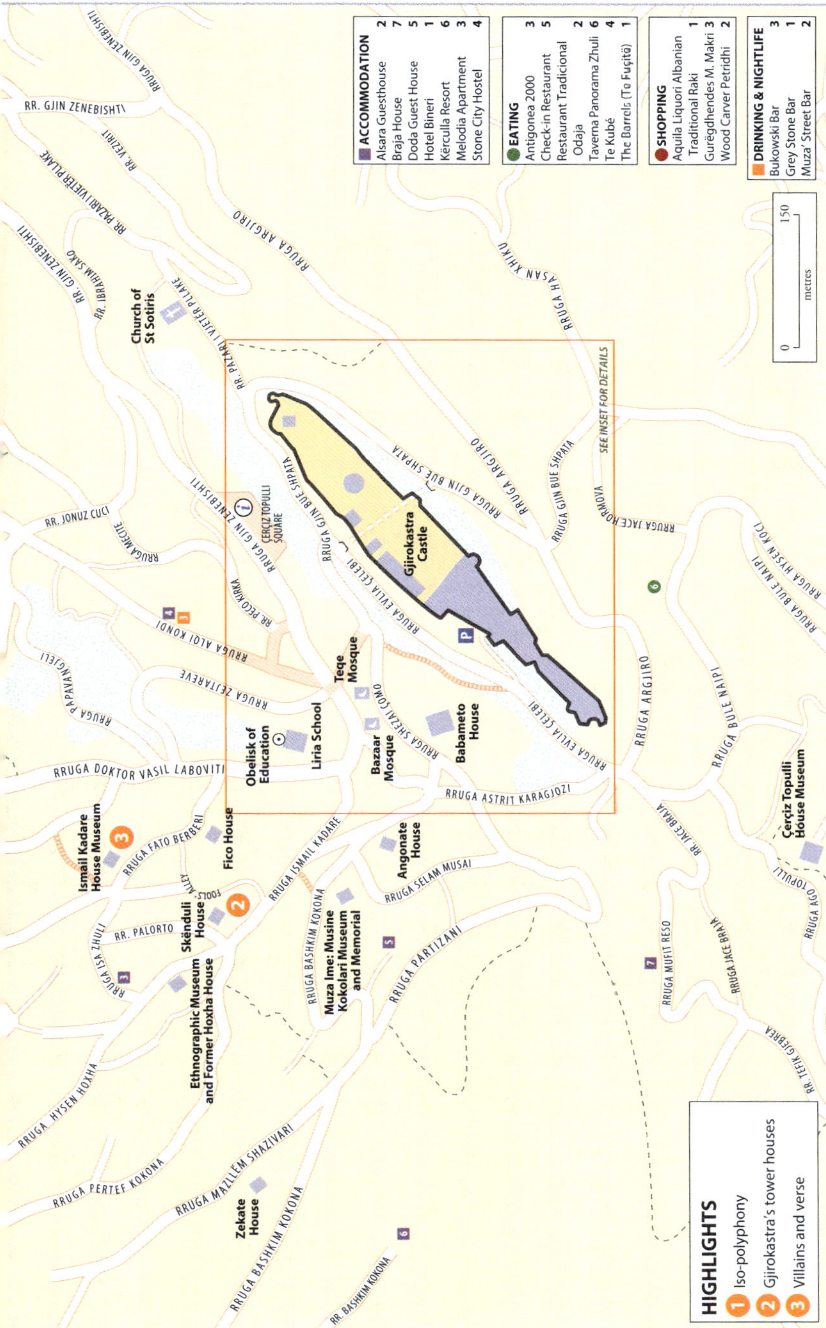
HIGHLIGHTS
1 Iso-polyphony
2 Gjirokastra's tower houses
3 Villains and verse
ACCOMMODATION
Alsara Guesthouse 2
Braja House 7
Doda Guest House 5
Hotel Bineri 1
Kërculla Resort 6
Melodia Apartment 3
Stone City Hostel 4
EATING
Antigonea 2000 3
Check-in Restaurant 5
Restaurant Tradicional Odaja 2
Taverna Panorama Zhuli 6
Te Kubé 4
The Barrels (Te Fuçitë) 1
SHOPPING
Aquila Liquori Albanian Traditional Raki 1
Gurëgdhendes M. Makri 3
Wood Carver Petridhi 2
DRINKING & NIGHTLIFE
Bukowski Bar 3
Grey Stone Bar 1
Muza' Street Bar 2
0 150 metres
Gjirokastra Castle
Church of St Sotiris
Teqe Mosque
Liria School
Obelisk of Education
Bazaar Mosque
Babameto House
Angonate House
Fico House
Ismail Kadare House Museum
Skënduli House
Ethnographic Museum and Former Hoxha House
Muza Ime: Musine Kokolari Museum and Memorial
Zekate House
Çerçiz Topulli House Museum
Çerçiz Topulli Square
Ali Pasha Bridge (720m)
SEE INSET FOR DETAILS
Fools' Alley
RR. GJIN ZENEBISHTI
RRUGA GJIN ZENEBISHTI
RR. VEZIRI
RR. PAZARI I VJETËR PLLAKË
RRUGA ARGJIRO
RR. IBRAHIM SAKO
RR. JONUZ CUCI
RRUGA MECITE
RRUGA GJIN BUE SHPATA
RRUGA HASAN XHIKU
RRUGA JACE HORMOVA
RRUGA HYSEN KOÇI
RRUGA BULE NAIPI
RRUGA EVLIA CELEBI
RR. PECO KIRKA
RRUGA ALQI KONDI
RRUGA ZEJTAREVE
RRUGA PAPAVANGJELI
RRUGA DOKTOR VASIL LABOVITI
RRUGA SHEZAI ÇOMO
RRUGA ASTRIT KARAGJOZI
RR. JACE BRAJA
RRUGA FATO BERBERI
RRUGA ISMAIL KADARE
RRUGA SELAM MUSAI
RR. PALORTO
RRUGA ISA ZHULI
RRUGA BASHKIM KOKONA
RRUGA PARTIZANI
RRUGA MUFIT RESO
RRUGA JACE BRAJA
RRUGA AGO TOPULLI
RR. TEFIK GJEBREA
RRUGA HYSEN HOXHA
RRUGA PERTEF KOKONA
RRUGA MAZLLEM SHAZIVARI
RR. BASHKIM KOKONA

looks like, well, a house sticking its neck out. It was a café and post office before becoming a souvenir shop. The bazaar beneath the castle was developed as early as the twelfth century, but the current appearance mostly dates to the nineteenth and early-twentieth centuries.

It's an attractive enclave: the streets wiggle up and down the hillside, flanked by white, wood-trimmed buildings. It's the beating heart of local life and tourism, full of cozy cafés, pubs, boutique guesthouses, studios and shops.

Obelisk of Education

Rruga e Zejtarëve • Free • Enter through the arch with the sign reading 'Kompleksi Papavangjeli' and head up the stairs

Hidden from the street, the 7m-high stone **Obelisk of Education** (Obelisku i Arsimit) stands on a viewing platform that provides one of the best vantage points in a city full of them. Looking into the hills, you'll see the city springing up above the hillsides like a children's pop-up book.

The 'obelisk' is actually a statue of a rolled-up scroll etched with Albanian script, designed by artists Muntaz Dhrami, Ksenofon Kostaqi and Stefan Papamihali in 2008 to honour Gjirokastra's **first Albanian-language school**, next door.

Bazaar Mosque

Rruga Ismail Kadare and Rruga Astrit Karagjozi • Free

A rare surviving eighteenth-century **mosque** in Albania, the **Xhamia e Pazarit** was constructed in 1755 and restored in 2020. Like many structures built on Gjirokastra's wonky, sloped streets, it required some engineering ingenuity to make it stand level, in this case a vaulted stone substructure, which is now a cute coffee shop. To avoid putting too much weight on the stone foundations, the dome is squat compared to other mosques, but the whole thing is burlier than it looks from the bazaar side. The best angle to appreciate the tiered architecture and terrific polygonal roof is from Rruga Astrit Karagjozi, the street that curves sharply around and up to the west.

Cold War Tunnel

Sheshi Çerçiz Topulli • **Guided tours** Charge

The communist regime made anthills out of hills with their subterranean emergency shelters, tunnels and bunkers in cities around Albania – and Gjirokastra was no exception. In fact, the Hoxha government was especially invested in the project here: only the flat **Drino Valley** (Lugina e Drinos) separates it from Greece. At least one tunnel is visible aboveground, a passageway bored through the castle rock that connects its north and south sides.

What's now billed as the **Cold War Tunnel** (Tuneli i Luftës së Ftohtë) runs underground for around 800m in length, burrowed 80m beneath the castle, leading to a series of 59 rooms. Like the Bunk'Art complexes in Tirana (see pages 63 and 58), it was constructed in the 1970s and 1980s and sealed off with vault-style steel entrance portals, followed by a decontamination chamber, which looks like the airlock of a submarine in a naval disaster film. The tunnel's function was ultimately mundane, and it's filled with offices, meeting rooms and living quarters designed for the business of carrying on government as usual – even if an air raid or nuclear catastrophe is unfolding above.

Concrete and claustrophobic, it has no art or exhibitions, just rusted-out bedframes, the original power generator and some period furniture, providing an unvarnished snapshot of how the original bunker looked at the time. This quick detour is worthwhile if you can't make it to Bunk'Art 1.

In the bazaar area, it's also possible to duck inside the **Nostalgia Tunnel**, home to an eclectic private collection of World War II-era guns, helmets, gas masks and officers' coats, plus vintage TVs, dishware and newspapers (Rruga Shezai Çomo; tel: 069 327 9504).

Gjirokastra Castle

Rruga Evlia Çelebi • Charge

Gjirokastra Castle (Kalaja e Gjirokastrës) itself was never conquered by force, but it often found a way to insert itself into Albanian history. For the Byzantines and medieval Albanians, it was primarily a citadel and also a neighbourhood, like Berati Castle (see page 119). For Ali Pasha, it was the perfect venue to show off the array of wheeled cannons he'd acquired from the British. **King Zog I** built the Albanian government's first prison here, and it retained this role under occupying powers during World War II. **Enver Hoxha** declared his hometown a museum city in 1961, converting the brutal bastille into a display of weaponry.

Signs in the bazaar area, on Rruga Gjin Bue Shpata, point the way to the entrance, on the long north side of the castle. From here, you can first head right to check out the high vaulted gallery leading to the former south gate and even peep at a small **Bektashi tyrbe** (tomb or shrine) in a courtyard. From this part of the keep, you can climb up to the **southwest viewing platform** for an up-close look at the trademark angular and polygonal ramparts and towers masterminded by Ali Pasha's engineers. Though some of the castle walls have fallen into jagged disrepair, others retain a level of polish, and the whole thing glitters and glowers after rainfall. You can certainly grasp the likely etymology of 'Argyrókastro' – silver castle.

Back down at the main entrance, head northeast through a grand hall of arches, flanked by rows of World War II-era howitzers and mortars, until you reach the **Unknown Soldier** (Ushtari i Panjohur), a masterful monument sculpted by **Odhise Paskali**, at the far end. The Përmeti-born artist had a way with heroic statuary, and he gave his finest creation to Tirana – the mighty Skanderbeg on horseback in the main square (see page 57). The arches also shelter a rare Italian Fiat tank, while Enver Hoxha's museums are on your right.

Outside, you'll find a courtyard with Ali Pasha's cannon collection, along with another unusual weapon – a US Air Force **Lockheed T-33 Shooting Star jet**. In 1957, an American pilot performed an emergency landing at Tirana International Airport. Did he get lost in fog and run low on fuel, as the US version told it, or did Albanian anti-aircraft capabilities force a spy plane down, as the government here crowed? In any

ISO-POLYPHONY SINGING

It sounds discordant at first; you can't dance to it; and most of the early hits were howls of anguish – but people came around to Nirvana too. The genre in question is **iso-polyphony**, a centuries-old style of a-cappella music that can be heard all over Albania – but especially around Gjirokastra and the coastal southwest. Like most folk music, its roots are hard to trace, but iso-polyphony combines at least three ancient vocal traditions. One is the **vajtim** – a dirge for the dead once performed in Gjirokastra by families and professional mourners. The second is **polyphonic singing**, which consists of two or more simultaneous lines of independent melody, and probably originated in Illyrian times. The final piece is the **ison**, the drone or hum of Byzantine Orthodox church music and chanting.

Iso-polyphony has between two and four melodic parts, and a choir or voice backing them with the *ison* hum; harmonizing the melodies and the *ison* takes skill and range. The more complex, four-part versions were invented in the far south, and today both men and women perform. In the nineteenth century, clarinets, violins and lutes were added to create the **kaba**, which can be heard from **sazja** (or *sazet*) bands in Vlora, Delvina, Gjirokastra, Përmeti and Leskoviku.

Albanian iso-polyphony was inscribed on the **Intangible Cultural Heritage** list by UNESCO in 2008, giving it a push of renewed interest among younger generations, but it's not exactly open-mic material. Your best bet for hearing iso-polyphony is to attend a folk festival in Gjirokastra (see page 40), Himara, Vlora or a southern village.

event, the pilot was released, but Albania hung on to the plane, opting to display it at the armaments museum when it opened.

Finally, you can explore the ruined barracks and parapets and clamber around to get your perfect shot of the Drino Valley and the Lunxhëria massif, particularly fetching under snow caps. On the north side, an Albanian flag flutters where it was first raised in December 1912. From the south side – it is said – the mythological Princess Argjiro jumped, with her infant son, rather than be captured by Ottomans besieging the castle. The nineteenth-century clock tower stands at the far northeast point, jutting out in front of the city.

In the middle, a platform and metal bandshell overtake the scene. This is centre stage for the **National Folk Festival** (Festivali Folklorik Kombëtar), held every five years. It's the Olympics of Albanian folklore, where groups from around the country and the world don embroidered costumes, sing ancestral tunes and whirl in traditional *valle* dances. There is judging, there are winners. The category where Gjirokastra and the southwest really dominate is iso-polyphony singing (see box, page 205).

Museum of Armaments and Museum of Gjirokastra

Kalaja e Gjirokastrës • Charge (additional to castle entrance fee)

Despite the separate names, this is really one museum with two parts, set in the former prison. The **Museum of Armaments** (Muzeu i Armëve) doesn't have much in the way of signage in English, but you may find the weapons self-explanatory, mostly guns, mostly of World War II vintage: rifles, pistols, mounted automatic weapons and so on, along with helmets, tactical gear and interesting socialist realist statues. The **Museum of Gjirokastra** (Muzeu i Gjirokastrës), on the other hand, is highly informative, with English-labelled exhibits. Wide-ranging displays cover changing fashions in traditional regional dress; Ali Pasha's building programme; and the remarkable escape by 26 American nurses and medics whose plane crash-landed in Nazi-occupied Southern Albania.

The remainder of the museum has been preserved as the **prison** where those deemed enemies of the Axis occupation and communist party were left to rot in dank, dark, solitary 2m-by-3m cells, sometimes for years, subsisting on meagre servings of bread. Some accounts of the conditions are written on the walls in Albanian, but it is plain to see how nightmarish the place would have been.

Palorto

In old Gjirokastra, when wealth flowed, inevitably envy simmered and politics became personal. Centuries-long family vendettas were normal, and blood feuds were not unheard of. One way of keeping the peace was intermarriage. "*Kemi të bëjmë*", one aggrieved party would tell another – roughly, "we have something to do with each other", perhaps that the families intertwined seven generations prior.

Another was building the huge **fortified mansions** that pepper the Gjerë Mountain hillsides. Sometimes called **kulla** (also: kullë; tower house) or simply konak, these three- or four-storey villas – part hearth, part fort – are what give the city its wonderland appearance that has bewitched and baffled visitors for centuries. They are tucked into the twisted folds of the neighbourhoods of **Dunavati**, **Manalati** and **Palorto** – the latter, northwest of the bazaar, the place to start.

Mostly dating to the nineteenth century, the houses typically had stone-built lower levels that slotted right into the mountainside, designed for storage and cisterns. The upper floors, plastered and whitewashed in the style typical of wealthy Ottoman residences, were for welcoming visitors, dining, sleeping, gossiping, smoking pipes, drinking coffee and other everyday chores and pleasures. The most ornate room would be reserved for ceremony and pageantry, mostly surrounding weddings and deaths.

The structure would be crowned with **slate roof**, which in the largest houses could weigh 150-plus tons.

The **Zekate** and **Skënduli** houses are the best examples of early-nineteenth-century *kulla* that you can go inside. It's not a must to visit both, but if you're inclined to visit only one historic house in all of Albania, take your pick from these two.

And if you're inspired to delve deeper into the architectural quirks that made each tower house a home – lunette-topped windows, fairy-tale wrought-iron gable eaves – seek out the 1881 **Angonate House** (Banesa e Angonatëve; Rruga Bashkim Kokona), one of the biggest in the city; **Babameto House** (Shtëpia e Babametove; Rruga Shezai Çomo), from 1885; and the flamboyant yellow 1902-built **Fico House** (Shtëpia e Ficove; Rruga Fato Berberi), which belonged to a diplomat who carefully navigated Albanians and Jews to safety as an ambassador and consul in Germany in the late 1930s.

Zekate House

Rruga Bashkim Kokona • Charge • www.facebook.com/shtepiaezekateve

The handsome **Zekate House** (Shtëpia e Zekateve) was built in 1812 for **Beqir Zeko**, one of Ali Pasha's administrators. From the outside, it's much more tower than house. Inside, you can see how people actually lived in these behemoths. The cistern on the ground floor collected rainwater via a series of gutters and pipes during the wet winter and spring, saving fresh water for the hot, dry summer. Cool air from the cistern rose to the floor above, where it refrigerated a storage chamber for milk and other perishables. Wealthy families like those that lived here also enjoyed the luxury of a stone-insulated winter residential floor and a breezy summer floor above. The main event is the ceremonial room.

The restored fireplace frescoes curl out with floral-bouquet motifs, and frilly red trompe-l'œil curtains are painted around the hearth. Above head is one of the oldest geometric-patterned coffered wood ceilings in town, and – if that wasn't busy enough – even the windowpanes are tinted bright red, yellow and blue, like an unsolved Rubik's cube pattern. Pause at the *çardak* porch to smirk at all the other Gjirokastra houses looking small below.

Skënduli House (Shtëpia e Skëndulatëve)

Rruga Ismail Kadare and Rruga Palorto • Charge • Guided tours

A fortified house was wise in the Gjirokastra of yesteryear, but the sweetest victory over your neighbour-frenemies came from having the biggest, best fortified house. If you couldn't build the biggest, you could at least aim for the highest number of toilets. That appears to be the tactic the **Skënduli** family went for: six of them, with the holes dropping down through the tower. The house also boasts nine chimneys, a hammam and forty doors.

Built in the early eighteenth century and renovated in 1827, the house was seized from its original owners during the communist years. It has since been returned to Skënduli ownership, and family members serve as both the stewards and tour guides of the house. The **frescoes**, carved-wood ceilings and fanciful windows are only partially restored, so it's interesting to see decorative elements that haven't been modified in two hundred years. Hearing the story of the house straight from descendants of its first residents makes this experience unique. Ask before taking photos.

Muza Ime: Musine Kokalari Museum and Memorial

Rruga Selam Musai near Rruga Bashkim Kokona • Free; donations requested • www.facebook.com/p/Muzeu-Kokalari-100057066475945

In 2024, a small museum-memorial opened in Palorto near the bazaar, and it's now one of the most affecting places to visit in town. **Musine Kokalari** (1917–1983) discovered a passion for stories growing up in Gjirokastra, and she published her first book in her early twenties, around 1941. A collection of ten stories, vignettes and sketches, *As My*

Grandma Says unveils the then-hidden lives of Albanian women – sisters, mothers, daughters, friends and neighbours. Groundbreaking and experimental, the book made waves on the Albanian literary scene. Kokalari began penning political treatises and went on to co-found the **Social Democratic Party** (Partia Socialdemokrate e Shqipërisë) in 1943. Antifascist and pro-democracy, she openly dissented against the Communist Party in 1945, and, within weeks, she was jailed and tortured, then convicted in a show trial. Kokalari would be imprisoned, exiled and surveilled for the remaining 37 years of her life.

The museum is as much a celebration of her talent and courage as a testament to the tragedy of her life. Displays include archival photos, personal effects and first editions of her books. The highlight, though, is her voice: passages from her published works and her journals, touching on happiness, love, Gjirokastra, her politics and her ordeals, are painted on the walls, in both Albanian and English.

Ethnographic Museum

Rruga Hysen Hoxha near Rruga Palorto • Charge • www.facebook.com/p/Muzeu-Etnografik-Gjirokastër-100091605422684

After an extensive renovation and refresh, Gjirokastra's **Ethnographic Museum** (Muzeu Etnografik) reopened in 2023 with a series of smartly presented exhibitions about the art and culture of the city. Formerly the childhood home of **Enver Hoxha**, it burned down in 1916, but the latest reconstruction of its original rooms is faithful, even if they feel a little new and shiny. Informational placards with plans, diagrams and old photos of tower houses provide useful context for the region's favoured architecture, while a fine collection of Gjirokastrit woodcarving includes decorative rosettes, trunks and coffee tables.

This is one of a number of ways to experience the traditional costumes, customs and artisanship in Gjirokastra, and it may be the best one available in the low season. The museum does not cast aside Hoxha entirely; there's a small section about his childhood and how he transformed the house into a museum of antifascism.

Ismail Kadare House Museum

Rruga Fato Berberi 16 • Charge • www.facebook.com/p/Muzeu-Shtëpia-Kadare-100091634671207

Albania's most internationally acclaimed novelist by a mile, Ismail Kadare (see box, page 209) grew up in the house here, since rebuilt and turned into the **Ismail Kadare House Museum** (Banesa Muze Ismail Kadare), which was updated in 2022. There are some Kadare first editions and video interviews with the author, but the highlight is the publishing of snippets from his novels inside and outside the house, particularly if you are not already familiar with his work. Translated into English, they include his many rich (and funny) descriptions of his own topsy-turvy Gjirokastra. To reach the museum from the Muzeu Etnografik, you'll blunder down Fools' Alley (Sokaku i të Marëve) – "As if looking for trouble with other streets, [it] tumbled around the district with sudden, sharp turns," Kadare.

Dunavati, Manalati and around

A paved road passing the castle along the south side (Rruga Argjiro) now climbs up to the **Dunavati** and **Manalati** neighbourhoods in the south of the city, though you'll run up against cobblestones and rocky roads bang on arrival. Here, you're nearing the crest of the Gjerë Mountain, with fine views unfurling before you.

You'll pass a small *teqe* (Bektashi Sufi lodge) and the ruins of a mosque, but these are overshadowed by the foreboding tower houses in these parts. Some cling precariously to the slopes, peering over the forested slopes. The most notable landmark, though, is the **Çerçiz Topulli House Museum** (Shtëpia-Muze e Heroit Çerçiz Topulli; Rruga Ago Topulli), which has been closed for some years but is worth a peep if you have the time and inclination.

ISMAIL KADARE, THE POSTER BOY FOR LITERATURE

Novelist **Ismail Kadare** earned comparisons to writers as diverse as Honoré de Balzac, of *La Comédie humaine* fame, and Gabriel García Márquez, the Nobel laureate behind literary masterpiece *One Hundred Years of Solitude* (1967). The only label Kadare consistently wore was 'Albanian'. But the material from his cultural roots was enough to fuel 76 years of stories, many about paradox – between tradition and absurdity, constraint and freedom.

Kadare was born in Gjirokastra in 1936, and the occupied city was a fantastical and macabre place to grow up in during **World War II**; we know, because he later described the experience in magical, horrible detail through the eyes of a young boy in his 1971 novel, ***Chronicle in Stone***. Kadare won a scholarship to study in Moscow and published what would be his breakthrough novel, ***The General of the Dead Army***, at just 26. The book was parcelled off to a translator in Paris and published in the French capital in 1970, turning Kadare into an international literary sensation. Hot on its heels came *The Siege* (1970), Kadare's fictionalization of the 1450 Siege of Kruja from the perspective of the Ottoman besiegers; *Chronicle in Stone* (1971); and *Broken April* (1978), set against the Northern Albanian culture of blood feuds.

By the late 1960s, however, Kadare had already been denounced and censored by the government for both his prose and poetry. But he continued to push the boundaries of allegory and obfuscation in describing what could certainly sound like contemporary communist dysfunction. In 1981, Kadare managed to sneak his most forthright book to date past censors and out into Albania. ***The Palace of Dreams***, a tale of dystopian totalitarianism in a setting that sure bore a resemblance to Tirana, sparked a panic within the party. How he escaped with his life through three decades of subversiveness is a minor mystery – skill and luck, then fame, and maybe an element of "Kemi të bëjmë" (see page 206) with fellow Gjirokastrit Enver Hoxha.

Kadare ultimately sought **political asylum** in France in 1990, a controversial move among Albanians, as the collapse of the regime seemed imminent. But in his final years, he returned to the motherland and could be found on quiet taverna terraces in **Tirana**, smoking, chatting and almost certainly regaling stories. Kadare was awarded the inaugural **Man Booker International Prize** in 2005 for his entire body of work, and he continued to publish novels, novellas, poetry and essays until his death in Tirana in 2024, at the age of 88.

Ali Pasha Bridge

Dunavati • Free

In pictures, the **Ali Pasha Bridge** (Ura e Ali Pashës) appears like it's secluded in a greenish-brown valley far from any city but, in fact, it is only on the far side of Gjirokastra's ridge, reachable from the Bazaar Pass (Qafa e Pazarit) in under forty minutes on foot. It's a trudge, for sure, but you're cheating yourself if you visit Gjirokastra and skip the bridge. You can reach fine viewpoints of the edifice from Rruga Baki Gjebrea or Rruga Hito Lekdushi, and from both, it's easy to follow trails down into the valley, where the bridge rears before you and the scale of the structure comes into focus.

Albanian brigand turned pasha Ali Pasha (c.1750–1822) controlled almost all of Southern Albania for decades, but he didn't conquer Gjirokastra city until late in his life, in 1811. Apparently smitten with it, he wasted no time bringing the castle up to the level of state-of-the-art fortress. The greatest feat of construction he undertook here, though, was an adjacent engineering marvel. Ali's **aqueduct** once spanned 12km from the Sopoti Mountain's (Mali i Sopotit) rivers and springs, culminating at the southwest end of the castle. Today, you can't see it from the castle at all: King Zog I dismantled most of it to pinch blocks to build his prison. What remains is this, the so-called 'bridge', 40m long and 16m high. Binding the valley under a single arch, it's especially wonderful in late spring when shrubs claw

5

their way through the cracks in the stone, and the surrounding valley is blanketed in yellow Jerusalem sage.

ARRIVAL AND DEPARTURE

GJIROKASTA

By bus or minibus Gjirokasta's bus terminal is on the east side of the roundabout where the SH4 meets Bulevardi 18 Shtatori, in the new city; it's about a 30min (1.6km) walk to Sheshi Çerçiz Topulli in the centre (uphill). Buses to other major cities are a bit sparse in all seasons, and some *furgon* (minibus) drivers may overcharge in the high season. Arrive at least 30min early; buses fill up.

Destinations Berati (1 daily; 3hr); Durrësi (many daily; 3hr 10min); Elbasani (several daily; 3hr 30min); Erseka (1 daily; 3hr 30min); Fieri (many daily; 1hr 25min); Korça (1 daily; 4hr 25min); Leskoviku (1 daily; 2hr 20min); Libohova (several daily; 30min); Lushnja (several daily; 2hr 10min); Përmeti (several daily; 1hr 10min); Saranda (several daily; 1hr 10min); Tepelena (many daily; 25min); Tirana (many daily; 4hr); Vlora (several daily; 1hr 45min).

There are also a few agencies that can get you to destinations in Greece. For Athens, try Lengo Travel (tel: 069 405 3333); for Ioannina, Dhropoli Tours (tel: 069 203 5015).

By car Driving to the base of Gjirokastra is a cinch. From north or south, you'll come in on the SH4, which is generally quiet in both directions. From a roundabout towards the south of the city, follow Rruga Gjin Zenebishti west to Sheshi Çerçiz Topulli, which is less than 5min from the motorway. Coming from the coast, you can drive the older, zigzagging mountain roads, SH78 through Delvina or SH99 past the Blue Eye (see page 262), or you can take Rruga Kardhiq–Sarandë, a mostly easy road built in 2022.

GETTING AROUND

On foot Everything in the old city can be reached on foot in under 40min from Sheshi Çerçiz Topulli. Wear sturdy shoes; most streets are cobblestone at best, and nothing is flat.

By bus Gjirokastra actually has a fleet of little vintage buses that manages to drive circuits up into the hills. Most leave every 30min–1hr from a stop on Bulevardi 18 Shtatori near Rruga Xhorxh Sorros, about 700m from the intercity bus terminal; or from Sheshi Çerçiz Topulli on the return journey. Ask the driver if they are going near where you want to end up.

By car Old Gjirokastra is all rocks, inclines, hairpin turns and pedestrianized streets streets – avoid driving beyond the main square if you can. The underground car park under Sheshi Çerçiz Topulli is a decent location for a modest fee, and it's best to then explore on foot. There's also a small free car park down the street (east) on Rruga Gjin Zenebishti. If your accommodation is far up in the hills, ask staff for specific directions; your GPS will lead you astray.

If you're looking to explore the Drino or the broader South, you have some trustworthy car rental options here: Rental Car Ksera (tel: 069 987 6900) and Rent.Car.Gjirokastër (tel: 068 444 5644), both on SH4 next to the bus terminal, and Rent-a-Car Az (Rruga Doktor Vasil Jorgji; tel: 068 216 7470).

By taxi You'll find many taxi drivers around the bus station. They can be a little pushy, but there are more taxi ranks close by, every few blocks along Bulevardi 18 Shtatori; taxis also come and go from Sheshi Çerçiz Topulli frequently. If you don't have a car, a taxi may be your most convenient option for reaching Drino Valley (Lugina e Drinos) spots like Libohova, Antigonea or Hadrianopolis. Some drivers are also happy to arrange longer trips to destinations around the riviera and beyond. Call or message Taxi Krenari (tel: 069 363 6697), Taxi Alketi (te: 069 282 2121) or Taxi Service Aurel (tel: 069 225 1495) to make plans and ask for rates.

INFORMATION

Tourist information There's a tourist information kiosk on Sheshi Çerçiz Topulli, the castle side near the Cold War Tunnel entrance. Staff can provide details on things to see in the city, and they sell maps. If the office is closed, much of the information is online, and the map too. See below.

Websites www.gjirokaster.al; www.visit-gjirokastra.com; www.bashkiagjirokaster.gov.al.

TOUR OPERATORS

Blerim Topulli (tel: 069 478 1552) is a sixteenth-generation Gjirokastrit with an encyclopaedic knowledge of these parts. For a walking tour of the city and free-ranging discussion about Gjirokastra life and culture past and present, he's the guy you want. Trips to other heritage sites in the greater region can be arranged as well.

Experience Gjirokastra (www.experiencegjirokastra.com) operates a range of tours in the city and the Drino Valley, including culture-focused trips to Labova e Kryqit and Libohova, and adventure experiences in the Zagoria Valley, which is difficult to access without a 4WD. The young guides also host the Experience Gjirokastra podcast in the off-season, bringing on musicians, artisans and other interesting guests.

C-Adventures & Tours and Caravan Horse Riding (www.c-adventures.al; www.horseridingalbania.com) together provide the most diverse options for adventure travel in the Drino, especially single- and multiday excursions on horseback, year-round. The team also facilitate traditional cooking classes, wine tasting and woodcarving classes.

GJIROKASTRA'S FESTIVALS

Gjirokastra's best folklore and village festivals are either very infrequent, new as of this publication, or one-offs. The **National Folk Festival** (Festivali Folklorik Kombëtar) was last held in 2023 and, before that, 2015. A springtime fest, **Walking with History**, made for a perfectly nice replacement in 2024, offering visitors the chance to watch artisans at work on traditional crafts or take in a folk concert. The best way to find out what's coming up is to check the Instagram accounts of the three sites listed under Websites above.

ACCOMMODATION

SEE MAP PAGE 202

Mass tourism is new to Gjirokastra, and hotels and guesthouses in the old city are striving to meet both international demand and standards. Not all are there yet. Most of the really special places to stay are restored rooms in Palorto, Dunavati and Manalati tower houses. They are fantastically atmospheric, generally inexpensive and book up quickly. Owners will sometimes be able to fetch you from the centre or bus terminal if their place is tough to reach. There are also many solid, larger options right in the Gjirokastra Bazaar, though you'll usually pay a premium to be in the centre.

Alsara Guesthouse Rruga Ismail Kadare, opposite the Xhamia e Pazarit; tel: 069 318 7558. This is a clean, pleasant, very comfortable choice if you want to stay right in the middle of the bazaar area, at a very fair price. Rooms are nicely appointed with modern amenities and traditional touches, but the highlight is the rooftop terrace, where you can take breakfast or relax at night watching the bustle of Gjirokastra below. €€

★ **Braja House** Rruga Mufit Reso; tel: 068 468 7877. For the price point, it's one of the best places to stay not just in Gjirokastra but all of Albania. The room (just one) is set within a superb 1831-built tower house, and the family lives there as well. You'll be welcomed with home-made liqueur and *gliko* (sweet preserve) in a courtly sitting room, much like those in the museum houses. You can explore the garden and gawk at the neighbours, who managed to build arguably the most ridiculous *kulla* in town. The room itself, with a fireplace and traditional decor, is cosy and comfortable in all seasons. €€

Doda Guest House Rruga Bashkim Kokona; tel: 069 471 1401. A young Gjirokastrit couple opened this renovated property as a two-bedroom guesthouse in 2024, and it's about as close to a luxe mountain villa experience as you can find here, with a lot of attention given to the handmade and heirloom furnishings. The romantic two-person room occupies a stone-domed space that may have been a hammam, and the veranda of the family suite overlooks the castle from the heights. €€€

Hotel Bineri Rruga e Zejtarëve; www.facebook.com/HotelBineriofficial. This updated hotel in the bazaar area is fairly big and has the conveniences of a larger property – 24hr reception, excellent wi-fi – without losing the charm factor of the stone city. Rooms sleeping one to four are kitted out with carved wooden ceilings, exposed stone and archival photos; each is named for a local notable. €€€

Kërculla Resort Rruga Bashkim Kokona; www.kerculla.al. Hard to believe, but they somehow managed to squeeze into little old Gjirokastra a resort complex with two pools, a spa, a gym and a restaurant. The setting is impeccable, service is professional, and rooms for one to four are chic and comfortable, with Ottoman-style trim that's not over the top. It's tricky to get up here, but you can recoup in the pool hanging right over the Gjerë Mountain. €€€€

Melodia Apartment Rruga Isa Zhuli and Rruga Hysen Hoxha; tel: 069 540 2219. A top option for groups who are keen to stay overnight in a historic *konak*, this two-bedroom apartment lies beyond the clamour of the bazaar, but not too far up the hills. It's been restored with both eclectic and traditional accents, and the host goes above and beyond to welcome visitors. Home amenities like a full kitchen and washing machine are a plus. €€€€

Stone City Hostel Rruga Alqi Kondi; tel: 069 348 4271. With dorms sleeping between four and ten guests in a historic property right in the bazaar, this is an excellent place to lay down your backpack. Accommodation is clean, the common room is chipper, the terrace has excellent views, and the owners offer some very choice perks, especially walking tours of the city and hiking trips beyond. €

EATING

SEE MAP PAGE 202

Gjirokastrit food is as good as any in Albania, but it is a small town, and many perfectly fine restaurants have similar menus. In addition to the typical roasted lamb, veal and grilled *qofte* (meatballs) be sure to try dairy here, whether it's ice cream, cheese or the local *oshaf* pudding made from milk, sugar and figs. *Qifqi*, a type of fried rice ball made with eggs, herbs and sometimes cheese, is a popular starter. *Shapkat*, a cornflour casserole with feta and spinach, is another local favourite.

Antigonea 2000 Rruga Ismail Kadare and Rruga Doktor Vasil Laboviti; tel: 069 664 7733. This centrally located patisserie and café, perfect for picking up goodies to go,

5

is a top snack spot for those with a sweet tooth. You'll find Greek-inflected local desserts here, including *bakllava* and *portokalopita* (sweet-orange cake), plus *shëndetlie*, the dense, syrupy Albanian cake. It's a favoured local hangout; prices are better and scoops of ice cream, bigger. Order a combo of cake and two scoops. €

Check-in Restaurant Rruga Astrit Karagjozi; tel: 069 414 7626. A big, lively outdoor space right by the Xhamia e Pazarit mosque, *Check-in* attracts both tourists and locals to its expansive menu and live music. Filled peppers, stuffed eggplant, moussaka and *qifqi* (fried rice balls) are all crowd-pleasers, but you can also plump for pizza, risotto or thick, tender cuts of lamb with almost-as-thick fries. €€

Restaurant Tradicional Odaja Rruga Gjin Bue Shpata; www.facebook.com/odajarestaurant. This spot is among the best in the bazaar for a hearty Gjirokastrit lunch or dinner, in an ambient little upstairs room tucked among the storefronts. Mezes are a standout, especially *qifqi*, *qofte* with yoghurt and *Odaja's* take on baked sesame-crusted cheese. Portions are big, prices are friendly, and if your timing is right, you can snag a table on the balcony above the street. €€

Taverna Panorama Zhuli Rruga Bule Naipi near Rruga Jace Hormova; tel: 069 573 3011. Opposite the castle on the south side, this family-run place a bit off the tourist track offers warm hospitality, excellent veggie options and superlative castle views from a trellised terrace shaded by grapevines. The fruit and salads are particularly fresh, and *Zhuli* is the place to go in town for *shapkat* (feta and spinach casserole). It's an unfussy menu, and vegetarians can eat well at old-fashioned Albanian prices. €

★ **Te Kubé** Rruga Ismail Kadare; tel: 069 607 4631. In the barrel-vaulted stone corridors beneath the Xhamia e Pazarit, you'll find a lovely little café-bookstore where you can brush up on your Kadare (see page 209) and sip fresh plum, strawberry or cranberry juice. Rainy days call for coffee or lavender tea (no alcohol; you're right under a mosque), and the food is mostly vegetarian, with vegan options as well. The omelettes, especially, are a fine way to start a brisk-paced day. €

★ **The Barrels (Te Fuçitë)** 6km northeast of Gjirokastra on Rruga Valare, Valareja village; www.facebook.com/fucite. Just outside town across the Drino River, *The Barrels* sets the standard for Gjirokastrit cuisine, and you can try a little bit of everything at this laidback agritourism-style spot. A *meze* platter of stuffed peppers, *lakror* (meat, vegetable or cheese pie), *qifqi* (rice balls) and more is the way to start, and then you can dig into huge slabs of lamb or pork on the bone or *qofte* over rice. Tables are set up next to the vineyards for maximal romance, and you should try the wine and *raki*. Reserve ahead. €€€

DRINKING AND NIGHTLIFE

SEE MAP PAGE 202

This wasn't always a party city, but in the summer, the bazaar area gets pretty spirited, pretty late. In other seasons, the pace slips down a few gears. Something fun can usually be found.

★ **Bukowski Bar** Rruga Alqi Kondi; tel: 068 565 5959. A watering hole inspired by the hard-living American poet, this extremely friendly two-storey spot on a busy bazaar drag is cosy inside, with kilim-draped sofas dotted around to encourage mingling. Chess, Uno and cards are at your disposal, but don't miss out on the live music; the upright piano sees plenty of action. Try the signature *Bukowski* cocktail, but everything's good.

Grey Stone Bar Rruga Gjin Bue Shpata; tel: 068 220 1900. Personable service and tasty snacks make this an excellent cooldown spot after you've conquered the castle. Coffee (hot or chilled) provides a caffeine boost, and the bar has a solid selection of international beers. *Grey Stone Bar* has just about perfected the Aperol spritz – that global go-to for sipping at pavement tables watching the world go by.

Muza' Street Bar Rruga Shezai Çomo; www.instagram.com/muza_street_bar. Just around the bend from the bazaar, this summer outdoor bar concept opened in 2024 to dispense cool drinks on warm nights. The vibe is laidback, the music is good, and the bartender is more than happy to get creative for you. Come around sunset.

SHOPPING

SEE MAP PAGE 202

Gjirokastra has a long, proud tradition of craftsmanship, and you can see it everywhere in the city. It can be enjoyable to bop around the bazaar's trinket shops, and there are many, but it is possible to find more authentic local handicrafts to take home too. Don't be afraid to browse the wares of folks who make and sell lace or stone carvings on the streets leading up to the castle; they're the real deal.

Aquila Liquori Albanian Traditional Raki Rruga Gjin Zenebishti at the Qafa e Pazarit; www.aquilagroup.net. This shop is an outpost of one of Albania's larger distillers, but that does make it a good spot to sample a whole array of specialty *rakis* in one place. It has plum, pear and grape varieties, plus versions aged eighteen months in oak barrels. Wines, liqueurs and *gliko* (sweet preserves) are sold here too, and you can purchase drinks by the pour before committing to a bottle.

★ **Gurëgdhendes M. Makri** Rruga Gjin Bue Shpata; tel: 069 327 0276. Muhedin Makri was among the masters of decorative stonework here in Gjirokastra, and his son, Ermal, continues the tradition at this shop and studio. There are plenty of smaller engravings you can fit in your suitcase, including renditions of the city, Orthodox icons and Albanian eagles, but Ermal can also sculpt bespoke pieces; you can even watch his process.

Wood Carver Petridhi Rruga Gjin Bue Shpata; www.facebook.com/Anastas.Petridhi. A woodcarver in Gjirokastra for nearly four decades, Anastas Petridhi makes and sells frames, handheld mirrors and wall decorations, such as ornate rosettes, but you can also pick up carved cityscapes or smaller souvenirs – keychains, ornaments, bracelets and the like. Or start with a blank piece and commission some custom pyrography.

DIRECTORY

Banks and currency exchange Most major Albanian banks have branches on Bulevardi 18 Shtatori, up the street from the bus terminal. In the old city, there are just a few ATMs in Sheshi Çerçiz Topulli and the bazaar area, and all have high withdrawal fees. Regardless, make sure you retrieve cash somewhere before you start climbing up the city, as most businesses, including hotels and restaurants, do not accept credit cards. There's also a Western Union and some currency exchanges on 18 Shtatori.
Emergencies Call tel:127 or tel: 112 for medical, tel: 129 or tel: 112 for police.
Hospital The city hospital is Spitali Rajonal Omer Nishani, at Bulevardi 18 Shtatori 28 (tel: 069 582 7475).
Immigration and visas For visa issues, visit the DVKM office off the SH4 north of town, take the left turning west after *Green Park Camping Gjirokastra*.
Pharmacies Pharmacy Albana (tel: 069 697 1917) and Farmaci Ada (tel: 069 320 4066) are near the main hospital, towards the east end of Bulevardi 18 Shtatori.
Police The regional police station is at Bulevardi 18 Shtatori and Rruga Zeman Haska (tel: 069 411 0230).
Post office There's a DHL service point on Bulevardi 18 Shtatori in the building across the street from Rruga Zeman Haska (tel: 04 240 6666). The Posta Shqiptare office is just up the street past the intersection with Rruga Rauf Fico.

Around Gjirokastra: the Drino Valley

Tucked between the Gjerë Mountain (Mali i Gjerë, meaning 'Wide Mountain') to the west and the Lunxhëria and Bureto (or Buretos) massifs to the east, the **DRINO VALLEY** (Lugina e Drinos) has been a fertile, attractive place to settle for millennia. The first important city in antiquity here was **Antigonea**, founded by King Pyrrhus of Epirus in the third century BC. When the Romans conquered the city, they burned it to the ground and enslaved the inhabitants. A long history of violence would plague the valley thereafter. Enver Hoxha heavily fortified the Drino (definite form: Drinos or Drinosi), and the fall of communism left many people unemployed and at a loose end. In the 1990s, the villages emptied out, Gjirokastra's bazaar was burned and vandalized, and the rural economy turned toward some rather less traditional crop varieties. But today, things have quietened down. In this evocative landscape, you will find Byzantine and post-Byzantine **monasteries**, the ruins of Antigonea and **Hadrianopolis**, and a few quaint historic villages – all easy excursions from Gjirokastra. Solitude-seekers with sturdier 4WDs can rattle all the way up the mountains to hike and meditate at the **Çajupi Field** (Fusha e Çajupit), and venture off grid to the untouched **Zagoria Valley** (Lugina e Zagorisë) to the east.

Antigonea Archaeological Park

Asim Zeneli village • Charge

Like many other sites in Albania, the **Antigonea Archaeological Park** (Parku Arkeologjik i Antigonesë) may be as attractive for the ambience of its setting as the ruins themselves, which are mostly foundations. In the early third century BC, **King Pyrrus of Epirus** triumphed, infamously, over the Roman republic on the Italian peninsula – 'infamously' because his wins were the original Pyrrhic victory, by his own admission. Though Pyrrus was better at wars and quips than governing, he did establish a great urban centre, naming it for his first wife, Antigone. It's still a large site, covering around a hundred acres. But the Romans did not forget Pyrrhus, and the town made a fatal error in opposing them during their conquest of Southern Albania. After the legions destroyed the Greek city in 167 BC, it was never rebuilt.

Today, the site is well signed, with maps, reconstructions and English-language explanations of what you're looking at. You can easily identify the orderly layout

5

of the town plan, and even see how individual houses were set up, with living and working quarters surrounding peristyle inner courtyards. Also worth a stop is the stoa, a large portico on the agora, with a panorama of the valley. It likely functioned as a marketplace. The 4km perimeter wall wrapping around the city can mostly be tracked, and you'll spot a smattering of the slabs of Lunxhëria limestone that made up the ramparts at the south gate.

ARRIVAL AND DEPARTURE — ANTIGONEA

By car or taxi From the Gjirokastra bus terminal on SH4, head east on Rruga Kryepiskopi Anastas through the villages of Arshi Lëngo and Asim Zeneli towards Sarqinishti and follow signs south to Antigonea Archaeological Park (Parku Arkeologjik i Antigonesë) from there. The road is paved, though many of the ruins are around 1.2km south of the park entrance. From Gjirokastra, the park takes around 30min to reach by car or taxi. See page 210 for Gjirokastra taxi info.

Libohova

Tucked into the folds of the Bureto foothills, **Libohova** is a fine stop for a quick Gjirokastra escape by bus. There is no shortage of places serving traditional regional food in town, and you'll have a great panorama over **Doftia Lake** (Liqeni i Doftisë) and, beyond, the yawning Drino Valley. Plus, the town has a famous tree, which is fun. The **Libohova Plane Tree** (Rrapi i Libohovës) is around 500 years old, and it is indeed a beast. But it'll graciously throw shade your way if you're taking coffee on the terrace around it.

Libohova Castle

Rruga Cupreli east of the centre, or walk 500m up from the square or tree • Free

The big quadrangular **Libohova Castle** (Kalaja e Libohovës) just above the town is an **Ali Pasha** original, finished in 1798. He built it as a gift or dowry for his sister Shanisha, who was portrayed by the great French novelist Alexandre Dumas as almost as cunning and even more creatively cruel than the pasha in his history-inspired tales, *Celebrated Crimes: Ali Pacha* (1839). Contemplate what the truth might be as you wander the quiet, empty grounds of the fortress and survey the valley unfolding before you.

ARRIVAL AND DEPARTURE — LIBOHOVA

By bus Buses head from Gjirokastra to Libohova and back daily, roughly hourly until afternoon (several daily; 30min).
By car or taxi From the SH4 south of Gjirokastra, take the SH96 (Rruga e Libohovës) east, and turn right (east) at the exit signposted Libohova. Keep left at the fork on Rruga e Libohovës as you're about to enter town, and exit via Rruga e Zhepës. The drive is around 30min from Gjirokastra. See page 210 for Gjirokastra taxi info.

Labova e Kryqit

Overnighting in a hamlet in the heights is a wonderous occasion after a day in the Gjirokastra crowds. You can unlock some of the best *bujtinës* (guesthouses) in the Drino by picking **Labova e Kryqit** as your village. It is a tiny, but idyllic spot with just a few streets in one 'neighbourhood', and a handful more streets in another, 200m above. Labova's historical claim to fame is right in the name: Labova e Kryqit translates as Labova of the Cross, a nod to the fact that the village church was, until recently, the guardian of a piece of the **True Cross**.

Church of St Mary (Kisha e Shën Mërisë)

Labovë e Vogël e Kryqit village • Free • www.facebook.com/groups/labova.e.kryqit

A Byzantine gem, the **Church of St Mary** (Kisha e Shën Mërisë) is among the oldest churches in the region (and the country) in this excellent state of preservation. Researchers have posited that the current building dates from between the eleventh and thirteenth centuries. Things get murky delving back that far, but it is said that a shard of the **True Cross** – a Christian relic on which Jesus of Nazareth was believed to have been crucified – was stashed here for safekeeping for hundreds of years. (No one could really confirm the provenance of True Cross pieces until radiocarbon-dating tech, but it was a sacred totem nonetheless.) Things became even more muddied in recent Albanian history: the fragment allegedly disappeared around 1990.

At any rate, the church itself is a marvellous relic, with a complete narthex and frescoes that are as old as the standing structure – a rarity in Albania. Masonry alternates between square and diamond bricks, and a few large blocks have square chunks scooped out, intended to host **beehives** – symbolic in Christianity, with the church a figurative hive and the worshippers as the bees.

ARRIVAL AND DEPARTURE — LABOVA E KRYQIT

By car or taxi From the SH4 south of Gjirokastra, follow the SH96 (Rruga e Libohovës) northeast past Libohova; continue for 3.5km then turn right on the paved road towards Labova e Kryqit. It's another 4.5km on narrow, curvy mountain roads, but they're paved and any car can make the trip. Labova e Kryqit is around 40min from Gjirokastra by car. See page 210 for Gjirokastra taxi information.

ACCOMMODATION AND EATING

A few quiet getaway spots have opened in Labova e Kryqit, fairly close to Gjirokastra but even closer to nature. Visit during the Orthodox holidays to watch folkloric dances – and join in if you wish. Both of the following have fine on-site restaurants with farm-fresh food, which are open to all.

Bujtina Maria Labovë e Vogël e Kryqit, follow signs; tel: 069 704 5551. More a genteel manor than rustic cottage, this guesthouse has clean, spacious rooms sleeping one to four, all kitted out with kilims, exposed stone and big windows framing views of the church, the village and the valley below. Welcoming staff, excellent food and a swimming pool. Highly recommend. €€€

★ **Bujtina Sophie** Labovë e Vogël e Kryqit, follow signs; tel: 069 700 3353. An ultra-peaceful spot far removed from the tourist bustle, *Bujtina Sophie* has an elegant, romantic atmosphere, with lace window trim and a flower garden with chirpy birds. The terrace overlooking the Drino Valley is a sublime spot to relax with a glass of wine or a coffee. €€

Hadrianopolis

Sofratika village • Free

Not much is left of the Roman city of **Hadrianopolis** (Hadrianopoli). Unlike Antigonea (see page 213), it's a small site, but what remains is better preserved. The city was established as the administrative and population centre of the Roman Drino in the second century AD by the emperor Hadrian, and it was arranged in a grid plan, with houses, shops, a forum and the like. Today, the **theatre** is most impressive, with a diameter of 58m and a capacity of roughly four thousand spectators. Nearby, you can also see the ruins of the **baths**, featuring solid examples of Roman and Byzantine brick- and stonework in a herringbone pattern. Note the contrast to the foundation of the **Hellenistic temple** in the **forum** area, which is all hefty limestone blocks, precisely fitted about seven or eight centuries earlier.

Around 4km south beyond the SH4 turnoff to the site, follow the grassy road around the north side of a factory to discover what's been dubbed the '**Field of Bunkers**'. It's pretty much what it says on the tin, a green space fitted with underground shelters commissioned by paranoid dictator Enver Hoxha in case of attack.

ARRIVAL AND DEPARTURE — HADRIANOPOLIS

By car or taxi Follow the SH4 south and exit west to Sofratika village, then turn left (east) to drive under the motorway, and the site is about 800m on. The final section is dirt road, but it's manageable even with a small car. The trip takes about 25min from Gjirokastra; see page 210 for Gjirokastra taxi info.

Gjerë Mountain monasteries

You can't spot them from the motorway, but a smattering of incredible Byzantine and post-Byzantine **monasteries** dapple the slopes of the **Gjerë Mountain** (Mali i Gjerë, meaning 'Wide Mountain') in the Drino Valley (Lugina e Drinos). Some are among the most joyful religious places in the country, with cupolas like ornate lanterns and gloriously vivid frescoes, set in undisturbed wilderness. You can reach a handful by 4WD, but the trek is as much the experience in this pristine corner of Albania. Hikes partially follow old military tracks, passing communist-era tunnels, caves, cliffs and springs. Initiatives to mark walking trails – and restore faded churches – were well underway at the time of writing, in the mid-2020s. Still, some of the more scenic paths aren't too difficult to follow, and a 12km route from the side-by-side villages of **Vanistra** and **Goranxia** makes for a bracing half-day trek up and down the Gjerë Mountain; most of the trail is well marked.

You can start from either village, climb to the summit, loop around the **Monastery of Ravena** and the **Monastery of the Evangelization** and return. The Monastery of Ravena (Manastiri i Ravenës) was built in 1600, and it's not at all demure like later post-Byzantine churches; it flaunts fine-tuned decorative pilasters and arches around the apses and cupola. Fairly close by, though down somewhat hair-raising cliff trail, the Monastery of the Evangelization (Manastiri i Ungjillëzimit) dates from 1582 and is notable for its largely intact seventeenth- and eighteenth-century frescoes. It's not essential to go inside either church, but one or both are usually left open until late afternoon.

Download hiking app Wikiloc (www.wikiloc.com) and search for 'Vanistër' and 'Goranxi' to find a route that appeals. More charming churches that don't require a trek can be found in the villages of **Bodrishta** and **Bularati** near the Greek border.

ARRIVAL AND DEPARTURE — GORANXIA AND VANISTRA

By car Goranxia and Vanistra are right next to each other and just off the SH4, on the west side. Goranxia is 9.3km from Gjirokastra and can be reached in 15min by car.

By bus or minibus Buses from Gjirokastra to Jorgucati (sometimes marked as 'Dropull', the municipality name) will usually drop you off on the SH4 by either village if you ask the driver (many daily; 15min). Minibuses on the route will almost certainly oblige you.

EATING

★ **Kalimera Patisserie** SH4, Vanistra; www.instagram.com/kalimera_patisserie_official. *Kalimera* has a few locations in Gjirokastra and Saranda now, but the original café is a Route 66-style roadside stop in tiny Vanistra. It's become quite a holy place itself among dessert devotees. Crêpes with Nutella, banana and walnut crumble are excellent. *Bakllava*? You know it. Ice cream is made fresh, in house, and frappés are served tall and thick. €

The Myzeqeja plain

The **MYZEQEJA PLAIN** (indef: Myzeqe, sometimes Fusha e Myzeqesë) is an oddity in Albanian geography – it is flat. The area can be very roughly traced from Kavaja in the north, south to Vlora and east to Berati, with the Adriatic to the west. The landscape of crop swatches and low-slung villages is most obvious west of **Fieri** and **Lushnja**, where the communist government drained the wetlands, planted grains and built several forced-labour camps. The two mid-sized cities will probably only interest real Albania-heads, but if you're travelling without a car, you may need to pass through to pick up a ride to the pristine ruins of **Apollonia** (Apolonia) and **Byllis** (Bylisi), the resplendent medieval monastery at **Ardenica** and the **Divjaka-Karavasta National Park** (see page 152).

The story of this place comes into focus with the Romans, who elevated Apollonia to a city of wealth and grandeur. As Christianity made its way to the uppermost echelons of Rome in the fourth century AD, major basilicas and ecclesiastical hierarchies were established in what was then the province of Epirus Nova – now this part of Albania. Like much of Roman culture, it spread from Dyrrachium (Durrësi), the capital, and the Myzeqeja is full of relics spanning 1700 years of Christianity.

The current iterations of most churches and monasteries in Myzeqeja date to the eighteenth and nineteenth centuries, and they largely remain active as places of worship, cemeteries and, in a couple of cases, functioning monasteries. Except for those at Apollonia and Ardenica, they aren't really tourist destinations, they aren't near cities, and they may or may not be open. The Church of St George (Kisha e Shën Gjergjit) in Libofsha, Church of St Nicholas (Kisha e Shën Kollit) in Vanaj and the Monastery of St Kosmas (Manastiri i Shën Kozmait) in Kolkondasi, surrounding a church built on the order of Ali Pasha, are serene spots for contemplation among cypresses but not particularly suited to itinerary-ticking travel.

Fieri

Unlike most of Albania's larger cities, **Fieri** is relatively new. In the wake of the 1851 earthquake that ravaged Berati, members of the most powerful family in the region, the **Vrionis**, officially established Fieri in 1864. The city underwent a makeover after the fall of communism, with shiny new places of worship for Orthodox Christians and Sunni Muslims, and brightly painted squares, parks and pedestrianized boulevards in the centre. Construction began on a new university, the enormous wedding-cake building that borrows heavily from the United States Capitol, in 2012.

The paint has since faded, the planks on park benches have rotted, and the university is unfinished. Its grand lawn acts as a paid car park. But if you're killing time on the way to Apollonia, grab a bite to eat at the **Central Park** (Parku Qendror) next to the truly peculiar postmodern building that houses the **Vilson Kilica Art Gallery** (Galeria e Arteve Vilson Kilica; www.facebook.com/Artgallery-Fier-104065361333994), filled with contemporary artwork.

Fieri History Museum

Rruga Leon Rei and Rruga Llambi Bego • Charge • www.facebook.com/MuzeuHistorikFier

The 1970s facade could use a touch-up, but **Fieri History Museum** (Muzeu Historik Fier) conceals a substantial collection, covering archaeology, ethnography and archival photography. Its gallery of socialist realist paintings is worth the stop, where **Vilson Kilica**, one of Albania's most talented painters of the twentieth century, takes pride of place. His *Këngë në Mbrëmje* (Evening Song) of partisan fighters unwinding in the twilight of a hard day, is extraordinarily expressive. The artist caught the attention of the party for 'bourgeois influences' in his work, but he lived long enough to colour outside the lines after 1990.

ARRIVAL AND GETTING AROUND — FIERI

Fieri is an excellent base for day-trips by taxi and/or bus to a number of highly worthwhile destinations that are otherwise difficult or impossible to reach without your own car. It's the most efficient point of access to Apollonia, Ardenica and Byllis.

By bus or minibus Fieri connects to most of Central, Southwestern and Northwestern Albania with frequent buses, but intercity buses come and go from various points around the city. The primary terminal is near Rruga Shenjt Leonardo Murialdo about 2km from the city centre (25min walk). Catching an urban bus at the roundabout where Rruga Shenjt Leonardo Murialdo and Rruga Jani Bakalli meet can cut down on your walking time; the bus for/from Berati also stops at this roundabout. The Tirana bus arrives at the defunct Stacioni i Trenit, closer to the centre. The one for/from Vlora is at the roundabout where Rruga Ramiz Arianitasi and Rruga Unaza Nuredin Aliu meet. Finally, the bus stop for Apollonia (alight at Pojani village) is at the corner of Rruga Leon Rei and Rruga Brigada IX Sulmuese (several daily; 20min). It helps to ask for help wherever you arrive.

Destinations Berati (many daily; 1hr 25min); Çorovoda (several daily; 2hr 50min); Dhërmiu (several daily; 1hr 15min); Durrësi (many daily; 1hr 45min); Elbasani (many daily; 1hr 50min); Gjirokastra (many daily; 1hr 30min); Himara (several daily; 2hr 30min), Korça (several daily; 4hr 5min); Lezha (several daily; 3hr 25min); Librazhdi (several daily; 2hr 15min); Lushnja (many daily; 45min); Përmeti (many daily; 2hr 10min); Pogradeci (several daily; 3hr 10min); Saranda (several daily; 2hr 40min); Shkodra (several daily; 4hr 5min); Tepelena (many daily; 1hr 15min); Tirana (many daily; 2hr 15min–2hr 45min); Tirana International Airport (many daily; 1hr 50min); Vlora (many daily; 40min).

By car The A2 highway loops right around Fieri, and the SH4/SH8 motorways lead directly to the centre. Follow

5

signs for exits to Fieri (Qendër) from either direction. Street parking on side streets near the centre is usually available and free, and there's a paid underground car park beneath Sheshi Europa Plaza, in front of *Hotel Fieri*.

By taxi Most of Fieri county's points of interest are tricky or impossible to reach by bus, but the city has many taxi services that can take you for a fair rate. If you're after a return trip, nail down the time and price in advance. There's a large taxi rank in the centre on Rruga Ramiz Aranitasi in front of the Teatri Bylis. To arrange in advance, call or message a reliable operator like Taxi Qamili (tel: 069 218 5801), Delux Taxi (tel: 068 505 5500), Taxi Sharra (tel: 068 541 0001), Malasi Taxi (tel: 068 890 0888) or Bylis Taxi (tel: 069 356 0970). Albes Taxi has the biggest fleet of cars (tel: 08 003 333 or tel: 069 809 8719).

ACCOMMODATION

Albes Hotel Rruga Teodor i II Muzaka; www.albes.al/en/portfolio/albes-hotel. Clean, modern hotel with friendly and helpful staff, and a 24hr reception. Rooms accommodate one to three people, breakfast is included and there's an EV charging station. The Albes taxi service operates from here, a nice bonus for getting around the region. €€€

Apartments Natalia 4.2km west of Fieri via SH94 (Rruga e Semanit), then right (north) into Çlirimi. With four one-bedroom apartments, this is a basic but comfortable option for the region at a very affordable price. All units have modern amenities, plus parking, kitchens or kitchenettes, and washing machines. You're close to the city but even closer to nature. €

Hotel Fieri Rruga Jakov Xoxa; www.hotelfieri.com. The original elite hotel of the city, built in 1966, this 55-room high-rise is right on Sheshi Europa Plaza in Fieri centre. Staff are professional and helpful; rooms are well kept and ambient – the best with decent views of the city. Underground parking is included, as is breakfast; there's a solid restaurant on site. €€€

EATING

Toska Fish Restaurant Rruga Llambi Bego and Rruga Hasaf Dishnica; www.facebook.com/toskafishrestaurant. A minimalist modern space with lids from cases of pricey French and Italian cult wines affixed to the walls, so you know what you're getting into. *Toska Fish*'s menu is an encyclopaedia of seafood dishes, pasta plates and seafood pastas, with some particularly intricate and delicious crudos and carpaccios. Alternatively, ask what's fresh that day. The wine list features fine Albanian selections among the more broad-shouldered bottles too. €€€

Lushnja

A medium-sized city of mostly communist and post-communist architecture 30km north of Fieri, **Lushnja** has a few museums that may entice those inclined to get more immersed in Albanology. It's also where you can pick up a bus or minibus to Divjaka and Divjaka-Karavasta National Park (see page 152).

Congress of Lushnja Museum

Pedestrian boulevard leading from Shëtitorja Kongresi i Lushnjës • Charge • www.facebook.com/kongresi.i.lushnje.9

In the aftermath of World War I, Albania's new, fragile independence continued to be contested, with Greece and Italy laying claim to most of the south and west of the country. In January 1920, statesmen from around Albania gathered at this house in Lushnja to devise a plan. Independent Albania needed a capital, and delegates decided it should be built in a hinterland backwater town called Tirana; they also drafted the outlines of a constitution. The house was restored and reorganized, opening as the **Congress of Lushnja Museum** (Shtëpia Muze Kongresi i Lushnjës) in 2020. Displays featuring maps and explanatory text drive home just how difficult the task of creating an independent, functioning nation-state in the Balkans really was.

Lushnja Historical Museum

Shëtitorja Kongresi i Lushnjës and pedestrian boulevard, north corner • Charge • www.facebook.com/p/Muzeu-Historik-Lushnje-100030921472227

A small municipal museum, **Muzeu Historik Lushnjë** showcases Neolithic ceramics and stone tools, medieval stonework from Ardenica Monastery (see page 219) and a large wall mural painted by Prime Minister **Edi Rama**. The highlight, though, is not as dusty as the exhibits: archaeologist and historian Dr Niko Ferro – director of Lushnja's museums – guides visitors through the exhibits and the archaeology of the region and can even take you on a short drive to sites and structures he's excavated. Niko is an expert on all things Myzeqeja and speaks confidently and fascinatingly on everything from the mobility-enhancing helmet designs of Illyrian warriors to the paranoia of life under communism. Ask for him at the ticket desk or message him on Facebook via www.facebook.com/p/Lushnja-Histori-Tradita-100060821679933.

ARRIVAL AND GETTING AROUND — LUSHNJA

By bus or furgon Buses for Lushnja follow the same north–south and central routes as Fieri (for destinations see page 217). Additional services from Lushnja run to Divjaka (several daily; 30min) and Fieri (many daily; 45min). The station is at the western end of Ypsiloni; walk east 800m to Lushnja centre via Ypsiloni and Rruga Vedut Do Kollari. *Furgons* (minibuses) also leave from here for the visitor centre in Divjaka-Karavasta National Park (35min).

By car Lushnja is at the juncture of SH4 going north–south and SH72 northwest of Berati. Follow signs for exits to Lushnja (Qendër).

Ardenica Monastery

SH67, Ardenica village • Charge • www.facebook.com/ManastiriiArdenices

The **Ardenica Monastery** (Manastiri i Ardenicës) is a rare active monastery, but it keeps fairly regular visiting hours. Dominant on a hilltop, it's an extraordinary site centred on one of the most beautiful churches in the country in this excellent state of preservation, inside and out. There was likely a pagan temple here dedicated to Artemis (the multihyphenated Greek goddess of hunting, the wilderness, wild animals, childbirth and childcare), which would explain why it's 'Ardenica', and later a paleo-Christian church. The monastery followed in the thirteenth or fourteenth century, and lore has it that a certain **Gjergj Kastrioti Skënderbeu** (Skanderbeg) hosted his wedding here in 1451. That is, in any event, what the presiding bishop told communist soldiers in 1967, and perhaps the reason there's any monastery left at all.

The focal point today is the **Church of St Mary** (Kisha e Shën Mërisë), a grand post-Byzantine basilica built in 1743 with funds from merchants of Voskopoja. They sent their best guys for the job: revered painter-brothers **Kostandin and Athanas Zografi**, with assistance on the iconostasis from **Kostandin Shpataraku**. In addition to the frescoes, far better preserved than most remaining in Albanian churches, the woodcarving is also worth a snoop up close. The bishop's throne, pulpit and iconostasis are all eighteenth-century originals – gold-trimmed and very much in sync with the Baroque style that enamoured the Catholics across the sea. Most of the outbuildings can't be accessed, so you can make this a pretty quick detour if you're driving. Knock on the wooden door to be let in, and ask before taking photos.

ARRIVAL AND GETTING AROUND — ARDENICA

By car or taxi Exit the SH4 west near the village of Kolonja, via the SH67. Ardenica is about midway between Lushnja and Fieri, and there are signs for the monastery on the motorway and throughout the village. From the motorway, it's about 4km (10min) to the monastery; mind the steep roads up the hill. If you're tempted to try a 'shortcut' from the west side of the hill instead of the motorway, bin that idea. You can also grab a taxi from Fieri; see page 218 for options.

ACCOMMODATION AND EATING

Albanica Wine Kolonja village, follow signs; www.albanicawine.com. This is a super-hospitable winery and restaurant poised on the crest of the hill, with elevated food to match the views. Stop by for a glass of Debinë e Bardhë with bruschetta and olives, or tuck into something more substantial like steak or sausage. Wander the thirty acres of vines, and you can even park your campervan overnight. €€

Hotel Nature SH67, Kolonja village; tel: 069 338 7409. A friendly budget option, *Hotel Nature* actually has an intriguing history. The building is a former military office, and the hill behind it conceals communist-era bunkers and tunnels, which you can visit. Rooms are spartan but clean and comfortable, and the hotel is surrounded by fruit gardens, so breakfast and dinner are very good. €€

5

Apollonia Archaeological Park

SH66, Pojani • Charge • www.apolloniaarchaeologicalpark.al • Virtual tour via 'Apolonia & Byllis Parks' app in the Google Play Store and Apple App Store

Never sacked nor built over, **Apollonia** is a very fine example of an important Greek and Roman colonial city. The archaeological site, **Parku Arkeologjik Apoloni**, is easy to reach by car en route from Durrësi to Vlora, and it's not at all overwhelming. The orator **Cicero**, writing in 44–43 BC, called it a '*magna urbs et gravis*' (great and important city), but today, the most impressive excavated monuments in the 1700-acre park are clustered around the forum, near the entrance. You can see them, along with the museum, in under two hours, or you can spend half a day tracing the walls and finding ruins you'll likely have to yourself. There's not too much left standing, so don't expect the likes of Pompeii. But do imagine what could remain undiscovered beneath your feet – less than ten percent of Apollonia has been excavated.

Brief history

The hill on which Apollonia was established was likely uninhabited by Illyrians when Greek colonists from **Corinth** and **Corcyra** (now Corfu) chose the area to settle around 600 BC. Evidence suggests the Greeks and Illyrians in the area eventually got on well enough that there was substantial intermarriage at Apollonia. With a port to the Adriatic on the **Vjosa River** (Lumi i Vjosës), the city grew as a hub of trade and agriculture during the fourth and third centuries BC. The **stoa** (portico), linking the north and south centres of the city, dates to this period, as does the **theatre**, which could seat 11,000 spectators.

Absorbed by Rome in 229 BC, Apollonia earned special status as a favoured city of a very promising young man. The teenaged **Octavian** was studying oratory here in 44 BC when he learned his great-uncle, Julius Caesar, had been assassinated. When Octavian became Emperor Caesar Augustus, he granted Apollonia increased autonomy as a '*civitas libera*' (free city). Connected to Rome's primary trade route through Albania – the **Via Egnatia** – the city flourished until an earthquake in the third century AD altered the course of the Vjosa, its economic lifeline. Detached from the river, Apollonia became a malarial swamp of no strategic importance. Inhabitants relocated to Aulona (Vlora), and Apollonia carried on primarily as an episcopal centre.

The city ruins

Built in the late second century AD, the six-columned **bouleuterion** is what you see on the postcards of Apollonia. In Hellenic Roman cities, the **boule** was the city council, and its meeting place here once sat about 160 people in a semicircular auditorium. The facade, of course, is the distinguishing feature, but it's more than just a pretty face. Above the Corinthian capitals of the columns, the architrave is inscribed in Greek, not Latin – it was a free city, after all. It reads, in part, that 25 pairs of gladiators battled here on the day of its inauguration: it was also a Roman city.

The **odeoni**, across the street, was built around the same time and was once the stage for oratory and musical performances, seating an audience of five hundred. Scattered around the odeoni, you'll also discover the foundations of temples, a library, an obelisk and storefronts. To your left, follow a trail past the stoa (portico), preserving the pediments of its 36 columns. Down the hill, if you have time, check out a larger venue, the theatre, where both plebeians and aristocrats enjoyed bread and circuses. The orchestra bit and a section of the stage were likely converted in Roman times to a small 'arena' for bloodsport. A bit further afield is the **nymphaion**, an unusual system of terraced canals for catching and 'filtering' runoff water. Hiking east and uphill, you can head to either the **acropolis** or the house of French archaeologist Léon Rey (1887–1954), now a café. Both spots have few ruins but fairly enchanting views of the Myzeqeja plain, stretching as far as the Adriatic on a clear day.

Dormition of the Virgin Mary Monastery and Apollonia Archaeological Museum

You can visit the monastery complex (Manastiri Fjetja e Shën Marisë) and the archaeological museum (Muzeu Arkeologjik Apoloni) at the start or end of your tour of Apollonia, as it's located just to the right of the park entrance. Next to the ruined ancient city, the **Dormition of the Virgin Mary Monastery** feels new and even a little intrusive, but it's a genuine medieval artefact representing eight hundred years of Roman and Byzantine Christianity in Albania. The Romanesque narthex vestibule of the **thirteenth-century church** merits closer inspection: check out the column etched with birds, human faces and a few monsters *with* human faces. Opposite, to the right is the door, to the refectory, easily overlooked by visitors but adorned with thirteenth-century **frescoes** and **fourth-century AD mosaic floors**.

The **Apollonia Archaeological Museum** is small but well curated, and it might be the country's finest archaeological museum until the Archaeological Museum of Durrësi (see page 145) reopens. In the exhibition space, wend your way from seventh-century BC black-figure pottery and bronze figurines to third-century AD statues and busts of gods, men and a mermaid. (Larger statues and sarcophagi are in the pavilions downstairs.) The luxuries and necessities of everyday life in Apollonia two millennia ago bring the site to human scale; there are bronze brooches, bracelets, styluses, strigils (a curved tool used to scrape moisture and oil off the body after bathing), tweezers and little clay toys shaped like birds and dogs. The prize of the collection, however, is an intact **fourth-century BC Illyrian shield**, around 70cm in diameter, marvellously embossed from top to bottom, with a jolly gorgon head lolling its tongue in the centre – a unique artefact in the country.

ARRIVAL AND DEPARTURE — APOLLONIA

By car or taxi Apollonia is right off the A2 highway that connects Fieri and Vlora, and it's a popular place to take a break on drives between Tirana and the riviera. From Fieri, take the highway and leave at the Apollonia exit, which is well marked; then follow the SH66 through Pojani village to the park's main car park or overflow lot. The drive is less than 20min. Fieri taxi drivers are used to ferrying people to Apollonia as well; see page 218 for Fieri taxi info.

By bus Pojani village is within the network of Fieri's urban buses. Services to Pojani depart from the corner of Rruga Leon Rei and Rruga Brigada IX Sulmuese (several daily; 20min). From the Pojani bus stop at the village centre (SH66), walk southwest about 1.2km (15min) to the gate of the park, following signs.

Byllis

Rruga e Bylisit, Hekali village • Charge • www.apolloniaarchaeologicalpark.al • Virtual tour via 'Apollonia & Byllis Parks' app in the Google Play Store and Apple App Store

Butrint is evocative and Apollonia is mysterious, but **BYLLIS** is the most enchanting archaeological site in Albania, its ancient ruins tumbling across a sloping bluff 550m above sea level in the Mallakastra hills. Byllis (Bylisi) was an important city for hundreds of years, an **Illyrian capital** and **early Byzantine ecclesiastical centre**. Large-scale monuments of both periods are rare in Albania, as many were razed and built over later, so it's a treat to find the impressive and intact collection in this remote location. Byllis isn't hard to reach, though. it's just out of the way – but the detour is a rich reward for archaeology fans and nature lovers. The 75-acre site peers over a giant bend in the Vjosa with scarce signs of modern life to blemish the panorama of deep green hills, swatches of farmland and the glinting river.

Brief history

In Greek mythology, the legendary founder of Byllis was **Neoptolemus**, son of warrior Achilles, who did not exactly cover himself in glory killing old men and babies during the Sack of Troy; an odd choice of ancestor. What is known, however, is that a

5

settlement existed here when an Illyrian tribe called the **Bylliones** began transforming it into a centre of power and population, most likely a capital of their territory, in the mid-fourth century BC. The large ashlar blocks of a 2.3km **fortification wall** that are scattered around the site date to this time.

The Bylliones interacted with their Hellenistic Greek counterparts in the area – Apollonia and Epidamnos (Durrësi) were Greek colonies – and developed a hybrid culture, minting bronze coins with the mug of Zeus but also incorporating more ancient symbols like sacred flames and horns of fertility. During its years as a **Roman colony**, Byllis was refreshed and modified, but in the fourth century AD, Visigothic invaders wrecked the city, and incursions became a growing threat. Nevertheless, the Romans and Byzantines built or rebuilt at least five **grand-scale basilicas** during the turbulent centuries to come, with one colossal cathedral complex stretching 67m long (the Hagia Sophia Grand Mosque in Istanbul is 82m long). In 586 AD, Slavs ravaged Byllis once more. Sick of being sacked, its inhabitants threw in the towel and fled.

The site

What has been excavated of the Illyrian and Roman city centre is fairly compact, and you could spend anywhere between an hour and half a day exploring **Byllis Archaeological Park** (Parku Arkeologjik Bylis). There's a restaurant by the site entrance, and the informational signage, in English, is pretty comprehensive, but that's it for facilities for now. In 2024, plans to build a museum were announced.

From the entrance on the west side of the park, you'll run into the cathedral, or **Basilica B**, to the left of the main path. The basilica, first built in the fourth century AD, is a big one, with three naves, a narthex, an exonarthex in front of the narthex, and an apse in the back. As you peer down the central nave to the apse, imagine that there would once have been porticos around the church and high galleries inside. The mosaics in the nave are kept covered, unfortunately. Scattered around the cathedral are crumbling outbuildings like a **baptistery** and an **episcopal palace**, plus odds and ends of stones, stairs and supersized storage amphorae. Columns at the entrance of a side building are of particular interest, as they've been restored to their upright position – look for the early Byzantine capitals that start with Ionic scrolls and scroll up to tropical-looking palm motifs.

Following the main path south, you'll reach the **agora**, the Illyrian city centre. Note the prytaneion on the right side of the path, which was the original seat of government, and then the Vjosa comes into view. From the jumble of buildings on the left, you can extract **Basilica A**, a **Roman bath** and the **third-century BC stadium** – unusual in that it only has one side, likely because the slope becomes too steep to fit a whole loop track. Excavations have turned up bronze 'tickets' to races and performances. A cistern just below the stands collected rainwater runoff. Together, the entire stadium complex is an ingenious number, ancient architects playing the hand they were dealt with this terrain.

Pass the gymnasium and **Basilica C** to the edge of the bluff, where you can take in the full panorama of the Vjosa horseshoe. Back on the path, on the east side, you can't miss the **third-century BC theatre**, carved directly into the hillside. You can see remnants of stone flowers, triglyphs and dentils from a former frieze, and portions of the seating rows, but you should hoof it up the hill to take in the full plan of the theatre against the backdrop of the river and valley.

ARRIVAL AND DEPARTURE — BYLLIS

By car From the SH4 or A2 coming from the north or south, exit towards Fieri and stay on the SH4 motorway loop east around the city, then head southeast on SH73 toward Portëzi. Exit SH73 right (south) towards Patosi, then right (south) again towards Banaj, Lalari and Ballshi. Continue south through Ballshi, and follow signs towards Parku Arkeologjik Bylis. The drive from Fieri centre takes about 45min. The roads are asphalted until the final ramp up to the site, but they are country roads, so drive cautiously. A road connecting the SH4 to Byllis (Bylisi) from the south was completed in 2024. Heading west on the SH4, it's a right (north) turn about 4.5km west past the intersection of SH4 and SH100 in Poçemi; follow signs. Don't take any other roads to Byllis from the south, as they are in poor condition.

By taxi From Fieri, taxis will take you to Byllis and back. It may be worth it if you're splitting the cost. See page 218 for Fieri taxi information.

By bus You can reach Ballshi from Fieri by bus (many daily; 40min), and you can usually find a taxi in Ballshi town that will take you the remainder of the way.

ACCOMMODATION AND EATING

Agroturizëm Bylis Rruga Hekal–Poçem, Hekali village; tel: 069 341 5337. A country house and five cabins, this property is easy on the eye and far from the noise. Rooms in the house are elegant; the cabins are cosy, and all are equipped with modern comforts. The owners make breakfast, lunch and dinner from local ingredients – rose and mandarin jam are specialities – and there are Vjosa viewpoints around the garden. Plus a pool. €€

Tepelena and the Kurveleshi highlands

TEPELENA straddles the junctions of the Vjosa, Drino and Bënça rivers, but the region is otherwise a forbidding landscape of hard-packed limestone, dizzying heights and sharp-toothed ravines. The Vjosa is about 100m above sea level here. Less than 9km southwest, the mountains loom 2100m above the landscape.

The highlands and valleys south and west of the town, called **Kurveleshi**, are beautiful and stark, reaching the **Nivica Canyon** (Kanionet e Nivicës) before rolling down to the coast. Tepelena itself is a little desolate too. It was once the northern headquarters of the storied Albanian warlord-turned-statesman, Ali Pasha, with a palace and fortress built to command awe. But only embers of grandeur remain.

Tepelena town

You'll run into echoes of **Ali Pasha Tepelena** (see box, page 224) and the ruins of his sweeping constructions all over Albania south of Tirana, but this is the town that lays claim to him. Ali was born here or in a nearby village, though he ruled from Janina (Ioannina), now in northern Greece. Tepelena was his northern stronghold and residence, where his presence wowed the young English traveller **Lord Byron**. It might not rank among Albania's great castle cities, but Ali's formidable **fortress walls** still menace and intrigue, and you can cross what remains of his mighty Vjosa **bridge**.

The inside of the citadel is a ramshackle residential area now, and there's not much else to see in the town itself. You'll find a statue of the pasha reclining at the southern 'entrance' to the city, at the roundabout from the SH4. The small **Muzeu Historik** (Rruga Ali Pashë Tepelena, west of the roundabout) has a handful of archaeological exhibits from the area, mostly ceramics, and some costumes typical of the nineteenth century. From Sheshi Lord Byron, you can access the best-preserved gates and ramparts of the castle, as well as the bridge and the pleasant enough riverwalk promenade along the Vjosa's west bank.

Tepelena Castle

Sheshi Lord Byron and Rruga Ali Pashë Tepelena • Free

Unlike those at Berati and Gjirokastra, **Tepelena Castle** (Kalaja e Tepelenës) was a whole-cloth project of one builder, Ali Pasha (see box, page 224). Figuring out where the ten-acre citadel begins and ends is not terribly easy, as the longest wall merges with a cliff over the Vjosa below, and the second-longest rampart is pretty ragged. But the **southern wall** is in good shape and accessible from an adjacent park that extends from Sheshi Lord Byron, in the town centre.

Ali Pasha captured his hometown in 1789, and built and renovated the fortress and palace between 1800 and 1819. As with most of his major projects, he entrusted architect **Petro Korçari** to take the lead. We don't know much about Petro, but at Tepelena, you can get the clearest up-close look at how he tackled defensive architecture on a grand

ALI PASHA

It's difficult to disentangle the facts about **Ali Pasha Tepelena** from the tall tales and exaggerations. That's partly on him: the 'Lion of Janina' had a talent for strategic showmanship and an inclination for spinning a yarn that his many subjects, enemies and guests from the West bought into. Despite piecing together a territory from Central Albania through the Peloponnese, he was, and still is, a figure on the fringes. As a Muslim Albanian who ruled from modern-day Greece in the Ottoman era with a ruthless brutal streak, he doesn't fit neatly into Albanian national narratives, and many Greeks would prefer to forget him entirely. You can see that attitude today in how few of his monumental constructions have been well preserved.

Born around 1750, Ali was the son of Albanian clan leader Veli Bej and his wife, **Hanko**. His father died when Ali was young, and Hanko stepped into the role of warlord, impressing on her son the virtues of courage and, perhaps, cruelty. In his rise to power, Ali subdued or savaged cities, wrestled for decades with Berati governors such as **Ahmet Kurt Pasha** (see page 111) and was recognized by the Ottoman government in Istanbul as the Pasha of Janina (Ioannina) by 1788.

In assembling the **Pashalik of Janina**, Ali allied with the French generals of Napoleon, who helped him take coastal positions he coveted, then subsequently turned on them. He had similarly turbulent relationships with Catherine the Great's Russia, various Greek tribes, and other pashas in Albania and Istanbul, whom he nominally answered to. The British, however, were always good in his book, according to his British visitors. **Lord Byron** met him in Tepelena in 1809. Ali spoke Greek, and his most famous wife, **Vassiliki**, was an Orthodox woman. He built a church in honour of a martyred preacher he'd known. He liked archaeology, or antique treasure at least, displaying statues excavated from Ancient Greek and Roman sites in his palaces. He tamped down the tradition of blood feuds in the Albanian South. He enlisted Albanian, British, French and Italian engineers and architects to help him construct fortifications like those at Tepelena, Gjirokastra, Porto Palermo, Saranda, Ioannina, Parga and Preveza but also roads, bridges, aqueducts, dervish lodges and places of worship. In the cosmopolitan cities of the pashalik, Christians, Muslims and Jews prospered as silversmiths, silk weavers and scholars. He had, some wrote, a travelling harem of women; others wrote he preferred men. In Greek folklore, he is remembered for massacring enemies and innocents, by burning, drowning, sledgehammer, you name it.

By 1820, Ali had overstepped the mark one too many times, and Ottoman **Sultan Mahmud II** ordered his resignation. After an open rebellion against Istanbul, the 'Mahometan Bonaparte' made his last stand in a monastery near his capital in 1822. He was in his seventies.

scale. Admire the primary entrance, the **south gate**, with its imposing double arch and barrel-vaulted portal. Check out Ali's favoured style of **tower**, neither round nor square but polygonal and slanted to better brush off cannonballs and other artillery rounds.

Inside the citadel, Ali installed a two-storey *seraglio* (palace) in which he lived and worked, gardens, a mosque, quarters for his retinue and guests, and barracks for his guard. William Martin Leake, the British consul to Ali Pasha's court, described the whole ensemble as a 'romantic and delightful country-house'. Within a century, it was in ruins, save the walls.

Beçishti Bridge

Access from Sheshi Lord Byron • Free

When the sun lights up the Vjosa in its signature cyan hues, the great, ruined **Beçishti Bridge** (Ura e Beçishtit), or Ali Pasha Bridge, set against a backdrop of undulating hills is a sight to behold. It was originally a Roman project, restored or rebuilt by **Ali Pasha**. Today, the 260m wooden span, supported by five partially intact stone piers and rusty suspension cables, looks a little more weather-beaten than you might feel comfortable trusting as a footbridge. However, you'll likely see a few brave souls cross it, so follow in their footsteps if you dare. From the bridge, you can take in a more zoomed-out view of the castle.

Tepelena Internment Camp

1.3km north of Tepelena via Rruga Ali Pashë Tepelena and unnamed roads • Free

Just outside the town of Tepelena, the communist regime built one of its first and most inhumane forced-labour camps in Albania. Between 1949 and 1954, 3380 people were imprisoned at **Tepelena Internment Camp** (Kampi i Tepelenës), the majority women, children and the elderly – relatives of those deemed 'enemies of the people'. Prisoners were deprived of food, medical care and sanitation, and hundreds died here. The concrete and brick shells of the factories, dormitories and guards' barracks remain, and a few **memorials** and plaques were added in 2022 to explain what happened here and to commemorate the victims. The site is unattended, but the gate is usually left unlocked.

Aqueduct of Ali Pasha

4.8km southwest of Tepelena centre via the Tepelena–Bënça road (asphalted); take the left uphill at the fork on Rruga Ali Pashë Tepelena north of Tepelena town • Free

The aqueduct straddling the gorge of the **Bënça River** (Lumi i Bënçës) is little known despite the size of the ruin, and it's well worth the short detour off the SH4 motorway. The valley is a dramatic landscape: greenish-brown and often shrouded in haze, with only a small stream trickling between the slopes. The **aqueduct** itself dates to Ali Pasha's reign, part of a network of channels that once carried water to Tepelena. It continued to be repaired and used for irrigation, and the most intact part of the original structure is on the east side near the road. You can pull over and climb the stairs down, where you'll see it's actually a two-level construction, with arches descending down to the stream – a welcome cool-down spot after a long drive.

ARRIVAL AND DEPARTURE — TEPELENA

By bus The Tepelena bus stop is on the SH4 at the roundabout near the statue of Ali Pasha. From here, it's about a 350m walk north to the castle via Rruga Ali Pashë Tepelena.

Destinations Berati (several daily; 2hr 40min); Durrësi (many daily; 3hr); Elbasani (several daily; 3hr 5min); Fieri (many daily; 1hr 15min); Gjirokastra (many daily; 25min); Libohova (several daily; 30min); Lushnja (many daily; 1hr 55min); Përmeti (many daily; 55min); Saranda (several daily; 1hr 25min); Tirana (many daily; 3hr 35min); Vlora (several daily; 1hr 25min).

By car The SH4 passes right by Tepelena, under the east wall of the castle. Drive in from the roundabout at the southern end of town. You can park in the square, Sheshi Lord Byron.

ACCOMMODATION

Lord Byron Agroturizëm 1.9km north of Tepelena on the SH4; www.lordbyron.al. A little bit country and a little bit fancy, *Lord Byron Agroturizëm* has all the accoutrements for chilling out. There's a pool, there's a 'beach' on the Bënça riverbank, there are gardens and there's a playground where you can park the kids. Rooms are intimate wood-panelled affairs, and you can book tours to Labova e Kryqit or the Peshtura Waterfall, or take a cooking class to learn the traditional recipe for chicken over *përshesh* stuffing (minced, meat-soaked cornbread, often slathered in butter). €€€

★ **Villa Goliku** 16.9km east of Tepelena via SH4 and SH75, Peshtani village; www.facebook.com/VillaGoliku. This warm countryside guesthouse on the slopes of Goliku Mountain is comfortable and well furnished, but the generous hospitality of the owners and the incredible views over the Vjosa gorge are what sets it apart. Poke around the orchards and groves to glimpse what'll be on the dinner table; even the butter is churned in house. €€

EATING

Zgara Tepelena Rruga Shullaz; tel: 069 828 0555. A no-frills grill focusing on what matters, and here, that's meat. A mixed plate of artfully seasoned pork chops, veal steak, chicken, sausages and more is the easy choice – and the correct one. Opened in 2024, this has quickly become a favourite local outdoor dining and drinking spot. €€

The Nivica canyonlands

West of Tepelena, you enter the **Kurveleshi** region along narrow mountainside roads, one of the most panoramic drives in southern Albania. First, you climb through the valleys and gorges of the **Bënça River** (Lumi i Bënçës), densely forested and misty, with peaks

5

puncturing clouds that stray too low – a slice of the Bolivian Yungas in Albania. Heading south, you'll pass through a string of high-altitude villages, likely having to brake to let sheep cross the road. Then, a particularly creative World War II lapidar (stone memorial) beyond the village of Progonati: shaped like a rocket on a launchpad, the monument is strapped with belts of rifle cartridges and wrapped in a bright red ring crowned with stars. From here, you can continue west along a 2022-built road all the way to Qeparoi on the Ionian coast, or head north to Nivica, an ethereal landscape of cliffs and canyons.

Nivica village, draped across a precipice of the Nivica Canyon (Kanionet e Nivicës), was very nearly abandoned, but it's been, well, pulled back from the brink. The cluster of white-grey stone villas, schoolhouse and plaza has been restored, some of the buildings now housing tavernas and guesthouses overlooking the magnificent maw below.

Nivica Canyon

Nivica or Progonati village • Free

An extraordinary landscape of cliffs, waterfalls and ravines, appearing out of nowhere, marks the arrival of **Nivica Canyon** (Kanionet e Nivicës), which stretch around 40km and are dotted with freefall waterfalls as high as 200m. The closest equivalent in Europe may be the gorges of the Haut-Var or Tarn in the South of France, and unlike other canyons in Albania, these aren't smooth-faced. The narrowest corridors and the best trekking areas are jagged, as if freshly cracked apart, and the pools beneath the waterfalls are translucent. You can follow a combination of hiking trails and shepherds' trails into the ravine, take a swim and return in just a few hours from Nivica. Another excellent option is a trek to the **Peshtura Waterfall** (Ujëvara e Peshturës) from **Progonati**. However, most trails are not well marked, and some passages could be dangerous. A guide, or at least guidance, is recommended. Some guesthouses and campsites in the region can help you out.

ARRIVAL AND DEPARTURE — NIVICA

By car From the SH4 just north of Tepelena, exit west near the Kastrati station to Rruga Ali Pashë Tepelena, and keep left (uphill) where the road forks. Follow the roads through Bënça, Lekdushi, Progonati and Gusmari to Nivica; the latter four are all strung along the canyons. Roads are mostly well paved but high, with switchbacks and some rockfall. It's 22km (40min) from the SH4 to Progonati and 31km (1hr) to Nivica village. Check your fuel before heading out.

ACCOMMODATION

Camping Lekdushi Shehu 1.7km east of Progonati; tel: 068 201 6919. If you've been travelling around rural Albania, you'll likely have spotted the conical straw hay bales peppering the fields. What if you could... sleep in one? That's the idea at this spot right near the Peshtura Waterfall, where straw huts with mattresses can sleep up to four. The bathroom is shared. There's also a roadside eatery here, and the owners sometimes offer off-road rides. €€

★ **Camp Nivica** Near Nivica village; www.campnivica.com. A seasonal campsite poised over one of the most picturesque spots in the canyonlands, *Camp Nivica* is not exactly roughing it. Guests hunker down in safari-style thatched-roof tents, each with a porch for canyon-gazing, private bathrooms, electricity and beds. You'll spend more time on the gazebo, munching spit-roasted meats and downing glasses of *raki*. It's a unique wilderness experience in Albania, and you can sign up for guided tours into the canyon. Reserve ahead. €€€€

EATING

Restaurant Vatra Lekdushi, near Progonati; www.facebook.com/p/Guest-house-Vatra-61560266819901. Serving local specialities of Albania and Kurveleshi, this roadside restaurant is a relaxing place to sip mountain tea while you wait for spit-roasted lamb, *kulaç* soda bread with poultry or *byrek* pie with wild cabbage. You'll find a friendly guesthouse here too, and you can camp on the picturesque premises. €€

Përmeti

PËRMETI has one key advantage over almost every other Albanian city: it's immersed in nature – all kinds of it. It's not something on the horizon. You can walk into the mountains, from the centre. You can swim in thermal springs. Përmeti is tucked away in one of the lushest, freshest corners of the country, with the crisp air to prove it. The Vjosa-side urban park is well manicured, the boulevards are lined with trees, and home gardens spill over with flowers, especially sweet-scented roses. You won't be assaulted by traffic. Or litter. Or noise.

Përmeti is mostly strung along the west bank of the upper **Vjosa River** (Lumi i Vjosës), which flows about 27km northwest from the Albania-Greece border. Parallel to Vjosa, the mountain ranges of **Dhëmbeli** and **Nemërçka** rise behind the city to the south, reaching nearly 2500m, while the highlands of the **Fir of Hotova-Dangëllia National Park** (Parku Kombëtar Bredhi i Hotovës-Dangëlli) unfurl to the north.

Përmeti is a wild place sculpted by saw-toothed mountains, shaggy with snow caps and conifers, **thermal springs** and a busy blue-green river. It's a year-round destination: blossoms and river rafting in the spring; horseriding and swimming in the summer; harvest in the autumn; and hot springs during winter. The city itself is brightly painted and cheerful, but the big-hitting sights would be here even without it. You can walk from one end to the other in twenty minutes.

Brief history

Archaeological evidence confirms there was at least a modest fortress here by the sixth century AD, and a population centre by the time of the **Ottoman** conquest in 1417.

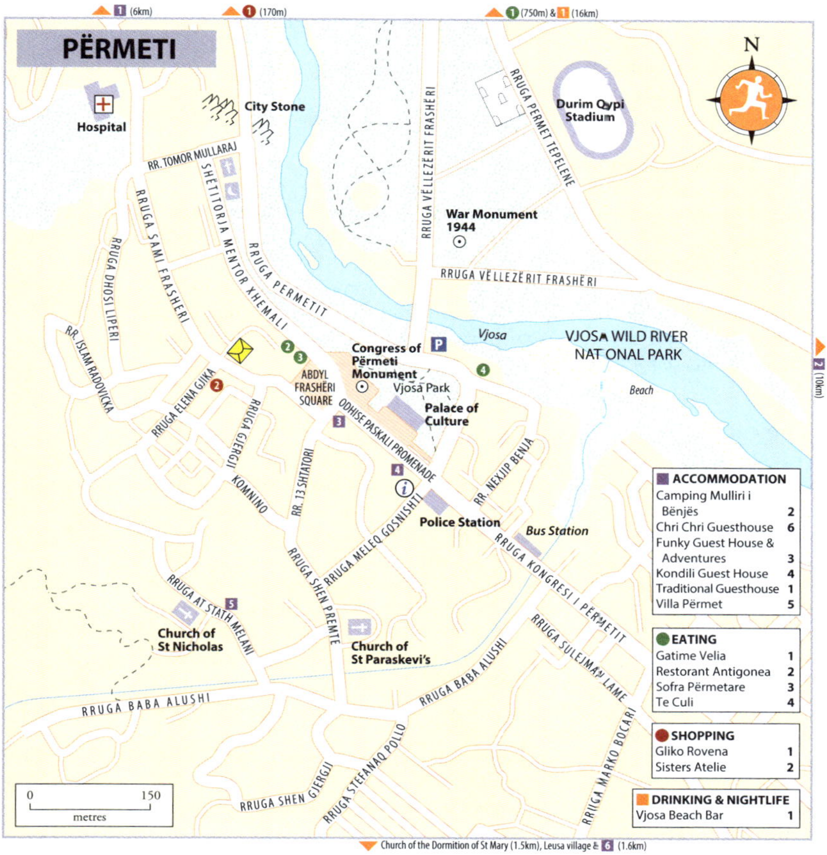

Under Ottoman rule, the Orthodox population was restive, resisting Islamization, and by the nineteenth century, the Islamic Sufi mystic order of **Bektashism** flourished here. The town's craftspeople distinguished themselves in shoemaking. The leather *opingë* shoes, with the upturned toe and wool tufts at the tip, that men wear with folkloric costumes were long made in Përmeti.

Despite cultural ties to Epirus and the Greek church, the Përmeti region was an incubator of **Albanian National Awakening** (Rilindja) ideas in the lead-up to independence, churning out poets, pamphleteers and, when the time came, revolutionaries. One village near Përmeti produced the lead figure in a major movement for Albanian autonomy; an author of an independence manifesto; and a future national poet – in the same family, in fact: brothers **Abdyl**, **Sami** and **Naim Frashëri** (see page 232).

The centre

The municipal offices, *Hotel Përmeti* and other *pallats* of the communist city square (see page 131) surround **Sheshi Abdyl Frashëri** on three sides. It's now a pedestrianized area paved with a trippy lava-lamp pattern. The **Shëtitorja Odhise Paskali** promenade leads east from the square, running parallel to the large **Vjosa Park** (Parku i Vjosës). Stretching five blocks along the river, the park has a streetside and a riverside level connected by several broad stairways, fountains, gardens, cycling and walking paths, some light topiary, springs with drinkable water, and a monument to a World War II-era antifascist congress held in Përmeti. At the north end of the park, you'll reach a Përmeti icon, the mighty **City Stone** (Guri i Qytetit).

City Stone

Rruga e Përmetit and Rruga Tomorr Mullaraj • Free

Përmeti may lack a castle hill, but it does have a very large rock. The bulbous **City Stone** (Guri i Qytetit) is 25m tall and around 30m in diameter. Some of the ruins from late antiquity and medieval Përmeti are scattered around and on top of the rock: fragments of stone walls and a tower.

Local lore says that during the Ottoman invasion the leader of the city jumped from the rock, along with his daughter, rather than fall into enemy hands. That fellow, named **Premt**, supposedly gave the city its name. You can indeed climb up the rock via a metal staircase for fine views of the city.

The old city

If you're looking for a UNESCO-approved historic quarter with a gaggle of museums, you should keep it moving to Gjirokastra. **Përmeti's old city** is worth taking a lap through, but you won't find much Ottoman statement architecture or any grand basilicas. You will find a little sachet of stone villas, humble cottages and brightly coloured doors on the gates of tiny walled fiefdoms.

A handful of post-Byzantine churches should also be on your radar. The 1776 **Church of St Paraskevi** (Kisha e Shën Premtes; Rruga Shën Premte), just a couple blocks from the centre, is the most likely to be open. It's architecturally interesting because the naos, narthex and portico sections are all set beneath one long, tapering roof. The **Church of St Nicholas** (Kisha e Shën Kollit; Rruga At Stath Melani) dates to 1757, and the portico and campanile, though rebuilt, give a fine appearance of completeness.

From here, you can follow shepherds' trails up to the ridge of **Dhëmbeli Mountain** (Mali i Dhëmbelit), one of several bucolic escapes into the hills straight from the city. Pick up a map of hiking routes at the **visitor centre** before you set off, and mind the sheepdogs.

Church of the Dormition of St Mary

2.1km southeast of Përmeti on Rruga e Leusës, Leusa • Free • Hike 45min from the centre; don't drive Rruga e Leusës without an off-road vehicle

One of the more extraordinary post-Byzantine basilicas in Albania is the **Church of the Dormition of St Mary** (Kisha Fjetja e Shën Marisë) near the village of **Leusa**, just southeast of Përmeti city. It's the total package. The short but stiff hike up on a country road is easy to follow, offering panoramas over Përmeti and sublime views across to the church itself, wreathed in forest. The two-storey edifice, built from mountain pumice in the late eighteenth century, preserves its cupola, portico, bell tower and curved bloom of stone steps to the churchyard.

The **frescoes** steal the show, though. They panel the exterior portico wall and garnish the entranceway, and the interior is entirely plastered in them, up across the big barrel vault over the nave. An **ornate coffered wood ceiling** is a special artefact of its time and place, with a geometric pattern resembling those you see in the reception rooms of wealthy Ottoman homes, but the focal point is a small hexagonal **icon of Christ Pantocrator**. To get in, you can ring the bell (seriously), ask around the village for the key master, call the number posted on the door (tel: 069 691 7314 at the time of writing) or loiter for a beat until a custodian shows up.

ARRIVAL AND GETTING AROUND — PËRMETI

By bus The bus stop for Përmeti is on Bulevardi Kongresi i Përmetit opposite Rruga Agathokli Xhitomi. The main boulevard becomes Shëtitorja Odhise Paskali, and then you're at Sheshi Abdyl Frashëri in 250m. You can find buses to other cities here, as well as to the Thermal Waters of Benja (signposted Llixha Bënjë, the Bënja spa), which also marks the entrance to the Lëngarica Canyon. It's best to confirm the times for those buses in advance (tel: 068 252 8833).

VJOSA WILD RIVER NATIONAL PARK

The **Vjosa River** (Lumi i Vjosës) beats a path 270km from its source in the **Pindus Mountains** in Northern Greece, where they call it the Aoös River, to its mouth at the Adriatic just north of Vlora. With 400km of waterways in Albania alone, you're bound to come across the Vjosa at some point. It's one of the few undammed and unrestricted rivers in Europe – that's what makes it 'wild' – and it's a showy, mostly languorous river, a turquoise ribbon of both gentle and dramatic bends. The Vjosa rises and recedes in the catchment of the southeast around **Përmeti**, carves ravines like the 1000m **Këlcyra Gorge** (Gryka e Këlcyrës) between Përmeti and Tepelena, then pronounces itself with broad arches around farmland and hills near the ancient city of **Byllis** (see page 221). In the flat wetlands north of the **Narta Lagoon** (Laguna e Nartës), it empties into the sea.

There are somewhere in the vicinity of 1200 plant and animal species that call the watery habitat home, including European otters, eels, stone curlews and the endangered **Egyptian vulture**. In the 2010s, plans were announced to build hydropower plants and dams in the region. A loud and vigorous Albanian and international conservation campaign revved up; even Leonardo DiCaprio put in a word urging preservation. In 2023, the whole length of the river in Albania was granted protected **national park** status – and Parku Kombëtar i Lumit të Egër Vjosa (www.vjosanationalpark.al) was born.

Rangers and volunteers are marking trails for hiking and biking, and three visitor centres are in the pipeline, with the primary one near Tepelena and two other info points in Përmeti and near Vlora. Until then, the best way to experience the river is on a **rafting trip,** and the best spot to dip in an oar is near Përmeti. You can tackle light rapids, float beneath cliffs and through gorges, and even meet a wayward cow or two. Trips usually run for around three hours. Vjosa Explorer (www.vjosaexplorer.com) is a top provider, and it has also mapped many hikes in the region (www.wikiloc.com/wikiloc/user.do?id=4790740). Vjosa Albania Rafting & Kayak is Albania Rafting Group's Përmeti outpost (https://www.albrafting.org), and Rafting Vjosa (tel: 068 302 8000) also runs excellent, informative raft tours. For a landlubber valley experience, the gold standard is Funky Adventures, which leads off-road tours and horseback trips around the Përmeti region (www.funky-permet.al/activities.html).

5

Destinations Berati (1 daily; 3hr); Durrësi (several daily; 3hr 55min); Erseka (several daily; 2hr 20min); Fieri (several daily; 2hr 10min); Gjirokastra (several daily; 1hr 10min); Korça (several daily; 3hr 30min); Leskoviku (several daily; 1hr 10min); Lushnja (several daily; 2hr 50min); Saranda (1 daily; 2hr 10min); Tepelena (several daily; 55min); Tirana (several daily; 4hr 30min); Thermal Waters of Benja (several daily; 25min); Vlora (several daily; 2hr).

By car The SH75 passes the city on the east bank of the Vjosa, and there are exits to the centre, over the river, from both the north and south. The motorway is in good condition, but it does become very wiggly heading southeast along the mountains toward Çarshova. You can find a car park on Rruga e Përmetit just left (east) of the bridge into the city, or at another car park on Rruga Kamber Bënja.

By taxi Find taxis in the centre at Rruga e Përmetit and Bulevardi Kongresi i Përmetit, across the street from Shëtitorja Odhise Paskali. It's another option for getting to Bënja.

On foot Everything in the city centre is within a 10min walk.

INFORMATION

Tourist information Find maps and brochures and get recommendations for things to do and places to eat at the visitor centre (Qendra Kulturore Multifunksionale Odhise Paskali; the yellow building at the southeast end of Shëtitorja Odhise Paskali). Perhaps most useful are the topographic hiking maps (charge). If the centre is closed, there's good info online; see below.

Websites www.permet.al; www.bashkiapermet.gov.al

ACCOMMODATION

SEE MAP PAGE 227

To explore the Përmeti region, it's more convenient to stay in the city, but a village or hillside *bujtinë* (guesthouse) may be the vibe you want out here in God's country.

Chri Chri Guesthouse 2.5km southeast of Përmeti, Leusa village; www.instagram.com/chrichripermet. A village oasis near the city, this stone guesthouse is a just-rural-enough escape, with valley-facing terraces to take your coffee amid the olive and pine groves. Rooms are simple, snug stone affairs with modern amenities, and the host can whisk you back and forth to the city in his Jeep. Breakfast and dinner are excellent, and you can take them at shared or secluded tables. €€

Funky Guest House & Adventures Sheshi Abdyl Frashëri; www.funky-permet.al. Centrally located and clean, with 24hr reception and parking nearby, this ten-room guesthouse serves as a one-stop shop for almost all things Përmeti: breakfast *gliko* (fruit preserve), afternoon Aperol, friendly and knowledgeable owners, 4WD trips into the Fir of Hotova-Dangëllia National Park, horseriding excursions into highlands. Rooms are eclectic, modern and comfortable, and prices are very fair. €€

Kondili Guest House Shëtitorja Odhise Paskali; tel: 068 416 1411. A decent budget option in the heart of the city, *Kondili Guest House* is a cute little place with character, modern amenities and a pizzeria downstairs. The owner is accommodating, and you can people-watch the evening walkers on the promenade. €

★ **Traditional Guesthouse** 6.4km northwest of Përmeti by road, Buali village; www.instagram.com/traditional_guesthouse_permet. This can be a family spot or a romantic getaway, but however you play it, you won't leave hungry. A century-old villa steeped in nature and staring straight down the Vjosa, it's a perfect place to experience Përmeti cuisine, plucked from the garden, cooked by the owners and served over many courses. Rooms are traditionally decked out with wood paneling, *qilims* and exposed stone. The hosts can pick you up if you don't have a 4WD. €€

Villa Përmet Rruga 13 Shtatori; www.villapermet.com. Relatively large and luxe for Përmeti, this beautifully restored nineteenth-century stone mansion in the old city gazes out over the rooftops, with particularly fine views from the upper floors. Rooms are very spacious, with elegant wood floors and ceilings, fireplaces, lace decor and plush couches. Staff are friendly and can help you book tours and excursions. Try a cooking class and learn to make *gliko* (fruit preserve). €€€

EATING

SEE MAP PAGE 227

Some of Përmeti's best restaurants are all-in on the slow-food movement of cooking with locally grown, organic ingredients. As for what to try, the signature dessert, without question, is *gliko*. It's essentially just preserved, candied fruit or vegetables: soaked in water, mixed with sugar, boiled in copper and stashed in glass jars. *Gliko* comes in many varieties, including (deep breath) cherry, white plum, fig, mandarin, apricot, kumquat, rose, unripe walnut, watermelon, pumpkin, eggplant and more. Many restaurants and guesthouses make their own, and you can also buy directly from local producers (see Shopping).

★ **Gatime Velia** Rruga Mendul Zavalani; www.instagram.com/gatime_velia. More a homely dining room than a restaurant, this spot on the east side of the river serves up traditional Përmetar cuisine, making use of whatever's fresh that day. Try whole-grilled fish from the Vjosa, or *kolloface*, a local sausage made with liver, onion, leek and oregano. But most of all, it's where to go for house-made *gliko* – walnut, rose, even whole-apple versions. It's top-notch food all around, and very inexpensive. €

★ **Restorant Antigonea** Rruga Mentor Xhemali 10; www.restorantantigonea.com. The restaurant that kicked off Përmeti's reputation for fine food, *Antigonea* has been a dining destination in Albania for some years and hasn't lost a step. Come here for chef-owner Urim Jace's creative take on hard-to-find traditional dishes: *salcë kosi*, yoghurt fermented in goat-skin sacks; roasted wild hare or boar; partridge over *përshesh* stuffing; and veal stew in wine and mushroom sauce. Staff are attentive; they'll walk you through what you're eating and how it's made. €€€

Sofra Përmetare Rruga Mentor Xhemali 1; www.instagram.com/soframpermetare. With a stylish patio near the park, *Sofra Përmetare* has a friendly vibe and becomes lively in the evenings. Stuffed eggplant, rich soups and anything with beets make for a fine starter, and meat lovers can take their pick of pork and veal chops and ribs. Delicious mezes and pastas have vegetarians covered too. €€

Te Culi Rruga Nexhip Bërja; tel: 068 630 3487. Hearty portions of traditional Përmetar cooking in a small diner-like setting make this an intimate spot to settle in, and locals do too. Try chicken over *rosnica* pasta, stuffed peppers, *dollma* (dolmadakia), moussaka and your choice of *gjellë*, a creamy soup typical of the region. It's a family kitchen with welcoming staff and wallet-friendly prices. €

DRINKING AND NIGHTLIFE

SEE MAP PAGE 227

Vjosa Beach Bar 16.6km from Përmeti on SH75, near Këlcyra; www.instagram.com/vjosaecoresort. '*Vjosa Eco Resort*' is, first of all, a petrol station. It's also a mechanic shop, makes sense. There's a café – a little off brand. And a pizzeria, even more left field. And an organic food shop, and a bar, and a riverside bar. You expect to find this sort of hybrid in, say, America, less so in rural Southern Albania. But the beach bar has sand, sun, stones and spritzes; the owners bring in DJs; there are sun loungers; and staff drive a free shuttle to and from Përmet centre.

SHOPPING

SEE MAP PAGE 227

★ **Gliko Rovena** Rruga Ali Irfan Përmeti; www.instagram.com/gliko_rovena_permeti. You can find a few *gliko* producers in the north of the city, in the *Ramis Hotel* and along Rruga Ali Irfan Përmeti. Rovena Hamataj's version is now available around Albania, and she also runs an artisanal cooperative with the women who work with her. You can find virtually any type of *gliko* here – fig, walnut, rose and Cornelian cherry are particularly tasty – along with *reçel* (jam), juice and other fruit treats. Consider calling ahead.

Sisters Atelie Lagjja Naim Frashëri; www.instagram.com/sistersatelie_aa. If you're looking for folkloric costumes or a *fustanellë* (Balkan kilt), sisters Anila and Arjeta make high-quality designs in their shop and workshop. Also find modern skirts, dresses, vests, coats and bespoke items.

DIRECTORY

Banks and currency exchange There are a handful of banks and ATMs right in the centre on Shëtitorja Odhise Paskali and Sheshi Abdyl Frashëri, as well as a currency exchange. Find a Western Union on Rruga Gjergj Komnino near the square.

Emergencies Call tel: 127 or tel: 112 (medical); tel: 129 or tel: 112 (police).

Hospital The local hospital is Spitali Bashkiak Përmet, and the entrance is on Rruga Tomorr Mullaraj, near Rruga Amerika (tel: 08 132 2369).

Pharmacies A handful of pharmacies can be found on Rruga Sami Frashëri, within a few blocks of Sheshi Abdyl Frashëri.

Police The police station is on Rruga Meleq Gosnishti and Bulevardi Kongresi i Përmetit.

Post office No international express mail here, but there's a Posta Shqiptare on Rruga Sami Frashëri less than a block from the square.

Fir of Hotova-Dangëllia National Park

Many of the natural attractions associated with Përmeti today are not in the city proper, but more broadly in the region historically called **Dangëllia**. Much of that is now protected as part of the **Fir of Hotova-Dangëllia National Park** (Parku Kombëtar Bredhi i Hotovës-Dangëlli) – 360 square kilometres of it, to be more precise. It's the second-largest national park in the country, after the Albanian Alps. Far from Tirana and the coast, it's a truly remote area, and the vast majority is difficult or impossible to access quickly. There are no hotels or restaurants in the heart of the park and only a few campsites along the one asphalted road going in, which lasts all of 6km. Bredhi i Hotovës-Dangëlli is as lonesome as it gets, and if that's your jam, you'll love it.

The hills of the park, reaching more than 1600m in altitude, don't resemble the grim, grey rock faces of the Tomorri and Korabi mountains. The clue's in the name, after all: this place is all about trees. **Macedonian firs** and **European silver firs** are the giants that swallow up little hikers, though they deign to share space with black pines and maples.

At lower elevations and in the meadows, you'll find wild juniper, cherry, blackberry, rose and even strawberry trees and bushes, along with wild herbs like oregano, rosehip and chicory. Bears, badgers, tortoises, frogs, eagles, owls and humans all eat good here.

Some of the villages, especially **Frashëri**, were once towns of modest importance, but most are nearly uninhabited today. If you have a 4WD, you can reach the **Tekke of Baba Ali** (Teqeja e Baba Aliut) near Alipostivani village. The current **Bektashi** complex was built in 1920, and it's a captivating sight, with its white, green and gold domes peeking above the peaks and fog.

Frashëri

Frashëri village was one outpost of the scholarship and strategizing that helped foment the **Albanian National Awakening**, or **Rilindja.** Brothers Abdyl, Naim and Sami Frashëri were born here at what is now the **House Museum of the Frashëri Brothers** (Shtëpia Muze e Vëllezërve Frashëri), and the **Tekke of Frashëri** (Teqeja e Frashërit) served as a meeting place for the members of the autonomy-minded League of Prizren in the late 1870s and early 1880s. Rebuilt versions of the house and *teqe* (definite form: *teqeja*) can be visited, but you may have to ask around the village, or at the Përmeti visitor centre, to enter. On the road to Frashëri, you can stop for a quick hike to the lookout over the **Kamencka Canyon** (Kanioni i Kamenckës).

ARRIVAL AND DEPARTURE — FRASHËRI

By car The route to Frashëri is on the main road into the heart of the park. It's 30km into the mountains to reach the village – and it's entirely unpaved. A 4WD is definitely recommended, but you can drive as far as you feel comfortable to enjoy whatever spot catches your fancy. You could also trek it, and camp or picnic anywhere.

To enter the Fir of Hotova-Dangëllia National Park at Frashëri, follow the SH75 northwest from Përmeti for

THE FRASHËRI BROTHERS

You see their names on streets and schools in Përmeti, Vlora, Tirana, Durrësi and Shkodra, and their faces on sculpted busts in the capital. One of them, Naim, is printed on the 200 lek note. Three of the most prominent leaders of the nineteenth-century **Rilindja** – a political movement for Albanian culture, values, identity and nationhood – brothers Abdyl, Naim and Sami Frashëri hold founding father status. Think of them as, roughly, the Samuel Adams, Walt Whitman and Benjamin Franklin of Albania, in that order – if the American trio had shared a bedroom growing up.

Abdyl (1839–1892), the eldest, became a leader and statesman. In 1878 he helped found, and led, the **League of Prizren**, an assembly of local leaders from Albanian communities that sought a unified, protected Albanian territory within the Ottoman Empire – at first. Within three years, Abdyl and others had declared an autonomous state, raised an army and seized several towns from the military. Istanbul crushed that revolution, and Abdyl was jailed.

Naim (1846–1900) took a different tack, as a writer. He published history books and textbooks and promoted the first **Albanian-language schools**. But he was especially drawn to the Bektashi and Sufi mysticism of his childhood, and **poetry** would be Naim's highest calling. One of Albania's **national poets**, he penned the line that would become a patriotic and romantic motto: "You, Albania, give me honour, and you name me as Albanian," he wrote, "and my heart you have replenished both with ardour and desire."

Sami (1850–1904), the youngest of the three, was a true polymath. He founded the **Society for the Publication of Albanian Writings** to disseminate Albanian-language texts and wrote a new encyclopaedia in Ottoman Turkish, nudging Turks to think on the question of their own national identity too. He's best known in Albania for the 1899 treatise, *Albania: What It Was, What It Is and What Will Become of It?* The last of the three brothers living, he died just eight years before independent Albania began its journey of figuring out the answers to his question.

8.8km, past Kosina, and turn right (north) before Piskova village. Expect to drive 2–3hr to reach Frashëri.

Information If you're visiting the Fir of Hotova-Dangëllia National Park, you can find informational placards dotted around and an info point with some faded maps on the SH75 roadside, 1.5km northwest of the Vjosa bridge into Përmeti. The rocky old dirt roads serve as hiking paths, and the visitor centre (see page 230) sells more in-depth maps.

Thermal Waters of Benja

Rruga e Bënjës, Bënja village • Free

The **Thermal Waters of Benja** (Ujërat Termale e Bënjës), also called the **Llixhat** or **Banjat e Bënjës** (Spas or Baths of Bënja), is by far the easiest part of Fir of Hotova-Dangëllia National Park to visit. Plus, it has something for everyone: willowy canyons, historic architecture, spring-fed thermal pools, hiking, climbing, swimming and perhaps traditional trance music if you stay late enough. The **natural springs** have attained scientifically improbable hues of azure on social media, but in person, the thermal waters are still alluring. Eight sources of mineral-rich water are corralled into six pools here. The water isn't unbearably hot, rising to the surface through limestone fissures at temperatures between 23°C and 30°C, nor is it as sulphuric as other mineral pools in Albania. The medicinal case for the springs goes as far as claiming that you're supposed to drink the stuff – knock it back at your own risk.

The first and biggest pool, a manmade one right beside the Ottoman-era Kati Bridge (Ura e Katiut), does get a lot of use, never a strong selling point for a hot tub (please don't drink the water). The bridge itself, a svelte single-arched span over the **Lëngarica River** (Lumi i Lëngaricës), dates to 1700. The most enjoyable way to experience the baths is to pass beneath the bridge and splash along the river until you find a pool to your liking. All are within 1km, but you'll need water shoes.

Lëngarica Canyon

Rruga e Bënjës, Bënja village • Free

The **Lëngarica Canyon** (Kanioni i Lëngaricës) starts, more or less, at the biggest pool and really gets going within just a few hundred metres. One option is to hike up above the gorge and then loop back to the bridge through the 5km canyon. It's a super-scenic but substantial trek. A shorter out-and-back is a 30min uphill hike from Rruga e Bënjës to Bënja, a silent one-alley mountain-hued village with views across the Dhëmbeli range. Find good routes at www.wikiloc.com/trails/hiking/albania/gjirokaster/benje-novosele.

Alternatively, from the Kati Bridge, you can simply head straight into the gorge along the riverbed. The limestone walls flare out at some points, then narrow dramatically to widths of just 3m, in a canyon more than 100m deep. In the broader sections, a few rockfaces are equipped for **climbing**, and you'll find the smaller thermal pools, a handful of **caves** and some **waterfalls**. You may need to swim in a few places. The river is usually shallower than those in other canyons, but the riverbed hike is best attempted in summer or fall before it rises; some of the baths, however, can be accessed all year.

ARRIVAL AND DEPARTURE — THERMAL WATERS OF BENJA

By bus Shuttle buses from Përmeti head to the Thermal Waters of Benja a few times a day, mostly in the morning, and return in the afternoon (several daily; 25min). See page 230.

By car or taxi From Përmeti, follow the SH75 southeast, turn left at the sign for the Thermal Waters of Benja (Ujërat Termale e Bënjës), and continue on Rruga e Bënjës to the car park. The roads are asphalted up to the parking, and the trip takes about 25min. See page 230 for Përmeti taxi info.

ACCOMMODATION — SEE MAP PAGE 227

Camping Mulliri i Bënjës 2.3km south of the Thermal Waters (Ujërat Termale) on Rruga e Bënjës, Bënja village; tel: 069 631 2827. There are a handful of atmospheric campsites near the thermal baths, most with restaurants on site and adequate facilities, but this thirty-pitch one has the edge. You can park or pitch right on the banks of the Lëngarica and enjoy swimming and tanning away from any crowds upriver. It's family-friendly, pet-friendly and owners can organize rafting trips. €

The Albanian riviera

ZVËRNECI ISLAND

The Albanian riviera

6

The stretch of coast ribboning from the city of Vlora down to the Greek border is known as the Albanian riviera. It's a popular holiday destination for sun-seekers, thanks to its abundance of pretty beaches lapped by calm, turquoise waters that are ideal for swimming and snorkelling. But relaxing by the seaside isn't the only attraction this area offers: with gorgeous scenery, imposing fortresses and some of Albania's finest ancient ruins, the riviera is an unmissable part of the country.

At the northern end of the riviera is **Vlora**, the third-biggest city in Albania and jumping-off point for boat trips to the beautiful **Sazani Island** and **Karaburuni Peninsula** (Gadishulli i Karaburunit). From here, two roads lead south: the inland route through a pristine mountain valley offers little-visited sites such as the hilltop ruins of **Amantia** and the elegant Ottoman Bridge of Brataj, while sticking to the coast will bring you to **Orikumi** and then up the dramatic **Llogara Pass** (Qafa e Llogarasë). From here, there's a lovely string of beaches to take your pick from, with standouts being **Dhërmiu** and **Gjipeja** (or Gjipe). The town of **Himara** makes a great place to overnight, with a historic hilltop old town as well as top-notch hotels and restaurants, before you head south again past the imposing fortress of **Porto Palermo** (Kalaja e Porto Palermos). Further beaches await on the route down to **Saranda**, a busy and welcoming city that makes a handy base for visiting the ruins of **Butrint**, one of Albania's most popular sights. Round off with a trip up into the mountains to check out the stunning turquoise pool of the **Blue Eye**, or simply relax on the beaches of Saranda and **Ksamili**. All in all, there's more than enough to keep you exploring for a week or more.

Brief history

Though settlements in the region appear to have existed up to four thousand years ago, the area first made its mark on history around the fourth-century BC, when it became the home of the **Chaonians**. The Chaonians were an ancient Greek people whose capital may have been at Phoenice near Saranda, and who also established settlements which include Butrint, Saranda and possibly others as far north as Vlora. The Chaonians were active in the Hellenistic period but succumbed to **Roman invasion** in around 168 BC.

The Romans continued to use and expand the cities established by Chaonians, with Butrint in particular becoming a centre of greater importance in this era. The **Byzantine Empire** subsequently absorbed the area, though it became a frontline in the increasingly fractious relationship between eastern and western Christianity, and as Byzantium went into decline, the gap was filled by expanding Western European states, notably the Venetians.The **Venetians** remained in control of important outposts around the region for several hundred years, regularly coming into conflict with the Ottoman Empire, which finally established complete rule over this coast through the machinations of local governor-adventurer **Ali Pasha Tepelena** (see page 224) eventually annexed the riviera. Under the Ottomans, Albanian nationalism surged, until tensions erupted in the 1910s, triggering Albania to declare independence in Vlora in 1912. The first half of the twentieth century witnessed instability, with the region undergoing regular incursions by the Italians and full-scale invasion during **World War II**.

Under the **communist regime**, the riviera's natural beauty was largely left untouched, with vast pockets of land designated closed military zones owing to the submarine base at Porto Palermo and the naval base at Orikumi. In the years since the collapse of communism, the region has seen rapid and sometimes ill-advised development as it has pivoted to accommodate increasing numbers of tourists seeking a dose of sun and sea.

WORLD HERITAGE SITE OF BUTRINT

Highlights

❶ **Zvërneci Island** Just north of Vlora, this tiny forested speck is home to an attractive Orthodox church, fascinating communist-era bunkers, and unspoiled beaches. See page 246

❷ **Brataj Bridge** A little off the beaten track, this multi-arched stone Ottoman-era bridge leaps across an inviting turquoise river. It's a lovely spot for a swim in the summer. See page 248

❸ **The Llogara Pass** For a bird's-eye view of the riviera coast, head up the winding road into the mountains over the Llogara Pass and enjoy the fabulous panoramas. See page 250

❹ **Qeparoi Beach** There are endless beaches to choose from along the riviera, but the well-kept Qeparoi is one of the best: calm and pretty waters, backed by a tidy promenade with welcoming cafés and restaurants. See page 254

❺ **The Blue Eye** Up in the hills east of Saranda, the stunning teal waters of the Blue Eye are cradled in an idyllic wooded valley. See page 262

❻ **Butrint** Unquestionably one of Albania's highlights, the picturesque ruins of Butrint span the centuries from the ancient Greek period through to the Venetian era. See page 264

HIGHLIGHTS ARE MARKED ON THE MAP ON PAGE 238

Vlora

Albania's third-biggest city, **VLORA** has a long, storied history that dates back potentially to the first millennium BC. Known in antiquity as Aulon or Aulona, its natural harbour made it an ideal site for trading, and it has been occupied over

the centuries by Greeks, Romans, Byzantines and Ottomans. From the eighteenth century onwards, agitators for Albanian independence increasingly based themselves in the city, and it was here, in 1912, that the **Albanian Declaration of Independence** was proclaimed.

During World War II, Vlora was seized by Italian forces, who were briefly succeeded by Germans in 1944 before the advancing communists wrestled control of the city. During the communist reign, Vlora was almost a flashpoint in the deteriorating relationship between Albania and the Soviet Union: the latter, resentful at having been evicted from the nearby Pashalimani base at Orikumi, threatened to invade the city. Following the downfall of the communist regime, Vlora became the epicentre of the **civil unrest** that engulfed much of the country: in February 1997, a student protest against pyramid schemes invested in by the government sparked widespread revolt. As in several other cities across the country, Vlora fell under the control of rival criminal gangs, and it remained unstable until the resignation of the government in July that year.

Vlora is a rather curious city today. Much effort has gone into gentrifying its small **old town**, and the area around **Ri Beach** (Plazhi i Ri, 'New Beach') is also fairly upmarket, but the areas in between are large and pretty scrappy. Although the city has a couple of small **museums** and **monuments**, it's largely a place to pass through rather than linger.

6

Seafront

Most visitors to Vlora will be found along the seafront, attracted by the beaches and the strip of hotels, restaurants and bars close at hand. The Vjetër and Ri beaches are separated by the city's port, close to which is the National Museum of Independence.

National Museum of Independence

Off Rruga Çamëria • Charge • tel: 069 6347 498

In the centre of a rapidly developing and bizarrely landscaped hotel zone, the attractive old building housing the **National Museum of Independence** (Muzeu Kombëtar i Pavarësisë) cuts an odd figure as the sole surviving structure from an earlier era. Inside is plenty of memorabilia from the years leading up to the declaration of independence in 1912, and it's something of a place of pilgrimage for Albanians. Unless you're hugely interested in this particular chapter of history, though, it can't be said to be enormously compelling.

Note that the museum keeps rather strange hours: Monday to Saturday 9am until noon and 5pm to 10pm, Sunday 6pm to 10pm.

The Lungomare

Rruga Çamëria • Free

A short way east of the National Museum of Independence is the seafront promenade known as the **Lungomare**. It begins at a large square which is home to a big wheel and a couple of sculptures – including, oddly, two oversized Coca-Cola bottles – but is otherwise a rather bare concrete space, with a couple of cafés and restaurants on its western edge. It livens up a little at night, and you can also pick up boat trips to Sazani Island and the Karaburuni Peninsula from here.

Heading southeast, the Lungomare passes along a grassy area, on which you can find a couple of information boards with details of various World War I and II ships that sank in the vicinity. Notable among them was the SS *Principe Umberto*, an Italian merchant cruiser sunk by the Austro-Hungarians in 1916. More than 1900 people died, making it World War I's heaviest single naval loss of life. Note that many simply refer to the whole beach-and-boulevard stretch running south to the Vlora Tunnel as the 'Lungomare'.

Ri Beach

Rruga Murat Tërbaçi (SH8) • Free

South of the promenade, **Ri Beach** (Plazhi i Ri, 'New Beach') is sandy and intersperses section of public beach with private areas full of sun loungers (to rent) owned by restaurants on the opposite side of the road. The latter are generally well kept and litter-free; the public stretches a little less so but still reasonably clean.

Vjetër Beach

Off Rruga Sazani • Free

Vlora's western **beach**, Plazhi i Vjetër ('Old Beach') is a long stretch of sand, which extends from the port all the way up towards Zvërneci Island (see page 246). At the town end, it's a bit grim, strewn with litter and backed by scrubby bush and a couple of desultory beach bars. It gets much better if you venture further up the coast; those determined to enjoy some toes-in-the-sand time while in Vlora are best off heading towards Zvërneci and stopping at one of the small beach bars such as *Venus*, which has a pleasant stretch of sand (see page 246).

Old town

Around 2.5 kilometres inland from the Lungomare, the couple of pedestrianized streets that make up Vlora's **old town** have been smartened up to the point of feeling somewhat artificial, but even so, they're colourful and attractive and make a welcome retreat from the busyness of Vlora's centre. Most buildings in the old town are now restaurants, bars, hotels or all three, and in the very close vicinity you'll find two of Vlora's museums as well as the important historical site of Independence Square.

Ethnographic Museum

Rruga Perlat Rexhepi • Charge • tel: 069 3341 387

Vlora's small **Ethnographic Museum** (Muzeu Etnografik i Vlorës) exhibits pieces largely from the medieval and Ottoman eras, with an emphasis on tools used in everyday life. Given Vlora's coastal location, there's a fair representation of fishing equipment – including some fun model ships – as well as copperware and farming tools. Up the sweeping wooden spiral staircase are examples of national costumes, weaving looms and further artefacts from the early twentieth century.

The building itself has some historical significance: in the early 1900s it was the headquarters of the Labëria Club, whose members were dedicated to the establishment

BOAT TRIPS TO KARABURUNI AND SAZANI

Visitors to Vlora keen to explore the beautiful beaches of the riviera coast could consider taking a **boat trip** to the **Karaburuni Peninsula** and **Sazani Island**. Available from kiosks along the Lungomare (see page 239), or bookable through most accommodation, boats tend to follow a tried-and-tested route across from Vlora to Sazani, an attractive wooded island with a string of pretty beaches as well as the ruins of a naval base, where an old school and cinema still stand in picturesque decay.

From Sazani, boats then putter across the water to the Karaburuni Peninsula, which juts out from the mainland south of Vlora, forming a large natural harbour around the town of Orikumi. Some trips stop off at **sea caves** en route, the most popular being the **Cave of Haxhi Ali** (Shpella e Haxhi Aliut), a hiding place used by an eighteenth-century pirate. The final stopping point will likely be a beach on the peninsula, where you can spend the rest of the day **swimming** and sunbathing.

Depending on the beach the boat takes you to, there will probably be sun loungers and parasols available, though you may have to pay for them. There is usually a small café or bar to hand as well for drinks and food. It's worth briefly shopping around the various boat touts in Vlora and clarifying exactly where the tour is going if you've got your heart set on a particular place. Most trips leave about 10am and return to the city by 5pm. Among the many operators, Aquamarine Adventure (www.aquamarine-adventure.al) is particularly recommended.

The waters around Karaburuni and Sazani form Albania's only national marine park (Parku Kombëtar Detar Karaburun-Sazan), with some excellent snorkelling, but best to visit soon, as developers have designs on the island in particular.

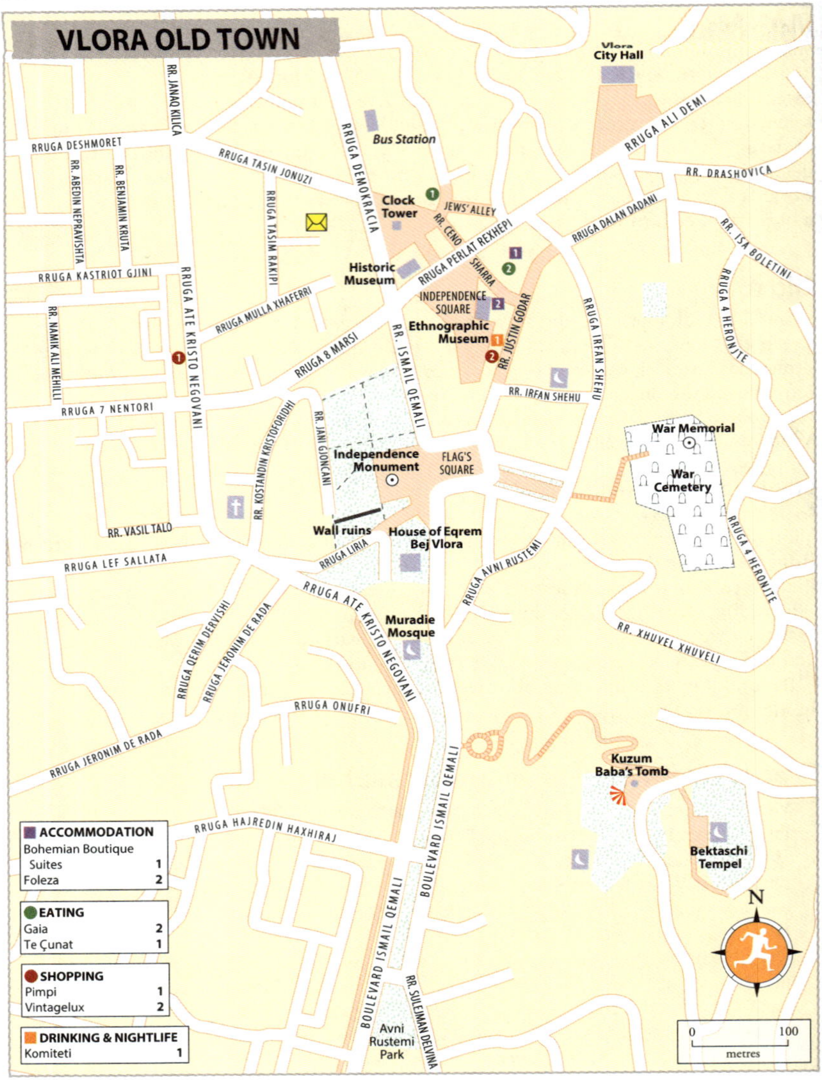

of Albania's independence. One such member was Marigo Posio (1882–1932): under cover of alleged embroidery classes here in this building, she taught many people how to read and write in the Albanian language. There's a statue of her in Hope Park, approximately one kilometre south of the Muradie Mosque (Xhamia e Muradies).

Historic Museum

Rruga Perlat Rexhepi • Charge

Sheltered within an elegant old house, the small **Muzeu Historik** walks you through the history of Vlora and the surrounding region, with displays starting in the prehistoric period and continuing up to the twentieth century. The room on the left as you enter contains some interesting archaeological pieces from Amantia (see page 247) and Orikumi (see page 248), including tombstones and amphorae, while the room on the right is filled with artefacts from the Byzantine, medieval and Ottoman periods. There's a small but diverting range of ethnographic items on display too, including silverware, national costumes and a beautifully carved fork for wool processing.

The upper floor is perhaps less essential viewing: the first room contains detailed information – in Albanian only – about the struggle for independence in the early twentieth century, as well as reproductions of artworks by English artist Edward Lear, who travelled in Albania in 1848. The second room is home to a selection of musical instruments, radios, a magnificent gramophone and a monstrous TV from the mid-twentieth century.

Independence Square

Rruga Ismail Qemali • Free

Vlora's **Independence Square**, or **Flag Square** (Sheshi i Flamurit) is dominated by a magnificent socialist realist **monument** commemorating the country's independence in 1912. Slightly to the north is a rather more modest concrete **statue** bearing the Albanian double-headed eagle, as well as the date 28 November, 1912: this stands upon the site of the now-demolished building where the Albanian flag was first raised. At the square's northernmost edge is the **tomb** of Ismail Qemali, the principal author of the Declaration of Independence and the country's first prime minister.

If your tastes stretch more to the ancient than the modern, check out the square's southwest corner where you'll discover some minor remnants of the city's **walls**, dating back to the fourth century AD. Just south of here is the **House of Eqrem Bej Vlora** (Banesa e Eqerem Bej Vlorës), a well-kept nineteenth century mansion which is not open to the public but can be admired through the gates. Eqrem Bej was one of the architects of Albania's independence in 1912.

On the hill to the east of the square is another blocky **monument**, this one a memorial to the fallen of World War II. It stands above a large cemetery of war graves, which can be reached by a staircase along a short boulevard from Independence Square. Once up here, you can follow the road around to Kuzum Baba's tomb as an alternative to the path up from Muradie Mosque.

Muradie Mosque

Rruga Ismail Qemali • Free

At the centre of a modern square just south of the House of Eqrem Bej Vlora sits the **Muradie Mosque**, dating from the 1540s and thought to have been designed by the eminent Ottoman architect Mimar Sinan. It's a lovely elegant little building, with yellow stone blocks interspersed with layers of red brick, and topped with attractive tiles. The interior is relatively plain, but it's worth popping in to take a look at the small section of calligraphy on the ceiling dome.

THE ALBANIAN DECLARATION OF INDEPENDENCE

In the early years of the twentieth century, **Ottoman power** in the Balkans was on the decline. Attempts to reform the Ottoman political system led to a **widespread revolt** in Albania from January until August 1912, which ended with the Ottomans granting all the Albanians' demands. Emboldened, Albanian nationalists declared **independence** from the Ottoman Empire in Vlora on 28 November, 1912. It took until July the following year for the European great powers to recognize Albania's independence, and the country's early years were plagued by **political instability**, not helped by the outbreak of World War I.

Kuzum Baba's tomb

Off Rruga 4 Heronjtë • Free • Best accessed via staircase near Muradie Mosque

Steps from the Muradie Mosque lead up to a hilltop complex housing the **tomb of Kuzum Baba**, the leader of the Albanian Bektashi sect (see page 127) during the fifteenth century. Set in immaculate gardens, the tomb is found within a modest green-domed building, next to a smaller pavilion used for lighting incense candles. Even if you're not hugely interested in the mausoleum, it's worth hoofing it up here for a drink at the gorgeous café, which offers excellent city views stretching across to the Karaburuni Peninsula and Sazani Island.

Just outside the complex and a little further up the hill is a modern Bektashi administrative centre, housed in an attractive building with a terrace that also offers top-notch views.

It is usually kept locked, but you can peek through the glass doors to see the central hall overlooked by a bust of Kuzum Baba.

Clock tower

Rruga Ceno Sharra • Free

A small square lined with cafés just north of the old town centre is home to a blocky modernistic **clock tower**, now occupied by a little supermarket. Off to the east, the **Jews' Alley** – which commemorates the Jews of the city and Albania's generally successful efforts during World War II to save its Jewish population from the Holocaust – leads back to the main road.

Vlora City Hall

Rruga Zigur Lelo • Free

An attractive grey and white paved square a block or two east of the old town is home to Vlora's impressive **City Hall**, a large Italianate rose-pink building. It's not open to the public but worth a quick glance if you're passing by; the best views of it can be taken in from the top of the triangular stepped seating area opposite.

Further afield

If you're heading south, the fairly slow coastal road to Orikumi is lined with private hotels and beach clubs. An alternative route is to pick up the Vlora bypass, a faster road which offers the added bonus of a side trip to the ruins of Kanina Castle.

Kanina Castle

Vlora–Kanina highway • Charge • tel: 033 230 665 • No public transport; best reached by taxi

In its prime, **Kanina Castle** (Kalaja e Kaninës) must have been an extremely imposing fortress. It sits at the top of a large hill, dominating the surrounds, with 360-degree views of Vlora, across the bay and into the mountains to the east.

Dating back to antiquity, it's sheltered Byzantines, Normans, Serbians, Albanians and Ottomans, and has witnessed plenty of action in that time, most recently in twentieth-century conflicts in which it sustained major damage. It now consists of a sole remaining tower and an impressive set of walls, around which you can stroll and admire the vistas.

ARRIVAL AND DEPARTURE — VLORA

By bus Vlora's bus terminal is on Rruga Demokracia, which is convenient if you're staying in the old town but not if your accommodation is on the seafront – you'll need to complete your journey by taxi or city bus. Long-distance destinations from Vlora's bus station include Tirana (every 30min), Tirana Airport (6 daily), Durrësi (every 30min), Gjirokastra (several daily), Himara (several daily) and Saranda (several daily).

By ferry Ferries from Brindisi, Italy, arrive at Vlora's port, operated by A-Ships (www.a-ships.com) in the summer and Starlines (www.starlines.it/en) year-round. Tickets can be purchased online, or at the offices near the port.

By plane At the time of writing, Vlora International Airport was still under construction, with a target opening date of March 2025. It is expected to operate low-cost flights to numerous countries.

By car Self-drivers from the north will most likely be coming along the A2, which heads straight into the city, depositing you near the old town. Those approaching from the south will usually take the Vlora bypass and then enter the city from the north, but it's also possible to take the somewhat-slower coast road (SH8) from Orikumi which will bring you out on the Lungomare.

GETTING AROUND

The spread-out nature of Vlora means that if you want to visit the old town and the beaches, you'll almost certainly want to use some form of transport to nip between the two: it is walkable, but it's a long way and not enormously exciting.

By bus Vlora has a couple of city bus routes, of which the handiest is the Uji i Ftohtë: this service runs all the way along the Lungomare and up past the Muradie Mosque to the old town. It's relatively frequent; you shouldn't have to wait longer than 15min at most times of day.

By taxi Taxis are easy to come by and can be particularly useful if you want to venture to far-flung spots such as Kanina Castle or Zvërneci Island. Make sure the meter is on, or negotiate a price beforehand.

By car Vlora is quite busy, but driving poses few problems other than finding a sensible place to park, which can be particularly problematic near the old town. You may have to settle for a spot some distance from where you actually want to go.

INFORMATION

Vlora doesn't have a tourist information office, although you'll come across the occasional kiosk claiming to be one: these are usually places to buy tours or boat trips. You can find some fairly vague information at www.albania.al/destinations/vlora, and it's always worth asking in your hotel for advice.

ACCOMMODATION

SEE MAPS PAGES 240 AND 242

Most accommodation in Vlora can be found either on the seafront or in the old town; in the latter, the majority of places have (generally pretty good) restaurants attached. Accommodation on the seafront promenade can be very noisy at night, so it can be worth choosing a place a block or two back.

Bohemian Boutique Suites Rruga Justin Godard; www.bohemian.al. An old-town boutique hotel with beautifully decorated rooms, featuring exposed stone walls and big comfy beds. The pick of the bunch has a balcony with good views over the square below. €€

Foleza Rruga Perlat Rexhepi; tel: 069 248 1402. A spotlessly clean bed-and-breakfast with three rooms above a restaurant in the old town. The rooms are all decorated with lovely rustic and homely touches, which feel traditional yet modern at the same time. Two overlook the square; if you're a light sleeper, try to score the Olive Room at the back. €€

Hotel Semajo Rruga Francesko Krispi; www.hotelsemajo.al. This friendly family-run hotel is set a couple of blocks back from Ri Beach on a quiet street. Rooms on the lower floors are clean and functional but a little small; if you've got cash to splash, ask for one of the suites on the fourth floor, which are much larger and come equipped with corner baths. €€

Vlora Backpackers Hostel Rruga Leka Gjiknuri; www.facebook.com/vlora.backpackers.hostel. There aren't many hostels in Vlora, so this place is probably the best in town if you're looking for budget accommodation where you can meet up with other travellers. There are several dorms and a communal kitchen, and it's close to the beach. €

EATING

SEE MAPS PAGES 240 AND 242

Bujar Rruga Murat Tërbaçi; tel: 069 553 7476. This upmarket fish-focused restaurant on the seafront by Ri Beach is a great choice for a classy meal. There are plenty of fish and seafood options, as well as a decent range of pasta dishes and a couple of meaty options. Portions are not huge – the emphasis is on quality rather than quantity – but that means you'll have room for one of the tempting desserts. There's an extremely extensive wine list to work through as well. €€€€

Gaia Rruga Justin Godard; tel: 069 305 8308. Of the many restaurants on and around Vlora's old town square, *Gaia* is one of the best. The menu is primarily traditional Albanian plates, with the barbecued sea bass and chargrilled vegetables a particularly good choice. It also has a vast list of cocktails. The downside is that service is at best indifferent. €€€€

La Nonna Rruga Shaban Demiraj; tel: 069 377 7000. This Italian-style place right on the seafront, complete with classic red-and-white checked tablecloths, is where you'll find Vlora's best pizza. Aside from a couple of seasonal salads, pizzas are the only thing on the menu – and when they're this good, you likely wouldn't want anything else anyway. €€

Te Çunat Rruga Ceno Sharra. Cheap and cheerful fast-food joint on the clock tower square offering tasty and good-value gyros (meat and salad in pita), as well as other choices including sandwiches, burgers and hot dogs. A good spot for a quick and easy lunch. €

6

DRINKING

SEE MAPS PAGES 240 AND 242

Café del Mar Rruga Çamëria; tel: 069 221 7822. One of the café-restaurants on the edge of the Lungomare, *Café del Mar* is a pleasant spot to pause for a coffee if you're wandering along the promenade, though sadly the views are more of the concrete plaza than of the sea. Alcoholic drinks are available too, as are decent meals of the pizza and pasta variety.

★ **Komiteti** Rruga Justin Godard; tel: 068 507 6671. A meticulously decorated bar, with antique sewing tables, stylishly mismatched chairs, and an entire wall bedecked with driftwood. There's a rather tropical garden out the back for warm summer evenings, and a fantastic old stove (much appreciated by the resident cats) which keeps the place toasty warm if you happen to be here in winter. Also has a great selection of *rakis*, and is justly proud of its excellent sweet and smoky *raki* Marigo cocktails.

Seasons Rruga Murat Tërbaçi; tel: 069 209 2603. This seafront bar is a popular spot for Vlora's young and beautiful set, who are drawn by the extensive range of delicious cocktails, chilled soundtrack and friendly service. If cocktails aren't your thing, there are also ice-cold beers available.

Venus Beach Off Rruga Sazani; tel: 069 291 8847. Right up at the top end of Vjetër Beach, this great little beach café offers alcoholic and non-alcoholic drinks – including some excellent cocktails – as well as tasty light meals. It's accessed via a short track through pine forest, with its own area of beach that's sufficiently far from the town centre to give you a lovely uncrowded experience.

SHOPPING

SEE MAPS PAGES 240 AND 242

La Boutique d'Alcohol Rruga Murat Tërbaçi; tel: 069 660 9066. Just off the Ri Beach seafront is this very classy liquor store, boasting a marvellous array of *raki*, grappa, gin, vodka and tequila, among much else. There's also a small selection of local wines, so the only question really is how many bottles you can squeeze in your luggage.

Pimpi Rruga Atë Kristo Negovani. Unappealing name aside, this little shop just outside the old town is a great place to pick up a bottle of Albanian wine, *raki* or brandy. There's also a decent range of Italian wines, and the friendly owner can help you choose.

Vintagelux Rruga Justin Godard. A good choice if you're looking for an interesting Albanian souvenir. There's a decent selection of goods on offer, from the fridge magnet and baseball cap standards to more unusual choices such as musical instruments, jewellery and rugs. There are a couple of genuine antiques on sale here too.

DIRECTORY

Banks ATMs are pretty easy to find both in the old town and along the Lungomare. Should you need an actual branch of a bank, they're mostly found along the length of Bulevardi Ismail Qemali, which connects the seafront and the old town.

Hospital Vlora's hospital, Spitali Rajonal Vlorë, is about a kilometre northeast of the old town on Rruga Mitaq Sallata (tel: 03 322 2631).

Pharmacies There are plenty of pharmacies across the city, including a cluster of them just south of Independence Square.

Post office The central post office is on Rruga Demokracia (tel: 03 323 3675), close to the clock tower. There's a DHL service point on Rruga Kosova.

Zvërneci

The large **Narta lagoon** just north of Vlora is an important habitat for birds, with many visitors hoping to spot the local colony of **flamingos**. The area is under threat from the construction of the Vlora International Airport, which is north of the lagoon and well within the ostensibly environmentally safeguarded Vjosa-Narta Delta Protected Area. A gravel road provides access to the lagoon's northern shore for **birdwatchers**, though most visitors tend to head for the peninsula and island of **ZVËRNECI** instead, easily accessible from Vlora centre.

St Mary's Monastery

Zvërneci • Free • No public transport; best reached by taxi

On a small island off the Zvërneci peninsula is the fourteenth-century **St Mary's Monastery** (Manastiri i Shën Mërisë), which has an extremely attractive Orthodox church with an arched porch and a beautiful tower. Inside is a gorgeously carved iconostasis, while in the churchyard outside you'll find the **grave** of Marigo Posio (see page 242). In the later years of the communist regime, the monastery and island were used as a prison camp.

The monastery is accessed via a lovely sweeping boardwalk from a car park on the mainland, at which you'll also find a welcome drinks kiosk and a good example of a communist-era concrete bunker.

Zvërneci Lighthouse and bunkers

Zvërneci • Free • No public transport; best reached by taxi

Accessible via an unpaved but driveable road, **Zvërneci Lighthouse** on the summit of the western edge of the peninsula offers lovely views over to Sazani Island. More interesting, though, is the series of four communist-era **bunkers** lining the coast just beneath the lighthouse, the exteriors of which have been painted with impressive environmentalist-themed street art. You can still enter them to take a look at the Cold War iconography on the walls: the first bunker you reach has a fascinating pictorial guide to enemy naval vessels. Be careful poking about in here, though: the interiors are very dark, and there are uncovered holes in the floor.

There are also a couple of isolated beaches tucked away up this end of the peninsula, which you can explore if you're hoping for a bit of solitude away from Vlora's busier urban beaches.

Vlora to Qeparoi

Most travellers heading south from Vlora take the coastal road, but the good-quality inland road to Qeparoi offers an interesting – if slightly lengthier – alternative, with the chance for stops at sights including the ancient ruins of **Amantia** and the gorgeous **Brataj Bridge** en route. Above all, it's a hugely picturesque route, threading down the Shushica River valley between towering mountains on either side – though, as there's very limited public transport, it's best suited for self-drivers.

Drashovica Monument

SH76, Drashovica • Free

As the road passes the small village of **Drashovica**, stop at the enormous concrete **monument** just by the bridge. A huge arch, decorated with carved socialist realist figures, frames a statue commemorating the fallen of the 1920 Italian invasion as well as a 1943 battle against the Germans. It's among the most impressive war memorials in Albania.

Amantia

Past Ploça village, off SH76 • Charge

The crumbling remnants of the ancient city of **Amantia** are scattered across a hilltop, accessed via an asphalted side road. The city, which was the home of the Amantes people, seemed to gain prominence in the mid-fourth century BC, with particular

RIVIERA BEACHES

At almost every beach along the riviera, you'll find hotels and bars have staked their claim to prime spots by setting up **sun loungers** on the seafront, which they'll then **charge** you a daily fee of about €10 to use. These do offer much-needed shade in the hot summer, but if you've got your own parasol then consider seeking out the **public beach areas** that exist on most stretches; at these you can simply pitch up in your chosen spot for **free**.

prosperity from around 230 BC, and it was still a populous place by the time of the Byzantine Emperor Justinian I in the mid-sixth century AD.

From the car park, the nearest remains are those of the third-century BC **stadium**, once used for sporting events: it's an elongated horseshoe shape which still retains several rows of seats. From the stadium, return to the car park and drive or walk the gravel track to the hill's summit, emerging in a small farmyard. Take the first turning right and head along the track to reach a viewpoint over the ancient **Temple of Aphrodite** and the later Byzantine-era **basilica** – if you're feeling energetic, you can scramble down to explore them. Otherwise, return to the farm and strike out on the path around the front of the hill to a marvellously picturesque **archway**. On your way back down, stop at the farmyard again, where the family may show you a few artefacts found on the site, and offer fruit and home-made drinks.

Lepenica footbridge

SH76, Lepenica • Free

A short diversion for the adventurous awaits at **Lepenica**, a small village worth a stop if you dare to cross the river on its rackety swaying **suspension bridge**. Some 12m above the water at its lowest point, the bridge swings and creaks rather alarmingly even in the slightest of breezes.

Brataj Bridge

SH76, Brataj • Free

The elegant three-arched **Brataj Bridge** (Ura e Bratajt) dates from the eighteenth century and was formerly one of the main crossing points of the river in this valley. It spans a beautiful section of gorge, and the pools beneath it are popular with locals for swimming. You may see local lads testing their courage by leaping from the bridge into the waters below. Access is via a short walk downhill from a convenient car park which also contains a small roadside café; it's a lovely spot to enjoy a drink while taking in the expansive mountain scenery.

Brataj to Qeparoi

SH76 • Free

From Brataj, the road heads south back towards the coast, passing a few more sights of minor interest. Primary among them, just a few kilometres south of Brataj Bridge, is a striking and well-kept **war memorial**. Continuing along the road will bring you to the turn-off for **Kuçi**, a small village that offers a few walking trails up into the mountains. Thereafter, there's little to detain you until you reach the coastal road again at Qeparoi.

EATING **VLORA TO QEPAROI**

Mondial SH76, just west of Kota village; tel: 069 675 5827. A convenient little roadside restaurant, in between Drashovica and Amantia, which offers traditional Albanian dishes, mostly veering towards the barbecued meats end of the scale. Seating is either in the tavern-like interior or the pleasant breezy garden. **€€€**

Orikumi

If, instead of taking the inland road, you travel along the coastal route from Vlora, the first place of any size that you'll reach is **ORIKUMI**, a fairly sleepy town which makes a decent enough place to stop overnight if you're taking it slow. As well as its beach, it has a couple of points of interest, notably the nearby minor **archaeological ruins** of ancient Oricum and the interesting **Marmiroi Church** (Kisha e Marmiroit).

Orikumi Beach

Rruga Pashaliman • Free

A little quieter than many of those along this stretch of coast, Orikumi's narrow pebbly stretch of **beach** (Plazhi i Orikumit) is directly opposite the Karaburuni Peninsula, making it rather picturesque, particularly toward sunset. There are sun loungers available (charge) and a couple of restaurants close at hand.

Orikumi Archaeological Park

Rruga Pashaliman • Charge

The **ancient site** of **Oricum**(Parku Arkeologjik i Orikumit), some five kilometres along the coast from the modern town, was first settled in around the fifth century BC by Greek colonists. The ruins are fairly scanty, though the large semicircular **nymphaeum** – reached by turning left from the map near the parking area – is pretty impressive. There's also an attractively eroded staircase leading up to further remains, including a small dwelling place containing a very deep well. The site is most unusual, however, for its setting – it's within an active naval base that is a restricted military zone.

To visit the archaeological site, drive up to the naval base gates and show your passport to the staff in the tourist information kiosk to your left; you'll then be escorted through the military base to the ruins. This unique access arrangement makes a visit here rather memorable.

Marmiroi Church

Off Rruga Pashaliman • Free

Just before entering the naval base, there's a rough road that swerves left and circles the wetlands of the **Pashalimani Lagoon**, where birdwatchers may be rewarded with sightings of herons and cormorants, amongst other. The road runs for three kilometres before ending at the **Marmiroi Church** (Kisha e Marmiroit), a twelfth-century Orthodox church sheltering some attractive Byzantine-era frescoes.

Marina Orikum

SH8, Orikumi • Free

Just outside the town centre, the shiny **Marina Orikum** is home to large and expensive-looking pleasure yachts. It's a pleasantly cool and breezy place for a drink at the waterside café, and boat trips to Karaburuni can be arranged from here.

ACCOMMODATION AND EATING — ORIKUMI

Hotel Adriatik Orikum Off Rruga Kaonët; www.facebook.com/p/Hotel-Adriatik-100032787320343. A centrally located and very friendly small hotel with eclectically decorated and spotless rooms, a welcome swimming pool in the courtyard, and a well-stocked bar. The evening meals at the poolside restaurant come highly recommended. €€€

Orikumi to Himara

The main road south from Orikumi loses sight of the coast for some distance as it passes the Karaburuni Peninsula, after which it begins to climb up into the mountains to the **Llogara Pass**, from which you can enjoy lovely views and several walks of varying lengths. Thereafter, the road snakes past several of the riviera's nicest **beaches** and prettiest **villages**, before reaching the town of **Himara**. If you're behind the wheel for the length of the winding coastal road down the riviera, drive cautiously and mind the many drivers who don't take care.

6

CAESAR'S PASS

From the Llogara National Park Visitor Centre, head slightly up the road and take the track to the left of the *Sofo Hotel* for an enjoyable 45min ramble through the woods. The path – which follows a route **Julius Caesar's army** once allegedly stomped along – is well maintained and can be followed easily; the only point of confusion comes about five minutes in, at a ruined house, where you should take the right-hand paved path, not the unpaved left one. You'll head steadily uphill through pine forest until you reach a fork in the trail; take the left route to emerge at a stunning viewpoint which looks all the way back down the **Llogara Pass** and to the **Karaburuni Peninsula** beyond. You can either return by the same route or take the other path at the fork for a slightly longer circuit back down to the road.

Llogara Pass

SH8, Llogara Pass • Free

The quickest way to follow the south road is to head through the 6km-long tunnel – completed in July 2024 – which burrows through the Ceraunian Mountains (Malet e Vetëtimës), but the older **Llogara Pass** (Qafa e Llogarasë; definitive form Llogaraja) is a far more enjoyable drive. Bending up along switchbacks, you'll eventually reach the visitor centre of the **Llogara National Park** (Parku Kombëtar i Llogarasë), where staff can advise on short and long hikes in the area.

Heading on from the visitor centre, you'll reach the top of the pass and then descend a little to the **Llogara Panorama**, a large plaza with ample car parking where you can stop and drink in the splendid views down to the sea and the mountains beyond. It's a popular spot for paragliding, boasting a long and scenic descent to the beaches below. Reliable paragliding operators include SkySports (www.skysports.al/paragliding-from-llogara).

Drymades Beach

Gjileka village • Free

The first beach after the Llogara Pass, **Drymades** (Plazhi i Drimadhës) offers a wide stretch of pebble shoreline and beautiful turquoise waters. There's an attractive and largely litter-free promenade, behind which loom the mountains to form a great backdrop. The beach has sun loungers (charge) and beach bars aplenty, and there are also several outlets for hiring sea canoes and stand-up paddleboards. As with so many spots along the coast, there's a lot of development underway, but for now it's a pleasant place to soak up the sun.

Dhërmiu Beach

Dhërmiu village • Free

The SH8 road passes straight through the village of **Dhërmiu**, an attractive place with a couple of pretty blue-and-white painted churches. For most visitors, though, the real draw is the long and pebbly stretch of **beach** (Plazhi i Dhërmiut), which is backed by a pleasant, largely pedestrianized, promenade offering an excellent range of hotels and restaurants. Sun loungers can be rented, and boat trips along the nearby coast are easily available too. By and large, the further along the beach you venture, the quieter it becomes: if you head all the way to the southeastern end, you can take a boardwalk over a small cape to a very picturesque rocky cove.

Gjipeja Beach

Off SH8 • Free, though mandatory car parking charge

Despite being reached by what is quite possibly the most ridiculous single-track road in Albania – the high kerbs make it impossible for vehicles to pass each other – and thereafter by a twenty-minute walk down a dirt track, **Gjipeja (or Gjipe) Beach** (Plazhi i Gjipesë) remains very popular. With good reason: it's a small, pleasant cove of pebble and sand, lapped by calm, sparkling waters that are ideal for swimming. There are sun loungers (charge) aplenty and a smattering of beach cafés which – despite having cornered the market – are very reasonably priced. Overnight camping on the beach is permitted.

St Theodore's Monastery

Off SH8 • Free, though mandatory car parking charge

Begun in the fourteenth century and continually added to for the next five hundred years, **St Theodore's Monastery** (Manastiri i Shën Theodorit) was taken over by the military in the communist period. It is accessible along a short path from the Gjipeja Beach parking area – ask at the car park for the key to enter the inner courtyard.

Vunoi

SH8 • Free

The coastal road next wends through the pretty village of **Vunoi**, worth a quick stop to check out its collection of interesting churches, all bedecked with impressive frescoes. Just off the main square, the 1783 **Church of St Mary** (Kisha e Shën Mërisë) is often kept locked, and its frescoes suffered major damage under communism.

More rewarding is the **Church of St Spyridon** (Kisha e Shën Spiridhont), accessible via a walk through winding picturesque alleys down from the main square on Rruga Orest Vasili. Here, the gorgeous frescoes have survived, despite years of neglect under communism and a fire in 1998. Those on the stone iconostasis directly ahead of you as you enter are particularly impressive, but make sure also to take a look at the murals above the arches to the left and right.

Just across the small square from St Spyridon, you'll find further brightly coloured frescoes on the iconostasis of the **Church of St Michael** (Kisha e Shën Mëhillit), though otherwise the interior is of rather less interest.

Jale Beach

Jale village • Free

The small cove of **Jale (or Jala)** has a pleasant **beach** (Plazhi i Jalës) with the usual gorgeous clear water and small pebbles, but the promenade behind – which could have been lovely – is unfortunately rather scrappy and litter-strewn, and is packed with uninspiring bars and restaurants.

There's major construction work ongoing here too, with large hotels and apartment blocks springing up along the waterfront. All in all, there are better beaches along the coast at which to spend your time.

ACCOMMODATION AND EATING — ORIKUMI TO HIMARA

Nassau Beach Hotel Rruga Plazhi, Dhërmiu; www.nassau.al. One of the best choices of hotel along Dhërmiu's seafront: designed with a stylish blocky architecture, it boasts a spa, a well-supplied bar and a lovely infinity pool facing right onto the seafront. The rooms are clean and comfortable, if not hugely exciting, though the gorgeous sea views make up for the slightly corporate style. €€€€

Shotgun Hostel Vunoi village; https://shotgunhostelvuno.my.canva.site. A friendly hostel in the centre of quiet Vunoi village, with an eight-person dorm as well as a private double room. Good food is on offer, and the owner can arrange transport and tours around the region. €

Vela e Bardhe Rruga Plazhi, Dhërmiu; tel: 069 249 5207. A friendly seafront restaurant in Dhërmiu, with a menu offering tasty seafood, fish, pasta, pizza and much else besides. Its position on the promenade makes it a perfect spot for people-watching. €€€

Himara

HIMARA is the largest place between Vlora and Saranda, and makes a decent place to overnight if you're travelling between the two. Its **old town**, draped across the hill above the beach, is a relaxed and pleasantly atmospheric knot of cobbled alleys leading up to the castle walls, while the more happening new town unfurls along the coastline below. The road through the centre can get clogged and busy, but the **beaches** escape the traffic noise.

The town's beaches are separated by a small cape: the more central option is at the western end of town, set back from the road in a semi-pedestrianized area, while Plazhi i Prinos and Plazhi i Potamit can be found further southeast with plenty of parking immediately to hand.

Old town

Off SH8 • Free

Himara's old town sits three kilometres uphill from the new town, and it would be a stiff hike without transport. Picturesque stone alleys wind up through semi-abandoned houses to the summit, where you'll find the ruins of the **castle**. Inside the walls is the **Church of Sts Sergius and Bacchus** (Kisha e Sergjit dhe Bakut), which conceals attractive painted murals on the iconostasis, though arguably more compelling are the marvellous views out across the bay.

Himara Beach

Himara • Free

Backed by a well-kept promenade, the short stretch of public central **beach** (Plazhi i Himarës) on Himara's front is a very pleasant place to swim and catch some rays. Enclosed on the western edge by a small and wooded headland, it's sandier and less packed with sun loungers (charge) than many riviera beaches and boasts calm turquoise waters. Paddleboards are available for rent, and boat trips are touted along the promenade, offering visits to sea caves, isolated beaches and even a communist era submarine bunker.

Prinos and Potami Beaches

Himara • Free

Himara's southernmost beaches, **Plazhi i Prinos** and **Plazhi i Potamit**, are pebbly rather than sand, and are ideal for swimming as the water – which gets deep very quickly – is lovely and clear. Both beaches are lined with sun loungers (charge) owned by various nearby hotels and restaurants.

Livadhi Beach

Himara–Livadhi road, Himara • Free

Accessed by a road just south of the old town, **Livadhi Beach** (Plazhi i Livadhit) is a less-frequented stretch of sand and pebble than Himara's other beaches. Even so, it does still get busy, and parking is both expensive and limited. The sea here is clear, calm and inviting, and the shore is lined with shaded sun loungers (charge) and beach bars.

ARRIVAL AND DEPARTURE — HIMARA

By bus Two buses a day leave Himara for Vlora; these can also be used to reach Vunoi and Dhërmiu. Heading south, there are two daily buses to Saranda, which will also stop at the Porto Palermo fortress, Qeparoi or Borshi, if you ask. The stop is located on the main road (SH8) in the centre of the new town.

By car Himara is on the main road between Vlora and Saranda, and there's no bypass, so you can't miss it, especially since you're likely to get caught in a traffic jam in the centre. Parking at the old town is easy, but a little more chaotic by the beaches: aim for Prinos and Potami for your best chance.

GETTING AROUND AND INFORMATION

Himara isn't a huge place, and getting around the new town is by and large best achieved on foot. It's a bit of a trek up to the old town on foot, though; the easiest option is to pick up a taxi, which should take no more than five minutes. If you're self-driving, there's plenty of parking at Prinos and Potami beaches, though it st ll gets busy.

Information There's no tourist information office in town. Official, if cursory, information can be found at www.albania.al/destinations/himara.

ACCOMMODATION

★ **Alex Boutique Hotel** Rruga Spiro Milo; tel: 069 578 9266. Just a little way down the hill from the old town is this lovely place, which occupies a beautifully converted traditional house. The rooms are all done out in a stylish nautical blue-and-white colour palette, and there are fantastic views out across the sea. €€

Rea Boutique Hotel Himara seafront; tel: 069 935 6181. In a peaceful spot at the end of Himara's seafront, *Rea Boutique Hotel* is a love y little bolthole, at which real care has gone into ensuring that every detail is perfect. Try to score one of the rooms with a sea view. Breakfast, on a terrace overlooking the beach, is delicious. €€€

Sun Bakers Hostel Plazh i Potamit; tel: 068 458 0819. The *Sun Bakers Hostel* is an excellent sociable choice for travellers on a budget. The owners rent out canoes, as well as arranging events such as barbecues and boat parties. €

EATING

★ **Fig and Olive** Himara–Livadhi road; tel: 068 905 0872. Attached to the *Aphrodite's Garden* hotel, this top-notch restaurant just downhill from the old town is one of Himara's best places to eat. The setting is gorgeous, with expansive views over the bay making it extremely popular at sunset, and the menu – highlights of which include seafood risotto, shrimp *saganaki* (or *saganaq*; dish with tomato sauce and feta) and grilled Mediterranean sea bass – is extremely good value and outstanding quality. Don't skip the garlic bread for starters – it may well be the best you ever have. €€€€

Himara '28 Rruga Dhjetori; www.himara28.al/restaurant.html. In an attractive stone building on Himara's promenade, this ocean-focused restaurant offers a variety of seafood and freshly grilled fish. It looks right out onto the seafront and is a lovely place for a relaxed lunch. €€€

Lui Potam Plazhi i Potamit; tel: 069 442 2533. A good choice for lunch or dinner at the Potami Beach end of town, *Lui Potam* offers the usual range of grilled fish, seafood, pizza and pasta. It's right on the seafront and makes a great spot for an evening cocktail €€

DRINKING

Café Butterfly Old town; tel: 069 306 1212. Tucked away among the ruins of Himara's old town, *Café Butterfly* boasts a beautiful vine-covered terrace and stunning panoramas across the bay. It's a perfect spot to pause your explorations for a coffee, fresh juice or glass of wine while enjoying the view. Light meals are also available.

Ice Land Gelato SH8, Plazhi i Potamit; tel: 069 655 6315. A cheerful little place offering not just a fine selection of ice-cream flavours but also tasty cakes, good coffee and plenty of alcoholic drinks. It's just a stone's throw from Prinos and Potami beaches.

Himara to Saranda

Following the coastal road south from Himara offers access to further pretty riviera beaches, with **Qeparoi** a particular standout. This stretch of coast is also packed with interesting historical attractions to explore, notable among them the prominent fortress of **Porto Palermo** and the gorgeous **St Mary's Monastery**.

Porto Palermo Fortress

SH8 • Free

On a small spit of land, visible from some distance away along the road, stands the **Porto Palermo Fortress** (Kalaja e Porto Palermos), a triangular-shaped stone edifice built on the orders of Ali Pasha Tepelena (see page 224) in the nineteenth century.

You can explore its pleasantly cool interior, noting the immensely thick and defensible walls, before clambering up onto the battlements for views across to Corfu. The final stop is the very well-fortified dungeon, a dark and foreboding room from which escape would be very unlikely. Beneath the castle is a small, popular **public beach** with calm and clear waters, and a restaurant with a fine terrace, which rather lets itself down with outstandingly surly service. In August, the **Porto Palermo Festival** (www.portopalermofestival.com) means there are musical performances at the fortress.

Qeparoi Beach

Qeparoi village • Free

The wide cove of **Qeparoi** has a lovely stretch of **pebble and sand beach** (Plazhi i Qeparot), with calm waters and a much gentler slope into the water than many other beaches along the coast. There are the usual array of sun loungers (charge) and a smattering of excellent beachfront bars. It's litter-free and backed by an immaculate palm-lined promenade. All things considered, it's a very good choice of beach.

You can see another side to Qeparoi by heading uphill to the pretty **old village**, a charming warren of cobbled alleys overlooked by a picturesque church tower. The views from up here down to the coast are gorgeous. The drive up is not for acrophobes.

Borshi Beach

Rruga Plazhi, Borshi • Free

The village of **Borshi** boasts a wide **beach** (Plazhi i Borshit) of coarse sand and pebble, with the usual attractive blue water, beach bars and sun loungers (charge). There are also sea kayaks and paddleboards available to hire here. It's a pleasant enough choice, but a bit scrappier than some: it feels like a little more care could go into its maintenance.

Borshi Castle

Off SH8, above Borshi village • Free

Visible on a rocky outcrop far above Borshi, the **castle** (Kalaja e Borshit) site was inhabited as far back as the fourth century BC. Most of the current remains, though, date back to the Byzantine and medieval periods, with the mosque – the most picturesque and intact building – having been added around the sixteenth century: check out its atmospherically decaying interior to admire the fine pillar carvings and the faint artwork on the ceiling dome. The castle, surrounded by beautiful mountain peaks and offering views straight down to the sea, is a peaceful and relatively rarely visited spot, and you're free to pick your way among the fairly substantial ruins. Access is via a surprisingly well-paved path from a turnoff above Borshi; it'll take you about ten to fifteen minutes to hoof it up to the castle from the car parking spot.

Buneci Beach

Off SH8, east of Piqerasi village • Free

Accessible down a rough but driveable road, **Buneci Beach** (Plazhi i Bunecit) is one of the most undeveloped along the coast. The pebble and sand shore is largely free of sun

THE SOUTH OUTDOOR FESTIVAL

Borshi hosts the annual **South Outdoor Festival** (https://southoutdoor.al/en), which is a showcase for the region's culture, tradition, sports, food and adventure activities. It's usually held in April or May, and is well worth checking out if you're passing through at the time.

SHËN E PREMTE

From the village of Lukova above the beach, you could seek out the ancient **Shën e Premte**. This tiny and picturesque church sits in a delightful spot on a wooded hillside just outside the village. It's a tad difficult to find: follow Rruga Shën Premte downhill until you reach a post with yellow hiking signs; turn right here, and take the rough track to the left of a villa. The church is in a little clearing about three minutes on.

loungers and there are only a couple of cafés; the water is gorgeous and clear, and at the near end, by *Beach Bar Naza*, there's a beautiful – almost tropical – landscaped little stream. The downside is that litter is something of a problem, particularly in the areas not owned by beach bars.

Lukova Beach

Lukova–Shpella road, Lukova village • Free

Accessed by a long and beautiful road, **Lukova Beach** (Plazhi i Lukovës) is a delightful stretch of seafront. The sea is clean and clear, and there's relatively little development – no high-rise hotels and just a few beach bars. Sun loungers (charge) can be found on the sand, but they don't fill every square inch as they do elsewhere. The surrounding scenery is idyllic, with wooded hills rising from the sides of the bay.

St Mary's Monastery

Off SH8, signposted 3km south of Nivica village • Free

St Mary's Monastery (Manastiri i Shën Mërisë) is an abandoned but well-preserved Orthodox religious complex nestled into the hillside a few kilometres off the main road. Take the signposted turn and follow the asphalted side road to its end at a blue gate, then pick up the obvious path, which is clearly indicated with red and white waymarks. It takes about fifteen minutes to reach the monastery on foot, and the path is easy to follow. The only point of confusion comes about ten minutes in, at a fork where you should take the left-hand route (signed to Lost Paradise) and then right at the next junction.

Once at the monastery, you'll likely have it to yourself. The main draw is the outstanding medieval frescoes, a rare and fortunate survival of the anti-religious campaign under communism. The images can be found within the church to the right of the entrance gate, and cover every inch of the interior walls, with beautiful colours and detailed artwork still apparent. The rows of angels and saints lining the dome are particularly intricate. After, explore the picturesque ruined cloisters and admire the views down to the cove below.

St George's Monastery

Off SH8, 4km south of turn for St Mary's (Shën Mërisë) • Free

About five kilometres before Saranda, just off the main road on a driveable gravel track, is the pretty **St George's Monastery** (Manastiri i Shën Gjergjit), a perfect little Orthodox church. Inside, there are faint traces of frescoes still to be seen, and there are lovely views across the valley from the terrace.

ACCOMMODATION AND EATING — HIMARA TO SARANDA

Caffe Borbone Qeparoi promenade; tel: 069 520 3459. A friendly restaurant at the corner of the promenade on Qeparoi Beach, offering good-value and tasty meals that run the gamut from barbecued fish to pizzas. It goes by the name of Gjika on some mapping apps. €€

★ **Vila Panorama** SH8 Piqerasi; www.vila-panorama.al. Welcoming family-run hotel with spotless rooms, the upstairs ones equipped with balconies framing fine bay views. On the terrace below, you can tuck into top-notch wood-fired pizzas while gazing across to Corfu. €€

Saranda

SARANDA is one of Albania's principal seaside resorts. It hooks around an attractive bay, backed with a pleasant promenade, and has been extensively developed with hotels, restaurants and bars where the party continues until the early hours. The city has a pair of small **beaches** which somehow manage not to feel crowded, even in the summer months, as well as several minor **museums** and **ancient remains** to explore. On top of this, it's an ideal place to base yourself for a day-trip to the ruins of Butrint (see page 264).

Although Saranda appears to have been settled up to four thousand years ago, today there's little evidence of its early history. Under the name of Onchesmos, it began to gain prominence in the third or fourth century BC, as a port city of the ancient Greek Chaonian people.

During the early Byzantine era, the city was still inhabited, but it went into decline in the later medieval period, and was just a small village by the time the Ottomans took control of the area. It passed between Albanian, Italian, Greek and – briefly – British hands during the twentieth century, and underwent rapid development into the busy seaside city it is today.

The promenade

Saranda seafront • Free

A walk along Saranda's **seafront promenade** will take you around fifteen minutes. Starting at the western end, by the port, the first sight of note is a small fairground, in which the only vaguely tempting diversion is the **big wheel**, thanks to its great views over the bay. Continuing along the waterfront, you'll spot a chunk of ancient stone-and-brick **masonry** standing on the beach; this is a lonely remnant of the old city wall.

Shortly thereafter, you'll pass **busts and statues** of various Albanian political and literary heroes, most notably Hasan Tahsini, a nineteenth-century rector of Istanbul University who was prominent in the development of growing Albanian nationalism in the declining years of the Ottoman Empire. The official name of this part of Saranda's promenade is Bulevardi Hasan Tahsini. At night, rows of souvenir stands set up opposite the statues.

On both sides of the harbour arm hosting *Restaurant Limani*, **boat trip** touts ply their trade, offering day and half-day excursions to various beaches and coves up and down the coast. Passing the Museum of Tradition (see page 256), the promenade then continues pleasantly, though without any specific sites, to the eastern public beach.

Saranda Beach

Saranda seafront • Free

There are two stretches of public **pebble beach** on Saranda's seafront. The section at the eastern end is busier and is a popular place to catch some rays, swim and snorkel in the sea, and enjoy activities such as jet skiing and bouncing about on an inflatable aqua-run. At the western end, things tend to slip down a few gears, with calm and clear water, and sunbathers relaxing on the shore. There may be better beaches along the riviera, but Saranda's are both perfectly passable for a lazy afternoon.

Museum of Tradition

Rruga Jonianët • Charge, joint ticket with Archaeology Museum and Galeria Art

The ground floor of the small **Museum of Tradition** (Muzeu i Traditës) on the seafront consists of two mostly empty rooms, with a few exhibits including ethnographic items such as a large wooden chest, metalwork tools and pieces of amphorae. The old sepia pictures of Saranda in days gone by are perhaps the most interesting of the bunch. The

SARANDA
ACCOMMODATION
Austin Boutique 4
Julia Hotel 5
LaFe Boutique 1
Relax Mea 2
Saranda Backpackers 3
EATING
La Banana 3
Limani 4
Manxurane 7
Oda e Babës 2
Summer 6
Tako Taco 1
Taverna JoAn 5
DRINKING & NIGHTLIFE
Blue Moon Bar & Crêperie 1
Jericho Cocktail Bar 2
Old House 3
Vino Vibe 4
Kaleja e Lëkurësit & Monastery of the Forty Saints (2km)
War Cemetery
N
0 150 metres
(450m)
Brindisi, Corfu
(900m)
Bay of Saranda
IONIAN SEA
Eastern Beach
Western Beach
Saranda Beach
Era Beach
Saranda Port
Saranda Terminal
Police Station
Town Market
Municipality of Saranda
Basilica and Synagogue ruins
Bus Station
Friendship Park
Saranda Bunker
Museum of Tradition
Archaeology Museum
Galeria Art Saranda
Church of St Charalampos
Hospital Petro Nako
RRUGA TEKI HADERI
DORA D'ISTRIA
RRUGA BUTRINTI
RRUGA NAIM FRASHËRI
RRUGA 40 SHENJTORËT
SHËTITORJA NAIM FRASHËRI
RRUGA LEFTER TALO
RRUGA QAZIM DEMI
RRUGA GJERGJ ARANITI
RR. APOSTOL QENDRO
RRUGA FEIZO MEHMETI
RRUGA E FLAMURIT
RRUGA SKËNDERBEU
RRUGA ONHEZMI
RR. TELAT NOGA
RRUGA FLAMURIT
RRUGA JONIANËT
BULEVARDI HASAN TAHSINI
RRUGA ADEM SHEME
RRUGA ABEDIN DINO
RR. SALI CEKA
RRUGA MITAT HOXHA
RRUGA APOSTOL CUNI
RRUGA ISMAIL QEMALI
RRUGA BILAL XHAFERRI
RRUGA IDRIZ ALIDHIMA
RR. ONHEZMI
RRUGA STUDENTI
RRUGA JANAQ KUMI

upstairs is marginally more exciting, with dummies adorned in national costume and further black-and-white photos on the wall. Explanatory text is minimal.

Archaeology Museum

Rruga e Flamurit • Charge, joint ticket with Museum of Tradition and Galeria Art

The centrepiece of Saranda's **Archaeology Museum** (Muzeu Arkeologjik) is a large and relatively well-preserved Byzantine mosaic, which was once the floor of a basilica which stood on this site. The remainder of the museum's exhibits are a little limited, consisting of a few pieces of masonry and clay pot fragments, and photos of finds that are on display elsewhere.

6

Galeria Art Saranda

Shëtitorja Naim Frashëri • Charge, joint ticket with Museum of Tradition and Archaeology Museum

Saranda's little **art gallery**, tucked away beneath *Bar Riviera*, is a couple of pleasantly air-conditioned rooms that host temporary exhibitions, usually with a local theme and by local artists. It's generally worth popping by to see what's on show.

Church of St Charalampos

Rruga e Flamurit • Free

The attractive white **Church of St Charalampos** (Kisha e Shën Harallambit) makes a refreshing change from the soulless high-rises clustered along Saranda's seafront. Although the interior is of limited interest, and the door is often kept locked, the church's pretty garden and pleasant terrace offers a welcome retreat from the busy city.

Basilica and Synagogue ruins

Rruga Skënderbeu • Free

Looking a little incongruous in the town centre is a small block of ruins, the foundations of a **basilica and synagogue complex** dating to the fifth century AD. The remnants are pretty scanty, though archaeologists did unearth impressive mosaics here, which are regrettably not on display. There's also a small stretch of the old castle wall running along the eastern edge of the site.

Just down the street, tucked away in a little park behind the *Mr Chef* restaurant, is a small bust of Hillary Clinton. It was placed here in 2016, in recognition of the former US Secretary of State's support for Albania in the international arena.

Saranda Bunker

Rruga e Flamurit • Free

Outside the *Diamond Hotel* is a typical example of the concrete **bunkers** that can be found all over Albania. Pop down through the staircase to the edifice's left-hand side to look through the doorway, and you'll see a poster that acts as a handy cut-out-and-keep guide to the various types of bunker scattered across the country.

Lëkurësi Castle

Off Rruga Skënderbeu • Free • Best reached by taxi

The old **Lëkurësi Castle** (Kalaja e Lëkurësit) above Saranda has been converted into a restaurant with an enormous terrace boasting stunning views across the city, the lagoon towards Butrint, and over the sea to Corfu. It's an excellent spot for a sundowner, or simply to come up to admire the panorama.

DAY-TRIPS TO CORFU

Saranda's proximity to Corfu and the existence of frequent fast ferries between the two means that you could easily take a day-trip over to the Greek island.

PRACTICALITIES

Ferry tickets can be bought online or at the port. Passport control on arrival in Corfu can be a bit of a free-for-all; position yourself near the boat's exit and be prepared to move quickly if you're in a rush. Remember that Greece is in a different time zone to Albania, so you will lose an hour when you reach Corfu and regain it when you return to Albania. It'll take you about half an hour to walk from the port to Corfu's old town, or you could take bus No. 15. Taxis are also easy to pick up.

SIGHTS

Corfu's **old town** is a pretty little place, packed with cobbled alleyways draped in bougainvillea, which rewards aimless wandering and frequent stops at tavernas. You'll likely eventually make your way to the **Old Fortress** (https://visit.corfu.gr/sights/old-fortress), which occupies the easternmost spit of land: it's a sprawling fortification that warrants exploration. Make sure to head to its summit for great views over the town and sea. Nearby, the **Archaeological Museum of Kerkyra** (https://tinyurl.com/32p6y4bj) boasts a wealth of artefacts from Corfu's ancient past, and a little way north is the outstanding **Corfu Museum of Asian Art** (www.matk.gr), housed in a lavish palace originally designed to be the home of the British High Commissioners of the Ionian islands.

Monastery of the Forty Saints

Off Rruga 40 Shenjtorët, Gjashta • Charge • Best reached by taxi

On a hill above town, you'll find the ruins of the **Monastery of the Forty Saints** (Manastirit të 40 Shenjtorëve), which was built in the sixth century AD. The Greek translation is *Iera Moni ton Agion Saranta Martyron*, from which Saranda's current name is derived.

Clearly once a religious establishment of some size, it is now largely reduced to rubble following British bombardment during World War II and subsequent demolition during the communist era.

The external remnants are picturesque, and if you have a torch you can venture into the dark inner sanctum in the heart of the monastery: the arched entrance is not immediately obvious but sits opposite an enclosed copse of pine trees. It's a good spot to visit at sunset for lovely views over the city below.

ARRIVAL AND DEPARTURE — SARANDA

By bus Most buses arrive and depart from the bus terminus on Rruga e Flamurit, near Friendship Park (Parku Miqësia), which is nice and central.

Destinations Gjirokastra (2 daily); Himara (2 daily); Ksamili-Butrint (every 30min); Tirana (7 daily); Vlora (2–3 daily).

By ferry Corfu is just a short hop across the water from Saranda, and numerous ferries ply the route with multiple daily sailings, taking between 30min and 2hr. Among the operators are Finikas Lines (www.finikas-lines.com) and Ionian Seaways (www.ionianseaways.com). Tickets are most easily bought online, but you can also pick them up at the offices at Saranda's port.

By car The SH8 from Vlora reaches a roundabout in the village of Gjashta just outside Saranda, from which you can head towards the coast to enter the town itself along a busy road that runs steadily downhill and arrives at another roundabout, where the usual rules of traffic are regarded as guidelines at best. From here, depending on where you're staying, you can enter Saranda's one-way system along Rruga Onhezmi or head to the strip of hotels south along Rruga Butrinti.

GETTING AROUND

Saranda is small enough that most places can be reached on foot, though you could make use of the Ksamili-Butrint bus to travel in and out of the centre if your accommodation is along Rruga Butrinti heading south. Self-drivers will have few problems, though the one-way system can get slightly confusing, and parking is a challenge. Don't be tempted to park in taxi ranks to nab a good spot at the beach: the police are free and easy with fines.

INFORMATION

Saranda's small tourist information office (Rruga Skënderbeu) can be found opposite the Basilica and Synagogue ruins. The team can supply town maps and details about Saranda's attractions as well as onward travel. Online, both the official Saranda tourism website, www.saranda.al, and www.visitsaranda.net are excellent resources, with extensive coverage of tourist sites in Saranda and the surrounding region, plus events listings, restaurant recommendations and a wealth of practical information.

6

ACCOMMODATION

SEE MAP PAGE 257

There's no shortage of accommodation in Saranda, but some of it is pretty shabby, and it's worth being a little cautious of apparent bargains. Note, also, that hotels along the promenade may offer lovely sea views, but they're also often noisy, given the music and general party atmosphere on the seafront in the evenings. Between October and April, some hotels and restaurants close, as elsewhere on the riviera.

Austin Boutique Rruga Ismail Qemali; tel: 069 292 3208. The stylish minimalist rooms in this small hotel are clean, comfortable, good value and come with a warm welcome. It's in a quiet part of town so your sleep should be undisturbed by the partying along the seafront. Breakfast not included. €€€

Julia Hotel Rruga Bilal Golemi; tel: 069 945 6767. Well situated a block back from the main coastal road, just south of the eastern end of the beach, *Julia Hotel* offers smart and spotless rooms, some with sea views. There's also a small swimming pool if you've had enough of saltwater, and as an added bonus, breakfast is taken on the roof terrace overlooking the bay. €€€

LaFe Boutique Rruga Mitro Dhimetrika; www.lafehotel.al. An excellent hotel, on a quiet side street just off the promenade, *LaFe* has just five rooms, all decorated in classy muted colours. It's something of a rarity in Saranda, as it occupies an older house, rather than being a purpose-built hotel, so it has more character than many. The breakfast is top-notch. €€€€

Relax Mea Rruga Idriz Alidhima 72; www.relaxmeahotel-saranda.com. A good budget choice, with clean and well-kept rooms, some offering views down to the sea. It's out along the road to the west, about a twenty-minute walk to the promenade. There's a good fish restaurant underneath the hotel if you don't fancy straying too far for dinner. €€

Saranda Backpackers Rruga Mitat Hoxha; https://saranda.inn.fan. A sociable, friendly and well-located hostel which can arrange trips out to Butrint, the Blue Eye or any other destination around Saranda. A great place for solo travellers to meet. €

EATING

SEE MAP PAGE 257

La Banana Rruga Ismail Tatzati; tel: 069 849 0419. Just off the seafront on a quiet side street, *La Banana* is set in a lovely little garden packed with – what else? – banana trees. It has an extensive menu, with a particular emphasis on locally sourced seafood: it's a good place to try Butrint mussels or eels, for example, or you could go for the frogs' legs from the nearby Bistrica River. €€

Limani Rruga Jonianët; tel: 08 522 5858. *Limani* is a longstanding fixture on Saranda's seafront, occupying a perfect position on the harbour arm. Despite a slightly odd policy not allowing people to eat on the prime waterside seating area – reserving this section for drinks only – it's still a good choice, offering the usual array of seafood, grilled fish, pizzas and pastas. €€€

Manxurane Rruga Butrinti; www.mydigitalinovation.com/menu/manxurane-restaurant. One for a bit of a splurge, *Manxurane* is an upmarket restaurant with a marvellous array of local seafood – the Butrint mussels are excellent – as well as a vast menu of delicious meaty options, including rabbit cooked in honey, white wine, herbs and spices. There's also what has to be Saranda's best selection of Albanian wines to pair your chosen dish with. €€€€

Oda e Babës Rruga Lefter Talo; www.facebook.com/odaebabes. A far cry from Saranda's glitzy seafront options, *Oda e Babës* is decorated as a traditional Albanian home – with a menu to match. Start with a sharing platter of delicious appetizers, then choose from the regularly changing main courses that might include moussaka, grilled fish or beef stew. There's sometimes live traditional music to add to the experience. €€€

Summer Shëtitorja Naim Frashëri; www.summer-restaurant.al. On the eastern end of the seafront, *Summer* is a popular and friendly restaurant specializing in fish and seafood, though meat, pizza and pasta are also on offer. Try to snag one of the side tables on the upper terrace to enjoy views over the beach and the happening promenade. €€€

Tako Taco Rruga Sali Çeka; https://tinyurl.com/5n8c8c6e. Here's an unexpected find: a small place serving delicious and authentic Tex-Mex tacos on a rather unlikely side street a few blocks up from the front. It also has a fine range of classic and flavoured margaritas, so if you're searching for something a little different from the usual Albanian fare, this is a good choice. €

Taverna JoAn Rruga Mitat Hoxha; tel: 069 232 3239. A friendly little spot just up from the port, making it ideal for breakfast if you've just stumbled off the ferry from Corfu. The yoghurt and honey is an excellent choice. €

DRINKING

SEE MAP PAGE 257

Blue Moon Bar & Crêperie Rruga Skënderbeu; www.facebook.com/Blue.Moon.Bar.Creperie. A friendly place that successfully combines the roles of coffee shop, bar and crêperie, *Blue Moon* is just off the seafront and offers a relaxed spot to have a drink or a light lunch. In case you missed the name, there's a large picture of a bright blue moon on the wall.

Jericho Cocktail Bar Shëtitorja Naim Frashëri; www.jerichorooms.com/jerichococktailbar. Of the many cocktail bars lining the seafront, *Jericho* is arguably the best. The concoctions are well made, reasonably priced and, in many cases, quite imaginative, and the staff are welcoming and friendly. Okay, the music's perhaps a little loud, meaning you wouldn't want to be staying in a hotel anywhere nearby, but if your night is just getting started, *Jericho* can't be faulted. Try to score a seat on the balcony bar for prime people-watching over the promenade below.

Old House Rruga Mitat Hoxha; tel: 069 890 7955. A laid-back, effortlessly cool bar with a hippy-ish vibe, the interior of *Old House* looks like a wooden beach hut bedecked with souvenirs accumulated over years of travelling: foreign number plates, coloured cassette tapes, and statues of figures such as the Buddha and Queen Nefertiti.

Vino Vibe Rruga Mitat Hoxha; tel: 068 525 3330. A little way out towards the western end of town, *Vino Vibe* is probably Saranda's most stylish and relaxed wine bar. The pavement seating is on carefully mismatched furniture, wine crates are artfully attached to the wall, and there's an antique television nestled in the corner. There are only a few wines available by the glass, but it doubles as a wine shop with a much wider selection for taking home as a souvenir.

6

DIRECTORY

Banks ATMs can easily be found along the promenade and on Rruga Skënderbeu. If you need a bank branch, try along Rruga e Flamurit.

Hospital Saranda's hospital (tel: 08 522 2312) is pretty central, on the corner of Rruga Onhezmi and Rruga Studenti.

Pharmacies Plenty of pharmacies can be found along Rruga Onhezmi, not far from the hospital.

Post office The post office is conveniently sited on Rruga e Flamurit, just opposite the *Diamond Hotel* and the concrete bunker.

Around Saranda

Most visitors to Saranda make a beeline to Butrint (see page 264), but that's by no means all the area has to offer. If you have your own wheels, heading east from Saranda for a day's exploration will yield a variety of diversions, including the ancient ruins of **Phoenice**, the translucent waters of the **Blue Eye**, and the attractive **St Nicholas Monastery Church**.

Phoenice

Above Finiqi village • Charge

The ancient site of **Phoenice** was first settled in the fifth century BC, and as the likely capital of the Chaonian people it became a town of some importance. After the Roman conquest of the region, however, Phoenice went into decline, though it was still sufficiently prosperous to become the see of a bishopric in the early Byzantine period. Although the ruins are now fairly limited, it's still worthwhile exploring the remains thanks to their commanding position atop a ridge with views in every direction. Interestingly, although Phoenice was abandoned sometime in the sixth century AD, it came back into military service during the communist period and, as a result, the site now spans more than two millennia of usage. The site suffered a fire in July 2024, and at the time of writing, much of the vegetation was burned and black, giving the ruins a slightly apocalyptic feel.

From the car park, head up the slope and turn left at the top, following the path to the end of the outcrop, where you'll find a small surviving section of the **ancient wall**, built with enormous stone blocks. Nearby are fortifications of a far more modern nature: a cluster of communist-era **bunkers** overlooking the valley below. They're all connected by a tunnel, which you can explore if you have a torch and don't mind narrow spaces.

Return to the junction of walkways and pass another bunker and a Roman **water cistern** to reach a plateau on which you can find the bare remains of a third century BC Greek **temple**, which was reworked in the early medieval period into a basilica. From here, take the signposted track down the rather treacherous gravel slope to the scant remains of the **theatre**.

It's thought it could seat up to 17,000 people, an indication of Phoenice's former importance, but there's now very little remaining: the foundations of the stage and the front row of seats are pretty much all there is left to see.

Back at the ridge, you can press on to the remains of a set of ancient residential buildings, which are the last ruins of any substance on the site; although the scarp does continue for some distance further, there's nothing more of particular interest to see.

Gjin Aleksi Mosque

Rruga Rusan, Rusani village • Free

In the village of Rusani is the **Gjin Aleksi Mosque** (Xhamia e Gjin Aleksit), a pretty sixteenth-century complex with a central mosque surrounded by smaller *tyrbes* (tombs). It's most attractive from the outside, but there's pleasant calligraphy round the interior dome, and it's also possible to climb the narrow spiral staircase of the minaret for views over the complex from above.

An entirely different flavour of mosque can be seen in nearby **Bamatati** village: this delightfully space-age gleaming white edifice, with a groovy avant-garde minaret, was built in 2017 by local architect Martin Shameti. It's as interesting as it is incongruous, and is well worth a quick stop.

St Nicholas Monastery Church

Off SH99, Mesopotami village • At time of writing free, but expected to charge when restoration complete

In a pretty setting just outside the village of Mesopotami is the late Byzantine **St Nicholas Monastery Church** (Kisha e Manastirit të Shën Kollit), a very attractive building of brick and stone thought to have been constructed on the site of a much earlier temple. The interior is undergoing extensive renovations, expected to be completed in around 2027, which should restore the medieval frescoes hidden beneath layers of whitewash on the walls. It's still worth dropping by in the meantime, though, to admire the beautiful facade, adorned with several bas-reliefs of mythical creatures: there are a couple to the right of the entrance door, though the more impressive ones can be found if you walk around the church and check out the rear wall.

The Blue Eye

SH99, near Krongji village • Charge

Up in the hills on the road to Gjirokastra is the **Blue Eye** (Syri i Kaltër), a beautiful natural pool formed by the effects of limestone karst stone, which gives the water a stunning turquoise hue as it bubbles up from beneath the surface. It's surrounded by lush tropical vegetation and has an idyllic feel. A viewing platform directly above provides the best vantage point, but there are several other spots from which you can admire the natural wonder: take the rough path from the viewing platform for about five minutes to pass a number of such viewpoints.

The Blue Eye is no secret: it's a very popular excursion from both Saranda and Gjirokastra, and there's a car park which, despite its enormous size, fills pretty quickly, so don't expect to have the site to yourself, especially not on summer weekends. It's accessed by a well-paved path that takes around 25 minutes to walk, or you could opt to hire an e-bike or e-scooter, or take the dotto train (extra charge), which trundles back and forth from the ticket office to the pool. There is a large café near the Blue Eye for refreshments before the walk back. Finally, note that many people flout the no-swimming rule: be responsible and don't join them.

Into the mountains

Dhivri road, off SH97 • Free

For an enjoyable afternoon's exploration in a less touristed corner of Southern Albania, take the road signposted to Dhivri (or Dhivër) off the SH97. As you climb the pretty mountain road, you'll pass numerous points of minor interest, first among them the **St George's Monastery** (Manastiri i Shën Gjergjit), a small cave church built into the rockface. A few kilometres on is the pretty village of **Dhivri**, the main square of which is dominated by an outstanding communist-era monument depicting a huge white hand grasping a red torch bearing the Albanian flag.

About six kilometres further, in the rather rundown village of **Cerkovica**, is another fine communist war memorial. The road becomes a rough gravel track shortly after Cerkovica, but if you have a 4WD, you could press on to check out the attractive churches in the villages of **Malçani** and **Leshnica**.

ACCOMMODATION AND EATING — AROUND SARANDA

Shëna the Farm Mesopotami; tel: 069 690 4387. This conveniently sited restaurant is at the roadside in the village of Mesopotami, making it a sensible stop en route to or from the Blue Eye. The menu's highlights include grilled lamb and chicken, though be aware that service can be very slow. Rooms are also available. €€

Taverna Kamara Dhivri With a lovely flower-filled terrace offering magnificent views over the valley and down to the Butrint lagoon, this small tavern in Dhivri is a great place to stop for a coffee, or for a meal of Greek salad or grilled meat. €€

South of Saranda

The road **south from Saranda** leads towards the archaeological site of **Butrint** (see page 264), but en route there are a couple of stops you could consider making. The little-visited Monastery of St George occupies a lovely hilltop position, while the small resort town of Ksamili makes a potential alternative to overnighting in Saranda.

Monastery of St George

Off SH81 • Free

Accessed from the main road up a signposted gravel track – not suitable for most vehicles – the **Monastery of St George** (Manastiri i Shën Gjergjit) is a large and pretty complex, the centrepiece of which is a church that dates back to the fourteenth century. Inside, faded frescoes adorn the inner chamber, alongside multiple images of St George having his famous difference of opinion with the dragon. The monastery is often kept locked, but the guardian can usually be found nearby and will happily unlock it for you. Even if you can't get in, it's a fine point for views over the sea.

Ksamili

SH81 • Free

Excitable news reports in the early 2020s described **Ksamili** as the 'Maldives of Europe', inspired by its blue waters, sandy beaches and dinky wooded islands dotting the sea. This was perhaps an ambitious label, as Ksamili – though undoubtedly once an extremely attractive place – is regrettably overdeveloped, with a seemingly endless dusty sprawl of average hotels and restaurants, and hopelessly crowded beaches. The boat trips around the nearby islands are enjoyable, but otherwise you're probably better advised to seek out beach time elsewhere.

ACCOMMODATION AND EATING — KSAMILI

6

Castle Hotel Rruga Riviera, Ksamili; www.hotelcastle.al. *Castle Hotel* gets a pass for daring to be different. Instead of the standard, bland architectural style favoured by most hotels in Ksamili, *Castle Hotel* has really gone the extra mile and looks like a small chateau, albeit one designed by someone who'd never seen an actual castle. The rooms aren't as exciting as the exterior, but they are comfortable, and the hotel also offers a decent restaurant and a private strip of beach, so all things considered, you could do worse. €€€€

Oxhaku Rruga Riviera, Ksamili; www.oxhaku-restaurant.al. Most of Ksamili's restaurants serve up similar menus of fish, seafood, pasta and pizza, and while *Oxhaku* doesn't exactly vary that theme, its food is reliably tasty and extremely reasonably priced. The soft-crust pizzas are generously topped, and the grilled fish is lovely. €€

Butrint

Four kilometres south of Ksamili, and an immensely popular day-trip from Saranda, is the fascinating archaeological site of **Butrint**. It's unquestionably one of Albania's highlights, with ruins spanning centuries of occupation, and its importance has been acknowledged by its inclusion on UNESCO's World Heritage List. The wider **national park** (Parku Kombëtar i Butrintit) in which it stands is a wetlands frequented by migratory birds, protected as part of the Ramsar List (www.ramsar.org).

The site is a perfect encapsulation of the faultline between Eastern and Western Europe, having been fought over and developed by every civilization that's had a stake in this region: Greeks, Romans, Byzantines, Angevins, Venetians and Ottomans have all played their part. If you have even the vaguest interest in Albania's history, you'll want to pay a visit.

Archaeological site

SH81, Butrint National Park • Charge • www.butrint.al • Bus every 30min from Saranda or Ksamili

Occupying a strategic spot which allowed the occupants to defend both the Straits of Corfu and the entrance to the large Butrint Lagoon, it's no surprise to learn that **Butrint** was first occupied several millennia ago. There's evidence of habitation dating back to around the eighth century BC, though it seems to have first become an important settlement around the fourth century BC, when the Chaonians – an ancient Greek people – developed it, establishing the **theatre** and the **Sanctuary of Asclepius**. Butrint was subsequently seized by the Romans – under whom, on the orders of **Julius Caesar** and his successor, **Augustus**, it was made into a colony for loyal veteran soldiers – before suffering an earthquake in the third century AD.

BUTRINT LAGOON

The archaeological site of Butrint occupies the western side of the Vivari Channel, a narrow outlet linking the saltwater **Butrint Lagoon** (Liqeni i Butrintit) to the sea. The lagoon is a large body of water, with a surface area of around sixteen square kilometres, and is home to a wide variety of **birdlife**. **Seals** and **turtles** are also not uncommon sightings here. The lagoon is particularly well known for its **mussels**, which are cultivated here and available in many **restaurants** in Saranda and Ksamili. The *Mussel House* (www.facebook.com/@musselhouse.al), off SH81 just north of Ksamili, is the place to try the molluscs – sautéed, fried, in cream sauce, in a *saganaki* preparation (with tomatoes and feta); the outdoor seating terrace hovers directly over the lagoon, with next season's catch burbling up from the rocks beneath your feet.

THE GODDESS OF BUTRINT

Found during excavations in the theatre, the **Goddess of Butrint** is a masterpiece of **ancient sculpture**. Luigi Ugolini, the Italian archaeologist leading the expedition, was so taken with the statue that upon its discovery, he considered that it must depict a goddess. What happened next is not entirely clear: it seems that Ugolini attempted to **smuggle** the sculpture back to Italy but was **caught** in the act, though the Albanian authorities at the time decided to gift the Goddess of Butrint to the Italians anyway. It was returned in 1982, and is now on display in the **National History Museum** (see page 56) in Tirana.

The **Byzantine era**, despite challenges posed by Slavic and Norman invaders, saw Butrint undergoing another surge of growth, with some of the site's most impressive buildings constructed in this period. As Byzantium went into decline, Butrint – and the wider riviera region – came under the control of the Angevins and, subsequently, the **Venetians**, whose expansion in the area brought them into conflict with the burgeoning Ottoman Empire. Butrint became a frontline in the near-constant skirmishes. The result: the Venetians built numerous forts on the site.

Butrint was finally taken for the **Ottoman Empire** by **Ali Pasha Tepelena** (see page 224) in 1798, and it remained part of the empire until Albania's independence in 1912. Archaeological work began in 1928, with expeditions funded by Italy's Fascist government. In the post-war communist period, further excavations were undertaken from 1956 onwards, and the site was inscribed on the UNESCO World Heritage List in 1992.

The site is spread over a large area, so give yourself several hours to explore. The recommended route is clearly marked on signs as you go, and you can also pick up a map at the ticket office.

Toilets are found near the theatre and up at the Venetian castle, and there's also a café on the Acropolis at the top of the site.

Venetian tower

Directly opposite the ticket office stands a blocky **tower**, which dates from the fifteenth century, a period in which the Venetians had occupied Butrint and needed to defend it against the Ottoman Empire. On the opposite side of the river – outside the archaeological site – you can see the larger Venetian triangular fortress (see page 267).

The Sanctuary of Asclepius and theatre

Head between the two columns and follow the path up past souvenir stalls to the **Temple of Asclepius**, which dates back to the fourth century BC; the **theatre**, immediately adjacent, was added to the Sanctuary of Asclepius complex a century later. Take the staircase down into the flooded temple area and cross the wooden bridge into the theatre itself; initially built by the Greeks, it was modified by the Romans in the second century AD.

The Goddess of Butrint statue, the head of which is now on display in Tirana's National History Museum (see page 56), was found here in the 1920s. You can climb the rows of seats to get a good look down at the stage, then return to the main path and peer in at the **Roman baths**, now containing somewhat stagnant water and looking distinctly uninviting.

Around the next corner is the **Roman forum**, a public space built around the first century BC. Once very grand, it was largely destroyed by an earthquake in the fourth century AD.

The Gymnasium and the Triconch Palace

Follow the path around the corner to the **Gymnasium**, a reasonably extensive cluster of Roman remains containing an early medieval basilica which appears to have been converted from an earlier temple. This area is often a little flooded, and you may see small turtles in the water.

At the fork in the path, head right to arrive at the **Triconch Palace**, which started life as a Roman villa in the second century AD before being upgraded into an even more luxurious palace two centuries later. Unfortunately, its riverside location was the grand abode's undoing: as water levels rose, living here became unsustainable, and the residence was abandoned. Even in its now-ruined state, it's clear to see the size and former grandeur of the palace, despite the majority of the remaining walls being just knee-high. A walkway from here runs back to the entrance along the riverfront, but don't take it: there's more to see in the heart of the site. Retrace your steps to the Gymnasium and turn right.

The Baptistery

Next up is one of Butrint's main calling cards: the **Baptistery**. This elegant circular place of worship contains two concentric rings of pillars, arranged around a central pool once used as a baptismal font. Dating from the early Byzantine period, this was a building of considerable ceremonial importance, demonstrated by the presence of a magnificent mosaic on the floor, depicting animals, plants, trees and geometric shapes. Regrettably, the mosaic is usually kept covered; there is at least a picture of it on the information board.

The Great Basilica

Follow the path marked to the **Merchant's House**, which brings you to a stretch of the old **city walls** that line the channel bank. Trace the ramparts until you reach a gateway, which you can pass through to arrive at the substantial remains of the magnificent **Great Basilica**. This once-grand church, built in the Byzantine period and extended further during the medieval era, was the city's main place of worship and the seat of Butrint's bishop.

The enormous main hall was initially floored with a fine mosaic, but this was covered during the medieval expansion work: a corner of the mosaic can still be glimpsed at the eastern end.

The city gates

Exiting the basilica at the western end, take the path through the trees to the waterfront. Turn left and follow the line of the city walls; a Roman aqueduct once crossed the lagoon at this point to supply fresh water to Butrint. Just around the corner is the **Lake Gate**, a Greek-era entrance to the city which is notable for the intricacy with which the stone blocks are fitted together; no mortar was used to secure them.

Continue around the ramparts to reach the **Lion Gate**, built in the Roman era. It takes its name from the bas-relief of a lion carved into the enormous block above the gateway, which was removed from a nearby temple and placed here in the fifth century AD.

The Acropolis and Venetian Castle

At the top of the staircase, take the left turn and head up to the **Acropolis**, which may have been the earlier inhabited area of the site, as far back as the eighth century BC. There are some rarely visited ruins on the hill's summit here, but the principal attraction these days is the coffee shop, which offers welcome – if pricey – refreshments after your exploration of the site. Although not splashy, the Acropolis has been the focus of some of Butrint's most recent excavations. Archaeologists still dig at the ancient city every September or October.

From the café, strike out across the hill to reach the well-preserved Venetian-era **castle**; you can climb its tower for decent views, but otherwise it's most notable for housing the site's small **museum**. Here you'll find an interesting run-through of

Butrint's history, accompanied by a wealth of artefacts discovered on the site, but you're unlikely to want to stay too long, as it tends to get stiflingly hot. A vast ultramodern visitor centre is scheduled to be completed near the site in 2025 or 2026.

From the castle, steps lead down to the theatre, from which you can take the path back to the exit.

Ali Pasha Castle

Vivari Channel • Free, though charge for boat

Boating folk in the Butrint car park can take you on an enjoyable trip up the channel to the **Ali Pasha Castle** (Kalaja e Ali Pashës), built on a defensible island at the lagoon's outlet. Keep an eye out for birds in the marshes as you go, and you may also see fishermen at work catching mussels. The castle itself is a squat little fortification, enjoyable enough but of interest mostly for its location and the novelty of arriving by water. Although it bears Ali Pasha's name, an earlier fort already existed here before he made upgrades.

Venetian Triangular Castle

SH81 • Free

Across the lagoon from Butrint is the **Venetian Triangular Castle** (Kalaja Trekëndore Venedikase), built by the Venetians as part of their efforts to defend their territory from the encroaching Ottomans. The fort is well preserved, and you can scramble around the battlements for decent views of its interior. Access is on the small cable ferry (charge), which chugs back and forth across the channel.

South of Butrint

SH98 • Free

If you've taken the car ferry over to check out the Venetian Triangular Castle and have time to spare, there are a couple of sights to be found by driving a little way south. About six kilometres from the fortress, just outside the village of Xarra, is a **memorial complex** to 2900 Cham Albanians, who were killed in an ethnic-cleansing campaign in the latter years of World War II. About 2.5km further is the village of **Mursa**, where another memorial commemorates Albanians who tried to escape to Greece during the communist years. Below Mursa is a large lake, where migratory birds can sometimes be seen.

FRESCOED ST ATHANASIUS CHURCH

Contexts

History

As is the case with all Balkan nations, Albania's history is a complex tapestry woven by a long list of civilizations. From the Illyrians to the Roman Empire through the Byzantines, Slavs and finally Ottomans, waves of invasion swept in from all points of the compass. During the five centuries of Ottoman occupation, strong nationalist sentiments bubbled beneath the surface. Despite resistance, most notably under celebrated hero Skanderbeg, Albania remained under Ottoman control until the early twentieth century, when the Rilindja movement gained momentum, culminating in the country's declaration of independence in 1912. The twentieth century was a period of political turmoil, from a self-declared monarchy, to Italian and German occupation during World War II and, later, an era of brutal dictatorship under paranoid communist Enver Hoxha. After the fall of communism in 1991, Albania made a shaky transition to democracy, though economic struggles and political instability persisted, as they do to this day.

Prehistory

Archaeologists in Albania have unearthed a wealth of ancient finds with evidence of human activity in the region dating back to the **Paleolithic** period, around 40,000 years ago. This is supported by the discovery of stone tools and artefacts in various caves and open-air sites, including the well-known **Rrëza e Dajtit** near Tirana, Xarra in the south and Mati River caves in the north.

Beginning around 7000 BC, the **Neolithic** period marked significant developments in the region with the emergence of agriculture, animal domestication and permanent settlements. The prehistoric inhabitants of Albania cultivated crops such as wheat and barley and raised livestock, mostly sheep and goats (a practice that continues to this day). Archaeological finds from sites such as Maliqi, Buqeza and Cakrani suggest the existence of organized communities, with fragments of pottery, tools and figurines indicating a settled and complex society.

In the **Bronze Age** (c.3000–1200 BC), Albania's ancient ancestors developed advanced metallurgy, indicated by the discovery of bronze tools, weapons and various pieces of jewellery at sites across the country. Trade routes linked the region to other parts of the Balkans as well as to the Aegean and the Adriatic coast to the north. Albania's strategic location facilitated the exchange of goods and ideas, nurturing cultural connections with other civilizations that existed at that time.

The discovery of *tumuli* (burial mounds) in Southern Albania, such as those near Apollonia and Kamenica, provided fascinating insights into the burial practices and social structures of Albania's Bronze Age communities.

7000 BC

Hunter-gathers have moved through the area for tens of thousands of years; now, agrarian settlements begin to appear around the Korça Plain and Lake Ohrid.

2000 BC

Bronze Age peoples begin to form the tribal societies that eventually rule much of Albanian territory (Illyrians).

7th century BC

The ancient Greeks establish colonies along the Adriatic, including Epidamnos, the future port city of Durrësi.

Enter the Illyrians

The **Illyrians** were an ancient group of tribes who inhabited a vast region stretching across the Western Balkans. Albania was one of the main cores of Illyrian settlement. Over the centuries, the link between the Illyrians and present-day Albanians has been the subject of much academic deliberation, with some theories claiming the Albanians are direct descendants of the Illyrians. This view is by no means universally accepted.

Illyrian tribes of Albania

The Illyrians were not a single, unified nation, but a collection of tribes, each with its own customs and leadership but united by a common language and culture. Ancient Greek and Roman scholars lumped all the groups in the area together and dubbed them the Illyrians, but the people around at the time probably never used a common name for themselves. In the region that is now Albania, the most prominent Illyrian tribes were the Taulantii, the Parthini, the Albanoi and the Dassaretii.

The **Taulantii** were one of the most powerful Illyrian tribes and inhabited the coastal region of what is now Central Albania, including the areas around Durrësi, known in ancient times as **Epidamnos** (the Romans later called it **Dyrrachium**). Coastal settlements made them a force in seaborne trade, and they came into frequent contact with the Greeks, who established colonies along the Albanian coast. The Taulantii are also mentioned in the works of ancient historians such as Herodotus and Thucydides who describe their interactions with other peoples in the region. The **Parthini** occupied territory further inland, particularly the region between the Shkumbini and Mati rivers in Central Albania. They are often mentioned in connection with their struggles against the expanding Macedonian and Roman empires. The **Albanoi** were another Illyrian tribe whose name is often suggested as a potential etymological root for 'Albania'. They inhabited the northern and central parts of present-day Albania, especially around what is now Kruja. The last in the list are the **Dassaretii** who inhabited the southeastern reaches of Albania, bordering the region of Epirus. They were known for their military organization, joining larger coalitions of Illyrian tribes that occasionally banded together to resist outside powers, including Macedonia and Rome.

Economy and society

The economy of the Illyrians in Albania was diverse and included **agriculture**, animal husbandry, **metalworking** and trade. Archaeological discoveries have revealed that they were skilled in working with iron and bronze, crafting weapons, helmets, tools jewellery and ornaments with unique and intricate designs. Their geographic location also enabled maritime trade, as well as commerce with Greek coastal cities such as the afore-mentioned Epidamnos (Durrësi) and Apollonia. The latter was an important Greek colony founded in the sixth century BC. It became one of the most significant trading hubs in the region and played a crucial role in the spread of **Greek culture** and **political influence** among the Illyrians. But it also served as a meeting point for various Illyrian tribes who used the trade routes to their advantage. The cultural exchanges between the Illyrians and the Greeks were significant, though the Illyrians managed to retain their distinct identity. Some of Albania's finest archaeological sites were once substantial Illyrian cities and monuments, including Byllis, Amantia and the royal

229 BC

Rome begins its slow conquest of Illyria, incorporating modern Albania into the Roman Republic and Empire. Augustus Caesar studies at Apollonia in 44 BC

5th century AD

Albania becomes part of the Byzantine Empire. Eastern Orthodox Christianity is the state religion.

Late 14th century

The Ottoman Empire launches its conquest of modern-day Albania.

tombs at Selca e Poshtme, and many of the country's great castles began life as Illyrian hillforts. Socially, the Illyrians had a **hierarchal society**, which included chieftains or kings who wielded significant power over their people. Some of these leaders, such as King Agron and Queen Teuta, played crucial roles in repelling foreign invasion. The Illyrian social structure was relatively egalitarian compared to contemporary cultures such as Rome or Greece, with women sometimes holding prominent positions of power, as seen in the case of Queen Teuta who led her people in wars against the Romans in the third century BC.

Wars with Greece and Rome

Throughout their history, the Illyrians had frequent interactions – both friendly and hostile – with Greek colonies on the Albanian coast, the Macedonians to the east and the Romans from all sides. In the fourth century BC, Philip II of Macedon, father of Alexander the Great, launched campaigns against various Illyrian tribes, bringing some of them under Macedonian control. However, the Illyrians were often able to maintain their autonomy or regain it after periods of foreign domination.

By the third century BC, the growing power of Rome led to ever-more frequent conflicts with the Illyrians. One of the key figures during this time was **Queen Teuta**, the widow of King Agron, who ruled over the Ardiaei tribe. Under her leadership, the Illyrians engaged in piracy along the Adriatic Sea which provoked the Romans to intervene. The subsequent Illyrian Wars (229–168 BC) marked a turning point in Albanian history. Despite initial successes, the Illyrians were eventually subdued by Rome, and the region that is now Albania was gradually incorporated into the Roman Republic and Empire. The Chaonian Greeks, Illyrian contemporaries who thrived south of the Bay of Vlora, were too brought under Roman control.

Illyrians under Roman rule

The Roman conquest did not mean the immediate end of Illyrian identity, but it did trigger profound changes. Illyrian tribes were incorporated into the Roman provincial system, with much of today's Albania falling under the province of **Illyricum**. Roman infrastructure, such as roads and fortifications, was built to secure control over the region. One of the most famous Roman roads, the **Via Egnatia** crossed Illyrian lands, connecting Dyrrachium (Durrësi) to Byzantium (later Constantinople), thus facilitating trade and swift military transport. Roman influence brought about urbanization and the spread of Roman culture, though elements of Illyrian culture persisted for several centuries. The process of Romanization was gradual, with Illyrian customs, religious practices and languages coexisting alongside the official Roman systems (as in many other parts of the Empire). Illyrian warriors became highly valued in the Roman military and several Illyrians rose to prominent positions, most notably emperors **Diocletian** and **Constantine the Great**, who had Illyrian ancestry.

Albania's Illyrian identity

The legacy of the Illyrians in Albania is a matter of ongoing debate among scholars. After the fall of the Roman Empire, new groups such as the Slavs and later the Ottomans invaded and settled in the region, further complicating the ethnic, genetic and cultural landscape. However, some historians and archaeologists argue

1405

Gjergj Kastrioti, aka Skanderbeg, is born in Sina. His resistance to the Ottomans' attempted takeover of Albania makes him the national hero.

1468

Skanderbeg dies and is buried in the cathedral in Lezha. His final resting place is ransacked by the advancing Turks.

1479

The Ottomans complete their conquest of Albanian principalities by capturing Rozafa Castle near Shkodra.

that many of the ancient Illyrian tribes were never fully assimilated or displaced, and they continued to form the basis of the local population. This theory suggests that modern Albanians are, at least in part, directly descended from Illyrian ancestry. Linguistically, Albanian is considered by some academics to be the obvious heir of the ancient Illyrian language, though the evidence for this is circumstantial. Albanian is an Indo-European language with no close relatives, and while many believe it evolved from Illyrian, others argue that it could have originated from Thracian or Dacian, other ancient languages once spoken in the Balkans.

Roman times

Roman Albania refers to the period when parts of modern-day Albania were under Roman domination, from the mid-second century BC until the fifth century AD. During this time, Albania became an integral part of the **Roman Empire**, and the legacies of Roman influence can still be seen in Albania's archaeological sites, architecture, language and culture to this day.

Roman cities

Having subdued the Illyrians, the Romans launched a campaign of urbanization, establishing and expanded several cities in the region. **Dyrrachium** and **Apollonia** became important urban centres, serving as hubs for trade, culture and the military. Dyrrachium in particular became a key Adriatic port, an essential transit point for Roman armies heading east. Apollonia under Roman rule continued to flourish as a centre of learning and culture. It was home to a prominent philosophical school; and Octavian, the future Emperor Augustus, studied in the city. In addition to Dyrrachium and Apollonia, other Roman settlements also played vital roles in the region. Butrint, near the border with modern Greece, had been a Greek colony before coming under Roman control. It became a prominent Roman city, complete with an amphitheatre, temples, baths and aqueducts, much of which can still be seen today (see page 264). Along with Durrësi (Dyrrachium), several of modern Albania's other major cities grew in prominence in the Roman period, including Vlora, Shkodra and Elbasani. However, despite Latin being the official language and Romans commanding trade and politics, the Illyrian people maintained many of their customs and there was a merging of Roman and Illyrian traditions.

Arrival of Christianity

One of the longest-lasting legacies of Roman rule in Albania was the introduction of **Christianity**. By the first century AD, Christianity began to spread throughout the Roman Empire, including in the provinces of **Illyricum** and **Epirus** (now Southern Albania and Northwestern Greece). Roman Albania became an early epicentre of Christian activity, with the establishment of churches and Christian communities.

Dyrrachium and **Apollonia** were important early Christian centres. Bishops from these cities are known to have attended several early church councils, and the region played a role in the spread of Christianity throughout the Balkans. The eventual adoption of Christianity as the official religion of the Roman Empire in the fourth century obviously further consolidated its presence in Albania.

1480s

Many Albanians flee to escape the Muslim Ottomans, some to Italy, where they establish the Arbëresh communities that still thrive today.

1788–1822

Ali Pasha rules over Southern Albania and Northern Greece as Ottoman pasha, creating a near-autonomous entity.

Mid-19th century

Albanians revolt against Ottoman rule three times between 1833 and 1847.

Decline of Roman rule

Roman power began its slow decline in Albania in the late fourth and early fifth centuries, as the Roman Empire faced internal instability and external invasions. The division of the empire into East and West in 395 AD further weakened the western provinces, including parts of Roman Albania. The region became vulnerable to **invasions** by the Visigoths, Huns and later the Slavs, which greatly contributed to the decline of local Roman influence. By the end of the fifth century, much of the Western Balkans had fallen under the control of various barbarian tribes, marking the end of ancient Roman rule in Albania. However, the Eastern Roman (Byzantine) Empire would continue to govern much of the region, at least in name, for several centuries.

The Byzantine period

Rome's influence had faded by the fifth century AD and from then until the fall of Constantinople in 1453, Albania fell under the pull of the Byzantine Empire. The capital of the Eastern Roman Empire, Constantinople inherited the territories that comprised the modern-day Balkans after the division of the Roman Empire in the late fourth century. Due to its geographical location Albania became a frontier region, exposed to both Byzantine and external influences, especially from the Southern Slavs surging into the Balkans.

During the early Byzantine period, Albania was part of the provinces of **Epirus Nova** and **Praevalitana**. These areas were part of the empire's larger Balkan defence system designed to ward off invasions by Slavic tribes. The coastal cities of Albania, in particular **Durrësi**, remained strategic points in both trade and military operations. Durrësi was one of the most important ports in the region and served as a gateway for trade and military campaigns across the Adriatic, linking the Byzantine Empire with Italy and the broader Mediterranean world.

Byzantine influence

The Byzantine bureaucracy was highly centralized: the regions of Albania were governed by local Byzantine officials who answered directly to the emperor in Constantinople. These officials were responsible for maintaining military defences, collecting unpopular taxes and ensuring the local population remained 'loyal'. However, as a frontier, Albania was often subject to competing influences, which sometimes made direct rule from relatively distant Constantinople complicated. On the other hand, Emperor Anastasius I was born in Durrësi, reigned for three decades and tremendously enriched the city. A key feature of the Byzantine reign was the sprouting of Christianity. Albania had already been Christianized by the Romans, but it was under Constantinople that **Orthodox Christianity** put down roots in the region. Byzantine clergy played a crucial role in overseeing ecclesiastical affairs in Albania, building churches and promoting customs. This religious influence left a lasting legacy, with the Orthodox Church remaining a significant institution throughout the Ottoman era.

Military significance and conflicts

Albania's mountainous terrain and strategic coastal cities made it a **military hub**. It was often used as a base for Byzantine operations against Slav, Avar and, later,

1878	**1887**	**Late 19th century**
The League of Prizren is established to protect Albania's integrity and potential nationhood.	The first secular Albanian-language school opens in Korça, though some religious academies in the north had previously taught in Albanian.	The Albanian National Awakening, the *Rilindja*, sparks a cultural renaissance, a surge in national pride and a clamouring for independence.

Norman invasions. The **Via Egnatia**, the Roman road that crossed Albania, was vital for the movement of troops and goods between the western and eastern parts of the Byzantine Empire. In the ninth century, the **Bulgars**, a rising power in the Balkans, frequently clashed with the Byzantines over control of Albania. The Byzantine-Bulgar wars resulted in periods of shifting power, with parts of Albania falling under Bulgar influence for a time. However, Constantinople reasserted dominance during the reign of **Emperor Basil II**, known as the 'Bulgar Slayer', in the early eleventh century.

His military campaigns re-established Byzantine dominance in Albania and much of the Balkans. In the eleventh and twelfth centuries, Albania experienced a new wave of invasions, this time from the **Normans** from southern Italy. The Normans, under leaders such as feared warlord Robert Guiscard, sought to expand their influence into the Byzantine-held territories of the Adriatic. Durrësi was a prime target due to its wealth and strategic location and it was captured and recaptured multiple times during the Norman-Byzantine conflicts. Despite these challenges, Byzantine influence remained strong until the empire began to decline in the thirteenth century.

Decline of Byzantine control

By the late twelfth and early thirteenth centuries, the Byzantine Empire began to lose its grip on Albania. Internal strife, including civil wars and power struggles in Constantinople, weakened the empire's ability to defend its frontiers. The **Fourth Crusade** in 1204 dealt a major blow to the Byzantine state, as Constantinople itself was captured by the crusaders, leading to the establishment of the Latin Empire.

In the power vacuum that followed, Albania became a battleground for competing local and foreign powers. The **Despotate of Epirus**, a successor state of the Byzantine Empire, established control over parts of Southern Albania, while the **Serbian Empire** under Stefan Dušan – AKA Dušan the Mighty – conquered Northern Albania during the fourteenth century. Local Albanian leaders also began to assert more autonomy during this turbulent period, often playing larger regional powers against each other.

Byzantine cultural legacy

Despite the political instability, Byzantine cultural and religious influence continued to shape Albania. The **architecture** of churches and monasteries in Albania during this period reflects Byzantine styles, and many religious texts and liturgical practices followed the **Byzantine Orthodox tradition**. The use of Greek as a ceremonial language further welded Albania to the Byzantine world. Byzantine artistic traditions, such as **iconography**, also left a deep imprint on Albania. Many surviving icons from this period are of Byzantine origin or are heavily influenced by the period's artistic conventions. The Orthodox Christian identity that thrived under Byzantine rule continued to play a role in Albanian society throughout the Ottoman reign, even as Islamic influences began to take root. The current Albanian Orthodox Church was established not long after independence, in 1922.

Conquest by the Ottoman Empire

The conquest of Albania by the **Ottoman Empire** was a gradual process that unfolded over several decades, starting in the late fourteenth century and culminating in the early

1909

Edith Durham publishes *High Albania* about her travels in the north.

1910

Ethnic Albanian Mother Teresa is born in Skopje, now North Macedonia, then part of the Ottoman Empire.

1912

Following more uprisings against the Ottomans, while much of Albania is occupied by Greece and Serbia, Ismail Qemali declares Albanian independence on 28 November.

WHY IS KOSOVO NOT PART OF ALBANIA?

Despite having a mostly Albanian-speaking population, Kosovo is not part of Albania. An important piece in the jigsaw of Serbian national identity due to its historical importance in the medieval Serbian Kingdom and its role in Serb resistance to the Ottomans, Kosovo became part of Serbia when the Turks left the region, and then part of Yugoslavia. When the Serbian state removed Kosovo's autonomy and brutalized the local Albanian population in the 1990s, Kosovan Albanians resisted, eventually forming their nation in 2008, a country recognized by most of the world. The decision not to join Albania was part of a move to preserve regional stability. However, Kosovo and Albania enjoy perhaps the closest link of any two states in Europe and share everything from pop singers to groceries.

sixteenth century. Albania's strategic location on the Adriatic Sea, close to Italy and at the crossroads between Europe and the Ottoman territories in the Balkans, essentially placed it in the crosshairs. So the Ottomans unleashed a series of military campaigns and political manoeuvring, all of which met with fierce resistance from local leaders and most of the Albanian populace.

Early Ottoman campaigns

The Ottoman Turks began their incursions into the Balkans in the late fourteenth century. The first significant advances into Albania occurred after the pivotal Battle of Kosovo in 1389, which allowed the Ottomans to consolidate their hold over much of the Balkans. By the early fifteenth century, the Turks had secured a foothold in parts of Albania, especially the south and east, seizing some territories and demanding tribute from local leaders. At this time, Albania was fragmented into a number of small principalities and feudal lordships. These regional rulers, such as the Thopia, Muzaka, Balšić (or Balsha), Zenebishi, Dukagjini and Kastrioti noble families, often fought among themselves for control and this internal strife made it much easier for the Ottomans to exert their influence.

Some Albanian leaders initially submitted to the Turks and agreed to pay tribute in exchange for being allowed to maintain their local authority. Others resisted, sparking a spate of imperial military campaigns aimed at bringing the entire region under direct control.

The rise of Skanderbeg and Albanian resistance

The most legendary chapter in the Ottoman conquest of Albania centres around the figure of Gjergj Kastrioti, better known as **Skanderbeg** (Skënderbeu or Skënderbej in Albanian), the Albanian national hero whose statue dominates the main square in Tirana named in his honour (see page 56). Skanderbeg was taken hostage by the Ottomans as part of the *devşirme* system, a practice where Christian boys were forcibly removed from their families, converted to Islam, and trained as soldiers or administrators. Skanderbeg was trained in the Ottoman military and rose to a high rank, but in 1443, during a campaign in Hungary he defected and returned to Albania. He renounced Islam, reclaimed his family's ancestral lands and initiated a celebrated rebellion against the Turks.

1913

The London Conference of the Ambassadors delineates the borders of the newly independent Albania, leaving many Albanians outside the country. This is still a source of problems to this day.

1914–1918

The new state is plunged into chaos by the outbreak of World War I, with neighbours carving up the country once again.

For the next 25 years – from 1443 until 1468 – Skanderbeg led one of the most sustained and successful resistances to Ottoman expansion in the Balkans. Under his leadership, the **League of Lezha**, a confederation of Albanian nobles, fought off numerous Ottoman invasions. Skanderbeg's forces, using guerrilla tactics and taking advantage of Albania's mountainous terrain, repeatedly defeated larger and better-equipped Ottoman armies. His defiance of the empire earned him the support of several European powers, including the Papacy and the Kingdom of Naples, which viewed him as a bulwark against Ottoman (read: Muslim) expansion into Western Europe.

Despite many famous victories over imperial forces, Skanderbeg's rebellion could not be sustained after his **death** in 1468. Without his leadership, the Albanian resistance weakened, and many local leaders who had followed him either submitted to Ottoman rule or fled. The Ottomans gradually regained control of Albanian territory, and by 1479 they captured the last major stronghold of resistance, Rozafa Castle near Shkodra.

Final conquest and consolidation

After the fall of Shkodra, the conquest of Albania was effectively complete. However, unrest continued in the region under Turkish rule, and rebellions occasionally flared up. The Ottoman authorities implemented measures to secure their control, including the resettlement of loyal Muslim populations, the construction of fortresses and the appointment of Ottoman officials to administer the region. Over time, Albania became fully integrated into the **Ottoman Empire**.

Albania under the Ottoman Empire

Once Albania was incorporated into the Ottoman Empire, it was organized into several administrative units called *sanjaks*, which were part of larger provinces known *eyalets* or *pashaliks*, and later as vilayets. The local **Albanian nobility**, many of whom nominally converted to Islam, were often integrated into the Ottoman ruling class, allowing them to retain local power and influence. Some of these families would go on to play significant roles in politics and the military, with Albanians serving as high-ranking officials, including grand viziers, in the Ottoman government. In the eighteenth and nineteenth centuries, the powerful *pashaliks* of Shkodra, Berati and Janina flexed a great deal of autonomy, and all were governed by Albanian pashas. Ali Pasha of Tepelena, ruling from Janina, was perhaps the most famous, openly rebelling against Istanbul.

Many ordinary Albanians also converted to **Islam**, both as a way to avoid heavy taxation on Christians and to gain access to greater opportunities within the Ottoman administration. By the sixteenth century, a large proportion of the population had embraced Islam, and Albania became an important and compliant province within the empire. Bektashism, a Sufi order that permitted drinking, dancing and less structured worship, gained a foothold as a natural choice for converts. By the nineteenth century, the majority of Albanians were Muslim, although sizable Christian communities – both Catholic and Orthodox – remained.

Social and cultural impacts

Ottoman rule brought significant changes to Albanian society. The Ottomans introduced new social hierarchies, legal systems and institutions. The **millet system**,

1920

Tirana becomes the capital of Albania despite other cities such as Durrësi and Shkodra being more developed centres.

1920

Albania's first theatre opens in Shkodra.

1925

Ahmet Zogu becomes president following two years as prime minister, a brief period of exile and a reclamation of Tirana by force.

IS ALBANIA A MUSLIM COUNTRY?

Well, yes and no. Albania is, barely, a majority-Muslim country, but it is known for its secularism and religious tolerance. Just over fifty percent of Albanians identify as Muslim, with the majority being Sunni, and a smaller proportion adhering to the local Bektashi order. However, Albania has a history of religious diversity, including significant Orthodox Christian and Roman Catholic communities. The country's secular policies ensure that religion does not play a dominant role in public life or governance. Under the communist regime from 1946 to 1991, Albania was officially declared an atheist state, a fact that has had a lasting influence on religious observance.

which allowed religious communities to govern themselves in matters of certain laws, enabled Christians and Muslims to coexist relatively peacefully, though social divisions remained. Islam became a major component of Albanian identity, though it did not erase earlier Christian and folk traditions entirely.

Albania's cities, such as Shkodra, Berati and Gjirokastra, were transformed under Ottoman rule, with the construction of bazaars, mosques, bridges, paved roads and public buildings that reflected the Islamic style of **architecture** across the empire. The Ottoman legal system based on **Islamic law** became the framework for governance, though local customary laws, especially in rural areas, remained influential.

The rise of Albanian nationalism

By the nineteenth century, the Ottoman Empire began to weaken, and independence movements were spreading across the Balkans. In Albania, nationalist sentiments were growing, spurred on by a desire for greater autonomy, resistance to the centralizing Ottoman state and the efforts of similar movements across Eastern and Central Europe. Established in 1878, the **League of Prizren** was one of the first significant expressions of **Albanian nationalism**. The league sought to protect Albanian lands from being divided among neighbouring Balkan states and demanded greater recognition of Albanian autonomy within the Ottoman Empire.

During this period, the Ottoman administration was also engaged in efforts to modernize and reform the empire, a package of measures known as the **Tanzimat**. These reforms, which aimed to centralize authority and create a more uniform system of governance, often conflicted with the the self-determination previously enjoyed by local Albanian leaders.

As a result, simmering tensions between the Ottoman state and Albania bubbled to the surface.

Independence and the end of Ottoman rule

Albania's path to independence was shaped by both internal and external factors. The weakening of Ottoman authority in the Balkans, coupled with the rise of Albanian nationalism and the geopolitical interests of European powers, set the stage for Albania's eventual break from the Ottoman Empire. The **Balkan Wars** (1912–1913) in which the Ottoman Empire lost most of its European territories triggered Albania's declaration of independence.

1928

Ahmet Zogu declares Albania a monarchy and himself King Zog I.

1930s

Albania becomes ever more dependent on Mussolini's Italy, which eventually controls much of the economy.

1939

Italy invades Albania after King Zog I increasingly takes a stance against Mussolini's meddling in the country's affairs. King Zog flees into exile, for good.

The empire ruled Albania for nearly half a millennium, leaving a lasting imprint on the country's political, religious and cultural landscape which can still be felt today. While Ottoman rule introduced Islam and pulled Albania into the broader Eastern world, it also forged a sense of national identity that ultimately stoked the country's struggle for independence in the early twentieth century.

Declaration of Independence

The **Albanian Declaration of Independence** was proclaimed on 28 November, 1912 in Vlora – for Albanians a truly historic event that marked the country's emergence as a sovereign nation for the first time. The pronouncement was driven by a desire to preserve Albanian identity, language and culture, which were under threat from a fragmenting Ottoman Empire and the power-hungry Balkan neighbours snapping at its heels.

The declaration was the culmination of the long process of **Albanian National Awakening**, or *Rilindja*, which had taken root in the mid-to-late nineteenth century. Intellectuals, patriots and leaders from across Albania and the Albanian diaspora began advocating for national unity and independence. The deteriorating situation within the Ottoman Empire, the Albanian revolts of 1910–1912 and the Balkan Wars of 1912 further galvanized the Albanian elite to act.

Under the leadership of **Ismail Qemali,** a prominent Albanian statesman, representatives from various Albanian regions convened in Vlora. On 28 November, Qemali raised the red flag with the black double-headed eagle, symbolizing Albania's independence and its historic links to the medieval national hero Skanderbeg. This act was a clear message to both the international community and Albania's neighbours that the Albanian people were intent on establishing a distinct and autonomous nation state. While the declaration did not immediately result in full recognition by the great powers of Europe, it set the foundation for Albania's eventual establishment as an independent state at the **London Conference of 1912–1913**, also known as the Conference of the Ambassadors. Despite facing immense challenges, including territorial disputes and the threat of partition, the Albanian Declaration of Independence remains a symbol of national pride and resilience. The day (28 November) is celebrated annually as **Albanian Independence Day**. The following decade of turmoil included resistance against land grabs by neighbouring countries and European powers, the formulation of a standardized nationwide written language and the establishment of a capital and parliament in Tirana.

Albania under King Zog I

King Zog I of Albania, born Ahmet Muhtar Bej Zogolli (1895–1961) was a prominent figure in Albanian history and the first monarch of the modern Albanian state, albeit a self-declared one. He rose to power during a tumultuous period for Albania, a country that had just gained independence from the Ottoman Empire in 1912 but was still struggling to establish a stable government and administration.

Zog came from a noble family in Northern Albania and was involved in politics from a young age. In 1920, at the age of just 25 he became interior minister and quickly

1943

Italy capitulates, and Nazi Germany occupies Albania.

1946

After forming a provisional government near the end of World War II, the Hoxha-led communist party declares Albania a People's Republic.

1947

Under pressure from the USSR, Albania turns down participation in the Marshall Plan, an economic aid plan for Western Europe, a mistake with repercussions to this day.

asserted himself as a prominent leader in the political world. He became prime minister in 1922 and, after navigating several political crises, was elected president in 1925. His presidency marked a period of relative stability, but it also revealed his slightly absurd ambitions for more centralized power. In 1928, Zog dissolved the republic, declared Albania a **monarchy** and crowned himself King Zog I.

As self-appointed monarch, Zog attempted to modernize Albania, a country that was still largely rural, poor and underdeveloped. He introduced legal reforms, improved infrastructure and encouraged economic development. However, his reign was also stained by **authoritarianism** – Zog relied heavily on his personal power and a loyal police force to maintain control. He faced opposition from various factions within the country, including republican, ccommunist and tribal leaders, who resisted his centralizing tendencies, and suppressed dissenters brutally.

On the international stage Zog navigated Albania's precarious position between the growing influence of Italy and the geopolitical struggles that were beginning to emerge in Europe. He initially sought to balance relations with both Italy and Yugoslavia, but Italy's influence became increasingly dominant as the years passed. By the late 1930s, Benito **Mussolini's Italy** wielded enormous control over Albania's economy and military.

Zog's reign came to an abrupt end in 1939 when Mussolini's forces invaded Albania. With little support from the global community, Zog was forced to **flee into exile** with his family. After leaving Albania he lived in various countries, including Britain and Egypt, but he was never again in a position to regain his throne. His efforts to return to power after World War II were thwarted by the establishment of a communist regime under Enver Hoxha in 1946. King Zog died in exile in France on 9 April, 1961. Despite his controversial rule, he is remembered as a symbol of Albania's early struggles for national identity and sovereignty.

Albania during World War II

During **World War II**, Albania played a significant role in the way the conflict played out in the Balkans, despite the country's relatively small size. Albania became a theatre of **resistance** against foreign occupation, enduring a complex web of political, military and social challenges. Albania's experience during the war was marked by **fascist occupation**, opposition and the eventual establishment of a brutal **communist regime**.

Italian occupation (1939–1943)

Albania's strategic location on the Adriatic Sea made it attractive for Italian expansionism, and **Mussolini** saw its occupation as a means to bolster his empire and demonstrate power as he sought to match Adolf Hitler's ambitions in Europe.

With King Zog I in exile, Albania was swiftly absorbed into the Italian sphere of influence. It became a protectorate of Italy, and **Victor Emmanuel III** of Italy was proclaimed King of Albania. The Italian government set up a puppet regime, placing pro-Italian Albanian leaders in power. Despite Italian promises of modernization and integration, the Albanian people were largely resistant to foreign control. While some collaboration existed, especially among the elite who benefited from Italian

1961	**1966**	**1968**
Albania breaks with the Soviet Union and turns to communist China for economic support.	Llogara, Mount Dajti, Thethi, Butrint and the Lura Lakes become protected natural areas, effectively Albania's first national parks.	Albania leaves the Warsaw Pact in protest at the Soviet-led invasion of Czechoslovakia.

patronage, many Albanians resented the loss of sovereignty, and Italian cultural domination. Notably, they assisted Jews fleeing other parts of Europe, in defiance of the Axis government. The situation grew worse when Italy, seeking to use Albania as a springboard for further territorial expansion, launched an ill-fated invasion of Greece in October 1940 from Albania. The Greek army successfully repelled the Italians and even pushed into Southern Albania, humiliating Mussolini's regime. It was only after German intervention in 1941 that Greece fell, and Albania once again came fully under Axis control.

Resistance and German occupation (1943–1944)

As World War II progressed and Italy's doomed military ambitions fell away, Albania opened up as a hotbed of resistance. Two major factions emerged in opposition to the Axis powers: the **National Liberation Movement** or LANÇ (Lëvizja Antifashiste Nacional-Çlirimtare), which was a communist-led group, and the **National Front** (Balli Kombëtar), a nationalist organization that sought to create a Greater Albania by uniting all Albanian-inhabited territories, including parts of Kosovo and Macedonia.

Under the leadership of **Enver Hoxha** and supported by the **Communist Party of Albania**, the LANÇ grew in strength as it received backing from the Allies, most notably the British. The LANÇ was highly organized and effective in guerrilla warfare, particularly in the mountainous regions of the country. The National Front, on the other hand, initially cooperated with the Italians and later the Germans in the hope of achieving nationalist goals, but their collaboration eroded popular support.

Once Italy had capitulated to the Allies in 1943, Albania fell under **Nazi control.** Hitler looked to exploit internal divisions within the Albanian resistance and established a nominally independent Albanian government, hoping to use the country as a buffer zone against advancing Allied forces in the Balkans. However, the LANÇ refused to cooperate with the German occupiers and continued its guerrilla campaign, intensifying attacks on both German forces and Albanian collaborators.

Throughout 1943 and 1944, the communist partisans of the LANÇ clawed control over the countryside. By the end of 1944, they were in a strong position as German forces began to retreat under pressure from the advancing Soviet and Yugoslav forces. The LANÇ eventually emerged as the dominant force, thanks to its military successes and its ability to capitalize on fervent anti-Nazi sentiment.

The rise of communism

By November 1944, the partisans had liberated most of Albania without the need for direct Allied military intervention. Enver Hoxha and the communist leadership seized control of the government and Albania was declared a **People's Republic** in 1946. The post-war period saw the establishment of a Stalinist **dictatorship** under Hoxha, who would rule Albania with an iron fist for four decades until his death in 1985. His regime cooperated closely with the Soviet Union initially, though later broke with the USSR and aligned instead with Maoist China during the Sino-Soviet split.

The communist takeover was accompanied by a brutal crackdown on political dissent, and those who had collaborated with the Italians or Germans were either executed or imprisoned. The National Front and other nationalist groups were disbanded, and Albania became one of the most reclusive and repressive states in Eastern Europe.

1950–1989

The paranoid Albanian communist regime builds tens of thousands of concrete bunkers across the country.

1985

Dictator Enver Hoxha dies and is succeeded by Ramiz Alia. Under his rule communism begins to collapse.

Hoxha's government implemented radical land reforms, collectivized agriculture, and built a centralized economy based on self-reliance, but Albania remained impoverished and isolated from the international community.

Legacy of World War II in Albania

The impact of World War II on Albania was profound. The war not only triggered the end of the country's monarchy but also shaped its political future for decades. Albania's resistance during the war remains a defining point of national pride, particularly the role played by communist partisans in liberating the country. However, the war also set the stage for the rise of a dictatorship that would isolate Albania from the rest of Europe and suppress political freedoms for nearly half a century.

Enver Hoxha and the communist decades

Albania's **communist era**, which lasted from the end of World War II until the early 1990s, was a period marked by extreme political repression, isolation and radical social and economic transformation. This period is chiefly associated with one man, Enver Hoxha, the country's paranoid communist dictator who eradicated opposition and cultivated an atmosphere of permanent fear of threat from outside. The first decade of his rule was characterized by the consolidation of power, the execution of political opponents and the establishment of a one-party state.

Economic and social policies

In the years following the war, the Hoxha regime sought to transform Albania into a **socialist state** through radical economic reforms. The government nationalized all major industries, including agriculture, and herded agricultural workers into ham-fisted collective farms. By the late 1940s, most private property was abolished (Albanians were not allowed to own cars or even chickens), and the economy was centrally planned in the clumsiest of ways. The ruling party focused on heavy industry and attempts at self-sufficiency, often at the expense of consumer goods, agricultural productivity and food in the mouths of ordinary people. Hoxha's government also invested in literacy and education. Significant amounts of attention were paid to teaching and health, resulting in increased literacy rates and some improvements in wellbeing among the populace. However, these achievements came at a high cost. The regime tightly controlled what children were taught, promoting Marxist-Leninist ideology while suppressing dissent and any alternative viewpoints.

Cultural repression and isolation

During the 1950s and 1960s, Albania became increasingly isolated from the West and even from its former communist allies. Hoxha initially aligned Albania with the **Soviet Union**, benefiting from economic and military aid. However, after the death of Joseph Stalin and the subsequent de-Stalinization policies under Nikita Khrushchev, Hoxha **broke ties with the USSR** in 1961. He criticized Khrushchev's approach as revisionist and embarked on a path of ideological puritanism. Hoxha's paranoid regime was also on poor terms with neighbouring Yugoslavia which, under , under Josip Broz Tito, established the Non-Aligned Movement.

1988

The Pyramid of Tirana is built in the capital, initially as a museum dedicated to Enver Hoxha.

1991

The communists allow Albania's first multiparty elections.

THE PARANOIA OF ENVER HOXHA

Albanian communist dictator **Enver Hoxha** had a complex psychological profile shaped by a blend of ideological fervour, acute paranoia and obsessive authoritarianism. His intense devotion to Marxist-Leninist principles and his deeply ingrained distrust of both internal and external forces heavily influenced his leadership 'style'.

Hoxha exhibited strong **authoritarian** tendencies, demanding absolute loyalty from his subordinates and the Albanian people. He fostered a cult of personality where dissent or opposition was met with harsh repression. His leadership was characterized by **paranoia**, particularly after the death of Stalin and Albania's break from the Soviet Union (he saw Khrushchev as a revisionist). In the 1960s and 1970s Hoxha grew increasingly suspicious of both domestic rivals and pretty much all foreign powers. This fear of betrayal led him to sever ties with allies such as Yugoslavia and China, and to implement a repressive regime that purged enemies – real and imaginary – within the state.

His obsessive need for control was reflected in Albania's extreme isolationism, which he justified as a necessity to protect the nation from capitalist and revisionist threats. His insistence on ideological purity displayed an inflexible mindset, unable to tolerate deviation from orthodox Marxism-Leninism. Hoxha's mental rigidity and paranoia created an environment of fear and oppression, where political and personal freedoms were stamped out in the name of safeguarding the 'socialist revolution'. This insularity and his brutal tactics significantly stunted Albania's development, bequeathing a legacy of authoritarianism and economic stagnation after his death.

The cultural landscape in Albania was marked by severe repression. The ruling party controlled all forms of creative expression including literature, art and music. Intellectuals, artists, writers and anyone perceived as a dissenter faced persecution, imprisonment, forced-labour sentences, torture and even execution.

The regime sought to promote unique Albanian identity based on Marxist-Leninist principles, leading to the erasure of cultural diversity and historical nuance, the destruction of monuments and the eradication of religious institutions and expression. Unlike in many other communist countries such as Czechoslovakia and Poland, there was only a very small dissident movement within the country's borders. The most prominent figure to emerge in opposition to Hoxha's regime was the writer, **Ismail Kadare** (1936–2024).

The cult of personality

Hoxha cultivated a strong cult of personality, promoting himself as the embodiment of the Albanian state and its ideology. **Propaganda** portrayed him as an infallible leader and his image was ubiquitous in public spaces. The regime organized huge, North Korea-style rallies to celebrate his leadership and reinforce loyalty to the party. Education systems were infused with reverence for Hoxha, and loyalty to the regime was mandatory for social and professional advancement.

Enver Hoxha died in 1985, leaving a power vacuum. The party limped on for another few years, but as democracy began to put out shoots across Eastern Europe, its days were numbered.

1992

Butrint becomes Albania's first UNESCO World Heritage Site. (The country now has four, including parts of Berati, Gjirokastra and Lake Ohrid.)

1995

Albania joins the Council of Europe as its 35th member.

ALBANIA'S DISASTROUS PYRAMIDS

There are a few countries around the world known for their pyramids – Egypt, Mexico, Sudan… and Albania. In the small Balkan country's case, these were not magnificent stone structures but financial schemes (see page 284) whereby investors were encouraged to recruit members to generate profit. Participants earned money primarily by enrolling others rather than selling products or services. Each level of the pyramid profited from the investments of the new recruits below them but as the scheme expanded, it became increasingly difficult to find interested parties, leading to inevitable collapse. But why did these enterprises have such an impact on the Albanian economy? Because, sadly, around two-thirds of the population lost all their savings.

Fall of communism

The late 1980s marked a turning point for Albania. Economic mismanagement combined with the abandonment of all allies and trading partners led to severe shortages of food and basic goods. By the end of the 1980s, the Albanian people had grown disillusioned with the regime, sparking public marches and calls for reform.

In December 1990, Albania witnessed its first major **anti-communist protests**, fuelled by the wave of democratization sweeping through Eastern Europe. The regime's response was brutal, but the cracks in the system were there for all to see. Amid growing, violent unrest, in 1991 the regime announced **multiparty elections**, leading to the establishment of a **democratic government** and the eventual resignation of Hoxha's successors.

The legacy of communism in Albania is complex and multifaceted. On the one hand, the period resulted in significant advancements in education and health, with notable improvements in literacy and life expectancy. On the other, the oppressive regime left a profound psychological and social impact, characterized by mistrust, trauma and economic hardship. Like all post-communist societies, Albania will need several generations to heal. Unlike people living under other regimes, Albanians had been completely isolated from the culture and influence of the broader world, making the post-communist transition even more disorienting. Many Albanians grapple with the repercussions of decades of isolation and tyranny, while the process of reckoning with the past remains ongoing and, to some extent, incomplete and neglected.

The 1990s

The 1990s marked a transformative decade for Albania as it shifted from rigid communist control to a **multiparty democracy** and unfettered **capitalism**. The events of this period were characterized by political upheaval, economic turmoil and profound social change, much of which gave Albania a reputation for lawlessness it no longer deserves.

Political transition

The **Democratic Party of Albania** or PD (Partia Demokratike e Shqipërisë) emerged as a key player in 1991, advocating for a transition to a market economy and democratic rule of law. In March 1991, Albania held its first free elections in over 45 years; the

1995

Dua Lipa is born in London to Kosovan-Albanian parents. As an award-winning singer, she goes on to be arguably the most famous person of Albanian heritage in the world.

1997

Anarchy erupts as scam pyramid schemes begin to collapse and Albanians lose all their savings. The international community steps in to calm the situation.

second parliamentary elections one year later resulted in a victory for the PD. However, the political environment remained volatile, marked by infighting among political factions and widespread public disillusionment with the slow pace of reform.

Economic challenges

The transition from a centrally planned economy to a market-oriented system posed immense challenges for Albania. The country faced severe economic difficulties, including hyperinflation, rising unemployment and a plunge in living standards. State-owned enterprises were privatized, but the process was often marred by corruption and mismanagement. In 1991 GDP (gross domestic product) contracted significantly, leading to widespread poverty and social unrest.

The collapse of the communist regime also triggered the withdrawal of state subsidies, leaving many Albanians without a safety net. As a result, people turned to informal and often illegal means of survival, including smuggling, black market activities, robbery and worse.

Pyramids and anarchy

The 1990s were marked by increasing social unrest as frustrations over economic hardship mounted. Following the toppling of the communist party, in 1992 the new democratic government was failing to address the rising – and essentially impossible – challenges. This sparked widespread protests and strikes, particularly among workers in formerly state-owned industries.

By the mid-1990s, the situation worsened as **scam pyramid schemes** (see box) promising high returns on investments swept through the country. These ventures attracted millions of naive Albanians, offering hope for financial stability amid economic turmoil. However, in 1997 the schemes inevitably collapsed, leading to massive monetary losses for the population. The resulting economic mayhem ignited protests, culminating in a state of violent and often armed anarchy that engulfed the country.

In March 1997, the government declared a **state of emergency** as riots and worse erupted across Albania. Armed groups seized control of various regions, and the authorities struggled to maintain order. Alarmed by the instability in an already war-torn Balkans, the international community intervened by sending in troops as part of a humanitarian mission to restore peace.

International intervention and reconstruction

The chaos of 1997 prompted global intervention, with the Organization for Security and Co-operation in Europe (OSCE) and NATO stepping in to help stabilize the country. The international community recognized the urgent need for reconstruction and development in Albania, which was on the brink of disintegration. In 1999, during the **Kosovo War**, Albania became a significant place of **asylum** for Kosovo-Albanian refugees, further straining its already-fragile infrastructure. Worldwide aid poured in, supporting both humanitarian efforts and financial recovery.

The Albanian government, under the leadership of prime minister **Fatos Nano**, worked to implement reforms aimed at rebuilding the economy and establishing a more stable political environment.

1999

Around 450,000 Kosovan refugees flood into Albania during the Kosovo War and NATO bombing of Yugoslavia.

2009

Albania joins NATO on 1 April alongside fellow Balkan nation Croatia.

EDI RAMA

Edi Rama (1964–) has served as the **Prime Minister of Albania** since 2013. Educated at the Academy of Arts in Tirana and with a degree in painting from the University of Tirana, he is also known to have played basketball at a high level. Before entering politics, he had established a reputation for his work as a painter and his contributions to the cultural scene in Albania.

Rama began his political career in the late 1990s and was elected **Mayor of Tirana** in 2000. During his tenure he kickstarted several urban renewal projects that transformed the city, focusing on public spaces, infrastructure and the arts. His leadership in this role garnered widespread recognition and laid the foundation for his future political success.

In 2013 Rama led the **Socialist Party** to victory in the parliamentary elections, becoming prime minister in the process. His government has prioritized economic reforms, EU integration and anti-corruption measures. He has also focused on social policies aimed at improving healthcare and education. Rama's leadership style is often described as charismatic and assertive, and he is known for his use of social media to communicate with the public.

Rama has faced criticism for various issues, including media freedom, alleged cronyism and curtailment of political opposition. However, he remains a pivotal figure in Albanian politics, advocating for modernization and European integration.

Culture and emigration

The 1990s also witnessed a cultural renaissance in Albania. The newfound political freedom allowed for greater expression in the **arts, literature and media** for the first time in half a century. Albanian intellectuals, artists, writers and other creatives began to explore themes of identity, history and the experience of living under a repressive regime. Western influence became more pronounced, with an influx of foreign media, music and design.

Youth culture flourished, as a new generation of Albanians embraced alternative forms of expression, including pop music and fashion from abroad. But amid the turmoil of the 1990s, many young Albanian voted with their feet and departed for Western Europe, most notably Italy, the UK and Germany.

Post-millennium Albania

In the past quarter-century, Albania has emerged from post-communist anarchy and found its feet as a relatively stable Balkan state. It is a long way down the road to becoming a member of the EU, with a number of deep-rooted social, political and economic challenges it needs to first address.

At the turn of the millennium, Albania was still grappling with the aftermath of the **1997 financial crisis**, which had led to widespread chaos and political instability. The country transitioned from a one-party state to a multiparty system in the early 1990s, but the issue of political polarization continued to bubble under the surface. The Democratic Party, led by **Sali Berisha**, and the Socialist Party or PS (Partia Socialiste e Shqipërisë) traded power after 1997 and through the 2000s. Leadership was often marred by allegations of **corruption** and mismanagement.

2011

The Albanian women's national football team is established.

2013

Socialist Party leader Edi Rama becomes prime minister, a post he holds to this day.

GHEG VS TOSK

The **Albanian language** is divided into **Gheg** and **Tosk** dialects, each spoken in different regions of Albania and among the Albanian diaspora. Gheg is primarily spoken in the northern regions and Kosovo, while Tosk is the language of the south. They differ in pronunciation, vocabulary and grammar. The Tosk dialect forms the basis of standard Albanian taught in schools and as a foreign language. Despite these differences, speakers of both dialects generally understand each other with no difficulty.

In 2013, the **Socialist Party** under **Edi Rama**, won the parliamentary elections, and Rama's administration focused on anti-corruption measures and public administration reforms, gradually improving governance. This trend continued through 2010s, as Albania made progress in enhancing its democratic institutions. Despite these advancements, political instability persisted, with protests and political crises often challenging the government's legitimacy.

The 2017 elections were significant for Albania, as the Socialist Party secured a strong majority. Rama prioritized economic growth, infrastructure development and European integration. Albania's path towards EU membership gained momentum, with Brussels granting candidate status in 2014 and starting accession negotiations in 2020. However, the process was complicated by various internal and external challenges, including the need for judicial reforms and addressing the rule of law.

Economic transformation

The Albanian economy has undergone substantial changes since 2000. After the financial meltdown of the late 1990s, the government implemented reforms to stabilize the economy and attract foreign investment. The liberalization of trade and investment policies contributed to economic growth. Albania's GDP growth rate fluctuated over the years, but the country generally experienced positive financial trends, particularly in the early 2000s and mid-2010s.

Key sectors driving economic growth included agriculture, tourism and, it has to be said, money sent home from the Albanian diaspora. The government focused on improving infrastructure, including road networks, and enhancing energy production capacity. The discovery and exploitation of oil and natural gas reserves also played a role in boosting the economy. However, challenges remained, including high unemployment rates, particularly among youth, and a reliance on the grey economy (not formally registered, taxed or monitored by the authorities). Corruption and bureaucracy hindered business development, prompting the powers-that-be to continue their efforts to improve the business climate. The World Bank and International Monetary Fund (IMF) provided support and guidance to strengthen economic governance and encourage sustainable growth.

Social challenges

Socially, Albania underwent significant transformations as it integrated into Europe. The rise of civil society organizations and **activism** played a crucial role in advocating for **human rights**, **gender equality** and **environmental protection**. The younger

2016

The first budget airline flight, operated by easyJet, lands at Tirana International Airport Nënë Tereza.

2020

Albania begins accession talks with the EU on full membership.

generation, influenced by globalization and access to information, have become increasingly vocal about their rights and aspirations.

However, social issues persist. High levels of poverty and inequality remain, particularly in rural areas. Access to education, healthcare and civil infrastructure varies widely, with urban hubs experiencing better services than rural regions. The government has made efforts to improve social welfare and access to education, but many citizens are still plagued with economic difficulties.

The issue of **emigration** also still looms large, with many Albanians seeking better opportunities abroad. Brain drain is still a concern, as educated and skilled individuals leave the country, impacting the labour market and economy.

European integration

One of Albania's priorities after the fall of communism has been integration into the Western geopolitical order; NATO membership in 2009 and talks with the European Union (EU) are the result of political determination over the past two decades. The EU integration process has been a primary goal for successive Albanian governments. In addition to gaining candidate status in 2014, the announcement of accession negotiations in 2020 marked a key step in the right direction. The powers-that-be are focused on aligning their laws and regulations with EU standards, particularly in areas such as the judiciary, anti-corruption measures and human rights. However, the EU is not entirely satisfied with Albania's performance and recent spats with Greece have put a spanner in the works. Until 2024, Albania's membership was coupled with that of North Macedonia, but to the relief of many in Tirana, this was ditched as Skopje's negotiations have ground to a halt. There is still no firm date set for Albania to join the EU.

Albania today

In late 2024, political unrest reared its head again when opposition parties demanded the resignation of Prime Minister Edi Rama and the establishment of a caretaker government ahead of 2025's parliamentary elections. Allegations against the ruling Socialist Party of corruption and manipulation of the judiciary sparked the protests. Meanwhile, the Albanian economy is showing mixed signals, with projected GDP growth of around 3.8 percent amid concerns over inflation, particularly when it came to food prices, which disproportionately affect low-income households.

2024

Anti-government protests erupt in Tirana amid allegations of corruption in the ruling Socialist Party.

Books

There are a growing number of books concerning Albania. Travel accounts and histories are particularly well represented, and Albanian culture and society has long had the potential for great stories. There is a smattering of titles on other subjects such as cookery and architecture, but sadly coverage of the region's environment and natural history is sparse.

TRAVEL AND ADVENTURE

Rudolf Abraham *The Peaks of the Balkans Trail.* Cicerone's excellent guide to this long-distance trail that runs through the mountainous areas of Albania, Kosovo and Montenegro is a must if you are aiming to tackle the whole thing or just a section.

Robert Carver *The Accursed Mountains: Journeys in Albania.* Amusing, adventurous and sometimes absurd account of a journey through Albania just after the fall of communism and a fascinating, if often irreverent, snapshot of life in Europe's most isolated country in the early 1990s.

Edith Durham *High Albania.* The classic Albania travelogue by the undeterrable Edith Durham who spent months in Northern Albania documenting the traditional way of life of the locals before it disappeared forever. Published in 1909 and written in the style of the day.

Robin Hanbury-Tenison *Land of Eagles: Riding through Europe's Forgotten Country.* Join Hanbury-Tenison and his wife on an epic horse ride from the mountainous north to the country's southern reaches. Packed with incidents and insights into the Albanians and Albania.

Henry Holland *Travels in the Dominions of Ali Pasha, 1812–1813.* Holland was among quite a few curious young Brits who visited the Epirus region during the *pashalik* era. This slender excerpt is a lively account of a nearly mythical Albania and its legendary ruler, through the eyes of an innocent abroad.

Peter Lucas *Rumpalla: Rummaging Through Albania.* The son of an Albanian, American reporter Peter Lucas was granted a rare visit behind the veil of communist Albania in 1986, and returned repeatedly, collecting tales of rollicking encounters during the Wild West years of the post-communist 1990s.

John Watkins *Enver Hoxha's Long Shadow: Travels in Albania.* Writer John Watkins returns to locations he visited in the late 1980s to document the changes the country has gone through since the fall of communism. An interesting read for those who are perhaps already acquainted with the country and its historical context.

Rose Wilder Lane *Peaks of Shala.* Possibly inspired by Edith Durham, South Dakota-born Wilder Lane also travelled into the mountains of Northern Albania and wrote this book about her journey.

HISTORY AND POLITICS

Robert Austin *Royal Fraud: The Story of Albania's First and Last King.* The tale of Albania's bizarre king, Zog, the self-proclaimed monarch whose reign came to an abrupt end when the Italians invaded just before World War II. Published in 2024, the book examines his rise to power and his short, decidedly lacklustre rule.

Marin Barleti *The History of George Castriot Scanderbeg, King of Albania.* Painstakingly researched biography of Skanderbeg examining his life and heroic deeds. A good read, even for the armchair traveller to Albania. Barleti interviewed eyewitnesses to the events of the book, first published in 1508.

Robert Elsie *Albania in a Nutshell: A Brief History and Chronology of Events.* A concise overview of Albanian history for time-pressed readers, written by one of the leading Western scholars on Balkan history. Elsie also maintained the most comprehensive online English-language resource of Albanian-culture research at www.elsie.de.

Blendi Fevziu *Enver Hoxha: The Iron Fist of Albania.* The first biography of Enver Hoxha available in English, this expertly written book published in 2022 is a must for anyone interested in Albania's decades under authoritarian communist rule.

Colin Imber *The Ottoman Empire, 1300–1650: The Structure of Power.* Recently written study of the Ottoman Empire, examining its rise, structures and administration. At least some of the book deals with the specifics of Albania.

Margo Rejmer *Mud Sweeter than Honey: The Voices of Communist Albania.* This collection of oral histories, published in 2022, gives voice to the repressed during the decades of communist rule. These are stories that needed to be told and are essential reading to truly understand modern Albania.

Miranda Vickers & James Pettifer *Albania: From Anarchy to a Balkan Identity.* Excellent overview of the turbulent 1990s in Albania and the country's painful and often chaotic transition penned by two of the leading writers on the region.

Miranda Vickers *The Albanians: A Modern History.* Dealing with twentieth-century Albania, this is arguably the best book to read for an insight into the turbulent past of this Balkan nation.

Tom Winnifrith *Nobody's Kingdom: A History of Northern Albania.* A very readable history of this until recently isolated region, which has a fascinating past quite different from the rest of Albania.

Tajar Zavalani *History of Albania.* Excellent and concise overview of Albanian history written by one of the most prominent Albanian exiles in London during the decades of communism and edited by leading experts on Albanian history. Only goes up to the communist takeover.

CULTURE AND SOCIETY

Phil Harrison *Inside the Hermit Kingdom: Football Stories from Stalinist Albania.* The history of football in Albania from 1945 to 1991 may not sound like a gripping read, but this 2024 title examines life in communist Albania through the prism of football, one of the only communal outlets people had.

Margaret Hasluck *The Hasluck Collection of Albanian Folktales.* Around a hundred Albanian folktales translated into English by Margaret Hasluck, a scholar who spent sixteen years in Albania before World War II studying archaeological ruins, folk culture and language.

Ismail Kadare *Selected Works.* The most famous of Albania's writers of the late twentieth and early twenty-first centuries, all of Kadare's novels offer fascinating glimpses into Albanian life during the days of communism. Many have been translated into English.

Edward Lear *Edward Lear in Albania – Journals of a Landscape Painter in the Balkans.* Edward Lear is famed for his nonsensical verse, but few know that he was a landscape painter and even fewer are aware that he spent a decade in Albania in the mid-nineteenth century.

Marcus Tanner *Albania's Mountain Queen: Edith Durham and the Balkans.* Published in 2014, Marcus Tanner tells the story of Edith Durham, the British writer and anthropologist who in some respects put Albania on the map. A great read for anyone interested in this obscure but fascinating story of adventure.

FICTION

Robert Elsie *An Elusive Eagle Soars: Anthology of Modern Albanian Poetry.* Albania's great twentieth-century poets are granted fine English-language translations in this volume. The best collection of verse by the likes of Lasgush Poradeci, Ismail Kadare, Martin Camaj, Migjeni, Natasha Lako and others.

Robert Elsie *Classical Albanian Literature: A Reader.* During the *Rilindja* and early independence years, Albanian literature experienced a jubilant golden age. Find the masters in English here: Naim Frashëri, Andon Zako Çajupi, Ndre Mjeda, Gjergj Fishta and more.

Gjergj Fishta *The Highland Lute.* Albania's national epic poem, by one of its greatest verse writers, *The Highland Lute* renders heroic, tragic and poignant the nineteenth- and twentieth-century struggles toward independence.

Ornela Vorpsi *The Country Where No One Ever Dies.* The first novel by the now-acclaimed Albanian author, it's a dark – and darkly funny – ramble through sex, death, disorientation and imagination in a crumbling society that feels inescapable all the same.

FOOD AND COOKERY

Liam Luxe *Albanian Cookbook: Traditional Recipes from Albania.* A traditional cookbook for that post-trip Albanian night with your friends and family.

LANGUAGE

Anila Mayhew *Beginner's Albanian.* Arguably the best crash course in basic Albanian if you want to learn a few phrases before your trip. Albanian is a difficult language for several reasons, but this book does the best job possible.

Language

Albanian is a hard language to learn, the main hurdle being that it doesn't resemble any other language and sits alone in its own one-tongue language group. Acquiring a few niceties is easy enough and welcomed by locals, but when it comes to Albania's complex grammar system, you would have to dedicate years of study to speak any at all. The good news is that in places where tourists gather, English (as well as Italian and German) is now increasingly spoken and most signs you might need to read are bi-lingual at the very least.

The complexity of Albanian comes from its high level of inflection and complicated morphology. Verbs are highly inflected, with conjugations depending on tense, mood, voice, person, and number. There are three main tenses (present, past, future) and various moods, including indicative, subjunctive, and imperative. Nouns in Albanian have definite and indefinite forms and are conjugated according to gender (masculine, feminine) and number (singular, plural). Cases (nominative, accusative, genitive, dative, and ablative) play an essential role in sentence structure. Even if you have studied some of the more complex Slavic languages such as Czech or Ukrainian, some elements of Albanian will still leave you scratching your head… Possibly the best you can hope for is to learn a few "hellos" and "goodbyes" for your trip and fall back on English. Even these will bring a smile to locals' faces and break the ice with older people, for instance, who normally only speak Albanian.

Pronunciation

Albanian pronunciation is mostly phonetic, meaning words are pronounced as they are written. The language has 36 letters, including unique ones like "ë," "xh," and "gj." Stress usually falls on the last or second-to-last syllable. Vowel sounds are clear and distinct, while consonants can have soft or hard variations.

Stress

Usually on the penultimate syllable, eg Warszawa, przyjaciel, matka.

Vowels

a: as "a" in "father".
e: "e" in "neck".
ë: "a" in "sofa" (schwa)
i: "ee" in "see", never as in "I".
o: "aw" in "saw"
u: "oo" in "boot".
y: unknown in Standard English; like "u" in "manicure"

Consonants

b: "b" in "book"
c: "ts" in "cats"
d: "d" in "day"
dh: treated as a single letter – like "th" in "this".

THE ALBANIAN LANGUAGE QUESTION

Albanian is an ancient and unique language, and if you find it frustrating to learn, you may be comforted to know that it caused all kinds of conundrums for the Albanian leaders, intellectuals, writers and educators of the nineteenth and early twentieth centuries who tried to hammer out a standardized, teachable tongue and script. By the nineteenth century, Albanians north of the Lumi i Shkumbinit spoke several dialects of **Gegërishtja** (Gheg), while Albanians south of spoke variations on **Toskërishtja** (Tosk). Those who could write recorded it in Latin, Greek, Cyrillic and Arabic, more or less following the influences of the powers that controlled the regions they lived in. In 1685, **Pjetër Bogdani** published the first lengthy Albanian prose work, *The Band of the Prophets*, mostly using the Latin alphabet and an archaic version of the Gheg tongue; he was from the Prizren area of modern-day Kosovo and worked in Padua, Italy.

By the mid-nineteenth century, Albanian thinkers realized that a written, pan-dialect, pan-religion, single-script language was needed if Albanian stories, values and identity were to survive. Mass education would bolster the feeling of Albanian unity – and the aspiration for an independent Albanian nation. A lawyer named **Naum Veqilharxhi**, from Vithkuqi, invented an **Albanian-language alphabet** whole-cloth, giving no favour to Greek, Latin or Arabic, and published it in 1845. His bespoke script had the right spirit and helped light the fire of Albanian education in the Korça region, even if it proved too cumbersome to catch on. Working in the late nineteenth century, Elbasani-born translator **Kostandin Kristoforidhi**, sometimes called the 'father of Albanian grammar', published the **New Testament** in both Gheg and Tosk, and the first modern dictionary of Albanian. The 1908 Congress of Manastir in what is now Bitola, North Macedonia, popularized a Latin script, and the follow-up Congress of Elbasani led to the widespread expansion of Albanian education, including the **first secondary school** in Elbasani. Bringing prominent Albanians from far and wide together – Gheg and Tosk, Muslim and Christian – these events rightly alarmed Ottoman authorities. Albanian **independence** was just a few years away.

In the centre of Albania, Elbasani spoke the closest thing to a **Gheg-Tosk hybrid dialect**. More language conferences followed independence, and Elbasanas scholar **Aleksandër Xhuvani** argued that his town's version of Albanian was best suited to be the national standard – he won. But the communist leaders who took power after World War II were mostly southerners, and they imposed Tosk across the country for educational and administrative purposes. That's where things stand today, but the thorny debate over language continues.

f: "f" in "fresh"
g: "g" in "girl"
gj: "dj" in "adjust"
h: "h" in house
j: "y" in "yes"
k: "k" in "kiss"
l: "l" in "live"
ll: treated as a single letter – so-called "dark L" like "ll" in "ball"
m: "m" in "man"
n: "n" in "nice"
nj: treated as a single letter – like "n" in "new"
p: "p" in "penny"
q: "t" in "tune"
r: rolled "r" like in Spanish or Czech
rr: treated as a single letter – highly trilled "r". No English equivalent.
s: "s" in "son"
sh: treated as a single letter - "sh" in "ship"
t: "t" in "ten", not aspirated

PLACE NAMES

Note that the dual nature of Albanian nouns – all have definite and indefinite forms – can cause some confusion with place names. In this Guide, we have used the definite form, except in cases where the indefinite is far more widely used in English. Please find below a list of common place names, with their definite and indefinite forms.

Bashtova Bashtovë
Durrësi Durrës
Gjirokastra Gjirokastër
Llogara Pass Llogaraja or Llogarja
Mount Korabi Mount Korab
Saranda Sarandë
Shiroka Shirokë
Tomorri Tomorr
Vlora Vlorë
Berati Berat
Fishta Fishtë
Kanina Castle Kaninë Castle
Lushnja Lushnjë
Peshkopia Peshkopi
Shebeniku-Jabllanica Shebenik-Jabllanicë
Tirana Tiranë
Vjosa-Narta Vjosë-Nartë
Vunoi Vuno

th: treated as a single letter – like "th" in "thick"
v: "v" in "very"
x: "ds" in "ads"
xh: treated as a single letter – like "j" in "jail"
z: "z" in "zoo"
zh: treated as a single letter – like "s" in "treasure"

ALBANIAN WORDS AND PHRASES

BASICS

Hello/Good day Tungjatjeta
Goodbye Mirupafshim
Excuse me Më falni
Yes Po
No Jo
Please Ju lutem
Thank you Faleminderit
How are you? Si jeni ju?
My name is... Emri im është...
How much is…? Sa kushton…?
What time is it? Sa është ora?
I don't understand Unë nuk kuptoj
Do you speak English? A flisni anglisht?
Where? Ku?
Open I hapur
Closed Mbyllur
Today Sot
Yesterday Dje
Tomorrow Nesër
Doctor Mjek
Police Policia

NUMBERS

One Një
Two Dy
Three Tre
Four Katër
Five Pesë
Six Gjashtë
Seven Shtatë
Eight Tetë
Nine Nëntë
Ten Dhjetë

ACCOMMODATION

Guesthouse Bujtinë
Farm stay Agroturizëm
Do you have a..? A keni një..?
Double room Dhomë dyshe
Single room Dhomë teke
Accessible room Dhomë e aksesueshme
I have a reservation Kam nje rezervim
Do you have wi-fi? A keni wi-fi?
What time is breakfast? Në çfarë ore është mëngjesi?

AT THE RESTAURANT

Can I have the menu please? Mund ta kem menunë ju lutem?
What do you recommend? Çfarë rekomandoni?
I am vegetarian/vegan Unë jam vegjetarian/vegan
Can I order please? Mund të porosis ju lutem?
The bill, please Fatura, ju lutem
Do you take card? A merr karton?
White wine Verë e bardhë
Red wine Verë e kuqe

Beer Birrë
Beef Viçi
Lamb Qengji
Chicken Pulë
Fish Peshku
Salad Sallatë
Pizza Picë
Waiter Kamarier
Knife Thikë
Fork Pirun
Spoon Lugë
Salt Kripë
Pepper Piper
Olive oil Vaj ulliri
Dessert Ëmbëlsirë

TRANSPORT AND DIRECTIONS

Car Makinë
Where is? Ku eshte?
Left Majtas
Right Drejtë
Straight on Drejt në
Mechanic Auto servis
Petrol Benzinë
Diesel Dizel
Minibus Furgon
Karrotrec towing service

Glossary

Baba Tomorri The father of gods and humans in Albanian folklore
Bakllava Honey and nut filo pastry
Bashkia Town hall
Byrek Pastry filled with spinach, cheese or meat
Çorbë Rice and milk dessert
Djathë në furrë Baked cheese
Fustanellë Balkan kilt
Gjakmarrje Albanian blood feud
Gliko Fruit preserved in syrup
Kanioni Canyon
Kanun Ancient code of honour
kisha Church
konak Traditional Ottoman-style house
kulaç Soda bread
Kulla Tower house
Lugina Valley
Lumi River
Mali Mountain
Manastiri Monastery
Opingë Leather folk shoes
Parku Park
Passeggiata Evening stroll
Plazhi Beach
Qilim Kilim rug
Raki Fruit brandy
Reçel Jam
Rilindja Albanian National Awakening
Saç Lidded metal pan set over hot coals
Shëndetlie Honey and walnut cake
Sheshi Square
Sufi Followers of an ascetic Sufi Muslim order
Teqe Bektashism house of worship
Tumuli Burial mounds
Tyrbe Tomb or shrine
Ujëvara Waterfall
Ura Bridge
Xhamia Mosque

ON THE MENU: CLASSIC ALBANIAN DISHES

Fërgesë Ricotta-style cheese baked with tomatoes, onions and spices, often with bell peppers, beef or liver
Kadaif Shredded dough with a sweet filling
Kolloface Local sausage made with liver, onion, leek and oregano
Lakror Meat, vegetable or cheese pie
Petka Home-made pasta, dried for days and broken into small pieces, often served with chicken, eggplant or mushrooms
Pispili Spinach and leek pie spiked with mint
Pite Layers of pastry filled with pumpkin or apple
Qifqi Fried rice ball
Salcë kosi Yoghurt fermented in goat-skin sacks
Speca të mbushura Stuffed peppers
Tavë kosi Lamb, marinated with garlic and spices, combined with yoghurt and rice
Tullumbë Albanian doughnut soaked in syrup

Small print and index

ABOUT THE AUTHORS

Marc Di Duca has been a full-time travel guide author for over two decades, during which he has contributed to almost two hundred guides to destinations as diverse as Siberia, Brazil and the Caribbean for all major travel publishers. Based in the Czech Republic, Marc is a regular visitor to the Balkans, where hiking in the remote and largely undiscovered mountains of Northern Albania comes a close second to lounging on the beaches of the Adriatic as his favourite activity.

Owen Morton is based in North Yorkshire, and has written or contributed to numerous Rough Guides, ranging from Orkney to the Philippines. He particularly enjoyed working on the Albanian riviera chapter for this book. When not exploring the world, he entertains himself by writing a blog about 1980s cartoons. His favourite animal is the wonderfully expressive and permanently furious manul, which is native to Central Asia and sadly not Albania. Follow him on Instagram @owenmortonmanul.

Ben O'Donnell grew up in Florida and spent most of his career as a magazine writer and editor in New York City. More recently, he has contributed to outlets such as National Geographic Traveller and Archaeology Magazine as a freelance journalist and photographer. He is based in Tirana or near the beach (most any will do). Find him on Instagram at @odonnalbania.

A ROUGH GUIDE TO ROUGH GUIDES

Published in 1982, the first Rough Guide – to Greece – was a student scheme that became a publishing phenomenon. Mark Ellingham, a recent graduate in English from Bristol University, had been travelling in Greece the previous summer and couldn't find the right guidebook. With a small group of friends he wrote his own guide, combining a contemporary, journalistic style with a thoroughly practical approach to travellers' needs.

The immediate success of the book spawned a series that rapidly covered dozens of destinations. And, in addition to impecunious backpackers, Rough Guides soon acquired a much broader readership that relished the guides' wit and inquisitiveness as much as their enthusiastic, critical approach and value-for-money ethos. These days, Rough Guides include recommendations from budget to luxury and cover more than 120 destinations around the globe, from Amsterdam to Zanzibar, all regularly updated by our team of roaming writers.

Browse all our latest guides, read inspirational features and book your trip at **roughguides.com**.

Rough Guide credits

Editor: Joanna Reeves
Cartography: Carte
Picture editor: Piotr Kala
Picture Manager: Tom Smyth
Layout: Ankur Guha
Publishing Technology Manager: Rebeka Davies
Production Operations Manager: Katie Bennett
Head of Publishing: Sarah Clark

Publishing information

First edition 2025

Distribution
UK, Ireland and Europe
Apa Publications (UK) Ltd; mail@roughguides.com
United States and Canada
Two Rivers; ips@ingramcontent.com
Australia and New Zealand
Woodslane; info@woodslane.com.au
Worldwide
Apa Publications (UK) Ltd; mail@roughguides.com

Special Sales, Content Licensing and CoPublishing
Rough Guides can be purchased in bulk quantities at discounted prices. We can create special editions, personalized jackets and corporate imprints tailored to your needs. mail@roughguides.com.

roughguides.com

EU Representative
LOGOS EUROPE, 9 rue Nicolas Poussin, 17000, LA ROCHELLE, France; Contact@logoseurope.eu; +33 (0) 667937378

Printed by Omur in Turkey

ISBN: 9781835292150

This book was produced using **Typefi** automated publishing software.

A catalogue record for this book is available from the British Library.

Help us update

We've gone to a lot of effort to ensure that this edition of **The Rough Guide to Albania** is accurate and up-to-date. However, things change – places get "discovered", transport routes are altered, restaurants and hotels raise prices or lower standards, and businesses cease trading. If you feel we've got it wrong or left something out, we'd like to know, and if you can direct us to the web address, so much the better.

Please send your comments with the subject line "**Rough Guide Albania Update**" to mail@roughguides.com. We'll send a copy of the next edition (or any other Rough Guide if you prefer) for the very best emails.

Acknowledgements

Owen would like to thank the fantastic team at Rough Guides, particularly editor Joanna Reeves and fellow authors Ben O'Donnell and Marc Di Duca. Thanks to all the many hugely welcoming people we met on the road – a special shout-out to the family-run Hotel Panorama Piqeras. And finally, thanks to travelling companion Katherine Morton; it was a pleasure exploring the Albanian seaside with you.
Ben would like to thank Rezarta Bare, Yevgeniy Zelenko, Isuf Braho, Fjoralba Prifti, Brunilda Liçaj, Blerim Topulli and so many others in Albania for their generosity with their time, expertise and recommendations over the years – as well as the many, many folks who have shown me warm hospitality everywhere. Special thanks to Jayne, Ed, Jacquie and Alex for their unfailing encouragement overall and high tolerance for my more questionable ideas; to Vasil for tractor-towing my car out of the olive grove the day before his own wedding; and to Ani, who first showed the way.

Photo credits

(Key: T-top; C-centre; B-bottom; L-left; R-right)

All images **Shutterstock** except **Ben O'Donnell** 10, 199

Cover: The Valbona Valley **Shutterstock**

Index

A

B

C

D

N

O

P

U

V

W

Z

Map symbols

The symbols below are used on maps throughout the book

International boundary	Ferry route	Statue	Church
Chapter boundary	Wall	Gate/entrance	Mosque
Motorway	Place of interest	Ruins	Market
Major road	Airport	Monastery	Building
Minor road	Bus/taxi stop	Castle	Stadium
Pedestrian road	Parking	Museum	Park
Steps	Post office	Mountain peak	Beach
Railway line	Tourist office	Mountain range	Cemetery
Footpath	Hospital	National park	
Cable car	Vineyard	Viewpoint	

Listings key

- Accommodation
- Eating
- Drinking/Nightlife
- Shopping

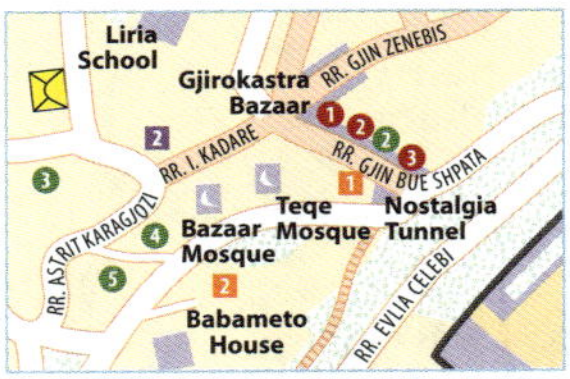